Sengan Baring-Gould

Sams **Teach Yourself**

Cocoa Touch™ Programming

in 24 Hours

SAMS 800 East 96th Street, Indianapolis, Indiana, 46240 USA

Sams Teach Yourself Cocoa Touch™ Programming in 24 Hours

ISBN-13: 978-0-672-33125-1

ISBN-10: 0-672-33125-X

Library of Congress Cataloging-in-Publication Data:

Baring-Gould, Sengan.

Sams teach yourself Cocoa touch programming in 24 hours / Sengan Baring-Gould.

p. cm.

Includes bibliographical references and index.

ISBN 978-0-672-33125-1

1. Cocoa (Application development environment) 2. Application program interfaces (Computer software) 3. iPhone OS. 4. iPhone (Smartphone) I. Title.

QA76.76.A63B37 2010

005.3–dc22

2009035325

Printed in the United States of America

First Printing October 2009

Trademarks

All terms mentioned in this book that are known to be trademarks or service marks have been appropriately capitalized. Sams Publishing cannot attest to the accuracy of this information. Use of a term in this book should not be regarded as affecting the validity of any trademark or service mark.

Warning and Disclaimer

Every effort has been made to make this book as complete and as accurate as possible, but no warranty or fitness is implied. The information provided is on an "as is" basis. The author and the publisher shall have neither liability nor responsibility to any person or entity with respect to any loss or damages arising from the information contained in this book or from the use of the programs accompanying it.

Bulk Sales

Sams Publishing offers excellent discounts on this book when ordered in quantity for bulk purchases or special sales. For more information, please contact

U.S. Corporate and Government Sales

1-800-382-3419

corpsales@pearsontechgroup.com

For sales outside of the U.S., please contact

International Sales

international@pearson.com

Associate Publisher

Greg Wiegand

Acquisitions Editor

Laura Norman

Development Editor

Daniel J. Richcreek

Managing Editor

Kristy Hart

Project Editor

Betsy Harris

Copy Editor

Karen Annett

Senior Indexer

Cheryl Lenser

Proofreader

Kathy Ruiz

Technical Editor

Christian Kenyeres

Publishing Coordinator

Cindy Teeters

Book Designer

Gary Adair

Compositor

Bronkella Publishing

Contents at a Glance

PART VI: Interacting with the World

PART VII: Completing Your Application

Appendixes A, B, and D are online-only bonus materials. You can access them at www.informit.com/title/9780672331251.

Table of Contents

PART III: Advanced User-Interface Elements

Appendixes A, B, and D are online-only bonus materials. You can access them at www.informit.com/title/9780672331251.

About the Author

Dr. Sengan Baring-Gould earned his Ph.D. in Artificial Intelligence (Natural Language Processing) and has published a number of papers in this field. Prior to that, he wrote a seminal series of articles reverse engineering the video hardware of the Atari ST, which are still quoted today. He has coauthored two patents in the field of x86 debugging hardware.

He is the owner of Ansemond LLC, a small Mac and iPhone software company based in Colorado.

Its current products include Tetratile (an iPhone puzzle board game) and Find It! Keep It! (a Mac web browser that captures web pages reliably and saves them to a fully searchable database).

Dedication

To my wife, to my cats, and to the beautiful planet we all share.

Acknowledgments

As is so often the case, to write this book, I stood on the shoulders of giants far too numerous to acknowledge. However, I'd like to mention a few people whose writings or code taught me a lot about Cocoa: Peter Ammon, Mike Ash, Bill Bumgarner, Mark Dalrymple, Aaron Hillegass, Matt Gallagher, Matt Gemmell, Bob Ippolito, Christopher Lloyd, Nat of mulle-kybernetik.com, and Scott Stevenson. I would also like to thank the cocoadev.com community for sharing their knowledge so freely.

I'd like to thank my friends, teachers, and parents for all they have taught me and give a big thank-you to my wife, Simone, for emotional support and practical help while writing this book.

Finally, I'd like to thank the staff at Sams who helped me dot all the i's and cross all the t's.

We Want to Hear from You!

As the reader of this book, *you* are our most important critic and commentator. We value your opinion and want to know what we're doing right, what we could do better, what areas you'd like to see us publish in, and any other words of wisdom you're willing to pass our way.

You can email or write me directly to let me know what you did or didn't like about this book—as well as what we can do to make our books stronger.

Please note that I cannot help you with technical problems related to the topic of this book, and that due to the high volume of mail I receive, I might not be able to reply to every message.

When you write, please be sure to include this book's title and author as well as your name and phone or email address. I will carefully review your comments and share them with the author and editors who worked on the book.

E-mail: feedback@samspublishing.com

Mail: Greg Wiegand
Associate Publisher
Sams Publishing
800 East 96th Street
Indianapolis, IN 46240 USA

Reader Services

Visit our website and register this book at informit.com/register for convenient access to any updates, downloads, or errata that might be available for this book.

Introduction

About This Book

Sams Teach Yourself Cocoa Touch Programming in 24 Hours teaches you how to create reliable applications for your iPhone or iPod touch in as little as 24 hours. By the time you have finished reading this book, you'll know everything you need to create and sell your own applications on the iPhone App Store!

iPhone applications are written in Objective-C using system-provided libraries called Cocoa. You might wonder why Apple did not adopt a more standard developer environment already known to more programmers. Why learn yet another language and application programming interface (API)? By the end of this book, I hope that you'll agree that Objective-C and Cocoa are very powerful tools for building applications and graphical interfaces quickly, that they would be hard to translate to another environment, and that they are well worth learning.

The power of Cocoa and Objective-C comes from splitting graphical user interface (GUI) tasks into a few well-chosen abstractions that reduce the amount of code we have to write. Once understood, these abstractions seem obvious, so most books simply introduce them as the way things are done in Cocoa, leaving beginners bewildered: They adopt a top-down approach. Apple's documentation falls into this category, discussing each topic deeply without explaining how it fits into the overall picture.

This book adopts a bottom-up approach. I start with the basics, and show you recurrent code patterns that can be generalized into an abstraction, which will simplify client code. Because you understand the mechanics of each task, you'll be able to quickly resolve most problems you encounter on your own.

Understanding the mechanics of each task is a double-edged sword. Although it helps you debug problems and gain confidence that you know what your code is doing, the more your code assumes it knows how the libraries work, the more it is liable to break when Apple upgrades the iPhone OS. I judge this trade-off to be worthwhile. Reverse engineering system libraries to debug your application takes a lot of time for little transferable knowledge. Learning to see what code assumes too much about other code's behavior also takes time, but the gain is immense: You learn how to build loosely coupled complex systems.

To further help you, throughout the book I place a strong emphasis on debugging. I want you to be able to deliver working software once you've completed this book. You'll also see that I place emphasis on what works rather than hiding behind how things "should" be done, and leaving you stranded.

Finally, I list sources of information that helped me understand what was really going on when I was totally stumped.

About You

Who is this book for? I assume you know C but neither Objective-C nor Cocoa. Even if you know some Objective-C and Cocoa, I hope you find this book valuable because of the depth of its presentation.

If you know a C-like language such as Java or JavaScript, I have provided a short primer in Appendix A, "C Primer," to help you get up to speed (available online at www.informit.com/title/9780672331251). If that proves insufficient, you'll have to learn C first. 24 hours is simply not enough time to learn C, Objective-C, and Cocoa.

Because I assume some previous programming experience, I won't go through each API method by method giving an example of each. Instead, I'll give a few examples of the main functionality, and summarize the rest so that you remember where to look when you encounter a new task.

About Objective-C

Objective-C is a thin extension to C which adds reflective and object-oriented features. Reflection lets Objective-C programs observe and modify their class hierarchies and methods dynamically. Object-oriented programming provides a means of dividing programs into simple parts. This book starts with an in-depth introduction to Objective-C.

Stylistically, Objective-C programs emphasize simplicity. Fewer lines of code is better. Because common tasks take little code, if you find yourself writing a lot of code for a simple task, check whether Cocoa does not already provide large parts of the solution.

What You Need

The software development kit (SDK) requires an Intel Mac running the Leopard or Snow Leopard OS, but I will not be giving guidance on how to use a Mac. David Pogue's *Mac OS X: The Missing Manual* series of books provides a popular introduction to Mac OS X. I do encourage you to download the SDK and to actively try the examples. Although I explain how to use the development tools, I encourage you to explore the tools further yourself. They come with good in-built documentation.

How to Read This Book

Each hour builds on the previous one, so it's best to read the book from front to back unless you already understand a topic. However you may wish to read the "Applications Must Enhance, not Sully Apple's Image" section of Hour 24 earlier to understand the kinds of applications Apple will not sell via the App Store.

Conventions Used in This Book

This book uses the following typefaces to distinguish code, computer input and output, from the text and new concepts:

- New concepts use a green font.
- Code is shown in `monospace`.
- Things you should type are displayed in **`bold monospace`**.
- Keys are marked Shift for Shift, Option for Option, and ⌘ for Command.
- The computer's response is in `shaded monospace`.
- Code to be replaced appears in ~~`stricken through monospace`~~: Some of the examples build upon previous code, and the stricken-through code will help you locate the code to change.
- Placeholders are shown in *`italic monospace`*.

HOUR 1

Starting Your First Application: A Calculator

What You'll Learn in This Hour:

- Setting up your development tools
- Using Xcode
- Using Interface Builder

Welcome to the world of iPhone development! To get started you'll need to set up the development tools and learn how to use them. This hour, you'll learn how to use Xcode, Interface Builder, and the iPhone simulator. Please turn on your Mac and try things out: This book is a map, and you'll only really gain confidence by making the journey yourself. Xcode is the development environment used for writing, compiling, installing, and debugging iPhone applications. Interface Builder is a visual design tool used to create and test iPhone application user interfaces. The iPhone simulator is a software simulator of an iPhone, which improves turnaround time by eliminating the time it would take to install the application on the device itself.

Setting Up Your Development Tools

Apple's basic iPhone developer program is free. It lets you develop applications you can run on the iPhone simulator. However, you must pay a yearly fee if you want your applications to run on a real iPhone or iPod Touch. Apple details the programs it offers at http://developer.apple.com/iphone/program/. Apple will take a number of weeks to process your payment, so sign up early! Apple also takes a long time to switch registrations from individuals to companies, so it's best to register as a company if you intend to sell your software as a company.

To get ready to begin your first application, start by downloading the iPhone software development kit (SDK) from http://developer.apple.com/iphone/. This SDK contains the tools needed to develop iPhone applications. Apple requires you to become a registered iPhone developer before letting you download these tools. After you've signed up, log in and download and install the iPhone SDK.

This book covers developing iPhone applications on an Intel Mac running Leopard.

Although Apple's iPhone simulator is very useful, it does not replace testing on an actual iPhone: It does not simulate the iPhone's hardware accurately. The iPhone's performance is significantly lower than the simulator's, and the simulator lacks devices such as the camera or the accelerometer.

Did you Know?

> If you can't log in to download the tools, check Appendix B, "Troubleshooting Xcode"—Apple might be rejecting your Internet service provider (ISP). After you have been accepted as a paying developer, if you can't figure out how to install the certificate to run programs on your iPhone or iPod Touch, go to Appendix B.

The next few pages give you a quick tour of one of the main applications you'll be using to develop iPhone applications and the key tasks you'll be performing.

Using Xcode

Xcode is an Integrated Development Environment (IDE). It subsumes project management, project building, code editing, and debugging into one giant tool. IDEs improve productivity by making common operations easier.

Not everyone likes IDEs because they require people to learn a whole new unfamiliar environment. By making common tasks easier, they tend to obfuscate (render incomprehensible) rarer tasks, either by hiding needed settings in some far-flung options page or by hiding what they are doing. People who prefer using their own text editors will be relieved to know they can continue to do so: Xcode recognizes when files are edited externally and will ask you what it should do. When Xcode builds a project, it uses external command-line tools, so you can also use makefiles if you want. You will, however, need to run your applications from Xcode.

Starting Xcode

Your development tools are installed in `/Developer`. Open the Finder and press Shift-⌘-G. Type **`/Developer`** and click OK. Now drag the Developer icon in the title bar to Places for quick access. Xcode is in the Applications folder and can be dragged to your Dock.

Launch Xcode. If you have an iPhone or iPod Touch connected to your machine when you launch Xcode, you might see a message asking if you want to use the device for development. Click the Ignore button for now.

On launch, Xcode shows a Welcome screen introducing itself. Clicking on a link opens documentation you can read at your leisure later. For now, close this page.

Creating an Empty Project

Choose File, New Project, select Application under the iPhone OS heading in the left pane, and then choose Window-Based Application in the upper right pane (see Figure 1.1). Now choose a directory and give the project the name **Calculator**. This sets up a number of template files common to Window-Based Applications. The other project types set up other template files.

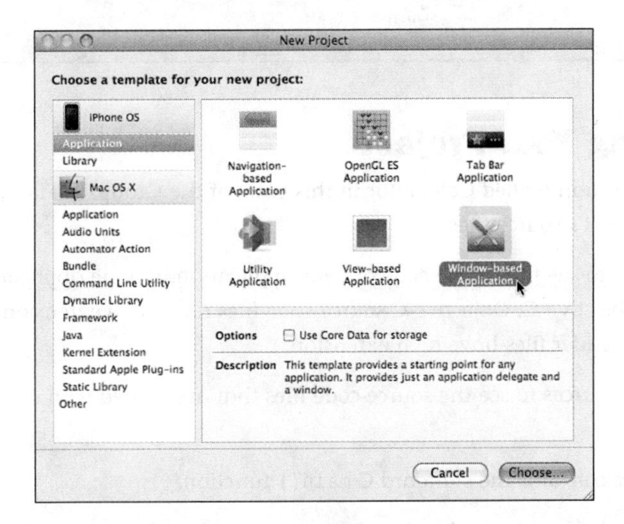

FIGURE 1.1
New Project window

A new window appears (see Figure 1.2). The Groups & Files pane on the left contains all the project information. The upper-right pane is called the Detail View and shows information corresponding to the selected item in the Groups & Files pane. This information is often a list of files. Missing files are shown in red. Selecting an editable file in the Detail View shows it in the Editor in the lower-right pane.

The template files can be built into a functional application. Click the Build and Go icon in the toolbar (at the top of the window) to run the application. The iPhone simulator will run and display a white background. To exit your application, click the button at the bottom of the iPhone simulator as you would on a real iPhone. The simulator comes with a number of built-in applications you can play with.

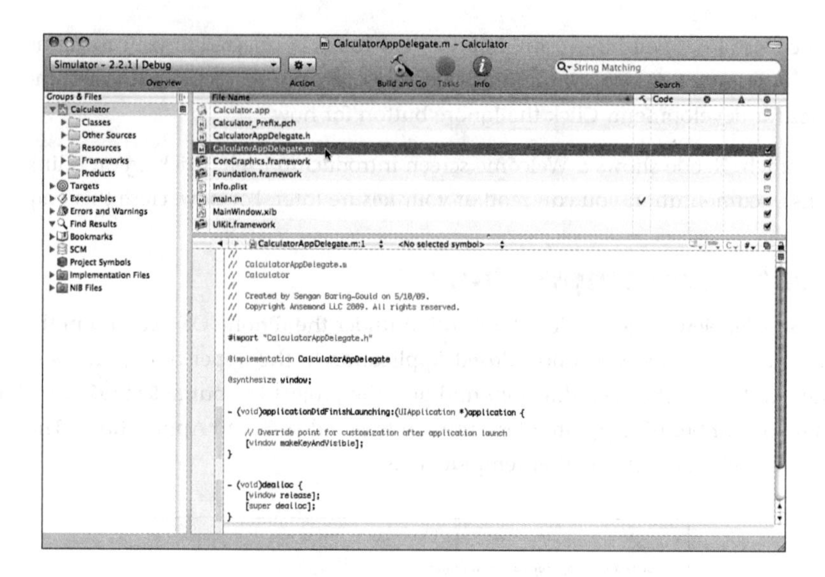

FIGURE 1.2
Main development window

Exploring Your Project

The Project section (called Calculator in this case) of the Groups & Files pane contains the project's source files.

Select Classes to see the source code of your application. iPhone applications are written in Objective-C. Objective-C source-code files have a `.m` extension. Like C, Objective-C header files have a `.h` extension.

Select Other Sources to see the source-code files that are shared with other applications:

- `main.m` contains the standard C `main()` function.
- The `.pch` file specifies header files to precompile to boost compilation speed.

Select Resources to see files that will be included in your application, such as pictures and sounds:

- `Info.plist` is a list of your application's properties such as its version.
- `MainWindow.xib` is an Interface Builder file, which specifies where user-interface (UI) elements should be placed on the screen.

Select Frameworks to see the frameworks used by your application. Frameworks are Objective-C's extended version of libraries. Frameworks contain binary libraries, header files, and optional resources, such as sounds and images.

- The `Foundation` framework provides basic Objective-C class functionality: basic data types, collections, and operating system services.
- The `UIKit` framework provides tools to build and manage iPhone user interfaces.
- The `CoreGraphics` framework provides lightweight 2D rendering.

Select Products to see the files the project will or has built: `Calculator.app` is the calculator application. Other product types include libraries and frameworks.

The Targets section contains the files to process. Click the Target disclosure triangle. The Calculator subsection specifies the rules used to build the `Calculator.app` product. Click its disclosure triangle to see the three build phases:

- **Copy Bundle Resources**—Copy these files into the application.
- **Compile Sources**—Compile these files and build them into the application binary.
- **Link Binary with Libraries**—Link the application binary against these libraries and frameworks.

The Executables section shows products that are applications and can be run.

Other self-explanatory categories follow. The SCM section refers to Xcode's ability to integrate a source-control system.

Using Information Panels

Control-click or right-click the Project section of the Groups & Files pane to reveal a context menu. Remember that the Project section will use the name of your project. In this case it will appear as Calculator in the Groups & Files pane. Choose Get Info (see Figure 1.3). This displays an information panel about the project. Options set at the project level are inherited to every target, unless explicitly overridden. Choose the Build tab (see Figure 1.4). This tab shows all the build options for each build configuration. Most iPhone projects have two build configurations: a Debug configuration, which produces an executable that is easier to debug, and a Release configuration, which produces an executable that runs faster. Many settings are shared between these configurations, and can be set when the All Configurations option is chosen in the Configuration field. The search field in the upper right helps narrow down build options to specific properties. The button with the icon of spectacles lying on two books in the lower left brings up documentation for each build option (see Figure 1.5).

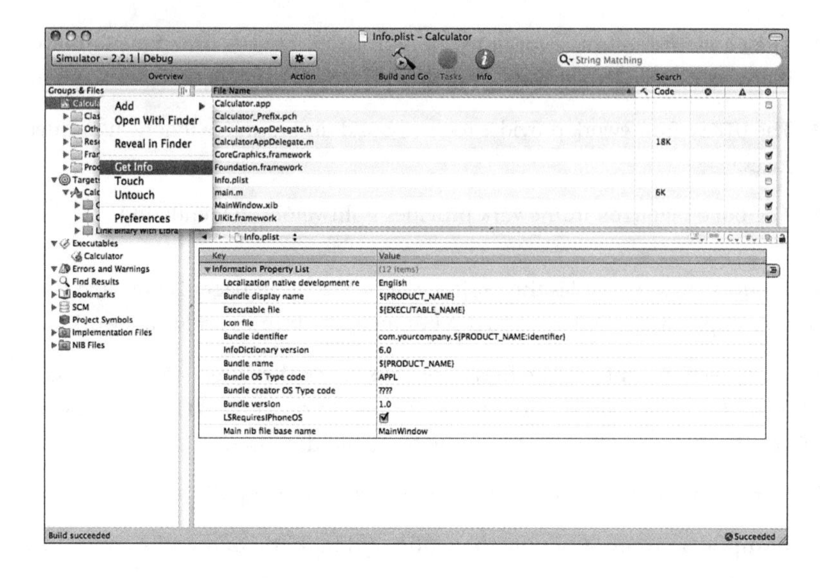

FIGURE 1.3 Get Info context menu

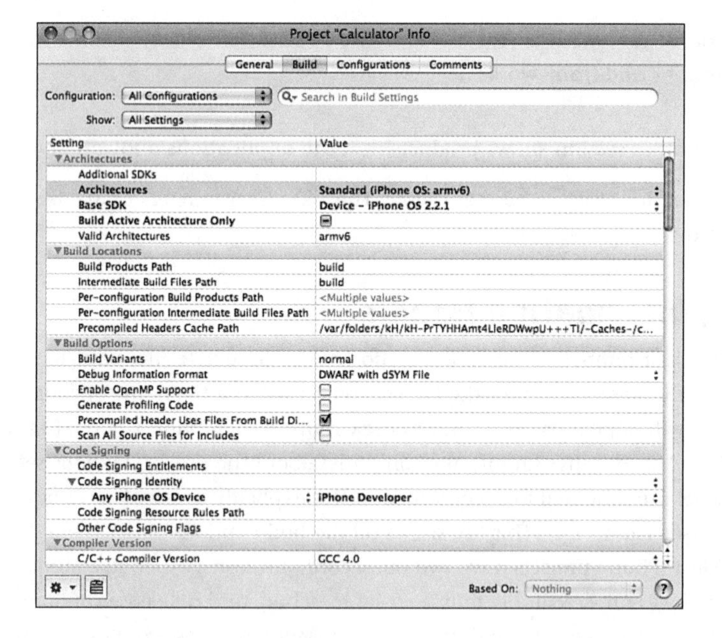

FIGURE 1.4 The Build tab of the Project information panel

Open Targets' context menu in the Targets section. Again choose Get Info. This time, the information panel shows you the build options for a target, letting you override the project defaults.

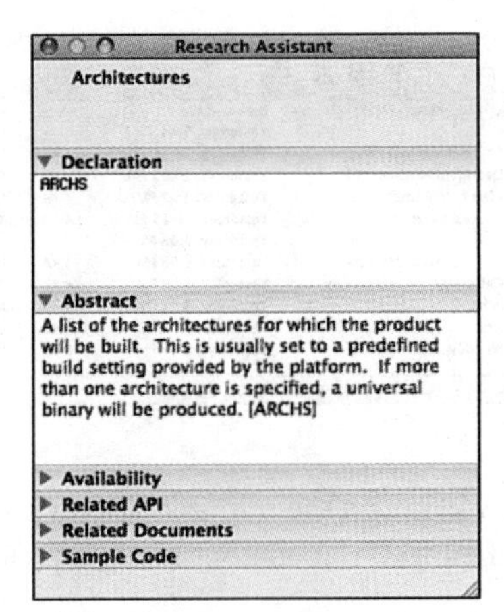

FIGURE 1.5
The Research Assistant

Open Executables' context menu in the Executables section. Again choose Get Info. This time, the information panel lets you modify the context in which the application will run when launched from Xcode.

Exploring the Project Directory Structure

Open the project's context menu, and choose Open With Finder (see Figure 1.6). Inside the project, you'll see the following:

- The build directory contains the Xcode products and can be deleted to guarantee a complete rebuild.
- Any new classes you create with Xcode will appear in the Classes directory.
- The resources (`MainWindow.xib`, `Info.plist`) and the Other Sources (`Calculator_Prefix.pch` and `main.m`) are not by default in their own directories.
- `Calculator.xcodeproj` is Xcode's project file. Double-clicking it from the Finder will open it in Xcode.

To add an existing source-code file, either drag it into Classes or Other Sources sections of the Groups & Files pane, or open one of these section's context menus and choose Add, Existing Files. You'll be asked whether to copy the file into the project. If you choose not to copy a file into a project, it can be shared with other projects.

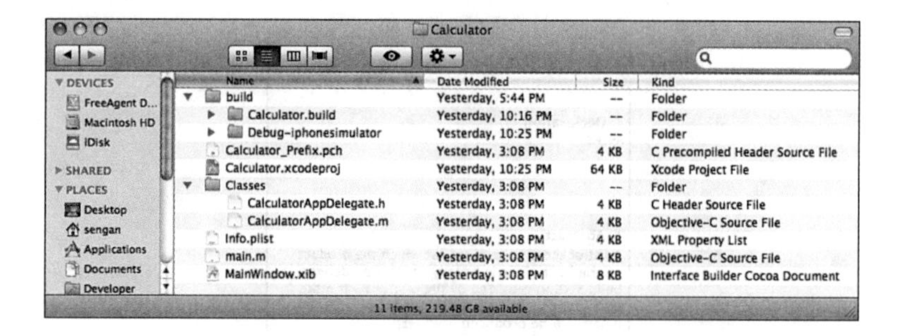

FIGURE 1.6
The project in the Finder

To add an existing framework, open the framework section's context menu and choose Add, Existing Frameworks. You do not usually copy frameworks into projects.

Using Help

Xcode comes with integrated documentation. Choose Documentation from the Help menu. This brings up a documentation window (see Figure 1.7). If you have not downloaded the documentation for a specific SDK already, a GET button will appear next to the topic. Click it to download that documentation.

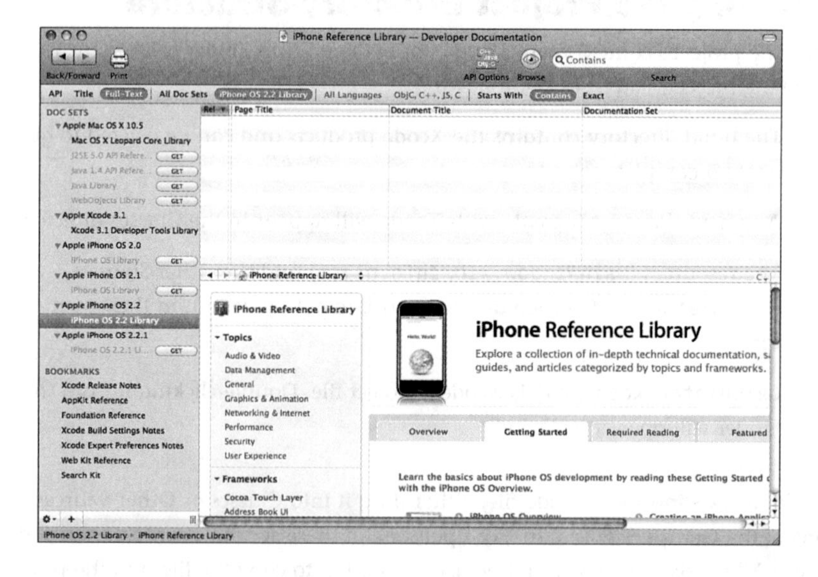

FIGURE 1.7
Xcode documentation window

To search for something, choose the search field in the upper right to find things and type something. The search bar below the toolbar lets you choose the kind of search: by API, by Document Title, or by Full-Text. API search is useful for finding Objective-C methods and classes. It lets you narrow the search to a particular document set or language.

The upper-right pane shows the search results; the bottom pane shows the text of a particular result. The bar at the top of the bottom pane lets you choose different functions within a document and return to recently viewed documents.

Using Interface Builder

Interface Builder is a visual design tool used to create and test user interfaces.

Interface Builder documents are called *NIB files*. NIB stands for NeXT Interface Builder, named after the 1988 incarnation of Interface Builder, which shipped on the NeXTSTEP 0.8 operating system. Older versions of Interface Builder edited NIB files directly. Interface Builder now uses XIB files, which are compiled during the build process into NIB files. XIB stands for XML-Based Interface Builder, but don't let the word XML fool you. These files are not made for people to edit.

First, we'll take a quick tour of the tool. Then, we'll start making something with it: a simple calculator. By Hour 8, "Drawing User-Interface Elements," the calculator will look like the one shown in Figure 1.8.

FIGURE 1.8
The finished calculator

Using the Document Window

Double-click `MainWindow.xib` to open this file in Interface Builder. The Interface Builder Document Window (see Figure 1.9) shows the objects the NIB file contains:

- File's Owner represents the `UIApplication` object, which is responsible for handling user-interaction events (see Hour 6, "Understanding How the User Interface Is Built"). Every application has a `UIApplication` object.

- First Responder is a fictional object used to route user-interaction events. It is explained in Hour 7, "Understanding How Events Are Processed."
- Calculator App Delegate represents the `CalculatorAppDelegate` object that decides how the application will behave. We will implement this object's class in Hour 7.
- Window represents a `UIWindow` object that will contain the user-interface elements that will be drawn to the screen.

Double-clicking the Window object brings a canvas of the iPhone's screen to the front (see Figure 1.9). We will be adding user-interface elements to this canvas to create a calculator.

FIGURE 1.9
Interface Builder Windows

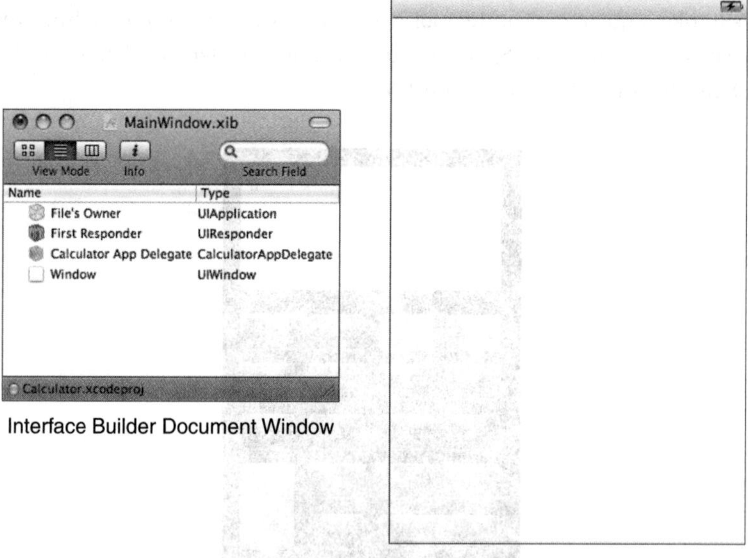

We can rename the window to something more descriptive by selecting it, and then choosing the Tools, Inspector menu item. This opens the Inspector panel (see Figure 1.10), which lets you edit the selected object's properties. The top part of the Inspector panel contains four icons that let you choose between the object's attributes, connections, layout, and identity. Click an icon to choose what you want to see. The pane below the icons will display the relevant information and the Inspector panel's title will change. Switch to the Identity pane. The Inspector's title will change to Window Identity. Enter **BasicCalculator** in the Name text field of the Interface Builder Identity section (see Figure 1.10).

Notice that `BasicCalculator` also appears in the Document Window.

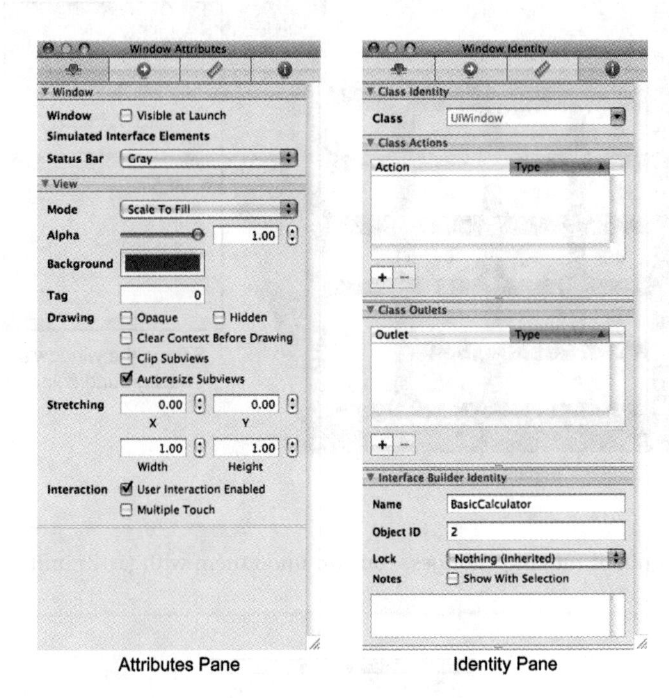

FIGURE 1.10 Interface Builder's Inspector Panel's Attributes and Identity panes

Creating a Calculator

The first version of your calculator will be very simple: a screen, a keypad, and a background (see Figure 1.11). iPhone users appreciate simple applications, as most applications are only used a few minutes at a time.

Select the Window object in the Interface Builder Document Window. Choose the Attributes pane in the Inspector panel. Click the background color button (see Figure 1.12). It is now selected as shown by its darkened edge. A color picker will appear. Adjust the color to a dark gray: 34% (see Figure 1.11). The color picker only affects a color button if it is selected, which can be confusing: Clicking the color button deselects it, without closing the color picker.

The Attributes pane of the Inspector panel is also known as the Attributes Inspector. Similarly, there is a Connections Inspector, a Size Inspector, and an Identity Inspector, corresponding to the Connections, Size, and Identity panes of the Inspector panel.

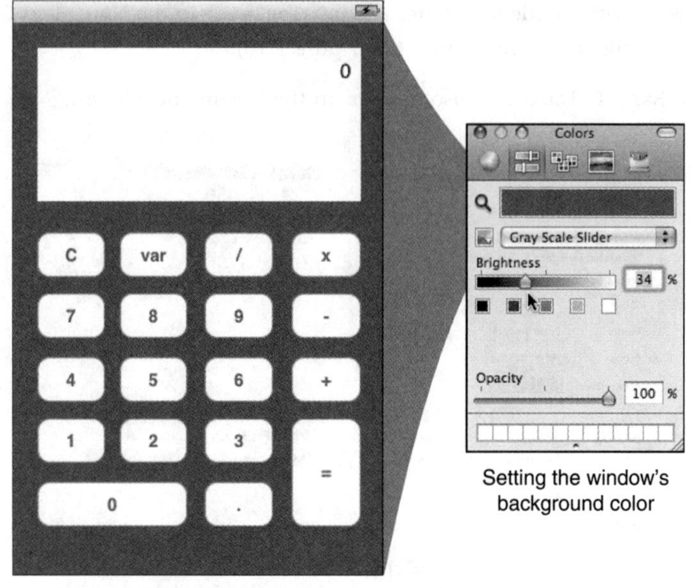

FIGURE 1.11 Initial Calculator's background color

Don't worry about making changes. You can undo them with (⌘-Z) and redo them with (Shift-⌘-Z).

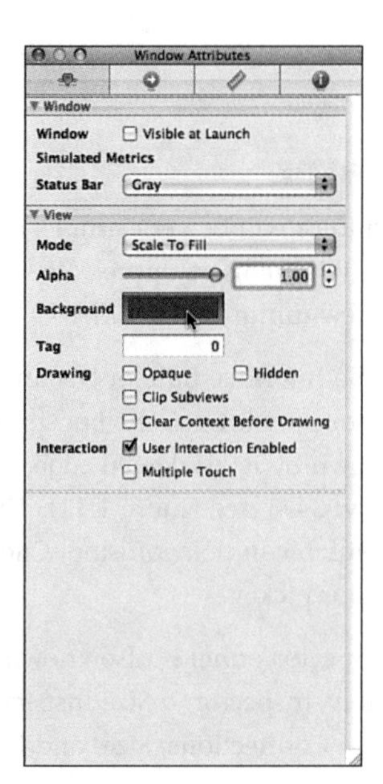

FIGURE 1.12 Selecting the background color

Creating the Calculator's Screen

Now we'll add the calculator's screen, where the results will be displayed. It will be a Text View: an area in which text can be displayed or edited.

Interface Builder provides a library of user-interface (UI) elements. Choose the Tools, Library menu item to access them. A Library window will appear. As you can see, Cocoa provides many UI elements. Text Views are Data Views, so select Data Views in the Objects section (see Figure 1.13). Now, to add a Text View to your application, drag one onto the canvas (see Figure 1.14).

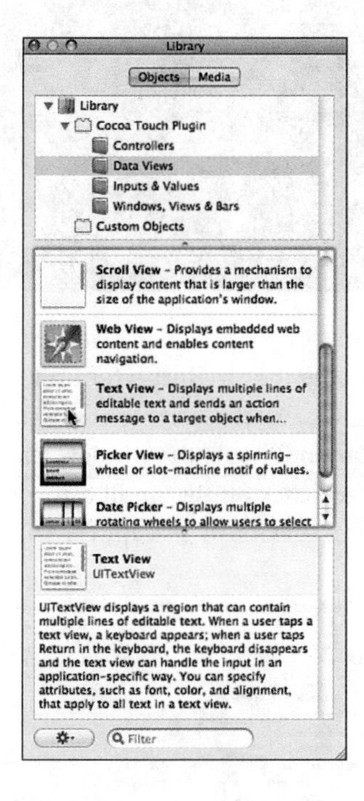

FIGURE 1.13 Interface Builder's Library window

The Text View has a transparent background, but we want it to have a white background: Ensure the Text View on the canvas is selected (the blue dots should be visible), as seen in Figure 1.14. Choose the Attributes Inspector, and adjust the background to opaque white (see Figure 1.15). Opacity is adjusted by the slider at the bottom of the color picker (see Figure 1.11). We also want the alignment to be right-justified so we change it, as shown in Figure 1.15. Finally, double-click the text to change it to a 0.

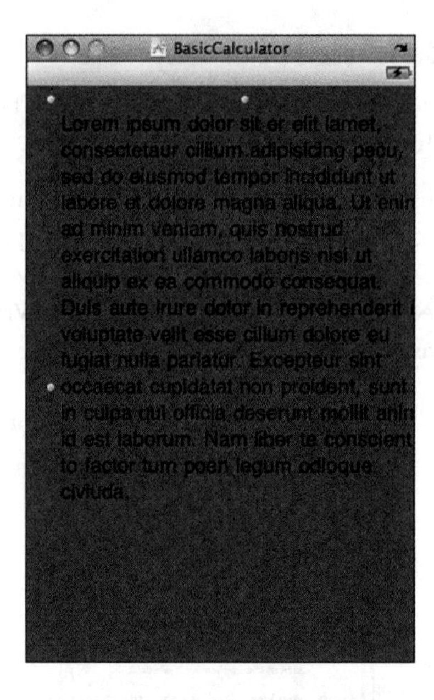

FIGURE 1.14 Adding a Text View to the canvas

The Text View is too big. Choose the Size Inspector and change the sizes, as shown in Figure 1.15. On a Mac, you can ask Cocoa to resize the contents of a window if the window size changes. On an iPhone, the window changes size if the display is rotated. To simulate this effect, click on the small arrow at the right end of the canvas window's title bar (as seen previously in Figure 1.14).

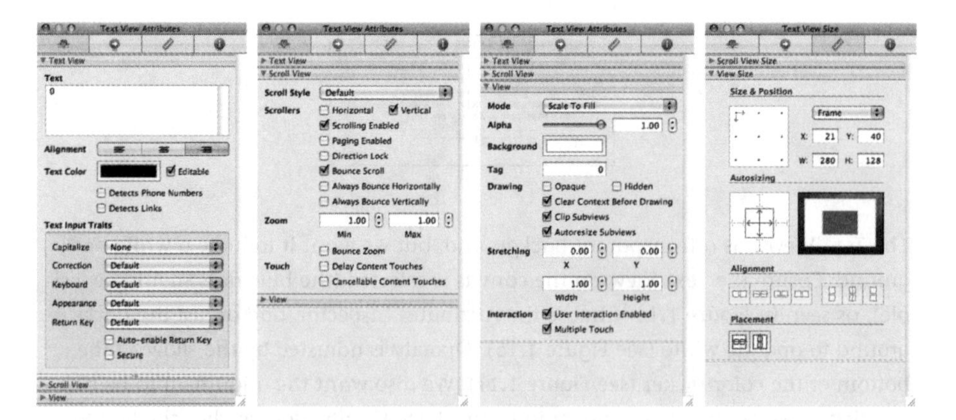

FIGURE 1.15 Text View settings

Did you Know?

For simplicity, this book uses the term iPhone to refer to any iPhone OS compatible device: an iPhone or an iPod Touch.

Adding the Calculator's Buttons

Now we'll add the calculator's keypad. We'll create it out of buttons. Buttons are inputs, so select Inputs & Values in the Library window. Drag a button onto the canvas, so that it lines up with the Text View's left edge but is below it. You'll notice a blue guideline appears and the button snaps to it. These lines help you line interface elements up to create a pleasing interface that is consistent with Apple's Interface Guidelines (see Figure 1.16).

The button's size is too large. Select it on the canvas and adjust it in the Size Inspector to a width of 59 pixels, and a height of 37. Turn to the Attribute Inspector and make sure that the horizontal and vertical alignment options are selected, as shown in Figure 1.16.

Blue positioning guidelines

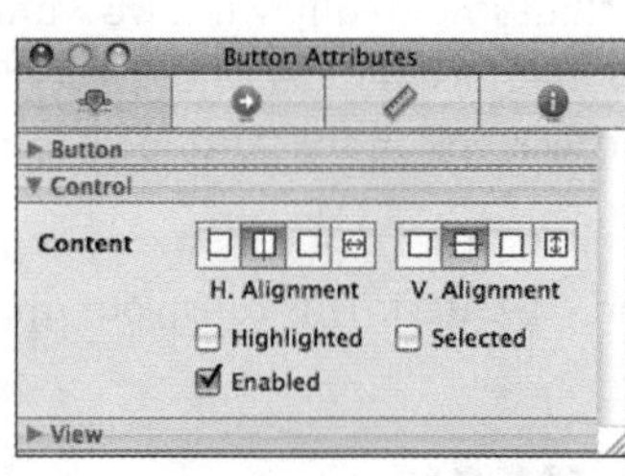

Button attributes

FIGURE 1.16
Placing and sizing a button

To create the keypad, we'll copy (⌘-C) and paste (⌘-V) our original button to create a row. Use the guidelines to align the buttons correctly. Repeat until you have four buttons in a row. Notice that the buttons do not align with the edges of the Text

View, so adjust their coordinates in the Size Inspector such that their x coordinates are 21, 93, 167, and 242. Now select all four buttons, and paste four more copies below, vertically aligned with the Text View. Select four buttons at a time, and adjust their y coordinates to 194, 245, 298, 349, and 402. You can do this because the buttons recognize that the x coordinate contains a minus sign because they do not share a common value.

We want the bottom-left button to be wider. Delete the second button on the bottom row by selecting it and pressing the delete key. Now adjust the bottom-left button's size by selecting it, and dragging the middle-right blue dot to the right until it lines up with the right side of the second button row. Merge the two lowest buttons of the rightmost column in the same way.

Now we need to label the buttons. Double-click the buttons and change the titles appropriately.

Trying Out the Interface

You can play with an interface you've designed by choosing File, Simulate Interface (⌘-R) in Interface Builder. This starts the iPhone simulator and shows your design. It looks good. The buttons can be clicked. It's often a good idea to behave like a four-year-old child at this point. Click on everything to see what happens. For instance, click on the Text View. A keyboard comes up and lets you edit the Text View. However, that's not really what we wanted. We wanted a noneditable Text View. Return to Interface Builder and select the Text View on the canvas. Disable the Editable check box in the Attributes Inspector (shown enabled in Figure 1.15).

Now, let's build the application and run it. Switch to Xcode and click the Build and Go button (⌘-Enter). This runs your application in the iPhone simulator.

Summary

In your first hour, you've set up your development tools, created your first project, and designed a calculator's user interface. In the next hour, you'll add code to make the calculator calculate.

Workshop

The Workshop consists of quiz questions and answers to help you solidify your understanding of the material covered in this hour. You should try to answer the questions before checking the answers.

Quiz Questions

1. What is Xcode?
2. What is Interface Builder?
3. What is the iPhone Simulator?

Quiz Answers

1. Xcode is the development environment used to create projects, edit code, and build applications.
2. Interface Builder is a visual user-interface design tool.
3. The iPhone Simulator provides a rough simulation of an iPhone so that you can run and debug your applications on your Mac.

Exercise

In Interface Builder, open the Library window and select Data Views, Inputs & Values, and Windows, Views and Bars. Create a new window by dragging a Window out of the Library window. Try adding different UI elements to this new window. Try it out in the simulator. In a project with multiple windows, one of the windows with the Window Set at Launch option's checkmark set will be shown.

HOUR 2
Handling Interaction

What You'll Learn in This Hour:

- Understanding Objective-C objects
- Binding an object to the user interface
- Managing memory
- Invoking methods on `nil`
- Understanding Objective-C type checking

Now that you've installed the development tools and you've built a basic Calculator UI, it is time to make it useful. You'll write code to give your calculator the ability to do arithmetic. As all iPhone code is written in Objective-C, you start learning Objective-C this hour. I cover the Objective-C objects, memory management, invoking methods on `nil`, and Objective-C type checking. You'll also learn how to bind an object to the UI and how to debug with `NSLog()`.

Objective-C

Objective-C adds a thin layer of object-oriented support to C.

The C language was designed to support procedural programming. In procedural programming, programs consist of procedures that contain a series of computational steps to be carried out. Procedures can even call other procedures to carry out subtasks. When a procedural programmer designs a program, he begins by dividing its behavior into simpler subtasks then builds the program up from these subtasks.

Object-oriented programming provides a different way of designing programs. Instead of thinking of subtasks as the building blocks, programmers think of objects as the building blocks. Objects consist of data and methods (behavior) that make them useful, just like numbers consist of data (the number's value) and arithmetic operations. In object-oriented parlance, objects are sent messages that tell them to do something (run one of their methods). You can write object-oriented programs in C, but it's burdensome: C only supports numbers, structures, and pointers as data values, whereas object-oriented programmers would like to think of objects as data values. Objective-C simplifies using objects as data values.

As graphical user interface (GUI) programs are naturally modeled by objects, using a language that provides support for object-oriented design simplifies iPhone application development. However, Objective-C also includes C, and for good reason: In many situations, procedural programming provides more natural solutions.

Declaring Objects

We would like our calculator to keep track of our calculation. We can model this with an object. Objects consist of data and methods. An object is declared as follows in Objective-C:

```
@interface Name : Parent
{
  Type name;                    // Zero to many
}

+ class method declaration;     // Zero to many
- instance method declaration;  // Zero to many

@end
```

Let's take it line by line:

```
@interface Name : Parent
@end
```

This declares `Name` as a new type of object, derived from an existing `Parent` object. This means that `Name` objects have all the data and methods that `Parent` objects have. `Name` objects might, however, reimplement a `Parent` object's methods in different ways. `Name` objects might also define additional data and methods that `Parent` objects do not have. `Parent` is known as `Name`'s superclass. Objective-C classes cannot have more than one superclass: that is, there is no multiple inheritance.

```
{
  Type name;                    // Zero to many
}
```

This declares the data (called **instance variables**) that `Name` objects have, but `Parent` objects do not. The notation here follows that of a structure because the data storage aspect of objects is similar to a structure that inherits some of its members from Parent, and Parent's superclass, and so on. If Name objects add no data, you do not need to include this section.

```
+ class method declaration; // Zero to many
```

This declares class methods. Notationally, class methods are prefixed with a (+) to distinguish them from instance methods, which are prefixed with a (-). Class methods operate on classes rather than on specific objects.

```
- instance method declaration; // Zero to many
```

This declares instance methods that operate on objects.

Consider a real example. A calculator remembers the current and saved values of a calculation. This allows you to perform an arithmetic operation on the current value. Listing 2.1 declares the methods our Calculator will support.

LISTING 2.1 CalculatorModel.h

```
#import <Foundation/Foundation.h>

@interface CalculatorModel : NSObject
{
  float      value;
  float      savedValues[16];
}

- (float)   value;
- (void)    setValue:(float)value;

- (void)    saveValue:(float)value atIndex:(int)i;
- (float)   savedValueAtIndex:(int)i;

- (void)    add:      (float)value;
- (void)    subtract:(float)value;
- (void)    multiply:(float)value;
- (void)    divide:  (float)value;

@end
```

We import Foundation because NSObject is defined there. You'll learn the role of NSObject later this hour. For now, just note that CalculatorModel has NSObject as its superclass. #import is like #include, except that it guarantees that the header file will be included exactly once.

Note these three points:

- CalculatorModel keeps track of the currentValue and of 16 saved values.
- The syntax of the method declarations is new.

- The return type is specified before the method name. `value` returns a `float` and takes no arguments:

```
- (float) value;
```

If a method takes an argument, the method name (called a **selector**) will end with a colon—`setValue:` takes a `float` as an argument.

```
- (void) setValue:(float)value;
```

Selectors have as many parts as there are arguments—`saveValue:atIndex:` takes two arguments:

```
- (void) saveValue:(float)value atIndex:(int)i;
```

This notation makes Objective-C functions self-documenting, at the cost of more typing.

To create and add this file to your project, choose the File, New File menu item, and then Cocoa Touch classes, `NSObject` subclass from the New File Template window that appears. Click Next, and change the name to `CalculatorModel.m`. This creates two files: `CalculatorModel.h` and `CalculatorModel.m`. Type Listing 2.1 into `CalculatorModel.h`. Click Build and Go. You'll notice `Succeeded`, followed by a small yellow triangle and a 9 in the status bar, as shown in Figure 2.1. This tells you that building your application caused nine warnings. Choose Build, Build Results (Shift-⌘-B) to see the warnings (see Figure 2.2). Xcode is telling you the methods you need to implement. Clicking an error in the build results shows the location of the error in the lower pane of the Build Results window.

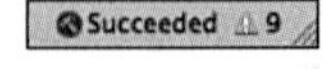

FIGURE 2.1
Status bar

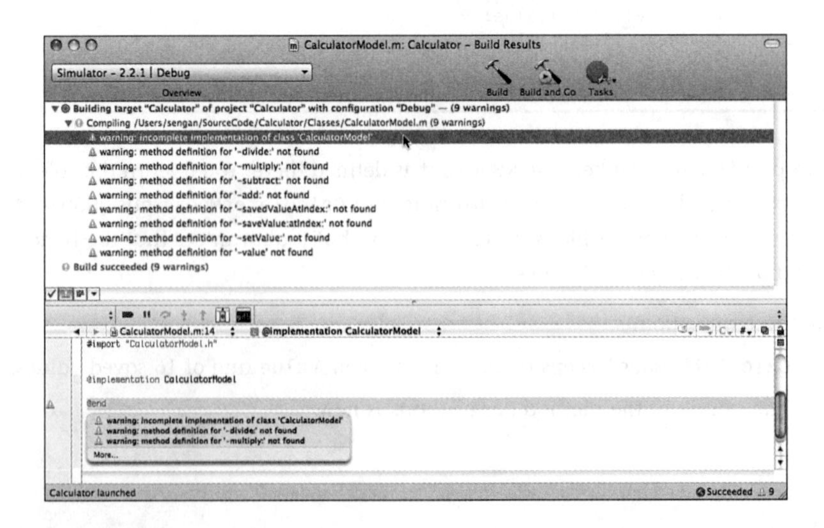

FIGURE 2.2
Build Results window

Xcode reformats the errors and warnings to make them more readable. You can see the tools it invoked and the raw errors by clicking the third small button below the error list (see Figure 2.3). This will help you understand the build process.

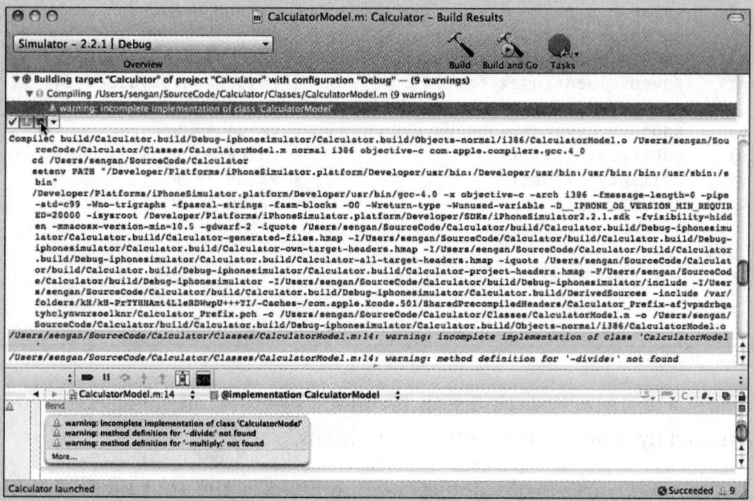

FIGURE 2.3
Raw error list

Implementing Objects

We now need to implement our object's methods. Object methods are defined in an implementation block, and must appear after the interface definition:

```
#import "Name.h"

@implementation Name

+ class    method definition  // Zero to many
{ ... code ... }

- instance method definition  // Zero to many
{ ... code ... }

@end
```

The code sections are laid out just as in C. The compiler does not enforce any layout rules. Listing 2.2 implements the calculator's arithmetic functionality.

LISTING 2.2 CalculatorModel.m

```
#import "CalculatorModel.h"

@implementation CalculatorModel

- (float)   value                             { return value;           };
- (void)    setValue:(float)v                 { value = v;              };
- (void)    saveValue:(float)v atIndex:(int)i { savedValues[i] = v;     };
- (float)   savedValueAtIndex:(int)i          { return savedValues[i]; };

- (void)    add:      (float)v                { value += v; };
- (void)    subtract:(float)v                 { value -= v; };
- (void)    multiply:(float)v                 { value *= v; };
- (void)    divide:   (float)v                { value /= v; };

- (id) init
{ /* SEE DEFINITION BELOW */ }

@end
```

Notice that `CalculatorModel`'s instance variables `value` and `savedValues` are simply referenced by name in the method definitions.

`CalculatorModel`'s instance variables are initialized by the `init` method, which we'll define in the "Initialization" section later in this hour.

Did you Know?

Applications that use classes derived from Cocoa Touch classes, and define or use methods prefixed by an underscore, are liable to break when users upgrade their iPhone firmware. Apple reserves the right to start or stop using any method name prefixed by an underscore without warning. Your application might crash if you use a method that Apple has removed. It will also misbehave if you override a method that Apple now expects to have Apple-defined behavior.

Method Invocation

Objective-C invokes an object *receiver*'s method *method* with the following syntax:

```
[receiver method];
```

A receiver is a pointer to an object to which a message is sent. So, if `calculator` is a pointer to a `CalculatorModel` object, we can write the following:

```
float value = [calculator value];
```

Arguments follow the same syntax as in method declarations:

```
[calculator setValue: 99.0           ];
[calculator saveValue:99.0  atIndex:15];
```

Be aware that the order of the arguments does matter. Writing

```
[calculator atIndex:15 saveValue:99.0];
```

would try to use the `atIndex:saveValue:` method, which does not exist. Method invocation is how Objective-C performs object messaging.

A common complaint about the use of square brackets for method invocation is that you must balance them correctly, which is difficult when deeply nesting method invocations. This is a feature, not a bug, because it forces you not to nest method invocations deeply. Source level debuggers can only step through code on a statement by statement basis. Deeply nested method invocations constitute a single statement that cannot easily be teased apart using a source level debugger. Instead, use temporary variables to document each step. These temporary variables will be optimized away by the compiler when you ship your application, but can be examined while debugging.

Creating Objects

Objects need memory in which to store their instance variables. Creating an object is, thus, a two-step process. First, obtain some memory and then initialize the object. This is discussed in detail in the next section.

Allocating Objects

Instead of using `malloc` as we would to reserve memory for a structure, Objective-C classes use `alloc` class methods. `alloc` is a class method that knows how to determine how much memory must be reserved for each instance of the class.

```
CalculatorModel* model = [CalculatorModel alloc];
```

`NSObject` implements `alloc`, and `CalculatorModel` inherits it. All objects are allocated on the heap. Objects cannot be built on the stack as local variables to a function, nor can they be built statically.

Initialization

By convention, instance methods prefixed by `init` initialize the objects' instance variables. Creating a `CalculatorModel` is, thus, a two-step process:

```
CalculatorModel* model = [CalculatorModel alloc];
[model init]; // BAD
```

For convenience, `init` returns a pointer to the object, so that we can write the following:

```
CalculatorModel* model = [[CalculatorModel alloc] init];
```

Did you Know?

> This book uses the comment `// BAD` to tell you that the code in question is lacking a detail that you'll learn about in the next few paragraphs. The comment is designed to help you when you refer back to code in the book and to avoid overwhelming you with details as you learn.

A class's `init` must not only set up its own instance variables, but also those of its superclass(es): Every `init` method is required to call its superclass' `init` method. Our first attempt looks like this:

```
- (id) init
{
  [super init]; // BAD

  self->value = 0.0;
  for (int i = 0; i < 16; ++i)
    self->savedValues[i] = 0.0;

  return self;
}
```

`self` is a pointer to the method's object (just like `this` in C++, JavaScript, and Java). `super` also points to the method's object, but tells the compiler to invoke the method from the object's superclass. The `id` type is a pointer to any Objective-C object.

Did you Know?

> You might notice the local variable `i` is declared within the `for` statement. This is not enabled by Objective-C but by the C99 dialect of the C language which iPhone Objective-C programs use.

For more flexibility, superclass `init` methods are allowed to return `nil` in case of error or a different pointer. `nil` is Objective-C's null pointer. Clearly, assigning to `self->value` will crash if `self` is `nil`, so we check the following:

```
- (id) init
{
  self = [super init];

  if (self)
  {
    self->value = 0.0;
    for (int i = 0; i < 16; ++i)
      self->savedValues[i] = 0.0;
  }

  return self;
}
```

> A number of Objective-C tutorials incorrectly suggest not assigning to `self`. Do not follow this advice! It is wrong because `init` can return a different pointer than the value of `self` at the beginning. For instance, Core Data does this.

Did you Know?

For convenience, Objective-C does not require the `self->` pointer. Instance variables can be accessed directly as follows:

```
- (id) init
{
  self = [super init];

  if (self)
  {
    value = 0.0;
    for (int i = 0; i < 16; ++i)
      savedValues[i] = 0.0;
  }

  return self;
}
```

What Is `NSObject`?

`NSObject` is the root class for most Objective-C classes: It has no parent, and most Objective-C classes derive from it. `NSObject` defines many methods, such as `alloc` that Cocoa frameworks expect all objects to respond to. By inheriting these methods from `NSObject`, objects avoid reimplementing them. If you want, you can override any of these methods in your own classes with your own implementation. You can even create your own root classes if that proves necessary.

Adding Power Without Adding a Lot of Syntax

Objective-C adds support for object-oriented programming, using very little additional syntax. For instance, both `alloc` and `init` are simply methods, and could have been called something else.

Binding an Object to the User Interface

Cocoa uses a variant of the Model View Controller (MVC) architecture for its GUI. There are a number of variants of the MVC idea, which partition functionality between the view and the controller objects differently. Here, we describe Cocoa's variant. Cocoa's MVC architecture separates a user interface into three parts:

- Model objects contain the data and functionality specific to the application.
- View objects display the state of the model to the user and collect his input.

- **Controller** objects mediate between Model and View objects: They tell the view classes what to draw and the model classes what to do.

The UI elements we used to create the Calculator's UI in Interface Builder are implemented by View classes. For instance, the buttons of the keypad draw themselves, but also receive taps and highlight accordingly. The buttons then inform their controller object that they were tapped, which lets the controller change the model accordingly and refresh the view if necessary.

Creating a Controller

Each user-interface element provided by Cocoa Touch lets you choose a message to send to a controller object of your choice. We'll create a simple `CalculatorController` class with a `pressButton:` method as shown in Listings 2.3 and 2.4.

LISTING 2.3 `CalculatorController.h`

```
#import <Foundation/Foundation.h>

@interface CalculatorController : NSObject

- (void) pressButton:(UIButton*)sender;

@end
```

LISTING 2.4 `CalculatorController.m`

```
#include <stdio.h>
#import  "CalculatorController.h"

@implementation CalculatorController

- (void) pressButton:(UIButton*)sender;
  { fprintf(stderr, "Button pressed!\n"); }

@end
```

Create these files and add them to your project as before. They are `NSObject` subclasses, and type in the listings.

Did you Know?

Objective-C lets you place a semicolon between the function declaration and the code block in function definitions:

```
- (void) pressButton:(UIButton*)sender;  // <- semicolon!
{ fprintf(stderr, "Button pressed!\n"); }
```

This lets you copy and paste function declarations from your header file.

Instantiating `CalculatorController` in Interface Builder

Recall that Interface Builder's Document Window shows objects: a `UIApplication` object, a `CalculatorAppDelegate` object, and a `UIWindow` object. How does Interface Builder know these objects exist? Because it makes them: When your application loads an NIB file, it builds the objects specified by the NIB file. You, too, can tell the NIB file to create objects by dragging them to the Document Window.

Double-click the `MainWindow.xib` file to start Interface Builder.

We would like to create a `CalculatorController` object. However, Interface Builder does not know about `CalculatorController` objects because we just invented them. To tell Interface Builder about custom objects, choose the File, Read Class Files menu item (Option-⌘-R) and select the header file containing the custom object's interface declaration. In this case, choose the `CalculatorController.h` file.

To create an object, open the Library window—choose Library from the Tools menu or type (Shift-⌘-B). Select the Controllers section, and drag an `NSObject` to the document window. Now select the object, and choose the Identity Inspector (the Identity pane of the Inspector panel) and replace the class with the desired custom class. In this case, choose `CalculatorController` (see Figure 2.4).

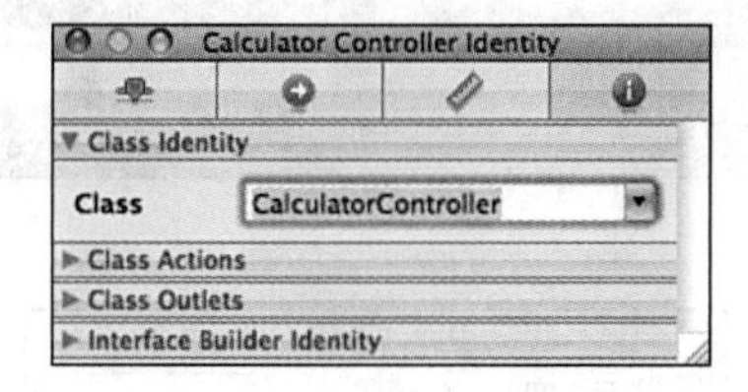

FIGURE 2.4
Class Identity Inspector

To check if `CalculatorController` truly was created, you can define its `init` method:

```
- (id) init
{
  fprintf(stderr, "CalculatorController created");
  return [super init];
}
```

Choose Console from the Run menu (Shift-⌘-R) to open the console window. Click Build & Go on the console window. You should see the message:

```
[Session started at (some time)]
CalculatorController created
```

Actions: Making `pressButton:` a Button Action

We want `pressButton:` to be called when a button is pressed. Methods that can be triggered by UI elements are called actions. Interface Builder provides an easy way to bind a user-interface element to actions: Choose a button on the canvas, press the Ctrl key, and drag the mouse to the Calculator Controller object in the document window (see Figure 2.5). A small menu will appear on the Calculator Controller letting you select the `pressButton:` method (see Figure 2.6). Connect all the buttons in this manner.

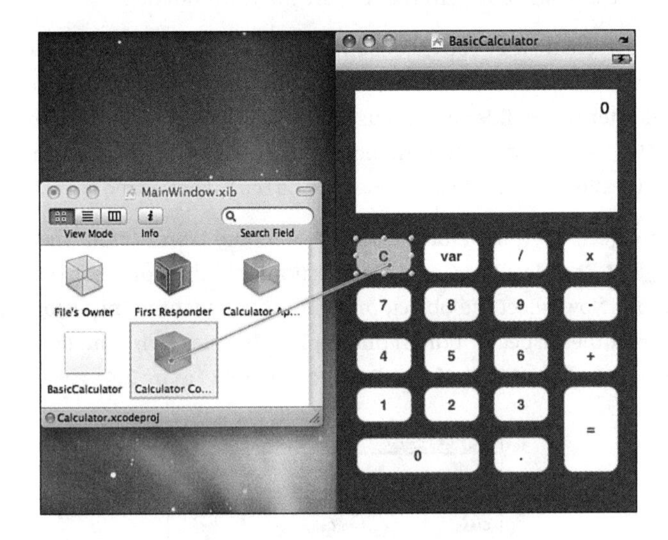

FIGURE 2.5
Binding a button to an action (step 1)

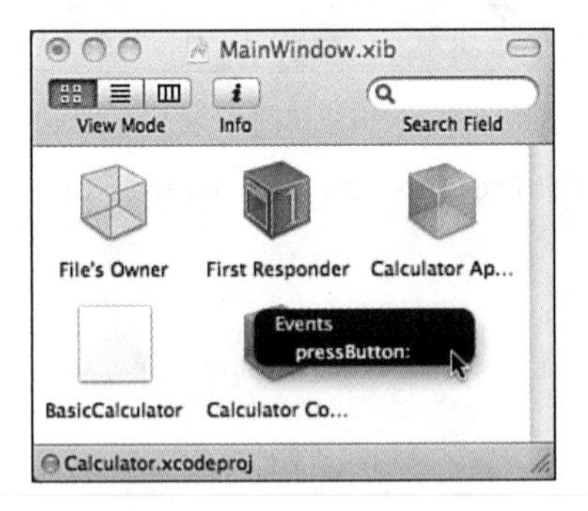

FIGURE 2.6
Binding a button to an action (step 2)

Now rebuild and run from the Console Window. Each time you click a button, you should see a new "Button pressed!" message in the Console.

To see all the buttons connected to the `pressButton:` method, control-click (right-click) the Calculator Controller. A small black window will appear. Click Multiple to see all the buttons (see Figure 2.7). Hovering over a button in the list highlights it on the canvas.

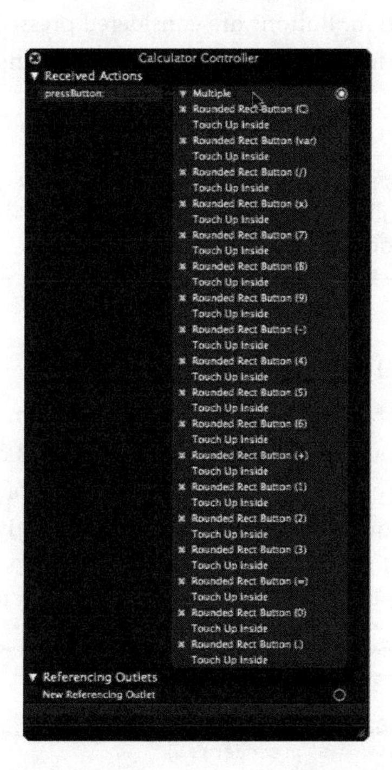

FIGURE 2.7
Calculator Controller's actions

Now control-click (right-click) a button to reveal a window showing all the button's connections (see Figure 2.8). There are two kinds of connections: events and outlets. Events can be bound to object methods, which will be invoked when the event occurs. Outlets are discussed later this hour.

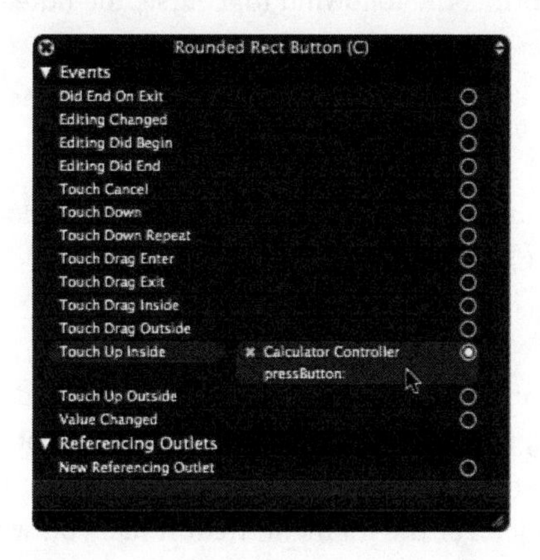

FIGURE 2.8
Button's action

To bind an event to an object's method, control-drag from the event's circle to the controller object as before. When you drag from the UI element to the controller, you set up the default action. Buttons are considered pressed if the user's finger was lying on the button prior to being lifted: This "Touch up, inside" event is the buttons' default action.

Did you Know?

> On a single-button mouse, control-drag means press the Ctrl key and the mouse button and drag. On a many-button mouse, control-drag means press the Ctrl key and the left mouse button and drag.

`sender` and `NSLog()`

We've been using `fprintf` to print the "Button pressed!" message. `NSLog` serves the same purpose in Cocoa, but takes an Objective-C string as an argument, and provides richer conversion specifiers than the `printf` family of functions. Whereas C strings appear between double quotation marks `""`, Objective-C strings appear between `@"` and `"`: One of the new conversion specifiers is `%@`, which is used to print a description of an object. Replace `pressButton:` with the following:

```
- (void) pressButton:(UIButton*)sender;
{ fprintf(stderr, "Button pressed!\n"); }

- (void) pressButton:(UIButton*)sender;
{ NSLog(@"Button pressed: %@\n", sender); }
```

Did you Know?

> This book strikes through source code that is to be replaced so that you know to delete it.

Now pressing buttons prints the following (of course, the date and the number after Calculator will vary):

```
2009-05-16 21:58:02.602 Calculator[67152:20b] Button pressed:
<UIRoundedRectButton: 0x525030>
```

In general, I will omit the first part of the message from the logs, and just show what you asked `NSLog()` to print:

```
Button pressed: <UIRoundedRectButton: 0x525030>
```

The `sender` is the button that received the event and invoked `pressButton:`. We'll see in Hour 4, "Making the Calculator Calculate," why the object is a `UIRoundedRectButton` rather than a `UIButton` as you might have expected from its name in Interface Builder. For the moment, treat it like you would a `UIButton`.

Did you Know?

> Interface Builder understands that `pressButton:` might only be an action for `UIButtons` and classes that inherit from `UIButton` because `sender` is declared to have the type `UIButton*` in the `Calculator Controller`'s interface file. To check this, drag a Segmented Control onto the canvas from the Library window, and try to bind it to `Calculator Controller`. Nothing happens. You can, however, bind it to `First Responder`, which tells you that Segmented Controls can trigger actions.

The API documentation (see Hour 1, "Starting Your First Application: A Calculator," for how to use the documentation) lists `UIButton`'s methods. The button's title is provided by the `currentTitle` method. This lets us print the button's title:

```
- (void) pressButton:(UIButton*)sender;
{ NSLog(@"Button pressed: %@\n", [sender currentTitle]); }
    Button pressed: C
```

Outlets: Writing to the Text View

We'd like `pressButton:` to write to the calculator's screen. The screen is a `UITextView`, whose text is modified by the `setText:` method. Assuming `textView` is known, we can change `pressButton:` to the following:

```
- (void) pressButton:(UIButton*)sender;
{
  NSLog(@"Button pressed: %@\n", [sender currentTitle]);
  [textView setText:[sender currentTitle]];
}
```

For `pressButton:` to access `textView`, we declare it as an instance variable of `CalculatorController`:

```
#import <UIKit/UIKit.h>

@interface CalculatorController : NSObject
{
  IBOutlet UITextView* textView;
}

- (void) pressButton:(UIButton*)sender;

@end
```

You can now compile and run the calculator. Clicking a key prints the debug message, but does not change the `textView`: We need to set `textView` to point to the `UITextView` object that the NIB file will build. To do this, we will use the other kind of connection provided by NIB files: outlets. Outlets are instance variables that point to objects. Update Interface Builder's class definitions by choosing Reload All Classes from the File menu. Control-drag from the `Calculator` object to the Text View: A small black window will appear, letting you choose the textView outlet. Interface Builder will only show outlets prefixed in the header file by IBOutlet as possible outlets. IBOutlet has no effect on the compiled code as it is defined to nothing with #define:

```
#define IBOutlet
```

You can now rebuild. The buttons will now change the textView.

Applications that use classes derived from Cocoa Touch classes and define or use instance variables prefixed by an underscore are liable to break when users upgrade their iPhone firmware. Apple reserves the right to start or stop using any instance variable name prefixed by an underscore without warning. If Apple adds an underscore prefixed instance variable you are using, the instance variable might contain the data you expect, or the data Apple expects. Either way, your application will most likely misbehave.

Accessor and Mutator Methods

NIB files can create objects and set their instance variables directly, using something known as the Key-Value-Coding protocol, which you learn about in Hour 5, "Adding Variables to the Calculator." Accessors, also known as getters and setters, let other classes get and set instance variables. Cocoa Touch frameworks expect getters to have the name of the instance variable and setters to capitalize the first letter of the instance variable and prefix it with set:

```
- (id) init
{
  self = [super init];
  if (self)
    textView = nil;
  return self;
};

- (UITextView*) textView;
{ return textView; }

- (void)        setTextView:(UITextView*)view; // BAD
{ NSLog(@"setTextView : %@", view);           // BAD
  textView = view; };                         // BAD
```

Add these methods to the interface and implementation files and then run. You will see setTextView appear in the console window. However, as you'll learn next, it leaks memory which is why I commented it with // BAD.

Basic Memory Management

The standard C libraries provide minimal memory management: `malloc` lets you request memory from the operating system, and `free` lets you return it to the operating system. Depending on the operating system, using too much memory either causes `malloc` to return `NULL`, or causes your program to be terminated. The iPhone is a memory-starved device, and using too much memory is one of the main reasons applications quit unexpectedly.

The difficulty with the C style of memory management is that memory chunks have only one owner, which decides when to free the memory. A better way is to have each pointer to the memory chunk share partial ownership: Memory should be freed as soon as no pointers point to it, but not before. Think of a time-share. Each owner of a time-share would be very unhappy if the time-share manager sold the property without warning. However, if the time-share owners all foreclose, the time-share manager is free to dispose of the property. Pointers behave similarly. If you're lucky, a pointer that references `freed` memory will crash the program when it is dereferenced. This is nice because the debugger will stop at the offending statement. If you're unlucky, it will point to memory that has not been returned to the OS. In that case, the value obtained by dereferencing the pointer is undefined. The consequences depend on how the value is used, meaning the bug may remain undetected for a long time, corrupting user data. This kind of bug is hard to find.

`NSObject` solves this problem by introducing reference counting. The reference count of an object is the number of owners the object has. Pointers to objects can claim ownership by retaining the object and can release ownership by releasing the object. Once an object has no owners (zero reference count), the memory it occupies is freed. Before the memory is freed, however, the object's `dealloc` method is called. The `dealloc` method closes any files the object owns and releases any objects it owns.

`Calculator Controller` expects `textView` to be accessible every time someone presses a button. Therefore, it should claim ownership in the setter:

```
- (void) setTextView:(UITextView*)view;
{
  NSLog(@"SetTextView from: %@ to %@", textView, view);
  if (view != textView)
  {
    [textView release];
    textView = [view retain];
  }
}
```

```
  SetTextView from: (null) to <UITextView: 0x526af0>
```

The nonequality test ensures that views are not freed before they are retained, which can happen if `textView` and `view` are the same object. You will find out why `[textView release];` works when `textView` is `nil` in the next section.

The retain count of an object can be obtained by sending it a `retainCount` message:

```
NSObject* obj = [NSObject alloc];
NSLog(@"Retain count after allocation: %d", [obj retainCount]);
[obj init];
NSLog(@"Retain count after initialization: %d", [obj retainCount]);
[obj release];
NSLog(@"Retain count after release: %d", [obj retainCount]); // BAD
```

```
Retain count after allocation: 1
Retain count after initialization: 1
FREED(id): message retainCount sent to freed object=0x520970
```

The object returned by `alloc` is assumed to have an owner (otherwise, it would be freed before it could be initialized): Its retain count is one. `init` does not change the retain count. `release` decrements the retain count to zero and, therefore, frees the object.

Invoking methods on freed objects is an error. With the previous code, we were lucky and Objective-C detected the error. It caused the program to stop in the debugger. (We discuss using the debugger in more detail in Hour 3, "Simplifying Your Code.")

Before `CalculatorController` is freed, it should release ownership of `textView`: Once it is freed, no pointers should point to the `textView`, which will therefore also be freed:

```
- (void) dealloc;
{
  [self  setTextView:nil];
  [super dealloc];
}
```

This implementation of `dealloc` uses an Objective-C stylistic pattern of using `textView`'s setter to release ownership. This pattern keeps all `retain` and `release` invocations in a single, simple, often-repeated function, reducing the chance of error. This pattern is so common that more advanced functionality such as the Key-Value-Observing protocol (explained in Hour 5, "Adding Variables to the Calculator") and Core Data (explained in Hour 18, "Using Core Data") rely on it.

You will find out why `[self setTextView:nil];` works in the next section.

> Beware! Terminating an application does not automatically release its objects. You must release them yourself in your Application Delegate's `applicationWillTerminate:` method. Application Delegates are described in Hour 6 "Understanding How the User Interface Is Built." You can check this yourself by adding a call to `NSLog` in `dealloc`.

Invoking Methods on nil

In Objective-C, sending messages to nil is safe and harmless: Nothing happens.

If the message returns an object, the result is guaranteed to be nil. This is what makes the following line in dealloc work.

```
textView = [view retain];
```

Although the result is not guaranteed to be zero for any nonobject result, in practice, it is zero for pointers, Booleans, integers, and floating-point numbers but not for structures.

Did you Know?

On both the simulator and the iPhone, the return value is zero (nil, 0, 0.0, or NO) for integral types, pointers, and floating-point values. However, the simulator zeroes out structures smaller than 8 bytes (such as NSRange), whereas the iPhone does not. Another difference is that the iPhone does not support long doubles, whereas the simulator does. This difference is a source of bugs that appear only on the iPhone and not in the simulator.

Objective-C's nil behavior can be confusing: If you have written code that should do something, but nothing is happening, check to see if the object is nil. A particularly nonobvious incarnation of this error occurs when you forget to connect an outlet in Interface Builder. We encountered this error in the "Outlets: Writing to the Text View" section when we implemented setTextView: but had not yet bound textView to the UITextView in Interface Builder.

Type Checking Rules

A strength of Objective-C is that it lets you use as much static and as much dynamic typing as you want. Objective-C's attitude is very pragmatic: Static type checking is not always necessary—use it where it is useful and avoid it where it causes more difficulty than benefit.

Static Typing

Static typing helps you find bugs where you thought a variable contained one kind of object but it really contained another. Compilers type check programs and report errors or warnings if the program contains any type error. Most of the time, static typing is useful. Sometimes, it is not. In C, you can escape type checking by explicitly casting variables to different types.

Objective-C extends C's static type rules by allowing you to use class names as variable types in code.

Type Equivalence

A variable declared to be of a given class type may only point to an object of that class or to an object that inherits from that class. This rule allows subclasses to be used wherever the superclass is used.

```
NSObject*               nsObject;
CalculatorController* calcObject;
nsObject   = [[NSObject             alloc] init];  // OK
calcObject = [[CalculatorController alloc] init];  // OK
calcObject = nsObject;                             // Error
nsObject   = calcObject;                           // OK
```

Because `CalculatorObject` is a child of `NSObject`, `nsObject` can point to it. Because `NSObject` is not a child of `CalculatorObject`, `calcObject` cannot point to it. Although the Objective-C compiler does not abort compilation if it detects a class type mismatch, it produces a warning:

```
  warning: assignment from distinct Objective-C type
```

In most cases, you should consider this warning to be an error and determine its cause. In the extremely unlikely event that you know better than the compiler, you can use a C-cast to override the error.

Type Checking

Pointers to objects of a particular class type should only be used as receivers of methods declared or inherited by that class. This rule guarantees that every object that the pointer can reference has the methods invoked by the code.

For instance, although `CalculatorController` declares `setTextView:`, `NSObject` does not:

```
NSObject* oops = [[CalculatorController alloc] init];
[oops setTextView:nil];
  warning: 'NSObject' may not respond to '-setTextView:'
  warning: (Messages without a matching method signature will be assumed to
return 'id' and accept '...' as arguments.)
```

Even if you disagree with the compiler, generally assume that it is right.

Dynamic Typing

Dynamic type checking determines whether an object has the methods invoked at runtime. If the object lacks the method, an exception is generated:

```
- (void) pressButton:(id)sender;
{ [textView setYoyo:[sender currentTitle]]; }
  # *** -[UITextView setYoyo:]: unrecognized selector sent to instance 0x526af0
```

We examine this mechanism in more detail in Hour 13, "Adding Undo and Redo Functionality." The application then terminates as no user defined exception handler caught the exception. Objective-C always performs dynamic type checking, even if the program was statically type checked.

Escaping Static Typing: `id`

As Objective-C always performs dynamic type checking, it is safe to drop static type checking. Furthermore, source code filled with type-casts is unpleasant to read and write. Although Objective-C's static typing rules would not appear to allow it, the `id` type provides the solution to the restrictions associated with static typing. Instead of writing the following:

```
NSObject* oops = [[CalculatorController alloc] init];
[oops setTextView:nil];
  warning: 'NSObject' may not respond to '-setValue:'
  warning: (Messages without a matching method signature will be assumed to
return 'id' and accept '...' as arguments.)
```

We write:

```
id oops = [[CalculatorModel alloc] init];
[oops setValue:9.0];
```

`id` causes no warnings because `id` is not a pointer to an Objective-C class, so the compiler does not check method invocations against known method declarations. Instead, `id` is a pointer to a structure whose first element is a pointer to a class structure:

```
typedef struct objc_class                *Class;
typedef struct objc_object { Class isa; } *id;
```

All Objective-C objects have this layout. This means that `id` can even point to those rare objects that are not derived from `NSObject` such as `NSProxy`. The `isa` pointer is used for method lookup, dynamic type checking, and instance variable access.

Objective-C lets `id` be cast into any Objective-C class silently, so that you can write the following:

```
NSObject* oops = [[CalculatorController alloc] init];
```

Recall that init returns an id. However, this also means you can write the following without causing an error:

```
CalculatorController* calcObject = [[NSObject alloc] init];  // No error
detected!
```

The Objective-C compiler emits an invalid receiver type warning if a method's receiver is not a pointer to an Objective-C object or to a structure objc_object. You might encounter this error when using toll-free bridging (described in Hour 7).

Argument Types

Escaping static typing has a downside: If a method is invoked on an id receiver or argument, all the methods that share its name must agree on the type of each argument and the type of return value. The compiler performs a consistency check, and issues a warning if any of the methods' argument lists or return types conflict, or if no method declaration can be found. This limitation exists to guarantee that the compiler can build a single kind of argument list on the stack that will satisfy whichever method ends up being invoked, and to guarantee it can do something useful with the result. This also goes some way toward explaining Objective-C's extremely long, pedantic, and verbose method names.

Because typing extremely long Objective-C names is painful, Xcode provides Code Sense to reduce the amount of required typing. It tries to guess what you're typing and complete it for you. Typing Return accepts the current completion. Typing Ctrl+. provides another autocompletion, letting you step through the possibilities. To see the entire list, press the Esc key. Many autocompletions come with placeholders, such as the arguments of a function, which are highlighted in blue. Typing Ctrl+/ jumps to the next placeholder. Xcode's preferences let you customize Code Sense.

Summary

Objective-C supports object-oriented programming with a few simple, but well-chosen additions to the C language: objects, object method invocation syntax, and extensions to the type rules. The Foundation object NSObject provides the basic pattern used for memory management: reference counting. In the next hour, you learn an extension to this pattern, which further simplifies memory management.

Interface Builder lets you instantiate objects and bind them to the user interface. It is able to glean user-defined actions and outlets from source files, and it uses static type checking to ensure actions can only be bound to the correct UI elements.

To learn how to use object-oriented programming to architect your applications, consider reading *Object-Oriented Analysis and Design* by Grady Booch.

Q&A

Q. ***Do all Objective-C objects have a parent?***

A. No, `NSObject` has no parent. There is no requirement that every object must have a parent. However, the Objective-C runtime does expect most of `NSObject`'s methods to be defined. As `NSObject` provides all these methods, there's no good reason to rewrite them.

Workshop

The Workshop consists of quiz questions and answers to help you solidify your understanding of the material covered in this hour. You should try to answer the questions before checking the answers.

Quiz Questions

1. What is an `@interface` block?
2. What is an `@implementation` block?
3. What syntax is used to invoke a method?
4. What is a receiver?
5. What is dynamic type checking?
6. What is static type checking?

Quiz Answers

1. An `@interface` block declares the data (instance variables) and methods a class provides.
2. An `@implementation` block provides the implementation of a class's methods.

3. Method invocations use square brackets. The first item is the object whose method is being invoked. For methods with no arguments, the second item is the selector. For instance to invoke the method `sleep` on the object `john` you would write

   ```
   [john sleep]
   ```

   The selectors of methods with multiple arguments use a colon (`:`) to specify the location of each argument (and must be terminated by a colon). In method invocations, each argument is written after the appropriate colon.

   To invoke the method `eat:with:` on the object `john` using the arguments `theFish` and `theKnife` you would write:

   ```
   [john eat:theFish with:theKnife];
   ```

4. The receiver is the object that receives the message: the object on which the method is invoked.

5. At runtime, Objective-C dynamically checks the receiver of each method invocation to see whether it implements the invoked method. If it does not, an exception is generated.

6. The compiler statically checks your program to ensure that only objects whose types match are used interchangeably. It emits errors or warnings if your program does not type check.

Exercise

This exercise is designed to check your understanding of classes and inheritance. Consider a role-playing game with a number of characters. Each character needs to eat and drink. Create a `Character` class which provides the `eat:` and `drink:` methods. Create `Food` and `Liquid` classes that provide the `calories` and `hydration` methods. Create two subclasses of `Characters` for male and female characters who need different amounts of nourishment and `hydration`. After a character eats food, his stored calorie count should increase—similarly with drinking. Test this using `NSLog()`. For now, you can place your test code in the `pressButton:` method and run it by pressing the button.

HOUR 3
Simplifying Your Code

What You'll Learn in this Hour:

- **Managing memory with** `NSAutoReleasePools`
- **Using Objective-C strings**
- **Using the debugger**
- **Understanding object messaging**
- **Debugging a real bug**
- **Using shorthands: the dot notation and properties**

A key Objective-C idea is to recognize commonly occurring code patterns and to replace them with library functions. This helps you keep fewer details in mind, and reduces the amount of code you must write and debug. `NSAutoReleasePools` simplify memory management. `NSStrings` simplify string handling by providing good Unicode support. Messaging, dot notation, and properties simplify method invocation.

This hour also introduces the debugger, another tool to help you understand how Objective-C works.

Managing Memory with `NSAutoReleasePools`

So far, if a function or a method wants to return an object, it must return it with a nonzero retain count because it is deallocated as soon as its retain count reaches zero. Releasing the object becomes the caller's responsibility. As a programmer, you must release objects created by the functions you call, leading to more code—and more memory leaks.

In the rest of this section, you'll use an example based on `NSString`, which we discuss in more detail in the "Objective-C Strings" section later in this hour. To understand the example, you only need to know that NSStrings can be created from C strings with the initWithCString: initializer.

For instance, if we are limited to using retain and release, and we want to convert a C string to an Objective-C string to use with NSLog(), we have to write the following:

```
char      test[] = "Test";
NSString* oTest  = [[NSString alloc] initWithCString:test];
NSLog(oTest);
[oTest release];
```

Instead, wouldn't it be nice if we could avoid releasing oTest? Then we could write:

```
char test[] = "Test";
NSLog([NSString stringWithCString:test]);
```

In this section, you'll discover how to do this.

Using Sample Code

In this hour, you'll create the smallest legal iPhone program. Begin by making a new Window project and calling it SimpleTest. Type Listing 3.1 into main.m.

LISTING 3.1 main.m

```
int main(int argc, char *argv[])
{
  char      test[] = "Test";
  NSString* oTest  = [[NSString alloc] initWithCString:test];
  NSLog(oTest);
  [oTest release];

  sleep(1);
  return 0;
}
```

Choose Console from the Run menu. Set the target to Simulator | Debug. Click on the Build and Go button in the Console Window. As in C, main() is invoked. NSLog() prints Test to the Console Window.

The sleep(1) line gives Xcode the chance to connect to the test application before it exits so that Xcode does not get confused.

Xcode sometimes does not recognize that a program has stopped, and will print Cannot launch in simulator while it is already in use to the console. Simply exit the simulator to fix the problem.

The Idea Behind NSAutorelease Pools

We want functions that return an object to be able to specify that the returned object should be released after their callers have run. To do this, we can require such functions to add returned objects to a global pool, which will retain them temporarily:

```
[pool   addObject:result];
[result release];
return  result;
```

As the pool must remember objects, its memory consumption depends on the number of objects added to it.

The pool must be created before it is used and then be `released` afterwards. Therefore we'll set it up before invoking any functions that use it, and release it once they have returned:

```
static ReleasePool* pool = nil; // global variable

int main(int argc, char *argv[])
{
  pool = [[ReleasePool alloc] init];

  // Do some work, calling our functions

  [pool release];
  return 0;
}
```

Now every object that is added to the pool will be freed. The callers' code is simplified, at the price of a small increase of complexity in the callee. This is a good tradeoff, as many callers will call the same callee.

NSAutoReleasePool

The `Foundation` library provides an efficient version of the `ReleasePool` described previously, called NSAutoReleasePool.

Instead of writing

```
[pool   addObject:result];
[result release];
return result;
```

you can write

```
return [result autorelease];
```

The autorelease method adds the object to the global pool, releases it, and returns it. autorelease is an NSObject method, and as every Objective-C object must derive from NSObject, autorelease is available to all Objective-C objects.

Using NSAutoReleasePool, main() is rewritten as follows:

```
int main(int argc, char *argv[])
{
  NSAutoreleasePool* pool = [[NSAutoreleasePool alloc] init];

  char test[] = "Test";
  NSLog([NSString stringWithCString:test]);

  [pool release];

  sleep(1);
  return 0;
}
```

Did you Know?

Errors are reported if you run code without an NSAutoReleasePool in place:

```
2009-05-05 12:12:44.901 SimpleTest[14665:20b] *** _NSAutoreleaseNoPool():
Object 0x508710 of class NSCFString autoreleased with no pool in place - just
leaking
Stack: (0x90a9073f 0x9099ce32)
```

In most situations, you will not encounter this error.

Naming Conventions

NSAutoReleasePools are widely used throughout Cocoa. The convention is that any new object created by a function or method is autoreleased, unless the method name starts with init or is new.

```
NSString* surname   = [[NSString alloc] initWithString:@"Baring-Gould"];
NSString* firstName = [NSString stringWithString:@"Sengan"];
```

surname must be released, but firstName is already autoreleased, and should not be released again. Errors of this form are sometimes automatically detected as demonstrated by Listing 3.2.

LISTING 3.2 main.m

```
int main(int argc, char *argv[])
{
  NSAutoreleasePool* pool = [[NSAutoreleasePool alloc] init];

  char test[] = "Test";
  NSString*     crash = [NSString stringWithCString:test];
  NSLog(crash);
  [crash release]; // BAD
```

LISTING 3.2 Continued

```
  [pool release];

  sleep(1);
  return 0;
}
```

Listing 3.2 returns the following error:

```
SimpleTest(15042) malloc: *** error for object 0x509410: double free
*** set a breakpoint in malloc_error_break to debug
```

You'll learn to set breakpoints later this hour.

Sometimes, however, releasing auto-released objects is not detected, and causes a bad access fault (`EXC_BAD_ACCESS`) in `NSPopAutoreleasePool()`, which tries to release it again when releasing the autorelease pool.

> **Did you Know?**
> It is difficult to debug `EXC_BAD_ACCESS` faults in `NSPopAutoreleasePool()`. You'll learn how to do this in Hour 22, "Debugging."

Downsides to NSAutoReleasePools

`NSAutoReleasePools` have a few downsides: They increase your application's memory usage, and they are slower than calling `release`.

Memory Usage Increases

Autoreleased objects are only released once the autorelease pool is drained. If your code creates many temporary objects, only to autorelease them, you might run out of memory. In such cases, you can either insert more autorelease pools into your code or avoid using autoreleased objects. Judicious positioning of autorelease pools into your code can reduce the number of temporary objects kept at a time. However, I prefer to avoid using autoreleased objects where possible in such cases.

Your Application Slows Slightly

Adding objects to a pool and then releasing them later takes longer than simply releasing them. Therefore, you should prefer the following

```
- (void) setProperty:(id)p
{
  if (property != p)
  {
    [property release];
    property = [p retain];
  }
}
```

to the following shorter version:

```
- (void) setProperty:(id)p
{
  [property autorelease];
   property = [p retain];
}
```

Exception Handling Is Made More Complex

Exceptions are rarely used in Cocoa, but it is worth noting that they are autoreleased. This section explains how they interact with `NSAutoReleasePools`, but this will be most useful to you when you encounter a bug of this form.

If you are concerned that an exception might be thrown after a pool was created but before it was released, you can release the pool in a `@finally` block. But as releasing the pool will also release the exception, you cannot safely rethrow. Instead, retain it, and then autorelease it and rethrow:

```
NSAutoreleasePool* pool          = [[NSAutoreleasePool alloc] init];
id                 autoreleaseMe = nil;

@try
{ /* do some stuff */ }

@catch (id) exception
{ autoreleaseMe = [exception retain];
  @throw; }

@finally
{ [pool release];
  [autoreleaseMe autorelease]; };
```

Exceptions are discussed further in Hour 4, "Making the Calculator Calculate."

Objective-C Strings

The `NSString` class provides Cocoa's support for Unicode text strings. Unicode strings can display the text of most of the world's languages. However, the power of `NSString` comes at a cost: It has over 120 different methods. In this hour, you'll learn the most commonly used methods.

Creating `NSStrings`

`NSStrings` can be created with literals, from C-strings or UTF-8 strings, or by using a formatting string just as is done with `sprintf()` in C.

NSString **Literals**

The compiler recognizes literals that use the notation `@"string"`, and creates `NSString`s for them:

```
int main(int argc, char *argv[])
{
  NSString* test = @"test";
  NSLog(test);
  sleep(1);
  return 0;
}
```

The compiler concatenates sequences of string literals:

```
NSLog(@"Hello" @" " @"World");
```

Unicode literals are supported in two ways. Using the notation, or by simply typing them into a Unicode source file:

```
NSLog(@"\u00e9 é");
```

Did you Know?

In Xcode, you can type é by typing (Option-e-e) and ß by typing (Option-s). Apple documents these keyboard shortcuts at the following URL: http://www.apple.com/pro/tips/type_european.html

Did you Know?

You cannot use the notation for values less than 0x20, or in the range 0x7F-0x9F inclusive, or if the value designates a character in the basic source character set. The compiler will reject the program with the following error:

```
\u0085 is not a valid universal character
```

Creating NSStrings

`NSString`s can be created from C strings, UTF-8 strings (a form of Unicode that uses an 8-bit encoding), or raw data. The `init` methods are all of the form `initWith`*`something`*. We've already used `initWithCString` in Listing 3.1. There are `stringWith`*`something`* variants to obtain autoreleased strings, as shown in Listing 3.2.

`NSString`s can be built using a format string. Format strings contain characters and conversion specifiers. Characters are simply copied to the result. The *n*th conversion specifier converts the *n+1*th argument to a string, which is added to the result.

```
int main(int argc, char *argv[])
{
  NSAutoreleasePool* pool = [[NSAutoreleasePool alloc] init];

  NSLog([NSString stringWithFormat:@"Was passed %d arguments", argc]);

  [pool release];
```

```
  sleep(1);
  return 0;
}
```

NSLog() uses the same format. We can write the following:

```
NSLog(@"Was passed %d arguments", argc);
```

Table 3.1 shows common conversion specifiers.

TABLE 3.1 Common Conversion Specifiers

Specifier	Description
%@	Objective-C object, printed as the string returned by descriptionWithLocale: if available, or description otherwise; also works with CFTypeRef objects, returning the result of the CFCopyDescription function
%%	'%' character
%d, %D, %i	Signed 32-bit integer (int)
%u, %U	Unsigned 32-bit integer (unsigned int)
%x	Unsigned 32-bit integer (unsigned int), printed in hexadecimal using the digits 0-9 and lowercase a-f
%qX	Unsigned 64-bit integer (unsigned long long), printed in hexadecimal using the digits 0-9 and uppercase A-F
%o, %O	Unsigned 32-bit integer (unsigned int), printed in octal
%f	64-bit floating-point number (double)
%e	64-bit floating-point number (double), printed in scientific notation using a lowercase e to introduce the exponent
%g	64-bit floating-point number (double), printed in the style of %e if the exponent is less than -4 or greater than or equal to the precision, in the style of %f otherwise
%c	8-bit unsigned character (unsigned char), printed by NSLog() as an ASCII character, or, if not an ASCII character, in the octal format \\ddd or the Unicode hexadecimal format \\udddd, where *d* is a digit
%C	16-bit Unicode character (unichar), printed by NSLog() as an ASCII character, or, if not an ASCII character, in the octal format \\ddd or the Unicode hexadecimal format \\udddd, where *d* is a digit
%s	Null-terminated array of 8-bit unsigned characters. %s interprets its input in the system encoding rather than, for example, UTF-8.
%p	Void pointer (void *), printed in hexadecimal with the digits 0-9 and lowercase a-f, with a leading 0x

If there are more arguments than conversion specifiers, no harm is done. However, if there are more conversion specifiers than arguments, invalid data can be shown. Be aware that these functions can crash during conversion if a conversion specifier does not match the object's type.

Did you Know?

The compiler will type check conversion specifiers if you add GCC_WARN_TYPE-CHECK_CALLS_TO_PRINTF to the User-Defined Settings in the Build Settings. Right-click the project and click the Get Info item in the context menu. Click on the lower-left button and choose Add User-Defined Setting. Create the setting with key GCC_WARN_TYPECHECK_CALLS_TO_PRINTF and value YES.

Objects' Description Methods

The object conversion specifier (%@) works because `NSObject` defines a `description` method, which returns the string to print. You can override this method to tailor it to objects you define. Listing 3.3 defines a complex number class and shows an example implementation of `descriptionU`.

LISTING 3.3 `main.m`

```
@interface Complex : NSObject
{
  float imaginary;
  float real;
}

- (id) initWithRealComponent:(float)r imaginaryComponent:(float)i;
@end


@implementation Complex
- (id) initWithRealComponent:(float)r imaginaryComponent:(float)i
{
  self = [super init];
  if (self)
  { imaginary = i;
    real      = r; }
  return self;
}

- (NSString*) description
{
  return [NSString stringWithFormat:@"Complex Number (%g, %g)",
                                                real, imaginary];
}

@end

int main(int argc, char *argv[])
{
  Complex* c = [[Complex alloc] initWithRealComponent:1.0
                                   imaginaryComponent:2.0];
```

LISTING 3.3 Continued

```
    NSLog(@"Object is : %@", c);
    [c release];
    sleep(1);
    return 0;
}
```

Decomposing Strings

NSString provides a variety of methods to help cut strings into pieces. For each method, I'll give an example and show the corresponding output.

Slicing Strings

`substringWithRange:`*range* returns a string of the characters lying within *range*. *range* is an `NSRange`, which is a structure consisting of a `location` (the beginning of the range) and a `length`:

```
typedef struct _NSRange
  { NSUInteger location;
    NSUInteger length; } NSRange;
```

The function `NSMakeRange(`*location*`,` *length*`)` builds a range. Returning a structure is rare in C or C++, but is very common in Objective-C.

```
NSString* fullString = @"The quick brown fox jumped over the lazy dog";
NSLog([fullString substringWithRange:NSMakeRange(16,3)]);
Fox
```

Splitting Strings Up

`componentsSeparatedByString:`*separatorString* splits the string wherever it finds *separatorString*. It returns an array of strings. You'll study arrays in Hour 5, "Adding Variables to the Calculator." For now, you just need to know that `NSLog()` can display arrays.

```
int main(int argc, char *argv[])
{
  NSAutoreleasePool* pool = [[NSAutoreleasePool alloc] init];
  NSString*  rockyPlanets = @"Mercury, Venus, Earth, Mars, Pluto";
  NSLog(@"%@", [rockyPlanets componentsSeparatedByString:@", "]);
  [pool release];
  sleep(1);
  return 0;
}
```

`componentsSeparatedByCharactersInSet:`*characterSet* splits the string wherever it finds a character that belongs to *characterSet*. *characterSet* is an instance of the class `NSCharacterSet`, which provides shorthands for many commonly used sets, such as whitespaceAndNewlineCharacterSet. You can also build your own character set from a string using characterSetWithCharactersInString:*string*.

```
NSString*       text = @"There\tare\nalmost\u30007\u00a0billion people";
NSCharacterSet* ws   = [NSCharacterSet whitespaceAndNewlineCharacterSet];
NSLog(@"%@", [text componentsSeparatedByCharactersInSet:ws]);
(
There,
are,
almost,
7,
billion,
people
)
```

Individual Characters of an NSString

Characters can be accessed using the characterAtIndex: method:

```
NSString*  decomposed = @"e\u0301";
unichar    char0      = [decomposed characterAtIndex:0];
unichar    char1      = [decomposed characterAtIndex:1];
NSLog(@"Character at index 0 : 0x%x,  at index 1 : 0x%x", char0, char1);
```

The number of characters returned by length is not the same as the number of glyphs that are drawn:

```
NSLog(@"Length of é and é : %d %d", [@"\u00e9" length], [@"e\u0301" length]);
```

Comparing Strings

String comparison is used not only to check for equality or to find a substring within a string, but also to sort strings. The following sections discuss some common methods used to compare strings.

NSString Equality

NSString's isEqualToString: method checks literal equivalence: Do the two strings contain the same characters and are they of the same length?

```
NSLog([@"Hello" isEqualToString:@"H" "ello"] ? @"Equal" : @"Not");
Equal
```

Two strings might not be equal even if they result in the same glyphs being drawn. For instance, there are two ways of writing an é: \u00e9 and e\u0301. (The next section explains this in detail.) They are not equal:

```
NSLog([NSString stringWithFormat:@"\\u00e9 is equal to e\\u0301 : %@",
      [@"\u00e9" isEqualToString:@"e\u0301"] ? @"YES" : @"NO"]);
\u00e9 is equal to e\u0301 : NO
```

The `hasPrefix` and `hasSuffix` methods indicate whether strings share the beginning or ending characters of the argument:

```
NSLog([@"colorado" hasPrefix:@"color"] ? @"YES" : @"NO");
YES
```

Sorting `NSStrings`

The rules for sorting words (lexographic sorting) differ in different languages. For instance, "ch" is treated as a single letter for sorting purposes in Spanish. `compare:options:range:locale:` sorts strings appropriately for the chosen locale (an instance of `NSLocale`):

```
- (NSComparisonResult) compare:(NSString*) searchString
                       options:(NSStringCompareOptions) mask
                         range:(NSRange) range
                        locale:(id) locale
```

Options are available to modify the search to support case insensitive search, or natural ordering of numeric values embedded in text. *`range`* specifies the part of the receiver that will be compared against *`searchString`*. *`locale`* specifies the language rules to use.

For instance, comparing the first four characters of "`File3`" with "`file`" returns identical when case insensitive search is used:

```
NSComparisonResult up = [@"File3" compare: @"file"
                                  options: NSCaseInsensitiveSearch
                                  range:   NSMakeRange(0,4)
                                  locale:  [NSLocale currentLocale]];
NSLog(@"subrange %@", up == NSOrderedSame ? @"Identical" : @"Different");
subrange Identical
```

Without numeric search, `file3` is sorted after `file25` because 3 comes after 2. With numeric search, `file3` is sorted before `file25` because 3 is smaller than 25:

```
NSComparisonResult up;

up = [@"file3" compare: @"file25"
               options: 0
                 range:   NSMakeRange(0,5)
                locale:  [NSLocale currentLocale]];

NSLog(@"nonNumericSearch -- file3 %@ file25",
      up == NSOrderedAscending ? @"<" : @">");

up = [@"file3" compare: @"File25"
               options: NSCaseInsensitiveSearch | NSNumericSearch
               range:   NSMakeRange(0,5)
               locale:  [NSLocale currentLocale]];
```

```
NSLog(@"Numeric search -- file3 %@ file25",
     up == NSOrderedAscending ? @"<" : @">");
```

```
nonNumericSearch -- file3 > file25
Numeric search -- file3 < file25
```

Two shorthands are provided to encourage you to use the `currentLocale` wherever the ordering is visible to the user.

`[str localizedCompare:searchString]` is a shorthand for

```
[str compare:searchString options:0
       range:NSMakeRange(0, [str length]) locale:[NSLocale currentLocale]];
```

`[str localizedCaseInsensitiveCompare:searchString]` is a shorthand for

```
[str compare:searchString options:NSCaseInsensitiveSearch
       range:NSMakeRange(0, [str length]) locale:[NSLocale currentLocale]];
```

Finding Substrings

`rangeOfString:`*`searchString`* returns the location in the string of the first occurrence of *searchString*:

```
NSString* str   = @"LondonOsloParisMunich";
NSRange   range = [str rangeOfString:@"Oslo"];
NSLog(@"Oslo is at (%d,%d)", range.location, range.length);
Oslo is at (6,4)
```

It returns `{NSNotFound, 0}` if *searchString* does not appear.

`rangeOfString:`*`searchString`* `options:`*`options`* provides case insensitive search:

```
NSString* str   = @"LondonOsloParisMunich";
NSRange   range = [str rangeOfString:@"osLo" options:NSCaseInsensitiveSearch];
NSLog(@"Oslo is at (%d,%d)", range.location, range.length);
Oslo is at (6,4)
```

`rangeOfString:`*`searchString`* `options:`*`options`* `range:`*`range`* searches substrings:

```
NSString* str   = @"LondonOsloParisOsloMunich";
NSRange   range = NSMakeRange(8, [str length]-8);
          range = [str rangeOfString:@"Oslo" options:0 range:range];
NSLog(@"Oslo is at (%d,%d)", range.location, range.length);
Oslo is at (15,4)
```

The `rangeOfString:` methods return a structure. As mentioned in Hour 2, “Handling Interaction,” when invoked on `nil`, such methods return undefined values.

Transforming Strings

Converting Case

The rules for converting between upper- and lowercase letters are language dependent. For instance, a lowercase 'ß' in German is converted to an uppercase 'SS', but the conversion is not guaranteed to be symmetric:

```
NSLog([[@"Straße"  uppercaseString] isEqualToString: @"STRASSE"]
      ? @"YES" : @"NO");
NSLog([[@"STRASSE" lowercaseString] isEqualToString: @"strasse"]
      ? @"YES" : @"NO");
YES
YES
```

Adding NSStrings

New strings can be created by adding strings together using `stringByAppendingString` or `stringByAppendingFormat`:

```
NSString* quickFox  = [@"Quick" stringByAppendingString:@" Fox"];
NSLog(quickFox);
Quick Fox
```

In the next hour, you'll learn how to modify strings, which is the usual way strings are added together.

Replacing Substrings

`stringByReplacingCharactersInRange:`*range* `withString:`*replacementString* replaces the characters in the range *range* with *replacementString*:

```
NSString* dotMac   = @"Dot Mac is Apple's online service";
NSString* mobileMe = @"MobileMe";
NSRange   range    = NSMakeRange(0, 7);
NSLog([dotMac stringByReplacingCharactersInRange:range withString:mobileMe]);
mobileMe is Apple's online service
```

`stringByReplacingOccurrencesOfString:`*searchString* `withString:`*replacementString* finds occurrences of *searchString* and replaces them with *replacementString*:

```
NSString* sentence = @"This is a four-colour book";
NSString* english  = @"colour";
NSString* american = @"color";
NSLog([sentence stringByReplacingOccurrencesOfString:english
withString:american]);
This is a four-color book
```

Combining Substrings into an NSString

Just as componentsSeparatedByString:*separatorString* splits an NSString into pieces, NSArray's componentsJoinedByString:*string* combines them into a string:

```
NSArray *innerPlanets = [NSArray arrayWithObjects:@"Mercury", @"Venus", nil];
NSLog([innerPlanets componentsJoinedByString:@" "]);
Mercury Venus
```

Multilanguage Support with Unicode

C strings represent text as an array of 8-bit characters, using 1 byte per character. This works well for English, which only needs 7 bits per character (allowing 128 distinct characters to be shown). It does not work well for other languages, such as Traditional Han Chinese, which has over 70,000 characters. Over time, many standards evolved to support the languages of the world. Unicode is an effort to provide a single encoding for any script in any language.

NSStrings are conceptually arrays of 16-bit characters, using 2 bytes per character. These 16-bit characters are called UTF-16 units. Each English character corresponds to a UTF-16 unit. However, this is not true for other languages: 16 bits can only represent 65,536 distinct characters, still not enough for Traditional Han Chinese.

The character set is extended by using many UTF-16 units for a single character. For instance, rarer characters are represented by pairs of UTF-16 units called **surrogate pairs**. Alternatively, characters can be built from a base letter plus an accent or other decoration, as we saw for é: The base letter is e and the accent is \u0301. A similar idea applies to Korean and Indic languages where many UTF-16 units are combined to build a character. Unicode-aware string libraries must be able to identify the range of UTF-16 units for each composite character called a **grapheme cluster**. You can find the boundaries of a grapheme cluster using NSString's rangeOfComposedCharacterSequenceAtIndex: method, which returns the index of the first character and the length of the character.

For instance, to count the number of grapheme clusters in a string, use the following:

```
int main(int argc, char *argv[])
{
  NSString* frenchSummer = @"été";

  int characterCount = 0;
  for (int i=0; i < [frenchSummer length]; ++characterCount)
    i += [frenchSummer rangeOfComposedCharacterSequenceAtIndex:i].length;

  NSLog(@"%d characters", characterCount);

  sleep(1);
  return 0;
}
```

There might be many equivalent grapheme clusters for a given character as the order of the UTF-16 units is not always specified. Some characters that can be drawn using a grapheme cluster also exist as a single UTF-16 character. The UTF-16 character is called a **precomposed form**, whereas the equivalent grapheme cluster is called a **decomposed form**.

Unicode recognizes two types of equivalence. Two strings are canonically equivalent if they result in the same glyphs being drawn. They are compatibly equivalent if the glyphs that are drawn are not identical but are equivalent (for instance, an *H* in different fonts, or a subscript versus a superscript).

`NSString` lets you normalize a string into one of the forms. For instance, to convert between precomposed and decomposed forms using a canonical mapping, use `precomposedStringWithCanonicalMapping` and `decomposedStringWithCanonicalMapping`:

```
NSString* precomposed = [@"e\u0301" precomposedStringWithCanonicalMapping];
NSString* decomposed  = [@"\u00e9"  decomposedStringWithCanonicalMapping];
NSLog([@"\u00e9"  isEqualToString:precomposed] ? @"YES" : @"NO");
NSLog([decomposed isEqualToString:@"e\u0301"]  ? @"YES" : @"NO");
```

Introducing the Debugger

Reload Listing 3.3.

Place a breakpoint at the second line of `main.m` by clicking in the same place as shown by the mouse pointer in Figure 3.1. Make sure that the build target setting is set to Simulator | Debug Build. The build target is shown in the upper-left corner of the Project Window. Open the debugger window by choosing the Run, Debugger menu item.

Click the Build and Go button, and you'll stop at your breakpoint, as shown in Figure 3.2.

> If the application did not stop in the debugger, you must click on the Activate button in the toolbar. This will switch it to Deactivate.

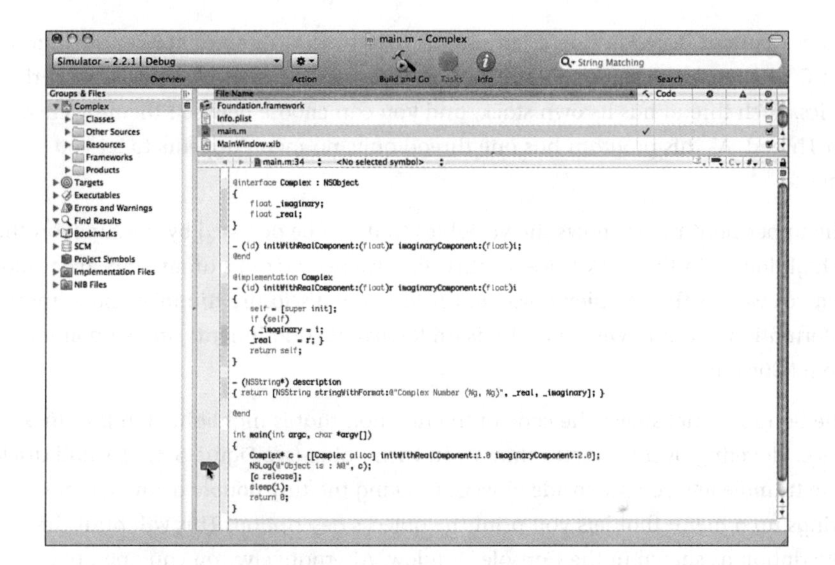

FIGURE 3.1 Placing a breakpoint

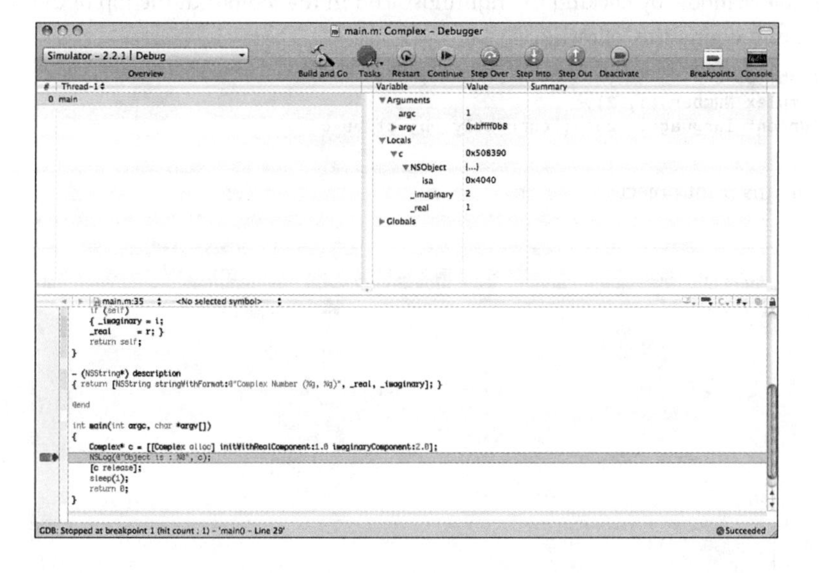

FIGURE 3.2 Stopping at a breakpoint

The upper-left panel shows the stack trace of each thread of your program. When you call a function, you expect it to return to the caller, and for the next instructions to be executed. The way the computer does this is to record on the **stack** the address of the instruction following the call. Then, the function that is called can read the address on the stack to return to the correct instructions. A stack is a data structure to which data can be added (pushed) or read and removed (popped). The last data added to a stack is the first data retrieved. The stack is maintained by the CPU using a stack pointer stored in a register (esp on your Intel Mac, `sp` or `r13` on the iPhone). For C programs, the stack contains not only return addresses, but also local variables. Each thread has its own stack, and you can choose between them by clicking on Thread. As this program has one thread only, no menu appears to let you choose.

The upper-right panel shows the variables that can be accessed by the function that is highlighted in the stack trace. In this case, we see `main()`'s arguments `argc` and `argv` as well as the complex object `c`. Clicking the disclosure triangles shows more information about `c`. We see that `c` is an `NSObject`, and inherits an `isa` pointer from `NSObject`.

The bottom panel shows the code of the function that is highlighted in the stack trace. Hovering over variables shows you their value (see Figure 3.3). A small disclosure triangle lets you see inside objects. Clicking the tiny double-arrow symbol brings up a menu that lets you print the object's description. This will print the description as shown in the Console Window. Alternatively, you can open the Console Window by clicking the rightmost icon in the toolbar at the top of the window, and typing the following:

```
(gdb) po c
Complex Number (1, 2)
Current language:  auto; currently objective-c
```

po means print object.

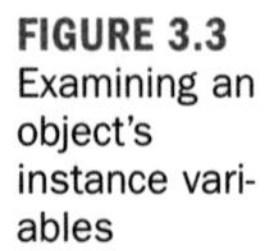

FIGURE 3.3
Examining an object's instance variables

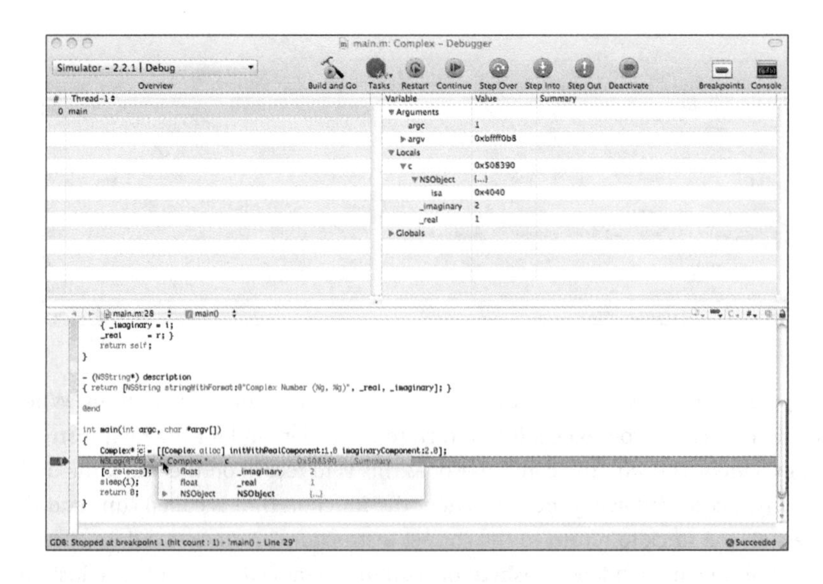

Finally, notice the status bar at the bottom of Figure 3.2. It tells you why the program stopped. The Xcode debugger provides both a GUI for simple tasks and a command-line interface for complex tasks. UNIX users will recognize the command-line interface as gdb.

Understanding Messaging

Understanding the mechanics of Objective-C messaging helps debug errors that appear in framework code.

Creating a Message

To send a message to an object, Objective-C introduces specific object-messaging syntax that is understood by the compiler. For instance:

```
int main(int argc, char *argv[])
{
  NSAutoreleasePool* pool = [[NSAutoreleasePool alloc] init];

  NSString* obj      = @"Ham";
  NSString* hamburg;                                    // NEW

  hamburg = [obj stringByAppendingString:@"burg"];     // NEW
  NSLog(hamburg);

 [pool release];
 sleep(1);
 return 0;
}
```

```
Hamburg
```

Object messaging is implemented by the `objc_msgSendfunction` which takes the object pointer as first argument, a `selector` as second argument, followed by all the method's arguments. The `selector` uniquely identifies the method. The Objective-C compiler creates a selector with the `@selector(methodName)` notation. So, the selector for the method `stringByAppendingString:` is created with `@selector(stringByAppendingString:)`. We can call `objc_msgSend` ourselves:

```
#import <objc/message.h>                                      // NEW

typedef NSString* (*s2s)(id, SEL, NSString*);                 // NEW

int main(int argc, char *argv[])
{
  NSAutoreleasePool* pool = [[NSAutoreleasePool alloc] init];

  NSString* obj      = @"Ham";
  NSString* hamburg;
  hamburg = [obj stringByAppendingString:@"burg"];
  hamburg= ((s2s) objc_msgSend)(obj, @selector(stringByAppendingString:),@"burg");
  NSLog(hamburg);
```

```
  [pool release];
  sleep(1);
  return 0;
}
Hamburg
```

The s2s type helps objc_msgSend take and return the right types.

On the iPhone, a selector is simply a pointer to a C string containing the method's name and can be printed out:

```
NSLog(@"stringByAppendingString: is %s", @selector(stringByAppendingString:));
  stringByAppendingString: is stringByAppendingString:
```

This is useful to know when debugging, if you find yourself within objc_msgSend and you want to know what the selector is.

Using Object Methods

The Objective-C compiler converts object methods into C callable functions that take an object as the first argument, a selector as the second argument, followed by all the method's arguments. These functions are expected to return an object. Pointers to these functions have the type IMP (implementation):

```
typedef id (*IMP)(id, SEL, ...);
```

For instance, we can obtain a direct pointer to NSString's stringByAppendingString: method and call it:

```
#import <objc/runtime.h>                          // NEW

typedef NSString* (*s2s)(id, SEL, NSString*);

int main(int argc, char *argv[])
{
  NSAutoreleasePool* pool = [[NSAutoreleasePool alloc] init];

  NSString* obj     = @"Ham";

  // NEW From here

  IMP imp = class_getMethodImplementation([NSString class],
                                          @selector(stringByAppendingString:));

  NSString* hamburg;
  hamburg = ((s2s) imp) (obj, @selector(stringByAppendingString:), @"burg");

  // NEW To here

  NSLog(hamburg);
  [pool release];
  sleep(1);
```

```
  return 0;
}
Hamburg
```

The compiler gives the name `self` to the first parameter of the C callable function, and the name `_cmd` to the second parameter: `self` is just a simple function parameter. `[NSString class]` returns a `Class` object for `NSString`.

Understanding `objc_msgSend`

`objc_msgSend` looks up the implementation for the selector it is given and jumps to it. To do this, it needs to know the class of the receiver object. Objective-C objects are structures that all have the same first field: `isa`. `isa` points to the object's class.

```
NSString* obj      = @"Ham";
IMP       imp      = class_getMethodImplementation([NSString class],
                                        @selector(stringByAppendingString:));
NSString* hamburg
       = ((s2s) imp) (obj->isa, @selector(stringByAppendingString:), @"burg");
NSLog(hamburg);
Hamburg
```

Apple discourages direct access to the class' `isa` field, and may change the layout of Objective-C runtime information at any time, so this code is for demonstration purposes only. `objc_msgSend`, therefore, looks like this:

```
id objc_msgSend(id receiver, SEL name, arguments...)
{
  if (receiver == nil)
    return nil;

  IMP function = class_getMethodImplementation(receiver->isa, name);
  return function(arguments);
}
```

Figure 3.2 shows the `isa` pointer in the `NSObject` structure in the variable pane of the debugger.

In reality, `objc_msgSend` is highly optimized assembly code, which makes a lot of assumptions. Rather than calling functions, it jumps directly to them, avoiding copying stack information and providing better stack traces. For instance, `@selector()` returns a unique pointer, which is hashed to find the implementation:

```
NSLog(@"stringByAppendingString: is %x", @selector(stringByAppendingString:));
NSLog(@"stringByAppendingString: is %x", @selector(stringByAppendingString:));
Selector 92691400
Selector 92691400
```

Using a C string directly will throw the same exception as invoking a nonexistent method would:

```
// Will throw an exception
NSString* hamburg
          = ((s2s) objc_msgSend) (obj, "stringByAppendingString:", @"burg");
```

Using `super`

`super` is implemented by calling the function `objc_msgSendSuper` instead of `objc_msgSend`. This function finds the object's superclass, and looks for the method implementation there.

Using Variants

There are a number of `objc_msgSend`-like functions, which are optimized for returning floating-point values, structures, using the superclass as a receiver, or taking a variable number of arguments. They all start with `objc_msg`. To find out more about them, read Apple's *Objective-C 2.0 Runtime Reference*.

Debugging a Real Bug

We'll now debug a simple program and apply our understanding of Objective-C messaging:

```
int main(int argc, char *argv[])
{
  NSLog(@"Was passed %@ arguments", argc);
  sleep(1);
  return 0;
}
```

First start the debugger by selecting Run, Debugger.

This brings up the debugger. Make sure the build target is the simulator, not the iPhone. Click on the Build and Go button on the toolbar. The application starts the simulator, and stops, as shown in Figure 3.1. You'll see `GDB: Program received signal: "EXC_BAD_ACCESS"` appear in the status bar at the bottom of the window.

If the application did not stop in the debugger, but instead you saw an alert panel stating `The application xxxx quit unexpectedly`, you must click on the Activate toolbar item so that it shows Deactivate.

If you know assembly language, you'll notice that the code is x86 assembly when running on the simulator and ARM assembly when running on the device. The simulator does not emulate an ARM processor. Instead, it mainly emulates the touch screen and forwards touch screen events to your application, which is essentially a normal Macintosh application linked against custom iPhone frameworks.

The code stopped inside `objc_msgSend`. We know that the second argument of `objc_msgSend` is a selector, which is pointer to a C string. gdb can print strings. Type the following into the Console Window:

```
(gdb) print (char*)(((int*)($esp))[2])
$1 = 0x926a1164 "respondsToSelector:"
```

Within `objc_msgSend`, on an x86 processor, the arguments are offset from the stack pointer register `esp`. The third argument also happens to be a selector:

```
(gdb) print (char*)(((int*)($esp))[3])
$2 = 0x926a38e0 "descriptionWithLocale:"
```

So `objc_msgSend`'s caller is trying to figure out if the receiver supports the `"descriptionWithLocale:"` method. Looking at the stack trace, we see that the caller is `_NSDescriptionWithLocaleFunc` and that it is called by `NSLog()`.

Click on `main.m` on the stack trace and you'll see in the code window that the following code called `NSLog()`:

```
NSLog(@"Was passed %@ arguments", argc);
```

We know that the first argument to `objc_msgSend` is the object. We can obtain its type by typing into the Console Window:

```
  (gdb) print (char *) object_getClassName(((int*)($esp))[1])
  Program received signal EXC_BAD_ACCESS, Could not access memory.
  Reason: KERN_INVALID_ADDRESS at address: 0x7073657a
  0x92601058 in _class_getName ()
  The program being debugged was signaled while in a function called from GDB.
  GDB remains in the frame where the signal was received.To change this
behavior, use "set unwindonsignal on".
  Evaluation of the expression containing the function (object_getClassName)
will be abandoned.
```

You will notice that the receiver is not a valid object. When gdb reports a signal error due to something you typed into the Console Window, the program's state is usually invalid. Restart the program by clicking on the Build and Go button. Return to the Console Window and type the following:

```
(gdb) print ((int*)($esp))[1]
$1 = 1
```

1 is not a valid object address.

We learned in this hour that `descriptionWithLocale:` is used to convert objects into strings for printing. For `descriptionWithLocale:` to be called, we must have asked `NSLog()` to print an object...but `argc` is an integer. Let's check again:

```
NSLog(@"Was passed %@ arguments", argc);
```

And there's our error. We used `%@` when we should have used `%d`.

Using Shorthands

A very common pattern in object-oriented design is the use of accessors (getters and setters) to change object state. The dot notation provides a simpler syntax for using accessors. Objective-C provides a way to automate the process (this is good because writing accessors can be quite boring).

Using the Dot Notation

Dot notation provides a simple notation to invoke accessors. Assuming `controller` is an instance of `CalculatorController` and `CalculatorController` has a getter `model` that returns a `CalculatorModel`, then the following lines are equivalent and compile to the same executable:

```
double v = [[controller model] value];
double v = controller.model.value;
```

Similarly,

```
[[controller model] setValue:1.1];
controller.model.value = 1.1;
```

The notation understands compound assignments:

```
[[controller model] setValue:(1.0 + [[controller model] value]) ];
controller.model.value += 1.0;
```

A warning will be emitted if accessors do not use the following type pattern. For instance, setters that return values (such as a BOOL) will cause a warning:

```
- (Type) value;
- (void) setValue:(Type)v;
```

Using this notation, we can write `CalculatorController`'s `dealloc` as follows:

```
- (void) dealloc;
{
  self.textView          = nil;
  [model release]; model = nil;  // model has no setter
  [super dealloc];
}
```

Dot notation has the same pitfalls as accessors do. In the following example, you'll get 0 on the simulator and a random value on the iPhone because `str` is `nil` and `rangeOfString:` returns a structure.

```
NSString* str = nil;
int       oslo = [str rangeOfString:@"Oslo"].location;
```

The implementation of dot notation is extremely simpleminded. If something looks like a getter, it can be used like one. For instance, `retain` looks like a getter:

```
CalculatorModel* model = controller.model.retain;
```

This is not a recommended practice, but you might encounter it when reading other people's code.

Advantages of Dot Notation

If a property only has a getter, and you try to write to it with dot notation, the compiler will signal an error:

```
error: object cannot be set - either readonly property or no setter found
```

If a property only has a setter, you cannot read it or write it with dot notation:

```
error: request for member '...' in something not a structure or union
```

On the other hand, invoking a getter or a setter directly might or might not generate a warning.

Disadvantages of Dot Notation

There are three disadvantages to dot notation:

- It makes searching for properties in source-code files harder (search for "`.property =`" versus `setProperty:`).
- It encourages you to chain many properties, which, like nesting method invocations, makes debugging `nil` issues harder.
- It does not work with `id` types.

Although Apple claims dot notation works with the `id` type, it does not. You can't write

```
[array objectAtIndex:0].text = @"foo";
```

but you can write

```
[[array objectAtIndex:0] setText:@"foo"];
```

Property Specifications and Synthesis

Property specification lets you specify how accessors behave. For instance, you can state whether a property will be retained. Synthesis automatically generates accessors based on the specification. Again this saves you from writing boring code.

Property Specification

A problem with simply declaring a setter is that its users cannot know how it behaves. For instance, although most setters retain their argument, some don't, and some copy it. Programmers must rely on the source code (if available), the documentation (if correct), or reverse engineering to know what happens.

Property specifications are placed in interfaces and are written as follows:

```
@property (attributes) type name;
```

The optional list of *(attributes)* is comma separated. Default attributes need not be mentioned. *type* is the type of the value being accessed, and *name* is its name. For instance:

```
@interface CalculatorModel : NSObject
{ float     value;
  ... }

@property float value;

...
@end
```

The property specification replaces the accessor declarations. If you implement the accessors yourself, be aware that the property specification is simply a declaration of intent, and is not enforced by the compiler.

The following sections examine the three ways in which accessors can differ.

Writability

By default, all properties are `readwrite`—that is, they have both a setter and a getter. You can, however, specify that they only have a getter with the attribute `readonly`. For instance:

```
@interface CalculatorController : NSObject
{ CalculatorModel* model;
  UITextView*      textView; }

@property (readonly, retain) CalculatorModel* model;
@property (retain)           UITextView*      textView;
...
@end
```

Memory

By default, all properties are assigned. A copy of the argument is made. This makes sense for all nonpointers.

However, pointers are generally qualified either by `retain` or `copy` attributes. Usually, objects want to own the objects to which their pointers reference, so that they know their pointers are valid. They can do so either by retaining the object (as we did in `setTextView:`) or by copying the object. We will encounter a rare counterexample of an `assign` to a pointer property specification in Hour 11, "Displaying Tables."

Atomicity

By default, all properties are assumed to be atomic—that is, the accessors are thread safe. Thread safe accessors guarantee that when you use the getter, you obtain a pointer to a valid object. They do not guarantee that other threads will not change the contents of the object you are given.

If you know your objects will not be used by multiple threads, use the `nonatomic` attribute. Thread-unsafe accessors make no guarantees with respect to threads, but they are faster.

Synthesis

As property specifications completely define the behavior of accessors, Objective-C can generate code for them. To do this, add the following to `@implementation`:

```
@synthesize name, name2...;
```

For instance, the three nonatomic memory variants are as follows:

```
@property   (nonatomic, memory attribute) id pointer;
@synthesize pointer;
```

memory attribute	Generated Code
`ASSIGN:`	`{ pointer = p; };`
`RETAIN:`	`{ if (p != pointer)`
	`{ [pointer release]; pointer = [p retain]; } }`
`COPY:`	`{ if (p != pointer)`
	`{ [pointer release]; pointer = [p copy];   } }`

Atomic getters and setters use a lock on the object to guarantee thread-safe access. Furthermore, getters retain, then autorelease the result, so that it is still available if other threads release it.

In the next hour, you'll learn about the different variants of `copy`. If you need to use a different way of copying, such as `mutableCopy`, you must implement the getter and setter by hand.

Summary

Properties are a useful shorthand. You'll learn more about them in Hours 4, 5, and 18. We do not discuss the more esoteric aspects of properties because they only work on the iPhone and not on the simulator. These aspects are covered in Apple's *The Objective-C 2.0 Programming Language* book.

In the next hour, you'll use what you've learned to make a functioning calculator.

Q&A

Q. ***If I* `autorelease` *an object, does its* `retainCount` *go down immediately?***

A. No, it only goes down when the autorelease pool is drained.

Q. ***If I use a property specification, must I* `@synthesize` *the properties?***

A. No, you can write your own accessors.

Q. ***If I request accessors to be* `@synthesize`*, must I use a property specification?***

A. Yes, `@synthesize` uses the property specification to generate the accessors.

Workshop

The Workshop consists of quiz questions and answers to help you solidify your understanding of the material covered in this hour. You should try to answer the questions before checking the answers.

Quiz Questions

1. What is an auto-release pool?
2. In what way do Objective-C strings differ from classical C-strings?
3. What is `objc_msgSend()`?
4. What is the dot notation?

Quiz Answers

1. An auto-release pool is a data-structure which retains objects until it is released. It is used to simplify cross-method boundary memory management.
2. Objective-C strings provide full Unicode support.
3. The compiler uses `objc_msgSend()` and functions like it to implement Objective-C's method invocation.
4. The dot notation is a shorthand to invoke a property's accessor or mutator without using method invocation syntax.

Exercises

- You've learned the key `NSString` methods, but there are more. Read the Tasks section of the `NSString` documentation in Xcode by choosing the Documentation item on the Help menu. Choose the Apple iPhone OS 2.2 section and type **`nsstring`** into the search box. Choose NSString Class Reference. Scroll down to tasks. Clicking on a method shows you its definition.
- On most UNIX systems, header files are located in standard directories such as /usr/include. In Cocoa, they are included in frameworks, which also include binary library files. For instance, `NSRange` and `NSString` belong to the Foundation framework. It's in `/Developer/Platforms/iPhoneOS.platform/Developer/SDKs/iPhoneOS2.2.sdk/System/Library/Frameworks/Foundation.framework/` on my system. `Foundation` is the binary file. Headers/ is a directory of includes. To learn more, read the `NSRange.h` file.

HOUR 4
Making the Calculator Calculate

What You'll Learn in This Hour:

- Creating a simple calculator
- Using mutable classes
- Using dynamic features: protocols, categories, class methods, and objects

The first part of this hour is dedicated to making the calculator calculate. You'll learn how to use mutable strings, strings you can change, and why Objective-C provides two mutable and immutable variants of many common data-structures. To illustrate their use, you'll add a history of calculations to the calculator using strings. Attempting to change an immutable string generates an exception, leading to a discussion of error handling in Objective-C.

The second part concentrates on the dynamic aspects of Objective-C that distinguish it from other languages.

Protocols specify methods objects must implement. Many Cocoa Touch classes use protocols to specify the methods they expect other classes to implement. As you'll be writing some of these other classes, you need to understand protocols.

Categories let you extend existing classes with new methods. This is extremely useful, as it lets you extend Cocoa Touch classes while minimizing the changes to your client code. Other languages extend classes using subclassing, but this adds spurious classes. For instance, if you wish to use extension methods defined by two subclasses, you need to declare a third class which has both sets of methods. Categories avoid this problem entirely by adding new methods to the original class.

A Simple Calculator

We now have all the tools we need to build a simple calculator.

We'll split `pressButton:` as follows:

- `pressDigit:` for 0–9
- `pressOperation:` for C, +, –, x, /, and =
- `pressDot:` for the . key
- `pressVar:` for the var key

As you can see, the code is quite straightforward. The calculator controller is quite complex because it simulates the user interface of the calculator:

- `current` is the number being typed in.
- `decimalPlace` is the decimal place of the digit being typed in.
- `lastOperation` is the last operation the user typed.

Listing 4.1 defines the interface of the `CalculatorController` class you'll use to implement the calculator controller. Listing 4.2 provides `CalculatorController`'s implementation.

Did you Know?

Listing 4.1 includes the line `@class CalculatorModel`. This is a forward declaration. It tells the compiler that there is a `CalculatorModel` class. Without this declaration the compiler would report an error at the first reference to `CalculatorModel`.

LISTING 4.1 CalculatorController.h

```
#import <UIKit/UIKit.h>

@class CalculatorModel;

@interface CalculatorController : NSObject
{
  IBOutlet UITextView* textView;
  float               current;
  float               decimalPlace;
  unichar             lastOperation;
  CalculatorModel*    model;
}

@property (retain, nonatomic)           UITextView*      textView;
@property (retain, readonly, nonatomic) CalculatorModel* model;
```

LISTING 4.1 Continued

```
- (void) pressVar:     (UIButton*)sender;
- (void) pressDigit:   (UIButton*)sender;
- (void) pressDot:     (UIButton*)sender;
- (void) pressOperation:(UIButton*)sender;

@end
```

LISTING 4.2 CalculatorController.m

```
#import  "CalculatorController.h"
#import  "CalculatorModel.h"

@implementation CalculatorController

@synthesize textView, model;

- (id) init
{
  self = [super init];

  if (self)
  {
    textView      = nil;
    lastOperation = 0;
    decimalPlace  = 1.0;
    current       = 0.0;
    model         = [[CalculatorModel alloc] init];
  }

  return self;
};

- (void) dealloc;
{
  self.textView          = nil;
  [model release]; model = nil;  // model has no setter
  [super dealloc];
}


- (void) updateScreen:(float) value;
{ textView.text = [NSString stringWithFormat:@"%g", value]; }


- (void) pressVar:(UIButton*)sender;
{};


- (void) pressDigit:(UIButton*)sender;
{
  NSString* button       = [sender currentTitle];

  if (lastOperation == '=')
    lastOperation = 'C';
```

LISTING 4.2 Continued

```
  if (decimalPlace >= 1.0)
    current = (current * 10.0) + [button floatValue];
  else
  { current = current          + [button floatValue] * decimalPlace;
    decimalPlace  *= 0.1; }

  [self updateScreen:current];
}


- (void) pressDot:(UIButton*)sender;
{
  if (lastOperation == '=')
    lastOperation = 'C';

   if (decimalPlace == 1.0)
    decimalPlace = 0.1;
}


- (void) pressOperation:(UIButton*)sender;
{
  NSString* button       = [sender currentTitle];
  unichar   buttonChar   = [button characterAtIndex:0];

  if      (lastOperation == '+')  [model add:current];
  else if (lastOperation == '-')  [model subtract:current];
  else if (lastOperation == 'x')  [model multiply:current];
  else if (lastOperation == '/')  [model divide:current];
  else if (lastOperation != '=')  [model setValue:current];

  lastOperation = buttonChar;
  decimalPlace  = 1.0;
  current       = 0.0;

  if (buttonChar == 'C')
    model.value = 0.0;

  [self updateScreen:model.value];
}
```

In Interface Builder, reload all class files. You'll notice a warning at the bottom of the Document Window (see Figure 4.1). This is due to the deletion of `pressButton:`. Open the connection context menu on the Calculator Controller object and delete all the connections to `pressButton:` by opening the Multiple Values disclosure and clicking the small *x* on the left of each `pressButton:` (see Figure 4.2a). Now connect the buttons appropriately by control-dragging as was explained in Hour 2, "Handling Interaction," in the section, "Instantiating `CalculatorController` in Interface Builder" (see Figure 4.2b).

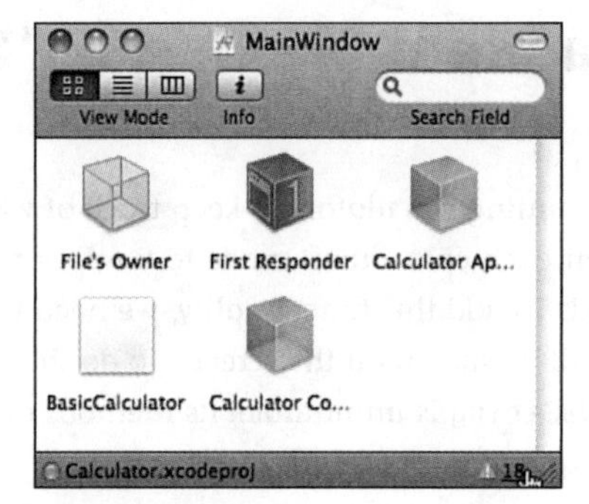

FIGURE 4.1
Interface Builder shows warnings.

(a) Obsolete connections

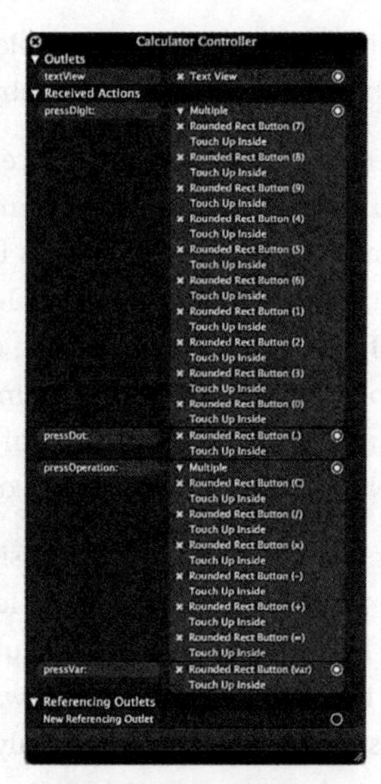

(b) New connections

FIGURE 4.2
Calculator Controller connections

The `floatValue` method converts a string to a `float` or 0.0 if the conversion fails. Because `pressNumber:` is only connected to buttons labeled with a button, we know that the conversion never fails.

You might have noticed that `updateScreen:` is not declared in the interface. By defining it before using it in the object implementation, you can hide it from `CalculatorController` clients. You'll learn a better way of hiding methods from clients later this hour.

Mutable Classes: Making a "Printing" Calculator

Many accountants use printing calculators to keep track of what they've typed. Printing calculators print each calculation made to a roll of paper, providing a history that can be checked. To add this functionality, we need to add each new calculation to the text that will be shown on the screen. To do this, we need to append to an `NSString`. Because `NSString` is immutable, its methods only let you create new strings. Immutable strings can be modified.

Immutable Versus Mutable Objects

Objective-C distinguishes between mutable and immutable objects. Whereas mutable objects can be changed, immutable objects guarantee that their state is fixed.

Immutable objects are useful. For instance, if many objects share a reference to the same object *o*, any one of them could change *o* without the others knowing. This is problematic if one of the objects assumes it knows *o*'s state. For instance, if *o*'s location in a data structure depends on its value (such as its location in a sorted list), changing its value will not move it to the correct, new location. This kind of bug is hard to find. Objects that only reference immutable objects are protected from this kind of bug. Immutability is also useful in multithreaded applications as immutable objects can safely be shared between threads.

You can implement entire applications using immutable objects. For instance, the computational model of pure functional languages such as Haskell involves no mutability. The main reason for using mutable objects is because they are faster: The time taken to build a new string grows linearly with its length, whereas the time taken to add a string to another often only grows linearly with the length of the appended string.

Objects that reference mutable objects should either not share their mutable object, or not assume that they know anything about the object's state.

In Cocoa, mutable objects are subclassed from their immutable variants. For instance, the mutable variant of `NSString` is its child class `NSMutableString`. This pattern lets mutable strings be used wherever immutable strings are expected. Static type checking guarantees that if a function requests an immutable object, it will not try to mutate it.

Adding History

To simulate the history captured by the printing calculator's paper roll, we will model history with an NSMutableString that only CalculatorController will reference.

Add the following line to init:

```
history = [[NSMutableStringalloc] initWithCapacity:4096];
```

Add the following line to dealloc:

```
[history release]; history = nil; // history has no setter
```

initWithCapacity: lets you define how much initial space the history should take. Each time the user taps an operation key, the following code adds state to the history string. The code should be added pressOperation: before the assignment to lastOperation:

```
[history appendString:[NSStringstringWithFormat:@"%g %c\n", current,
buttonChar]];
if (buttonChar == '=')
  [history appendString:[NSStringstringWithFormat:@"%g  \n\n", model.value]];
```

Also add the following method:

```
- (void) updateScreen:(float)value;
{ textView.text = [NSStringstringWithFormat:@"%@%g", history, value]; }
```

Scrolling to the Bottom of the Text

As soon as the text no longer fits on the screen, you'll notice that only the top of the text is visible. scrollRangeToVisible: fixes this by letting us scroll down to the bottom of the text:

```
- (void) updateScreen:(float)value;
{
  textView.text = [NSString stringWithFormat:@"%@%g", history, value];
  [textView scrollRangeToVisible:NSMakeRange([history length], 0)];
}
```

Unfortunately, UITextView jumps to the top of the text each time we change the text. scrollRangeToVisible: then scrolls down to the bottom of the text. As this happens each time we tap a key, the text jerks up and down. To solve this, we remember where the text was positioned within the space reserved for it on the screen, update the text, and restore the position. This is explained in more detail in Hour 6, "Understanding How the User Interface Is Built."

```
- (void) updateScreen:(float)value;
{
  CGPoint p = [textView contentOffset];
  textView.text = [NSString stringWithFormat:@"%@%g", history, value];
  [textView setContentOffset:p animated:NO];
  [textView scrollRangeToVisible:NSMakeRange([history length], 1)];
}
```

Of course, you can still drag the text view up and down to see your previous calculations.

Other NSMutableString Methods

Appending strings created by `stringWithFormat:` is so common that `Foundation` provides an `appendFormat:` method:

```
[history appendFormat:@"%g %c\n", current, buttonChar];
```

`insertString:atIndex:` inserts strings into other strings:

```
NSMutableString* hello = [NSMutableString stringWithString:@"Hello World"];
[hello insertString:@" beautiful" atIndex:5];
NSLog(hello);
Hello beautiful World
```

`deleteCharactersInRange:` elides parts of strings:

```
[hello deleteCharactersInRange:NSMakeRange(5,10)];
NSLog(hello);
Hello World
```

`replaceCharactersInRange:withString:` combines the two last methods, whereas `replaceOccurrencesOfString:withString:options:range` behaves like `stringByReplacingOccurrencesOfString:withString:` but in place. The entire string can be replaced with `setString:`.

Exceptions: Checking Mutability

Cocoa does not provide a means to test whether an object is mutable: The types of your methods' arguments state whether you expect an object to be mutable. If you state that you will not mutate an object, static type checking should prevent you from doing so. If a Cocoa framework says it will give you an immutable object, you should believe it, rather than check: It might have avoided making an immutable copy of a mutable object for efficiency reasons, but it is liable to break if you change the value.

Having said that, if you try to invoke `setString:` on an immutable `NSString` object, you'll cause an `Attempt to mutate immutable object with setString:` exception.

Exception Syntax

Exceptions provide an additional way to leave functions using an @throw statement. Just like return, @throw takes an argument. Unlike return, @throw does not return to the calling function, but unwinds the stack until a suitable @catch is found (in a function that directly or indirectly called the function that threw the exception). The notation for catching exceptions is as follows:

```
@try
{
  // Exception causing code
}
@catch (NSException* exception)
{
  // Exception handling code
}
@finally
{
  // Code to run whether an exception is thrown or not
}
```

As in other languages, you can have multiple @catch blocks each with a different exception type. The @catch blocks should be ordered from most specific to least specific.

Exceptions are thrown with @throw:

```
NSException *exception = [NSException exceptionWithName:@"EndOfTheWorld"
                          reason:  @"Vogon Hyperspace Bypass Construction"
                          userInfo:nil];
@throw exception;
```

As mentioned in Hour 3, "Simplifying Your Code," exceptions are expected to be autoreleased: They must survive until the @catch block, and @catch blocks do not release them.

Objective-C Provides Many Ways to Handle Errors

Abstraction is one of the main tools for designing applications. Handling error conditions and efficiency are the two biggest impediments to abstraction. For instance, you can abstract the data persistence part of an application so that it works with local storage or online storage. However, the kinds of error these two forms of storage can encounter are quite different.

The low-level persistence code doesn't know what to do about errors so it forwards them up to its clients. Thus, the clients need to know about every kind of persistence error; however, that breaks encapsulation.

Exceptions do not solve the encapsulation problem, but they try to mitigate it. If low-level functions return special "error values" to indicate errors, every function that directly or indirectly called them needs to either forward the error to its calling function, or do its job despite the error. Exceptions remove the need for forwarding code. Only the code that knows how to deal with the exception needs to catch exceptions.

Objective-C's `nil`-rule provides another mechanism to avoid forwarding code: Methods can return `nil` to indicate an error. Indeed, this pattern is so widespread that Objective-C programmers structure their code to work with both `nil` and valid objects. Because they know that invoking a method on `nil` returns `nil` a false condition, or a zero value, they rarely need to add any `if` statements to handle the error.

Error delegates provide a third mechanism for error handling. In the case of an error, an error method is invoked on a user-supplied object, called a delegate. You'll learn more about delegates in Hour 6. The details of the error are often specified in an `NSError` object. The error delegate method can then decide what to do. Consider an error delegate that must handle a failure to save data to online storage. It has many options. It could try to contact the server again. It could save the data locally to a transaction file and try again later. It could alert the user and ask to use a different server, or name and password.

Because of the `nil` rule and the use of error delegates, exceptions are only used as a last resort in Objective-C, typically for exceptional cases where no local recovery is possible. The `@try` statement creates slow `setjmp`-based code. Most Objective-C programs have as little to do with exceptions as possible.

Appendix D (online at www.informit.com/title/9780672331251) discusses exceptions further, showing you how to set the default exception handler and how exceptions are implemented, which is useful to know when interfacing with C++ code.

Copying Objects

Immutable Copies

As mentioned earlier, objects should reference immutable objects if they assume any knowledge of those objects' state. For instance, the `NSDictionary` and `NSMutableDictionary` classes associate keys with values. They are implemented with hash tables: The value's position in the table is determined by the key's hash. Clearly, the key should be immutable. However, nothing stops you from building a dictionary using a mutable key:

```
NSMutableString* value = [NSMutableString stringWithString:@"key"];
NSDictionary*    dict  = [NSDictionary dictionaryWithObject:value
                                                      forKey:value];
```

Indeed, we can change value, even though it's also used as a key:

```
[value setString:@"value"];
NSLog(@"Dictionary : %@", dict);
```

This will print

```
Dictionary : { key = value; }
```

We obtained key = value, not value = value. NSDictionary wasn't fooled. It made an immutable copy of the key. This can be verified:

```
id k = [[dict allKeys]   objectAtIndex:0];
id v = [[dict allValues] objectAtIndex:0];

#define mutable(X) isMutableString(X) ? @"" : @"im"

NSLog(@"Original is %@mutable %@ (%x)", mutable(value), value, value);
NSLog(@"Key      is %@mutable %@ (%x)", mutable(k), k, k);
NSLog(@"Value    is %@mutable %@ (%x)", mutable(v), v, v);
```

and will print

```
  Original is mutable value (509970)
  Key      is immutable key (a01480a0)
  Value    is mutable value (509970)
```

allKeys returns an array of all the keys in the dictionary, and objectAtIndex:*i* returns the *i*th object of that array.

Making Copies

You can obtain an immutable copy by invoking any object's copy method. You can obtain a mutable copy by invoking an immutable object's mutableCopy method, if the object provides a mutable variant.

These methods are inherited from NSObject and try to invoke copyWithZone: or mutableCopyWithZone:, respectively, on self with a nil zone. An exception is raised if the copyWithZone methods do not exist. It is up to each class to implement copyWithZone: and mutableCopyWithZone: because each class knows which instance variables should simply be copied and which should also be retained. Again, like init methods, if the superclass has a copyWithZone: method, it should be invoked; otherwise, invoke allocWithZone:. For instance, our complex number class can be copied as follows:

```
- (id) copyWithZone:(NSZone*)zone
{ return [[Complex allocWithZone:zone]
                initWithRealComponent:real
                   imaginaryComponent:imaginary]; };
```

The convention is that copy and mutableCopy perform shallow copying and do not copy objects they externally reference. Internally referenced objects are objects that are not visible to other classes. For instance, the history string is an internal object. In Hour 12, "Adding Navigation and Tab Bar Controllers," you'll learn how to perform deep copying with NSCoder.

Did you Know?

NSZones are the arguments of allocWithZone:, copyWithZone:, and mutableCopyWithZone:. They are discussed in more detail in Appendix D (online at www.informit.com/title/9780672331251).

Dynamic Objective-C

Although Objective-C does not support multiple inheritance, it provides **protocols**, which specify methods classes should have. It also provides **categories**, which let you extend existing classes with your own methods.

Protocols

A protocol is simply a list of methods that some code expects objects to provide. This list is determined by the code's behavior. For instance NSDictionary expects its keys to be copyable: It will invoke copy on keys.

As with type checking, Objective-C also provides a way to statically require that a class implement certain methods. This is called a **formal protocol**.

Dynamic Type Checking: Protocols

As soon as you write a piece of code that expects an object to provide a method, you have created an unnamed protocol. For instance, because eat expects its argument food to provide the calories method, it expects objects passed as food to follow an unnamed protocol that includes the method calories:

```
- (void) eat:(id)food
{ energy += [food calories]; };
```

Protocols can include optional methods: methods that will be invoked if they exist. For instance:

```
- (void) eat:(id)food
{
  energy += [food calories];

  if ([food respondsToSelector:@selector(waterContent)])
    hydration += [food waterContent];
};
```

The respondsToSelector: method, inherited from NSObject, checks whether an object implements a method. Here, we check whether food implements (or inherits) the waterContent method before invoking it. Because food is declared to be of type id, the compiler issues no warning when waterContent is invoked on food.

Protocols are a strength of Objective-C. They are used in many places where subclassing would be used in other languages. They neatly sidestep the ambiguities inherent in multiple inheritance while providing all the necessary power. Optional methods simplify writing objects that support protocols: If you don't care to track waterContent, you don't need to add hydration methods to your objects. Patterns such as delegates (explained in Hour 6) and data sources (explained in Hour 11, "Displaying Tables") rely heavily on protocols.

Static Type Checking: Formal Versus Informal Protocols

Dynamic protocol checking always happens. However, it is useful to detect missing methods at compile time using static type checking. Method can explicitly state what methods they expect their argument to provide using a formal protocol. Alternatively they can assume the object provides these methods without stating so explicitly. This is called an informal protocol.

Formal protocols specify that a class has certain methods. For instance, all objects that obey the Nourishes protocol must define or inherit a calories method:

```
@protocol Nourishes
- (float) calories;
@end
```

By default, all methods declared in a formal protocol are required: They must be implemented by classes that comply with the protocol. However, methods can be marked as optional using the @optional keyword:

```
@protocol Nourishes
- (float) calories;
@optional
- (float) waterContent;
@end
```

As before, the existence of optional methods must be checked at runtime before they are invoked.

Method declarations can specify arguments that require compliance to one or many protocols:

```
@interface Animal : NSObject
{ ... }
- (void) eat:  (id<Nourishes, NSCopying>)        food;
- (void) drink:(NSObject<Nourishes, NSCopying>*) liquid;
@end
```

Classes must state that they comply with protocols in their interface to avoid a compilation warning. Simply declaring the protocol's methods in the interface is insufficient.

```
@interface Food : NSObject <Nourishes, NSCopying>
...
@end
```

Having stated their compliance, classes do not need to declare the methods specified by the protocol in the interface block, but they must implement them in the implementation block, or they must inherit them.

An object's compliance to a formal protocol can be tested at runtime with the `conformsToProtocol:` method. The protocol argument is obtained using the `@protocol()` notation:

```
BOOL canEat = [object conformsToProtocol:@protocol(Nourishes)];
```

As formal protocol verification is a form of static typing, passing an object of type `id` to an argument that requires a protocol defeats the type check.

Categories

Categories let you add new methods to existing classes without creating subclasses. For instance, suppose that we stored the calculation in a string as it was typed. Then, we want to calculate the result. We can do this by adding a `calculate` method to `NSString` so that it is also inherited by `NSMutableString` by declaring a `Calculator` category:

```
@interface NSString (Calculator)
- (float) calculate;
@end
```

We can implement it with the following notation:

```
@implementation NSString (Calculator)

- (float) calculate;
{ ... };

@end
```

To achieve this result using multiple inheritance, we would have to create a "mixin class" and two derived classes. However, unlike multiple inheritance, categories cannot add any new instance variables to a class. Using categories to override existing methods is discouraged because it renders the original method inaccessible.

Reducing Coupling

A key observation of the object-oriented methodology is that slack is key for the survival of complex systems. The more different parts of a program use their knowledge of how other parts of the program work, the more tightly bound they are, making it difficult for the program to survive changes.

One way in which Apple tries to reduce coupling is to underdocument how things work, giving you abstract recipes rather than telling you how things really work or why things are designed the way they are. This book explains the reasons and the mechanisms because understanding them is essential to debug problems. However, you should avoid relying on this knowledge in your programs because Apple is free to change the implementation of any class, and, historically, has done so quite often.

One kind of tight-coupling problem is called the fragile base class problem. It arises any time derived classes assume anything about the implementation of their superclasses: Any modifications to the superclasses that break these assumptions cause the derived classes to malfunction. As the author of the superclass cannot guess all the assumptions the authors of subclasses made, any changes to the superclass will probably break some subclasses. Hiding implementation details from subclasses clearly signals that they should not assume these details will not change.

Tight-coupling is insidious because it is hard to detect. To see tight-coupling it is not sufficient to know the API to a class. Instead, you must understand how it works and what part of its behavior is specified and will not change and what part of its behavior is implementation dependent and subject to change. Only then, by understanding how the client software uses it, can you determine if a system is tightly coupled. Because loosely coupled and tightly coupled systems work equally well, tight-coupling is rarely detected and is a prevalent problem in software. It is only detected when the software has become unmaintainable, and needs to be rewritten. For instance, tight-coupling is the key reason Microsoft struggles to release new versions of its operating system. While Apple routinely breaks any software that is too tightly coupled when it updates its libraries, Microsoft tries to maintain compatibility so its users are not inconvenienced. Recognizing and preventing unnecessary tight-coupling is a key skill of experienced programmers.

Hiding Methods from Subclasses

Unnamed categories are called **extensions** and are commonly used to hide private methods from subclasses, so that the authors of subclasses don't rely on their existence. For instance, we didn't want clients to be able to write to `model`, so we declared `model` to be read-only:

```
@interface CalculatorController : NSObject
...
@property (retain, readonly, nonatomic) CalculatorModel* model;
...
@end
```

We can override the readonly property and add methods to the extension:

```
@interface CalculatorController ()
@property (retain, readwrite, nonatomic) CalculatorModel* model;
- (void) updateScreen:(float) value;
@end

@implementation CalculatorController
...

- (void) updateScreen:(float)value;
{
  CGPoint p = [textView contentOffset];
  textView.text = [NSString stringWithFormat:@"%@%g", history, value];
  [textView setContentOffset:p];
  [textView scrollRangeToVisible:NSMakeRange([history length], 0)];
}

@end
```

Instance Variable Scope: Hiding Instance Variables from Subclasses

Another means of reducing the fragile base class coupling is to limit who can access the instance variables of an object. Limiting access to instance variables is called encapsulation.

By default, Objective-C instance variables are protected: They can only be accessed by objects of the class that declares them or its subclasses. You can specify that an instance variable should be private (only accessible by objects of the class that declares it) if you want to prevent subclasses from accessing it. Instance variables that could be removed at some point in the future or that would cause bugs if accessed inadvertently should be marked private. Public instance variables are accessible by all, which breaks encapsulation. For instance:

```
@interface Music : NSObject
{
  @public
    NSString* tag;

  @protected
    Score*    score;
    float     playbackSpeed;

  @private
    int       position;
}
```

Most user-defined Objective-C classes do not declare any scope and just rely on the default. The possible presence of private instance variables does, however, reinforce the need for your `copyWithZone:` methods to call their superclass's `copyWithZone:` methods.

Class Objects and Class Methods

In Hour 2, we briefly mentioned that classes can have methods, and that class methods could be inherited. For instance, the `alloc` method is inherited from `NSObject`. Because class methods are not instances, you might think that class methods would not have a `self` pointer. However, without a `self` pointer, the inherited `alloc` method would not know how much memory to reserve for an object, only how much memory to reserve for an `NSObject`. Therefore, Objective-C invokes class methods on class objects, and class methods' `self` points to a class object.

Class Objects

Class objects are shared by all instances of a class. They are pointed to by the object's `isa` pointer, but the documented method for obtaining an instance's class is to use the `class` method it inherits from `NSObject`. Class objects contain information shared by all instances of a class, such as the following:

- The class's name (used by `description`)
- The class's superclass (used by `super` and `superclass`)
- The class's metaclass
- The size of instances of the class (used by `alloc` and `allocWithZone:`)
- The methods supported by class instances (used by method invocation and `respondsToSelector:`)
- The instance variables of class instances (used by NIB instantiation)
- The protocols complied to by the class (used by `conformsToProtocol:`)

Just as instance method invocation uses the list of methods provided by the class object, class method invocation uses the list of methods provided by the class's metaclass object. Class's `isa` pointer points to their metaclass. However, invoking the `class` method on a class object returns the class itself: There are two implementations of `class`. The class `class` method (`+ class`) returns `self`, whereas the instance `class` method `- class` returns the contents of `((id)self)->isa`.

Did you Know?

Sometimes, you will encounter errors like the following:

```
*** +[NSString initWithString:]:
                    unrecognized selector sent to class 0xa00acf20
```

Looking at the source code, the problem might not be obvious. `NSString` does have an `initWithString:` method. The problem is that you invoked an `initWithString:` method on a class object. The Objective-C runtime does not find `initWithString:` in the metaclass's list of methods, and throws an exception. A common cause is forgetting to call `alloc`:

```
id oops = [NSString initWithString:@""];
```

All metaclasses' `isa` pointers point to `NSObject`'s metaclass. This catches errors where an application somehow ended with a pointer to a metaclass instead of to an object.

`NSString` is defined in the `Foundation` library, whereas our `Calculator` category is defined in our application. After the application is fetched from storage (or Flash on the iPhone), its frameworks are loaded. Then the Objective-C runtime finds the categories in the application and adds their methods to the appropriate class objects: It adds the `calculate` method to the list of methods in `NSString`'s class object.

Similarly, overriding inherited methods is simply a matter of adding the method to the class object's method list. `objc_sendMessage` iterates up the superclass hierarchy (using the class object's superclass field) checking whether a method exists in the class objects' method lists, and invokes the first matching method it finds.

Dynamic Behavior Based on Object Class Type

`NSObject`'s `isKindOfClass:` method checks whether the receiver is an instance of a class or a class that derives from it by using the class object and the class object's `superclass` field. `isMemberOfClass:` checks whether the receiver is an instance of a class. If the answer is `YES`, you can safely cast objects to that class:

```
NSObject* object;

if ([object isKindOfClass:[CalculatorController class]])
{
  CalculatorController* obj = (CalculatorController*) object;
  obj.textView = textView;
}
```

The `class` method returns a `Class` object, which represents the object's class. As mentioned earlier, do not mutate an object that was declared immutable. Mutating an object that is not supposed to be mutated results in inconsistent program state, which leads to unexpected program behavior. The precise bad behavior depends on your program.

Did you Know?

Appendix D (online at www.informit.com/title/9780672331251) shows you how to create singletons and extend objects by overriding `allocWithZone:`.

What You See Is NOT What You Get: Class Clusters

Many of Cocoa's classes provide a vast array of static settings. Although every method could modify its behavior based on the settings, subclassing leads to simpler, faster code. For instance, subclasses of `UIButtons` such as `UIRoundedRectButton` can use their own specialized drawing methods. Similarly, subclasses of `NSString` can optimize processing of Unicode, ASCII, and other types of strings.

Class clients do not want to be burdened with selecting the specialized class best suited to their needs: Specifying you want a string should be sufficient. Class clusters hide the implementation classes (called concrete classes) behind a unified façade. Thus, `NSStrings` created from C strings using `initWithCString:` are different objects from `NSStrings` created from UTF-8 strings using `initWithUTF8String`. `NSString`'s `alloc` method returns a pointer to a static `NSPlaceholderString` object. Then `NSPlaceholderString`'s `init` methods allocate and build the appropriate subclass.

Because no objects of class clusters' façades are created, you cannot subclass them to add functionality. For instance, if you were to subclass `NSString`, your class's inherited `alloc` method would return an `NSPlaceholderString` and the subsequent `init` method would return a standard concrete class. You can, however, extend `NSString` and its subclasses with a category.

The only reason to subclass a class cluster façade is to add your own concrete class. Some of the `Foundation` classes are designed to allow this, distinguishing **primitive** methods that the concrete classes override from **nonprimitive** methods that are shared by all the subclasses and are implemented on the façade itself. Creating instances of your concrete class requires either overriding `allocWithZone` in your concrete class, and creating concrete instances directly, or adding methods to undocumented classes such as `NSPlaceholderString` to provide `init` methods from the façade for your classes.

Did you Know?

If you see undocumented classes in the debugger that resemble a documented class (such as `UIRoundedRectButton`), or classes containing the word `Concrete` (such as `NSConcreteArray`), you're looking at a concrete class from a class cluster.

Summary

You've now learned a few key concepts required to use Cocoa Touch. You know how to distinguish mutable and immutable objects. You know how to copy objects and which methods you must implement so that your objects will be copied. You understand protocols and the difference between a formal and an informal protocol.

You now understand how Objective-C categories use class objects to create a dynamically extensible class hierarchy. The ability to extend or even change a class' methods is a very powerful feature found in few compiled languages.

Q&A

Q. ***In what ways are immutable objects cheaper to use than mutable objects?***

A. Because they cannot be changed, immutable objects can safely be shared by many objects. For instance, NSNumber's `numberWithInt:` returns the same object for common numbers such as zero rather than building new ones. Immutable objects do not reserve additional memory in case data needs to be added. Mutable objects such as NSMutableString reserve enough additional memory to keep the computational complexity of adding to them low. You'll learn more about this in Hour 5, "Adding Variables to the Calculator."

Workshop

The Workshop consists of quiz questions and answers to help you solidify your understanding of the material covered in this hour. You should try to answer the questions before checking the answers.

Quiz Questions

1. What is a mutable object?
2. What is an immutable object?
3. Which type of object (mutable or immutable) should a class be careful about sharing with other objects?
4. What is a formal protocol?
5. What is an informal protocol?
6. What is a category?

7. What is an extension?

8. Should categories be used to override an existing object's methods?

Quiz Answers

1. Mutable objects are objects whose content can be changed.

2. Immutable objects are objects whose content cannot be changed.

3. Objects should only share mutable objects if they realize the other object may change it. The can share immutable objects safely.

4. A formal protocol is an explicit declaration of the methods a method assumes an object will provide.

5. An informal protocol is the undeclared list of methods a method assumes an object will provide.

6. A category is a means to add methods to an existing class.

7. An extension is an unnamed category, commonly used to add private method declarations to a class for the class' private use.

8. No, categories should not be used to override existing objects' methods. If two categories override the same method, which of the two implementations will be chosen is undefined.

Exercises

- Create a class whose superclass is `NSObject`. Do not add a `copyWithZone:` method. Try to use that object as a key to a `NSDictionary`. What happens? Do you get a compilation error? What message do you see written on the console? Do you break into the debugger? Add a `copyWithZone:` method. Does the error go away?

- Create a protocol and a class that says it obeys the protocol. Add an optional and a mandatory method to the protocol. Compile. Do you expect to see any errors or warnings? Does the compiler issue any errors or warning messages? Add a `test` method to the Application Delegate object which requires as argument an object that supports your protocol. Invoke that method from the `applicationDidFinishLaunching:` method. Do you get any new errors? Implement the optional method. Do any error messages change? Implement the mandatory method. Do any error messages change? Invoke your optional and mandatory methods from the `test` method without adding the `respondsToSelector:` test. Make sure the code works (using `NSLog()` if necessary). Remove the optional method. Do you get any error messages? What happens when you run it? Add the `respondsToSelector:` test. What happens now?

HOUR 5
Adding Variables to the Calculator

What You'll Learn in This Hour:

- Improving the split between the model and the controller
- Using an `NSDictionary` to add variables to the calculator
- Using the Key-Value Coding and Observing protocols

Currently the controller invokes the model to perform each calculation as you type numbers. It would be better if the controller knew less about mathematics, and concentrated on building expressions the Model can evaluate. You'll use NSScanner to perform simple parsing. You'll use Cocoa arrays to store the expressions for the calculator's history. To add variables to the calculator, you'll learn to use `NSDictionary`. Finally you'll learn about the Key-Value Coding and Key-Value Observing protocols. The Key-Value Coding protocol is used by NIB files to set outlets and provides a dynamic means of accessing your object's setters and getters.

A Better Model/Controller Split

Although the way we've divided responsibilities between model and controller is sufficient for a simple calculator, it will prove hard to extend. In this section, we'll retask each and introduce `NSScanner` and `NSArray`. Programming is like the real world: Solutions appropriate to small problems rarely extend to large ones, just like you can't build a passenger jet by scaling up a paper airplane.

Extracting the Finite State Machine

Our calculator is currently implemented as a finite state machine. Finite state machines model behavior in terms of a finite number of states, a set of legal transitions between these states, and actions triggered by entering or leaving a state. The states and the transitions form a graph. In this case, each key press corresponds to a transition and the states correspond to the state maintained by the calculator (such as the number you typed in).

A problem with our solution is that the finite state machine we have built is implicit in our code. Given the way different pieces of it are implemented in different methods, it cannot be made explicit in the code, which makes it difficult to extend. Instead, we will retask the controller to build up an explicit expression from the typed keys, and we will move the finite state machine into the model where it will parse the expression and calculate the result.

Moving the finite state machine to the model makes it clear that the problem is a parsing problem. Parsing problems can be split into subproblems: Recognizing numbers, recognizing arithmetic operations, and recognizing computations between parentheses can each be performed separately. In fact, certain tasks are so common that Cocoa provides `NSScanner` to perform them.

Another advantage of separating expressions from calculation is that we can reuse the expression to compute the result in a different domain (such as fractions versus floating-point numbers). We can also vary the interpretation of the expression, to add a mode to support Reverse Polish notation calculations.

Implementing `calculate` with `NSScanner`

To evaluate an expression, we need to tokenize it, distinguishing numbers from operations. Listing 5.1 shows the implementation. `NSScanner`'s `initWithString:` method specifies the string `NSScanner` should scan:

```
NSScanner* scanner = [[NSScanner alloc] initWithString:self];
```

For convenience, we'll ignore whitespace:

```
[scanner setCharactersToBeSkipped:[NSCharacterSet whitespaceCharacterSet]];
```

We'll scan through the string until it reaches the end (`isAtEnd`):

```
while (![scanner isAtEnd])
```

If an arithmetic operation starts at the scanner's current position, `scanCharactersFromSet:intoString:` returns a string of operations. We choose the last one, assuming that if more than one was pressed, it was in error:

```
if ([scanner scanCharactersFromSet:arithmetic intoString:&operation])
  lastOperation = [operation characterAtIndex:[operation length]-1];
```

If a number starts at the scanner's current position in the string, `scanFloat:` retrieves the entire number and we add the computation to the accumulator:

LISTING 5.1 NSStringCalculator.m

```
@interface NSString (Calculator)
- (float) calculate;
@end
static NSCharacterSet* arithmetic = nil;

@implementation NSString (Calculator)

- (float) calculate;
{
  NSLog(@"Calculate %@", self);
  NSScanner* scanner = [[NSScanner alloc] initWithString:self];
  [scanner setCharactersToBeSkipped:[NSCharacterSet whitespaceCharacterSet]];

  if (arithmetic == nil)
    arithmetic = [[NSCharacterSet characterSetWithCharactersInString:@"+-/*"]
                                                                        retain];

  float     accumulator   = 0.0;
  unichar   lastOperation = '+';
  float     current;
  NSString* operation = nil;

  while (![scanner isAtEnd])
  {
    if ([scanner scanCharactersFromSet:arithmetic intoString:&operation])
      lastOperation = [operation characterAtIndex:[operation length]-1];

    if ([scanner scanFloat:&current])
      switch (lastOperation)
      {
        case '+': accumulator += current; break;
        case '-': accumulator -= current; break;
        case '/': accumulator /= current; break;
        case '*': accumulator *= current; break;
      }
  }

  return accumulator;
}

@end
```

You'll notice that we are still using simple calculator rules without precedence for multiplication and division.

Instead of accumulating the number in calculator, this hour's example source code saves it in the NSMutableString currentNumber.

The source code is available at http:// www.informit.com/title/9780672331251. Because it's often easier to start by tinkering with a real working example, this book's source code includes complete programs. But because printing long listings kills trees, most of the examples' source code is provided electronically.

You use the free diffmerge tool to compare the Calculator's source code as it evolves from hour to hour.

Diffmerge is available from http://sourcegear.com

NSArray and NSMutableArray

When dealing with a collection of objects, it is convenient to have a single object to represent the collection. For instance, we would like to keep the calculator's history as a collection of expressions.

The way in which collection elements are accessed determines the type of collection. NSArrays are ordered collections of objects that are indexed by integers. NSMutableArrays are resizable and mutable NSArrays. Internally, NSArray contains pointers to objects. Adding an object to an NSArray retains it, while removing it releases it (as does deleting the array).

In Cocoa, NSArray is used where you might normally use a list: It has good performance characteristics when inserting to either of its ends. NSArray is a class cluster and must be subclassed carefully.

Nonobject Elements

NSArray can only contain objects. Primitive types such as numeric values must be placed in objects. Cocoa provides NSNumber to wrap numbers. For instance, to wrap a long:

```
NSNumber* answer = [NSNumber numberWithLong:42];
long      a      = [answer longValue];
```

Wrapping and unwrapping other numeric types follows a similar pattern using the type name.

NSValue wraps a number of other common entities such as pointers and objects that should not be retained. It also wraps system-defined structures, such as NSRange, CGPoint, CGRect, CGSize, and CGAffineTranform, which you'll learn about in Hour 6, "Understanding How the User Interface Is Built."

Inserting nil into an array will cause an exception, but you can use NSNull (a non-nil object representing nil).

Creating Arrays

initWithObjects: creates a new array containing the objects referenced in the argument list. The argument list must be terminated by nil:

```
NSArray* buttons = [[NSArray alloc] initWithObjects:button0, button1, nil];
```

`initWithArray:copyItems:` copies the array and every object inside it, whereas `copy` and `initWithArray:` only copy the array. `initWithObjects:count:` creates an `NSArray` from a C array of object pointers containing *count* objects. Autoreleased variants of the `init` functions start with `array`.

`NSMutableArrays` adds `initWithCapacity:` and `arrayWithCapacity:` to reserve enough memory to hold *capacity* objects. Adjust this value to boost performance.

New arrays can also be created by joining existing ones with `arrayByAddingObject:` and `arrayByAddingObjectsFromArray:`.

Accessing Elements and Slicing Arrays

`objectAtIndex:`*i* returns the *i*th object or throws an `NSRangeException`:

```
NSButton* b = [buttons objectAtIndex:0];
```

The returned object is typed `id`.

`subarrayWithRange:` uses the elements of the array within the argument range to create a new array. `objectsAtIndexes:` uses the elements of the array indexed by the argument `NSIndexSet` to create a new array. `getObjects` and `getObjects:range:` slice the array to the specified C array of pointers.

Traversing an Array

`count` returns the number of elements in an array, so you can write the following:

```
for (int i = 0; i < [buttons count]; ++i)
{ Button* b = [buttons objectAtIndex:i]; ... };
```

Alternatively, you can use an `NSEnumerator`. Enumerators work with many of Cocoa's collections, so the same code will work even if you change the collection.

```
NSEnumerator *enumerator = [buttons objectEnumerator];
Button*      b;

while (button = [enumerator nextObject])
{ ... };
```

The enumerator returned by `objectEnumerator` traverses the array forward, whereas that returned by `reverseObjectEnumerator` traverses it backward.

To further boost readability and performance, a third method of traversing arrays was added. Using the `NSFastEnumeration` protocol, you can write the following:

```
for (Button* b in buttons)
{ ... }
```

NSEnumerator also supports NSFastEnumeration, so to traverse the array backward, write the following:

```
for (Button* b in [buttons reverseObjectEnumerator])
{ ... }
```

The NSFastEnumeration protocol's countByEnumeratingWithState:objects:count: method copies blocks of object pointers to a C array through which for (Button* b in ...) iterates. By avoiding many calls to objc_msgSend, it boosts speed.

It is unsafe to add or remove elements from an NSMutableArray while traversing it.

Mapping and Sorting

makeObjectsPerformSelector: or makeObjectsPerformSelector:withObject: apply a method to every element of an NSArray. These methods do not replace objects within the array, but they might mutate them.

sortedArrayUsingFunction:context: creates a new sorted array using the comparator function. The *context* parameter lets you customize the comparison. Sorting an array of floats would look like the following:

```
NSArray* sortedArray = [floatArray sortedArrayUsingFunction:floatSort
                                                     context:NULL];

NSInteger floatSort(id lhs, id rhs, void *context)
{
  float v1 = [lhs floatValue];
  float v2 = [rhs floatValue];

  if      (v1 < v2) return NSOrderedAscending;
  else if (v1 > v2) return NSOrderedDescending;
  else              return NSOrderedSame;
}
```

I often use C arrays and qsort (in-place sort) for numerical values because the resulting code is simpler:

```
int compare (const void* lhs, const void* rhs)
{ return ((int) (*((float*)lhs) - *((float*)rhs)) );

qsort (array, arrayLength, sizeof(float), compare);
```

sortedArrayUsingSelector: lets you choose a method of the elements. Again, it should return NSOrderedAscending, NSOrderedDescending, or NSOrderedSame. For instance:

```
NSArray* sorted = [stringArray sortedArrayUsingSelector:@selector(compare:)];
```

sortedArrayUsingDescriptors: lets you combine different comparison functions: Sort alphabetically, then sort any values that compare equal by date, and so on.

Mutating

`NSMutableArray` provides in-place variants of the previous methods. It concentrates on adding, removing, and replacing elements.

`addObject:` adds an object to the end of the array, whereas `removeLastObject` removes the last object of the array. Stacks are easily implemented with `NSMutableArrays` using these two methods and `lastObject`, which returns the last object of the array.

`addObjectsFromArray:`, `insertObject:atIndex:`, and `insertObjects:atIndexes:` provide more generic means of adding objects within the array. `removeObjectAtIndex:`, `removeObjectsAtIndexes:`, `removeObjectsInRange:`, and `removeObjectsFromIndices:numIndices:` provide ways of removing (and releasing) objects from the array based on their location.

There are methods to find and remove all instances of an object from an array. `removeObject:` differs from `removeObjectIdenticalTo:` because it checks for equality with `isEqual:` versus checking pointer equality. Variants specify a subrange to process, or remove any object appearing in the argument array.

Elements can be replaced by index or range with other objects (for example, `replaceObjectAtIndex:withObject:` and `replaceObjectsInRange:withObjectsFromArray:`). The entire array is replaced with `setArray:`.

`NSMutableArray` provides in-place variants of the sorting functions.

Performance

Apple guarantees that access to an object in an array of *N* elements usually takes constant time, but can be at worst O(log *N*). Linear search operations are usually O(*N*) but at worst O(*N* * log *N*). Apple is guaranteeing that should it change the implementation of `NSMutableArray`, the new implementation will have equal or better amortized complexity, and equal or better worst case complexity to the current amortized and worst case complexities.

As currently implemented, `NSArrays` have the following properties:

- Immutable arrays are built as a single block of memory, and have constant read times.
- Small mutable arrays (smaller than 256Kb minus 4 bytes) are built as a single block of memory, and have constant read times. They are built as deques in the center of the reserved space, but are recentered from time to time as data is added. This means that adding to the front or the back of the array are

equally cheap (no cost until the edge of the array is reached, then a copy at a cost of the length of the array). Arrays are grown by rounding the required capacity up by a power of 2.

- Large mutable arrays are built using a tree structure—hence the O(log N) behavior. Converting between large and small mutable arrays is performance intensive.

Using `NSMutableArray` for stacks only allocates memory as the stack grows beyond its capacity. However, using `NSMutableArray` to keep track of a First In First Out (FIFO) type structure that does not grow will involve copying `sizeof(void*) * fifo_size` bytes every `fifo_size/array_capacity` additions. Increasing *array_capacity* will reduce this cost. Alternatively, you can build a circular FIFO.

Did you Know?

It would be difficult to remember all these application programming interfaces (APIs). In practice, you only need to remember the ones you use the most often. Look at Figure 1.10 from Hour 1, "Starting Your First Application: A Calculator." The search bar below the toolbar lets you choose the kind of search. Choose by API, and Starts With. Now, you can quickly find all `NSArray`'s methods by typing **nsar** into the search field at the upper right, and choosing `NSArray` in the upper-right pane.

Using an `NSDictionary` to Add Variables to the Calculator

Now we'll add variables to the calculator using `NSDictionary`. This section walks you through this process to show you some subtleties. We'll start with the `Hour5/Calculator` source code.

Tapping the Var Button

When the user taps the var button, we would like to change the button labels to show variables A–L, which can store values. To change the button labels, we need a handle to the buttons. Add the following outlets to `CalculatorController`'s interface file, and connect them to the relevant buttons, as shown in Figure 5.1:

```
IBOutlet UIButton    *buttonC, *buttonVar, *buttonDiv, *buttonMul;
IBOutlet UIButton    *button7, *button8,   *button9,   *buttonSub;
IBOutlet UIButton    *button4, *button5,   *button6,   *buttonAdd;
IBOutlet UIButton    *button1, *button2,   *button3,   *buttonEq;
IBOutlet UIButton    *button0, *buttonDot;
         NSArray     *buttons;
         BOOL        varState;
```

The title of each button can be set with setTitle:forState:. We'll set it for all three states:

- **Normal**—The button is at rest.
- **Highlighted**—The button is pressed down.
- **Selected**—The button is in an active state (like a Caps Lock key).
- **Disabled**—The button is disabled.

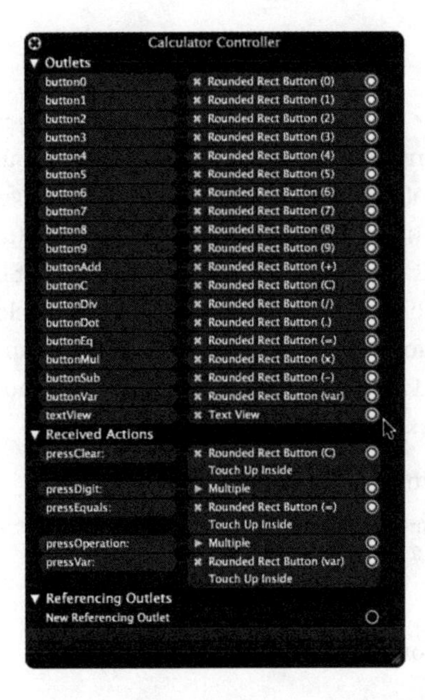

FIGURE 5.1 Outlet connections for KeyValueObserving example

addTarget:action:forControlEvents: lets you add an action for the button and removeTarget:action:forControlEvents: lets you remove the existing one. Invoking removeTarget:action:forControlEvents: with a NULL action removes all actions binding the button to this object.

```
- (void) pressVar:(UIButton*)sender
{
  varState = !varState;

  NSEnumerator* buttonIterator = [buttons          objectEnumerator];
  NSEnumerator* titleIterator  = [titles[varState] objectEnumerator];
  SEL*          sels           = selectors[varState];

  UIButton* button;
  NSString* title;
  int       i = 0;
```

```
    while (    (button = [buttonIterator nextObject])
           && (title = [titleIterator nextObject]))
    {
      [button setSelected:NO];
      [button setTitle:title forState:UIControlStateNormal];
      [button setTitle:title forState:UIControlStateHighlighted];
      [button setTitle:title forState:UIControlStateSelected];
      [button removeTarget:self action:NULL
                  forControlEvents:UIControlEventTouchUpInside];
      [button    addTarget:self action:sels[i]
                  forControlEvents:UIControlEventTouchUpInside];
      ++i;
    }
  }
```

Usually, we would create the `titles` and `selectors` arrays in the object's `init` method, but they are constants, so they do not need to be built each time. In C, you can create static arrays of constants at compile time. However, the Objective-C compiler does not recognize `NSArray`s or `@selector()`s as constants, so we must build them at runtime. Objective-C provides a class method, `initialize`, for this purpose. It is always the first method of a class to be invoked. Superclasses' `initialize` methods are invoked before subclasses'. Because of inheritance, if a subclass does not implement `initialize`, the inherited superclass's method will be invoked, so `initialize` can be invoked more than once.

Outside the implementation block, add the following:

```
static SEL      selectors[2][18] = {};
static NSArray* titles[2];
#define SL @selector
```

Inside the implementation block, add the following:

```
+ (void) initialize
{
  static BOOL initialized = NO;

  if (!initialized)
  {
    SEL sels[2][18] =
      {{SL(pressClear:),SL(pressVar:),  SL(pressOperation:),SL(pressOperation:),
        SL(pressDigit:),SL(pressDigit:),SL(pressDigit:),    SL(pressOperation:),
        SL(pressDigit:),SL(pressDigit:),SL(pressDigit:),    SL(pressOperation:),
        SL(pressDigit:),SL(pressDigit:),SL(pressDigit:),    SL(pressEquals:),
        SL(pressDigit:),SL(pressDigit:)},

      {           NULL,SL(pressVar:),              NULL,                NULL,
        SL(pressDigit:),SL(pressDigit:),SL(pressDigit:),                NULL,
        SL(pressDigit:),SL(pressDigit:),SL(pressDigit:),                NULL,
        SL(pressDigit:),SL(pressDigit:),SL(pressDigit:),    SL(pressStore:),
        SL(pressUse:),  NULL } };
```

```
    for (int i = 0; i < sizeof(selectors) / sizeof(selectors[0][0]); ++i)
      ((SEL*) selectors)[i] = ((SEL*) sels)[i];

    titles[0] = [[NSArray alloc] initWithObjects: @"C", @"var", @"/", @"x",
                                                  @"7", @"8",   @"9", @"-",
                                                  @"4", @"5",   @"6", @"+",
                                                  @"1", @"2",   @"3", @"=",
                                                  @"0", @".",   nil];

    titles[1] = [[NSArray alloc] initWithObjects: @" ", @"clc", @" ", @" ",
                                                  @"A", @"B",   @"C", @"D",
                                                  @"E", @"F",   @"G", @"H",
                                                  @"J", @"K",   @"L", @"STR",
                                                  @"USE", @" ", nil];

    initialized = YES;
  }
}
```

buttons is not constant, so we'll build it in the object's init method:

```
- (id) init
{
  self = [super init];

  if (self)
  {
    textView      = nil;
    varState      = NO;
    clearOnDigit  = NO;
    currentNumber = @"";
    model         = [[CalculatorModel alloc] init];
    buttons       = [[NSArray alloc] initWithObjects:
                               buttonC, buttonVar, buttonDiv, buttonMul,
                               button7, button8,   button9,   buttonSub,
                               button4, button5,   button6,   buttonAdd,
                               button1, button2,   button3,   buttonEq,
                               button0, buttonDot, nil];
  }

  return self;
};
```

Try this out, and tap the var key. Nothing happens!

What went wrong? Look at the pressVar: method: All the work is done inside the while loop. If either buttons or titles is empty, the while loop will stop. Let's print the two arrays in pressVar: as follows:

```
NSLog(@"buttons:%@\ntitles: %@", buttons, titles[varState]);
  buttons: ()
  titles:  (C, var, "/", x, 7, 8, 9, "-", 4, 5, 6, "+", 1, 2, 3, "=", 0, ".")
```

buttons is empty even though the source shows it has 18 elements. Perhaps the buttonC outlet is nil? Adding debug statements to init will show you it is, as are all the other outlets. We have a chicken-and-egg problem: The NIB loader cannot set up outlets before it has an object in which to set them up. To make such an object, it must call the object's `init` method. Thus, an object's outlets will be `nil` inside `init`. To solve the conundrum, after setting up an object's outlets, the NIB loader checks whether the object has an `awakeFromNib` method using `respondsToSelector:`, and if it does, the NIB loader invokes it.

```
- (void) awakeFromNib
{
  buttons = [[NSArray alloc] initWithObjects:
                                  buttonC, buttonVar, buttonDiv, buttonMul,
                                  button7, button8,   button9,   buttonSub,
                                  button4, button5,   button6,   buttonAdd,
                                  button1, button2,   button3,   buttonEq,
                                  button0, buttonDot, nil];

}
```

Set `buttons` to `nil` in the `init` method, and release them in `dealloc`.

NSDictionary

`NSDictionary`s are collections of objects that are indexed by keys (objects such as strings). `NSMutableDictionary`s are resizable and mutable. Keys must implement a `hash` method such that two keys that are judged equal by `isEqual:` must have the same hash. Two keys that are not judged equal may have the same hash value, but this should be minimized.

Adding a (key, value) pair to an `NSDictionary` creates an immutable copy of the key if it was not in the dictionary (see Hour 4, "Making the Calculator Calculate"), and retains the value. Overwriting the value or removing its key releases it, as does deleting the dictionary.

Creating Dictionaries

`initWithObjectsAndKeys:` creates a new dictionary containing the keys and values referenced in the argument list. Values are placed before keys. The argument list must be terminated by `nil`:

```
NSDictionary *french = [NSDictionary alloc];
french = [french initWithObjectsAndKeys:
                            @"mercure", @"mercury", @"terre", @"earth", nil];
```

`initWithObjects:forKeys:` creates a new dictionary from an array of objects and an array of keys. `initWithDictionary:copyItems:` copies a dictionary and every object inside it, whereas `copy` and `initWithDictionary:` only copy the dictionary.

`initWithObjects:forKeys:count:` creates an `NSDictionary` from a C array of object pointers and a C array of key pointers each containing *count* pointers. Autoreleased variants of the `init` functions start with `dictionary`.

`NSMutableDictionarys` add `initWithCapacity:` and `dictionaryWithCapacity:` to reserve enough memory to hold *capacity* objects. Fill your dictionary after using `initWithCapacity:` because it is liable to be resized to a lower capacity the first time you remove a value.

`NSDictionary` is a class cluster and must be subclassed carefully.

Nonobject Elements

As with `NSArray`, `NSDictionarys` can only contain objects. Use `NSNumber`, `NSValue`, and `NSNull` to wrap standard elements.

Accessing Elements

`objectForKey:`*k* returns the object whose key is `k` or `nil` if *k* was not found.

```
NSString* frMercury = [french objectForKey:@"mercury"];
```

The returned object is typed `id`.

The related method `objectsForKeys:notFoundMarker:` returns an `NSArray` of all the objects whose keys are in the first argument array. If no object is found for a key, the object specified by the second argument is used. `NSNull` is often used as a second argument. `allKeys` and `allValues` build new arrays to return keys and values in no predictable order. `getObjects:andKeys:` copies the dictionary's object and key pointers to two C arrays that should each contain at least `[`*d* `count]` elements for dictionary *d*.

`allKeysForObject:` searches the entire dictionary to find all the keys that share the specified value.

Traversing a Dictionary

`keyEnumerator` and `objectEnumerator` return `NSEnumerators` that traverse the dictionary. Similarly, `NSDictionary` supports the `NSFastEnumeration` protocol for keys:

```
for (id* key in dictionary)
{ ... }
```

It is unsafe to add or remove elements from an `NSMutableDictionary` while traversing it.

Mutating

The main methods for mutating are adding (or replacing) and removing keys and their associated objects. `setObject:forKey:` adds a (key, object) pair to a dictionary, replacing any previous object with the same key:

```
[mutableFrench setObject:@"le soleil" forKey:@"sun"];
```

`removeObjectForKey:` deletes a key and associated object from a dictionary.

Secondary methods include `addEntriesFromDictionary:` to merge a dictionary into the receiver, `setDictionary:` to replace a dictionary's content with another's, and `removeAllObjects` and `removeObjectsForKeys:` to remove objects from a dictionary.

Attempting to use any of these methods on an immutable `NSDictionary` causes an exception.

Performance

Apple guarantees that access to an object in a dictionary of *N* elements usually takes a constant time, but will be at worst O(log *N*). Inserting and deleting objects will also usually take a constant time, but can take O(*N* * log *N*) at worst. These guarantees assume the keys provide a good hash function.

`NSDictionary` is currently implemented using an open addressing scheme–based hash table. It hashes the key to obtain a bucket. Then, it linearly probes forward from this bucket until either the key is found, the probe encounters an empty (but not deleted) bucket, or the entire dictionary has been checked. For efficiency, the hash function must, thus, avoid clustering hash values. A hash function that always returns 1 will degrade lookup efficiency to O(*N*). A poor hash function will result in many calls to your keys' `isEquals` method.

`NSDictionary`s that are more than 75% full are resized larger when adding values, and those that are less than 25% full when removing values are resized smaller. This involves rehashing the entire contents of the dictionary.

The order of the keys or values obtained when enumerating a dictionary is the order in which they appear in the hash table: It depends on the hash function and the capacity of the dictionary in a nonobvious manner.

Adding Variable Keys

Users can either store data in a variable or retrieve it. Tapping a variable key selects it (like a Caps Lock key). Then, you can either choose `USE` or `STR` (store) to complete the action. The following code in awakeFromNib: ensures selected keys display red text:

```
for (UIButton* b in buttons)
  [b setTitleColor:[UIColor redColor] forState:UIControlStateSelected];
```

pressLetter: responds to a variable key being tapped and deselects any other selected key using unselectKeys, which returns the previously selected key.

Variables are stored in an NSMutableDictionary called variables. pressStore: stores the currentNumber (if there is one, zero otherwise) to the variable of the selected button.

```
- (void) pressStore:(UIButton*)sender
{
  UIButton* key = [self unselectKeys];

  if (key)
  { [variables setObject:([currentNumber length] ? [currentNumber copy] : @"0")
                  forKey:[key currentTitle]];
    [self      pressVar:buttonVar]; }
}
```

Similar code retrieves the current variable in pressUse:.

The Key-Value Coding and Observing Protocols

Cocoa's Key-Value Coding (KVC) protocol is a means of getting and setting object fields generically by name. This is how the NIB loader connects an object's outlets by name.

Key-Value Observation is also helpful as it will let us updateScreen: every time currentNumber is changed, so we don't have to remember to do it ourselves.

Key-Value Coding

Suppose you want to implement something like Interface Builder in C. Let's call it CIB. Like Interface Builder, CIB would generate CIB files that only contain data, no code. The CIB file loader would find it difficult to set data field values as C has no notion of introspection. You would have to write dispatch functions such as the following:

```
void set(char* structName, char* fieldName, void* structData, void* value)
{
  if (strcmp("CalculatorController", structName) == 0)
    setCalculatorController(fieldName, structData, value);
  else ...
}
```

```
void setCalculatorController(char* fieldName, void* structData, void* value)
{
  if (strcmp("textView", fieldName) == 0)
    setTextView((CalculatorController*) structData, *((UITextView**)value));
  else if (strcmp("button1", fieldName) == 0)
    ((CalculatorController*) structData)->button1 = *((UIButton**)value);
  ...
}
```

Writing such code is error-prone and uninteresting, so people have devised wizards to generate such code for them. This works as long as you don't have to debug the generated code or work around bugs in the generator.

Using Objective-C's Dynamic Aspects to Create Key-Value Coding

How would we build a dispatcher in Objective-C?. We know that `respondsToSelector:` (from Hour 4) checks whether an object supports a method. If we require every getter and setter to follow a naming convention, we can create a function to convert variable names to their getter and setter names:

```
// Prepend string by "set", capitalize the first letter, and append ":"

NSString* setterName(NSString* variable)
{
  int firstCharEnd = [variable
rangeOfComposedCharacterSequenceAtIndex:0].length;
  NSString*  firstChar    = [variable substringToIndex:  firstCharEnd];
  NSString*  rest         = [variable substringFromIndex:firstCharEnd];
  return [NSString stringWithFormat:@"set%@%@:",
                                   [firstChar uppercaseString], rest];
}

NSString* getterName(NSString* variable)
{ return variable; };
```

Using the conversion functions, we can create a generalized setter function that invokes the correct setter. `setterName` returns a string, which we need to convert to a selector. The runtime function `sel_getUid` converts a C string to a selector, so we use `NSString`'s `UTF8String` method to obtain the C string. Now we could call `objc_msgSend`. However, that involves using casts, so instead we'll use `NSObject`'s `performSelector:withObject:` as follows:

```
@interface NSObject(ToyKeyValueCoding)
- (void) setValue:(id) value forKey:(NSString*) key;
@end

#import <objc/runtime.h>

@implementation NSObject(ToyKeyValueCoding)
- (void) toySetValue:(id)value forKey:(NSString *)key
{
```

```
  NSString* setter   = setterName(key);
  SEL       selector = sel_getUid([setter UTF8String]);
  if ([self respondsToSelector:selector])
    [self performSelector:selector withObject:value];
}
@end
```

For objects that do not have setters and getters, the Objective-C runtime provides direct access to Objective-C instance variables via the `object_setInstanceVariable` function for pointers, and similar methods for other kinds of variables. Direct access occurs only if no setter or getter was found.

The following getter methods are tried in order: `get`*`Key`*, *`key`*, `is`*`Key`*. Only one setter method is tried: `set`*`Key`*. Then, the following instance variables are tried in order: `_`*`key`*, `_is`*`Key`*, *`key`*, or `is`*`Key`*.

Did you Know?

If an instance variable *i* is not being set, and you have not defined a setter and getter, it is possible that the Cocoa class from which you are inheriting defines an accessor method that is being inherited or a instance variable *_i* that is getting set instead. Try changing the instance variable name to something else to see if the problem goes away.

Access to Nonexistent Keys

If `setValue:forKey:` cannot find a key, it invokes `setValue:forUndefinedKey:` on the object. Unless you provide your own implementation, your object will inherit `NSObject`'s implementation, which raises an `NSUndefinedKeyException`.

If `valueForKey:` cannot find a key, it invokes `valueForUndefinedKey:` on the object and returns the result. Unless you provide your own implementation, your object will inherit `NSObject`'s implementation, which raises an `NSUndefinedKeyException`.

Did you Know?

The most useful breakpoint in Cocoa is `objc_exception_throw` because it shows you the stack trace of which function caused an exception. To set it, choose Breakpoints in the Show submenu in the Run menu or type ⌘-Option-B. Double-click on the new breakpoint and add it, as shown in Figure 5.2.

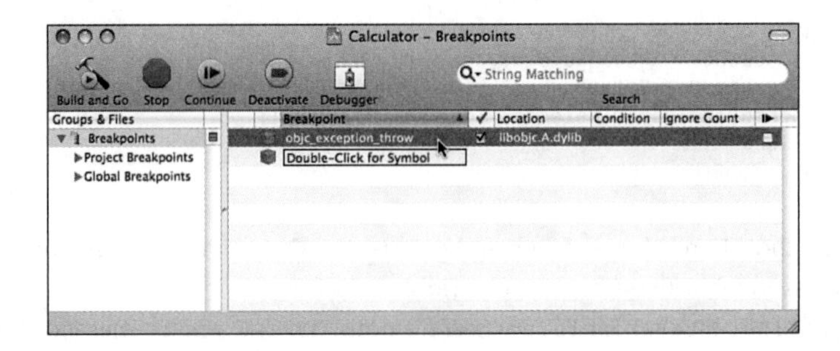

FIGURE 5.2
The most useful breakpoint in Objective-C

Primitive Value Setters and Getters

Our toy implementation of KVC is limited to getters and setters that use objects. Cocoa's KVC implementation checks method types and converts appropriately before invoking the setters and getters it finds. For instance, you can set the `CalculatorController`'s `clearOnDigit` boolean variable using the following:

```
[self setValue:[NSNumber numberWithBool:YES] forKey:@"clearOnDigit"];
```

If you pass a `nil` value, the object's `setNilValueForKey:` method will be invoked. Unless you provide your own implementation, your object will inherit `NSObject`'s implementation, which raises an `NSInvalidArgumentException`.

Guarding Access to Instance Variables

Even though KVC accesses the Objective-C runtime, it can access instance variables that are hidden with `@protected` and `@private`. Instance variable scope declarations are checked statically. Although you cannot prevent direct access to instance variables via the Objective-C runtime, the KVC protocol functions look for an object's class method `accessInstanceVariablesDirectly` and do not set instance variables directly if it returns `NO`. Adding it to `CalculatorController` causes an `NSUndefinedKeyException` when the NIB is loaded:

```
+ (BOOL) accessInstanceVariablesDirectly { NSLog(@"CALLED"); return NO; };
```

```
  CALLED
  *** Terminating app due to uncaught exception 'NSUnknownKeyException', reason:
'[<CalculatorController 0x523830> setValue:forUndefinedKey:]: this class is not
key value coding-compliant for the key buttonSub.'
```

The Key-Value Coding protocol assumes there is no value validation in the setters, and does not provide any means of enforcing it. It does, however, provide a convention that your code can use to check whether the value you are trying to set is valid. Some Cocoa libraries also use this convention. For each key that you would like to validate, define a `validateKey:error:` method. This method can accept the suggested value, correct it, or reject it. The methods can be invoked directly or via the following:

```
- (BOOL)validateValue:(id*) ioValue
              forKey:(NSString*) inKey
               error:(NSError**) outError;
```

For more details, refer to Apple's *Key-Value Coding Programming Guide*.

Using Key-Value Coding

The NIB loader uses KVC to deserialize NIB files without requiring users to write additional code. Although you can create a "poor-man's" deserializer using KVC, I do not recommend it because doing so breaks encapsulation: It will be difficult to change private instance variables if you want to maintain file compatibility. You'll learn how to solve this problem with versioned serialization methods in Hour 14, "Accessing the Network."

Another use of Key-Value Coding is to use naming to link a user-interface (UI) object with an instance variable. For instance, `pressStore:` uses button titles to access dictionary entries directly. Because titles might change in translation, all `UIView` elements have a **tag field** you can set in Interface Builder for this purpose. For instance, entering information into a text field triggers an action. In pre-KVC days, if you had a page of many text fields and you wanted each to store data in a different instance variable, you would have implemented a different action for each text field. With KVC, they can all share the same action, and you can place the instance variable name in the text field's tag.

Did you Know?

> To access a UI element's tag in Interface Builder, select the UI element on the canvas (such as a button), choose the Attributes Inspector, and look for Tag in the View section.

Unit testing can use KVC very effectively to set up the internal state of an object and check that a method changes it as expected. Different versions of a method can be run side by side and tested for divergence.

Did you Know?

> Use the following code to access instance variables in the debugger using KVC:
>
> ```
> po [self valueForKey:@"textView"]
> ```

Key Paths

Key paths extend the KVC mechanism to provide a means of accessing the instance variable of an instance variable. You can write the following code:

```
NSString* expression = [controller valueForKeyPath:@"model.expression"];
```

Because this invokes the `model` getter and then the `expression` getter, you can use the same syntax for methods that look like getters such as `length` or `lowercaseString`.

Similarly, if you have a dictionary, you can access its contents:

```
NSString* variable = [controller valueForKeyPath:@"variables.A"];
```

Key paths are useful as filter predicates. For instance, you can easily add a category to `NSArray` that will return objects whose key-path value matches some condition.

```
@implementation NSArray(Filter)

- (NSArray*) filterWithKeyPath:(NSString*)keyPath equals:(id)value
{
  NSMutableArray* result = [NSMutableArray array];

  for (id object in self)
    if ([[object valueForKeyPath:keyPath] isEqual:value])
      [result addObject:object];

  return result;
}
@end

NSLog(@"Planets belonging to the Milky Way %@",
      [planets filterWithKeyPath:@"solarSystem.galaxy" equals:@"Milky Way"]);
```

Key paths also let you invoke methods on each result and combine the results. More details are available in Apple's *Key-Value Coding Programming Guide* ("Set and Array Operators" section).

Key-Value Observing

Every time we change `currentNumber`, the screen needs to be updated by `updateScreen:`. This is a common problem for graphical user interfaces (GUIs), where changing a value needs to update UI elements. Cocoa's solution is the Key-Value Observing (KVO) protocol. Objects can register to be notified if a property of an object changes. Usually, a controller registers to observe changes in a model, so that the model need know nothing about the UI.

In our case, `currentNumber` is located in the controller, so we end up adding the following line to `CalculatorController`'s `init` method:

```
[self addObserver:self
       forKeyPath:@"currentNumber"
          options:NSKeyValueObservingOptionOld
          context:nil];
```

Changes are reported to the `observeValueForKeyPath:ofObject:change:context:` method of the observer:

```
- (void) observeValueForKeyPath:(NSString*)keyPath
                       ofObject:(id)object
                         change:(NSDictionary*)change
                        context:(void*)context
{
  if ((object == self) && [keyPath isEqualToString:@"currentNumber"])
    [self updateScreen:currentNumber];
}
```

The `NSKeyValueObservingOptionOld` option makes the `change` dictionary contain the value prior to the change. Don't forget also to remove the observer in the `dealloc` method!

```
[self removeObserver:self forKeyPath:@"currentNumber"]
```

The Mechanism

To record the change of a value, `willChangeValueForKey:` and `didChangeValueForKey:` are invoked before and after the change. `willChangeValueForKey:` saves the value before the change and `didChangeValueForKey:` saves the value after the change.

If a variable is changed directly without using getters or setters, the code that performs the change must invoke `willChangeValueForKey:` and `didChangeValueForKey:` itself. For instance, if `currentNumber` were a mutable string, you would have to bracket each mutation of it with these methods:

```
[self willChangeValueForKey:@"currentNumber"];
[currentNumber setString:something];
[self  didChangeValueForKey:@"currentNumber"];
```

However, when using getters and setters, you do not have to invoke these methods, even if you write your setters and getters: Key-Value Observation does it for you. When you invoke `addObserver:forKeyPath:options:context:` on an object, it creates a subclass `NSKVONNotifying_`*`ClassName`* of the object's class *ClassName*. The subclass redefines the methods of the setters you want to observe. Then, it replaces the object's `isa` pointer to point to this new subclass. Now, any invocation of a setter method on the object calls the replaced IMP.

Each IMP Key-Value Observation invokes its superclass's setter in between invocations of `willChangeValueForKey:` and `didChangeValueForKey:`. For instance, object setters are given `_NSSetObjectValueAndNotify` as IMP. This function figures out the name of the property that the setter is changing from the setter's selector, which is conveniently provided by its `_cmd` argument. This name is the argument required for `willChangeValueForKey:` and `didChangeValueForKey:`. The function looks something like this:

```
@implementation interface NSObject (Notification)
- (void) _NSSetObjectValueAndNotify:(id)object
{
  NSString* propertyName = findProperty( _cmd );
  [self willChangeValueForKey:propertyName];
  [super performSelector:_cmd withObject:object];
  [self didChangeValueForKey:propertyName];
}
@end
```

Summary

Congratulations! You've now finished Part I, "Understanding the Objective-C Language," the tools and the non-GUI libraries. We've concentrated primarily on the Model and Controller aspects of the Model View Controller design pattern, which is fundamental to all Cocoa iPhone applications. The next part is dedicated to the View aspect: how UI elements are drawn to the screen and how they react to user input.

Workshop

The Workshop consists of quiz questions and answers to help you solidify your understanding of the material covered in this hour. You should try to answer the questions before checking the answers.

Quiz Questions

1. What is `awakeFromNib:`?

2. What is Key-Value Coding?

3. What is Key-Value Observation?

Quiz Answers

1. `awakeFromNib:` is a method you can define on your objects if you need to initialize your object based on the values in its outlets.

2. Key-Value Coding provides a way to easily access properties using a string as key.

3. Key-Value Observation enables objects to be informed every time another object's property changes.

Exercise

Implement a Sieve of Eratosthenes to compute the primes smaller than 100. Create a one-hundred element `NSMutableArray` to store boolean `NSValues`: Each element will state whether the number at its index is a prime or not. Initially set all values to true. Create a for loop starting at p=2 and stopping at p=10. On each iteration, strike (set false) from the list all multiples of `p` greater than p and smaller than 100. Once the `for` loop has completed, the true elements state that the number that indexes them is a prime. www.wikipedia.org has a good explanation of Sieve of Eratosthenes and improvements to it.

HOUR 6

Understanding How the User Interface Is Built

What You'll Learn in This Hour:

- Views as the building blocks of user interfaces
- Building a user interface from views

In the model-view-controller architecture, views are user interface elements that are responsible for drawing themselves to the screen and reacting to user interaction. Before delving into how they work, which is the subject of the next two hours, you'll learn how to use them.

First you'll learn about windows, the canvas into which views are drawn. Then you'll learn how to combine views to create a complete user interface. The iPhone can display user interfaces in Landscape as well as Portrait mode. You'll learn how to create your own Landscape mode application, and the limitations of Landscape mode. Finally, we'll demystify the NIB file: You can write applications without it, but using it saves you from writing a lot of code.

User-Interface Building-Blocks: Views

Views are the building blocks of user-interface design. They have two responsibilities: drawing themselves and responding to user interaction. The following sections delve into the details of views.

View Hierarchy

The first UIView to be drawn is the UIWindow.

UIWindows cover the entire screen. Most applications work with only one visible UIWindow at a time, whose windowLevel is set to UIWindowLevelNormal. Figure 6.1 shows how the UIWindows that UIKit builds are stacked.

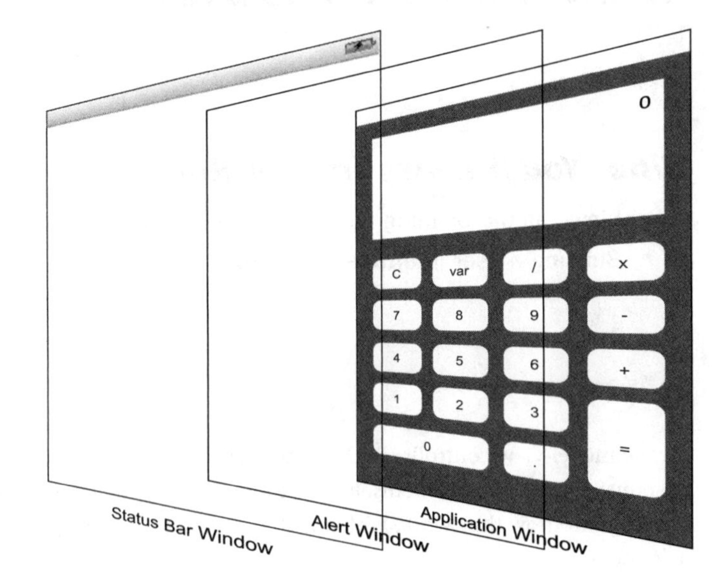

FIGURE 6.1
The UIWindow hierarchy that UIKit creates

Alerts that hover over your application's window are drawn to a second window whose windowLevel is set to UIWindowLevelAlert.

The status bar that hovers over everything else is drawn to a third window whose windowLevel is set to UIWindowLevelStatusBar.

UIWindows can have a background color or image, but by themselves they don't do very much. They must be populated by subviews added with addSubview:. When subviews are added to a superview, their position is specified relative to the coordinate system of the superview. This coordinate system is called the view's **frame**. The rectangle occupied by a subview in its superview is specified by its frame property.

UIWindows are a subclass of UIView, like all other views. UIView is an abstract class that provides the infrastructure to keep track of the view hierarchy and figures out which views need to be redrawn if part of the screen changes. It implements addSubview: to add a subview, subviews to return an NSArray of subviews, and superview to return the view's superview.

Drawing Views

UIKit invokes drawRect: on a view to draw it. drawRect:'s argument is a rectangle represented by a CGRect C structure, which is defined as follows:

```
typedef float  CGFloat;
typedef struct CGPoint { CGFloat x;      CGFloat y;      } CGPoint;
typedef struct CGSize  { CGFloat width;  CGFloat height; } CGSize;
typedef struct CGRect  { CGPoint origin; CGSize size;    } CGRect;
```

The rectangle specifies the part of the button to draw. The rectangle is specified in local coordinates, that is to say in a coordinate system whose origin is the top-left point of the view. The units of this coordinate system are usually pixels, although as you'll see in Hour 8, "Drawing User-Interface Elements," this is not always the case. This coordinate system is called the view's **bounds** (see Figure 6.2).

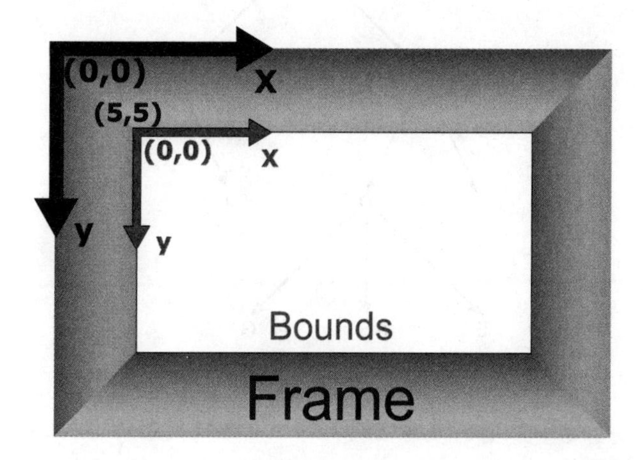

FIGURE 6.2 Frame versus bounds

The view's bounds are usually limited to the size of the view: If the superview's clipsToBounds property is set to YES (Clip Subviews in Interface Builder), UIKit prevents subviews from drawing outside their bounds. This is useful because it can be difficult to write code that only draws part of a view. You can render the entire view and let UIKit perform the appropriate clipping. Of course, there is a performance penalty for drawing things that won't end up on the screen. A view's bounds are specified by its bounds property.

UIViews that have subviews do not need to draw them because UIKit will invoke the subviews' drawRect: methods as needed. If your UIView does not override drawRect:, it will inherit UIView's drawRect: method (which does nothing).

UIKit draws UIWindows from the lowest-level window to the highest-level window. It traverses the subviews of each window and draws them in the order specified by the

NSArray returned by subviews. However, drawing each subview requires drawing its subviews, and so on. The result is a preorder tree traversal sequence (as shown in Figure 6.3). A simplified rendition of the drawing code looks like the following:

```
void drawView( UIView* view, ... )
{
  [self drawRect: ... ];

  for (UIView* subview in [view subviews])
    drawView( subview, ... );
}
```

This functionality is implemented by UIView.

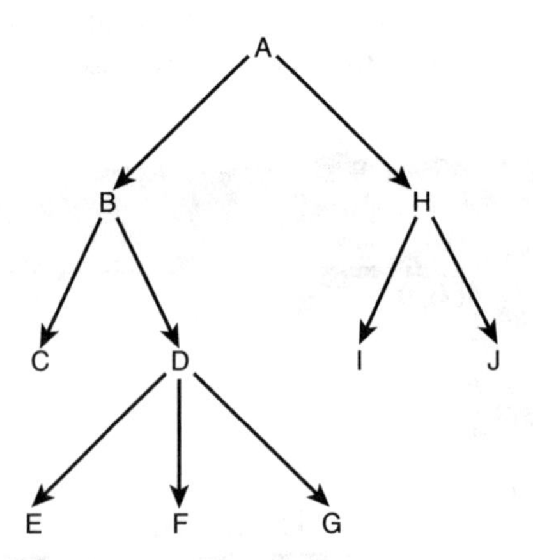

FIGURE 6.3 Preorder tree traversal sequence

UIViews that draw to their entire bounds can set their opaque property to YES. This property tells UIKit that it does not need to draw views behind the opaque view, which lets it optimize user-interface (UI) performance (see Figure 6.4).

Converting Between Coordinate Systems

Because every UIView is drawn in its own coordinate system, UIView provides a number of conversion routines to convert points and rectangles from one view to another. For instance, to convert a point from a superview to the local view, write the following:

```
CGPoint localPoint = [self convertPoint:p fromView:[self superview]];
```

FIGURE 6.4
Views are drawn over other views

Other methods include `convertPoint:toView:`, `convertRect:toView:`, and `convertRect:fromView:`.

To simplify the manipulation of `CGRects`, `CGGeometry` provides a number of utility functions. For instance, `CGRectIntersection` computes the intersection of two rectangles, whereas `CGRectIsEmpty` says whether the resulting rectangle is empty. Thus, we could write a hypothetical `displayRect:` method, which would look like the following:

```
@implementation UIView (DisplayRect)

  - (void) displayRect:(CGRect)rect
  {
    CGRect localRect = [self convertRect:rect fromView:[self superview]];

    for (UIView* subview in [view subviews])
    {
      CGRect toDraw = CGRectIntersection(subview.frame, localRect);
      [self drawRect:toDraw];

      if (!CGRectIsEmpty(toDraw))
        [subview displayRect: toDraw];
    }
  }

@end
```

Did you Know?

NSStringFromCGRect converts CGRects into strings, which can be printed by NSLog. For instance, if you add this line to CalculatorController's awakeFromNib method:

```
NSLog(@"Bounds: %@ Frame: %@", NSStringFromCGRect(buttonC.bounds),
                               NSStringFromCGRect(buttonC.frame));
```

the following will be printed to the console:

```
Bounds: {{0, 0}, {59, 37}} Frame: {{21, 194}, {59, 37}}
```

Reordering Views

Reordering a view's subviews changes the order in which they are drawn. A subview can be brought to the fore with `bringSubviewToFront:` or sent back with `sendSubviewToBack:`. `addSubview:` adds subviews to the fore (that is, it adds them to the back of the `subviews` list). Two subviews can be exchanged with `exchangeSubviewAtIndex:withSubviewAtIndex:` invoked on their superview.

For convenience, views can be given a tag, as discussed in Hour 5, "Adding Variables to the Calculator." You can retrieve a child view using a tag with `viewWithTag:`. This is safer than assuming each view is in a fixed position in the hierarchy, but is unnecessary if an outlet references the view.

Moving Subviews

You can move a subview by redefining its origin in its `frame`, or by moving its `center`. The two operations are equivalent as the `center` is simply the center point of the `frame`. Unless you set its `contentMode` property to `UIViewContentModeRedraw`, moving a subview does not redraw it. This improves its efficiency since nothing is redrawn.

Different Sized Bounds and Frames

Exactly what happens when the size of a view's bounds rectangle does not match the size of its frame depends on the specific `UIView`.

Some objects such as `UIButton` do not allow their frame and bounds sizes to differ. Change one, and the other is changed for you.

Objects such as `UIImage` allow their frame and bounds size to differ. These objects rescale the content they draw according to the value of `contentMode`:

- `UIViewContentModeScaleToFill` distorts the content to fit the view, without preserving its aspect ratio.

- `UIViewContentModeScaleAspectFit` scales the content to fit the view, while preserving its aspect ratio. As the entire content is shown, part of the view might not be drawn and might be transparent.
- `UIViewContentModeScaleAspectFill` scales the content to fit the view, while preserving its aspect ratio. As the entire view is drawn to, part of the content might not be drawn.

Figure 6.5 shows how content is rescaled.

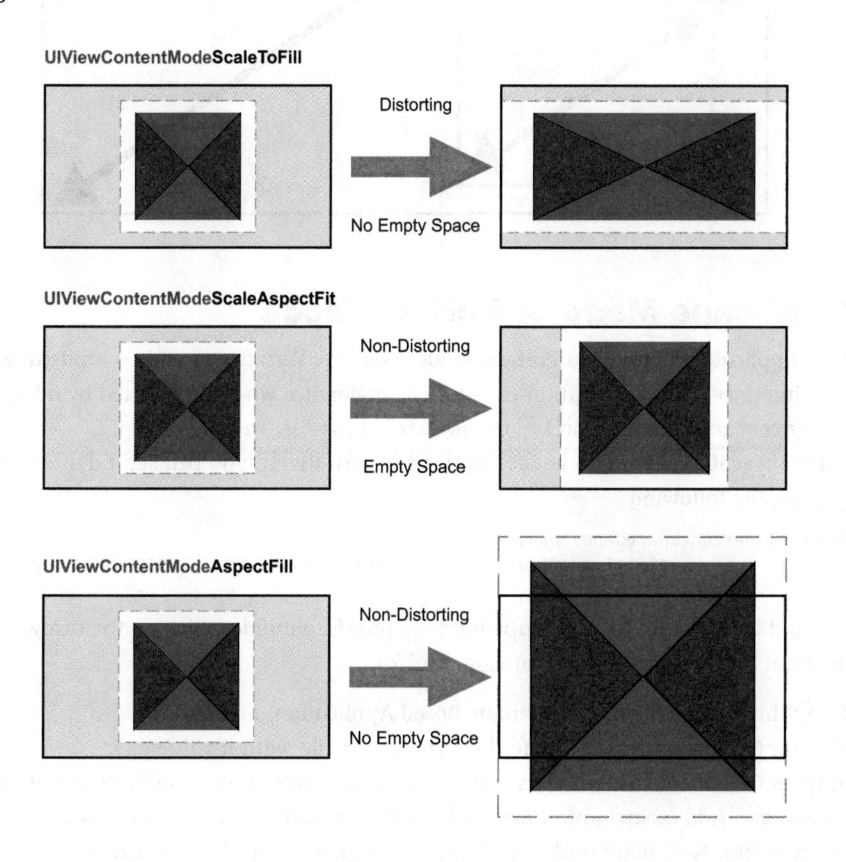

FIGURE 6.5 Image drawn according to `contentMode`

Some objects such as `UIScrollView` contain views larger than themselves. Rather than using the `frame` property, `UIScrollView` tracks the size of its subview object with the `contentSize` property. The `contentOffset` property specifies the (x,y) location within the content view that is shown at the origin of the `UIScrollView`, as shown by Figure 6.6. We encountered this method in Hour 4, "Making the Calculator Calculate."

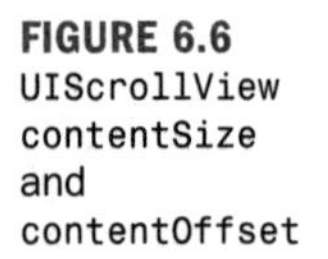

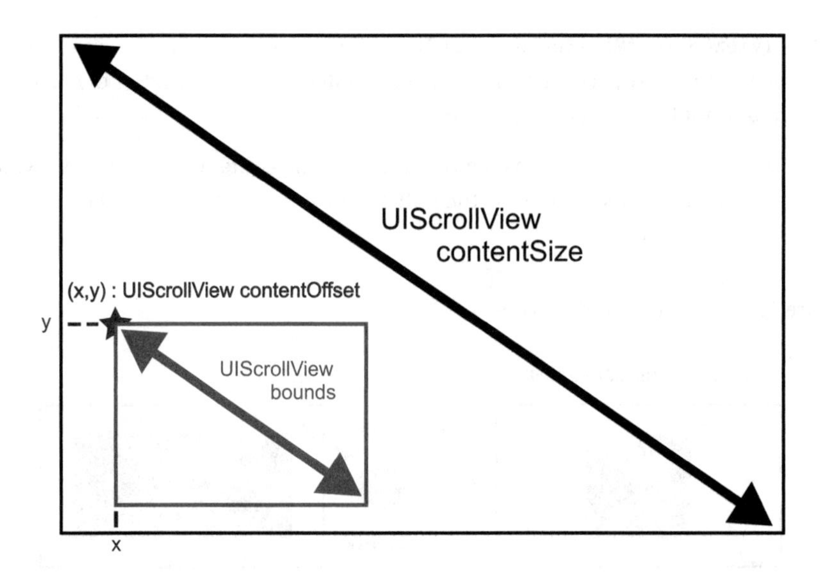

FIGURE 6.6
`UIScrollView` `contentSize` and `contentOffset`

Landscape Mode or Portrait Mode

Most applications provide a Portrait mode interface. Very few provide a landscape-only interface. Your application can state its preference when it is started by adding a `UIInterfaceOrientation` key to the `Info.plist` file, with a value of `UIInterfaceOrientationLandscapeRight`. Alternatively, you can set it dynamically using the following:

```
[[UIApplication sharedApplication]
                 setStatusBarOrientation: UIInterfaceOrientationLandscapeRight]
```

To build an interface in Landscape mode in Interface Builder, click on the arrow at the right of the titlebar shown in Figure 6.7(a).

To try this, just create a new Window-Based Application, and add the `UIInterfaceOrientation` key to the `Info.plist` file, with a value of `UIInterfaceOrientationLandscapeRight`. Build and run, and you'll see a horizontal window. Add a Navigation Bar and a Text View to `MainWindow.xib`, as shown in Figure 6.7(b). Now build and run. Oops! Although we built the interface to appear in landscape mode, our program shows it in portrait mode as shown in Figure 6.8.

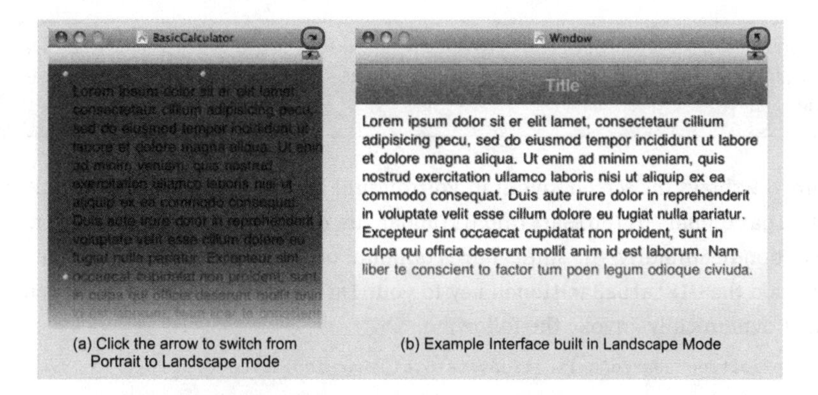

FIGURE 6.7 Using Interface Builder in Landscape mode.

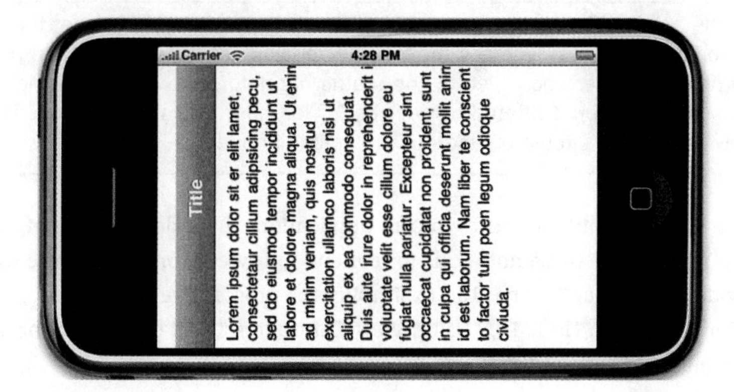

FIGURE 6.8 Incomplete rotation

The status bar window understood that it should be rotated. However, the user-interface window did not and is still in Portrait mode. It even left a gap for the status bar. You can force the user-interface window to adopt the correct orientation by adding the following lines to your application delegate:

```
- (void) awakeFromNib
{
  window.transform = CGAffineTransformMakeRotation(M_PI/2.0);
  window.bounds    = CGRectMake(0, 0, 480, 320);
}
```

The `transform` property is used to convert a view's coordinates from the superview to the subview. In this case, we are rotating the coordinates by 90° (or $\pi/2$). Then, we resize the window's bounds so it has the right shape. Now the view is properly drawn.

Did you Know?

When an alert is created, an alert window is created for it. As of the 2.2.1 SDK, the alert window does not reorient based on the `UIInterfaceOrientation` setting.

Figure 6.9 shows the screen layout in Portrait and Landscape modes. By default, the `UINavigationBar`, `UIToolBar`, and `UITabBar` are all 44 pixels high. These elements are optional. Similarly, the status bar is optional and can be hidden. To hide it statically, add the `UIStatusBarHidden` key to your `Info.plist` file and set it to `true`. To hide it dynamically, invoke the following:

```
[[UIApplication sharedApplication] setStatusBarHidden:YES]
```

Did you Know?

As of SDK 2.2.1, although the simulator rotates the phone when you set the status bar orientation, and it rotates the views when you set the window `transform`, the 20 pixels that were occupied by the status bar before the rotation do not produce touch events: on a rotated screen the 20 leftmost pixels are ignored. This bug only affects the simulator, and not the actual iPhone.

`UIDevice` provides notifications to inform applications if the device orientation has changed. You can use these notations to reorient your views, or you can use methods provided by `UIViewController` to simplify the process. We'll discuss `UIViewController` in Hour 10, "Using View Controllers," and orientation notifications in Hour 20, "Sensing the World."

FIGURE 6.9 Standard layouts

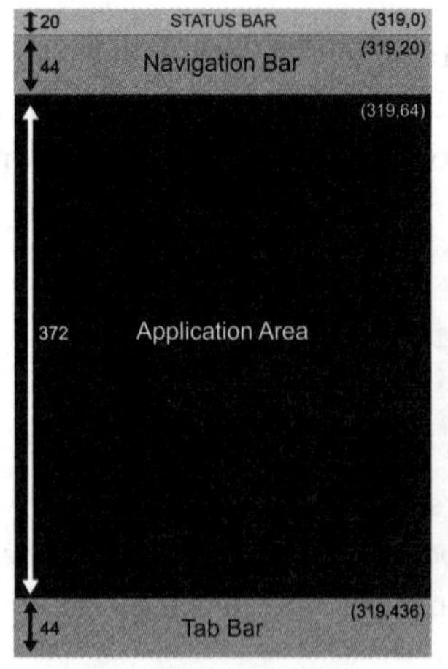

(a) Layout in Portrait Mode

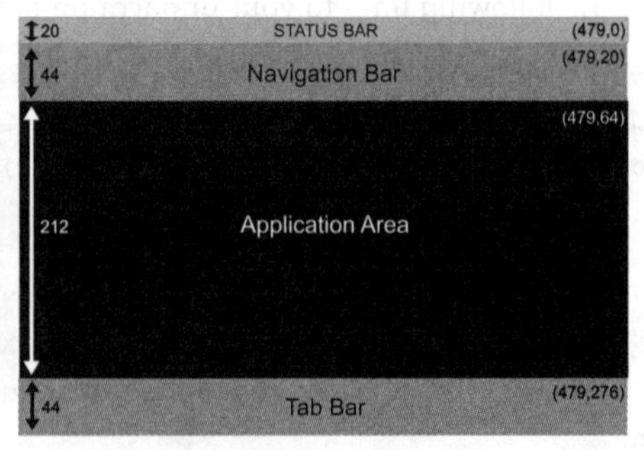

(b) Layout in Landscape Mode

View Layout

If a view is resized, for instance by zooming into it, its subviews will also need to be resized and moved. There are two ways of resizing views: programmatically and automatically.

Programmatic Layout

You could change the layout of your views' subviews in the `setFrame:` and `setBounds:` methods of your view. However, if you did this, each invocation of these methods would trigger a cascade of layout operations as all the subviews frames were adjusted. Instead, these methods invoke `setNeedsLayout`, which sets a flag that the view needs to be laid out.

Users' interaction is processed by code in event handlers. Once all event handlers have run, `UIKit` processes layout before drawing the views. Again, it performs a pre-order tree traversal, invoking `layoutIfNeeded` on each. `layoutIfNeeded` invokes `layoutSubviews` if layout is needed.

You can override your custom view's `layoutSubviews` method and define your own layout in three steps:

1. Call the superclass's `layoutSubviews` method.
2. Read the view's frame.
3. Adjust the subviews frames appropriately. The preorder tree traversal only works because `layoutSubviews` may only adjust their subviews' sizes and locations.

`layoutSubviews` is also invoked on the content view of a `UIScrollView` when the `UIScrollView`' `contentOffset` or `bounds` is changed. In this manner, the content view can use less memory by tiling a set of subviews. Subviews that are scrolled off one edge of the screen can be moved to the opposite edge to display new content.

Autoresizing Layout

A view can be marked as **autoresizing**. Autoresizing subviews change size proportionally to the change in size of their superview. So, if the superview increases width by 10 pixels, and the subview is 10% of the width of the superview, the subview will gain 1 pixel in width.

Autoresizing is enabled by setting the `autoresizesSubviews` property of a view to `YES`. Autoresizing can be refined by setting an autoresizing mask, which lets you specify the margins and bounds that should change size and those that should not. If the mask is set, the specified dimension is flexible.

You can specify these values programmatically by using `setAutoresizingMask:` and combining the constants specified in Figure 6.10 with the binary or operator (|). Alternatively, you can set them in Interface Builder, as shown in Figure 6.11. Interface Builder uses the term autosizing while Cocoa uses the term autoresizing. They refer to the same thing. The settings shown in Figure 6.11 correspond to the following code:

```
[superview setAutoresizesSubViews:YES];
[subview   setAutoresizingMask:   UIViewAutoresizingFlexibleWidth
                                | UIViewAutoresizingFlexibleWidth];
```

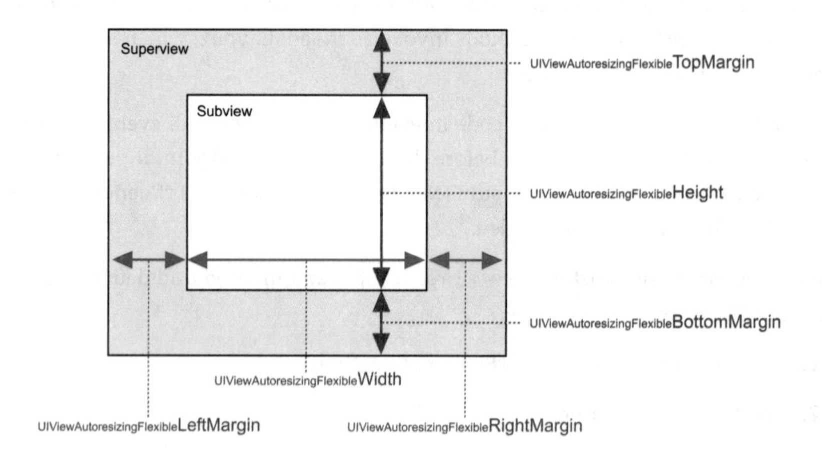

FIGURE 6.10
Autoresizing masks

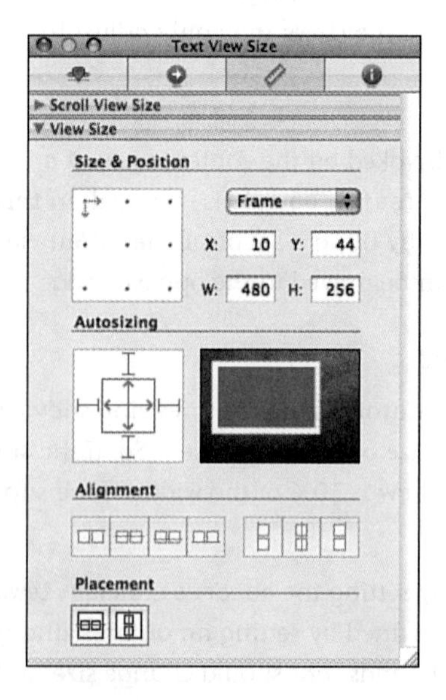

FIGURE 6.11
Autosizing in Interface Builder

Autoresizing is performed down the subview hierarchy until the first nonautoresizable subview is met. It is performed in `setBounds:` and `setFrame:`, which implies that repeatedly calling these functions could be expensive. It is, however, compatible with subviews that are laid out by `layoutSubviews`. Although autoresizing is often useful, the linearity of its layout algorithm results in poor layouts, if the subview contains more than a few elements. Remember that the space between user-interface elements will grow at the same rate as the UI elements themselves.

Did you Know?

This mechanism has an intermittent bug, at least on Mac Cocoa, if the subview being autoresized does not lie completely within its superview's frame. The symptoms are that the subview doesn't go back where you'd want it to be when you reexpand the superview after having collapsed it.

Handling Events

As `UIView` is derived from `UIResponder`, which deals with events, every instance of `UIView` inherits the methods `touchesBegan:withEvent:`, `touchesMoved:withEvent:`, `touchesEnded:withEvent:`, and `touchesCancelled:withEvent:`.

A view receives a `touchesBegan:withEvent:` message when one or more fingers touch down on the screen. We'll ignore the second argument, which is a `UIEvent` until Hour 7, "Understanding How Events Are Processed." The first argument is a set of distinct `UITouch` objects, each corresponding to the location of a finger on the screen.

`UITouch` objects can convert the coordinates of the finger on the screen to its location in the view with the `locationInView:` method. Pass `nil` as the view argument to obtain the coordinates in the window coordinate system. Each `UITouch` object also has a `phase`, which specifies whether its finger was

- Just placed on the screen (`UITouchPhaseBegan`)
- Moved (`UITouchPhaseMoved`)
- Not moved (`UITouchPhaseStationary`)
- Removed (`UITouchPhaseEnded`)
- Or the touch sequence was cancelled (`UITouchPhaseCancelled`)

Touch sequences can be cancelled by system events such as an incoming phone call.

Views receive the following:

- `touchesMoved:withEvent:` message when one or more fingers move.
- `touchesEnded:withEvent:` message when one or more fingers lift up from the screen.
- `touchesCancelled:withEvent:` message when the touch sequence is cancelled. We'll write our own methods to handling these events in Hour 8, "Drawing User-Interface Elements."

As `UIView` knows where each `UIView` subview is placed, and which subview appears above which other, it is also involved in dispatching events. We'll examine this mechanism in detail in Hour 7.

Building the UI from Views

Views are dynamically combined into a user interface using `addSubview:`. We can build entire interfaces in code without using Interface Builder. In this section, we'll build the calculator's interface without using Interface Builder. Doing so will show you what Interface Builder does behind the scenes, and will give you more confidence that you can solve any problems that arise with NIB files. It will also help you learn how to build custom interfaces to give your applications that extra shine.

Application Delegate

Before creating a NIB-less application, we need to understand what an **application delegate** is.

Every iPhone application has a `UIApplication` object, which represents the application. In Interface Builder, it appears as the `File Owner` object. When the operating system receives user events (such as touching the screen), it forwards these to specific methods on the application object. `UIApplication` decodes these events and dispatches them to the appropriate objects.As `UIApplication` is a complex class that could change in the future, subclassing it is likely to cause the fragile base class problem we discussed in Hour 4. Cocoa often uses **delegation** to avoid this problem: Another object is tasked with customizing behavior. Because delegate methods are called in well-defined circumstances, the architecture of the main class can be changed without breaking the delegates. A rarely used advantage of delegates is that they can be replaced at runtime, which is impossible with subclassing.

The methods a delegate should provide are often specified by a protocol. For instance, the `UIApplicationDelegate` protocol specifies the methods

UIApplication can invoke on the application delegate. The key method implemented by Xcode's CalculatorAppDelegate is applicationDidFinishLaunching::

```
@implementation CalculatorAppDelegate
@synthesize window;

- (void)applicationDidFinishLaunching:(UIApplication *)application
{
  // Override point for customization after application launch
  [window makeKeyAndVisible];
}

- (void)dealloc
{ [window release];
  [super dealloc]; }

@end
```

applicationDidFinishLaunching: is called when the application is ready to run. By this stage, the main NIB file has been loaded as the NIB file usually specifies the application delegate to build. Look at the application's outlets by right-clicking (Ctrl-clicking) the File Owner object in the Interface Builder document window. You'll see it has the CalculatorAppDelegate object as a delegate. You'll learn more about application delegates in Hour 7.

Building the Calculator UI with Code

First get rid of the NIB file: Open Resources in the Groups & Files pane and delete the Main nib file base name line by selecting it and pressing Delete (see Figure 6.12). Then delete the MainWindow.xib file from the Groups & Files pane by selecting it, pressing Delete, and choosing Delete References. Make sure you don't delete it without keeping a copy, as we'll need it later.

Now, we must tell the application launcher what application object and delegate to build. Choose main.m and change the line that launches the application:

```
int retVal = UIApplicationMain(argc, argv, nil, nil);
            int retVal = UIApplicationMain(argc, argv, @"UIApplication",
@"CalculatorAppDelegate");
```

The third argument specifies the class of the application object and the fourth argument specifies the class of the application delegate. Once the application has launched, we will get control in applicationDidFinishLaunching:. We will add the UI creation code here.

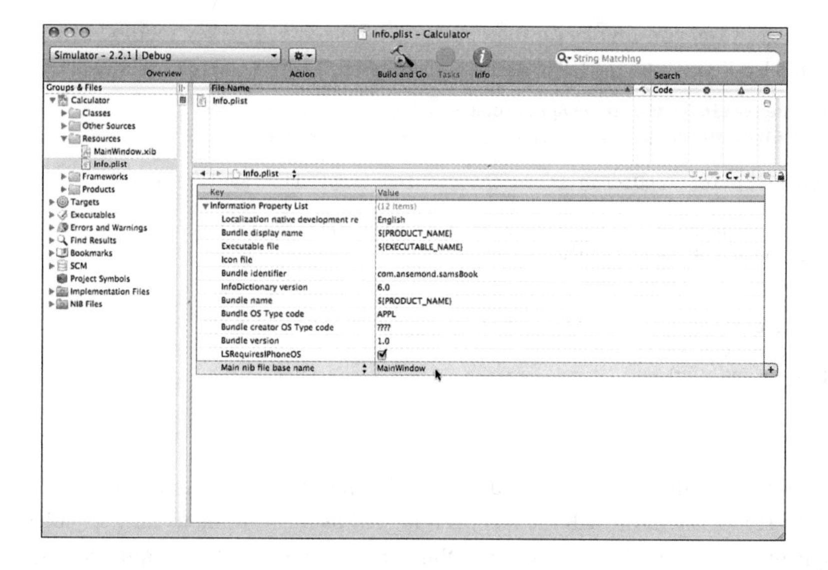

FIGURE 6.12 The `Main nib file base` name setting in the `Info.plist` file

First, we create a window and set its background color:

```
#define SL @selector

- (void)applicationDidFinishLaunching:(UIApplication *)application
{
  window = [[UIWindow alloc] initWithFrame:[[UIScreen mainScreen] bounds]];
  [window setBackgroundColor:[UIColor colorWithWhite:0.34 alpha:1.0]];
```

Then, we create the `CalculatorController` as we'll need to set its outlets:

```
CalculatorController* controller = [[CalculatorController alloc] init];
```

Then, we create the text view and add it as a subview to the window. We give it the settings we gave it in Interface Builder. We autorelease it because `addSubview` will retain it. We set it to be the text view of `controller`:

```
UITextView* textView
   = [[[UITextView alloc] initWithFrame:CGRectMake(21, 40, 280, 128)]
                                                          autorelease];
textView.textAlignment = UITextAlignmentRight;
textView.text          = @"0";
textView.editable      = NO;
textView.font          = [UIFont fontWithName:@"Helvetica" size:17];
[controller setTextView:textView];
[window addSubview:textView];
```

Then, we create the buttons, set the relevant outlets in the controller using KVC, and set up the methods to invoke when they are pressed:

```
SEL actions[18] =
  ={ SL(pressClear:), SL(pressVar:),   SL(pressOperation:), SL(pressOperation:),
     SL(pressDigit:), SL(pressDigit:), SL(pressDigit:),     SL(pressOperation:),
     SL(pressDigit:), SL(pressDigit:), SL(pressDigit:),     SL(pressOperation:),
     SL(pressDigit:), SL(pressDigit:), SL(pressDigit:),     SL(pressEquals:),
     SL(pressDigit:), SL(pressDigit:) };

NSArray* titles = [NSArray arrayWithObjects: @"C", @"var", @"/", @"x",
                                             @"7", @"8",   @"9", @"-",
                                             @"4", @"5",   @"6", @"+",
                                             @"1", @"2",   @"3", @"=",
                                             @"0", @".",   nil];

NSArray* outlets = [NSArray arrayWithObjects:
                    @"buttonC", @"buttonVar", @"buttonDiv", @"buttonMul",
                    @"button7", @"button8",   @"button9",   @"buttonSub",
                    @"button4", @"button5",   @"button6",   @"buttonAdd",
                    @"button1", @"button2",   @"button3",   @"buttonEq",
                    @"button0", @"buttonDot", nil];

NSEnumerator* titleEnum  = [titles  objectEnumerator];
NSEnumerator* outletEnum = [outlets objectEnumerator];
int i = 0;

for (float y = 194.0; y <= 402.0; y += 52.0)
  for (float x = 21.0; x <= 240.0; x += 73.0)
  {
    NSString* title      = [titleEnum  nextObject];
    NSString* outletName = [outletEnum nextObject];

    if ((title == nil) || (outletName == nil))
      break;

    UIButton* button = [UIButton buttonWithType:UIButtonTypeRoundedRect];

    float height = [title isEqualToString:@"="] ?  90.0 : 37.0;
    float width  = [title isEqualToString:@"0"] ? 131.0 : 59.0;

    if ([title isEqualToString:@"."])
      x = 167.0;

    [button setFrame:CGRectMake(x, y, width, height)];
    [button setTitle:title forState:UIControlStateNormal];
    [button setTitle:title forState:UIControlStateHighlighted];
    [button setTitle:title forState:UIControlStateSelected];
    [window addSubview:button];

    [controller setValue:button forKey:outletName];
    [button addTarget:controller action:actions[i++]
            forControlEvents:UIControlEventTouchUpInside];
  }
```

Finally, we call controller's awakeFromNib method and show the window.

```
    [controller awakeFromNib];
    [window makeKeyAndVisible];
}
```

As you can see, it's not complicated, just laborious. The nice thing about NIB files is that you don't have to write this kind of code.

Figure 6.13 shows the objects used by our Calculator application, distinguishing between model, view, and controller objects. Usually the NIB file instantiates most of these objects saving you from doing it.

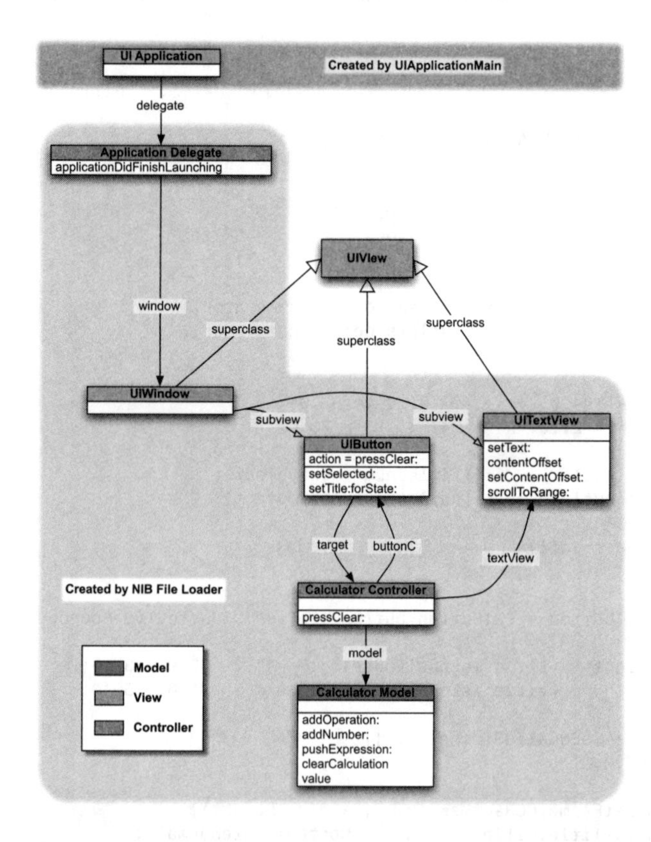

FIGURE 6.13 How view objects fit into the Calculator application

Did you Know?

We are using four closely related but different concepts:

- `text view` is the general concept of a view that can contain more than one line of text.
- `UITextView` is the class that implements text views in Cocoa Touch.
- `Text View` is Interface Builder's name for text views.
- `textView` is the name of an outlet we're using as a pointer to the text view of our calculator that serves as its screen.

The text view serving as a screen for our calculator is implemented by a specific `UITextView` object. In NIB-less code, we instantiate this object in code. If we use a NIB, we create this object by dragging a Text View object to Interface Builder's Document Window.

Building the Calculator UI with a NIB File

NIB files contain no code, so it is up to the NIB loader to dynamically build objects in memory and connect the outlets correctly. The NIB loader is a specialized interpreter that reads instructions from the NIB file and builds objects of the classes it names. Each class name is dynamically looked up in the Objective-C runtime. `NSClassFromString` returns a class object (or `nil` if the class was not found) from which the class can be built. KVC is used to set up the objects' settings and outlets. Subviews are added to their superviews and released. Top-level objects that have no superviews are retained by the NIB loader.

Objective-C's message logging lets you see this happen: Running an executable on a Mac with the `NSObjCMessageLoggingEnabled` environment variable set to `YES` causes the Objective-C runtime to log every Objective-C message to a file `/tmp/msgSends-`*`pid`*, where *pid* is the process identifier of the executable.

To set an environment variable, open the context menu on the Calculator executable in the Executables section of the Groups & Files pane, and choose Get Info. Now choose the Arguments tab and click on the + button in the lower-left corner of the window. Add **`NSObjCMessageLoggingEnabled`** as the name and **`YES`** as the value (see Figure 6.14). Ensure the check box is checked, and run the application. Exit the iPhone simulator, and choose Open from Xcode's File menu. Type Shift-⌘-G and then **`/tmp`** to see what's in `/tmp`. Choose the file prefixed by `msgSends-`. This shows you every method invoked during the execution of your application.

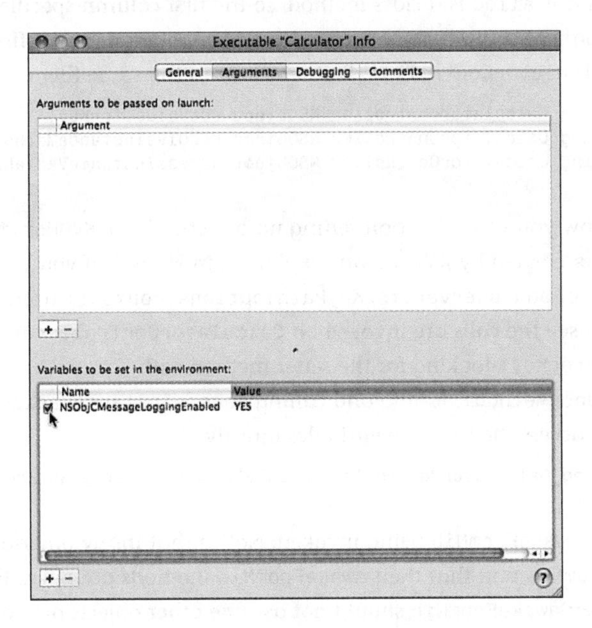

FIGURE 6.14 Setting an environment variable for the application

Run it on the Calculator project from Hour 5.

The first line,

```
- UIApplication UIApplication _loadMainNibFile
```

shows us that UIApplication's _loadMainNibFile method was called. _loadMainNibFile looks up the NIB filename from the application's Info.plist. (Open Resources in the Groups & Files pane, and click Info.plist). The Main nib file base name entry specifies MainWindow, which refers to the MainWindow.xib file.)

Further down in the file, you'll see the following line:

```
- UINib UINib initWithContentsOfFile:
```

This is the NIB loader opening the NIB file. Further down in the file, you'll notice CalculatorController being built:

```
+ CalculatorController CalculatorController initialize
+ CalculatorController NSObject alloc
+ CalculatorController NSObject allocWithZone:
- CalculatorController CalculatorController init
```

The first column specifies the object on which the method was invoked, the second column shows us on which object the method that was invoked was defined. For instance, CalculatorController has no alloc method, so NSObject's method is invoked. Similarly, alloc is a class method, so the first column specifies + CalculatorController, whereas init is a instance method, so the first column specifies – CalculatorController. Further down in the same file, you'll see:

```
- NSKVONotifying_CalculatorController NSObject setValue:forKey:
+ NSKVONotifying_CalculatorController NSObject resolveInstanceMethod:
+ NSKVONotifying_CalculatorController NSObject accessInstanceVariablesDirectly
```

These lines show you KVC in action setting up outlets. The NSKVONotifying_ prefix is the subclass created by KVO as was explained in Hour 5. If you were to remove the invocation of addObserver:forKeyPath:options:context: from the init method, you'll see the calls are invoked on CalculatorController instead. You can see setValue:forKey: looking for the setter method with resolveInstanceMethod:, failing and calling accessInstanceVariablesDirectly to see if it can access the instance variables directly.

```
- NSKVONotifying_CalculatorController CalculatorController awakeFromNib
```

Finally, we see awakeFromNib being invoked. Notice that many other objects implement awakeFromNib and that their awakeFromNib methods are not called in any particular order: awakeFromNib should not assume other objects are completely set up—just that they have been created and initialized. In other words, their init will have been called, but their `awakeFromNib` may not have been, so not all their instance variables may be ready to use.

If you continue to look around in the file, you'll see the buttons and text view being created.

Watch Out!

> The support library that provides logging is not available on the iPhone, but the Objective-C runtime will try to load it anyway because the environment variable is set. This causes a crash before `main()` is loaded with an `EXC_BAD_ACCESS` inside `instrumentObjcMessageSends`. The debugger becomes completely unresponsive and you'll be lucky to even get a crash log.
>
> Crash logs are not provided by the debugger, but by a process running on the iPhone. To see them, open the Xcode's Organizer Window by choosing the Window, Organizer menu item or pressing the Ctrl+⌘+O keys. Click your iPhone in the left pane, and choose the Crash Logs tab.

Supporting Multiple Views

Most applications display more than one view. Even Apple's Weather application shows two views: the weather and a settings screen.

Swapping Views

We can dynamically build views from other views with `addSubview:` in the same way we can take them apart. To swap any subviews, simply remove the existing subviews and add the new subviews. Although `addSubview:` adds a subview to a superview, there is no inverse function on the superview: You must invoke `removeFromSuperview` on the subview. However, we can create one ourselves. `subviews` returns an `NSArray` of a superview's subviews. Then, using `NSArray`'s `makeObjectsPerformSelector:` method, we can remove the subviews:

```
[[window subviews] makeObjectsPerformSelector:@selector(removeFromSuperview)];
```

Thus, we can create a `swapToViews:` method:

```
@interface UIView (Swapper)
- (void) swapToViews:(NSArray*)views;
@end

@implementation UIView (Swapper)

- (void) swapToViews:(NSArray*)views
{
  [[window subviews] makeObjectsPerformSelector:@selector(removeFromSuperview)];
  [window performSelector:@selector(addSubview:) withObjects:views];
}
```

```
@end

@interface NSObject (PerformSelectorWithObjects)
- (void) performSelector:(SEL)selector withObjects:(NSArray*)objects;
@end

@implementation NSObject (PerformSelectorWithObjects)

- (void) performSelector:(SEL)selector withObjects:(NSArray*)objects
{
  for (id o in objects)
    [self performSelector:selector withObject:o];
}
@end
```

You'll learn how to animate transitions between views in Hour 9, "Layers and Core Animation: Creating a Cover Flow Clone."

Dynamically Loading NIBs

Because `MainWindow.xib` is loaded and interpreted in its entirety each time you start the application, it is worth pruning down to the bare minimum. You can load other views dynamically when they are needed. This also helps you reduce your application's memory consumption.

`NSBundle`, which we'll describe in more detail in Hour 10, provides `loadNibNamed:owner:options:` to load NIB files. Each invocation of `loadNibNamed:owner:options:` creates a new graph of objects in memory. The top-level objects are returned in an autoreleased array. Top-level objects are those that are not subviews and appear in Interface Builder's document window (see Figure 6.15). If you don't retain them, they'll be released. On error, `loadNibNamed:owner:options:` returns `nil`.

```
NSArray* topLevelObjects = nil;
topLevelObjects = [[NSBundle mainBundle] loadNibNamed:@"myNib"
                                               owner:self
                                             options:nil];
```

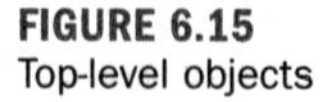

FIGURE 6.15
Top-level objects

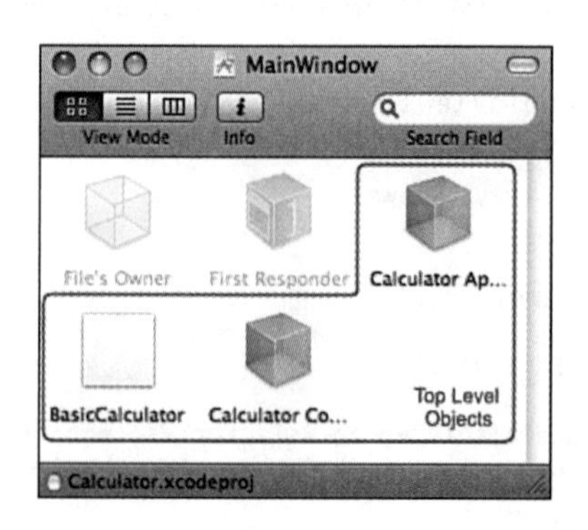

For instance, you can replace the current view with one from your NIB:

```
for (id object in topLevelObjects)
  if ([object isKindOfClass:[UIView class]])
  {
    [[window subviews] makeObjectsPerformSelector:
                                          @selector(removeFromSuperview)];
    [window addSubview:object];
    break;
  }
```

Proxy Objects

As mentioned previously, each invocation of `loadNibNamed:owner:options:` creates a new graph of objects in memory. For instance, if you place a new application delegate in each NIB file you load, you'll end up with many of new application delegates. Most of them won't be delegates to the `UIApplication` and won't do anything. You can, however, connect UI elements in a NIB to existing objects by using proxy objects.

Every NIB file contains at least one proxy object: `File's Owner`. This object is specified by the `owner` parameter of `loadNibNamed:owner:options:`. When `UIApplication` loads the main NIB file, it passes itself as `File's Owner`. You can specify any object you want when you invoke `loadNibNamed:owner:options:`. For Interface Builder to treat `File's Owner` as an object of the correct type, you must set `File's Owner`'s Class Identity in the Identity Inspector, as we did in Figure 2.4. For convenience, the figure is duplicated in this chapter as Figure 6.16. Now, the correct outlets will appear when you right-click `File's Owner`.

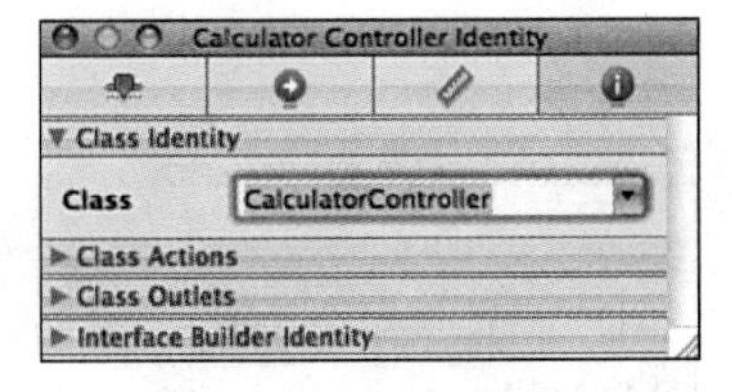

FIGURE 6.16 Class Identity Inspector

You can create new proxy objects by dragging them from the Controllers section of the Library window of Interface Builder (see Figure 6.17).

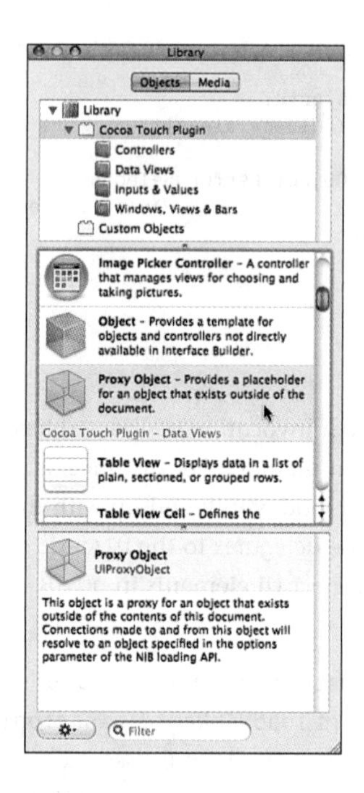

FIGURE 6.17
Creating proxy objects within Interface Builder

Again, `loadNibNamed:owner:options:` must specify the live objects to replace the proxy objects in the NIB. To do this, each proxy object created in Interface Builder must be given a Proxy Object Identifier (set in the Proxy Object's Attributes inspector; see Figure 6.18). Then, you must create a dictionary of proxy identifiers to live objects. Place this into the options dictionary, which is the third argument of `loadNibNamed:owner:options:`, using `UINibProxiedObjectsKey` as the key.

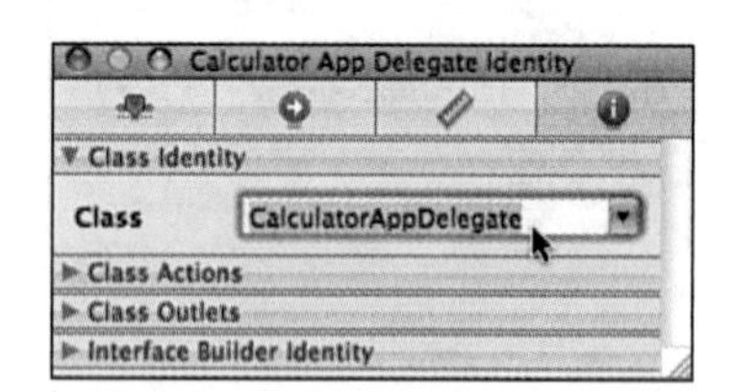

FIGURE 6.18
Setting a Proxy Object's type

For instance, if your application delegate wants to load a NIB file that uses a proxy object for `CalculatorController`, it could do so by implementing the following method:

```
- (NSArray*) loadNib:(NSString*)nibName
             withCalculatorController:(CalculatorController*)c
{
  NSDictionary* proxies = [NSDictionary dictionaryWithObject:c
                                        forKey:@"CalculatorController"];
  NSDictionary* options = [NSDictionary dictionaryWithObject:proxies
                                          forKey:UINibProxiedObjectsKey];
```

```
  return[[NSBundle mainBundle] loadNibNamed:nibName owner:self options:options];
}
```

`File's Owner` or `First Responder` are not included as top-level objects, shown previously in Figure 6.15, because they are proxy objects.

Summary

Views are the basic building blocks of user interfaces. This hour, you've learned how to build views from subviews, and how to lay them out. You've also learned how NIB files work, and that they save you from writing code. Views are the most easily recognized elements of the Model-view-controller architecture: They're user interface elements the user can interact with, and that are drawn to the screen. The next two hours investigate how they interact with the user and how they are drawn.

Q&A

Q. *When should I use autoresizing?*

A. Think of autoresizing as a great shortcut for simple superviews that only contain a few subviews and don't change too much. It reduces the amount of code you have to write for simple cases, but it does not scale to difficult cases. It is a useful tool because most of the time, one is dealing with simple cases. For anything more difficult, write layout code.

Q. *When should I use NIB files?*

A. NIB files are a handy shortcut and let nonprogrammers design UIs. The advantages of NIB files are the WYSIWYG editor and reducing the amount of code you have to write, which lets Cocoa engineers compete effectively with teams of engineers on other platforms.

As a beginner, it's all too easy to change a setting accidentally and not be able to figure out which one it was. The explicit textual format of code does not hide such changes in an inspector you don't remember seeing. It is always a good idea to save your work regularly and use version control for NIB files.

NIB files only scale to a certain level of interface complexity, beyond which it's easier to define and use reusable custom views. Interface Builder does not let you do this, so you must implement such views in Cocoa. Over time, you'll develop a feeling for the level of complexity for which NIB files are appropriate. Also remember to use many small NIB files, each for a different task, rather than one big one. Interface Builder contains a refactoring tool (File, Decompose Interface), which finds the different object graphs embedded in the NIB.

Again, NIB files simplify the common easy case, improving your productivity while not relieving you of the need to write code wherever they prove too simplistic.

Workshop

The Workshop consists of quiz questions and answers to help you solidify your understanding of the material covered in this hour. You should try to answer the questions before checking the answers.

Quiz Questions

1. Are there windows on the iPhone?
2. What is the view hierarchy?
3. In what order are views drawn?
4. In what order is programmatic layout performed?

Quiz Answers

1. Yes, but they occupy the entire screen. Applications rarely use more than one window.
2. The view hierarchy is the tree of subviews contained by views.
3. Views are drawn by performing a preorder tree traversal of the view hierarchy.
4. Views are laid out programmatically by performing a preorder tree traversal of the view hierarchy.

Exercise

In the "Landscape Mode or Portrait Mode" section, you learned how to build an application that starts in Landscape mode. Apply this knowledge to create this application. You will need to remember how to create a new project and use what you've learned to copy the correct code from the book. Change the application's NIB so that it looks like Figure 6.7(a) and make sure that the resulting application starts in Landscape mode with the views correctly rotated as shown in Figure 6.7(a).

HOUR 7
Understanding How Events Are Processed

What You'll Learn in This Hour:

- Understanding run loops
- Understanding Core Foundation and toll-free bridging
- Starting applications
- Dispatching events
- Understanding the `UIResponder` chain
- Understanding `UIControls`

This hour, we'll study how external events, such as the user touching the screen or a network packet arriving from the Internet, are handled and dispatched by your application. Misunderstanding the run loop is a common source of bugs among beginners. You'll also learn how touch events are dispatched to the correct `UIView` to provide user interface elements the user can interact with.

Run Loops and Core Foundation

Run loops are the backbone of any Cocoa application that responds to external events. Graphical user interface (GUI) applications are one such category, although there are other examples such as web servers.

A run loop is an infinite loop that waits for events to occur and dispatches them:

```
Event event;

while (getNewEvent(&event))
  process(&event);
```

Early GUIs such as Xlib would require programmers to write such a loop directly in their code. However, this does not allow the run loop to evolve and embrace additional functionality.

Therefore, Apple provides CFRunLoop objects, which provide a means to register new event sources, new timers, and new observers.

Understanding Event Sources

Cocoa Touch abstracts the sources of all external events into a single API: event sources.

Port Sources

The iPhone operating system (OS) kernel is Mach based. UNIX's fundamental idea was to treat everything as a file. Mach's fundamental abstraction is to treat everything as **interprocess communication** (IPC). IPC provides a communication channel between any two processes (programs). The advantage of this abstraction is that less code needs to be placed in the kernel. Programs in user space can communicate directly via IPC and can implement most of the functionality that would traditionally be placed in the kernel.

The run loop ties directly into IPC: All events that occur outside the application, such as touching the touch screen, rotating the iPhone, pressing the termination button, or receiving network communication, are communicated to the application via IPC. Thus, the application opens a different port for each kind of event it wants to receive.

Mach IPC is unidirectional and asynchronous: Messages are dispatched to the receiver without expecting any acknowledgement. The application that is the source for any IPC registers a port name. Applications that know the name and have permission can connect to the port and are given a port handle.

Mach's kernel function `msg_mach` is at the heart of the `CFRunLoop`. It blocks on a set of ports until one of them gets a message. During `msg_mach`, the thread that invoked it is said to be asleep. In a single-threaded application, the application is asleep. Once a new event is received, `msg_mach` returns and the run loop processes the event.

To register a source with a run loop, give it a `CFRunLoopSource` object. These objects contain the port they should listen to and a callback to be invoked should a message arrive on that port. The callback functions are responsible for decoding and handling the specific IPC message. The function that adds `CFRunLoopSources` to the run loop adds the port to the set of ports on which to block. Thus, the simplest incarnation of the run loop looks like this:

```
while (getMachMsg(timeout, portSet, &port, &msg))
{
  CFRunLoopSourceRef source;
  source = CFRunLoopModeFindSourceForMachPort(runloop, mode, port);
  if (source)
    source->callback(msg, source->context);
};
```

Did you Know?

A reference to Mach calls is available at http://web.mit.edu/darwin/src/modules/xnu/osfmk/man/.

Custom Input Sources

Custom input sources let applications use run loops to send messages from thread to thread. Threads might not share run loops, although they are not required to have one. If a thread has a run loop, another thread can send it a message, which will be invoked from the run loop. For instance, `NSObject` has `performSelectorOnMainThread:withObject:waitUntilDone:` and `performSelector:onThread:withObject:waitUntilDone:` methods that let you invoke operations on other threads.

Custom input sources do not require a port to be set up, and transmit their messages from thread to thread using traditional locks. Thus, `performSelectorOnMainThread:withObject:waitUntilDone:` and `performSelector:onThread:withObject:waitUntilDone:` do all the locking for you. However, a thread's run loop could be blocked waiting on its port set. The solution is that each run loop creates its own "wake up" port. A thread can wake another thread's run loop by sending a message to its wake up port. Once the run loop is running again, the custom input sources will be processed.

Creating Timers

`CFRunLoops` also allow you to create timers. The iPhone OS implements timers as an IPC connection that sends a message at the requested time. Thus, timers could be implemented as just another `CFRunLoopSource`. However, timers are considered to be time-critical events and are given special treatment: The run loop processes them first. As a result, `CFRunLoop` provides special `CFRunLoopTimer` objects, which create the appropriate IPC connections and add their port handles to the set of ports on which `mach_msg` blocks. The run loop, therefore, looks something like the following:

```
while (1)
{
  getMachMsg(timeout, portSet, &port, &msg);

  CFRunLoopTimerRef timer = CFRunLoopModeFindTimerForMachPort(mode, port);
```

```
    if (timer)
    {
      timer->callback(msg, timer->context);
      continue;
    }

    CFRunLoopSourceRef source;
    source = CFRunLoopModeFindSourceForMachPort(runloop, mode, port);
    if (source)
      source->callback(msg, source->context);
};
```

As timers are invoked from the run loop, they will be delayed if any callback invoked by the `CFRunLoop` takes too long.

Using Observers

Observers are callback functions that are called at particular points in the run loop. They are registered as `CFRunLoopObserver` objects, which also store a context pointer for them. Observers can be called at the observation points marked in Figure 7.1. Cocoa uses them extensively as you will see in "How Cocoa Uses the Run Loop" later this hour.

```
void runloop()
{
  callObserversOnEntry();

  while (getNewEvent(&event))
  {
    callObservers();
    process(&event);
  }

  callObserversOnExit();
};
```

Overall Run Loop Steps

The run loop performs the following steps, as shown in Figure 7.1:

1. Notify observers that the run loop has been entered.
2. Notify observers that any ready timers are about to fire.
3. Notify observers that any input sources that are not port based are about to fire.
4. Fire any non-port-based input sources that are ready to fire.
5. If a port-based input source is ready and waiting to fire, process the event immediately. Go to step 9.

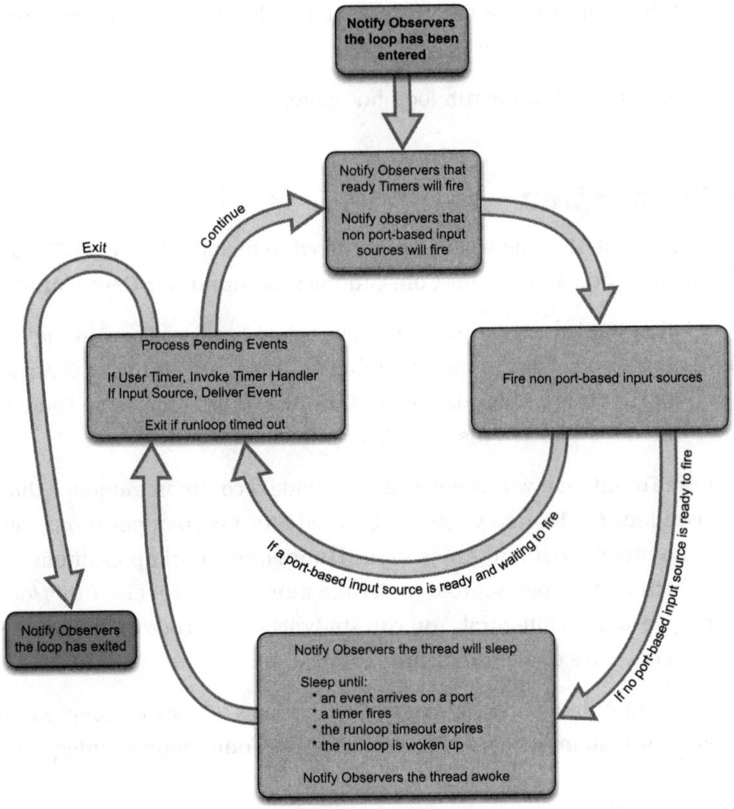

FIGURE 7.1
Run loop steps

6. Notify observers that the thread is about to sleep.
7. Put the thread to sleep until one of the following events occurs:
   - An event arrives for a port-based input source.
   - A timer fires.
   - The timeout value set for the run loop expires.
   - The run loop is explicitly woken up.
8. Notify observers that the thread just woke up.
9. Process the pending event and perform one of these events:
   - If a user-defined timer fired, process the timer event and restart the loop. Go to step 2.
   - If an input source fired, deliver the event.

- If the run loop was explicitly woken up but has not yet timed out, restart the loop. Go to step 2.

10. Notify observers that the run loop has exited.

Core Foundation

`CFRunLoop` is the latest name you've encountered to include the letters `CF`. Just as `UI` stands for `UIKit` and `CG` stands for Core Graphics, `CF` stands for **Core Foundation.**

Core Foundation implements many of the same data types you saw in the Foundation framework. For instance, there's a `CFString` for strings, a `CFArray` for arrays, and a `CFDictionary` for dictionaries. Unlike Foundation, Core Foundation is a C library and does not need the Objective-C runtime.

Initially, Core Foundation was developed to provide a common language that Mac OS 9, C-based Mac OS 10, and Objective-C-based Mac OS 10 applications could share. It's also proven useful to Apple for its iTunes and Safari applications on Windows. Much of it is open sourced under the name `CF-lite`. (See http://developer.apple.com/opensource/cflite.html. You can study its source code online at http://www.opensource.apple.com/source/CF/CF-476.18/.)

To maintain compatibility and save code, Foundation's `NSString`, `NSArray`, and `NSDictionary` are all implemented using their Core Foundation counterparts.

Toll-Free Bridging

To make Core Foundation even easier to use from Cocoa, the first element of every Core Foundation object is an `isa` pointer. The `isa` pointer points to a class object, which is filled with the appropriate methods for Objective-C to work properly. Some of these methods are implemented in C, and others in Objective-C. Now Objective-C can use Core Foundation objects as if they were native Objective-C objects.

We also want Core Foundation functions to accept Objective-C created dictionaries (and their subclasses) as if they were `CFDictionarys`. For instance, if a Core Foundation function discards an Objective-C created dictionary, it should invoke that dictionary's `release` method. Core Foundation checks whether the object was made by Objective-C and runs the appropriate method if it was.

These two mechanisms are called toll-free bridging. Although Core Foundation objects are toll-free bridged to their Foundation counterparts, you still need to type-cast them to prevent compiler warnings due to static type checking:

```
NSString*   nsString;
CFStringRef cfString;
```

```
nsString = (NSString*)   cfString;
cfString = (CFStringRef) nsString;
```

Not all classes are toll-free bridged. In particular, NSBundle (CFBundle), NSHost (CFHost), NSRunLoop (CFRunLoop), NSNotificationCenter (CFNotificationCenter), and NSSocket (CFSocket) are NOT.

Other classes, such as NSTimer's concrete implementation NSCFTimer and CFRunLoopTimer, are toll-free bridged.

The Power of Core Foundation

Reading the Core Foundation documentation, you'll notice it provides more data collection objects than Foundation, such as the following:

- CFBags—Sets that can hold duplicate values
- CFBinaryHeaps—Binary heaps that can be used as priority queues
- CFBitVectors—Ordered collections of bit values
- CFTrees—Tree nodes that can have multiple children
- CFUUIDs—Probabilistically unique machine dependent identifiers, which enable distributed systems to uniquely identify information with little central coordination

Core Foundation also provides network services that are unavailable in Cocoa and integrate into the Run Loop. For instance, the third-party AsyncSocket class currently maintained at http://deusty.blogspot.com/search/label/AsyncSocket uses these methods to provide a fire-and-forget asynchronous network operation. The key objects it uses are CFSocket, CFStream, and CFHost.

Foundation is described in terms of classes and objects, whereas Core Foundation uses the words opaque types and objects. Opaque types cannot be subclassed, but they do hide their implementation like classes. Some functions such as CFRetain and CFRelease can be invoked on any CFType compliant object. (CFType compliant objects are created by and registered with the appropriate Core Foundation administration functions.)

How Cocoa Uses the Run Loop

Much of Cocoa's functionality is implemented using the run loop, as shown in Figure 7.2.

The Cocoa Run Loop API

The CFRunLoop, CFRunLoopSource, CFRunLoopTimer, and CFRunLoopObserver objects are part of Core Foundation and are implemented in C. They, therefore, expect their callbacks to be C functions.

Although NSRunLoop and NSTimer provide a Cocoa application programming interface (API) to CFRunLoop and CFRunLoopTimer, code that uses CFRunLoopSource and CFRunLoopObserver must be written in C.

Timer Handling

Cocoa provides an API to create a timer and add it to the current runtime loop:

```
NSTimer* timer = [NSTimer scheduledTimerWithTimeInterval:0.1
                                                   target:self
                                                 selector:@selector(timer:)
                                                 userInfo:userInfo
                                                  repeats:YES];
```

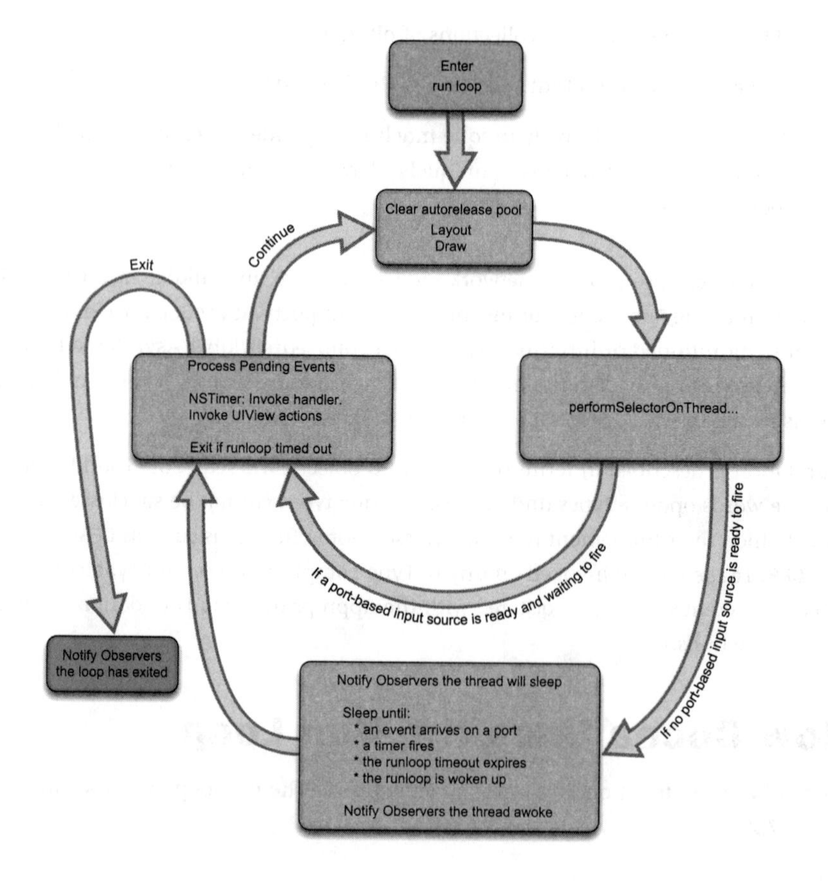

FIGURE 7.2
Cocoa's use of the run loop

This timer will invoke self's timer: method 10 times a second, with itself as the argument. userInfo is saved within timer, and can be retrieved with NSTimer's userInfo method. Here, we're telling the timer to repeat. Because of the kinds of input sources a typical run loop manages, do not expect to run a timer more than 10 times a second.

Timers trigger at fixed intervals, regardless of whether the timer handler has completed. Should the timer handler take too long, another timer event will be pending before it completes. Because Mach ports have a limited depth, in this situation your application will spend its entire time running the timer handler and will miss user-interaction events. Therefore, avoid performing large tasks inside timers.

Watch Out!

Releasing a pending timer will cause a crash. invalidate it first!

```
- (void) dealloc
{
  [timer invalidate];
  self.timer = nil;
  ...
}
```

Because the CFRunLoop functions are written in C, they expect C functions as callbacks. Cocoa defines C handlers, which set up an autorelease pool before invoking the appropriate Objective-C handler. For instance, NSTimer's undocumented __NSFireTimer function sets up an autorelease pool and catches any exceptions that occur while the timer is running. Any exceptions caused by your NSTimer handler will be logged with NSLog and discarded by __NSFireTimer before it returns to the run loop. Similarly, any objects autoreleased by your NSTimer handler will be released by __NSFireTimer.

Event Handling

UIKit uses CFRunLoopSource to set up port sources to be informed of touch events, accelerometer events, and system notifications such as application termination events and out-of-memory events.

For instance, touch screen messages are dispatched to an internal callback function, which converts the IPC message into a GSEvent, and invokes __UIApplicationHandleEvent. GSEvents are C structures the private GraphicsServices framework uses to keep track of interaction events. They contain the (x,y) coordinates of up to five fingers on the touch screen.

UIEvents are a more processed form of event used by Cocoa. UIEvents associate the UITouches encountered in Hour 6, "Understanding How the User Interface Is Built," with the windows and views at their coordinates. For instance, UIEvent's touchesForView: method returns the UITouches that belong to that view.

__UIApplicationHandleEvent figures out which UIWindows and UIViews were touched to create a UIEvent object. When users touch the screen, they expect to interact with the view they see, which is the one drawn on top. As discussed in Hour 6, the views they see are the deepest subviews in the view hierarchy. __UIApplicationHandleEvent invokes hitTest:withEvent: to step down the view hierarchy from each window and find the deepest subview in the view hierarchy for a UITouch coordinate.

hitTest:withEvent: descends the hierarchy and invokes pointInside:withEvent: on views to decide whether a point is in a view. hitTest:withEvent: ignores views that are hidden, that have disabled user interaction, or that are transparent (have an alpha level less than 0.1). By default, pointInside:withEvent: compares the point location with the view's bounds (which is rectangular). You can override it to provide better answers if your view is not rectangular.

Once __UIApplicationHandleEvent has created the UIEvent object, it creates an autorelease pool and invokes UIApplication's sendEvent: method on the UIEvent object. You will examine sendEvent: in more detail later this hour.

To improve performance, __UIApplicationHandleEvent reuses a small pool of UIEvent and UITouch objects. If you need to keep a copy of a UIEvent or UITouch object, make an immutable copy using their copy method.

Observers

NSRunLoop builds upon CFRunLoop and installs an observer to drain the current autorelease pool on every pass through the loop. This prevents CFLoopSource handlers that do not create an autorelease pool from leaking memory, and it improves performance: Because creating and destroying autorelease pools takes time, only handlers that perform significant work create them.

Similarly, the UIView display code that checks whether views need to be laid out and displayed is invoked by an observer. You'll learn the details of this in Hour 8, "Drawing User-Interface Elements."

Appendix D discusses in detail how UIApplicationMain starts your application.

One-Shot Invocation Versus Threads

Because the run loop is responsible for updating the user interface and responding to user interaction, your application will become unresponsive if the actions triggered by your user interface or if your timer handlers take too long. Worse than that, Mach ports queue messages but have a limited depth. If your application does not read its ports often enough, they will overflow and you will miss messages such as touch events, which will lead to poor interactivity.

Games that rely on NSTimer to render their content typify this problem: They miss touch events (and timer events) if their rendering takes too long. Missing timer events is less noticeable as they contain no information and occur regularly. Touch events that are lost are lost forever.The following sections discuss the two alternatives available to you, and recommend using one of them.

One-Shot Invocation

You can invoke the run loop directly from your code: The run loop functions are designed to be reentrant (they can be called from handlers they invoke). You can also specify how long they should wait for an event. Use a negative value if you want them to return as soon as there are no pending events. This is useful if you have updated your display but want UIKit to render your changes. NSRunLoop calculates the time to wait from a date, so the following code runs the loop from Cocoa once and will update your display:

```
[[NSRunLoop currentRunLoop] runUntilDate: [NSDate distantPast]];
```

Calling the run loop functions can provide smoother animation in OpenGL-based games. Instead of adding rendering code to a timer invoked 60 times a second, you can create a main loop as follows:

```
float               pollTime = 0.005;
BOOL                running  = YES;

while (running)
{
  NSAutoreleasePool* pool   = [[NSAutoreleasePool alloc] init];

  // Run until all pending events are processed
  while (CFRunLoopRunInMode(kCFRunLoopDefaultMode, pollTime, FALSE)
                                   == kCFRunLoopRunHandledSource )
  {};

  running = updateGame();
  renderGame();
  [pool release];
}
```

Increasing pollTime reduces the chances of missing an event at the cost of reducing the number of frames rendered per second. To reduce pollTime and maintain interactivity, insert the while loop into a few functions so that it is invoked at regular intervals.

```
while (CFRunLoopRunInMode(kCFRunLoopDefaultMode, pollTime, FALSE)
                                  == kCFRunLoopRunHandledSource);
```

> Adding threads can also improve rendering performance. Although creating threads is easy, debugging threaded programs is difficult. For this reason only experts should use multithreading. Appendix D includes a detailed discussion.

Touch Event Dispatching

Touch events occur when the user touches the iPhone's screen. They are dispatched first to the touched view by `UIApplication`'s `sendEvent:`. If the view does define event-handling methods, the event is forwarded along a chain of `UIResponders` until one claims it. Because tracking touches is actually quite hard, `UIControl` provides a standard mechanism to track finger positions, which triggers user-defined actions.

sendEvent:

`UIApplication`'s `sendEvent:` forwards the event to `handleEvent:withNewEvent:` to determine if the `UIEvent` is a system event (reorientation, suspension, touching the status bar, and the like). If it is not, it iterates through the `UIWindows` invoking their `sendEvent:` methods with the `UIEvent` as an argument.

`UIWindow`'s `sendEvent:` method invokes `_viewsForWindow:`, which returns the array of views the `UIEvent`'s `UITouches` reference that belong to the window. It steps through this array of views, and invokes `touchesBegan:withEvent:`, `touchesMoved:withEvent:`, `touchesEnded:withEvent:`, and `touchesCancelled:withEvent:` as necessary (in this order) on each of the views.

Behind the curtain, `UIWindow` also uses an undocumented `sendGSEvent:` method to handle more complex events that were processed by `GraphicsServices`, such as swipes, single finger events ("mouse" events), and so on. This method also knows about first responders and sends events to them. If your touch handlers are not getting called for gestures, it is because of `sendGSEvent:`. However, overriding `sendGSEvent:` is a bad idea because it is undocumented and liable to change.

> You can override `sendEvent:` by creating a subclass of `UIApplication`, say `DebugApplication` and changing the invocation to `UIApplicationMain` to build it.
>
> ```
> int retVal = UIApplicationMain(argc, argv, @"UIApplication",
>                                 @"CalculatorAppDelegate");
> int retVal = UIApplicationMain(argc, argv, @"DebugApplication",
>                                 @"CalculatorAppDelegate");
> ```
>
> Recall that `File's Owner` in Interface Builder is a proxy object, so that changing its class identity will not create a different object. You can declare a `sendEvent:` to see the events your application receives (drag your finger around on the screen).

```
- (void) sendEvent:(UIEvent*)event
{
  NSLog(@"Event %@", event);
  [super sendEvent:event];
}
```

You can use this to detect when the user is idle, to detect touches to the status bar, and to record user interactions for debugging.

Detecting idle users is simply a matter of recording the time between `sendEvent:` invocations.

You can record user interaction with your application by overriding `sendEvent:`. Later, you can replay the same events by invoking `sendEvent:`. This can be used with KVC to build unit tests. A less precise but more flexible method is to invoke `touchesBegan:withEvent:` and `touchesEnded:withEvent:` directly on views as this works even if you add UI elements to your window. http://cocoawithlove.com/2008/11/automated-user-interface-testing-on.html has the details and sample code.

`UIResponder`s and the Responder Chain

Every `UIView` is a `UIResponder`: It can respond to events or can forward them to another `UIResponder` (specified by its `nextResponder` property).

For instance, if the user touches a `UIImageView` (a subview that can display an image), a touch event will be sent to it. However, `UIImageView` does not define any methods to respond to touch events. Instead, its `nextResponder` specifies a UIResponder that might know how to service the touch. `UIResponders'` `nextResponder` is usually their superview, as the superview's area includes the subview's. However, the superview might also not define methods to respond to touch events, in which case its `nextResponder` is used, and so on, forming a chain. This is called the `UIResponder` chain. The steps are as follows:

1. Try the first `UIResponder` found by `handleEvent:withNewEvent:`.
2. If it does not have a touch event responder method, it passes the event to its view controller (if it has one), and then on to its superview.
3. Each subsequent view in the hierarchy similarly passes to its view controller first (if it has one) and then to its superview.
4. The topmost view passes the event to its `UIWindow`.
5. The `UIWindow` passes the event to the `UIApplication`.

Did you Know?

The UIResponder chain is implemented in a particularly elegant manner:

- UIView's nextResponder returns the view's view controller if it has one (by calling UIViewController's undocumented viewControllerForView: class method) or the view's superview otherwise.
- UIViewController defines nextResponder to return its view's superview.
- UIWindow defines nextResponder to return the UIApplication.
- UIApplication defines nextResponder to return nil.

This set of definitions just does "the right thing" without any complex management.

This ties in with an elegant solution to invoke nextResponder: UIResponder defines the four event responder methods touchesBegan:withEvent:, touchesMoved:withEvent:, touchesEnded:withEvent:, and touchesCancelled:withEvent:. If a view does not define these responder methods, it will inherit UIResponder's. At the UIResponder level, each of these methods simply invokes itself on its nextResponder:

```
- (void) touchesBegan:(NSSet*)touches withEvent:(UIEvent*)event
{ [[self nextResponder] touchesBegan:touches withEvent:event]; }
```

Becoming a First Responder

When a user touches a UITextView, a keyboard appears, and the UITextView maintains focus so that you can type text into it, rather than losing focus as soon as you tap a key on the keyboard. UITextView achieves this by invoking becomeFirstResponder in its touchesEnded:withEvent: method. A first responder is the user-interface element the user is interacting with.

UIResponder's becomeFirstResponder checks whether the view can become a first responder by invoking canBecomeFirstResponder, and then checks whether the current first responder is willing to resign being the first responder by invoking canResignFirstResponder. If both are true, it tells the old view to resignFirstResponder and sets the new view to being the first responder. On success, it returns YES.

UITextView's becomeFirstResponder invokes its parent's method, and on success shows the keyboard. To retract the keyboard, simply tell UITextView to resign its first responder status.

UIControl

Although the raw event responder methods touchesBegan:withEvent:, touchesMoved:withEvent:, touchesEnded:withEvent:, and touchesCancelled:withEvent: are all you need to respond to touch events, handling them is quite complex. UIControl is a subclass of UIView, which can detect a wide variety of user interactions and invoke methods (actions) on objects (targets) on detection.

Figure 7.3 shows the standard UIKit UIControls. Internally, UIKit also uses UIControls for buttons in the tab bar, the toolbar, to implement table view indexes and to implement the Emoji Keyboard.

Event Types

UIControl detects the following basic kinds of interaction:

- UIControlEventTouchDown—Triggers the event when the user touches the control
- UIControlEventTouchDownRepeat—Triggers the event when the user taps the control repeatedly
- UIControlEventTouchDragInside—Triggers the event when the user drags his finger within the control

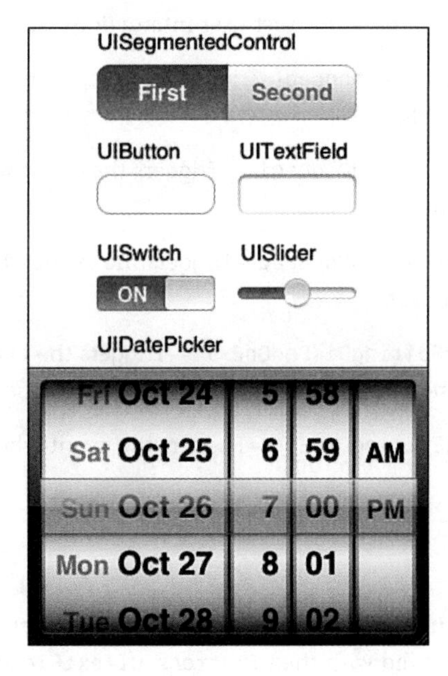

FIGURE 7.3 The standard UIControls

- UIControlEventTouchDragOutside—Triggers the event when the user drags his finger just outside the control

- `UIControlEventTouchDragEnter`—Triggers the event when the user drags his finger into the control
- `UIControlEventTouchDragExit`—Triggers the event when the user drags his finger out of the control
- `UIControlEventTouchUpInside`—Triggers the event when the user lifts his finger from the control
- `UIControlEventTouchUpOutside`—Triggers the event when the user lifts his finger from outside the control
- `UIControlEventTouchCancel`—Triggers the event when the system cancels touches for the control

`addTarget:action:forControlEvents:` tells a `UIControl` to invoke the action on the target if it detects the control events specified by the third argument. You encountered `addTarget:action:forControlEvents:` in Hour 5, "Adding Variables to the Calculator," when you associated `UIButtons` with their actions. `UIButtons` are subclassed from `UIControl`.

`UIControl` can trigger on more abstract user interactions, such as the following:

- `UIControlEventValueChanged`—Triggers the event when changing a value (such as a `UISwitch`)
- `UIControlEventEditingDidBegin`—Triggers the event when starting editing in a `UITextField`
- `UIControlEventEditingChanged`—Triggers the event when changing some text in a `UITextField`
- `UIControlEventEditingDidEndOnExit`—Triggers the event when ending editing by pressing the return key
- `UIControlEventEditingDidEnd`—Triggers the event when the keyboard is dismissed

Using `UIControls`

Using a `UIControl` is simply a matter of adding it to its superview, and wiring up its targets and outlets as we did with the `UIButtons`. `UITextField` is a little more complex in that you must dismiss it for it to go away. There are two ways to dismiss the keyboard: using a `UIControl` action or using `UITextField`'s delegate.

Building a `UITextView`**:**
To illustrate using a `UITextView`, create a new Window-Based Application project and call it `UIControls`. The final product will look like Figure 7.4. We'll just use the default NIB file and build the `UITextField` in code. Make sure you delete the `MainWindow.xib` entry from the `Info.plist` file.

```
@implementation UIControlsAppDelegate
- (void) applicationDidFinishLaunching:(UIApplication*) application
{
  window = [[UIWindow alloc] initWithFrame:[[UIScreen mainScreen] bounds]];
  [window setBackgroundColor:[UIColor colorWithWhite:0.34 alpha:1.0]];

  // Make the textField

  CGRect textFieldFrame  = CGRectMake(20.0, 68.0, 280.0, 31.0);
  UITextField *textField = [[[UITextField alloc]
                            initWithFrame:textFieldFrame] autorelease];

  [textField setBorderStyle:     UITextBorderStyleBezel];
  [textField setTextColor:       [UIColor blackColor]];
  [textField setFont:            [UIFont systemFontOfSize:20]];
  [textField setPlaceholder:     @"<enter text>"];
  [textField setBackgroundColor: [UIColor whiteColor]];
  [textField setReturnKeyType:   UIReturnKeyDone];
  [textField setKeyboardType:    UIKeyboardTypeDefault];
  [window    addSubview:         textField];
  [window    makeKeyAndVisible];
```

FIGURE 7.4
The `UIControls` application

UITextField and UITextView implement the UITextInputTraits protocol, which lets us customize the keyboard. We'll use a default keyboard, but replace the "return" key with "done".

```
  [textField setReturnKeyType:    UIReturnKeyDone];
  [textField setKeyboardType:     UIKeyboardTypeDefault];
}
```

Although you can type into the text field, you can't dismiss the keyboard.

Using UIControl **Actions to Dismiss the Keyboard**

We'll make the text field trigger an action when "done" is pressed. Add the following line to the end of applicationDidFinishLaunching::

```
[textField addTarget:self
              action:@selector(returnAction:)
    forControlEvents:UIControlEventEditingDidEndOnExit];
```

Add this method to the Application Delegate:

```
- (void) returnAction:(UITextField*)textField
{ [textField resignFirstResponder]; }
```

Now, you can dismiss the keyboard by pressing "done".

Using UITextField**'s Delegate to Dismiss the Keyboard**

UITextFields provides a delegate to further customize its behavior. The delegate must obey the UITextFieldDelegate protocol. The delegate decides whether to allow the text field to be edited, whether to accept the value that was entered, whether to allow the field to be cleared, and whether to accept the return key being tapped. It is also informed if users start or stop editing the text.

As every method of this protocol is optional, you only need to implement those you care about. In this case, we care about the return key being tapped. Change the code as follows:

```
@interface UIControlsAppDelegate : NSObject <UIApplicationDelegate>
@interface UIControlsAppDelegate
           : NSObject <UIApplicationDelegate, UITextFieldDelegate>

[textField addTarget:self
              action:@selector(returnAction:)
    forControlEvents:UIControlEventEditingDidEndOnExit];
[textField setDelegate:self];

- (void) returnAction:(UITextField*)textField
{ [textField resignFirstResponder]; }
- (BOOL) textFieldShouldReturn:(UITextField*)textField
{
  [textField resignFirstResponder];
  return YES;
}
```

Now, the delegate's `textFieldShouldReturn:` method is hiding the keyboard. If you decided to return `NO` from `textFieldShouldReturn:`, you wouldn't invoke `resignFirstResponder:`.

Watch Out!

`UITextField` does NOT retain its delegate to avoid potential retain cycles.

A retain cycle occurs whenever objects retain each other. Such cycles cannot be released. Suppose we have two objects A and B that retain each other. Because A is retained by B, its `dealloc` method, which releases B, will never be invoked because A's retain count is greater than zero. The same is true for B. So neither object will ever be released.

Delegates are controllers in the MVC sense. As it is common for controllers to retain views, if the view retained the delegate, it would likely cause a retain cycle. For example, I used the Application Delegate as the text field delegate previously. Had `UITextField` retained the delegate, there would have been a retain cycle through `window`'s subview.

`UITextField` specifies that it does not retain the delegate:

```
@property(nonatomic, assign) id<UITextFieldDelegate> delegate
```

`nil`-targeted Actions

If a `UIControl`'s target is set to `nil`, the action will be invoked on the current first responder. This is useful to know if you want to create buttons that affect the current first responder. For instance, copy and paste buttons use this mechanism to copy the currently selected text.

Summary

In this hour you learned about the run loop which is fundamental to the operation of many parts of Cocoa. Not understanding the run loop, and preventing it from running, trips up many beginners who wonder why their delegates are not being called as they expect. You also learned how events are forwarded to `UIView`s, knowledge that you'll use in the next hour to make your own custom `UIView`.

Q&A

Q. ***Why can't I `fork` a Cocoa application safely?***

A. Mach message port handles are not inherited across a `fork`, but once the run loop has been set up, its `CFRunLoopSources` have been assigned port handles to use. New port handles must be obtained by requesting IPC connections by name. However, the Cocoa frameworks only request port handles in their initialization code. Thus, you have to `exec` the binary to refresh the handle assignments. Apple's App Store bans all multiprocess applications.

Q. ***What's the difference between a thread and a process?***

A. Different applications run in different processes. Processes cannot access each other's memory unless they specifically agree to, which reduces their ability to crash each other. Threads run in the same process and share memory space. This means that a rogue thread can corrupt the data another thread is using. Debugging such bugs is horrendous. In the past, processes shared memory in this way, and computers would crash quite regularly.

Workshop

The Workshop consists of quiz questions and answers to help you solidify your understanding of the material covered in this hour. You should try to answer the questions before checking the answers.

Quiz Questions

1. What is a run loop?
2. How do timers fit into the run loop?
3. Why do I discourage you from using threads?
4. How are touch events forwarded to the correct `UIView`?

Quiz Answers

1. Run loops wait for events to occur and then dispatch them to the appropriate handler.

2. The run loop invokes timer handler functions when the timer count down reaches zero.

3. I discourage using threads because they are hard to debug if they share state. All Cocoa threads share state because they do not provide thread memory protection: Stray pointers, a common programming error, share data and are very difficult to debug.

4. Events are forwarded along the `UIResponder` chain to the first responder that claims them.

Exercises

- Build an application containing a `UISwitch` and trigger an event when it changes.
- Build an application containing a `UIDatePicker`. Set the date to your birthday, and record its changes.

HOUR 8

Drawing User-Interface Elements

What You'll Learn in This Hour:

- Adding images to buttons
- Writing your own control
- Drawing with Core Graphics

Although Apple provides standard UI controls, some of the most beautiful applications create their own interface elements to really stand out. In this hour you'll learn how to make interface elements. First, you'll learn how to customize the standard elements using the `UIImage` and `UIImageView` classes. Then, to better understand `UIViews`, we'll implement our own customized buttons, which we can animate for more polish. We'll learn all about Core Graphics, the powerful drawing framework provided by the iPhone, and use it to create the animation.

Adding Images to `UIButton`

`UIButton` can have eight images associated with each button: four for the foreground image and four for the background image. You can set one of these foreground images to serve as a label. The four different images for each class correspond to the key states we encountered in Hour 5, "Adding Variables to the Calculator": Normal (button at rest), Highlighted (button depressed), Selected (button selected), and Disabled (untappable button). Because the application behaves differently in these states, it's useful to be able to give visual feedback.

Before using an image, it must be added to your project's resources. In this way, it will get compressed and packaged into your application for deployment. Open the Add, Existing

File context menu in the resources by Ctrl-clicking (right-clicking) on Resources in Xcode's Groups & Files pane. Add the images files. Your Groups & Files pane should now look like Figure 8.1.

FIGURE 8.1
Adding images to the project's Groups & Files pane

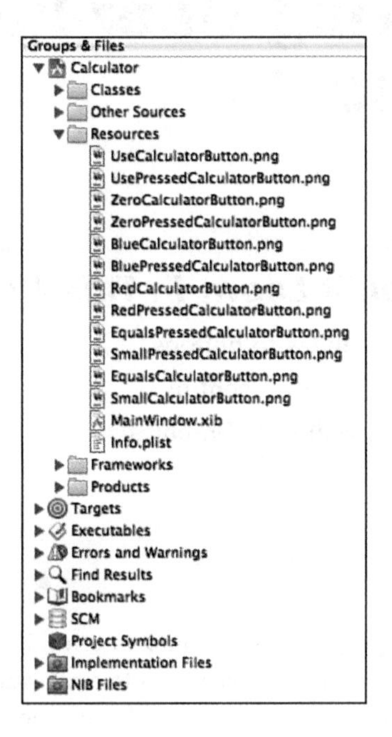

Adding Images with Interface Builder

Interface Builder (IB) recognizes the images you added as possible selections for a background image. To add images to buttons with Interface Builder, follow these steps:

1. Select all the numerical buttons (see Figure 8.2) and choose `SmallCalculatorButton.png`.
2. Change the type to Custom and change the title text to white (see Figure 8.2).

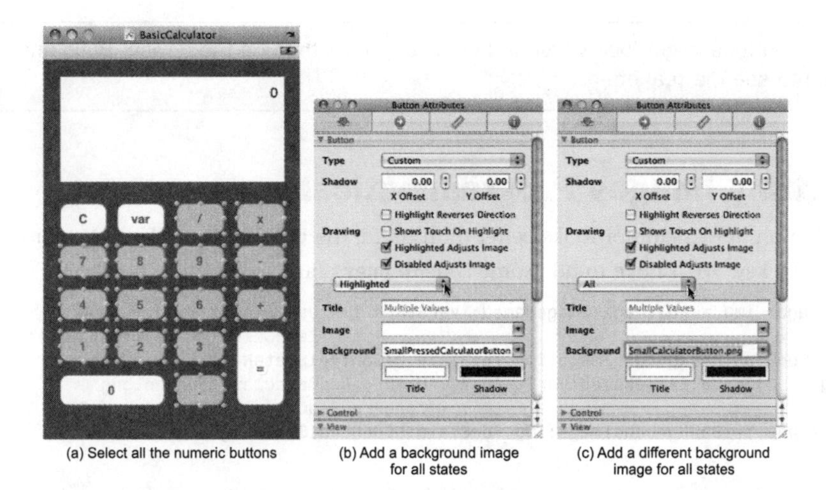

(a) Select all the numeric buttons (b) Add a background image for all states (c) Add a different background image for all states

FIGURE 8.2 Adding pictures to buttons with Interface Builder

3. Click All and replace it with Highlighted and choose `SmallPressedCalculatorButton.png` (see Figure 8.2).

Follow the same process for the other buttons using the large black button for the zero. I also adjusted the background color of the window to 5% brightness black. The resulting interface should look like the left side of Figure 8.3. When designing buttons, be aware that the results will look different on your iPhone than on your computer's screen. In fact, they even look different on different iPhones, so it's good to find friends with different models.

FIGURE 8.3 The resulting calculator in calculator and var modes

Your buttons might look worse in Interface Builder than on the device. Build and run to see the real effect.

Setting Images Programmatically

Although our calculator looks better than it did, the USE key is a different color from the STR key. We'll have to add some code to `pressVar:` to fix this:

```
UIImage* img = [UIImage imageNamed: varState ? @"UseCalculatorButton.png"
                                              : @"ZeroCalculatorButton.png"];
[button0 setBackgroundImage:img forState:UIControlStateNormal];
img = [UIImage imageNamed:varState ? @"UsePressedCalculatorButton.png"
                                   : @"ZeroPressedCalculatorButton.png"];
[button0 setBackgroundImage:img forState:UIControlStateHighlighted];
```

Depending on `varState`, we decide which image to show. `UIImage` is Cocoa's image class. Its class method `imageNamed:` reads the image from our application's resources into memory.

Experienced programmers might worry that `UIImage` will create and load an image each time it is invoked. In fact, `imageNamed:` loads the image and caches a copy in a dictionary. This is great for user-interface elements that are likely to be used often: Rather than remembering the images ourselves, we can let `UIImage` do it for us.

Images loaded by `imageNamed:` are, however, kept in memory for the entire lifetime of your application. If you do not want `UIImage` to cache the image, you can use `imageWithContentsOfFile:`, but be aware that it delays loading images until they are needed. Usually this is fine, but it can be a problem when many images need to be drawn to a view. An alternative is to load the image data with `NSData`'s `dataWithContentsOfFile:` and then convert them to images with `imageWithData::`

```
NSData*  data  = [NSData  dataWithContentsOfFile:name];
UIImage* image = [UIImage imageWithData:data];
```

As loading images from the iPhone's flash storage is much slower than loading them from memory, you should load them as little as possible while keeping your memory usage to a minimum.

`NSData` and `NSMutableData` are objects that wrap byte buffers, so that you can benefit from Objective-C memory management for raw memory instead of being thrown back into the world of `malloc` and `free`. They also provide methods to read from and write to files. `NSData` and `NSMutableData` are toll-free bridged with Core Foundation's `CFData`, which uses a `CFDataRef` pointer.

UIImage, UIImageView, and UIButton

In this section you'll learn about three classes: The UIImage class holds images; the UIImageView class displays them; the UIButton class uses UIImageViews to customize its appearance using images.

UIImage

UIImage provides a high-level Objective-C application programming interface (API) to image data. It is able to load TIFF, JPEG, GIF, PNG, BMP, and ICO formats (as well as the less-used Windows Cursor and XWindow bitmap formats). UIImages are immutable, so to manipulate them, we need to convert them to another format. Our options include Core Graphics' CGImages using CGImage, JPEGs using UIImageJPEGRepresentation, or PNGs using UIImagePNGRepresentation. Although you can load images larger than 1024x1024 pixels, you'll have to split them up into smaller images to draw them because of iPhone hardware limitations.

When we created the calculator, I provided images for each button size. UIImage provides a useful method to reduce the number of art assets you need: stretchableImageWithLeftCapWidth:topCapHeight:. The disadvantage of using it is that you cannot see your images in Interface Builder.

UIImageView

Although UIImage provides drawing methods, it is not an instance of UIView. If you want to add an image to the view hierarchy, use UIImageView:

```
UIImageView* imageView = [[UIImageView alloc] initWithImage:image];
[imageView setCenter: CGPointMake(x,y)];
```

Here, I'm setting UIView's center property, which automatically moves its origin. Alternatively, I could have written the following:

```
CGSize imageSize        = [image size];
CGRect frame            = CGRectMake(x - imageSize.width  / 2.0,
                                     y - imageSize.height / 2.0,
                                     imageSize.width, imageSize.height);
UIImageView* imageView = [[UIImageView alloc] initWithFrame:frame];
[imageView setImage:image];
```

UIImageView is an animatable view. You can easily achieve an animation by setting animationImages to the array of UIImages making up your animation. startAnimating starts the animation; stopAnimating stops it. By default, the animation runs at 30 frames per second, although you can change the speed with animationDuration. animationRepeatCount specifies how many times to run the animation (counterintuitively, 0 means forever). To show the static image again, set animationImages to nil.

UIButton

UIButton uses UIImageViews for its foreground and background images and uses UITextLabels for its label. It adds these elements as subviews, and exchanges them when you press a button (you highlight it), you select it, or you disable it. If you try to add a subview to a UIButton, your view will end up below the button's images. Nevertheless, adding subviews to buttons is a common request. One reason to do it is to create a button with a multiline label. Another is to create an animated button.

Adding Your View to UIButton's Superview

You can add your view to UIButton's superview and place it over the button, but you must also define its nextResponder to forward touch events to the button rather than to its superview. We'll define a HoverUIImageView class to be placed over the UIButton (see Listings 8.1 and 8.2). This class will let you display image-based animations over a UIButton.

LISTING 8.1 HoverUIImageView.h

```
#import <Foundation/Foundation.h>
#import <UIKit/UIKit.h>

@interface HoverUIImageView : UIImageView
{ id theNextResponder; }

@property (nonatomic, assign) id theNextResponder;
@end
```

LISTING 8.2 HoverUIImageView.m

```
#import "HoverUIImageView.h"

@implementation HoverUIImageView

@synthesize theNextResponder;

- (id) initWithFrame:(CGRect)frame
{
  self = [super initWithFrame:frame];
  if (self)
    theNextResponder = nil;
  return self;
}

- (id) initWithImage:(UIImage*)image
{
  self = [super initWithImage:image];
  if (self)
    theNextResponder = nil;
```

LISTING 8.2 Continued

```
  return self;
}

- (id) nextResponder
{ return theNextResponder ? theNextResponder : [super nextResponder]; };

- (BOOL) userInteractionEnabled
{ return YES; };

- (void) dealloc
{
  self.theNextResponder = nil;
  [super dealloc];
}

@end
```

Watch Out!

> Some UIViews are set up to discard user touches rather than forwarding them up the UIResponder chain. The idea is to prevent the superview from receiving spurious touches. UIImageView has this behavior. You can disable this behavior by returning YES from userInteractionEnabled. If a UIButton is a superview of this kind of UIView, it will not receive the necessary touch events.

You can create a category on UIButton for convenience (see Listings 8.3 and 8.4). Because UIButton is the superclass of all the classes of its class cluster, the method is accessible from all buttons.

LISTING 8.3 UIButtonEX.h

```
#import <UIKit/UIKit.h>
#import "HoverUIImageView.h"

@interface UIButton (UIButtonEX)
- (HoverUIImageView*) addHoverUIImageViewWithFrame:(CGRect)rect;
@end
```

LISTING 8.4 UIButtonEX.m

```
#import "UIButtonEX.h"

@implementation UIButton (UIButtonEX)

- (HoverUIImageView*) addHoverUIImageViewWithFrame:(CGRect)frame;
{
  HoverUIImageView* view = [[HoverUIImageView alloc] initWithFrame:frame];
  view.theNextResponder  = self;
  [[self superview] addSubview:view];
  return [view autorelease];
}

@end
```

Now you can create a HoverUIImageView with the following:

```
HoverUIImageView* hoverView = [button addHoverUIImageViewWithFrame:frame];
```

Writing Your Own Class

Another solution is to write your own button class. We'll do that in the last section, "Drawing Your Own Button" after learning how to draw.

Core Graphics

Quartz is the marketing name for Core Graphics, the powerful 2D graphics rendering engine used to render UIViews. Quartz mainly uses the CPU although some operations could be performed by the 3D graphics hardware.

Quartz's ancestry lies in the domain of desktop publishing software. Because printers have different resolutions to monitors, Quartz uses a floating-point-based coordinate system, which scales to any resolution. Because printers and monitors show colors differently, Quartz uses a device-independent color scheme and provides a means to specify colors on your device. All this information about the canvas being drawn on is bundled up into a graphics context. The iPhone provides graphics contexts for bitmaps, layers (which you'll learn about in the next hour), and PDFs. Yes, that's right, you can create or even modify existing PDFs on your iPhone!

The Current Transformation Matrix

Quartz uses two coordinate spaces. Applications draw into an abstract user space, which has no real-world constraints such as resolution or color depth. Quartz converts the drawing commands from user space to device space where it draws (as shown in Figure 8.4). Device space is limited by real-world constraints. For instance, the screen is a device space whose resolution is limited to 320x480 pixels.

A key element of this conversion is transforming the coordinate system: The same drawing will be rendered in higher resolution on your printer than on your iPhone. Each unit of distance in user space corresponds to more pixels on a printer than on an iPhone screen. Quartz uses an affine transformation, called the current transformation matrix (also known as CTM) to convert between device spaces. Affine transformations are nice because they provide a unique mapping between coordinate spaces: Any point in user space can only be mapped as a unique coordinate in device space. Affine transformations can flip, rotate, translate, and stretch user space to fit any reasonable device space. Every point you specify in user space will be transformed to device space using the CTM.

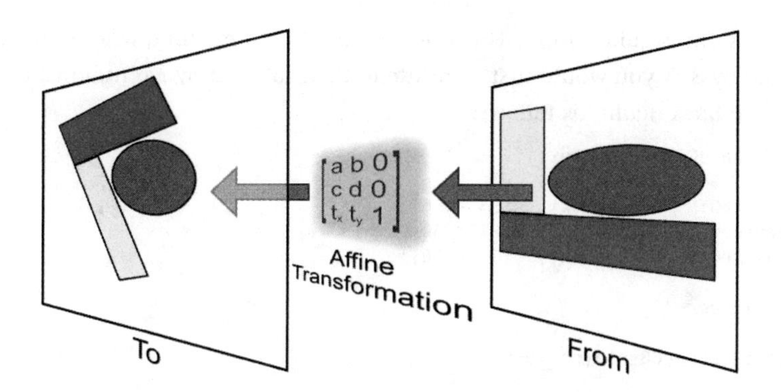

FIGURE 8.4
Converting coordinates from user space into device space

A very nice property of affine transformations is that you can combine any two affine transformations into a single transformation. Each affine transformation can be represented as a 3x3 matrix. Multiplying two 3x3 matrices results in a single 3x3 matrix: your combined transformation. This is very convenient as it lets you use a different coordinate system every time you want to draw a `UIView`. For instance, `UIView` uses affine transformations to transform bounds coordinates into frame coordinates. Even if a subview is 100 levels deep, only one affine transformation is needed to map it into screen space. Not only that, but scaling, flipping, and rotating the `UIView` is free. In Hour 6, "Understanding How the User Interface Is Built," when you set the `UIWindow`'s `transform` property to display information in Landscape mode, you were using this feature.

The CTM is stored in the graphics context. Quartz provides the following functions to manipulate it:

- `CGContextRotateCTM` rotates it by an angle specified in radians.
- `CGContextScaleCTM` scales it by (*sx, sy*).
- `CGTranslateCTM` translates it by (*tx, ty*).
- `CGContextSaveGState` pushes the current graphics state to an internal stack to save it.
- `CGContextRestoreGState` pops the previous graphics state from an internal stack to restore it.

The **graphics state** is part of the graphics context and includes information about the canvas, such as the CTM and the current region to be drawn to. The graphics context also contains information that is not saved, such as the drawing operation we're building up, which we'll discuss in the next section.

Using the CTM is quite simple. For instance, to rotate something whose center is at (123,456) by 30°, you would first translate it, then rotate it by π/6 radians, then translate it back again, as follows:

```
CGContextSaveGState(context);

CGTranslateCTM    (context, -123,-456);
CGContextRotateCTM(context, M_PI * 30.0 / 180.0);
CGTranslateCTM    (context,  123, 456);

// Draw it here!

CGContextRestoreGState(context);
```

Did you Know?

Cocoa Touch uses radians to specify angles. Just as angles vary between 0° and 360°, radians vary between 0π and 2π with 0° corresponding to 0π and 360° corresponding to 2π.

If you needed to scale something by 0.5 times along the x-axis, and by 2 times along the y-axis, you'd add the following line before your drawing code:

```
CGContextScaleCTM (context,  0.5, 2.0);
```

Did you Know?

This is a quick reminder how affine transformations work for people who know a little math. The following pair of equations define an affine transformation from user space (x,y) to device space (x',y'):

$x' = a * x + b * y + t_x$

$y' = c * x + d * y + t_y$

t_x and t_y correspond to translations. For instance, if the origin of the user space coordinate system is at (5,5) in the device space coordinate system, you'd write:

$x' = x + 5$

$y' = y + 5$

I.e.: $a = 1, b = 0, c = 1, d = 0, t_x = 5, t_y = 5$

Similarly a,b,c,d combine rotations, scaling and flipping coordinate systems. Here, the rotations are specified around the origin of user space ($t_x = 0, t_y = 0$):

$x' = s_x (x \cos \theta + y \sin \theta)$

$y' = s_y (-x \sin \theta + y \cos \theta)$

However, affine transformations are sufficiently powerful to capture rotations around any point in user space (p,q):

$$
\begin{aligned}
x' &= s_x ((x-p) \cos\theta + (y-q) \sin\theta + p) \\
&= (s_x \cos\theta)\, x + (s_x \sin\theta)\, y + s_x (p - p \cos\theta - q \sin\theta) \\
&= ax + by + t_x \\
&\text{where } a = s_x \cos\theta \\
&\qquad\quad b = s_x \sin\theta \\
&\qquad\quad t_x = s_x (p (1 - \cos\theta) - q \sin\theta)
\end{aligned}
$$

$$
\begin{aligned}
y' &= s_y (- (x-p) \sin\theta + (y-q) \cos\theta + q) \\
&= (-s_y \sin\theta)\, x + (s_y \cos\theta)\, y + s_y (p \sin\theta + q - q \cos\theta) \\
&= cx + dy + t_y \\
&\text{where } c = -s_y \sin\theta \\
&\qquad\quad d = s_y \cos\theta \\
&\qquad\quad t_y = s_y (p \sin\theta + q (1 - \cos\theta))
\end{aligned}
$$

To represent a,b,c,d, you only need a 2x2 matrix. But to include the two translations, you need a 3x3 matrix:

$$[x'\ y'\ 1] = [x\ y\ 1] \begin{bmatrix} a & b & 0 \\ c & d & 0 \\ t_x & t_y & 1 \end{bmatrix}$$

If you expand this out, you'll see we get the desired values for x' and y'. Matrix representation lets us combine successive affine transformations easily into a single matrix. If you need to, you can create an affine transformation directly. It is defined by Quartz as:

```
struct CGAffineTransform { CGFloat a, b, c, d, tx, ty; };
typedef struct CGAffineTransform CGAffineTransform;
```

To apply a transformation to the context, use `CGContextConcatCTM`:

```
CGAffineTransform scaleIt = { 0.5, 0.0, 0.0, 2.0, 0.0, 0.0 };
CGContextConcatCTM(context, scaleIt);
```

Quartz provides functions to create and manipulate such affine transforms outside of a context. Apple's `CGAffineTransform` reference provides the details. The function names are quite clear. The only new function is `CGAffineTransformInvert`. It inverts the transformation matrix, to let you retrieve user space coordinates from device space coordinates.

Device Spaces

The iPhone provides three device spaces:

- The bitmap device space to render to images
- The PDF device space to render to PDFs
- The layer device space to render to the screen

The default Quartz coordinate system assumes the y-axis points upward from the bottom of the screen (unlike UIViews, which assume it points down from the top of the screen).

Bitmap Device Space

CGBitmapContextCreate creates bitmap image contexts from the following arguments:

- *data*—The image's memory buffer should be at least (bytesPerRow*height) bytes. If you use NULL, CGBitmapContextCreate mallocs the needed memory itself.
- *width*—The width in pixels of the bitmap.
- *height*—The height in pixels of the bitmap.
- *bitsPerComponent*—The number of bits per color and alpha channel.
- *bytesPerRow*—The number of bytes taken by each row of the bitmap.
- *colorspace*—The color space to use for the bitmap.
- *bitmapInfo*—More details about the internal data representation.

Bitmap image contexts support many kinds of internal representations. The details are only useful to people who want to manipulate the data bitmap directly as an array. The only exception to this is that if you want an alpha channel, you must say so. Apple recommends using kCGImageAlphaPremultipliedLast as bitmapInfo to obtain an alpha channel:

```
CGContextRef c = CGBitmapContextCreate(NULL, width, height, 8,0, colorSpace,
                                         kCGImageAlphaPremultipliedLast);
```

Watch Out!

CGBitmapContextCreate only supports a subset of all the formats it could. This list tends to change with new releases of the operating system (OS), so you should refer to the supported pixel formats section of the *Quartz 2D Programming Guide* for more details. CGBitmapContextCreate returns a NULL pointer for unsupported formats, but prints out a message to the console. In particular, only 8, 16, or 32 bits per pixel are supported: not 24! For instance, the printed error message may be:

```
CGBitmapContextCreate: unsupported parameter combination:
8 integer bits/component; 24 bits/pixel; 3-component colorspace;
kCGImageAlphaNone; 1536 bytes/row.
```

PDF Device Space

PDFs are data. CGPDFContextCreate creates a PDF context with three arguments:

- A CGDataConsumer object. CGDataConsumer is an opaque type that supports appending data to a buffer (a memory buffer or a writable file buffer).
- A pointer to a CGRect, which specifies the size and location of the PDF page. Passing in NULL will create a page of 8 1/2 by 11 inches.
- A pointer to a CFDictionary of metainformation about the PDF (author, title, creator, passwords, usage rights, keywords, and so on).

Because PDFs are usually saved to file, CGPDFContextCreateWithURL provides a shortcut, creating a CGDataConsumer, and invoking CGPDFContextCreate on it. The CGDataConsumer saves data to a file. Similarly, PDF documents can be read from a file with CGPDFDocumentCreateWithURL, which builds on the opaque CGDataProvider type to read data from a buffer, and on CGPDFDocumentCreateWithProvider parse a PDF document from the data.

CGContextDrawPDFDocument draws a PDF document to a context. You can create an appropriate uniform resource locator (URL) with NSURL's initFileURLWithPath method.

```
CGPDFDocumentRef document = CGPDFDocumentCreateWithURL(url);
CGContextDrawPDFDocument( context, rect, document, pageNumber );
```

Layer Device Space

Layers are the topic of the next hour. For now, know that UIViews draw to layers. You can retrieve the graphics context to use for drawing by UIGraphicsGetCurrentContext inside your view's drawRect: method. UIGraphicsPushContext lets you save the current context and change to a new one, whereas UIGraphicsPopContext restores the old one.

Because UIViews assume that the y-axis grows down, whereas Quartz assumes it grows upward, you'll need to convert the coordinate system when using Quartz to draw the contents of a UIView. You need to flip the y coordinates, and then make them fit within the range [0..height]:

new_y = *height* - old_y;

As a result, most drawRect: methods will look like this:

```
- (void)drawRect:(CGRect)rect
{
  CGContextRef       context = UIGraphicsGetCurrentContext();
  CGAffineTransform reflect = { 1.0, 0.0, 0.0, -1.0, 0.0, rect.size.height };
```

```
  CGContextConcatCTM(context, reflect);

  // draw here!
};
```

Drawing Shapes

Drawing in Quartz is a two-step process. First, you define the path a line will follow. Then, you draw the line or fill the area defined by the path.

Defining Paths

A path consists of lines and/or curves. Paths are constructed incrementally within the graphics context by invoking C functions between `CGContextBeginPath` and the drawing code. As the graphics context can only contain one path at a time, calling `CGContextBeginPath` clears any existing path in the graphics context. However, paths might have gaps in them. Each contiguous part of a path is called a subpath.

`CGContextCloseSubpath` closes a path so that it is a loop without endpoints. If you don't close a path, even if the endpoints of your line overlap, Quartz will draw the endpoints in the style you specified.

`CGContextMoveToPoint(p)` sets the graphics context's current point to `p`, to create a new subpath. `CGContextAddLineToPoint(p)` adds a line segment to the path starting at the context's current point and ending at `p`. It also sets the current point to `p`. Thus, to create the path for a rectangle, you would write the following:

```
void createRectanglePath(CGContextRef context, CGRect rect)
{
  float X = rect.origin.x + rect.size.width;
  float Y = rect.origin.y + rect.size.height;

  CGContextBeginPath      (context);
  CGContextMoveToPoint    (context, rect.origin.x, rect.origin.y);
  CGContextAddLineToPoint(context,             X, rect.origin.y);
  CGContextAddLineToPoint(context,             X,             Y);
  CGContextAddLineToPoint(context, rect.origin.x,             Y);
  CGContextClosePath      (context);
}
```

`CGContextAddQuadCurveToPoint` adds a quadratic Bézier curve segment to the path. The curvature of quadratic Bézier curves is defined by a single control point. The line that passes through an endpoint and the control point defines the tangent of the curve at the endpoint. The distance from the endpoints to the control point determines how strongly the curve is pulled in that direction.

How does it work? Consider a curve with two endpoints p and r and a control point q, as shown in Figure 8.5. This forms two segments (p,q) and (q,r). Let a be a point on *(p,q)* that travels from *p* to *q* at a constant speed in the same time as a point *b* on *(q,r)* takes to travel from *q* to *r* at a constant speed. *(a,b)* also forms a line segment, which moves and changes length as *a* and *b* travel. Now as *a* travels from *p* to *q* and *b* travels from *q* to *r*, consider a third traveling point *c*, which travels from *a* to *b*, such that its fractional distance from *b* along *(a,b)* is the same as *a*'s fractional distance from *p* along *(p,q)*. *c* departs *a* when *a* is at *p* and arrives at *r* when *b* arrives at *r*. *c* travels along the cubic spline.

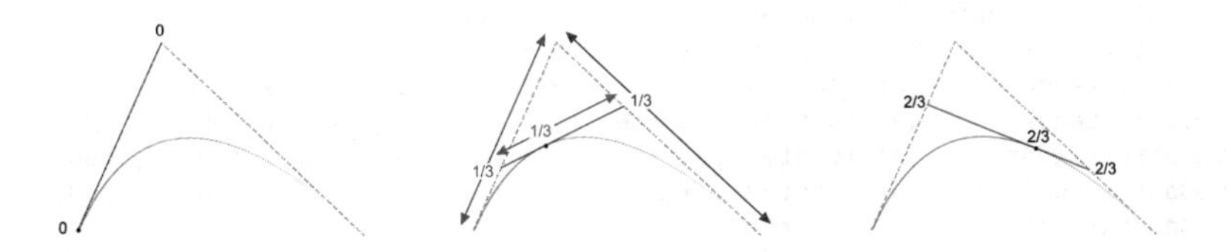

FIGURE 8.5 Quadratic Bézier curve

`CGContextAddCurveToPoint` adds a cubic Bézier curve segment to the path. The curvature of cubic Bézier curves is defined by two control points, as show in Figure 8.6. Each control point is paired with an endpoint of the curve. The line that passes though each endpoint and its control point defines the tangent of the curve at the endpoint. The distance from an endpoint to its control point determines how strongly the curve is pulled in that direction.

Cubic Bézier curves are created in the same way as quadratic Bézier curves, except that this time we start with three fixed segments. Three points travel along these segments, making two moving segments. Now, two points travel along the two moving segments to create a third moving segment. Then, the cubic curve follows a point that travels along this third moving segment.

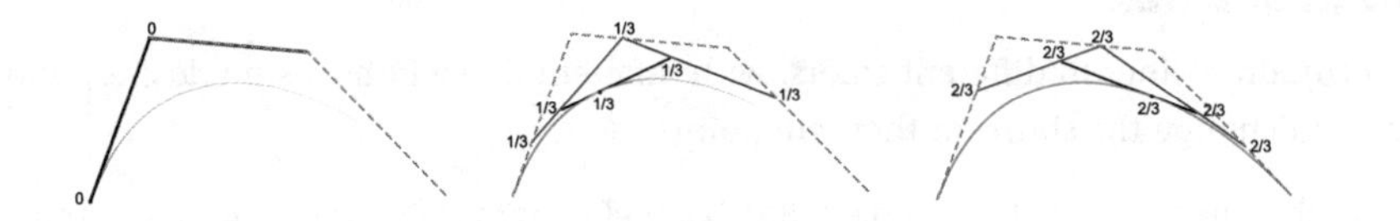

FIGURE 8.6 Cubic Bézier curve

Together, both types of Bézier curves can approximate most of the kinds of curves you could be interested in. Although higher-degree Bézier curves can display more curves, Quartz does not provide methods for them as they are slow to compute.

One kind of curve that cannot be drawn by Bézier curves are circles. Therefore, Quartz provides `CGContextAddArc` and `CGContextAddArcToPoint` to draw circles or circular arcs using standard trigonometry. We can use this method to create rectangles with rounded corners.

```
void createRoundRectanglePath(CGContextRef context, CGRect rect, float radius)
{
  if (radius == 0)
    return createRectanglePath(context, rect);

  float x = rect.origin.x;
  float y = rect.origin.y;
  float w = rect.size.width;
  float h = rect.size.height;
  radius  = min(radius, min(h/2, w/2));

  CGContextBeginPath      (context);
  CGContextMoveToPoint    (context, x     , y + h/2                         );
  CGContextAddArcToPoint (context, x     , y       , x + w , y       , radius );
  CGContextAddArcToPoint (context, x + w , y       , x + w , y + h   , radius );
  CGContextAddArcToPoint (context, x + w , y + h   , x     , y + h   , radius );
  CGContextAddArcToPoint (context, x     , y + h   , x     , y + h/2 , radius );
  CGContextClosePath      (context);
}
```

We're just passing the corners of the rectangle to `CGContextAddArcToPoint`, and it's drawing rounded corners of the specified radius.

A nice feature of lines, Bézier curves, and circular arcs is that applying affine transformations to their points and control points results in the same curve as you would get if you applied the affine transformation to each point of the curve. Quartz uses this property to transform the points and control points to device space before rendering lines, curves, and circular arcs.

If you need to reuse a path, use the `CGPath` functions; see `CAKeyframeAnimation` in Hour 9, "Layers and Core Animation: Creating a Cover Flow Clone," for an example.

Drawing Lines

You can draw lines in different colors, with different line widths, using dashes, and you can change the shape of their endpoints.

To set the line's color call `CGContextSetStrokeColorWithColor()`. We can obtain a color to use in Quartz from `UIColor`, using its convenience method `CGColor`. `CGColor` specifies both a color and its color space. For instance, to create red strokes, you can write the following:

```
CGContextSetStrokeColorWithColor(context, [UIColor redColor].CGColor);
```

Did you Know?

> Colors are defined with respect to a color space. You need at least three values to define a color because most people's eyes have three types of color receptors, which respond to three different spectra. The color space defines how these values are combined to produce a visible color. Commonly known spaces include the RGB color space, which is used for bright surfaces such as your iPhone's screen, and the CMYK color space, which is used for reflective surfaces such as this book. These color spaces are device dependent, but there are device-independent color spaces, such as LAB and DeviceN. You can read all about them in Apple's documentation. Generally, the iPhone just uses the RGB device space for speed to avoid doing any conversions.

`CGContextSetLineWidth` adjusts the width of line. Lines are defined by a path. They straddle this path, with half of their width lying on either side. The default width is 1.0 units.

```
CGContextSetLineWidth(context, 2.0);
```

`CGContextSetLineDash` sets a dash pattern consisting of dashes and spaces whose pattern is specified by the `lengths` C array. `phase` specifies how far into the dash sequence Quartz should start drawing.

```
CGContextSetLineDash(context,phase,lengths,sizeof(lengths)/sizeof(lengths[0]));
```

Now, you can draw a red rounded rectangle with `CGContextStrokePath`:

```
CGContextSetStrokeColorWithColor(context, [UIColor redColor].CGColor);
CGContextSetLineWidth           (context, 2.0);
createRoundRectanglePath        (context, CGMakeRect(10, 30, 300, 440), 20);
CGContextStrokePath             (context);
```

Quartz also provides methods to adjust the shape of line endpoints and the shape of sharp corners.

Filling Areas

Quartz can also fill areas (as shown by Figure 8.7). To fill the area defined by your path, Quartz needs to know which points are inside the area and which are outside.

The simplest case is a single, closed subpath that does not cross itself, such as a rectangle. Pretend that you're a point, and the path is a wall. If you're inside an area enclosed by a wall, you'll see the wall all around you. Otherwise, you'll see only part of the wall.

FIGURE 8.7
Stroke versus fill

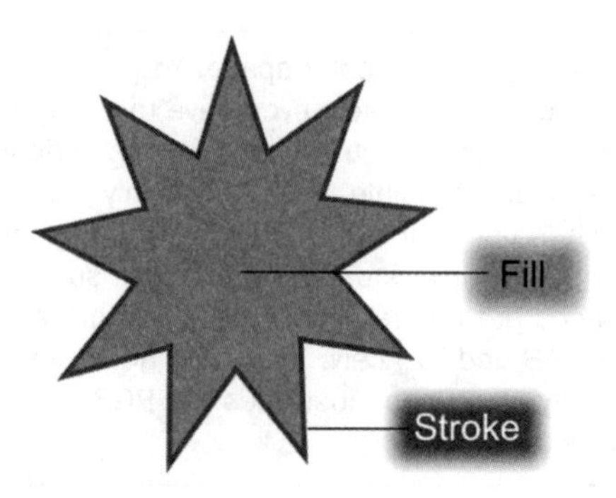

Now, what happens if we want to fill a shape that has a hole? Our rule will fill the shape, as every point in the shape sees a wall around it. But the hole will also be filled as it too is surrounded by a wall. Quartz solves this problem by requiring the shape's path and the hole's path to be built in opposite directions (clockwise and counterclockwise). Imagine that the walls are translucent and are marked with arrows to show their direction. Each point looks out and counts the number of arrows it sees in each direction surrounding it. It subtracts the two counts to obtain a **winding number**. If the winding number is not zero, it should be filled. Recall that this is done on a path by path basis, so you don't need to worry about the drawing's other paths. This process is called the **nonzero winding number rule** and also works for self-intersecting lines (see Figure 8.8).

FIGURE 8.8
Nonzero winding rule

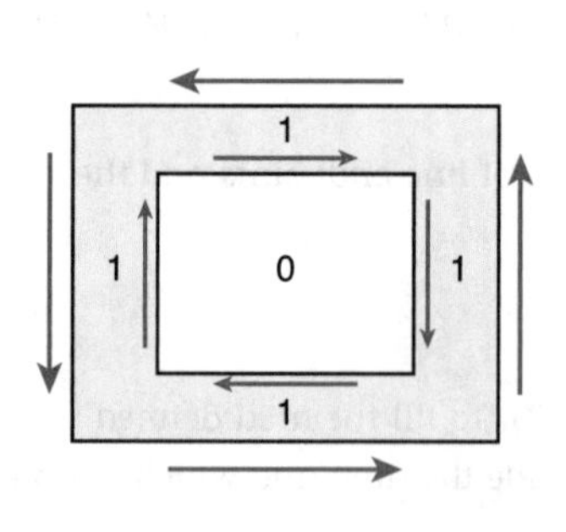

The two paths have opposite direction.

There is only one path, but it encompasses an area twice in the same direction.

As with drawing lines, shapes can be given a number of attributes, such as a color and a shadow. `CGContextSetFillColorWithColor` sets the fill color:

```
CGContextSetFillColorWithColor(context, [UIColor greenColor].CGColor);
```

Each shape can be associated with a shadow, which is a blurred copy of the shape drawn below it. The shadow has a color, the amount the shape should be blurred, and an amount by which the shadow should be offset from the shape. You can use the following:

```
CGContextSetShadowWithColor(context, offset, blur, color);
```

Quartz provides two means of creating gradients: `CGGradient` and `CGShading`. `CGShading` is the more flexible method as it lets you define your own shading function. `CGGradient` is more constrained but easier to use. You should refer to the "Gradients" section of Apple's *Quartz 2D Programming Guide* for more details on using them (available in Xcode's Leopard documentation set).

Invoking `CGContextFillPath` fills the current path:

```
CGContextSetFillColorWithColor(context, [UIColor greenColor].CGColor);
createRoundRectanglePath      (context, CGMakeRect(10, 30, 300, 440), 20);
CGContextFillPath             (context);
```

Because Quartz fills areas up to the path, and it draws lines straddling the path, you'll get different results depending on whether you fill a shape before or after drawing the line. In the first case, the line will be twice as thick as in the second.

Global Settings

A number of settings are not defined in a path, but must be set in the graphics context: clipping areas, anti-aliasing, and global alpha.

Clipping Areas

Closed paths can be used to limit all further drawing outside the area they enclose. The enclosed area behaves like the hole in a stencil. This process is called clipping. Quartz uses the same nonzero winding number rule to determine the enclosed area. `CGContextClip` sets the current path as the clipping path. For instance, we can limit drawing to occur within a round rectangle path by writing the following:

```
CGContextSaveGState(context);
createRoundRectanglePath(context, rect, diameter);
CGContextClip(context);

// draw here!

CGContextRestoreGState(context);
```

Before setting the clipping path, you should save any existing clipping paths by invoking `CGContextSaveGState`, and restore them with `CGContextRestoreGState` once you've finished drawing.

Aliased and Antialiased Rendering

There are two ways of converting a curve from continuous user space to pixelized device space: with aliased or antialiased rendering (see Figure 8.9). Each pixel corresponds to a rectangle in user space.

Aliased rendering considers each pixel, and asks itself a qualitative question: Does the center of the pixel's rectangle in user space lie on a curve or shape, or not? If it does, the pixel is given the color of the curve or shape. This leads to blocky output but renders quickly.

Antialiased rendering considers each pixel and asks itself a quantitative question: What percentage of the pixel's rectangle's surface in user space is occupied by the curve or shape? It uses the percentage to adjust the color assigned to the pixel. If a pixel lies on two shapes, each contributes according to the area of the pixel's rectangle in user space. This results in smoother rendering, but at a performance cost.

FIGURE 8.9
Antialiasing

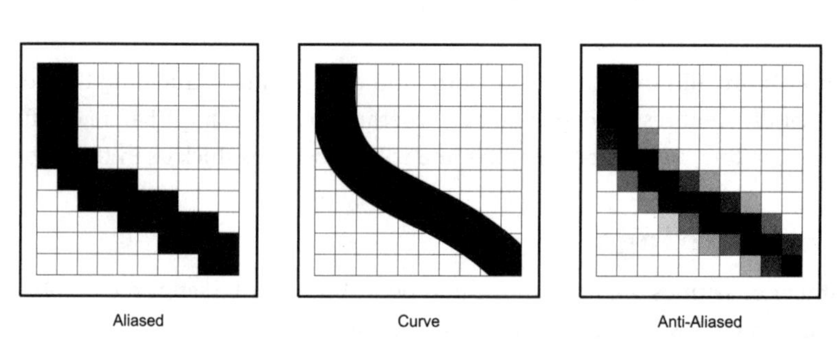

`CGContextSetShouldAntialias` disables or enables antialiasing where possible. Not all graphics contexts support antialiasing. For instance, a black-and-white laser printer can only draw jet-black dots.

Global Alpha

Although every color has an alpha channel, Quartz also has a global alpha setting, which applies to all its operations. `CGContextSetAlpha` sets its value (between 0 and 1). It's particularly useful for processing images.

Rendering Text

Quartz provides high-quality text rendering for glyphs. It does not lay text out and provides limited support for Unicode.

Choosing a Font

For simple MacRoman text encodings, `CGContextSelectFont` lets you choose the current font. It takes a font name, a font height, and the encoding, which must be `kCGEncodingMacRoman`. Be aware that `CGContextSelectFont` is slow.

```
CGContextSelectFont(context, fontName, fontHeight, kCGEncodingMacRoman);
```

Currently, the iPhone comes with the Arial, Courier New, Georgia, Helvetica, Marker Felt, Times New Roman, Trebuchet MS, Verdana, and Zapfino fonts. It has partial support (meaning certain kinds of typeface such as italic are missing) for the fonts American Typewriter and Arial Rounded MT Bold. You can enumerate the supported fonts using `UIFont`'s `familyNames` and `fontNamesForFamilyName:` methods. There are free apps at the AppStore that do this.

Alternatively, we can use `CGContextSetFont` and `CGContextSetFontSize`, but then we must draw with `CGContextShowGlyphsAtPoint` instead of `CGContextShowTextAtPoint`:

```
CGFontRef font = CGFontCreateWithFontName((CFStringRef)[uiFont fontName]);
CGContextSetFont(context, font);
CGContextSetFontSize(context, [uiFont pointSize]);
```

Getting Glyphs

Although Quartz can render the glyphs you want, you need to get the glyphs for `CGContextShowGlyphsAtPoint` yourself. Because `CGContextSelectFont` only works with a MacRoman encoding, this means you need glyphs for any Unicode string.

Unfortunately, the only function available to get glyphs, `CGFontGetGlyphsForUnichars`, is undocumented:

```
// Get glyphs

NSInteger length = [title length];
unichar chars[length];
CGGlyph glyphs[length];
[title getCharacters:chars range:NSMakeRange(0, length)];

// !!! UNDOCUMENTED !!!
extern void CGFontGetGlyphsForUnichars(CGFontRef, const unichar[],
                                       const CGGlyph[], size_t);
CGFontGetGlyphsForUnichars(f, chars, glyphs, length);
```

Where possible, use `NSString`'s `drawAtPoint:withFont:` or `UILabel`, `UITextField`, `UITextView`, and `UIFont` for Unicode strings.

Figuring Out the Text's Size

You often need to know the size of a piece of text before drawing it so that you can align it properly. The easy way to compute a text's size is to invoke `NSString`'s `sizeWithFont:` method that returns a `CGSize`.

The Quartz way of doing this is to draw the glyphs at (0,0) invisibly and see where the text ends:

```
CGContextSetTextDrawingMode(context, kCGTextInvisible);
CGContextSetTextPosition(context, 0, 0);
CGContextShowGlyphs(context, glyphs, length);
CGPoint textEnd = CGContextGetTextPosition(context);
```

`textEnd.x` now contains the width of the text, and you know the font height because you set it.

Drawing Text

Text is drawn in a mode specified `CGContextSetTextDrawingMode`. The `kCGTextInvisible` we encountered previously prevents all drawing. The other modes decide whether to give characters an edge (`kCGTextStroke`), an interior (`kCGTextFill`), or both (`kCGTextFillStroke`). Additional clipping modes let you create a clip path to be used as a stencil for future operations such as drawing a gradient.

Setting a text's color uses the same stroke and fill attributes we encountered for shapes:

```
CGContextSetTextDrawingMode(context, kCGTextFill);
CGContextSetFillColorWithColor(context, color.CGColor);
```

CGContextShowTextAtPoint shows text at a point if you are using CGContextSelectFont:

```
CGContextShowTextAtPoint(context, x, y, string, stringLength);
```

Otherwise, use `CGContextShowGlyphsAtPoint` for glyphs:

```
CGContextShowGlyphsAtPoint(context, x, y, glyphs, length);
```

An alternative is to use `CGContextGetTextPosition` to set text position and `CGContextShowText` or `CGContextShowGlyphs` to draw text. Consecutive calls to these two latter functions will place text in a line so that you can restyle or change font while staying on the same line.

The Text Matrix

To help you draw text at any angle, Quartz provides a text matrix, which is just another affine transformation, that is applied to text only. The advantage is that you can rotate the text independently of the coordinate system at which you will draw it. The text matrix is not changed by `CGContextSaveGState` or `CGContextSaveRestoreGState`.

Processing Images

Quartz can also process bitmaps. The key operation is drawing a bitmap to a context. All the primitives we've discussed so far will work on the bitmap.

Changing the CTM lets you rotate, scale, and flip the image any which way. Quartz uses interpolation to scale images to provide a less chunky result. However, this comes at a performance cost, so it is worth checking that the bitmaps used by your user interface avoid scaling wherever possible.

Setting a clipping path clips images. To fit an image into a round rectangle, create the round rectangle path, make it the clipping path, and then draw to your image.

Setting the global alpha value changes the transparency with which pictures are drawn. We'll use this to create a transition from our calculator's black 0 button to its yellow USE button. The transition consists of a series of images created by mixing the yellow and black buttons together.

```
#import "SBGButton.h"

void generateTransition(int transitionCount, UIImage** transitions, UIImage*
from, UIImage* to)
{
  CGColorSpaceRef   colorSpace = CGColorSpaceCreateDeviceRGB();
  CGRect                  rect = CGRectMake( 0, 0, to.size.width, to.size.height
);

  transitionCount -= 1;

  transitions[0]               = from;
  transitions[transitionCount] = to;

  for (int i = 1; i < transitionCount; ++i)
  {
    float     alpha = (float)(i) / transitionCount;

    CGContextRef ctx= CGBitmapContextCreate(NULL, to.size.width, to.size.height,
                          8,0, colorSpace, kCGImageAlphaPremultipliedLast);

    CGContextClearRect(ctx, rect);
    CGContextSetAlpha (ctx, alpha);
    CGContextDrawImage(ctx, rect, to.CGImage);
```

```
    CGContextSetAlpha (ctx, 1.0-alpha);
    CGContextDrawImage(ctx, rect, from.CGImage);

    CGImageRef img = CGBitmapContextCreateImage(ctx);
    CGContextRelease(ctx);

    UIImage *uiImg = [[[UIImage imageWithCGImage:img] retain] autorelease];
    CGImageRelease(img);
    transitions[i] = uiImg;
  }

  CGColorSpaceRelease(colorSpace);
};
```

We'll animate the transition by using a timer to step through the transition images.

Drawing Your Own Button

The SBGButton example source code shows to implement a button class from scatch: It draws the button and responds to user interaction itself. This section discusses the key methods.

Because the `SBGButton` class is a new class derived from `UIView`, Interface Builder knows nothing about it. Therefore, the example is built using the NIB-less version of the calculator. The `applicationDidFinishLaunching` method is responsible for adding `SBGButtons` to the calculator user interface.

Objective-C lacks namespaces. It is customary to prefix the names of reusable classes with a unique prefix such as one's initials.

The button has a different appearance depending on its state (enabled, highlighted, selected). Each of these states is either true or false, so 3 bits are sufficient to represent all state combinations. `state` represents the combined state and `0 < state < 8`. The images, transitions, titles, and title colors are stored in arrays of eight elements, one per possible state.

Responding to Touches

For simplicity, `SGButton` only responds to `touchUp` events. Other events follow the same pattern, so you can easily build from here. First, it saves the targets and selectors for `touchUp` events. I'm using `NSValue`'s `valueWithPointer` to save selectors to an array (you'll recall that they're pointers to C strings):

```
- (void) addTarget:(id)obj action:(SEL)selector
        forControlEvents:(UIControlEvents)event;
{
```

```
  if ((event != UIControlEventTouchUpInside) || (obj == nil))
    return;

  [touchUpTargets   addObject:obj];
  [touchUpSelectors addObject:[NSValue valueWithPointer:selector]];
}


- (void) removeTarget:(id)obj action:(SEL)action
         forControlEvents:(UIControlEvents)events
{
  if ((events != UIControlEventTouchUpInside) || (obj == nil))
    return;

  int i = [touchUpTargets indexOfObject:obj];
  [touchUpTargets   removeObjectAtIndex:i];
  [touchUpSelectors removeObjectAtIndex:i];
}
```

Touching a button causes it to be highlighted:

```
- (void) touchesBegan:(NSSet*)touches withEvent:(UIEvent*)event
{
  if (!self.enabled)
    return;

  self.highlighted = YES;
}
```

Dragging your finger off buttons causes them to be unhighlighted. You'll notice that touch events are sent to the button that was initially touched (until the finger is lifted or dragged off the screen).

```
- (void) touchesMoved:(NSSet*)touches withEvent:(UIEvent*)event
{
  if (!self.enabled)
    return;

  UITouch*    touch = [touches anyObject];
  CGPoint  location = [touch locationInView:self];

self.highlighted
  =  (     (location.x >= 0) && (location.x <= self.bounds.size.width)
       && (location.y >= 0) && (location.y <= self.bounds.size.height));

};
```

Lifting the finger triggers the action if the finger is still over the button:

```
- (void) touchesEnded:(NSSet*)touches withEvent:(UIEvent*)event
{
  if (!self.enabled)
    return;

  UITouch*    touch = [touches anyObject];
  CGPoint  location = [touch   locationInView:self];
```

```
  if (    (location.x >= 0) && (location.x <= self.bounds.size.width)
      && (location.y >= 0) && (location.y <= self.bounds.size.height))
  {
    int count = [touchUpTargets count];

    for (int i = 0; i < count; ++i)
    {
      id  target   = [touchUpTargets objectAtIndex:i];
      SEL selector = (SEL) [[touchUpSelectors objectAtIndex:i] pointerValue];
      [target performSelector:selector withObject:self];
    }
  }

  self.highlighted = NO;
}
```

A telephone call or a memory warning can cancel the touch sequence.

```
- (void) touchesCancelled:(NSSet*)touches withEvent:(UIEvent*)event
{
  if (!self.enabled)
    return;
  self.highlighted = NO;
}
```

Drawing the Button

Drawing the button is simple: We obtain the current graphics context and convert the coordinate space from `UIView` coordinate space to Core Graphics coordinate space by applying the `reflect` affine transformation. If there's an image for this state as returned by `imageForState:step:`, we draw it. Then, we draw the text.

```
- (void)drawRect:(CGRect)rect
{
  CGContextRef context = UIGraphicsGetCurrentContext();

  CGAffineTransform reflect = { 1.0, 0.0, 0.0, -1.0, 0.0, rect.size.height };
  CGContextConcatCTM(context, reflect);


  UIImage* image = [self imageForState:state step:step];
  if (image != nil)
    CGContextDrawImage(context, rect, image.CGImage);

  NSString* title = [titles objectAtIndex:state];
  UIColor*  color = [titleColors objectAtIndex:state];

  if (title != (id)[NSNull null])
  {
    float     fontHeight = 16.0;
    UIFont*   font       = [UIFont boldSystemFontOfSize:fontHeight];

    CGContextSelectFont(context, [[font fontName] UTF8String], fontHeight,
                                                    kCGEncodingMacRoman);
    CGContextSetTextDrawingMode(context, kCGTextFill);
    CGContextSetFillColorWithColor(context, color.CGColor);
```

```
    CGSize    size      = [title  sizeWithFont:font];

    float x = (self.bounds.size.width  - size.width) /2.0;
    float y = (self.bounds.size.height - size.height)/2.0 + fontHeight/4.0;
    CGContextShowTextAtPoint(context, x, y, [title UTF8String], [title length]);
  }
}
```

As our buttons are not opaque (they do not occupy the entire view because they are rounded rectangles), we made sure to set `self.opaque` to `NO` in our `initWithFrame` method.

Animating a Button Change

When we tap the var key, our calculator changes the color of the zero key from black to yellow suddenly. We can create a smoother transition by creating intermediate steps using the `generateTransition` function we wrote earlier. We'll keep track of the current step in the animation using `step`.

```
- (UIImage*) imageForState:(int)aState step:(int)aStep
{
  // Use transition array if it exists

  NSArray* fast = [transitions objectAtIndex:aState];
  if (fast != (id)[NSNull null])
    return [fast objectAtIndex:aStep];

  // Use main image if appropriate

  UIImage* from = [backgroundImages objectAtIndex:aState];
  if      (from == (id)[NSNull null])
    return nil;
  else if (aStep == 0)
    return from;

  // Use alternative image if appropriate

  UIImage* to   = [altImages objectAtIndex:aState];
  if      (to == (id)[NSNull null])
    return nil;
  else if (aStep == transitionCount)
    return to;


  // If both alternative and main images exist, create a transition

  UIImage* images[transitionCount+1];

  generateTransition(transitionCount+1, images, from, to);
  NSArray* transition = [NSArray arrayWithObjects:images count:transitionCount+1];
  [transitions replaceObjectAtIndex:aState withObject:transition];
  return [transition objectAtIndex:aStep];
}
```

`setUseAltImage:` switches between the main and alternative background images by starting a `NSTimer` and setting `delta` appropriately. `delta` is `-1` to animate from the alternative image to the main image, `0` for no animation, and `1` to animate from the main image to the alternative image.

```
- (void) setUseAltImage:(BOOL)useAltImage
{
  [self imageForState:state step:transitionCount/2];
  if (timer == nil)
    timer = [[NSTimer
             scheduledTimerWithTimeInterval:(transitionTime / transitionCount)
                                     target:self selector:@selector(animate:)
                                   userInfo:nil repeats:YES] retain];
  delta = useAltImage ? 1 : -1;
}
```

Animation is simply a matter of updating the current step, and requesting the view to be displayed again. We invalidate the timer if we're done to save battery power.

```
- (void) animate:(NSTimer*)t
{
  step = max(min(step + delta, transitionCount), 0);
  [self setNeedsDisplay];

  if ((step == 0) || (step == transitionCount))
  {
    delta = 0;
    [timer invalidate];
    [timer release];
    timer = nil;
  }
}
```

Applications on the iPhone share memory. Although user applications might not run in the background, system applications do. Because the iPhone has no virtual memory, if a system application requests memory and there is not enough memory to satisfy it, your application will be sent a memory warning: your application will receive a `UIApplicationDidReceiveMemoryWarningNotification`. If your application does not free enough memory to satisfy the system application's demand, your application might be terminated. Responding to memory warnings is, therefore, important to provide a pleasant user experience.

By default, `UIImages` that are loaded from bitmaps are freed if the iPhone OS sends the application a memory warning. Because `UIKit` knows their filenames, it can reload them later: This is a safe operation. On the other hand, `UIKit` cannot regenerate the button transition. Therefore, you have to respond to the memory warning and free the transition yourself. You can generate it again later if you need to:

```
- (void) handleMemoryWarning:(NSNotification*)notification
{
  NSLog(@"Memory warning");
  [transitions release];
```

```
  NSNull* n = [NSNull null];
  transitions = [[NSMutableArray alloc] initWithObjects:n,n,n,n,n,n,n,n,nil];
}

@end
```

SBGButton registers for memory warning notifications in its init method and unregisters for them in its dealloc method. Notifications are discussed in more detail in Hour 12, "Adding Navigation and Tab Bar Controllers."

Memory warnings are rare events. Choose Hardware, Simulate Memory Warning to test your code.

Summary

Core Graphics is incredibly powerful. It's a testament to the quality of Apple's standard user-interface (UI) elements that so few people need to use it. This power comes at the price of speed, but judiciously combining Core Graphics for rendering and layers (which you will learn about in the next hour) for animation gives you the tools to make visually stunning iPhone applications.

To learn more about Core Graphics, read the beautiful book *Programming with Quartz 2D and PDF Graphics in Mac OS X*. Although it's for Mac, it explains the concepts very clearly. It takes 650 informative pages to describe Core Graphics in its entirety, so we've only scratched the surface here.

Q&A

Q. ***How do should I prototype my Core Graphics widgets?***

A. It is often fastest to prototype them in a vector editing tool such as Xara on Windows, or Photoshop before writing code.

Workshop

The Workshop consists of quiz questions and answers to help you solidify your understanding of the material covered in this hour. You should try to answer the questions before checking the answers.

Quiz Questions

1. Why does Core Graphics use a device independent coordinate system?
2. What is the current transformation matrix?
3. What is a path?
4. What is the non-zero winding rule?
5. What types of curves does Core Graphics support?
6. Can Core Graphics manipulate bitmap images?

Quiz Answers

1. Core Graphics uses a device independent coordinate system to support the draw documents identically on your iPhone's screen as it would on a printer.
2. The current transformation matrix maps drawings from user space to device space.
3. A path specifies where a line will be drawn, a clipping area or an area to be filled.
4. The non-zero winding rule determines which areas are filled or clipped when dealing with a self intersecting path.
5. Core Graphics can draw lines, quadratic and cubic Bézier curves, and circular arcs.
6. Yes, you can use draw bitmapped images to user space, clip them or apply alpha blending to them. You can also stretch or rotate them using the current transform matrix.

Exercises

- Write a ruler application that draws a ruler to the screen. Tapping the screen should change units.
- Draw a fractal fern leaf (look up fractal fern leaf on the Internet; for instance, see http://local.wasp.uwa.edu.au/~pbourke/fractals/ifs_fern_a/).
- Load a PDF document and draw it to the screen.

HOUR 9

Layers and Core Animation: Creating a Cover Flow Clone

What You'll Learn in This Hour:

- Placing layers in 3D space
- Using Core Animation
- Creating a Cover Flow clone

In the previous hour, you started playing with animation. Because Core Graphics based animation is slow, the iPhone provides a Core Animation framework to create smoother and more complex effects using the iPhone's 3D hardware. To use Core Animation you must understand layers, the basic unit the 3D hardware can render. Then, you'll learn the Core Animation API and apply it to a new project: the Cover Flow clone shown in Figure 9.1.

FIGURE 9.1
Cover Flow (animal images courtesy of http://www.public-domain-image.com/)

Placing Layers in 3D Space

Whereas `UIViews` are the building blocks for your user interface, layers are the fundamental building block used by the iPhone's 3D hardware. Everything drawn to the screen is drawn to a layer: a two-dimensional bitmap image that can be placed in 3D space. Cocoa Touch uses the iPhone's 3D graphics hardware (called a graphics processor unit or GPU) to implement these layers as textures.

Layer Hierarchy

In Cocoa Touch, every `UIView` is drawn to its own layer. Layers are drawn to textures which are bitmaps that the GPU draws onto surfaces. Cocoa uses rectangular surfaces. The GPU can draw these rectangles at any angle and in any perspective in 3D space very quickly. However, updating textures is slow because when the GPU and the CPU both want to access a texture, the CPU has to wait. This is why Core Graphics based animations are slow: Core Graphics uses the CPU to draw to textures, causing the CPU to stall. Core Animation uses the GPU instead to provide smooth animations. The PowerVR GPU used in the iPhone limits layers to a maximum of 1024x1024 pixels, which is why no view can be larger than 1024x1024 pixels.

Layers follow a similar design to `UIViews`: Just as views are organized into a tree (the view hierarchy) layers are also organized into a tree (the layer hierarchy). Just like `UIViews`, layers have frame and bounds coordinate systems. The frame and bounds always have identical sizes. Unlike `UIViews`, layers use a coordinate system where the origin (0,0) is at the bottom left of the screen, rather than at the top left. Like `UIViews`, layers can have many sublayers, which are drawn following preorder tree traversal: A child appearing earlier in a layer's sublayers will be rendered under one appearing later, even if the 3D coordinates of the first layer should put it on top. It is up to you to sort each layer's sublayers appropriately.

The Quartz framework implements layers, using **Core Animation**'s prefix (the letters `CA`). All layers are either `CALayers` or its descendents. `sublayers` returns the list of sublayers, ordered from back to front. Like `addSubview:`, `addSublayer:` adds a sublayer to the fore (that is, the end of the `sublayers` array). Like `removeFromSuperview`, `removeFromSuperlayer` is used to remove layers. Similarly, methods to insert sublayers (`insertSublayer:atIndex:`, `insertSublayer:below:`, and `insertSublayer:above:`) and replace sublayers (`replaceSublayer:with:`) in `sublayers` are also available. It is an error to add a layer that already has a superlayer as a sublayer (it has a non-`nil` `superlayer`).

Updating Layers

Layer Content

Layers are textures and are stored in memory as bitmaps: as `CGImageRefs`. You can switch content by writing to the layer's `contents` property. Thus, you can create a layer with the following code:

```
CGImageRef image  = ...;
CALayer* layer    = [CALayer layer];
[layer setPosition: CGPointMake(50.0, 50.0)];
[layer setBounds:   CGRectMake(0.0, 0.0, 100.0, 100.0)];
[layer setContents: image];
```

To see this layer, you must add it to the layer hierarchy, as described previously.

Drawing to Layers

Because `UIViews` want to draw to a layer instead of providing prerendered bitmaps, Core Animation provides a means to draw to the layer's bitmap.

`CALayer` provides two ways of adding drawing code: by subclassing layers or by writing a delegate. Delegates are preferred.

If you opt for a delegate, you must either implement `displayLayer` or `drawLayer:inContext:`. Invoking `setNeedsDisplay` on a layer requests that `CALayer` later update the layer's contents by invoking one of these delegate methods. `displayLayer` is used to update the `CALayer`'s `contents` property with a prerendered `CGImage`. `drawLayer:inContext:` is used to draw to a context using Core Graphics. `drawLayer:inContext:` is much slower than `displayLayer` because it must create and draw the bitmap.

Instead of using a delegate, you can also subclass `CALayer`, and override its default `displayLayer` and `drawInContext:` methods. The default implementation of these methods just invokes the delegate's `displayLayer` and `drawLayer:inContext:` methods.

It is rarely necessary to subclass `CALayers`. A common reason for creating subclasses is to store arbitrary values in any instance. However, `CALayer` is a key-value coding compliant container class: It behaves like a dictionary. More precisely, it redefines `valueForKey:` and `setValue:forKey:` to store and retrieve values that it does not define itself using an auxiliary dictionary. As with categories, there is a danger that Apple could add properties to `CALayer` that clash with a key name you decided to use. Using unique key names reduces this risk.

Avoiding Drawing to Layers

As drawing to layers is slow, layers minimize the number of times they are drawn by postponing drawing until later in the run loop. Code that wants a layer to be redrawn invokes setNeedsDisplay on it, which sets a flag stating that the layer needs to be redrawn. After all pending user-interaction events have been processed, a CALayer run loop observer steps through the layer hierarchy and invokes the draw methods as needed. This is why invoking the run loop before starting an intensive computation updates the display.

```
[[NSRunLoop currentRunLoop] runUntilDate: [NSDate distantPast]];
```

UIViews integrate into CALayer's way of doing things in a number of ways. The UIView run loop observer, which is responsible for updating layouts, is executed before CALayer's run loop observer, which draws to the layers. Thus, changing UIView layouts results in redrawing resized views.

In Hour 6, "Understanding How the User Interface Is Built," we discussed hypothetical drawView and displayRect: functions, which traversed the view hierarchy and decided what to display. This functionality is provided by CALayer's run loop observer, which invokes UIView's drawLayer:inContext: method as needed: UIView is a delegate of the CALayer that it owns. (This is another example of why delegates are not retained so as to avoid retain cycles.) UIView's drawLayer:inContext: method invokes the view's drawRect: method after flipping the coordinate system and setting up the context you retrieve with UIGraphicsGetCurrentContext.

UIView's layout routines invoke its setNeedsDisplay: when they change the size of a view. UIView's setNeedsDisplay: method simply invokes the layer's setNeedsDisplay method, so that the views are redrawn.

By default, a layer's needsDisplayOnBoundsChange property is set to NO: Resizing a layer simply stretches it instead of redrawing it. The exception is that UIView's contentMode sets needsDisplayOnBoundsChange to YES to implement its UIViewContentModeRedraw mode. Thus, the layer will not be redrawn in the aspect resizing modes unless you change needsDisplayOnBoundsChange.

Using Texture Atlases

PowerVR recommends using texture atlases to reduce the time spent by the CPU waiting on the GPU. The idea is that rather than switching between many small textures to create an animation, you can put every frame of the animation into a single large texture. The task, then, is to only show part of this large texture in each frame. CALayer's contentsRect lets you select the part of the texture to show.

Placing Layers in 3D Space

The mathematics of placing objects in a 3D space are the same as those we encountered for 2D objects: transforms. Each layer is associated with two 4x4 matrices—how each point of the layer should be mapped into the superlayer's coordinate space. Just as with 2D transforms, these 3D transforms can rotate, scale, and flip objects. Unlike 2D transforms, they operate in 3D space and they include a term to apply perspective.

The first 4x4 matrix is called a `sublayerTransform` and applies to all a superlayer's sublayers. Because they apply to all sublayers, `sublayerTransforms` are mainly used to set up perspective. Each layer also has a `transform` matrix, which lets it be rotated or scaled independently from the other sublayers of its superlayer. As with `UIViews`, the 3D matrices are combined into a single transform by multiplying them as we step down the hierarchy.

Transforms are represented by `CATransform3D` objects. Core Animation provides the following functions to manipulate them:

- `CATransform3DRotate` rotates them by an angle specified in radians around an axis specified by a vector (*x,y,z*).
- `CATransform3DScale` scales them by (*sx, sy, sz*).
- `CATransform3DTranslate` translates them by (*tx, ty, tz*).

Alternatively, you can create rotation, scale, and translation matrices:

- `CATransform3DMakeRotation` creates a transform to rotate by an angle around an axis specified by a vector (*x,y,z*).
- `CATransform3DMakeScale` creates a transform to scale by (*sx, sy, sz*).
- `CATransform3DMakeTranslation` creates a transform to translate by (*tx, ty, tz*).

Because the iPhone can only display 2D content, it uses perspective to create the illusion of a 3D world. To create that perspective, the superlayer of all layers that will be in your 3D world must be told how far your eye is from the phone. I use 2500.0 for this, but you can play with the value to decide what works best for you.

```
CGFloat zDistance   = 2500.0;
CATransform3D threeDTransform = CATransform3DIdentity;
threeDTransform.m34 = 1.0 / -zDistance;
self.layer.sublayerTransform = threeDTransform;
```

By the Way

The units the iPhone uses for this distance are pixels, but in a third dimension. For instance, if you tend to hold your iPhone a foot away from your face, you would use 1920 because the iPhone screen is 7.5 cm long for 480 pixels, so 30 cm * 480 pixels / 7.5 cm = 1920 pixels distance. I chose 2500 because that corresponds to the distance at which I hold my iPhone from my face (see Figure 9.2).

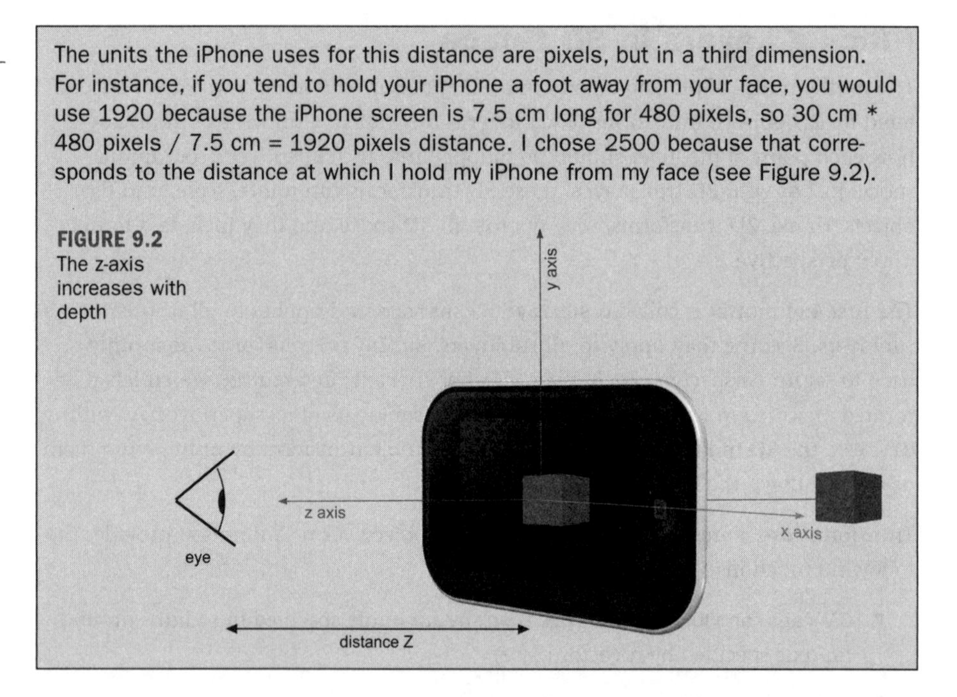

FIGURE 9.2 The z-axis increases with depth

Did you Know?

3D transformation matrices are commonly used by 3D application programming interfaces (APIs) such as OpenGL.

To scale a layer:

$$\begin{bmatrix} s_x & 0 & 0 & 0 \\ 0 & s_y & 0 & 0 \\ 0 & 0 & s_z & 0 \\ 0 & 0 & 0 & 1 \end{bmatrix}$$

To translate a layer:

$$\begin{bmatrix} 0 & 0 & 0 & 0 \\ 0 & 0 & 0 & 0 \\ 0 & 0 & 0 & 0 \\ t_x & t_y & t_z & 1 \end{bmatrix}$$

To rotate a layer:

$$\begin{bmatrix} r_{11} & r_{12} & r_{13} & 0 \\ r_{21} & r_{22} & r_{23} & 0 \\ r_{31} & r_{32} & r_{33} & 0 \\ 0 & 0 & 0 & 1 \end{bmatrix}$$

To multiply a vector by a 4x4 matrix, you need to use a four-element vector. Just as in the 2D case, using a 1 as a final vector element returns the correct result:

$$[x'\ y'\ z'\ 1] = [x\ y\ z\ 1] \begin{bmatrix} r_{11} & r_{12} & r_{13} & 0 \\ r_{21} & r_{22} & r_{23} & 0 \\ r_{31} & r_{32} & r_{33} & 0 \\ t_x & t_y & t_z & 1 \end{bmatrix}$$

3D also adds perspective. Consider two objects of the same size. If you place one twice as far away as the other, it will appear to be half the other's size: It will take half the visual angle that the first object takes. The center of your field of vision is the center of a coordinate system around which lengths shrink with distance in this manner.

As you'll be drawing on the screen, the screen's x/y plane is the center of origin for the z-axis, which grows out from the screen toward the user's face. To obtain the correct perspective, you need to guess where your eye is relative to the screen. Let's assume it's centered on the center of the screen and is at a distance *Z*: It has coordinates (*X*, *Y*, *Z*), where *X* = *Y* = 0 and *Z* is the positive distance to your face. Now, assuming the origin of the coordinate system is based at the center of the screen, the screen coordinates (*x"*, *y"*) for a point at (*x*, *y*, *z*) are as follows:

$$x'' = (x-X)\frac{Z}{Z-z}$$

$$y'' = (y-Y)\frac{Z}{Z-z}$$

Matrix multiplication cannot invert the z coordinate for division, so matrix multiplication cannot perform projection. However, if you set the third element of fourth column to the inverse of distance *Z*, the result of multiplying the vector with the matrix is a new vector (x' y' z' w), where *w* is not 1 but (1 - z/Z).

$$[x'\ y'\ z'\ w] = [x\ y\ z\ 1] \begin{bmatrix} r_{11} & r_{12} & r_{13} & 0 \\ r_{21} & r_{22} & r_{23} & 0 \\ r_{31} & r_{32} & r_{33} & -\frac{1}{Z} \\ t_x & t_y & t_z & 1 \end{bmatrix}$$

$$w = 1 - \frac{z}{Z}$$

All you must now do to obtain the desired (x", y") is to divide x' and y' by *w*:

$$x'' = \frac{x'}{w} = \frac{x'}{1-\frac{z}{Z}} = \frac{Zx'}{Z-z}$$

$$y'' = \frac{y'}{w} = \frac{y'}{1-\frac{z}{Z}} = \frac{Zy'}{Z-z}$$

This explains why we set `m34` to `1.0 / -zDistance`.

Did you Know?

Transparency comes at a cost on the iPhone: When the iPhone's GPU renders the screen, it avoids reading any texture data from layers behind opaque layers. This boosts its speed while reducing its power consumption. `CALayers` use the `opaque` flag to sort the layer list. If opaque layers are given to the GPU first, it can avoid unnecessary texture lookups. This hour focuses on standard `CALayers` because they are the most commonly use layers. Other types of layers (`CAScrollLayers`, `CATiledLayers`, and `CAEAGLLayers`) are discussed in detail in Appendix D.

Using Core Animation

Core Animation reduces the amount of code you must write while improving the fluidity of your animations. As we saw in Hour 7, "Understanding How Events Are Processed," timer handlers are invoked from the run loop and are at the mercy of all the handlers in your application running quickly. Core Animation uses multithreading to provide fluid animation that will not stall if a handler takes too long.

Core Animation Architecture

Animations are performed in a separate thread which will not block on the main thread. This means Core Animation can only animate properties that do not require main thread intervention. Your application can specify animations in a thread safe manner using transactions.

The Core Animation Thread

Core Animation creates a thread that is responsible for updating all current animations (see Figure 9.3). Animations are specified using objects of the `CAAnimation` class and its subclasses. Each animation that is committed is copied so that you cannot change it and passed to the Core Animation thread. The Core Animation thread then invokes private methods of `CAAnimation` to retrieve the properties to animate and their correct value at each point in time. Notice that animation delegate methods will receive a different animation object from the one you created. Animation delegates are discussed in more detail later this hour, but for now, know that they are invoked when an animation starts and when it stops.

Core Animation also hooks into the run loop:

- It redraws layers requested by the Core Animation thread.
- It invokes animation delegate methods (`animationDidStart:` and `animationDidStop:finished:`) as requested by the Core Animation thread.
- It dispatches queued transactions to the Core Animation thread.

This means your display and delegate calls are invoked from the main thread.

To keep track of properties, each layer has a twin called a presentation layer. The properties you see in the main thread are the layer's properties: a cache of the value you last set them to in the main thread. The actual value of the property (as seen on the screen) is maintained in the presentation layer and is accessed by the Core Animation thread. Thus, the main thread can access layer properties without locking, whereas the Core Animation thread can access presentation layer properties without locking.

In fact, there is a third thread called the render thread, which lurks in the background and is responsible for all compositing operations. Apple states that the render thread can run in a separate process, which seems to be the case on the iPhone since no render thread is visible in the debugger.

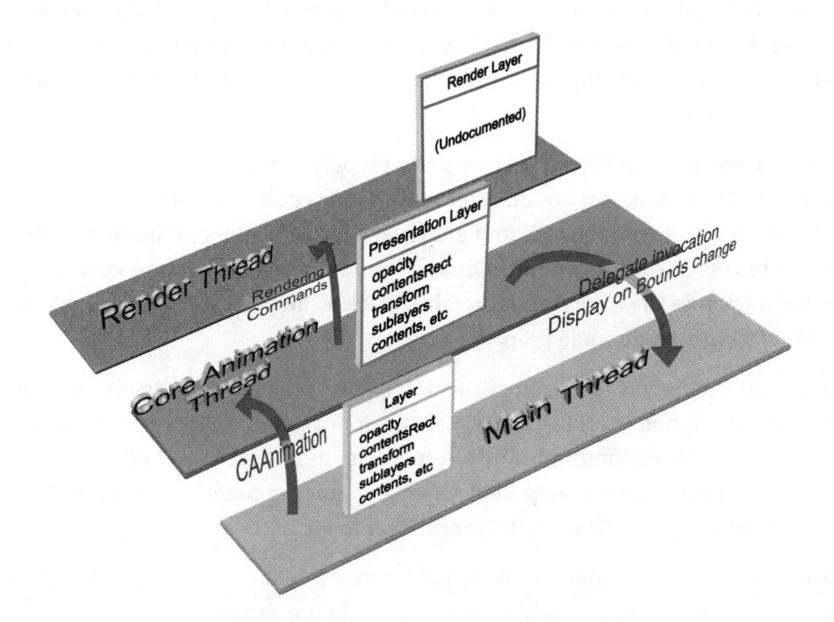

FIGURE 9.3 Core Animation threading architecture

Animatable Properties

Because animatable properties are updated by the Core Animation thread, only those properties that require no state to be changed on the main thread are animatable. In practice, this reduces the list to a few key presentation layer properties. If state had to be changed on the main thread, the Core Animation thread would run in lockstep with the main thread, negating any benefits of running in a separate thread.

Updating the opacity, color, presence, or double-sidedness of a surface are all GPU operations and require no main-thread intervention. Thus, `opacity` and `backgroundColor` are animatable. `hidden` lets you hide a surface, which means removing it from the GPU's list of surfaces to draw. GPUs use a technique called backface culling to reduce the number of surfaces they need to consider: As long as the camera does not enter a solid object, it is sufficient to model it with a single-sided surface that faces outward. `doubleSided` tells the GPU whether a surface has two sides.

`contents` is animatable, but requires the GPU to bind a different texture to the rectangle it will draw (which is slow).

Updating the location of a layer in 3D space requires no main-thread intervention as it is a GPU operation. The position of the layer in space is animatable using the properties `anchorPoint`, `position`, `sublayerTransform`, `transform`, and `zPosition`. `anchorPoint` is the point of the layer (usually its center) to which `position` refers. Rotating a layer rotates it around its `anchorPoint`, and scaling a layer expands it around its `anchorPoint`. You'll notice that the `anchorPoint`, `position`, and `zPosition` are encompassed by the `transform` matrix. `contentsRect` is similarly animatable.

`maskToBounds` lets you clip a sublayer so that it only occupies the bounds of its superlayer. By default, this option is set to `NO`, but because the Core Animation thread knows the layer's `bounds` and `sublayers` property, the appropriate `bounds` and `contentRect` can be computed and set without main-thread intervention. Similarly, because the Core Animation thread keeps track of each layer's `sublayers`, `sublayers` is an animatable property.

The `bounds` property is more complicated. If `needsDisplayOnBoundsChange` is set to `YES`, Core Animation invokes `displayLayer:` or `drawRect:inContext:` to update the layer. As these methods must be run in the main thread, Core Animation invokes them from the run loop (and suffers the time penalties associated with that). By default, `needsDisplayOnChange` is set to `NO`.

No other properties are animatable as their setters would need to be invoked from Core Animation's thread, which their setters would not expect.

Transactions

Transactions are the mechanism used to pass changes to animatable properties to the Core Animation thread, which maintains the presentation layer. Changing a layer property creates a transaction that is dispatched to the Core Animation thread by the Core Animation run loop observer. Such transactions are called implicit transactions. You cannot modify a property from a thread without a run loop using implicit transactions.

Explicit transactions are bracketed between `CATransition`'s `begin` and `commit` methods and are dispatched as soon as `commit` is invoked.

```
[CATransaction begin];
layer.opacity = 0.0;
[CATransaction commit];
```

Animation Objects

Animations are objects that specify the animation you would like to perform. They are examples of the object-oriented strategy pattern: They let you change animation algorithms without changing the Core Animation thread's code.

CAAnimation

All animations are CAAnimation classes or its descendents. CAAnimation specifies the basic features all animations share, although you can't use it directly to specify an animation.

CAAnimation obeys the CAMediaTiming protocol, which specifies when it starts (beginTime), its duration, how many times it should repeat (repeatCount) or how long it will repeat (repeatDuration), and whether the animation is always played forward or reverses direction on each repetition (autoreverses). Although most animations start at their beginning, timeOffset can be used to specify the point within the animation at which the animation should start. timeOffset is specified in seconds. fillMode specifies whether the values specified by the animation should apply before or after the animation.

CAAnimation extends CAMediaTiming to let you set a delegate that supports two methods animationDidStart: and animationDidStop:finished:. Its removedOnCompletion property states whether the animation will automatically be discarded once the animation is over.

> **Watch Out!** Animation delegates are retained by their animations!

CAAnimation's timingFunction lets you change the timing of the animation. You'd use timingFunction to model how a door slams: It starts moving slowly but gains speed. You can vary the door's angle linearly, but use timingFunction to model the increasing speed at which the door slams.

CAMediaTimingFunction's functionWithName: method provides four canned timing functions you'll encounter quite often:

- kCAMediaTimingFunctionLinear specifies that the animation stays at a constant speed.
- kCAMediaTimingFunctionEaseIn specifies that the animation speeds up (like the door slamming).
- kCAMediaTimingFunctionEaseOut specifies that the animation slows down (like an airplane landing).
- kCAMediaTimingFunctionEaseInEaseOut specifies that the animation starts slowly, accelerates until the middle of the animation, and then slows down again.

Setting timingFunction to nil also indicates a constant speed animation.

All timing functions are specified as cubic Bézier curves (discussed in Hour 8, "Drawing User-Interface Elements"). You can specify your own curve by using the `CAMediaTimingFunction`'s `functionWithControlPoints::::` method to specify a curve whose endpoints are (0,0) and (1,1) and whose control points are (*c0x, c0y*) and (*c1x, c1y*).

Did you Know?

> http://www.netzgesta.de/dev/cubic-bezier-timing-function.html lets you see how changing the control points affects the animation curve.

```
CAMediaTimingFunction *f;
f = [CAMediaTimingFunction functionWithControlPoints:c0x :c0y :c1x :c1y];
```

For instance, `functionWithName:kCAMediaTimingFunctionEaseIn` is equivalent to `functionWithControlPoints:0.42 :0 :1 :1` as can be determined by using `CAMediaTimingFunction`'s `getControlPointAtIndex:values:` method (see Figure 9.4).

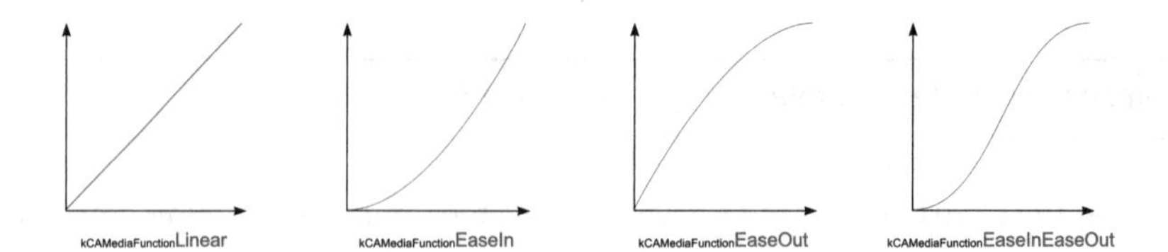

FIGURE 9.4
The animation curves (time flows from left to right).

`CABasicAnimation`: Linear Interpolation Between Two Values

`CABasicAnimation` is for animations that linearly interpolate from a beginning value (`fromValue`) to an end value (`toValue`). For instance, to make an object's opacity fade away, you could write the following:

```
CABasicAnimation *opacity  = [CABasicAnimation animationWithKeyPath:@"opacity"];
opacity.duration           = timeInterval;
opacity.fromValue          = [NSNumber numberWithFloat:1.0];
opacity.toValue            = [NSNumber numberWithFloat:0.0];
```

The key path specifies the animatable property (in this case, `opacity`).

Linear interpolation is also available for composite values such as `CGPoints` or `CATransform3Ds`.

```
CATransform3D transform     = CATransform3DMakeRotation(2*M_PI, 0, 0, 1.0);
CABasicAnimation* animation
   = [CABasicAnimation animationWithKeyPath:@"transform"];
animation.toValue           = [NSValue valueWithCATransform3D:transform];
animation.duration          = duration;
animation.cumulative        = YES;
animation.repeatCount       = 9999;
```

You might notice that I didn't specify a fromValue in the preceding code. If you don't specify a fromValue or a toValue, the current presentation layer value is used. If both fromValue and toValue are nil, the animation interpolates between the previous value of the property in the presentation layer and the current value of the property in the presentation layer.

When dealing with multiple repetitions of an animation, the cumulative property can be used to state that the animation should not be repeated starting at the fromValue, but from its current value. This is useful when working with values that can gain cumulative errors such as floating-point numbers.

CAKeyframeAnimation: Specifying More Than Two Values

CAKeyframeAnimations are used whenever you need to specify more than two values or need to use animation without any interpolation. Each of these values is called a keyframe value. You can specify the values in two ways: setting the values array or setting the path to a CGPathRef.

If the values array property is non-nil, the animation will step though its values. By default, keyframe values are equally spaced throughout an animation. The keyTimes array lets you associate each value of values with a time within the animation. These times are expressed as a fraction of the entire duration of the animation and fit within the range 0.0 to 1.0. The keyTimes array must start with 0.0 and end with 1.0. Each keyframe can also be associated with its own CAMediaTimingFunction using the timingFunctions array. This lets you create arbitrarily complex timing behavior. By default, linear interpolation is used to interpolate between keyframe values.

Alternatively, CAKeyFrameAnimation lets you specify a CGPathRef. This is useful to specify the path of a sprite animation using the Quartz path methods you encountered in Hour 8. In this case, you will manipulate a path directly rather than a context. The calls you will use are prefixed by CGPath instead of CGContext, and take as the first argument a path and as the second argument an affine transform. The affine transform is applied to the specified points before they are added to the path. For instance, CGContextAddLineToPoint becomes CGPathAddLineToPoint:

```
CGMutablePathRef path = CGPathCreateMutable();
CGPathMoveToPoint    (path, NULL, 160, 375);
CGPathAddCurveToPoint(path, NULL, 160, 375,
                                  160, 100,
                                  160, 100);

CAKeyframeAnimation* animation
  = [CAKeyframeAnimation animationWithKeyPath:@"position"];
animation.path                    = path;
animation.duration                = 5.0;
CFRelease(thePath);
```

By default, each path segment will be assigned an equal time through an animation. On the Mac, kCAAnimationPaced is used to assign each path segment a duration corresponding to its path length. This results in smooth movement along the path. Unfortunately, kCAAnimationPaced is not implemented on iPhone OS. Instead, you can use keyTimes to pace the animation correctly. Calculating the length of straight lines and arcs is easy (basic geometry). Calculating the length of a Bézier curve is hard, but in practice it is sufficient to approximate the curve as a set of segments and sum their lengths. *Graphics Gems V* states that only four segments are required to approximate the length of a cubic Bézier curve within an error margin of 0.1%. Quadratic Bézier curves require up to 12 segments to obtain the same accuracy. Hour 8 explained how points on the curve were computed (see pages 184-186).

Setting rotationMode to kCAAnimationRotateAuto specifies that the object should be rotated to match the tangent of the curve. This is useful to make a sprite, such as a spaceship, turn in the direction in which it is moving. Setting it to kCAAnimationRotateAutoReverse makes it face backward.

Although we usually want interpolation, sometimes it makes no sense. For instance, to animate a layer's contents, you need to provide a series of pointers to CGImages. You cannot meaningfully interpolate pointer values, so you can tell CAKeyFrameAnimation not to do so by setting calculationMode to kCAAnimationDiscrete. Its default value is kCAAnimationLinear.

CAAnimationGroup: Grouping Multiple Animations

At times, you might want to combine many animations and see them start and stop at the same time. CAAnimationGroup lets you do that. CAAnimationGroup provides an animations array property, which specifies the group of animations. Grouped animations behave as a single animation as far as their removedOnCompletion properties and their delegates are concerned: Only CAAnimationGroup's removedOnCompletion and delegate properties will be taken into account.

```
CAAnimationGroup *group = [CAAnimationGroup animation];
group.animations        = [NSArray arrayWithObjects:anim1, anim2, nil];
```

CAAnimationGroup is also used to assign a single timingFunction to a CAKeyframeAnimation: CAKeyframeAnimations ignore their inherited timingFunction property and use timingFunctions instead.

CATransition: Canned Animations

Because animations are so important to the iPhone user interface, Cocoa Touch provides canned animations you can use for common tasks. Transitions apply to entire layers. There are four types of transitions:

- kCATransitionFade to fade the layer in or out
- kCATransitionMoveIn to slide the layer over existing content
- kCATransitionPush to push existing content away as the layer slides into place
- kCATransitionReveal to reveal the layer gradually

Transitions involving movement have a subtype, which should be set to one of the following values: kCATransitionFromRight, kCATransitionFromLeft, kCATransitionFromTop, or kCATransitionFromBottom.

```
CATransition *transition = [CATransition animation];
transition.type          = kCATransitionMoveIn;
transition.subtype       = kCATransitionFromLeft;
```

startProgress and endProgress specify how far into the animation to start and stop (within a range 0.0 to 1.0).

```
CATransition *transition = [CATransition animation];
transition.type          = kCATransitionFade;
transition.startProgress = 0.0;
transition.endProgress   = 1.0;
transition.duration      = 0.25;
```

Playing Animations

Because animations are played in a different thread there is an API to add them to a thread and a delegate API to be informed when they terminate.

Adding Animations to Layers

To play an animation, add it to a layer using addAnimation:forKey:. The key should be a unique identifier you can use to remove or retrieve an animation at a later point (recall that animation objects are copied before being passed to the Core Animation thread). You can give the key any name you like:

```
[layer addAnimation:animation forKey:@"frodoBaggins"];
```

To stop an animation, remove it from the layer with removeAnimationForKey::

```
[layer removeAnimationForKey:@"frodoBaggins"];
```

If you do not set the final values of your animated properties in a delegate, you can set them after invoking addAnimation:forKey:. If the animation starts immediately (or uses an appropriate fillMode), changes to the layer property are not shown until the animation completes.

Delegates

The `animationDidStop:finished:` delegate is called after the animation completes. `finished` is true if the animation completed and false if it was stopped prematurely (because it was removed by `removeAllAnimations` or `removeAnimationForKey:`).

Because delegates are invoked on the main thread from the run loop, there can be a considerable gap of time between the moment the animation ends and the moment your animation delegate is called. If the animation restores the presentation layer property to its original value, and your delegate sets it to the new value, there will be a noticeable flicker at the end of your animation. The solution is to set the animation's `fillMode` to `kCAFillModeForwards` and to stop the animation from automatically being discarded when it completed by setting `removedOnCompletion` to `NO`.

```
animation.fillMode              = kCAFillModeForwards;
animation.removedOnCompletion   = NO;
```

Now your delegate can set animated properties' final values and then remove the animation, guaranteeing no flicker.

`fillMode` can take the following values:

- `kCAFillModeRemoved` restores the property to its original value once the animation completes.
- `kCAFillModeForwards` causes the final value of the animation to be used after the animation ends.
- `kCAFillModeBackwards` causes the initial value of the animation to be used until the animation starts.
- `kCAFillModeBoth` applies the initial value of the animation until the animation starts and the final value of the animation once the animation ends.

Animations Are KVC-Compliant Container Classes

Just like `CALayers`, `CAAnimations` are key-value coding compliant container classes. By adding a key-value pair to a `CAAnimation` object, you can pass information to the delegate methods. Again, use unique names. To set a value before launching an animation, use `setValue:forKey::`

```
NSNumber* indexN = [NSNumber numberWithInt:index];
[animation setValue:indexN forKey:@"SBGimageIndex"];
```

To retrieve a value from a delegate, use `valueForKey::`

```
int index = [[animation valueForKey:@"SBGimageIndex"] intValue];
```

Convenience Methods

Core Animation provides a number of convenience methods to reduce the amount of code you must write: actions and UIView animation methods.

Actions

Layer properties can be associated with default animations. The CATransaction mechanism checks for the existence of a canned animation by invoking the layer's actionForKey: method. The default implementation of actionForKey: performs the following search until it obtains a valid result (a CAAnimation) or an NSNull to terminate the search:

1. Invokes the layer's delegate's actionForLayer:forKey:
2. Looks up the animation in the layer's actions dictionary
3. Looks up an actions dictionary in the layer's style dictionary and looks up the animation in that dictionary should it exist
4. Invokes the layer's defaultActionForKey:

Returning NSNull from actionForLayer:forKey: lets you disable default animations.

CALayer's defaultActionForKey: method returns for all properties other than sublayers, a 0.25 second linear interpolation from their current value to their new value (using CABasicAnimation). The sublayers property is given a kCATransitionFade CATransaction.

For instance, you can override the standard action for changing opacity as follows:

```
- (id <CAAction>) actionForLayer:(CALayer*)layer forKey:(NSString*)key
{
  if (![key isEqualToString:@"opacity"])
    return nil;

  CABasicAnimation* a;
  a = [CABasicAnimation animationWithKeyPath:@"opacity"];
  a.duration = 0.5;
  return a;
}
```

Alternatively, you could set the layer's actions:

```
CABasicAnimation* a = [CABasicAnimation animationWithKeyPath:@"opacity"];
a.duration     = 0.5;
layer.actions = [NSDictionary dictionaryWithObject:a forKey:@"opacity"];
```

You can disable default animation by returning NSNull from actionForLayer:forKey:. Alternatively, you can use explicit transactions, and set kCATransactionDisableActions to True:

```
[CATransaction begin];
[CATransaction setValue:(id)kCFBooleanTrue forKey:kCATransactionDisableActions];
[layer removeFromSuperlayer];
[CATransaction commit];
```

UIView Animation Convenience Methods

UIView builds on top of Core Animation to provide its own class animation methods so that you don't need to worry about layers.

UIViews supports three kinds of animation:

- The predefined animation curves CATransition provides
- CABasicAnimations and CAKeyframeAnimations created by direct access to animatable UIView properties
- Some new transition effects (flipping and curling layers)

To create an animation, bracket your animation specifiers between beginAnimations:context: and commitAnimations. commitAnimations packages up your specification into the appropriate CAAnimation objects and commits them to be started either immediately, or when the queued animations for the UIView have completed (as determined by setAnimationBeginsFromCurrentState:). The *context* argument of beginAnimations:context: specifies additional information to be passed to the delegate.

To use a predefined CATransition curve, invoke setAnimationCurve::

```
[UIView setAnimationCurve:UIViewAnimationCurveEaseInOut];
```

To create a linear interpolation between a value's current value and the value it should have by the end of the animation, simply set it between beginAnimations:context: and commitAnimations:

```
[UIView beginAnimations:@"opacity" context:nil];
view.opacity = 0.5;
[UIView commitAnimations];
```

setAnimationDelegate:, setAnimationWillStartSelector:, and setAnimationDidStopSelector: define a delegate and start/stop methods corresponding to CAAnimation's delegate methods animationDidStart: and animationDidStop:finished:.

areAnimationsEnabled and setAnimationsEnabled: are used to disable animations, such as the autorotation animations used to switch between Portrait and Landscape mode. Be aware that some UIView user-interface elements reenable animations.

UIViews also provide new transitions, such as spinning an entire UIView about (UIViewAnimationTransitionFlipFromLeft and UIViewAnimationTransitionFlipFromRight) or peeling the bottom corner of the view upward to reveal a new view (UIViewAnimationTransitionCurlUp and UIViewAnimationTransitionCurlDown). setAnimationTransition:forView:cache: invokes these transitions. If *cache* is YES, the view is cached to improve performance. Caching it prevents it from being updated during the animation.

```
[UIView setAnimationTransition:UIViewAnimationTransitionFlipFromLeft
                                            forView:superView cache:YES];
```

setAnimationStartDate:, setAnimationDuration:, setAnimationDelay:, setAnimationRepeatCount:, and setAnimationRepeatAutoreverses: match their layer equivalents.

> Only UIView properties that correspond to an animatable CALayer property can be animated!

Watch Out!

Performance Is Good Enough for the Commercial Game Tetratile

Core Animation is not built to support hundreds of layers running simultaneously. It is designed to integrate well with UIKit and enable Cocoa programmers to achieve beautiful results quickly and effortlessly. It can be used for low-graphics intensity games, such as card games or board games. For instance, it worked well for the animations in my puzzle game Tetratile.

The single performance problem I encountered was when I tried to flip an entire board full of glass pieces and their lit shadows (around 80 layers; see Figure 9.5). The solution was to render the game screen to an image, and then to replace the game's view hierarchy with this image just before animating the flip. To render a view to an image, I used CALayer's renderInContext: method.

```
UIView* tmpFrame = [[UIView alloc] initWithFrame:self.bounds];
tmpFrame.backgroundColor = [UIColor blackColor];
[tmpFrame addSubview:board];

UIGraphicsBeginImageContext(tmpFrame.bounds.size);
[tmpFrame.layer renderInContext:UIGraphicsGetCurrentContext()];
```

```
UIImage *img = UIGraphicsGetImageFromCurrentImageContext();
UIGraphicsEndImageContext();

[tmpFrame release];

UIImageView* imgView = [[[UIImageView alloc] initWithImage:img] autorelease];
```

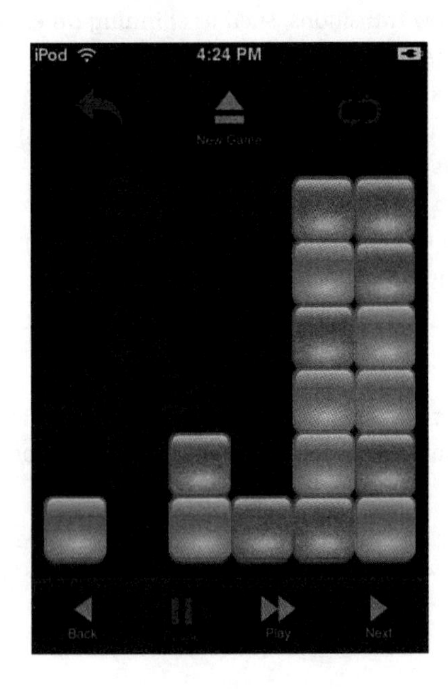

FIGURE 9.5 Tetratile: a puzzle game built with Core Animation

`board` contains the game board and pieces. By adding the board to `tmpFrame`, I can render `tmpFrame` to an image. `UIGraphicsBeginImageContext` creates a graphics context and its associated image of the size `tmpFrame` and pushes it onto the graphics context stack. `renderInContext:` renders the layer and its sublayers into the graphics context (including the 3D perspective). `UIGraphicsGetImageFromCurrentImageContext` returns the resulting image. `UIGraphicsEndImageContext` pops the graphics context back off the stack.

If your game requires a higher level of performance, use OpenGL.

Creating a Cover Flow Clone

Apple has made Cover Flow an iconic feature of the iPhone. It's the 3D graphical user interface you use to browse through your music's cover art in the iPod application. Yet, third-party application developers are forbidden to use it. The example source code for this hour is a simple version of Cover Flow. This section concentrates on its 3D and animation aspects.

The Cover Flow API

We'll build our Cover Flow using a `UIImageView` for each displayed image. Listing 9.1 shows its interface declaration.

LISTING 9.1 `CoverFlow.h`

```
#import <UIKit/UIKit.h>

@interface CoverFlow : UIView
{
  NSMutableArray* imageViews;
  id              delegate;
  CALayer*        moveToFront;

  int             savedOffset;
  float           xOffset;
  NSTimer*        relaxationTimer;

  id              theTouch;
  CGPoint         touchLocation;
  CALayer*        touchLayer;
}

- (id)   initWithFrame:(CGRect)frame;
- (BOOL) setUIImageViews:(NSArray*)imageViews;
- (BOOL) moveLayerToFront:(CALayer*)layer;

@property (nonatomic, assign) id delegate;

@end
```

`setUIImageViews:` sets the initial `UIImageViews`. `moveLayerToFront:` moves the specified layer to the central position. The `delegate` provides `leftView` and `rightView` methods to obtain a left and right image when the Cover Flow image carousel is scrolled right or left. If you use this source code in a different project, don't forget to add the `QuartzCore` framework!

Placing Layers in Space

`CoverFlow` displays five images. The front image is at `centralImageDistance` (-800), and the background images are at `backgroundImageDistance` (-2000).

The front image is not rotated, but the left background images are rotated by $\pi/6$ (30°) in either direction. To express this mathematically, the first transformation `imageRotationT` rotates the image by `imageAngle`, which is one of $-\pi/6$, 0, or $\pi/6$. The `0,1,0` vector basis specifies this is a rotation around the y-axis.

Background images are separated by `distanceBetweenBackgroundImages`. The `imageSeparationT` transform is a translation along the z-axis that pushes each image to its appropriate depth as calculated by `imageSeparation`. This is the transform `imageSeparationT`. `imageSeparation` is 0.0 for the central image, so it has no effect.

`imageSeparationT` translates along the z-axis rather than the x-axis. To fix this, `axisRotationT` rotates the axes by $\pi/2$ or $-\pi/2$ for the left and right background images.

Finally, `imageDistanceT` places the images at their respective distances from the viewer. Listing 9.2 shows the implementation.

This is shown in Figure 9.6, a view from above, which shows how the left (red), central (black), and right (blue) images turn and are moved by the different transforms. The gray area is the area that can be seen through the iPhone's screen (drawn in green). Your eye is at the bottom of the diagram where the two lines delimiting the grey area converge.

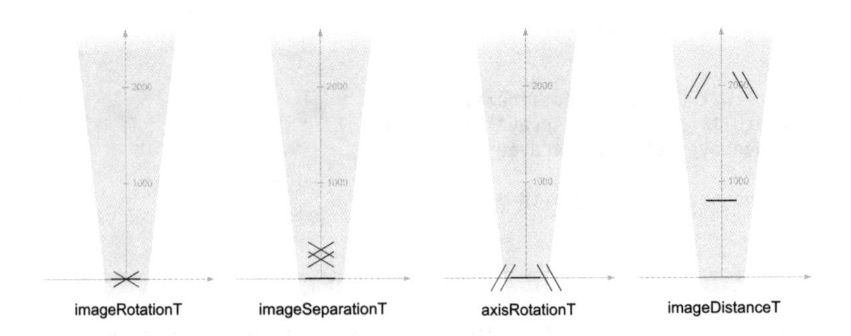

FIGURE 9.6 How layers are placed in space

The transforms are combined with `CATransform3DConcat` and the resulting transform is set as the `UIImageView`'s layer's `transform`.

LISTING 9.2 CoverFlow.m (continued)

```
const float distanceBetweenBackgroundImages      =   100.0;
const float distanceFromCenterToBackgroundImages =   200.0;
const float centralImageDistance                 =  -800.0;
const float backgroundImageDistance              = -2000.0;

- (void) placeIn3DSpace:(UIImageView*)view withIndex:(int)index
                                        withOffset:(float)offset;
{
  int count  = [imageViews count];
  int center = (count-1) / 2;

  if (index > center)
    offset *= -1;

  float imageSeparation = 0.0;
```

LISTING 9.2 Continued

```
  float imageDistance    = centralImageDistance;
  float axisAngle        = 0.0;
  float imageAngle       = 0.0;
  float x                = 0.0;

  if (index != center)
  { imageSeparation  = -distanceFromCenterToBackgroundImages;
    imageSeparation += offset;
    imageSeparation -= distanceBetweenBackgroundImages * abs(center - index);
    axisAngle        = M_PI / 2.0 * (center < index ? -1 : 1);
    imageAngle       = (-M_PI / 6.0) * (center < index ? -1 : 1);
    imageDistance    = backgroundImageDistance; }
  else
    x = offset;

  CATransform3D imageRotationT
    = CATransform3DMakeRotation   (imageAngle, 0, 1, 0);
  CATransform3D imageSeparationT
    = CATransform3DMakeTranslation(0.0,0.0,imageSeparation);
  CATransform3D axisRotationT
    = CATransform3DMakeRotation   (axisAngle, 0, 1, 0);
  CATransform3D imageDistanceT
    = CATransform3DMakeTranslation(x, 0, imageDistance );

  CATransform3D matrix = CATransform3DConcat(imageRotationT, imageSeparationT);
                matrix = CATransform3DConcat(matrix,         axisRotationT);
                matrix = CATransform3DConcat(matrix,         imageDistanceT);

  view.layer.transform = matrix;
}

              iewsIn3DSpaceWithOffset:(float)xdiff

              imageViews count];
              0; i < count; ++i)
              In3DSpace:[imageViews objectAtIndex:i]
              withIndex:i
              ithOffset:xdiff];



              mageViews:(NSArray*)array

      ([array count] & 1 == 0)
    return NO;

  for (UIImageView* imageView in imageViews)
    [imageView removeFromSuperview];

  [imageViews release];
  imageViews = [array mutableCopy];

  int i = 0;

  for (UIImageView* view in array)
  { [self addSubview:view];
    view.center = CGPointMake(480/2.0, 300 / 2.0);
```

LISTING 9.2 Continued

```
    view.layer.edgeAntialiasingMask = kCALayerBottomEdge | kCALayerTopEdge;
    [self placeIn3DSpace:view withIndex:i++ withOffset:0]; }

  return YES;
}
```

The view's layer's `edgeAntialiasingMask` is set to minimize aliasing. Unfortunately, the iPhoneOS dows not currently support antialiased textures.

Reacting to User Input

`CoverFlow` supports two kinds of user input: You can either drag your finger across the screen to scroll left and right, or you can touch an image on the left or right side to scroll in that direction.

`CALayer`'s `hitTest:` determines the sublayer containing the point passed as an argument: Tapping an image brings it to the central position.

Did you Know?

> As discussed in Hour 7, touch events that are sent to views that do not implement touch event handlers are instead propagated up the responder chain to their superview. This works well for the single touches we are interested in. However, if you place your fingers on two subviews, a single-touch event is dispatched to each of them. The events will propagate up the responder chain but won't be merged into a single multitouch event as would happen had the superlayer not had sublayers. A solution to this is to override the superview's `UIView`'s `hitTest:withEvent:` to return its view.
>
> A `UIView` that uses `hitTest:withEvent:` needs to know all its subviews. In practice, that means that it must have created them, making such classes dangerous to add subviews to.

`touchesMoved` uses `xdiff` to keep track of the how far the view has been dragged. First, it ignores all touches other than the first one. If touch movements update image locations while animations are in progress, the animations end with a visible jerk because the presentation layer cannot be updated during animations. Therefore image locations are not updated, but the distance traveled is updated so that if the user drags his finger at a constant rate, the animation will not stutter. If no animation is running and the user has dragged beyond a certain point, `addFromLeftside:` is invoked to add images from the left or right.

`touchesEnded` is responsible for invoking `moveLayerToFront:` if the operation was not a drag (5 pixels or less). It also starts carousel relaxation `relaxXOffset`, which is discussed next.

Relaxing to a Central Position

It is sometimes easier to use a timer than a Core Animation. `CoverFlow` uses a timer to make images spring back to their central position. `relaxationAnimation:` checks whether a Core Animation is in progress, and if not, causes the images to spring back by multiplying the offset by `0.75` at each timer tick.

Moving the Central Image

The movements of the image that takes the central position, and the image that leaves the central position, are quite complex:

- Both images immediately rotate from 0 to π/6 and from -π/6 to 0 at the beginning of the animation.
- Both images instantly spring from their current location to arrive gently in style at their destination.
- The destination of both images is moving along a line. To keep track of all of this, `CoverFlow` creates a `CAKeyframeAnimation` that contains five animation steps. `dx` and `dz` keep track of the linear movement from each image's starting point to its destination along the x- and z-axes. `dq` makes this movement nonlinear to make the images spring convincingly using the damping factor `fallPower`. You'll notice that I set `m41` and `m43` directly. This is because `CATransform3DMakeTranslation` will interpret the `x` and `z` value in terms of the rotated system of axes, which is not what we want.

LISTING 9.3 `CoverFlow.m` **(continued)**

```
const float animationTime  = 0.5;
const int   animationSteps = 5;

- (CAKeyframeAnimation*) centralKeyFrameAnimationFrom:(int)lhs to:(int)rhs
{
  BOOL left           = lhs < rhs;
  int  count          = [imageViews count];
  int  center         = (count-1)/2;
  BOOL becomingCenter = rhs == center;

  float fromX = xOffset;
  float toX   = (left ^ becomingCenter ? 1 : -1)
        toX  *= (  distanceFromCenterToBackgroundImages
                 + distanceBetweenBackgroundImages);
        toX  += xOffset;
  float fromZ = centralImageDistance;
  float toZ   = backgroundImageDistance;
  float fromA = becomingCenter ? M_PI/3.0 : 0.0;
  float toA   = becomingCenter ?        0 : -M_PI/3.0;
```

LISTING 9.3 Continued

```
  if (becomingCenter)
  {
    float tmp = fromX;  fromX = toX;  toX = tmp;
          tmp = fromZ;  fromZ = toZ;  toZ = tmp;
  }

  float totalDistance    = abs(toX - fromX);
  float rotationDistance = min(totalDistance, 150.0);

  NSMutableArray* path   = [NSMutableArray arrayWithCapacity:animationSteps];
  float fallPower= powf(1.0 / (totalDistance - distanceBetweenBackgroundImages),
                                                        1.0 / animationSteps
);
  float dq               = totalDistance - distanceBetweenBackgroundImages;

  for (int step = 0; step < animationSteps; ++step)
  {
    float  d  = 1.0 - dq / totalDistance;
    d -=   ((float)(animationSteps -1 -step) * distanceBetweenBackgroundImages)
         / ((float)animationSteps * totalDistance);
    float dx  = (toX - fromX) * d;
    float  x  = fromX + dx;
    float dz  = (toZ - fromZ) * d;
    float  z  = fromZ + dz;
         dq  *= fallPower;

    float a = (abs(dx) < rotationDistance)
                              ? fromA - toA * (dx / rotationDistance) : toA;

    if (!left)
      a *= -1;

    CATransform3D t = CATransform3DMakeRotation(a, 0, 1, 0);
    t.m41 = x;
    t.m43 = z;
    [path addObject:[NSValue valueWithCATransform3D:t]];
  }

  CAKeyframeAnimation* centralAnim;
  centralAnim = [CAKeyframeAnimation animationWithKeyPath:@"transform"];
  centralAnim.removedOnCompletion = NO;
  centralAnim.fillMode            = kCAFillModeForwards;

  centralAnim.duration            = animationTime;
  centralAnim.values              = path;
  centralAnim.calculationMode     = kCAAnimationLinear;

  return centralAnim;
}
```

Moving the Background Images

`animateIn:leftside:` animates images into their position. First, it checks whether an animation is in progress: `[self subviews]` will only be equal to `imageViews` once the animation completes.

The two central images are animated with centralKeyFrameAnimationFrom:to:. You'll notice I set their image index using the unique key SBGimageIndex. It is used by the animationDidStop:finished: delegate method to remove animations from their layers.

The CABasicAnimation transformA animates the translation movement of background images. To add polish, the opacity animation opacityA introduces the new image and removes the old image. If there are two animations, they are grouped together by the CAAnimationGroup groupA.

LISTING 9.4 CoverFlow.m (continued)

```
- (BOOL) animateIn:(UIImageView*)newView leftside:(BOOL)left
{
  if (![imageViews isEqualToArray:self.subviews])
    return NO;

  int   count    = [imageViews count];
  int   center   = (count-1)/2;

  // Swing the central image away

  UIImageView*          imageView = [imageViews objectAtIndex:center];
  int                   other     = left ? center+1 : center-1;
  CAKeyframeAnimation* animation
    = [self centralKeyFrameAnimationFrom:center to:other];
  NSNumber*             indexN
    = [NSNumber numberWithInt:center + (left ? 1 : 0)];
  [animation setValue:indexN forKey:@"SBGimageIndex"];
  animation.delegate             = self;
  [imageView.layer addAnimation:animation forKey:@"animateLayer"];

  // Swing the other image in

  other                = left ? center-1 : center+1;
  imageView            = [imageViews objectAtIndex:other];
  animation            = [self centralKeyFrameAnimationFrom:other to:center];
  indexN               = [NSNumber numberWithInt:other + (left ? 1 : 0)];
  [animation setValue:indexN forKey:@"SBGimageIndex"];
  animation.delegate = self;
  [imageView.layer addAnimation:animation forKey:@"animateLayer"];


  // Add in the new view with opacity 0

  newView.layer.opacity = 0.0;

  int   ignore   = left ? center-1 : center+1;
  float distance = (left ? 1 : -1) * distanceBetweenBackgroundImages;

  int   index    = 0;
  id    removeMe = nil;

  if (left)
  {
```

LISTING 9.4 Continued

```
    [imageViews insertObject:newView atIndex:index];
    [self insertSubview:newView atIndex:index];
    ++center;
    ++ignore;
    removeMe = [imageViews lastObject];
  [self placeIn3DSpace:newView withIndex:-1 withOffset:xOffset];

  }
  else
  {
    index = count;
    [imageViews addObject:newView];
    [self insertSubview:newView atIndex:index];
    removeMe = [imageViews objectAtIndex:0];
    [self placeIn3DSpace:newView withIndex:index withOffset:xOffset];
  }

  assert([self.subviews isEqualToArray:imageViews]);

  // The background images go left or right.

  int i = 0;
  for (UIImageView* view in [self subviews])
  {
    if ((i != center) && (i != ignore))
    {
      CATransform3D fromTranslation = view.layer.transform;
      CATransform3D toTranslation   = fromTranslation;

      // We want a left-right translation even though the pictures are pointed
      // at a 30° angle

      toTranslation.m41 += distance;

      BOOL needsOpacity = (view == newView) || (view == removeMe);

      CABasicAnimation *transformA;
      transformA = [CABasicAnimation animationWithKeyPath:@"transform"];
      transformA.duration    = animationTime;
      transformA.fromValue   = [NSValue valueWithCATransform3D:fromTranslation];
      transformA.toValue     = [NSValue valueWithCATransform3D:toTranslation];
      transformA.fillMode    = kCAFillModeForwards;
      transformA.removedOnCompletion = NO;


      CAAnimation* finalAnimation = nil;

      if (!needsOpacity)
        finalAnimation = transformA;
      else
      {
        float startOpacity = (view == newView) ? 0.0 : 1.0;
        float endOpacity   = (view == newView) ? 1.0 : 0.0;

        CABasicAnimation* opacityA
          = [CABasicAnimation animationWithKeyPath:@"opacity"];
        opacityA.duration          = animationTime;
```

LISTING 9.4 Continued

```
        opacityA.fromValue          = [NSNumber numberWithFloat:startOpacity];
        opacityA.toValue            = [NSNumber numberWithFloat:endOpacity];
        opacityA.beginTime          = (view == newView) ? animationTime/3.0 : 0.0;

        CAAnimationGroup* groupA    = [CAAnimationGroup animation];
        groupA.duration             = animationTime;
        groupA.animations
          = [NSArray arrayWithObjects:transformA, opacityA, nil];
        groupA.removedOnCompletion = NO;
        groupA.fillMode             = kCAFillModeForwards;

        finalAnimation              = groupA;

        if (view == removeMe)
          [imageViews removeObject:removeMe];
      }

      [finalAnimation setValue: [NSNumber numberWithInt:i]
                        forKey: @"SBGimageIndex"];
      finalAnimation.delegate = self;
      [view.layer addAnimation:finalAnimation forKey:@"animateLayer"];
    }

    ++i;
  }

  return YES;
}
```

Finally, the animation delegate method `animationDidStop:finished:` uses `SBGimageIndex` to retrieve the animation's layer, remove it, and set its final location and opacity, as shown in Listing 9.5. Because `animationDidStop:finished:` is invoked from Core Animation's run loop observer, `subviews` is not yet correct. Invoking `moveLayerToFront:` after 0 seconds causes it to be invoked after the Core Animation observer completes, and `subviews` is updated. We invoke `moveLayerToFront` to perform a second animation if the user touched an image that is not adjacent to the central image.

LISTING 9.5 `CoverFlow.m` **(continued)**

```
- (void) animationDidStop:(CAAnimation*)animation finished:(BOOL)finished;
{
  if (!finished)
    return;

  int index      = [[animation valueForKey:@"SBGimageIndex"] intValue];
  UIImageView* v = [[self subviews] objectAtIndex:index];

  int finalIndex = [imageViews indexOfObject:v];
  if (finalIndex != NSNotFound)
  {
```

LISTING 9.5 Continued

```
    [self placeIn3DSpace:v withIndex:finalIndex withOffset:xOffset];
    v.layer.opacity = 1.0;
  }
  else
    [v removeFromSuperview];

  [v.layer removeAnimationForKey:@"animateLayer"];

  if (moveToFront)
    [self performSelector:@selector(moveLayerToFront:)
               withObject:moveToFront
               afterDelay:0.0];
};
```

Summary

Core Animation lets you create stunning animations such as Cover Flow to create a signature user experience your users will come back to again and again. Cocoa Touch uses it pervasively to create animations between different views in your application, or to show animated alert panels. In this hour you learned how it works and how to use it. To learn more about it, I recommend Bill Dudney's *Core Animation for Mac OS X and the iPhone*. Although it is Mac centric, it is the reference text on the subject.

Q&A

Q. ***What is the difference between OpenGL and Core Animation Layers?***

A. Core Animation places 2D objects within a 3D space and provides animation services. OpenGL places 3D objects within a 3D space and provides no animation services.

Q. `CoverFlow`***'s source code contains an*** `IBOutlet` ***statement in a*** `@property` ***declaration. Is this legal?***

A. `IBOutlet` can either qualify instance variable declarations or a `@property` declaration. Most code uses `IBOutlet` to qualify instance variable declarations as `@property` declarations are a recent addition to Objective-C. However Apple now recommends qualifying `@property` declarations.

Workshop

The Workshop consists of quiz questions and answers to help you solidify your understanding of the material covered in this hour. You should try to answer the questions before checking the answers.

Quiz Questions

1. What is a layer?
2. How are layers positioned in 3D space?
3. What properties can be animated?
4. How are animations rendered?

Quiz Answers

1. A layer is a 2D surface placed in 3D space.
2. An affine transformation is associated with each layer to position it with respect to its superlayer. The `transforms` and `sublayerTransforms` are combined to position layers in 3D space.
3. Only properties that can be changed without the intervention of the main thread can be animated: properties that are implemented using the GPU.
4. Animations are rendered in the Core Animation thread.

Exercises

- To learn how to animate UIViews, change the calculator so that tapping the var key or the clc key causes the main view to flip. You'll need to add a window-sized `UIView` to the window, and add all the buttons and the screen to this `UIView`.
- To take pictures of Cover Flow in action, call `renderInContext:` , and save the pictures to your photo album by calling `UIImageWriteToSavedPhotosAlbum`:

```
UIImageWriteToSavedPhotosAlbum(image, nil, nil, nil);
```

- Apple's Cover Flow adds gradients to the images shown in the carousel. You can achieve the same effect by adding gradients to the images you'll show in the `UIImageViews`. Use the drawing methods we discussed and `CGContextDrawLinearGradient`. If you get stuck, consult the iPhone software development kit's (SDK's) Reflection example. You'll need to adjust Cover Flow's 3D transformations so that the images stay centered once their reflection has been added.

HOUR 10

Using View Controllers

What You'll Learn in This Hour:

- Understanding view controllers
- Adding a scientific mode to the calculator

Hour 2, "Handling Interaction," introduced the Model View Controller architecture, and Hour 5, "Adding Variables to the Calculator," reinforced the distinction between a controller and a model. So far, we've defined all the methods of our controllers, and our controllers have been derived from `NSObject`. Because controllers often implement the same methods in complex applications, Cocoa Touch provides standard view controller classes. By subclassing from these view controller classes, your controller can inherit their methods, reducing the amount of code you must write.

This hour's Calculator example source code uses view controllers to improve the calculator: It detects when the iPhone is rotated and displays a scientific calculator. Because handling complex formulas is complicated, it uses expressions to display what the user types and to compute the result.

View Controllers

View controllers handle common full-screen view controller tasks. They are designed to handle application-level views: the view that occupies the application area that is shown in Figure 10.1. They are not designed to be controllers for single user-interface elements such as buttons. All Cocoa Touch defined view controllers are implemented by `UIViewController` or its descendents.

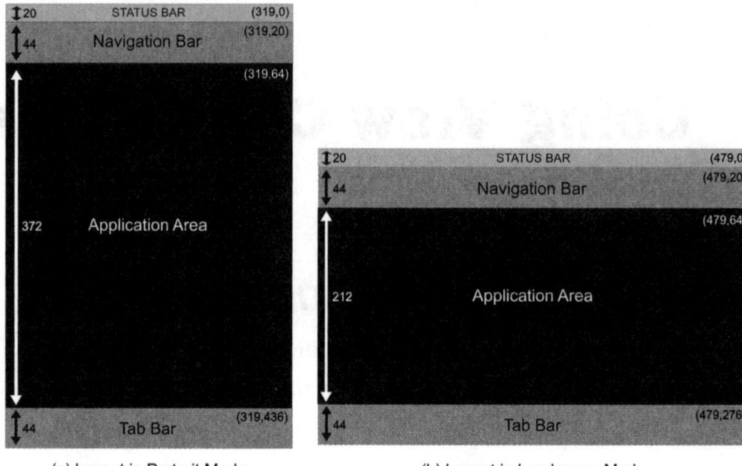

FIGURE 10.1 The application area in Portrait and Landscape modes

View controllers handle changing the view layout when the iPhone is rotated, they handle touches that were not handled by the view hierarchy, and they help create multiview applications.

Supporting Rotation

View controllers provide methods to help build interfaces that can be rotated when the iPhone is rotated. To add rotation to your application, your view controller must enable it, and then it must handle it.

Enabling Rotation

The `shouldAutorotateToInterfaceOrientation:` method specifies the layouts the application supports. The distinction between left (`UIInterfaceOrientationLandscapeLeft`) and right (`UIInterfaceOrientationLandscapeRight`) Landscape modes is rarely important. However, Apple recommends only supporting `UIInterfaceOrientationPortrait`, not upside down Portrait mode (`UIInterfaceOrientationPortraitUpsideDown`), because it can confuse iPhone users, leading them to answer the phone upside down. To declare that your interface supports both Landscape modes and the recommended Portrait mode, write the following:

```
- (BOOL) shouldAutorotateToInterfaceOrientation:(UIInterfaceOrientation)o
{
  switch (o)
  {
    case UIInterfaceOrientationLandscapeLeft:  return YES;
    case UIInterfaceOrientationLandscapeRight: return YES;
```

```
    case UIInterfaceOrientationPortrait:        return YES;
    default:                                    break;
  }
  return NO;
}
```

Handling Rotation

UIViewController registers for UIDevice's rotation notifications. The notifications are described in Hour 20, "Sensing the World." It decides to rotate the interface layout based on these notifications.

To provide a beautiful transition, UIViewController uses two half-rotation animations to create a complete rotation. The first animation rotates the original layout to 45°, whereas the second animation rotates the new layout to 90°. Because of the speed of the transition, we see a continuous motion.

The simplest case to implement is autoresizing: You simply set the autoresizing constants described in Hour 6 and the UIViewController lays the rotated interface out as specified. Unfortunately, the results are often less than perfect because the result is a vertically squashed, horizontally stretched version of your Portrait mode interface.

To create a better layout, you must either specify the position of each user-interface element or you must create a completely new layout and swap the views.

To specify new positions and sizes for each user-interface element, define a willAnimateSecondHalfOfRotationFromInterfaceOrientation:duration: method. This method is called by the first animation's completion delegate. The delegate creates the new animation for the second half of the rotation, by invoking UIView's beginAnimations:context and its commitAnimations. Because willAnimateSecondHalfOfRotationFromInterfaceOrientation:duration: is invoked between these two invocations, every property change you make will be animated.

```
- (void) willAnimateSecondHalfOfRotationFromInterfaceOrientation:
                                                (UIInterfaceOrientation)o
                                              duration:(NSTimerInterval)d
{
  if (o == UIInterfaceOrientationPortrait)
  {
    userInterfaceElement1.frame = CGRectMake(x1, y1, width1, height1);
    userInterfaceElement2.frame = CGRectMake(x2, y2, width2, height2);
  }
  else if (o == UIInterfaceOrientationLandscapeRight)
  ...
}
```

To swap layouts, define a willAnimateFirstHalfOfRotationToInterfaceOrientation:duration: method. Again, this method is invoked while creating the first half-rotation animation, so any property changes you make will be animated in the first half animation:

```
[source removeFromSuperview];
[superview addSubview:destination];
```

If you only want to target iPhone OS 3.0, you can use the single `willAnimateRotationToInterfaceOrientation:duration:` method instead. This creates an animation extending over the entire rotation rather than using two half animations.

If your application uses a navigation bar or a tab bar, `UIViewController` must also rotate and relayout these user-interface items. To do this, it expects the root view controller's `rotatingHeaderView` and `rotatingFooterView` properties to be correctly set. It does all the math for you, so you don't need to worry about rotating them.

Handling Touch Events

In Hour 6, you learned that views receive touch events. Although many views do capture these events and provide ways for you to customize their behavior, others, such as `UIImageView`, do not. To capture these events, you could subclass them, but that involves creating yet another class...

View controllers provide an alternative: In Hour 7, "Understanding How Events Are Processed," you learned about the responder chain. In particular, you learned that events that are not handled by views are forwarded along the responder chain. This means they are forwarded up the view hierarchy, but at each level up the hierarchy, a check is made whether the view has a view controller. If it does, the event is forwarded to the view controller. Because view controllers are only used as controllers for the highest views (application-level views) of the view hierarchy, they only receive the touch events that could not be handled by the rest of the view hierarchy. Remember that some views, such as `UIImageView`, discard touch events by default.

Handling Multiview Applications

So far, the example applications have used a single view. In Hour 6, you learned to swap views to create multiview applications. Because each view in your application usually has its own controller, you usually have as many controllers as views.

Multiview applications introduce a number of new problems. For instance, each view that cannot be seen consumes memory unnecessarily. View controllers can help to minimize this by reducing the amount of code you must write to manage your application's memory.

Because views do not provide a mechanism to inform their controllers that they were removed from their superviews, it is your responsibility to inform them as necessary. For instance, controllers need to know that their views are no longer visible, so that they can stop animating them. If `UIViewController` manages the application-level views, it informs them when it adds or removes them from the view hierarchy.

Building View Controllers' Views

View controllers are responsible for setting up their views. A view controller can build its view in two ways: programmatically or with a NIB file. In either case, layout is important because the views of view controllers that are used with tab bars or navigation bars (see Hour 12 "Adding Navigation and Tab Bar Controllers") will be resized.

Building View Controllers' Views Programmatically

View controllers can create the view programmatically by implementing the optional `loadView` method. They must set the `UIViewController`'s `view` property to the created view, as in the following example:

```
- (void) loadView
{
  CGRect  screenRect  = [[UIScreen mainScreen] applicationFrame];
  UIView* contentView = [[UIView alloc] initWithFrame:screenRect];
  self.view           = contentView;
  [contentView release];
}
```

Building View Controllers' Views Using a NIB File

View controllers can specify the NIB file that contains their view on initialization. For instance, to load the view defined by the `MainWindow` NIB file, write the following:

```
UIViewController* vc = [[MyViewController alloc]
                                initWithNibName:@"MainWindow" bundle:nil];
```

This sets the view controller's `nibName` and `nibBundle` properties. The view is later loaded by `loadView`. Because the default `loadView` method loads the NIB specified by the `nibName` and `nibBundle` properties, your view controller should not override this method if its view is specified by a NIB file. Instead, if you need to set any properties after the NIB file was loaded, you can override `viewDidLoad`. Once loaded, `view` returns the view controller's view.

Within Interface Builder, `File's Owner` will refer to your view controller, in this case, `MyViewController`. For `File's Owner` to have the correct outlets, read its class—File, Read Class Files or (Option-⌘-R)—and change its identity in the Identity

Inspector, as was explained in Hour 1, "Starting Your First Application: A Calculator."

If you do not implement `loadView`, the default `loadView` method is inherited from `UIViewController`. If no `nibName` or `nibBundle` was specified, this method uses `NSStringFromClass` to obtain your class's name. It derives a possible NIB filename from your class's name, and loads the corresponding NIB file if it exists. For instance, if your class is called `CloudViewController`, `loadView` tries to load a `CloudView` NIB file.

Bundles

To understand bundles, you need to understand where they came from. On the Mac, bundles are directories that appear to the user to be a single file. For instance, Mac applications are bundles: They appear to the user to be a single file to double-click, but they are directories containing the application executable, its resources (its NIB file, its graphic assets, any sounds to play, and so on), and its frameworks (any custom frameworks shipped with the application). Similarly, frameworks and plug-ins are bundles.

On the iPhone, Apple's App Store rules prevent you from shipping custom frameworks or plug-ins. Therefore, the only available bundles are the system frameworks (`Foundation`, `UIKit`, and so on), a preference bundle you'll learn about in Hour 16, "Adding Application Preferences," and your application. Because the system frameworks change between OS releases, you should not be loading resources from frameworks. This leaves your application bundle, which contains the NIB files and resources you added to it. `[NSBundle mainBundle]` returns the `NSBundle` object for your application. For convenience, `initWithNibName:bundle:` uses `[NSBundle mainBundle]` as the bundle if you pass a `nil` value as the second argument.

Managing View Memory

Complex applications can create so many application-level views that their memory consumption becomes an issue. Hour 6 recommended placing each view in its own NIB file, so that it could be unloaded when it is removed from the view hierarchy. In practice, because loading NIB files also takes time, they should only be discarded if memory is scarce. Thus, each controller should register to receive low-memory notifications, determine whether its view is still in the view hierarchy, and discard it if it is not. Hour 8, "Drawing User-Interface Elements," showed how to register to receive low-memory notifications.

View controllers automate this process. If a view controller builds its view using a NIB file (`nibName` is not `nil`) or by implementing `loadView`, when it receives a low-memory notification, it will check whether its view has a superview. If it does not, it will discard the view and rely on the NIB file or the `loadView` method to create a new one as needed. After discarding the view, it invokes the view controller's `viewDidUnload` method in iPhone OS 3.0 and more recent versions. Your view controller `viewDidUnload` method should release any view-related objects and set the outlets or variables referencing them to `nil`. As discussed in Hour 3, "Simplifying Your Code," the preferred way of doing this is to declare the outlets or variables as properties and to use the property setter method to set them to `nil`.

If no view is loaded, reading a controller's `view` property will create the view using `loadView` or the NIB file. iPhone OS 3.0 and more recent versions provide an `isViewLoaded` property you can use to check whether the view is loaded so that you don't inadvertently load it.

```
if (self.isViewLoaded)
  [self.view ...]; // do something with the view
```

The reason you set properties in `viewDidLoad` rather than setting them after the call to `initWithNibName:bundle:` is to allow `view` to reload the NIB. This creates a new set of view objects, requiring `viewDidLoad` to set the relevant settings. `viewDidLoad` and `viewDidUnload` should set the same properties.

Watch Out!

Do not cache references to a view controller's view. By retaining the view, you will defeat the view controller's memory management: The view it discards will not be discarded, but it will create a new view the next time it is referenced. Any changes you make to the old view will not be displayed because the old view will not be added back into the view hierarchy.

`UIViewController` Support for Multiple Views

`UIViewController` provides additional support for multiview applications. It provides a view controller hierarchy to simplify responding to users navigating through the user interface. It also provides the creation of modal views for context specific tasks.

`UIViewController` Hierarchy

`UIViewController`'s `parentViewController` property specifies the view controller that was responsible for displaying the current view controller: either a navigation controller or a tab bar controller. `parentViewController` can form a hierarchy of view controllers, similarly to `UIView`'s `superview` method.

Although `UIViewController` has no public analog to `UIView`'s `subviews` method, it has a private `childViewControllers` method, which performs this task. Thus, view controllers form a hierarchy.

Before a view controller removes a child view controller's view, it sends the child view controller a viewWillDisappear: message. After a view controller has removed a child view controller's view, it sends the child view controller a viewDidDisappear: message. The same sequence accompanies displaying a child view controller's view, using the messages viewWillAppear: and viewDidAppear:.

Your view controller can override these methods to reduce the computational cost of hidden views. For instance, you can ensure your view's animations only run when the view is visible. Similarly, you can ensure your view controller only observes model value changes using KVO (the Key-Value Observing protocol) when the view is visible. Your implementations of viewWillAppear:, viewWillDisappear:, viewDidAppear:, and viewDidDisappear: should invoke themselves on super, as follows:

```
- (void) viewWillAppear:(BOOL)animated
{
  [super viewWillAppear:animated];
  // Your code here
};
```

Watch Out!

viewWillAppear:, viewWillDisappear:, viewDidAppear:, and viewDidDisappear: are not always invoked as expected. Apple's documentation says they are not invoked if your view controller adds its view to the view hierarchy itself. However, that's not true, as addSubview: and removeFromSuperview do call these methods.

Watch Out!

In versions of iPhone OS prior to 3.0, viewWillAppear is invoked before the view is loaded. Because of this, your view's outlets will be nil, and any changes you make to the view will be ignored. To force the view to be loaded, simply read the view controller's view property before changing the view.

UIViewController hierarchies are shallow. For instance, consider the iPod application, which uses a tab bar and a navigation bar. The tab bar view controller is the root view controller because if you choose a different tab, the navigation bar and the table disappear. The navigation bar controller is the tab view controller's child because if you choose an artist, the table of artists is replaced by the artist's songs. This deep UIViewController hierarchy is only three levels deep. (The iPod application is called the Music application on iPod touches.)

Modal Views

Modal views are user-defined views that slide over your application-level view. They are commonly used to edit or add new fields. For instance, if you tap the + button in the iPhone Contacts application, a New Contact view pops up (see Figure 10.2). It is a modal view.

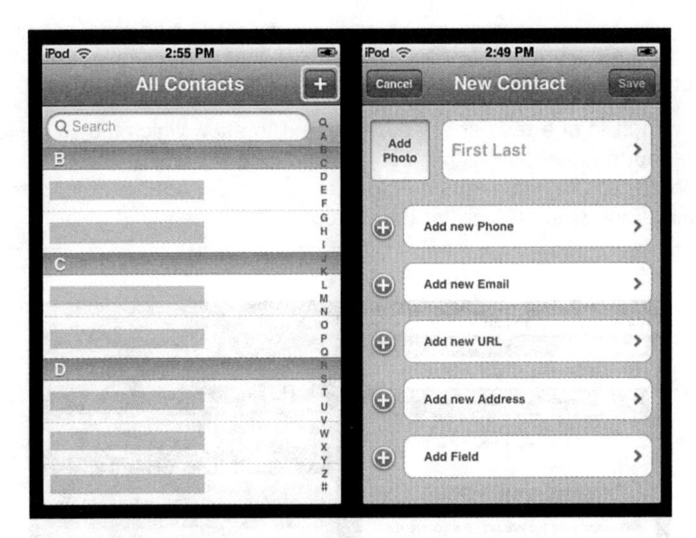

FIGURE 10.2
The Contacts application's modal view

To create a modal view, create a new view controller for the modal view. You can, of course, lay your modal view out using Interface Builder. To show the modal view, the user will tap a button (such as the + button in the Contacts application). Assuming the button action is defined on a view controller, it should invoke the following:

```
[self presentModalViewController:myModalViewController animated:YES];
```

To dismiss the modal view, you must dismiss it from the same view controller that caused it to be shown. Methods of the view controller that created the secondary view controller dismiss it with the following code:

```
[self dismissModalViewControllerAnimated:YES];
```

Methods of the secondary view controller can dismiss their own view controller with the following code:

```
[[self parentViewController] dismissModalViewControllerAnimated:YES];
```

The view controller that caused a modal view to be displayed can access that modal view's controller using the read-only `modalViewController` property.

Did you Know?

If you only want to create a modal view to ask a multiple-choice question, consider using `UIActionSheet`. The Safari application uses a `UIActionSheet` when you tap the + button to ask you whether you want to bookmark the page, add it to the home screen, and so on (see Figure 10.3). Using `UIActionSheet` is very simple: Create it with its `initWithTitle:delegate:cancelButtonTitle:destructiveButtonTitle:otherButtonTitles:` method. Show it with its `showInView:` method (or `showFromToolbar:` or `showFromTabBar:` if you want it to appear above a toolbar or a tab bar). `UIActionSheet`'s delegate informs you which button was tapped.

Whereas a button of a tab bar stays highlighted to show which tab you're looking at, toolbar buttons are only highlighted for less than a second to show the tool you tapped. The Safari application uses a toolbar at the bottom of its screen. The iPod application uses a tab bar at the bottom of its screen.

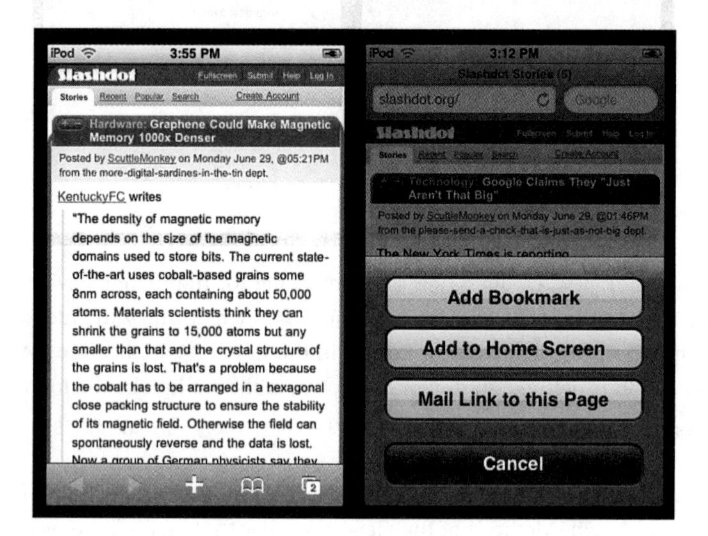

FIGURE 10.3
The toolbar in the Safari application shows a **UIActionSheet**

Adding a Scientific Mode to the Calculator

To demonstrate the process of creating a view controller–based application, this hour's sample source code converts the Calculator to use a view controller and adds a Scientific mode for Landscape mode.

Converting `CalculatorController` to Use a View Controller

Using view controllers does not radically change your application: view controllers simply invoke different methods. To better understand the differences, compare this chapter's implementation with that given in Hour 5.

Initialization

To use view controller methods, `CalculatorController` must have `UIViewController` as its superclass:

```
@interface CalculatorController : NSObject
@interface CalculatorController : UIViewController
```

The Calculator uses two view controllers for Portrait and Landscape modes. To make the behavior seamless between the two view controllers, most of the controller state is moved to a `ControllerState` object both view controllers can share.

Adding parentheses and mathematical functions (such as trigonometric functions) requires additional actions: `pressOpenParenthesis:` and `pressCloseParenthesis:`.

`CalculatorController` overrides `initWithNibName:bundle:` as `initWithNibName:bundle:` is `UIViewController`'s designated initializer. Many classes implement a number of initializer methods. For instance, `UIViewController` implements `init` and `initWithNibName:bundle:`. It would be reasonable to think a subclass should override every initializer of its superclass class to set up its instance variables. However, many Cocoa classes specify that one initializer is the **designated initializer**: All other initializers invoke the designated initializer. If we know the designated initializer, we only need to override it and `initWithCoder:`.

The NIB file loader uses `initWithCoder:`. You'll learn more about `initWithCoder:` in Hour 12.

Multiple View Management

`viewWillAppear:` replaces `awakeFromNib`. It is invoked as soon the view controller's view has been loaded and will be shown.

`viewWillAppear:` replaces `awakeFromNib`, as it is invoked as soon as the view controller's view has been loaded and will be shown. Notice that `CalculatorController` is observing `ControllerState`'s `currentNumber`. Recall that there are two view controllers—one for Portrait mode and one for Landscape mode. Both view controllers have been built, and both could observe `currentNumber`. However, only one should update the visible text view, which represents the calculator screen: The calculator is either in Portrait mode or in Landscape mode. By adding the KVO observer that updates the visible view's text view in `viewWillAppear`, and removing it in `viewDidDisappear`, we guarantee only one text view will be updated at a time.

`updateScreen:` updates the view's text view differently depending on whether the Portrait mode or Landscape mode view is visible: The Landscape mode layout is too small to provide any scrolling functionality.

Handling Rotations

`shouldAutorotateToInterfaceOrientation:` informs CalculatorController's UIViewController ancestor which rotation modes are supported:

```
- (BOOL) shouldAutorotateToInterfaceOrientation:(UIInterfaceOrientation)o
{
  switch (o)
  {
    case UIInterfaceOrientationLandscapeLeft:  return YES;
    case UIInterfaceOrientationLandscapeRight: return YES;
    case UIInterfaceOrientationPortrait:       return YES;
    default:                                   break;
  }

  return NO;
}


float orientationToAngle(UIInterfaceOrientation o)
{
  switch (o)
  {
    case UIInterfaceOrientationPortrait:       return  0.0;
    case UIInterfaceOrientationLandscapeLeft:  return -M_PI/2.0;
    case UIInterfaceOrientationLandscapeRight: return  M_PI/2.0;
    default:                                   break;
  }
  return 0;
}

- (void) willAnimateFirstHalfOfRotationToInterfaceOrientation:
                                              (UIInterfaceOrientation)o
                                             duration:(NSTimeInterval)d
{

  CalculatorAppDelegate* app = [[UIApplication sharedApplication] delegate];
  UIView                 *source, *destination;
  CGRect                 bounds;
  float                  angle  = orientationToAngle(o);

  if (o == UIInterfaceOrientationPortrait)
  {
    source      = app.landscapeMode.view;
    destination = app.portraitMode.view;
    bounds      = CGRectMake(0.0f, 0.0f, 320.0f, 460.0);
  }
  else
  {
    source      = app.portraitMode.view;
    destination = app.landscapeMode.view;
```

```
    bounds      = CGRectMake(0.0f, 0.0f, 480.0, 300.0);
  }

  UIView* superview = [source superview];
  [source removeFromSuperview];
  [superview addSubview:destination];
  destination.transform = CGAffineTransformMakeRotation(angle);
  destination.bounds     = bounds;
}
```

`orientationToAngle()` is a convenience function. It is convenient to declare C functions within an implementation block to place them near their clients.

`willAnimateFirstHalfOfRotationToInterfaceOrientation:duration:` swaps the views and creates the appropriate rotation.

Handling the Var State

The calculator provides a second mode for variables. To ensure that this mode is preserved during rotations, code from `pressVar:` is moved into `showVarState:` so that `viewWillAppear:` can update the new view to show the current calculator mode.

An Expression-Based Calculator

When using a scientific calculator, it is convenient to see the entire expression that you typed in. Similarly, scientific calculators are expected to provide parentheses to allow expressions such as `(5+6)*9` to be entered. This level of complexity requires a new approach: an expression-based calculator.

Expressions

Rather than parsing a string, the calculator builds a tree representing the expression the user typed in. The tree has four kinds of nodes:

- `Expressions`—Entire expressions or subexpressions
- `Arithmetic`—Arithmetic operations (+, -, *, /, power, and root)
- `Functions`—Functions (cos, sin, tangent, arc-tangent, logarithm, and exponential)
- `Numbers`—Implemented using `NSNumber`

To simplify the code, most of these nodes share the `eval` and `showToString` methods used to compute the result and used to show the expression.

Did you Know?

This source code uses Unicode characters. To insert characters such as e^X into the source code, or into Interface Builder labels, choose the Edit, Special Characters menu item. The window shown in Figure 10.4 will appear. Choose the Latin font (in the European Scripts category), and open Character Info. This shows you similar characters, such as the superscript x. Double-click it to insert it. The other characters you'll need are in the Mathematical Symbols section in the Symbols category.

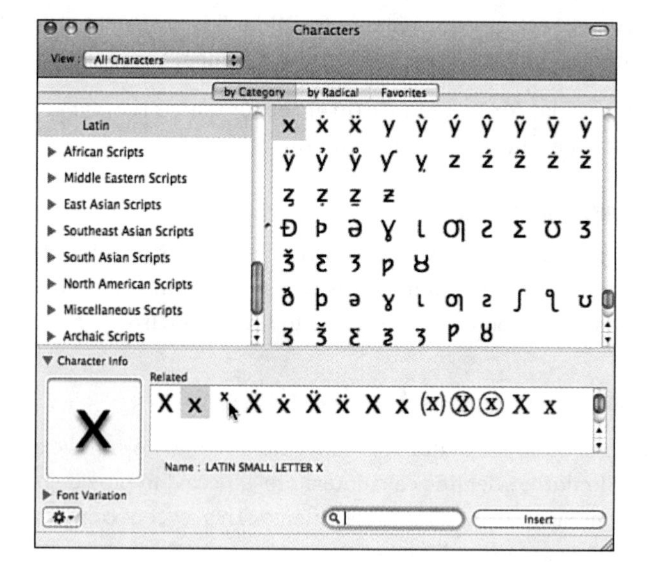

FIGURE 10.4 Creating a superscript x for e^X

The Model

The model manipulates expressions. It uses an expression stack to keep track of what users are editing. The expression at the last position of the stack is being edited by the user. The expression at the last but one position of the stack will be edited when the user closes one parenthesis. The expression at the last but two position of the stack will be edited when two parentheses are closed, and so on: Each time a parenthesis is opened, the stack grows down. Each time a parenthesis is closed, the lowermost element of the stack is removed.

This code is not perfect as it suffers from tight coupling: `CalculatorModel` needs to know a lot about expressions to create them. If other objects used expressions, it might be worth refactoring the code so that Expression provides more abstract operations for `CalculatorModel` to use. However, with the small number of use cases in this example, we are unlikely to identify the appropriate abstractions, which is why

I left the code as is. To learn more about refactoring, read *Refactoring, Improving the Design of Existing Code* by Martin Fowler.

The model also keeps track of the history of calculations. The expression being edited is the last element of the `history` array.

History displays all the saved expressions. `showToString` always returns a bracketed expression as this simplifies the rest of the code. However, it also brackets the entire expression. `trim` removes these additional parentheses. `value` returns the value of the current expression (the last one in the history). `pushExpression` adds a new expression to the history, thus creating a new current expression.

`invalidateExpressionStringCache` invalidates the string cache of the currently edited subexpression (and its parents).

To add a number to the current subexpression, `addNumber:` adds it to the expression at the bottom of the stack. To open an expression between parentheses, `openParenthesis` adds a subexpression to the current expression and to the bottom of the stack, creating a new current subexpression. By symmetry, `closeParenthesis` removes the subexpression from the bottom of the stack. Recall that the stack is used to know what the user will edit. The expressions that are removed from the stack are not lost. They are embedded in the expressions that were created so far.

`addFunction:` adds a mathematical function to the current expression and places its argument at the bottom of the expression stack, enabling it to be edited. `addArithmeticOperation:` deals with basic arithmetic. The precedence rules of basic arithmetic (`1 + 2*3 = 7` and not 9) make `addArithmeticOperation:` somewhat complex.

Using a NIB File

The Calculator uses a LandscapeMode and a PortraitMode NIB file. They were created by opening `Resources`' context menu (right-click or Ctrl-click) in the Groups & Files menu and choosing Add, New File: see Figure 10.5.

Figure 10.6 shows the `Autosizing` field of each button: All four struts are set. Struts and springs specify the layout of a view. The white box under Autosizing represents the view's superview. The view itself is represented by the inner box. The double-ended arrows (called springs) specify that the view should grow in the specified direction. The outer red I-like symbols (called struts) specify that view should not move with respect to the corresponding superview edge. Figure 10.6 states that the view should neither grow nor move.

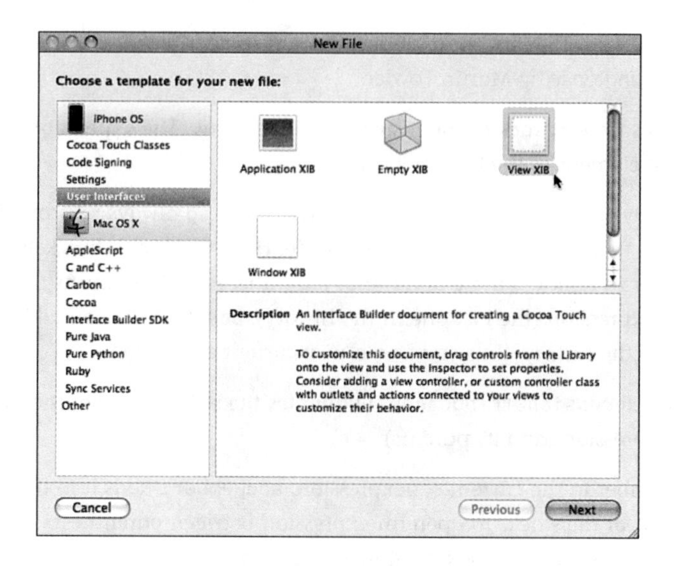

FIGURE 10.5
Creating an XIB file

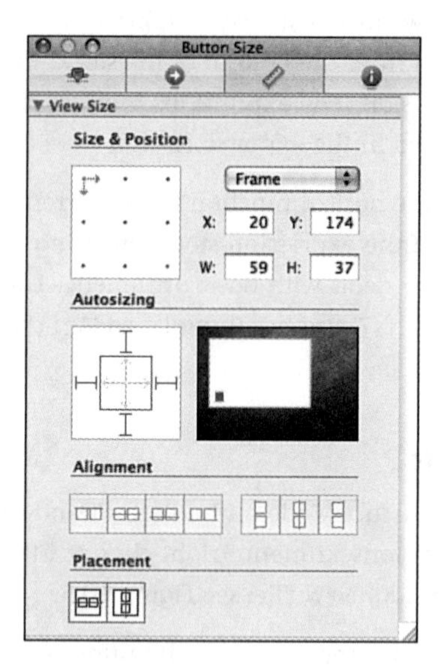

FIGURE 10.6
Calculator buttons autosizing

Figure 10.7 shows the `PortraitMode.xib` file. The `File's Owner's Class Identity` is set to `CalculatorController`.

Figure 10.10 shows the outline `View Mode`, which makes it easier to access the content of views: You can open the disclosure triangle next to `View` to see its content. Objects that are hard to select on the canvas are easily selected from the Document Window using this mode.

Figure 10.8 shows the calculators's user interface in Landscape mode.

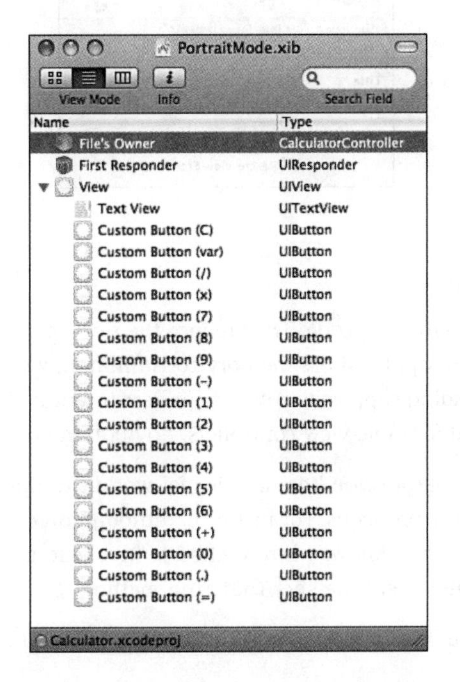

FIGURE 10.7 PortaitMode.xib's Document Window

FIGURE 10.8 LandscapeMode.xib's view

The MainWindow.xib file contains two view controllers for the PortraitMode.xib and LandscapeMode.xib files. Figure 10.9 shows how to set a view controller's Title and NIB Name in Interface Builder. The NIB Name specifies the name of the NIB file used to create the view controller's view.

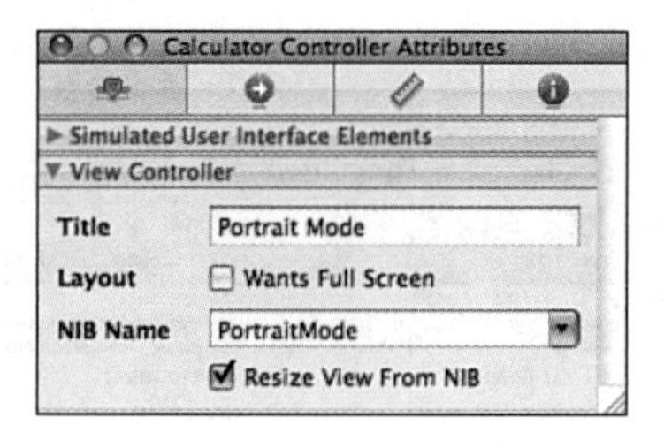

FIGURE 10.9 Setting Calculator Controller's `Title` and `NIB Name`

Summary

View controllers simplify your code. They reduce the number of objects you must build and reduce your application's memory consumption, while improving its appearance by providing support to rotate your user interface. They provide the basic support needed for table view controllers, navigation bars, and tab bars.

The calculator is now expression based. This real-world example shows how objects can be used to simplify problems. For instance, although an expression does not know how to print itself, it knows what method to invoke to print any of its constituents: They all implement the `showToString` method.

In the next hour, you'll learn how to use a common feature of iPhone applications: tables.

Q&A

Q. ***Are view controllers views, or are they controllers?***

A. View controllers are controllers. They are often associated with a view, and they receive some events views would normally receive, but they are controllers.

Q. ***The Calculator's expressions seem quite powerful. Can this serve as a general model of computation?***

A. Yes, lazy functional languages such as Haskell are implemented using this kind of expression. Laziness provides a different kind of modularity than encapsulation. In a lazy program, you can define a function that generates an infinite list of prime numbers. An unrelated part of the program might decide only to use the first 10 prime numbers. Laziness guarantees only those 10 prime numbers will be generated. To achieve this, each recursion of the prime generation function returns a new prime and creates an expression for its next recursion. If a new prime is needed, the expression is evaluated again, creating a new prime and a new expression. Thus, a different part of the program can decide how many prime numbers to generate without knowing anything about the original prime number function. To learn more about this topic, read *The Implementation of Functional Programming Languages* by Simon Peyton Jones.

Workshop

The Workshop consists of quiz questions and answers to help you solidify your understanding of the material covered in this hour. You should try to answer the questions before checking the answers.

Quiz Questions

1. What is a view controller?
2. How do view controllers participate in the responder chain?
3. How do view controllers help deal with iPhone rotation?
4. How do view controllers help reduce memory consumption?

Quiz Answers

1. A view controller is an abstract class your controller can subclass to gain additional functionality.
2. Touch events that do not reach the view controller's view but are not handled by it are forwarded to the view controller. If it does not handle them, they are forwarded up the view hierarchy.
3. View controllers register for device orientation events and provide animations to rotate your view. Autoresizing provides basic layout, but for a more polished result, override the animation methods.
4. View controllers lower memory consumption by discarding views that are no longer visible, and reloading them if necessary.

Exercises

- Use `NSTimer` to animate the `UIButton`'s background image. Use `showVarState:`'s `animate` argument to decide whether to start the animation. Use the code from `SBGButton` to create the transition images, and then animate `UIButton`'s background image by changing it with a timer.
- Improve the Calculator's C key: The first time the user taps it, it should set `currentNumber` to zero and update the expression. The second time the user taps it, it should remove the entire expression as it does now.

HOUR 11
Displaying Tables

What You'll Learn in This Hour:

- Creating tables
- Using table cells
- Creating a Twitter application

Tables are an essential component of most user interfaces. There are two kinds of tables—plain and grouped—which differ only in appearance (see Figure 11.1). In this hour, you'll learn how to make your own table based interfaces.

Grouped table

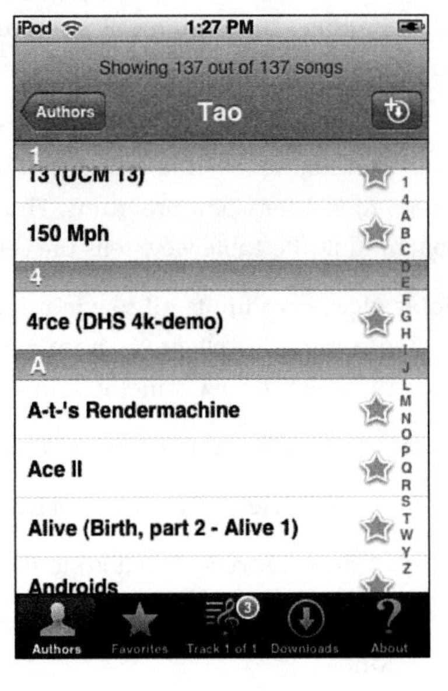

Plain table

FIGURE 11.1
Grouped and plain tables

Creating Tables

Table views are user-interface elements that display data in a table consisting of a single column of rows. Their main tasks are as follows:

- Displaying the data corresponding to a row in a row
- Displaying the table
- Providing support for rows to be manipulated (selected, edited, inserted, deleted, or reordered)

To display data, the table view needs to know what data it must show. A simple approach would require the data to be placed in a dictionary to be shown by the table view. This approach requires the data to be shown to fit in memory. Instead, in Cocoa Touch data is loaded lazily: Table views query a **data source** for each row they need to show.

To display the table, the table view could draw every row to a single giant layer. However, as tables occupy many times the screen size, doing so would waste a lot of memory. Instead, table views treat each row as a separate subview with its own layer called a cell. In this manner, scrolling only requires maintaining one more row than is visible on the screen. The cost is further minimized by recycling the cells that scroll off the screen and reusing them for the cells scroll onto the screen. This design also simplifies animating cell insertions, deletions, or changes: The graphics processor unit (GPU) simply moves cells whose content has not changed.

In fact, cells are responsible for drawing the table. Table views are symphony conductors, making sure the cells are playing in harmony, and providing a simpler usage model for client programs. Thus, for instance, if the user selects a table row by touching it, the table view tells the cell to change its appearance.

Table views coordinate all row manipulations, updating the cells' content as needed and informing the client program of state changes using delegates. For instance, if the user selects a row, a method on the delegate is invoked.

Three objects cooperate to create a table:

- **A table view**—The user-interface element displaying the table
- **A data source**—The data to be shown in the table
- **A delegate**—An object that customizes the table view's behavior and appearance

Table View Methods

Table view methods are used to build the table in the appropriate style, reload data, scroll the table, and select the row. Rows are identified by `NSIndexPaths`.

Styling the Table

Tables are created plain (`UITableViewStylePlain`) or grouped (`UITableViewStyleGrouped`) by their initialization method (`initWithFrame:style:`). Once set, the style cannot be changed (`style` is read-only).

Tables may have a header and a footer as specified by the read-write properties `tableHeaderView` and `tableFooterView`. These are not table elements, but will be scrolled as if they were part of the table. For instance, in Figure 11.2, the user's name and photo are a table header view, whereas the two buttons are a table footer view.

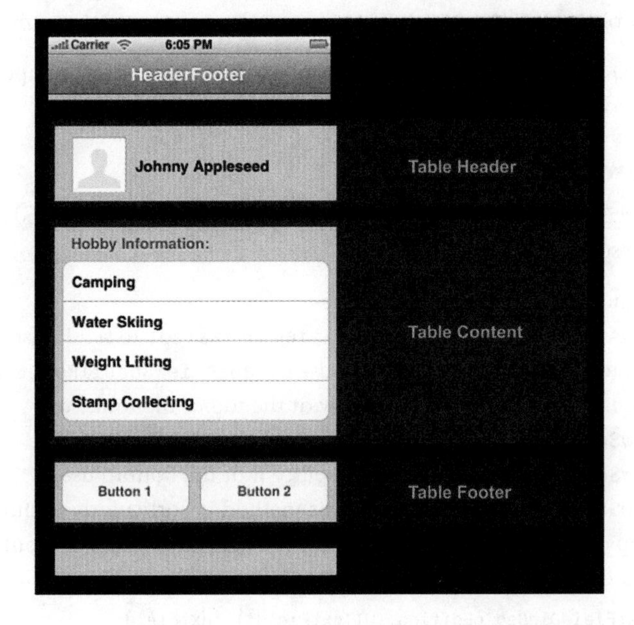

FIGURE 11.2
A table header and footer

Tables may separate rows using a separator. `separatorStyle` may either be `UITableViewCellSeparatorStyleNone` or `UITableViewCellSeparatorStyleSingleLine`. The separator can be given a color with the `separatorColor` property. Each cell draws its separator (as specified by the undocumented methods `setSeparatorStyle:` and `setSeparatorColor:`). The table uses its `separatorStyle` and `separatorColor` properties to set its cells' separator properties appropriately.

Sections and Rows

Table views assume tables consist of sections, each containing rows. Uniquely identifying a row requires knowing the index of the row within its section, and the index of that section within the table. The **NSIndexPath** class is used to capture this kind of multilevel indexing.

Reloading Data

Because `UITableView` requests data from a data source, it needs to be told if the underlying data has changed to update the screen: `UITableView`'s `reloadData` method queries the data source to update the rows visible on the screen.

iPhone OS 3.0 adds methods that animate changes to rows to show users the data changed: Invoke `reloadRowsAtIndexPaths:withRowAnimation:` to specify the rows that have changed and what animation to use. You have the choice of inserting rows from the top, left, bottom, or right of the screen and fading rows in or out. Similarly, invoke `reloadSections:withRowAnimation:` to update entire sections.

iPhone OS 3.0 also adds the `reloadSectionIndexTitles` method to update section indexes.

Scroll View

`UITableView` is derived from `UIScrollView`, and inherits all its methods: All table views can be scrolled vertically.

For convenience, `UITableView` also defines `scrollToRowAtIndexPath:atScrollPosition:animated:` to scroll a specific row. To request that the row simply be visible use `UITableViewScrollPositionNone` as *atScrollPosition* argument. To place the row at the top of the table, use `UITableViewScrollPositionTop`. To place it in the middle use `UITableViewScrollPositionMiddle`. To place it at the bottom use `UITableViewScrollPositionBottom`. This method is particularly useful to move a cell to the top of the screen when displaying the keyboard to edit its content. For instance, you can write the following:

```
- (void) textFieldDidBeginEditing:(UITextField*) textField
{
  UIView*      view = textField;
  NSIndexPath* path = nil;

  while ((path == nil) && (view != tableView))
  { view = [view superview];
    path = [tableView indexPathForCell:view]; }

  [tableView scrollToRowAtIndexPath:path
                   atScrollPosition:UITableViewScrollPositionTop
                           animated:YES];
}
```

If you need more control over a row's position, you can use the `rectForRowAtIndexPath:` method to determine a row's location and scroll the table view using the inherited `setContentOffset:animated:` or `scrollRectToVisible:animated:` methods.

Selecting Rows

`UITableViews` let users select a row, for instance to show the song that is playing. The `UITableView`'s `allowsSelection` property determines whether selection is enabled. If a row is selected, `indexPathForSelectedRow` returns the selected row.

When users select a row (and when they deselect it on iPhone OS 3.0), the delegate is informed (see "Tracking Selections with a Delegate" later in this hour). `selectRowAtIndexPath:animated:scrollPosition:` and `deselectRowAtIndexPath:animated:` update selections programmatically without invoking the delegate methods (or causing `UITableViewSelectionDidChangeNotification` notifications—Hour 12, "Adding Navigation and Tab Bar Controllers" discusses notifications). If `selectRowAtIndexPath:animated:scrollPosition:`'s `animated` argument is `YES`, the table view also scrolls to show the selection. The `scrollPosition` argument lets you adjust where the row will be shown (at the top, middle, or bottom of the screen).

Creating a Data Source

Data sources provide the data for table views. Without a data source, an empty table is displayed. Data sources must obey the `UITableViewDataSource` protocol. Data sources are not retained!

Sections

In tables, each section consists of an optional header, an array of elements, and an optional footer (see Figure 11.3).

Section headers are views just like cells. Table views are responsible for coordinating their movement. For instance, they stay at the top of plain table views as the user scrolls the table, as shown by the plain table example (the SC68 player) of Figure 11.1.

Your data source can implement the `numberOfSectionsInTableView:` method to specify the number of sections in the table view. If no method is implemented, the table assumes it has a single section. For instance, if `sections` is an array of the sections to display, you'd write the following:

```
- (NSInteger) numberOfSectionsInTableView:(UITableView*) tableView
{ return [sections count]; }
```

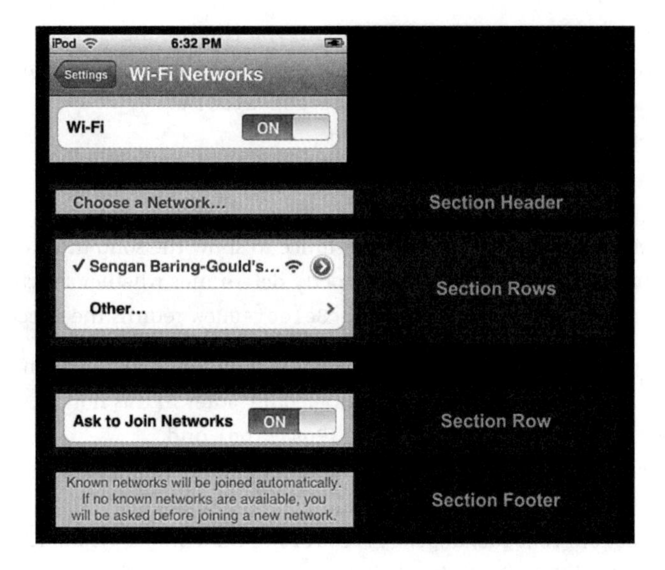

FIGURE 11.3 Section headers and footers

To display section headers, your data source should implement the optional `tableView:titleForHeaderInSection:` method. To display section footers, it should implement the optional `tableView:titleForFooterInSection:`. Both methods return an `NSString` that the table view will display in a fixed font style. For instance, if `sectionNames` is an array of the section names to display, you'd write the following:

```
- (NSString*) tableView:(UITableView*)t titleForHeaderInSection:(NSUInteger)n
{ return [sectionNames objectAtIndex:n]; }
```

Section Indexes

Section indexes provide a convenient way to navigate large, plain tables. They hover over the right side of a table, providing a list of sections the user can immediately jump to. For instance, the Contacts application uses them to provide users with instant alphabetic navigation. Section indexes are difficult to recognize when filled with few elements.

To display a section index, your data source should implement `sectionIndexTitlesForTableView:` to return an `NSArray` of `NSStrings` specifying the strings that should be displayed in the section index. Often, single-letter strings are used to minimize the space taken by the section index, but you can use longer strings. If you want, you can provide fewer strings for your section index than there are sections in the table.

```
- (NSArray*) sectionIndexTitlesForTableView:(UITableView *)tableView
{ return sectionNames; }
```

The section index needs to know which section to scroll to when the user taps one of its elements. It queries the optional data source method `tableView:sectionForSectionIndexTitle:atIndex:` for this information. The method is given the title and index of the element tapped in the section index. It should return the index of the section to jump to. If you do not implement this method, the index of the element tapped in the section index is assumed to be the same as the index of the section to jump to.

```
- (NSInteger) tableView:(UITableView*)tableView
             sectionForSectionIndexTitle:(NSString*)title
             atIndex:(NSInteger)index
{ return index; /* or [sectionNames indexOfObject:title]; */ }
```

Plain table views that use a section index are known as indexed table views.

Rows

Your data source must implement `tableView:numberOfRowsInSection:` to specify the number of rows in each section of the table. Not doing so results in an exception.

```
- (NSInteger) tableView:(UITableView*)v numberOfRowsInSection:(NSInteger)n
{ return [[sections objectAtIndex:n] count]; }
```

Your data source must implement `tableView:cellForRowAtIndexPath:` to return the cells that will be used for the table. Not doing so results in an exception.

```
- (UITableViewCell*) tableView:(UITableView*)tableView
        cellForRowAtIndexPath:(NSIndexPath*)indexPath
{
  static NSString* cellID = @"exampleTableCellIdentifier";
  UITableViewCell* cell;
  cell = [tableView dequeueReusableCellWithIdentifier:cellID];

  if (cell == nil)
    cell = [[[UITableViewCell alloc]
                                initWithFrame:CGRectZero reuseIdentifier:cellID]
                                autorelease];

  cell.text = [[sections objectAtIndex:indexPath.section]
                         objectAtIndex:indexPath.row];
  return cell;
}
```

This hour's "Using Table Cells" section discusses creating cells in more detail.

Creating a Delegate

Delegate methods let you dynamically customize the behavior and appearance of table views. Delegates are not retained by `UITableViews`.

Customizing Appearance with a Delegate

To customize the layout of group tables' headers or footers, override `tableView:viewForHeaderInSection:` and/or `tableView:viewForFooterInSection:`. You must also specify the header and footers' heights with `tableView:heightForHeaderInSection:` and `tableView:heightForFooterInSection:`. To create tables with rows of differing heights, override `tableView:heightForRowAtIndexPath:`.

Displaying a table with irregularly sized rows or headers requires the table view to accumulate these items' heights. If the user is scrolling quickly down the table, accumulating these heights is performance intensive. However, if your headers all have the same height, your footers have the same height, and your rows have the same height, the row indexes of the visible cells on the screen can be directly computed from the current position of the scroll view. To enable this optimization, set the `UITableView`'s `sectionHeaderHeight`, `sectionFooterHeight`, and `rowHeight` properties instead of overriding the corresponding delegate methods.

`tableView:indentationLevelForRowAtIndexPath:` lets you dynamically set the indentation level of a cell. It sets the `UITableViewCell`'s `indentationLevel` property. For instance, the following code will cause each row within a section to be indented more than the row above it:

```
- (NSInteger)                          tableView:(UITableView*)tableView
             indentationLevelForRowAtIndexPath:(NSIndexPath*)indexPath
{ return indexPath.row; };
```

`UITableView` invokes `tableView:willDisplayCell:forRowAtIndexPath:` before it draws a row. Overriding this method lets you customize the cell before it is drawn: You can change its state (such as its background color), but you should not change its content.

Because these methods work hand in hand with the data source, delegate and data source functionality are often combined into a single object.

Tracking Selections with a Delegate

The delegate is sent messages to inform it which row the user selected. When the user lifts their finger from a row, the delegate's `tableView:willSelectRowAtIndexPath:` method is invoked with the selected row as the argument. It can return a different row to cause a different row to be selected, or `nil` if no row should be selected. `tableView:didSelectRowAtIndexPath:` is invoked after the selection is made, enabling you, for instance, to set a check mark on the row. These methods are optional.

iPhone OS 3.0 introduces two new methods to respond to and control row deselection: `tableView:willDeselectRowAtIndexPath:` and `tableView:didDeselectRowAtIndexPath:`.

Scroll View Delegate

The `UITableView` delegate also serves as a scroll view delegate. This means it receives all the messages scroll views receive.

Most messages tell the delegate what the user is doing: If the user scrolled the table, the delegate's `scrollViewDidScroll:` is invoked. Similarly, when users start dragging the scroll view by placing a finger on the touch screen and dragging it, `scrollViewWillBeginDragging:` is invoked. When the users release their fingers, the table continues moving in the direction they dragged the table in but decelerates. These methods, and `scrollViewDidEndDragging:willDecelerate:`, `scrollViewDidScrollToTop:`, `scrollViewWillBeginDecelerating:`, and `scrollViewDidEndDecelerating:` are all optional methods: Only implement them if you want to respond to the user interaction they specify.

`scrollViewDidEndScrollingAnimation:` is invoked once a scrolling animation caused by `setContentOffset:animated:` or `scrollRectToVisible:animated:` completes.

By default, if a single scroll view is displayed, touching the status bar will scroll to the top of the scroll view. As scrolling can interfere with editing the table, the delegate can implement `scrollViewShouldScrollToTop:` to dynamically prevent this behavior. Alternatively, you can just set `UIScrollView`'s inherited `scrollsToTop` property to `NO`.

Using Table Cells

A table view consists of table cells. Each cell is a view with one or more subviews and displays a row or a section header. To reduce the amount of memory allocated and deallocated, cells are reused. You can create your own custom cells by adding your own subviews to each cell or by overriding cell drawing methods.

Reusing Cells

The data source method `tableView:cellForRowAtIndexPath:` creates cells for the table view to display.

The table view retains cells and keeps track of those that have scrolled off the screen. `tableView:cellForRowAtIndexPath:` can request a recycled cell from the table view rather than building a new one by using `dequeueReusableCellWithIdentifier:`. Because cells come in different sizes and can be instances of different classes, cells are assigned a reuse identifier, which specifies their class and size. If your table uses cells of different sizes or classes, it is important to use different identifiers for each.

If no cell is available to be recycled, `dequeueReusableCellWithIdentifier:` returns `nil`, and it is up to you to create it. This is implemented by the following code (previously introduced in the "Rows" section earlier this hour):

```
- (UITableViewCell*) tableView:(UITableView*)tableView
        cellForRowAtIndexPath:(NSIndexPath*)indexPath
{
  static NSString* cellID = @"exampleTableCellIdentifier";
  UITableViewCell* cell;
  cell = [tableView dequeueReusableCellWithIdentifier:cellID];

  if (cell == nil)
    cell = [[[UITableViewCell alloc]
                            initWithFrame:CGRectZero reuseIdentifier:cellID]
                            autorelease];

  cell.text = [[sections objectAtIndex:indexPath.section]
                      objectAtIndex:indexPath.row];
  return cell;
}
```

Recycled cells must be cleaned of all **noncontent state** before they can be reused. Noncontent state is state that is not set by `tableView:cellForRowAtIndexPath:`, such as alpha, editing, and selection state. `prepareForReuse` is invoked by `tableView:cellForRowAtIndexPath:` to reset this noncontent state. As `prepareForReuse` also clears undocumented state, all implementations that override this method should call their superview method.

Because the data source only knows how to create new cells, you should invoke `cellForRowAtIndexPath` to obtain a cell from the table, rather than trying to invoke the data source directly. Similarly, because the table knows which cell is assigned to each row, it provides `indexPathForCell` to find a cell's index path. It also knows which cells are visible (`visibleCells`).

Using `UITableViewCells`

Prior to iPhone OS 3.0, `UITableViewCells` could only display text, images, accessory views, and editing controls. The layout in editing mode and nonediting modes is shown in Figure 11.4.

FIGURE 11.4 UITableView Cell layout

Using Text in a `UITableViewCell`

`UITableViewCell` displays `text` in a `font` and `textColor` of your choice:

```
cell.text      = [[sections objectAtIndex:indexPath.section]
                      objectAtIndex:indexPath.row];
cell.font      = [UIFont boldSystemFontOfSize:[UIFont labelFontSize]];
cell.textColor = [UIColor redColor];
```

Because the background color of selected cells is usually either blue (`UITableViewCellSelectionStyleBlue`) or gray (`UITableViewCellSelectionStyleGray`) as specified by `selectionStyle`, it can be difficult to see the text when the row is selected. `selectedTextColor` lets you specify a different text color for selected rows.

```
cell.selectionStyle    = UITableViewCellSelectionStyleGray;
cell.selectedTextColor = [UIColor whiteColor];
```

The text's alignment `textAlignment` can be set left-aligned (`UITextAlignmentLeft`), center-aligned (`UITextAlignmentCenter`), or right-aligned (`UITextAlignmentRight`). `lineBreakMode` defines how text that is too long to fit in the row is handled. Apple's `UITableViewCell`'s class documentation specifies all its options.

Using an Image in a `UITableViewCell`

`UITableViewCells` can also display an `image` on their left side, as shown by the paper airplane in Figure 11.4. If your image is too tall, it will overlap the next row. Wider images push the text right. Set `selectedImage` to use a different image for selected rows.

Using Indentation

`tableView:indentationLevelForRowAtIndexPath:` lets you dynamically set the indentation level of a cell by setting the cell's `indentationLevel` to indent the cell. `indentationWidth` sets the indentation width per level.

Using Accessory Views or Types

Accessory views are drawn on the right side of cells. Standard accessory views are selected by setting `accessoryType` to be a disclosure indicator (`UITableViewCellAccessoryDisclosureIndicator`), a disclosure button (`UITableViewCellAccessoryDetailDisclosureButton`), or a check mark (`UITableViewCellAccessoryCheckmark`), as shown in Figure 11.5. Alternatively, you can set your own accessory view by setting the `accessoryView` property.

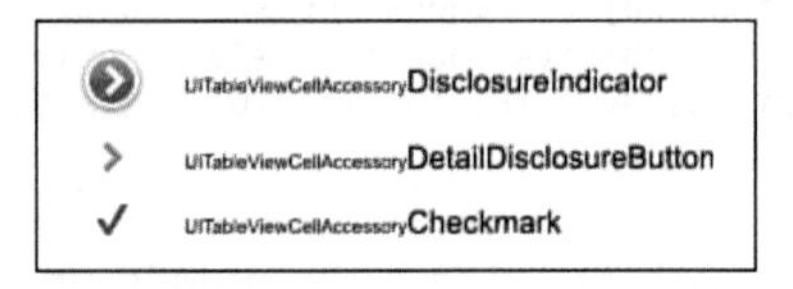

FIGURE 11.5 Standard accessory types

`UITableViewCell` Subviews

Selected cells and unselected cells have a number of subviews. Selected cells are easier to understand: Unselected cells, which constitute the majority of cells, have been optimized.

Selected Cells

If a cell is selected, it consists of a view with a number of subviews as shown in Figure 11.6:

- Background view
- Selection view
- Cell content view
- Accessory view
- Editing controls

For grouped tables, the background view (`backgroundView`) draws the cell background (white) and boundaries (gray) that are placed in front of the table's pinstripe background. For plain tables, there is no background view and `backgroundView` is set to `nil`.

If a cell is selected, a blue or gray selection view of the cell's shape is placed over the background view. If the cell is not selected, there is no selection view.

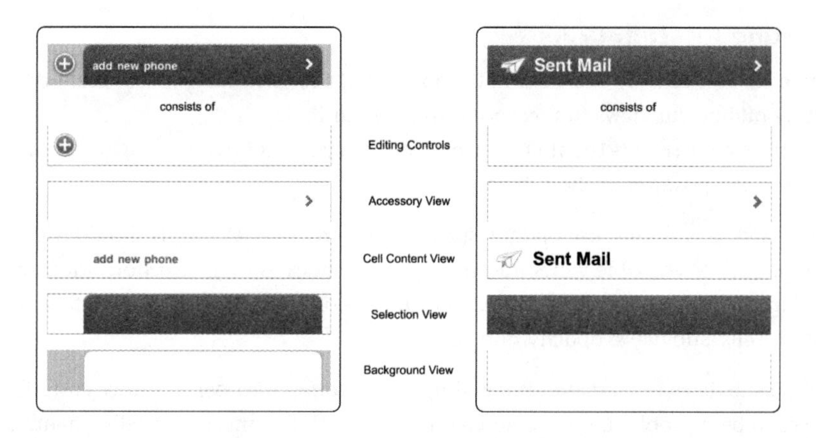

FIGURE 11.6
Table Cell subviews

The cell content view (contentView) overlays the cell background and selection. The cell content view and its subviews are set not to be opaque, allowing the background selection color to show wherever the content is not opaque. Cells that have labels have a UILabel as a subview of contentView. The UILabel's background color is set to [UIColor clearColor], making its background transparent. Cells that have images have a UIImageView as a subview of contentView.

Cells that have an accessoryType set have a nonopaque UIButton overlaying the cell content view. accessoryView is nil in this case. Alternatively, you can set accessoryView to be a view of your choice, in which case the nonopaque accessoryView overlays the cell content view.

Unselected Cells

Selected cells consist of many nonopaque views. As you'll recall from Hour 8, "Drawing User-Interface Elements," showing nonopaque views is performance intensive. As only one table cell is selected at a time, Apple optimized the drawing of unselected cells.

By default, unselected cells have no background view, no selection view, no image view, and no accessory view (for accessories set using accessoryType). Instead, the background view's content, its image, and its accessory view are drawn by UITableViewCell itself. Furthermore, the contentView and its subviews are set to opaque. The UILabel's backgroundColor is set to nil, resulting in a label with a white background.

However, you can set backgroundView and selectedBackgroundView yourself and UITableViewCell will use them correctly. For instance,

```
cell.backgroundView          = [[[UIImageView alloc] init] autorelease];
cell.backgroundView.image    = backgroundImage;
```

Creating Custom Cells

Create custom cells by subclassing `UITableViewCell`. The custom cells can add content by adding subviews to their `contentViews` in their `initWithFrame:reuseIdentifier:` method. They should override `layoutSubviews` to adjust the position of the subviews.

Unselected cells should use opaque subviews, whereas selected cells should use nonopaque views. Table views inform cells of changes to their selection status by invoking `setSelected:animated:`. You can override this method to update your custom cells' subviews' opacity and color.

Adding subviews to `contentView` is simple, but comes at a performance cost. If this proves to be a problem, you could create a fast path for unselected cells. Create a custom cell that overrides its `drawRect:` method, and use Core Graphics to draw all the content to a single content view subview. For selected cells, add your subviews to `contentView` as before: Override `setSelected:animated:` to change `contentView`'s subview hierarchy as needed.

Changes to `UITableViewCells` in iPhone OS 3.0

Apple decided to rearchitect `UITableViewCell` in iPhone OS 3.0. The changes are mostly improvements, but lead to some compatibility issues. From an end-result perspective, the new `UITableViewCell` makes its use of standard subviews explicit (`UILabel` and `UIImageView`) and provides new cell layouts.

New Cell Layouts

Cells are no longer built with `initWithFrame:reuseIdentifier:` (which is deprecated) but with `initWithStyle:reuseIdentifier:`. To obtain the same layout, use `initWithStyle:reuseIdentifier:` with the `UITableViewCellStyleDefault` style.

The three new styles display large text (`textLabel`) and small text (`detailTextLabel`) in three different layouts. `UITableViewCellStyleValue1` is the layout used Settings application, `UITableViewCellStyleValue2` is the layout used in the Contacts application, and `UITableViewCellStyleSubtitle` is the layout used in the iPod application.

Standard Subviews

`textLabel` and `detailTextLabel` are both `UILabels`. Because `UILabels` support `text`, `font`, `textAlignment`, `textColor`, `selectedTextColor`, and `lineBreakMode` properties, `UITableViewCell` no longer needs its `text`, `font`, `textAlignment`, `textColor`, `selectedTextColor`, and `lineBreakMode` properties, which are all deprecated.

Similarly, the new imageView property is a UIImageView , removing the need for image and selectedImage properties. Because UIImageViews can be animated, you can place animated images in a table view. Beginning with iPhone OS 3.0, UIImageView supports a highlighted property that displays a highlightedImage or a series of highlightedAnimationImages. Selected rows set this highlighted property.

Deprecated Delegate Method

Apple has also decided to remove the accessory type in the delegate method tableView:accessoryTypeForRowWithIndexPath:. You should set the accessory types when creating cells.

Working Around Deprecated Properties

On the Mac, support for deprecated methods is usually removed in the next major OS release. If the iPhone follows the same pattern, iPhone OS 4.0 will not support the methods that were deprecated in iPhone OS 3.0.

Did you Know?

The compiler emits warnings when you use deprecated methods.

To support more than one OS, you can use respondsToSelector: to check a method's existence before invoking it, or you can use Objective-C's runtime to add missing methods your code invokes. The first solution disperses complexity to your entire code-base, increasing testing requirements, whereas the second solution gathers it into a single location. Place your implementations of missing methods in a category, using unique names:

```
@interface UITableViewCell (UITableViewCellEX)
- (id) myInitWithStyle:(int)style reuseIdentifier:(NSString*)cellID;
@end

@implementation UITableViewCell (UITableViewCellEX)

- (id) myInitWithStyle:(int)style reuseIdentifier:(NSString*)cellID;
{ return [self initWithFrame:CGRectZero reuseIdentifier:cellID]; }

@end
```

Then, in the load class method of your view controller, change your methods' names so they stand in for the missing methods:

```
SEL s = @selector(initWithStyle:reuseIdentifier:);
if (![UITableViewCell instancesRespondToSelector:s])
  swizzle([UITableViewCell class], s,
                                    @selector(myInitWithStyle:reuseIdentifier:));
```

Swizzle uses the Objective-C runtime to either swap the implementation of two methods, or add the new one if the old one does not exist. Because the implementations are swapped, the old method's implementation is now called using the new method's selector, and vice versa. `swizzle` lets your categories replace existing methods while still letting you invoke them.

```
#import <objc/runtime.h>

void swizzle(Class c, SEL old, SEL new)
{
  Method oldMethod = class_getInstanceMethod(c, old);
  Method newMethod = class_getInstanceMethod(c, new);
  char*  encoding  = method_getTypeEncoding(newMethod);
  IMP    oldImp    = method_getImplementation(oldMethod);
  IMP    newImp    = method_getImplementation(newMethod);
  BOOL   addMethod = class_addMethod(c, old, newImp, encoding);

  if (addMethod)
    class_replaceMethod(c, new, oldImp, encoding);
  else
    method_exchangeImplementations(oldMethod, newMethod);
}
```

Creating a Twitter Application

To illustrate tables in more detail, this hour's source code is a Twitter application. Twitter is a popular communication service (see http://www.twitter.com) that lets you broadcast information to your fans, called followers. I recommend you study this hour's source code, available at http://www.informit.com/title/9780672331251, as the next hours build on it.

Building a Basic Application

For simplicity, the first incarnation of the Twitter application will show the messages (tweets) of the people you're following. To use the application, you'll need an account at Twitter and you'll need to follow some users. Such users are called your friends. For instance, the `BreakingNews` user is quite interesting.

The project was built with the name Twitter using the View-Based Application template. This created two NIB files and a `TwitterViewController` class. The initial `MainWindow.xib` file was automatically set to load the `TwitterViewController.xib` NIB file.

The project is based on the third party `MGTwitterEngine` from Matt Gemmell available at http://mattgemmell.com/source. Be sure to read the license conditions. `MGTwitterEngine` can use different libraries for parsing Twitter's responses. I'm using `NSXMLParser`.

Perusing MGTwitterEngine's source code, you'll notice a few oddities such as __weak: MGTwitterEngine also compiles on the Mac, and contains garbage collection annotations used on the Mac.

Merging Streams of Tweets

Visually, the first version of the Twitter application consists of a search bar and a table containing the history of your friends' tweets.

Although Twitter provides your friends' tweets sorted by date, the Twitter application merges your friends' tweets dynamically: This shows all their responses (including replies) and shows you how to merge multiple streams of data into a single table. To do this, it first obtains a list of your friends, and then loads each friend's image and tweet history. Tweet histories are loaded from the network on demand.

Because downloading information from twitter.com takes time, MGTwitterEngine downloads tweets in the background. twitter.com returns tweets in XML (Extensible Markup Language). When the tweets are received, MGTwitterEngine parses theXML and invokes a method on the delegate with the result.

To merge the different streams of tweets, each user is associated with a User class that is able to load the user's tweets on demand. User objects behave like enumerators: Each invocation of nextObject returns the next oldest tweet from the user's stream. topDate specifies the date of the next object to be returned by nextObject. Thus, each new row simply scans through every friend, and determines who made the most recent tweet which is then popped off that friend's tweet stream. As soon as a stream has been exhausted, no new rows can be output because the next tweet might be in the exhausted stream:

```
- (UITableViewCell*) tableView:(UITableView*)tableView
        cellForRowAtIndexPath:(NSIndexPath*)indexPath
{
  static NSString* cellID = @"messageCellID";

  UITableViewCell* cell;
  cell = [tableView dequeueReusableCellWithIdentifier:cellID];

  if (cell == nil)
    cell = [[[UITableViewCell alloc]
                             initWithFrame:CGRectZero reuseIdentifier:cellID]
                             autorelease];

  cell.text  = nil;
  cell.image = nil;

  int row = [indexPath row];
  while (row >= [messages count])
  {
    User* friend = nil;
```

```
    for (User* u in friends)
    {
      // Cannot proceed: need data from the network
      if ([u eof])
        return cell;

      // Choose the most recent message
      if ([u topDate] > [friend topDate])
        friend = u;
    }

    if (friend == nil)
      return cell;

    [messages addObject:[friend nextObject]];
  }

  NSDictionary* msg = [messages objectAtIndex:row];

  cell.image = [[msg objectForKey:@"user"] image];
  cell.text  = [msg objectForKey:@"text"];
  cell.font  = [UIFont systemFontOfSize:8];
  cell.lineBreakMode = UILineBreakModeWordWrap;

  return cell;
}
```

Notice the code uses the fact that `[nil topDate]` returns `0`. The code sets `cell.text` and `cell.image` to `nil` to guarantee that unfilled cells are empty. If `friends` is empty or a stream is exhausted, empty cells are returned.

The Twitter application specifies a large number (100000) as the number of cells in the table.

`MGTwitterEngine` Methods

The Twitter application uses the following three methods of `MGTwitterEngine` to query twitter.com:

- `getRecentlyUpdatedFriendsFor:startingAtPage:` starts retrieving a list of your friends.
- `getImageAtURL:` starts an image transfer.
- `getUserTimelineFor:sinceID:withMaximumID:startingAtPage:count:` starts downloading a user's tweets.

To download data from twitter.com you must provide `MGTwitterEngine` with your user name and password (in `TwitterViewController`'s `initWithCoder:` method).

The Twitter application uses four delegate methods of MGTwitterEngine:

- userInfoReceived:forRequest: is invoked with the downloaded list of your friends.
- imageReceived:forRequest: is invoked with the downloaded image.
- statusesReceived:forRequest: is invoked with the downloaded friends' tweets.
- connectionFinished: is invoked when the download completes.

Because MGTwitterEngine only supports a single delegate, I'm using the TwitterViewController as the delegate. Each User must register each request it makes with the TwitterViewController for its delegate to be invoked, using addConnection:delegate:. The final delegate methods are as follows:

- userInfoReceived:forConnection:
- imageReceived:forConnection:
- statusesReceived:forConnection:

The dispatch code is defined on TwitterViewController:

```
- (void) addConnection:(NSString*)connectionID delegate:(id)obj;
{
  [pendingConnections setObject:obj forKey:connectionID];
  ++networkActivityCounter;
  [UIApplication sharedApplication].networkActivityIndicatorVisible
                                              = networkActivityCounter > 0;
}

- (void) connectionFinished:(NSString*)connectionID;
{
  --networkActivityCounter;
  [UIApplication sharedApplication].networkActivityIndicatorVisible
                                              = networkActivityCounter > 0;
  [pendingConnections removeObjectForKey:connectionID];
}


- (void) userInfoReceived:(NSArray*)userInfo forRequest:(NSString*)connectionID
{
  id obj = [pendingConnections objectForKey:connectionID];
  [obj userInfoReceived:userInfo forConnection:connectionID];
}
```

It is the application's responsibility to update the status bar activity indicator to show when data is being downloaded. Setting networkActivityIndicatorVisible does this.

Reloading the Table

Each time more tweets are downloaded from twitter.com, the tweet table should be refreshed. However, because requests are issued in batches (when the application starts, or when the user scrolls), table refreshes tend to occur in batches. Because reloading the table is expensive, the Twitter application only reloads the table from a timer handler which is invoked 10 times a second.

```
- (void) timer:(id)sender
{
  if (needsDisplay)
    [table reloadData];
  needsDisplay = NO;
}

- (void) setNeedsDisplay
{ needsDisplay = YES; };
```

Adding a Search Bar

Search bars are separate user-interface elements provided by the `UISearchBar` class. Their `placeholder` property specifies the default string to be used. The Twitter application initializes `searchBar` in `viewDidLoad`.

Search bar delegates are informed of user interaction with the two delegate methods `searchBarCancelButtonClicked:` and `searchBarSearchButtonClicked:`. These methods take as argument the search bar. Invoke `resignFirstResponder` on the search bar in `searchBarCancelButtonClicked:`, and search for the search bar's `text` in `searchBarSearchButtonClicked`. Usually, the search bar only shows the rows that match the search term. Instead, for brevity, the Twitter application demonstrates their use by scrolling to the next tweet that matches the search term.

Summary

Tables are the most complex user interfaces we have encountered so far. They are a giant topic because they are so commonly used. This hour focused on giving you a strong understanding of how they work and how they avoid loading entire tables. This lets you create applications, such as the Twitter application, which can dynamically load data from the Web.

This hour did not cover adding, removing, and reordering data in tables. For instance, in the Contacts application, you can add or delete contacts. To do this, you define additional delegate methods and use additional table view methods. Apple's "Table View Programming Guide for iPhone OS" explains how to do this in detail. It's quite straightforward.

> The iPhone SDK comes with a suite of five table view applications, which you can use as a reference. Look for **TableViewSuite** in the iPhone SDK documentation.

Did you Know?

Q&A

Q. ***Can I add views to a section header or footer?***

A. Yes, you can.

Q. ***Why should I avoid overriding*** `UITableViewCell`***'s drawing methods in a subclass?***

A. Overriding cells' drawing methods is intrusive and is more likely to break with future OS releases. It should only be used when facing an unresolvable performance problem: `UITableCellView` manipulates its subview hierarchy to achieve effects like selection. Adding to a cell's existing subviews simply works in this case, whereas custom drawing requires additional code.

Workshop

The Workshop consists of quiz questions and answers to help you solidify your understanding of the material covered in this hour. You should try to answer the questions before checking the answers.

Quiz Questions

1. What is a table's data source?
2. What is a table's delegate?
3. What is a table view cell?
4. How do you add subviews to table view cells?

Quiz Answers

1. A table's data source provides the information to display in the table.
2. A table's delegate customizes the appearance and behavior of the table.
3. A table view cell is a row of the table. It is implemented as a view.

4. To add subviews to table view cells, add the subviews to the cells' `contentViews` in their `initWithFrame:reuseIdentifier:` (or `initWithStyle:reuseIdentifier:`) method.

Exercises

- Add subviews to `contentView` to create a better layout for the Twitter application showing the date and the entire message.
- Override `tableView:heightForRowAtIndexPath:` to create a layout that only uses enough space to display each tweet.
- Many of the images don't fit in the table. Use Core Graphics to create appropriately sized images.

HOUR 12

Adding Navigation and Tab Bar Controllers

What You'll Learn in This Hour:

- Using modal view controllers
- Saving application defaults
- Using tab bars
- Using navigation bars

Because the iPhone screen is small, many iPhone applications present information on multiple screens, each of which displays a different set of data. The simplest form of multiple-screen application uses animations to switch between two views.

Tab bars provide the next level of complexity: Tapping an item on the tab bar selects its view.

Navigation bars go further than tab bars, working with table view controllers to provide a hierarchical navigation structure.

Using Modal View Controllers

The simplest example of a multiscreen application consists of manually replacing the current application-level view by a new one. For instance, the Twitter application currently hard-codes your account information. Instead we'll use a modal view: Modal views are ideal interfaces for requesting the user's account information because the application is unable to do anything without this information.

Using Interface Builder

The first Twitter example source code for this hour (Twitter1) creates an account details form from a grouped table to illustrate how you can design static tables' cells using Interface Builder. The table consists of a single section, two rows, a header, and a footer, as shown by Figure 12.1.

FIGURE 12.1
Account details form

The view is a new View XIB file called AccountView.xib which is 460 pixels high, leaving space for the status bar. The view has as subview a table view of Grouped View type, whose scrolling is disabled (Scrolling Enabled checkmark disabled) and whose Show Selection on Touch is disabled.

To design the table view cells, drag a Table View Cell to Interface Builder's Document Window. Double-click it to see it. Drag contents such as a Label and a Text Field to its content view, as shown in Figure 12.2(a). AccountView.xib sets the Label's text to **Name,** the Text Field's Placeholder to **user name**, its Correction feature to **No**, and its Return Key to **Next**, as shown in Figure 12.2(b). The password's table cell sets its text field's Secure check mark to hide the password.

Setting table view cells' Identifiers helps distinguish table view cells in Interface Builder's Document Window: Each object's identifier is shown between brackets. File's Owner is an instance of AccountViewController which serves as delegate and dataSource for the table view and text field cells. Figure 12.2(c) shows its outlet connections.

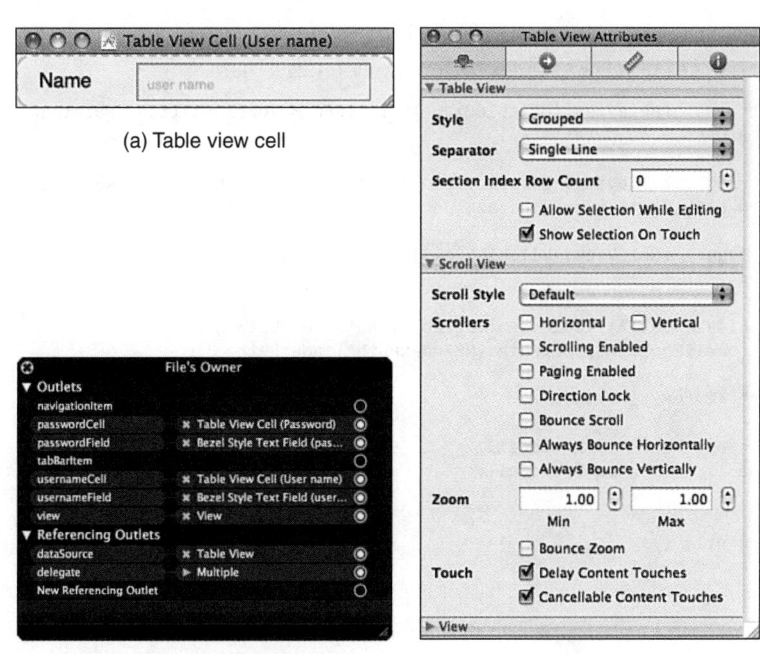

(a) Table view cell

(c) File's owner connections

(b) Text field attributes

FIGURE 12.2 Designing a modal view for Twitter account details

Implementing Account View Controller

AccountViewController's viewDidLoad sets up the username and password text fields (userNameField and passwordField) to the current values of username and password. It also stops table cells from being selected.

```
@implementation AccountViewController

#pragma mark Managing views

- (void) viewDidLoad
{
  [super viewDidLoad];
  self.usernameField.text = username;
  self.passwordField.text = password;
  self.usernameCell.selectionStyle = UITableViewCellSelectionStyleNone;
  self.passwordCell.selectionStyle = UITableViewCellSelectionStyleNone;
}
```

iPhone OS 3.0 calls viewDidUnload to release outlets that reference views within the discarded view's hierarchy. The #pragma mark line sets titles that appear within Xcode's function menu. (The second pull-down menu above the source code that shows the currently edited method.) Because our table only contains two cells, `tableView:cellForRowAtIndexPath:` simply returns them.

```
- (NSString*) tableView:(UITableView*)t titleForHeaderInSection:(NSInteger)n
{ return @"Account Details"; }

- (NSString*) tableView:(UITableView*)t titleForFooterInSection:(NSInteger)n
{ return @"All communications are encrypted with SSL."; };

- (NSInteger) tableView:(UITableView*)t numberOfRowsInSection:(NSInteger)s
{ return 2; };

- (UITableViewCell*) tableView:(UITableView*)tableView
        cellForRowAtIndexPath:(NSIndexPath*)indexPath
{
  switch (indexPath.row)
  {
    case 0: return usernameCell;
    case 1: return passwordCell;
  }

  return nil;
}
```

When the Next key is tapped on the iPhone keyboard, `textFieldShouldReturn:` moves input to the password field. When the Done key is tapped on the iPhone keyboard, `textFieldShouldReturn:` informs the view controller about the new username and password and dismisses the account view.

```
- (BOOL) textFieldShouldReturn:(UITextField*)textField
{
  if (textField == usernameField)
  {
    [usernameField resignFirstResponder];
    [passwordField becomeFirstResponder];
  }
  else
  {
    [passwordField resignFirstResponder];
    self.username = usernameField.text;
    self.password = passwordField.text;
    [controller setUsername:username password:password];
    [[self parentViewController] dismissModalViewControllerAnimated:YES];
  }

  return YES;
}

@end
```

Displaying the Modal View

Because `AccountViewController` is a view controller, it is initialized with its view's NIB file name. `presentModalView:animated:` slides its modal view over the table view of tweets.

```
- (void) requestAccount
{
  /* Put your username and password here */
  NSString *username = nil;
  NSString *password = nil;
  accountVC
    = [[AccountViewController alloc] initWithNibName:@"AccountView" bundle:nil];
  accountVC.username   = username;
  accountVC.password   = password;
  accountVC.controller = self;
  [self presentModalViewController:accountVC animated:YES];
}
```

Watch Out!

`presentModalViewController:animated:` does not work if its view controller's view has not been added to the window. This code invokes `requestAccount` from `applicationDidFinishLaunching`, rather than from `TwitterViewController`'s `initWithCoder`, `viewDidLoad`, or `viewDidAppear:` methods. These methods are invoked by the view controller's `view` method, which returns the view to add to the window: They are invoked before the view is added to the window.

Saving Application Defaults

On the iPhone, each application can save its settings to a private defaults file. `NSUserDefaults` provides access to this file. The Twitter application uses it to save the user's account details.

Using `NSUserDefaults`

To access the defaults, invoke `NSUserDefaults`' `standardUserDefaults` method:

```
NSUserDefaults *userDefaults = [NSUserDefaults standardUserDefaults];
```

`NSUserDefaults` is similar to `NSMutableDictionary`: It associates objects with keys. The keys must be `NSStrings`, and the objects may only be of the following types:

- `NSNumbers` (`objectForKey:` and `setObject:forKey:`)
- `NSDates` (`objectForKey:` and `setObject:forKey:`)
- `NSStrings` (`stringForKey:` and `setObject:forKey:`)
- `NSArrays` (`arrayForKey:` and `setObject:forKey:`)
- `NSDictionarys` (`dictionaryForKey:` and `setObject:forKey:`)
- `NSDatas` (`dataForKey:` and `setObject:forKey:`)

For convenience, the following methods wrap and unwrap NSNumbers:

- Booleans (boolForKey: and setBool:forKey)
- Integers (integerForKey: and setInteger:forKey:)
- Floats (floatForKey: and setFloat:forKey:)

removeObject:forKey: lets you remove an object from the defaults, whereas synchronize saves your changes to the defaults file. Reading an unknown key returns NO, 0, 0.0, or nil.

Watch Out!

> Everything you save will be stored as an immutable object.

The following lines read the username and password from the defaults:

```
NSUserDefaults *userDefaults = [NSUserDefaults standardUserDefaults];
NSString *username = [userDefaults stringForKey:@"username"];
NSString *password = [userDefaults stringForKey:@"password"];
```

The following lines are added to setUsername:password:

```
NSUserDefaults *userDefaults = [NSUserDefaults standardUserDefaults];
[userDefaults setObject:username forKey:@"username"];
[userDefaults setObject:password forKey:@"password"];
```

Defaults are generally saved on application exit, but you can save them earlier if you're concerned your application might crash or hang before exit. TwitterAppDelegate's applicationWillTerminate: invokes synchronize to save userDefaults:

```
- (void) applicationWillTerminate:(UIApplication*)application
{
  NSUserDefaults *userDefaults = [NSUserDefaults standardUserDefaults];
  [userDefaults synchronize];
}
```

> The user defaults are not encrypted and can be retrieved within a few minutes by jailbreaking an iPhone (see Hour 16, "Adding Application Preferences"). Applications that have access to sensitive passwords should store them to the keychain. Apple's *Keychain Services Programming Guide* explains how to use the keychain.

Property Lists

NSUserDefaults saves properties as a **property list**. Property lists can only use the types I listed for NSUserDefaults, they do not save full class information (such as the distinction between mutable and nonmutable classes), and they cannot handle cyclic object graphs. They can, however, be saved in the Extensible Markup Language (XML) platform-independent format.

Saving objects to a file is called **serialization**. Objects that refer to other objects create a graph. Often, objects refer to other objects that eventually refer back to them—creating a cyclic object graph. You encountered this problem in Hour 7, "Understanding How Events Are Processed," when I discussed retain cycles. Property list serialization follows a depth-first encoding strategy: It encodes each container by encoding its content within a type-specific block. For instance, XML property lists encode arrays between `<array>` and `</array>` tags. Property list serialization does not check whether it has already encountered an object and enters an infinite recursion loop when dealing with cyclic object graphs. The result is a stack overflow exception.

To encode a property list in XML, `propertyList`, write the following:

```
NSString *errorMsg = nil;
NSData* data = [NSPropertyListSerialization
                         dataFromPropertyList: propertyList
                                       format: NSPropertyListXMLFormat_v1_0
                             errorDescription: &errorMsg];
```

`data` will be `nil` and `errorMsg` will explain why if there's an error. You can also encode the property list in a faster binary format using `NSPropertyListBinaryFormat_v1_0`.

When decoding a property list, `NSPropertyListSerialization` detects the saved property list format automatically, and lets you specify the mutability of the objects it creates:

- `NSPropertyListImmutable` creates immutable objects.
- `NSPropertyListMutableContainers` creates mutable `NSDictionarys` and `NSArrays`, but immutable `NSNumbers`, `NSStrings`, `NSDatas`, and `NSDates`.
- `NSPropertyListMutableContainersAndLeaves` creates mutable objects (except `NSNumbers` and `NSDates`).

For instance, if your property list is stored in an `NSData` object named `data`:

```
NSPropertyListFormat  format;
NSString              *errorMsg     = nil;

id propertyList = [NSPropertyListSerialization
                              propertyListFromData: data
                                 mutabilityOption: NSPropertyListImmutable
                                           format: &format
                                 errorDescription: &errorMsg];
```

In case of error, propertyList will be nil and errorMsg will provide an explanation.

Archives and NSCoder

NSKeyedArchiver can save data to an **archive**. The archive format is able to save any object that obeys the NSCoding protocol. It also encodes data in a depth-first manner, but keeps track of objects that were previously encountered. Instead of reencoding such objects, it places a reference to their previous occurrence in the archive.

NSKeyedArchiver is a concrete subclass of NSCoder, which provides basic serialization for primitive C types (Booleans, integers, bytes), and a framework for serializing objects (the NSCoding protocol). Objects that can be serialized must support two methods: encodeWithCoder: for serialization, and initWithCoder: for deserialization. They use the coder passed as an argument to encode or decode their arguments:

```
- (void) encodeWithCoder:(NSCoder*)coder
{
  [super encodeWithCoder:coder];
  [coder encodeObject:territories forKey:@"territories"];
  [coder encodeInteger:population forKey:@"population"];
  [coder encodeConditionalObject:federation forKey:@"federation"];
}
```

To deal with cyclic object graphs, the NSKeyedArchiver object overrides encodeObject:forKey: and adds each object it encounters to a dictionary of unique identifiers. Objects that have not yet been encountered do not appear in the dictionary. NSKeyedArchiver creates a new identifier for each such object and adds the object and its identifier to the dictionary and to the archive. If NSKeyedArchiver has already encountered the object, it only adds the identifier to the archive. NSKeyedUnarchiver overrides decodeObject: to associate the address of each object it allocs with the object's identifier. If it encounters the identifier again, it looks up its object's address and returns that.

A further enhancement of NSKeyedArchiver is conditional encoding, which is a form of weak reference. If NSKeyedArchiver's encodeObject:forKey: has encountered this object, encodeConditionalObject:forKey: will save a reference to it. Otherwise, it will create a reference for it, but encode a placeholder for the object, until it encounters an encodeObject:forKey: for it. When the archive is decoded, objects that were not saved are assigned nil pointers. For instance, views archive their superview conditionally. This lets you archive a state and its territories without including the federation to which it belongs (or a view and its subviews, which are correctly connected to their superviews without archiving the entire view hierarchy).

Did you Know?

NSKeyedArchiver has a deprecated twin, NSArchiver, that does not use keys. Apple has not documented it on the iPhone because they don't want you to use it. However, it is the reason NSCoder defines methods without a key such as encodeObject: and encodeConditionalObject:.

You first encountered initWithCoder: in Hour 10, "Using View Controllers," where it was used to initialize CalculatorController. NIB files are archives that use initWithCoder: to deserialize their objects. Interface Builder uses encodeWithCoder to save the attributes of standard objects, but KVC (Key-Value Coding) to save the outlets of custom objects.

Did you Know?

Although property lists (and NSUserDefaults) cannot save many kinds of objects directly, if the objects support the NSCoding protocol, they can be serialized with NSKeyArchiver and saved as NSDatas. For instance, if color is a UIColor:

```
NSData *data = [NSKeyedArchiver archivedDataWithRootObject:color];
[[NSUserDefaults standardUserDefaults] setObject:data forKey:@"color"];
```

Deep copies can be made of objects that support the NSCoding protocol by using NSKeyedArchiver and NSKeyedUnarchiver. A deep copy is a copy of the object and the objects it references.

```
NSData *data  = [NSKeyedArchiver   archivedDataWithRootObject:object];
id objectCopy = [NSKeyedUnarchiver unarchiveObjectWithData:data];
```

Using Tab Bars

Tab bar user-interface elements are implemented by UITabViews. The UITabBarController class provides a standard tab view controller, which manages switching views.

Tab bars provide a fast interface for switching between up to five views. However, they take up space that could otherwise be used by a toolbar. Some interfaces flow better with a navigation bar and a toolbar.

Tab Bar View

UITabBarView is the view that appears at the bottom of the screen, which lets you choose different application-level views by tapping buttons. The buttons of tab views are called tab view items. Figure 12.3 shows how tab bar views are constructed in software.

FIGURE 12.3
Tab view objects

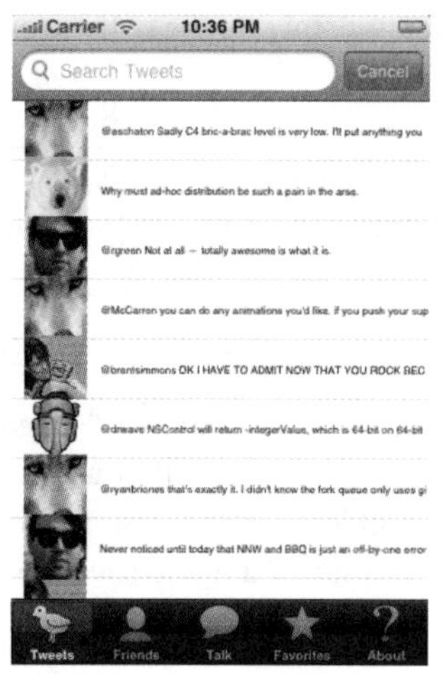

Tab Bar in Twitter Application

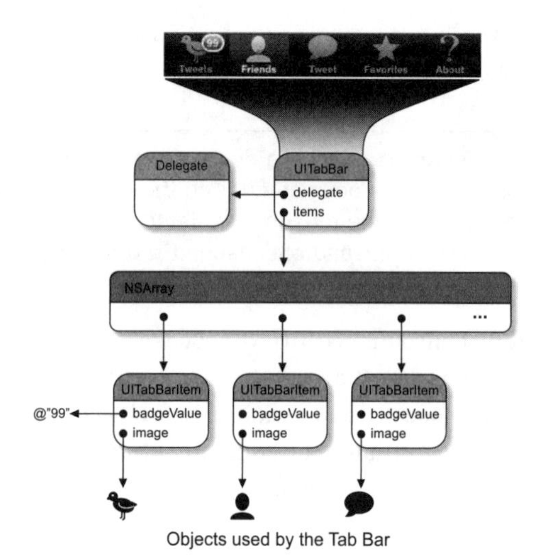

Objects used by the Tab Bar

Tab view items consist of an image and a possible badge. System-provided tab bar items have the images and titles specified in Figure 12.4(a). Your application will be rejected from the App Store if you use a system-provided icon for a different purpose.

```
UITabBarItem* more
  =[[UITabBarItem alloc] initWithTabBarSystemItem:UITabBarSystemItemMore tag:5];
```

FIGURE 12.4
Tab items and tab bar customization

(a) System provided tab items

(b) Images as Masks

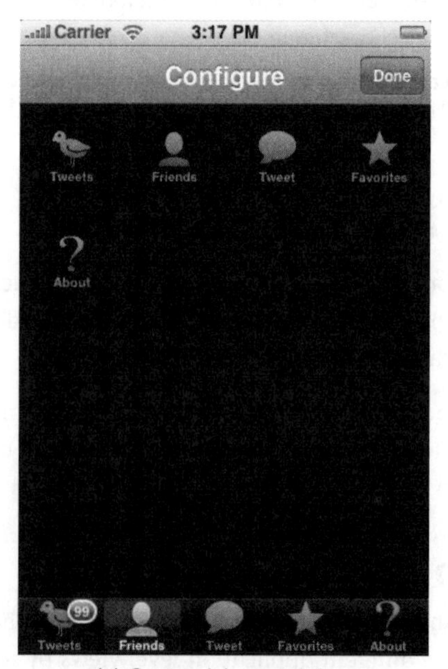

(c) Customizing a tab bar

User-provided images are 30x30 masks: The opacity of the image is used to create a mask that is combined with a gray or blue background to create the unselected or selected appearance, as shown in Figure 12.4(b). To avoid crowding the tab bar item text, leave a few pixels free at the bottom of your image.

```
UIImage*      bPic = [UIImage imageNamed:@"Bird.png"]
UITabBarItem* bird = [[UITabBarItem alloc]
                                 initWithTitle:@"Tweets" image:bPic tag:1];
```

badgeValue lets you add a badge to a tab bar item, such as the number of new tweets.

```
bird.badgeValue = @"99";
```

A tab bar's items are set using setItems:animated:, which can fade old items out and new items in if animation is requested. The read/write selectedItem property specifies the currently selected item. Tab bars can show more than five items, but it looks poorly designed. Apple only uses five items per tab bar in its applications.

```
UITabBar* tabbar = [[UITabBar alloc] initWithFrame:CGRectMake(0, 436, 320, 44)];
[tabbar setItems:[NSArray arrayWithObjects:bird, friend, talk, star, about,
                                                        more, nil] animated:NO];
tabbar.selectedItem = bird;
```

To respond to user input, set the delegate to an object obeying the UITabBarDelegate protocol. Its tabBar:didSelectItem: method is informed when users tap a tab.

```
- (void) tabBar:(UITabBar*)tabBar didSelectItem:(UITabBarItem*)item
{ [tabBar beginCustomizingItems:[tabBar items]]; }
```

To let your users customize a tab bar's items, invoke beginCustomizingItems: with an array of items. This will display a modal panel, as shown in Figure 12.4(c), letting the user drag and drop items and reorder the items in the tab bar. To close the modal panel, invoke endCustomizingAnimated:. Again, delegate methods inform you about user interactions.

Tab Bar Controller

Tab bar delegates all do the same thing: They swap between views and let you customize the tab bar. To reduce the amount of code you have to write, Cocoa Touch provides a tab bar controller class, UITabBarController, which is a delegate of the tab bar.

Using Tab Bar Controllers

When you tap a tab bar item, the tab bar controller will ask the corresponding view controller to create its view, and will replace the current application-level view with the new view. To do this, it needs to know which view controller is associated with which tab bar item. Set the tab bar controller's viewsControllers array to the view controllers that correspond to the tab bar items. Set each view controller's tabBarItem to the tab bar item to be displayed for its view.

If you add more items than can be displayed on the tab bar comfortably, a More tab bar item will appear to show the other tab bar items. This behaves like the tab bar's beginCustomizingItems: modal panel. However, only view controllers that appear in customizableViewControllers can be edited. As with the tab bar, setViewControllers:animated: lets you replace the tab bar items and their view controllers in the tab bar.

Because the tab bar controller will resize the application-level views to fit into the available space, either design your view for the correct size, or set the autoresizing mask of subviews appropriately.

The currently selected tab bar item is specified by selectedIndex, and delegate lets you use an object conforming to the UITabBarControllerDelegate protocol to manage tab bar item selections and customizations. For instance, you can define an updateTweets method on the tweet view controller to update the table of tweets each time the tweet view controller item is selected:

```
- (void)        tabBarController:(UITabBarController*)tbc
        didSelectViewController:(UIViewController*)vc
{
  if ([vc respondsToSelector:@selector(updateTweets)])
    [vc updateTweets];
}
```

The Twitter2 source code for this hour implements a tab bar controller.

Adding a Tab Bar Controller to a NIB File

Drag a Tab Bar Controller to Interface Builder's Document Window. By default, the tab bar comes with two view controllers for two tab bar items. To add another tab bar item, drag another view controller onto the tab bar in the canvas. Using the outline view mode, you can click a view controller to change its attributes, or its tab bar item to change its icon and text (see Figure 12.5).

You must set each view controller's Class Identity to the appropriate class name for an object of the appropriate type to be built. View controllers are initialized with a NIB, so you must also set the view controller's NIB Name. If the NIB Name is invalid, the application will crash on launch after printing an error to the console. If Xcode cannot install your application on the simulator after this error, exit the iPhone Simulator and Xcode before restarting them.

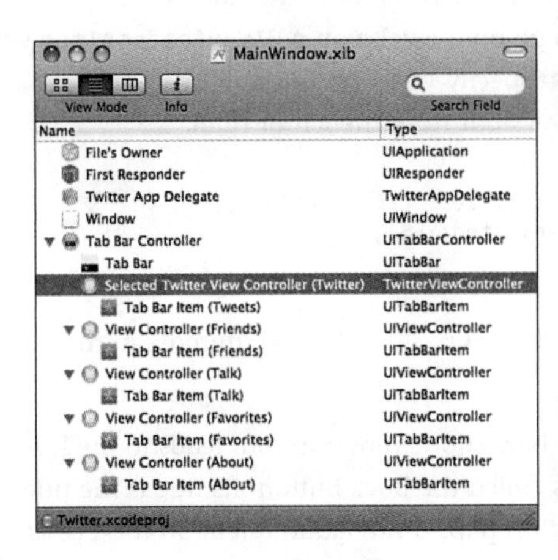

Tab bar controller bar Items

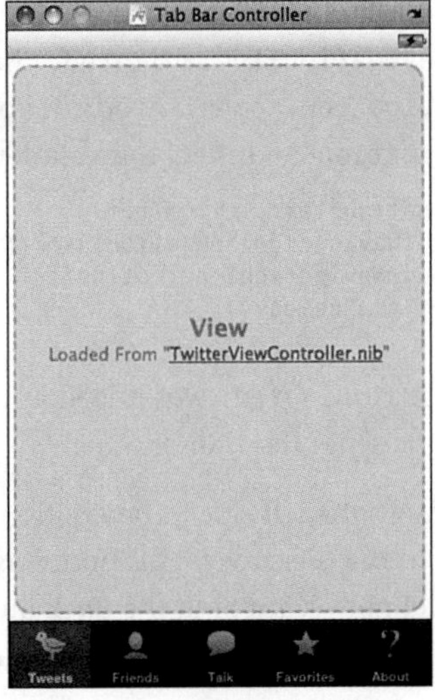

Canvas with tab bar Items

FIGURE 12.5
Twitter's `MainWindow.xib`

Using Navigation Bars

Tab bars only support one level of navigation depth: The tab bar shows users which view they are looking at. Navigation bars provide a multilevel navigation structure, by displaying a title for each level of the hierarchy, and showing on its left a named button, which lets the user return to the level above in the hierarchy.

Using `UINavigationBars` with `UINavigationItems`

Navigation bars are created like other views. `barStyle` lets you choose between a black and a colorable navigation bar (`UIBarStyleDefault` versus `UIBarStyleBlack`). Set `tintColor` to change the navigation bar's color, and `translucent` to change its opacity.

```
CGRect            rect = CGRectMake(0, 0, 320, 44)];
UINavigationBar*  bar = [[UINavigationBar alloc] initWithFrame:rect];
bar.tintColor = [UIColor redColor];
```

Navigation bars store a stack of traversed levels of the hierarchy in their `items` property. Each level is represented by a `UINavigationItem` object. Each navigation item stores the layout of the navigation bar for that level in the hierarchy. The current level is `items`' `lastObject`.

```
UINavigationItem* topItem = [[UINavigationItem alloc] initWithTitle:@"Friends"];
bar.items                 = [NSArray arrayWithObject:topItem];
[topItem release];
```

To go down a level, push a new `UINavigationItem` onto the stack with `pushNavigationItem:animated:`. To go up a level, pop a `UINavigationItem` with `popNavigationItemAnimated:`. If you specify you want animation, `UINavigationBar` inserts the next level's bar from the left or right.

```
UINavigationItem* bottomItem
  = [[UINavigationItem alloc] initWithTitle:@"newscientist"];
[bar pushNavigationItem:bottomItem animated:YES];
[bottomItem release];
```

`setItems:animated:` was added in iPhone OS 3.0 to let you animate a transition from one set of items to another.

By default, the left side of navigation bars shows a button that leads to the level above in the hierarchy. This button is called the Back button. Its title is the title of the level above. Tapping the Back button pops a navigation item off the `items` stack, and updates the navigation bar using animation.

The navigation bar's `delegate` lets you customize its behavior. Use the `navigationBar:didPushItem:` and `navigationBar:didPopItem:` methods to replace the view under the navigation bar. Use the `navigationBar:shouldPushItem:` and `navigationBar:shouldPopItem:` methods to prevent navigation. For instance, you can prevent a user from leaving a settings page that the user has left in an invalid state. The delegate should obey the `UINavigationBarDelegate` protocol.

Figure 12.6 shows how the navigation bar interacts with navigation items and the delegate in the `Twitter3` example.

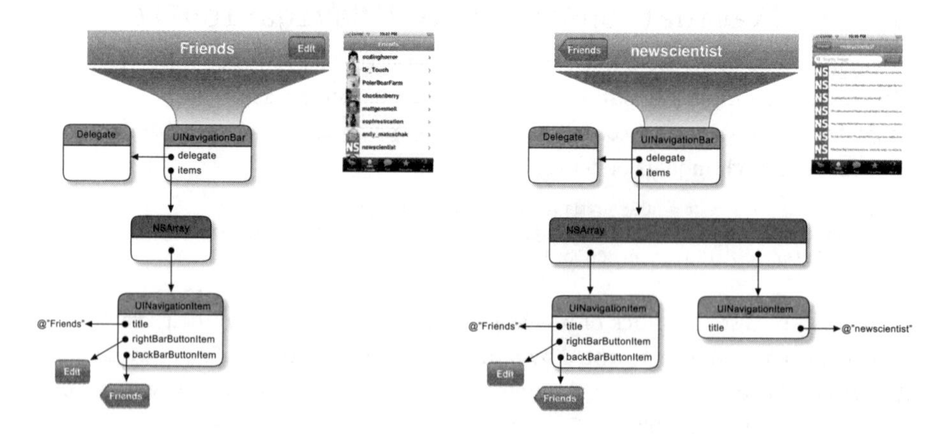

FIGURE 12.6
Navigation bar objects

Customizing `UINavigationItems`

Navigation items determine the layout of the navigation bar. The navigation bar usually displays three elements: a left element, a central element, and a right element.

The left element is usually a Back button (backBarButtonItem). UINavigationBar sets backBarButtonItem to a button containing the level's title. However, if leftBarButtonItem is not nil, it is displayed instead of backBarButtonItem. Both backBarButtonItem and leftBarButtonItem are set to UIBarButtonItems, which are discussed in the next subsection. Setting setLeftBarButtonItem:animated:'s animated argument to YES dissolves the button item when transitioning to a navigation item that does not have it.

The central element is the title, which is set with title. The title can be replaced with a fully customizable view by setting titleView, but this only works if leftBarButtonItem is nil.

The right element is another bar button item (rightBarButtonItem).

You can also add a message above the title by setting prompt, as shown in Figure 12.7.

FIGURE 12.7 Full navigation bar

Using UIBarButtonItems

Button bar items are the buttons you can add to a navigation bar or a toolbar. There are four kinds of UIBarButtonItems that display the following:

- A system image (created using initWithBarButtonSystemItem:target:action:)
- A custom view (created using initWithCustomView:)
- A custom image (created using initWithImage:style:target:action:)
- A title (created using initWithTitle:style:target:action:)

Touching most bar button items invokes a selector (action) on an object (target). If you use a custom view, the custom view must capture touches.

The style parameter changes the look of a button. Toolbar buttons can use a borderless style or a bordered style, whereas navigation bars only show buttons with borders. UIBarButtonItemStylePlain specifies a borderless button. UIBarButtonItemStyleBordered specifies a standard button with a border. UIBarButtonItemStyleDone specifies a button with a border in a lighter hue of blue, as shown by the Done button in Figure 12.8. Borderless buttons glow when touched, whereas buttons with borders look like they are pushed down when touched.

```
UIBarButtonItem* b
  = [[UIBarButtonItem alloc]
                      initWithBarButtonSystemItem:UIBarButtonSystemItemEdit
                                                  target:self action:@selector(edit:)];
topItem.rightBarButtonItem = b;
[b release];
```

Figure 12.8 shows the system-provided images you can use, while spacing is provided by `UIBarButtonSystemItemFlexibleSpace` and `UIBarButtonSystemItemFixedSpace`.

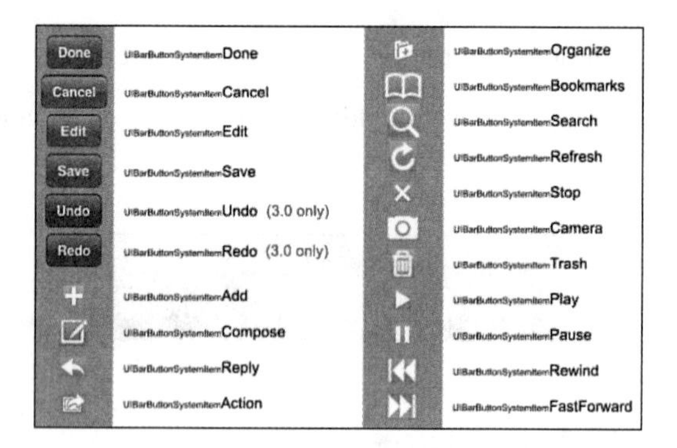

FIGURE 12.8
System UI bar items

Using `UIToolbars`

Toolbars look like navigation bars but are usually placed at the bottom of the screen instead of at the top. They display a number of buttons (tools), which the user can touch to invoke application-defined functionality. Touching a button makes it glow instead of making it darker.

The design of toolbars' APIs mirrors that of navigation bars. They support `tintColor`, `barStyle`, and as of iPhone OS 3.0 `translucent`. The comments made about these methods for navigation bars also apply to toolbars.

Unlike navigation bars, `items` and `setItems:animated:` take `UIBarButtonItem` objects instead of `UINavigationItems`.

Navigation Bar Controllers

Navigation bar delegates all do the same thing: swap views as the navigation bar steps through the navigation hierarchy. To reduce the amount of code you have to write, Cocoa Touch provides a navigation bar controller class, `UINavigationBarController`, which is a delegate of the navigation bar.

Using Navigation Bar Controllers

The navigation bar controller manages a stack of view controllers in its viewControllers property, which mirrors the stack of navigation items the navigation bar manages in items. It invokes the view controllers' view construction functionality when it swaps application-level views.

Navigation bar controller's views consist of an optional navigation bar (navigationBar) and an application-level view created by a view controller. The view controller used to create the top view of the hierarchy is called the root controller. Because navigation bar controllers always display an application-level view, they are initialized with the root view controller by initWithRootViewController:.

pushViewController:animated: and popViewControllerAnimated: mirror the navigation bar's pushNavigationItem:animated: and popNavigationItemAnimated: methods. Pushing a view controller that is already in viewControllers causes an exception. For convenience, navigation bar controllers also provide the popToRootViewControllerAnimated: and popToViewController:animated: methods to jump up a number of levels of the navigation hierarchy.

Because navigation bars manage navigation items, view controllers provide a read-only navigationItem property, which creates a navigation item from the view controller's title. Its title and backBarButtonItem are derived from the view controller's title. You can customize the navigation item yourself, by setting its backBarButtonItem, leftBarButtonItem, titleView, prompt, and rightBarButtonItem properties as desired. For instance, to override the Back button title with a shorter title, you could override the view controller's initWithNibNamne:bundle: method:

```
- (id) initWithNibName:(NSString*)name bundle:(NSBundle*)bundle
{
  self = [super initWithNibName:name bundle:bundle];

  if (self)
  {
    self.title = @"Long Title";

    UIBarButtonItem *backBarButtonItem
      = [[UIBarButtonItem alloc] initWithTitle:@"Back"
                                         style:UIBarButtonItemStyleBordered
                                        target:nil
                                        action:nil];

    self.navigationItem.backBarButtonItem = backBarButtonItem;
    [backBarButtonItem release];
  }

  return self;
}
```

Because UIBarButtonItem's action and target are nil, UINavigationBarController sets them appropriately.

You can change the appearance of the navigation bar (navigationBar) as before. However, navigation bar controllers can also hide their navigation bars (navigationBarHidden and setNavigationBarHidden:animated:).

As of iPhone OS 3.0, navigation bar controllers can also manage a custom toolbar for each level of the navigation hierarchy. View controllers have a toolbarItems property that the navigation view controller uses to construct a custom toolbar. By default, the toolbar is hidden but can be shown by invoking setToolbarHidden:animated:.

topViewController is the view controller of the current level of the navigation hierarchy. It's usually the visible application-level view, unless the screen is covered by a modal view. visibleViewController specifies the visible view.

Using Table View Controllers

Navigation bars are often associated with tables: To drill down the hierarchy, the user selects a row of the visible table. Because navigation controllers manage view controllers, Cocoa Touch provides a UITableViewController class, which is a UIViewController that adds a tableView property that references the table view.

If the UITableViewController is created with initWithNibName:bundle:, tableView will reference the table view in the NIB file. If it is created with initWithStyle:, tableView references a newly created table of the specified style (UITableViewStylePlain or UITableViewStyleGrouped).

The first time the table appears, UITableViewContoller's viewDidAppear method loads the table's data (reloadData). Every time the table appears, it clears the table's current selection and flashes the table view's scroll indicators.

The table view controller also implements setEditing:animated: to switch between the table's editing and nonediting modes when the user taps the Edit or Done button in the navigation bar.

Adding a Friend Table View

To illustrate navigation bars, the Twitter3 example uses a navigation hierarchy to show what your friends and followers are saying. The top level of the hierarchy is a table of your friends. Below that is a table of their tweets, as shown in Figure 12.6.

The table of friends appears within a navigation controller. The navigation controller is a child of the tab bar controller as shown in Figure 12.9. When you add a Navigation Controller in Interface Builder, it also adds a View Controller and a `Navigation Item`, whose title you can set. You can delete the `View Controller` and replace it with a `Table View Controller` to show a table.

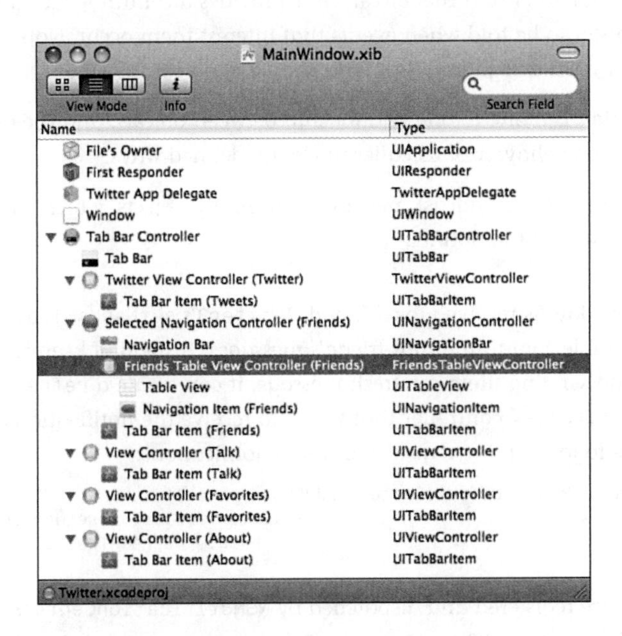

FIGURE 12.9
`MainWindow.xib`

Did you Know?

A figure showing the View Controller Hierarchy used in the Twitter application is available in Appendix D, in the "View Controller Hierarchy Used in the Twitter Application" section.

Hour 11, "Displaying Tables," introduced the User class to iterate through each users' tweets and to encapsulate information about each user. However, because `Twitter3` shows more than one table of tweets, it splits `User` into `UserIterator` to keep track of each table's current position in the user's list of tweets, and `User` to contain the user's name, image and tweets.

The new `FriendsTableViewController` class shows your friends. `tableView:didSelectRowAtIndexPath:` pushes a `TwitterViewController` onto the navigation hierarchy showing the tweets of the friend you selected.

```
- (void) tableView:(UITableView*)tv didSelectRowAtIndexPath:(NSIndexPath*)path
{
  User* friend     = [friends objectAtIndex:path.row];
  TwitterViewController* friendVC = [[TwitterViewController alloc] init];
  friendVC.friends = [NSArray arrayWithObject:friend];
  friendVC.title   = friend.name;
  [(UINavigationController*) [self parentViewController]
                              pushViewController:friendVC animated:YES];
}
```

Notifications

Cocoa Touch's NSNotificationCenter class provides a central location for your objects to register to be told when events that interest them occur. Notification is quite different from delegation, although people often confuse them:

- Delegation is a one-to-one relationship between objects, and the delegate can change the behavior of its caller in clearly defined ways.
- Notification is a broadcast mechanism to many objects, which cannot affect the behavior of the notifier.

Each time new data is received for a friend, Twitter3's setNeedsDisplay must refresh every table containing that friend's messages. Instead of keeping track of every view and sending them a refresh message, it can create a refreshTweets notification. Every view controller that wants to receive the notifications can register for them. The following line registers for these notifications:

```
[[NSNotificationCenter defaultCenter] addObserver:self
                                         selector:@selector(setNeedsDisplay)
                                             name:@"refreshTweets" object:nil];
```

Notifications are registered and dispatched by NSNotificationCenters. Cocoa Touch provides a default NSNotificationCenter you can use, defaultCenter, but you could have created your own if you wanted. Every object that registers for notification should stop observing notifications in its dealloc method with the following line of code because NSNotificationCenter does not retain objects, and will invoke released objects' methods:

```
[[NSNotificationCenter defaultCenter] removeObserver:self];
```

To create the notifications, use the following code:

```
NSNotificationCenter* defaultCenter = [NSNotificationCenter defaultCenter];
[defaultCenter postNotificationName:@"refreshTweets" object:self];
```

It is very important that the objects that register for a notification perform independent tasks when receiving a notification. This is harder than it might seem, as NSNotification does not randomize the order in which it invokes objects' methods. This leads to unseen dependencies as one method grows to rely on changes made by another previously invoked method. Then after you change some seemingly unrelated part of the application, the order in which objects register for the notification changes and the application stops working.

Summary

In this hour you learned how to switch views using view controllers. Because most applications display many views, this is a key topic. As you'll have noticed, it isn't hard, but it does involve a lot of details. Make sure you understand the difference between views (tab bars and navigation bars) and view controllers (tab bar controllers and navigation controllers), which was explained this hour. Navigation controllers and tab controllers are view controllers that manage other view controllers, which can build the appropriate subviews. This abstraction helps Cocoa Touch minimize memory usage while reducing the amount of code you must write.

In the next hour, you'll study how Cocoa Touch provides undo and redo functionality, and you'll learn how to edit tables.

Q&A

Q. ***I'd like to create a tab bar, but place every application-level view it displays in its own NIB file. Can I do this if one of these views contains a navigation bar?***

A. Yes you can, but your NIB's `File's Owner` cannot be a `UINavigationController`. Instead, use a `UIViewController` as `File's Owner`, and add a navigation controller to the NIB file. Add the navigation controller's view as a subview of the `UIViewController`.

Q. ***Should I use notifications?***

A. Yes, but sparingly. Many beginning Cocoa programmers fall in love with notifications, and overuse them until they are severely burnt by the experience. The problem is that you can easily lose track of all the code they invoke, which makes debugging nigh impossible. Explicit method invocations are easier to debug.

Workshop

The Workshop consists of quiz questions and answers to help you solidify your understanding of the material covered in this hour. You should try to answer the questions before checking the answers.

Quiz Questions

1. How do you display a modal view?
2. What kind of image do tab bars use?
3. What is a navigation item?
4. How does the navigation controller manage view controllers?
5. How do you create a navigation bar within a tab bar?
6. Do you have to use table view controllers with a navigation controller?

Quiz Answers

1. You can display a modal view by invoking `presentModalViewController:animated:` on the current view's view controller.
2. Tab bars use the tab bar item's image's alpha value as a stencil when drawing the tab bar item in its selected or unselected color.
3. A navigation item specifies the layout of the navigation bar at a particular level of the navigation hierarchy.
4. The navigation controller manages the view controllers representing the hierarchy of levels above the current level as a stack.
5. You can create a navigation bar within a tab bar by dragging a navigation controller to the tab bar on the canvas.
6. No, you can use any view controller with a navigation controller. However, table view controllers are often used.

Exercises

- If the phone rings, the user will lose his position in the navigation hierarchy. Each time the user changes tab, save which tab is currently displayed, and the current position in the navigation hierarchy using `NSUserDefaults`. Restore these settings when the user reopens the application.
- Create a table whose first row is a view of the user's profile, and whose next rows consist of the user's tweets. You'll need to change the height of the first row for the profile.

HOUR 13

Adding Undo and Redo Functionality

What You'll Learn in This Hour:

- Creating your own undo/dedo manager
- Using `NSUndoManager`

The first computers were considered unfriendly and hard to use because they were unforgiving of user error. You said you wanted to erase your hard drive? OK! I'm busy now; don't interrupt me! Users avoided exploring their application's user interfaces for fear of breaking something irreversibly. The result was that most software features were never used. Undo/redo is the unsung hero that led computers to be widely adopted. Although the Xerox Alto, the first computer to provide a GUI, introduced undo functionality in 1973, it took a long time to be widely adopted, partially because programmers did not know of a good abstraction for implementing undo and redo functionality. Cocoa provides a very nice abstraction for implementing undo and redo functionality.

Creating Your Own Undo/Redo Manager

Unless you understand the problem it is solving, using `NSUndoManager` appears to involve arcane method invocations. To understand the undo/redo problem, we'll create our own undo/redo manager. This will clarify the design of `NSUndoManager` and the problems it solves. Understanding these problems will help you simplify your applications' undo/redo support code.

A History of Changes

The simplest way of implementing undo would be to save a complete copy of the user's work, each time the user makes a change. This is too inefficient to be practical, but suggests we only need to save a history of the changes the user makes. To undo, we revert the change. To redo, we reapply the change.

It is easy to revert changes that add information. For instance, typing a word adds information. To undo the change, simply remove the word. It is a little less obvious how you should undo changes that remove information—the information was lost! The conundrum is solved by saving deleted information in the change. For instance, undoing a subtraction in the calculator is simply a matter of adding the number we subtracted back to the result.

For instance, consider the Calculator application's `pressEquals:` method. The following lines save `pressEquals:`'s state before it changes it. (`EqualsChange` just stores the data passed as arguments):

```
EqualsChange* change = [EqualsChange changeWithTarget:state
                                                model:model
                                         clearOnDigit:state.clearOnDigit
                                         lastWasDigit:state.lastWasDigit
                                      expressionStack:model->expressionStack
                                        currentNumber:state.currentNumber];
[[UndoManager defaultManager] saveChange:change];
```

Saving the application state before each change is an example of the memento pattern. Saving changes is an example of the command pattern. A good book to learn about object-oriented patterns is *Design Patterns* by Erich Gamma, Richard Helm, Ralph Johnson, and John Vlissides.

Creating an Undo Manager

For user-invoked actions to be undone, they must save enough information to reverse the change they make. This information is saved in objects of a history array. If all the change objects implement an `execute` method, we can create an `UndoManager` object that knows how to undo changes without knowing any details about the change. The `Change` protocol declares the required methods:

```
@protocol Change
- (void) execute;
- (void) invert;
@end
```

The simple undo manager's API is as follows:

```
@interface UndoManager : NSObject
{
```

```
  NSMutableArray* undoChanges;
  NSMutableArray* redoChanges;
}

+ (UndoManager*) defaultManager;
- (void)         saveChange:(id<Change>)change;
- (void)         undo;
- (void)         redo;
@end
```

The key routines are:

```
// Skipped init/dealloc which create and release undoChanges/redoChanges

- (void) saveChange:(id<Change>)change;
{ [undoChanges addObject:change];
  [redoChanges removeAllObjects]; }

- (void) undo;
{
  id<Change> change = [undoChanges lastObject];
  [change execute];
  [change invert];
  [redoChanges addObject:change];
  [undoChanges removeLastObject];
}
```

It is often useful to undo an undo. This is where the redo functionality comes in. We can save changes that have been undone to a redo stack. The only difference between the redo and undo stacks is that the redo stack is emptied as soon as a change is added to the undo manager.

As undo and redo do opposite actions, an `invert` method is needed to invert the change.

We can add an inverted flag to `EqualsChange`, which `invert` inverts, and use the flag in `execute`:

```
- (void) invert   { inverted = !inverted; }
// initWithTarget:clear:last:expression:currentNumber should set invert to NO.
// Example of how a naive approach to undo/redo functionality can lead
// to terribly tight coupling. The rest of this section explains how not
// to write code like this!

- (void) execute
{
  if (!inverted)
  {
    target.clearOnDigit  = clearOnDigit;
    target.lastWasDigit  = lastWasDigit;
    target.currentNumber = currentNumber;
    [model popExpressionStack:expressionStack];
  }
```

```
    else
    {
      state.clearOnDigit  = YES;
      state.lastWasDigit  = YES;
      [model pushExpressionStack:expressionStack];
      float value = model.value;
      state.currentNumber = [NSString stringWithFormat:@"%g", value];
    }
}
```

Unfortunately, this is a complex process. For a simple calculator, you'd need to repeat this exercise for `pressArith:`, `pressClear:`, `pressDigit:`, `pressStore:`, and `pressVar:`. Moreover, each change class is tightly coupled to the controller class: It goes so far as to change the controller's internal state, breaking encapsulation. The resulting code is bug prone and inflexible. Luckily, this is not the end of the story: We'll tame this monstrosity.

Moving Changes to the Model

At this stage of our design, each user action creates a single change in the undo/redo history. Our changes are being saved at the controller level, and break encapsulation. However, user actions often invoke a small set of methods to update the model. By saving state changes in mutators, we reduce the amount of undo/redo code we must write.

For instance, `setClearOnDigit:` becomes the following:

```
- (void) setClearOnDigit:(BOOL)c
{
  [[UndoManager defaultManager]
      saveChange:[ClearOnDigitChange clearOnDigit:self from:clearOnDigit to:c]];
  clearOnDigit = c;
}
```

Again, you must write a `ClearOnDigitChange` class, but it's a lot simpler. For instance, here are its `execute` and `invert` methods:

```
- (void) execute { target.clearOnDigit = from;  }
- (void) invert  { BOOL tmp = to; to = from; from = tmp; }
```

Because each user action may cause many changes to the model, `UndoManager` can no longer assume each change corresponds to a single action to be undone. For instance, replacing an object in an array consists of deleting the old object and adding the new object: two changes. The user does not expect to tap Undo twice to undo to this single change.

A simple solution is for each user action to create a change that the model methods can update. At exit, the user action adds the change to the undo history. The disadvantage of this simple solution is that every user action must create and save changes. It's easy to add an action but forget to write this additional code.

```
- (void) pressEquals:(UIButton*)sender;
{
  [[UndoManager defaultManager] beginUndoGrouping];
  state.clearOnDigit  = YES;
  state.lastWasDigit  = YES;
  float value = model.value;
  [model pushExpression];
  state.currentNumber = [NSString stringWithFormat:@"%g", value];
  [[UndoManager defaultManager] endUndoGrouping];
}
```

User actions are invoked by the run loop. Once the user action completes, it returns to the run loop. Therefore, the run loop could create the change before invoking the action and commit it afterward. In fact, there's no need to change the run loop: `UndoManager` can install an observer into the run loop and add the current change to the history if it was updated. Thus the `beginUndoGrouping` and `endUndoGrouping` lines can be deleted. Only code that creates changes need know about the undo mechanism.

Abstracting Changes: `NSInvocation`

Up to this point, every method that records a change must create its own change object. This results in a proliferation of change classes. Each change class contains the information needed to reverse the change and a method to reverse the change. It's not that different from a method invocation, except that method invocations occur immediately. Instead of creating a change object, we could add freeze-dried method invocations to the history. When `UndoManager` wants to undo something, it simply unfreezes the invocation and runs it.

In Hour 5, "Adding Variables to the Calculator," you learned about `performSelector:withObject:`, which invokes methods using a selector as an argument. We can easily create a freeze-dried invocation by creating a class that stores a method's selector and arguments. Indeed, `NSInvocation` does just this:

```
- (void) setClearOnDigit:(BOOL)c
{
  NSMethodSignature* signature
        = [self methodSignatureForSelector:@selector(setClearOnDigitNoChange:)];
  NSInvocation* invocation
         = [NSInvocation invocationWithMethodSignature:signature];
  [invocation setTarget:self];
  [invocation setSelector:@selector(setClearOnDigitNoChange:)];
```

```
    [invocation setArgument:&clearOnDigit atIndex:2];
    [[UndoManager defaultManager] saveChange:invocation];

    [self setClearOnDigitNoChange:c];
}

- (void) setClearOnDigitNoChange:(BOOL)c
{ clearOnDigit = c; };
```

`setClearOnDigitNoChange:` does not add a change to the undo manager: The change would be added to the undo history, so that the next invocation of undo would undo the change rather than the previous user action.

Because methods can use primitive types (`int`, `float`, `struct`) as arguments as well as pointers, `setArgument:atIndex:` needs to know the type of each argument of the method. It uses this type information to copy the correct number of bytes (primitive types) or retain the object (objects). The selector, target, and arguments do not provide this type information. Instead, it is provided by `NSMethodSignature*`, which is passed as an argument to `invocationWithMethodSignature:`. Although you can create signatures by hand, usually you simply invoke `methodSignatureForSelector:` on the object that declares the selector.

The first two arguments of a method invocation are the target (set with `setTarget:`) and the selector (`setSelector`). Therefore, the index of `setArgument:atIndex:` starts at 2. For efficiency, by default, `NSInvocations` do not retain their arguments, but you can invoke `retainArguments` to retain them (and to copy C strings).

Dispensing with Change Inversion

Although `NSInvocation` replaces change objects' argument storage and `execute` methods, it does not provide any support for inverting a change. This is not a problem because the undo manager knows the circumstances in which `saveChange:` is invoked. There are three possibilities:

- `saveChange:` is not invoked by the undo manager.
- `saveChange:` is invoked by the undo manager's `redo` method.
- `saveChange:` is invoked by the undo manager's `undo` method.

Because the undo manager can distinguish these three cases, it can tailor `saveChange:`'s behavior for each case. When `saveChange:` is invoked by user actions, or by `redo`, it should save changes to the undo history as before. However, when it is invoked by undo, it should save changes to the redo history. Now, mutators can always save changes and we don't need an invert method.

```
- (void) saveChange:(id<Change>)change;
{ [undoChanges addObject:change];
  [redoChanges removeAllObjects]; }

- (void) undo;
{
  id<Change> change = [undoChanges lastObject];
  [change execute];
  [change invert];
  [redoChanges addObject:change];
  [undoChanges removeLastObject];
}
```

Aside: Proxies and NSInvocations

Using NSInvocation has reduced the amount of code we must write. However, we can still improve on this solution. To learn how, we'll take a small detour to learn about proxies.

Proxies are objects that stand in for other objects. Proxies are often used to represent objects that will be loaded lazily. They can also be used to transparently invoke methods on objects running in different processes (or on different computers). This is how Cocoa on the Mac implements distributed messaging. To stand in for other objects, proxies must implement every method of the object they impersonate. However, writing methods that simply invoke another method is error-prone and unproductive.

Recall that in Hour 4, "Making the Calculator Calculate," you learned that objc_msgSend iterates up the class object hierarchy looking for the method implementation corresponding to the selector. You learned that if it fails to find the method, an exception is raised. This is true but skips a step.

If objc_msgSend cannot find a method for a selector, it tries to create an NSInvocation and invoke the object's forwardInvocation: method. Creating an NSInvocation requires the object to implement methodSignatureForSelector:. If it doesn't, an exception is thrown. If it does, forwardInvocation: is invoked. Proxies can override methodSignatureForSelector: and forwardInvocation: to forward messages to the objects they stand in for (NSObject's forwardInvocation: simply throws an exception):

```
- (void) forwardInvocation:(NSInvocation*)invocation
{
  SEL sel = [invocation selector];
```

```
  if ([objectImStandingInFor respondsToSelector:sel])
    [invocation invokeWithTarget:objectImStandingInFor];
  else
    [self doesNotRecognizeSelector:sel];
}

- (NSMethodSignature*) methodSignatureForSelector:(SEL)sel
{
  NSMethodSignature* result = [super methodSignatureForSelector:sel];

  if (result == nil)
    result = [objectImStandingInFor methodSignatureForSelector:sel];

  return result;
}

- (BOOL) respondsToSelector:(SEL)sel
{ return (    [super respondsToSelector:sel]
           || [objectImStandingInFor respondsToSelector:sel]); };
```

Simplifying NSInvocation Creation

The undo manager can use `forwardInvocation:` to reduce the amount of code needed to create `NSInvocations`: Instead of building an `NSInvocation`, we can simply invoke a nonexistent method of the undo manager, and `forwardInvocation:` will save the invocation it receives to the history. Because the method is invoked on the undo manager rather than the object that supports the method, we must tell the undo manager which object will be the receiver. `prepareWithInvocationTarget:` specifies the receiver.

Now `setClearOnDigit:` is reduced to the following:

```
- (void) setClearOnDigit:(BOOL)c
{
  [[[UndoManager defaultManager]
                 prepareWithInvocationTarget:self]
                 setClearOnDigit:clearOnDigit];

  clearOnDigit = c;
};
```

UndoManager's `forwardInvocation:` and `prepareWithInvocationTarget` are as follows:

```
- (UndoManager*) prepareWithInvocationTarget:(id)t
{
  target = t;
  return self;
};

- (void) forwardInvocation:(NSInvocation*)invocation
{
  [invocation setTarget:target];
  [self saveChange:invocation];
}
```

Notice that `target` is not retained. This prevents retain cycles because undo managers are often owned (directly or indirectly) by their targets.

An Elegant Final Design

Five separate refinements went into the final design of `UndoManager` to provide the simplest possible undo architecture: Methods only need invoke their inverse on `NSUndoManager`! Not only could it not be any easier, but it was done without any simplifying assumptions or requiring you to write change classes. Cocoa Touch's `NSUndoManager` class resembles the `UndoManager` described above. However, it replaces the class `defaultManager` method with an `undoManager` instance method. The next section explains why.

Using NSUndoManager

Using `NSUndoManager` requires understanding the context in which it is used. There are two aspects: user experience and the technical details of integrating it into your application.

Providing an Intuitive Experience for the User

Although you now have a nice tool, you must use it judiciously to create a pleasant user experience. This is more difficult than it sounds, and explains why Apple waited until the 3.0 SDK to provide undo functionality.

Associating an NSUndoManager with Views and View Controllers

On the iPhone, users only see one screen of information at a time. Users can change something, switch screens, and then invoke undo. It would be confusing if undo undid the last thing that was done chronologically as the data that was last changed is no longer displayed. For instance, consider a tab bar application. Each tab shows different information. Users expect undo to undo the last change made on the tab they are looking at, not the last change made anywhere in the application.

Every `UIResponder` has an `undoManager` property. When `UIResponder` receives an undo message, it searches up the view hierarchy until it finds the first `UIResponder` that returns a non-`nil` `undoManager`. It uses this undo manager for all undo/redo operations. As your view controllers create and manage views, they are a good place to also provide an undo manager. To return an undo manager, the view controller must become a first responder when its view appears and resign being first responder when its view disappears.

```
- (BOOL) canBecomeFirstResponder { return YES; }

- (void) viewDidAppear:(BOOL) animated
{ [super viewDidAppear:animated]; [self becomeFirstResponder]; }

- (void) viewWillDisappear:(BOOL) animated
{ [super viewWillDisappear:animated]; [self resignFirstResponder]; }
```

Undo Groups

Now consider editing a table. When users add a row to the table, a new screen is shown to let them edit the details. On the new screen, undo should not undo the last action performed on the table, but only what was done on the visible page. Once the users return to the main page, undo should undo the entire row addition, rather than each change the user made to the user details.

One way of achieving this functionality would be for the detail editing view controller to update two undo managers: its own and its parent table view controller's undo manager. Changes would be added individually to the detail editing view controller's undo manager, as usual. However, they would be combined into a single change for the table's view controller's undo manager. Although this would work, it does not scale well if you add more view controllers.

A better solution is to use undo groups. From the outside, an undo group looks like a single change. From the inside, the changes it contains look like individual changes. In this manner, the table view controller and the detail editing view controller use the same undo manager. However, the detail editing view controller creates a new undo group in `viewDidAppear:`, which it closes in `viewDidDisappear`. While the group is open, undo will only apply to the contents of the group, but once it is closed, the entire group appears to be a single change: The editing details view controller can only undo the changes it made, but once it is dismissed, the table view controller can undo its entire change in one step.

Undo groups scale to any number of view controllers: The undo history is no longer a stack of changes, but a tree of changes.

Providing Undo Names

When users shake their iPhones, an alert panel appears asking them whether they want to undo the last change or redo the last undone change. To help users remember the change they are undoing or redoing, you can specify the name of each action with `setActionName:`.

For instance, to change `pressClear:` to tell its undo manager instance that the last operation performed was pressing Clear, add an invocation to `setActionName:` to `pressClear:` as shown in the following code:

```
[undoManager setActionName:@"Press Clear"];
```

Integrating `NSUndoManager` into Your Application

Because pre-iPhoneOS 3.0 applications did not provide undo capability, it is off by default. To enable it, your application must set `UIApplication`'s `applicationSupportsShakeToEdit` property. This is usually done in `applicationDidFinishLaunching:`.

```
[UIApplication sharedApplication].applicationSupportsShakeToEdit = YES;
```

To limit the amount of memory used by an undo manager, invoke its `setLevelsOfUndo:` method with a number of undo levels as argument. Setting this value to zero creates an unlimited undo stack.

`NSUndoManager` provides a number of notifications to let observers keep track of its state which follow a similar pattern to Key-Value Observing notifications. Use these notifications to postpone updating the display until an undo change has completed.

To prevent retain cycles, `NSUndoManager` does not retain the targets of undo operations. If you delete a target object, be sure to remove it from any undo managers in which it might appear: Invoke `[`*`um`*` removeAllActionsWithTarget:self]` in the target's `dealloc` method, where *um* is the undo manager.

Summary

`NSUndoManager` provides a simple but powerful way of adding undo and redo functionality to your applications. Instead of saving snapshots of program state, `NSUndoManager` provides a way to save freeze-dried method invocations that will reverse user initiated state changes. By using a run loop observer to group model changes it simplifies your application's undo support code. In this hour you learned how it minimizes the amount of code you must write to implement undo functionality.

Q&A

Q. ***Do any other tools use similar ideas as*** `NSUndoManager`***?***

A. Yes, the `OCMock` framework available at http://www.mulle-kybernetik.com creates mock objects in the same way. Mock objects are used for testing code. For instance, you can create a mock network connection object to test your client when it encounters different server responses.

Q. ***Can I save the undo and redo stacks?***

A. `NSUndoManager` provides no means to save the undo and redo stacks.

Workshop

The Workshop consists of quiz questions and answers to help you solidify your understanding of the material covered in this hour. You should try to answer the questions before checking the answers.

Quiz Questions

1. How does Cocoa Touch implement undo functionality?
2. What must view controllers do to provide an undo manager?
3. What must you set to enable undo capability in your applications?

Quiz Answers

1. Cocoa Touch implements undo functionality by freezing method invocations that it can replay to undo or redo changes.
2. The view controllers must be willing to become first responders when their view is visible to provide an undo manager.
3. You must set the application's `applicationSupportsShakeToEdit` property to `YES` to enable undo capability.

Exercise

- Add undo/redo behavior to the calculator. Because the `Expression` class code is complex, build a test harness that checks undo works by randomly updating expressions, and verifying that undo restores expressions to their previous state. Use `beginUndoGrouping` and `endUndoGrouping` to demarcate each undo step.

HOUR 14

Accessing the Network

What You'll Learn in This Hour:

- How networks work
- How the Web works
- Using Cocoa Touch to access the Web
- Making the Twitter application deal with errors

The iPhone is a highly connected mobile device, providing users with access to any information available on the Internet. This hour shows you how to build applications that access the Internet. The iPhone supports wired and wireless networking via USB, Wi-Fi, and the telephone network. Because networks consist of many computers linked by fallible physical connections, your network code must be robust in the face of errors or unexpected latencies. By understanding how networks work, you can devise better error-handling strategies. You'll also learn how to easily access web servers, by using Cocoa Touch's HTTP connection APIs.

How Networks Work

To use the network effectively, you need to understand how networks work. Unlike other resources like memory and files, network access is not simple, not error free, and not instantaneous.

There are many possible causes of error. A short list includes the following: Your iPhone might not be connected to the network; the network might be suffering a temporary disruption; the server might be switched off; you might not have access to the resource you are requesting; or DNS might be returning the wrong Internet address.

Latency is also unpredictable: Simply because you received a response to your last request quickly does not mean the next one will be received quickly.

Routing Packets

Networks follow a similar design to the post office: Computers talk to each other in packets, the analog to letters. Each letter consists of an envelope and a message. The envelope says where the message came from and where it's going. Similarly, packets consist of layers. The outermost layers say where the packet is going and where it came from, whereas the innermost layers contain the message.

After you've dropped your letter off in a postbox, a mailman comes and takes it to a sorting center. There the address is read, and the letter is placed in a bin to be sent to the next sorting center. A mailman in Germany does not need to know the precise location of a small town in Japan. It is sufficient to know the letter should be sent to the International sorting center. Then, it is delivered to another sorting center. This happens a number of times. Each time, the letter is closer to its destination. The closer to the destination, the more of the address becomes important. Finally, it is delivered to its recipient. At each step, the letter can be lost or mangled.

Packets in a network follow the same process. They are delivered to a router, which forwards them to the next closest router to the destination. For instance, the router for your home network must only decide whether a packet goes to your Internet service provider (ISP), or to a computer in your house. At each step along the way, the packet can be lost or mangled. For instance, your neighbor's cordless phone can interfere with your iPhone's Wi-Fi connection, or a tractor might dig up a fiber-optic cable.

Routers constantly measure their distance apart. The distance to another router is measured as the round-trip time of a ping packet to that router and back. This continually updated notion of distance guarantees that packets are routed around congestion, but means that successive packets can take different routes to the same destination. Thus, packets can arrive in a different order than they were sent: They arrive out of order.

Packet Layers

Packets are built of many layers, like onions. Each layer uses the layers below to transmit its message to another device that can understand its layer's protocol. The advantage of this design is that the lowest layers need only know enough to correctly forward the message to the next recipient, and do not need to know anything about its content, or the wider world.

Layer 1: Physical Layer

Letters are carried by people, vans, trains, and airplanes to reach their destination. In the same way, a packet from your iPhone will travel over different kinds of network (USB, Wi-Fi, Ethernet, 3G, and so on) to reach its destination. This is called the Physical layer, and is implemented by hardware.

For instance, 10BASE-T Ethernet uses pairs of wires to send signals. If the current is flowing one way, a zero is transmitted; if it flows the other way, a one is transmitted. Ethernet's Physical layer specifies the precise series of ones and zeroes required to transmit a packet from one network interface to another. Most Physical layers limit packet length to minimize the probability of packet corruption while increasing the overall throughput.

At this level, there are no addresses. Messages are sent to the other end of the wire, just like letters are delivered to the next airport.

Layer 2: Data Link Layer

The Data Link layer provides a destination address for each packet and basic error checking.

Addresses specify the computer within a local network to which a message should be forwarded. In the letter example, this corresponds to the airport code used to specify a letter's destination airport. This airport code only makes sense as an address within the airport network. It would not make sense to use on a train network. Devices working at this level do not need to know anything about other networks.

Simple error checking is achieved by hashing the data in such a way that if one or more bits of the message were flipped, the hash would not match. These hashes are called cyclic redundancy checks and are sent with the packet so that its recipient can verify that it was correctly transmitted. For instance, recipients can request another copy when they receive a faulty copy.

Did you Know?

> Each layer may consist of other layers. For instance, Internet connectivity over the 3G network requires incoming packets to be routed to the cell phone tower that is closest to your phone. As you travel around, the closest cell phone tower changes. Sublayers of layers 1 and 2 are responsible for making this work.

Layer 3: Network Layer

The Network layer enables packets to be transmitted across multiple networks to reach their destination. To do this, it specifies network-independent addresses. The Internet Protocol (IP) is a Layer 3 protocol. It assigns an IP address to each computer on the Internet. In the letter example, trains, vans, and airplanes correspond to different networks. It is the job of routers (forklift trucks) to move packets from one network to another.

Because Data Link layers support different length packets, the Network layer also splits packets up into fragments that can be transmitted across the Data Link layer. The Network layer at the destination machine is responsible for reassembling these fragments into the original packets.

Layer 4: Transport Layer

The Transport layer sends packets to the correct application running on each computer. Although there are other Transport layers, I'll concentrate on the User Datagram Protocol (UDP) and Transmission Control Protocol (TCP) protocols of TCP/IP (Transmission Control Protocol/Internet Protocol).

Each application can request to listen to a port. If the port is available, the operating system accepts the request and forwards each message to the port to the application. Ports can only be used by a single application. This is similar to the front-desk person at a company who receives the mail and places it in individual employee mailboxes. Ports are identified by number. Specific port numbers are usually associated with a service. For instance, to display a page on my website, ansemond.com, your web browser sends a page request to whichever application on ansemond.com currently owns port 80.

The Transport layer merges the outgoing packets into a single stream to send over the network connection. For instance, ansemond.com sends responses to every web browser that is accessing it over the same wire.

Connection-oriented protocols also require the Transport layer to be responsible for making sure that messages are sent and received correctly. This is similar to tasking a secretary with sending an important fax as many times as it takes until it is received by the other party. Connection-oriented protocols at the Network layer are responsible for opening, maintaining, and closing connections, much like the telephone switchboard operators of the early twentieth century.

The two main Transport layers for the Internet are UDP and TCP. UDP is a connectionless protocol: No connection is created; messages are simply sent to their destination, which might or might not receive them. Packets will be received out of order. TCP is a connection-oriented protocol, which sends additional messages to guarantee packets arrive in order. TCP also provides a control-flow mechanism to ensure that neither the client nor the server send so much data as to overwhelm the other. Although TCP is much easier to use, lost packets result in transmission delays. Streaming video and audio services often use UDP because users prefer missing a little bit of the stream to waiting for the missing content.

UDP and TCP are accessed programmatically using the UNIX system calls. As mentioned in Hour 7, "Understanding How Events Are Processed," UNIX treats everything as a file. Sockets are a generalization of the file concept used for interprocess communication. The `socket()` system call creates a socket within a domain: A socket will act like a file in that it can be read or written. One such domain is the TCP/IP domain, used to communicate with the Internet.

Servers ask the OS to associate a socket with a port using the `bind()` system call, and then call `listen()` to wait for a client to connect to them. Clients call `connect()` to create a connection to the server. Once a server hears from the client, it `accept()`s the client's connection. `accept()` creates a new socket on the server, which is used to communicate with the client: The server sends the port number of the new socket to the client's `connect()`. This new socket is associated with a file descriptor, which the server can read (or write) to receive information from (or send information to) the client. The client's `connect()` creates a find handle for the client to read and write to communicate with the server. If the client does not care which port its socket is assigned, it does not need to call `bind()` before calling `connect()`.

Because `accept()` creates a new connection for each client, a single server can respond to many clients. Because the Transport layer only queues up a limited number of connections per port, new connections must be `accepted` relatively quickly. For this reason, web servers are often multithreaded, using different threads to manage active connections. However, the fastest web servers are single threaded (`lighttpd` and `nginx`), using one process per CPU. They use the equivalent of a run loop to manage pending connections.

Because sockets are not specific to Cocoa Touch, this book does not discuss them further.

Layers Beyond Layer 4

The Internet Protocol does not define layers beyond 4. However, the layering idea proves remarkably useful, and many Internet protocols use it. Most of the standard applications you use work at this level. Your email is sent and received using SMTP, POP, and IMAP protocols. You browse the web using the HTTP protocol. You might send files to co-workers using the FTP protocol, or log in to remote servers using SSH. Each of these protocols is incompatible with the others and works on very different principles, but they all use TCP.

Cocoa's `NSURL` classes provide support for the HTTP protocol, which is used by most services on the Internet. The second part of this hour discusses HTTP in more detail.

Whereas physical packet layers must be implemented in hardware, other layers can be implemented either in hardware or in software. At one extreme, software modems provided cheap Internet access in the 1990s: The sounds to send over the telephone wires (a Physical layer detail) were generated by software. At the other extreme, many governments mandate deep-packet inspection tools to monitor the Internet traffic passing through their country. Because so much information flows through the Internet, decoding packet layers in software is too slow: Hardware decodes the packet layers.

Network Irregularities

There are a few more wrinkles to mention because you'll encounter them when developing network code: firewalls, dynamic addresses, Network Address Translation, and HTTP proxy servers.

Firewalls

Most desktop computers run a number of servers. For instance, if you can access files on another computer, it is running a server. Flaws in software make it vulnerable to attack, and because unauthorized computer access can be lucrative for criminals, many companies and individuals install firewalls between their local network and the Internet. Firewalls only allow packets that have specified source addresses, source ports, destination addresses, and destination ports to flow through them.

Because the HTTP protocol is quite inflexible, there are many custom protocols. However, firewalls often block non-HTTP packets, creating unhappy users. For compatibility, it is best to use HTTP wherever possible. For instance, iPhoneOS 3.0 introduced HTTP live streaming, which uses simple HTTP file transfer for video streaming.

Dynamic Addresses

In the early 1990s, adding a computer to a network required manually assigning it an address on the local network. Today, network devices are automatically assigned an address when they connect to a network. Your iPhone has up to three different addresses: a USB address, a Wi-Fi address, and a cell phone address, which are all assigned dynamically. Your code should not assume that your iPhone's Internet address will not change.

Network Address Translation

Most iPhones are not directly connected to the Internet. Instead, they are connected to a local network. Their IP addresses are local and inaccessible from the Internet.

The local network is connected to the Internet by a router, which has an address accessible from the Internet.

When a computer on the local network opens a connection to a server on the Internet, the router receives the packet. Because local network addresses are invisible to computers on the Internet, it replaces the packet's source address with its own address: The server will send response packets to it. However, when it receives a response, it needs to know which computer on the local network the response should be sent to. To solve this problem, routers assign a unique identifier to each source address and port tuple. When the router receives a packet from the local network, destined to the Internet, it changes the source port of packets to the appropriate unique identifier. Because the server sends its responses back to the packet's source (port and address), the router can distinguish the computer on the local network to whom it must forward the response: It simply forwards all messages received on a port to the corresponding local network address and port.

Some routers allow all accesses to an IP address to be forwarded to a single machine on the local network, but this must be configured at the router. In general, you cannot expect to send information to your iPhone. For instance, Apple's "push notification" works by requiring the iPhone to open a persistent connection to a server. When the server has new information to deliver, it sends it to the client via that persistent connection.

HTTP Proxy Servers

HTTP proxy servers cache commonly accessed web content to reduce latency and bandwidth usage. Although some proxies are invisible and function transparently, others must be set up manually. Proxies that must be set up manually also require HTTP requests to be crafted differently.

Latency and Errors

Latency is a fundamental aspect of networking: It takes time to receive data from the server. Most programs assume they can access resources synchronously. For instance, programs usually access files synchronously: The `read()` system call blocks (does not return) until the data has been read from the file. Network access requires a significantly different design: A request is dispatched to the server, and the program continues running until a response is received. Once the response is received, an asynchronous handler is invoked to process it. Latency is dependent on bandwidth and distance to the server.

Errors are the other fundamental aspect of networking. At any time, packets might be lost, the network might go down, or the target server might suffer an error or be overloaded. Most errors are only detected because an expected response was not received within a preset time. The Twitter application you've written has been very cavalier about error handling. If it encounters a network error, it is unable to download any more tweets and needs to be restarted. You will fix this in this hour.

Did you Know?

> Trey Harris was a system administrator on a university campus, when the head of the Statistics department reported a very strange error: Nobody in his department could send email more than 520 miles away. Trey was shocked—email doesn't work that way. But the Statistics department had the data to back up their claim. The report was correct. A contractor had upgraded the server's operating system, but had downgraded the email server. The older email sever, not finding a suitable network timeout, defaulted the timeout to zero. In practice, a zero timeout would take 3 milliseconds to be aborted. Electricity travels approximately 550 miles in 3 milliseconds.

How the Web Works

The World Wide Web (WWW) is the Internet's killer application. I remember looking at the first browser back in 1993, and wondering whether it would take off. PostScript did a much better job of rendering content, and Gopher provided much more content. A few years and a good search engine (web crawler) made the difference.

The web is made from three main ingredients: uniform resource locators (URLs), Hypertext Transfer Protocol (HTTP), and Hypertext Markup Language (HTML). URLs provide a unique address for each resource. Resources are data. The HTTP protocol is the protocol used to talk to web servers. HTML specifies how a page should be rendered on the screen and is briefly discussed in Hour 15, "Showing a Web Page."

URLs

Uniform resource locators provide a unique path to resources. Resources are data. They follow this pattern:

```
scheme://user:password@host:port/url_path;params?query#fragment
```

This can be broken down as follows:

- The `scheme` specifies the protocol to use. The most common protocols are `http`, `https`, `ftp`, and `file`.
- The `user` and `password` specify the username and password to use for authentication on password-protected servers.

- The `host` is the name of the server with the resource. The name is converted to an IP address using DNS lookup. (DNS stands for domain name service and is another protocol that uses UDP and TCP.)
- The `port` specifies the TCP port to connect to for the service. Each protocol has a default port (80 for `http`, 443 for `https`), but you can run multiple web servers on the same machine by using a different port for each.
- The `url_path` specifies the location on the server of the resource you want to download or access.

Notice that in the scheme, the characters :/@;?# have a special meaning. In fact, the characters !*'();:@&=+$,/?%#[] are all reserved by URLs for special purposes. Any character other than the alphanumerical characters (A–Z, a–z, 0–9) and -_.~ must be **percent-encoded**: They are replaced by a percent character and their ASCII value (a two-digit hexadecimal number). For instance, a space is encoded as %20. Invoke `NSString`'s `stringByAddingPercentEscapesUsingEncoding:` method to perform this encoding.

The HTTP Protocol

Browsers communicate with web servers using the HTTP protocol: a text based protocol layered over a TCP/IP connection. This section describes the protocol in detail.

Requesting Data from the Server

The HTTP client sends requests for data to the server. The server responds with the requested data. Early versions of the HTTP protocol opened a new TCP connection for each requested resource. However, once pictures were added to web pages, creating a new TCP connection for each resource proved slow.

The HTTP/1.1 protocol added support for persistent connections: The client can request multiple resources over the same connection. HTTP/1.1 also added pipelining: The client does not need to wait for a requested resource to arrive before requesting another one. Up to eight requests can be pipelined. These two techniques help the server return data faster. TCP/IP only supports 65,536 ports per Internet address. Using fewer sockets means more clients can be served. Pipelining means the server does not need to wait for a new connection before returning the relevant data, improving cacheability and reducing disk access. (Think of a news article with a picture. If the client requested the news article, a request for the picture will follow.)

HTTP also supports multiple simultaneous connections. Because there are only 65,536 ports per server, server operators prefer you to use only two connections at a time. If your network is not bandwidth limited, you can use more connections. However, remember that creating new connections is slower than pipelining. To improve their loading times, many web pages load data from multiple servers. For instance, static images can be placed on different servers from text content, thereby increasing the effective number of simultaneous connections.

Request Format

Requests are sent to the server. They use a plain text format.

The first line of a request specifies the request: the method, the method's uniform resource identifier (URI), and the protocol used for the request. Usually, the URI is either an absolute URL path with query and fragment (when sending a request to a server) or a URL (when sending the request to a proxy server).

Headers follow. The headers form a dictionary of properties, associating a value with each key. For instance, the `Host` key specifies the host from which the data is accessed. Similarly, in HTTP/1.1, requests are considered pipelined by default. To close a connection once the request completes, the `Connection` header is assigned the value `close`. Other properties include cacheability, cookie state, the referring page, and the user agent string of the client.

Finally, the request may include a message body. The message body contains the data to send to the server, and must be accompanied by the `Content-Length` header to specify its length. Its encoding is specified by `Content-Type` and `Transfer-Encoding` headers.

Request Methods

You can request a resource from a server, or you can upload data to a server.

The GET and HEAD methods are used to request data from the server. The response will include status and headers (for both HEAD and GET) and the requested data (for GET). For instance, clients can use HEAD to decide whether to download a resource. GET and HEAD do not use message bodies.

For instance, to get `index.html` on `slashdot.org`, the following request is made:

```
GET /index.html HTTP/1.1
Host:slashdot.org
```

You can actually test this yourself using the `telnet` utility. Open the `Terminal.app` application, and type the following:

```
telnet slashdot.org 80
GET /index.html HTTP/1.1
Host:slashdot.org

HTTP/1.1 200 OK
Server: Apache/1.3.41 (Unix) mod_perl/1.31-rc4
...
```

(You must click return twice after the `Host:` line.) The server responds with `HTTP/1.1 200 OK`, a number of headers and the page.

The `POST` and `PUT` methods are used to upload data to the server. `POST` is used to send data to the server for processing (such as the contents of a web form you filled out), whereas `PUT` is used to upload a file. Both these methods have a message body.

Responses

Responses contain a status, headers, and possibly data.

The status specifies whether the request was successful, requires further action, or failed. The common codes are as follows:

- `200 OK`: The request was successful.
- `301 Moved Permanently`: Use the `URL` specified in the `Location` header for all future access. Redirect.
- `302 Found`: The resource was temporarily moved to the `Location` specified in the header. Ask the user whether to redirect.
- `401 Unauthorized`: The client has not specified correct credentials in the `WWW-Authenticate` header to access the resource.
- `403 Forbidden`: The client may not access that resource.
- `404 Not Found`: There is no such resource.
- `503 Service Unavailable`: The server is down.

To redirect means to issue the request again, sending it to the specified `Location`.

Response headers contain information about the response such as the message, whether the server will close the connection after completing the request (`Connection`), the message's date, cacheability, and so on.

The message body is simply the requested data. Its length is defined by the `Content-Length` header, and its encoding is specified by the `Content-Type` header.

Cookies

Because many clients may share an IP address, and have multiple open connections, the server does not know the client's state. However, servers wanted to provide services such as shopping baskets that track users. Cookies solved the problem.

The client associates each server with a dictionary of cookies. The cookies are key-value pairs. The values must be 4Kb or smaller. Cookies may be qualified by an expiration date, a path, and a domain, which specify which pages on a server (or set of servers) may receive the cookie.

When the client makes a request from the server, it includes a `Cookie` header for each cookie, specifying the cookie's name and value. The server can then use this cookie to display the appropriate data. The server sets a cookie on the client either using a JavaScript script or by adding a `Set-Value` header to a response.

Caching

Web pages are large, around half a megabyte each. To reduce network traffic, HTTP uses caching:

- If the data is not in the cache, it is fetched from the network.
- If the data is in the cache, and its expiry date is in the future, or it was fetched recently and was modified a long time ago, the data from the cache is used.
- Otherwise, a request is made to the server to check whether the data is still valid, by sending the date (or etag) of the cached resource. If the server has a newer copy of the page, it can return it. Otherwise, it tells the client to use its cached page by returning the `304 Not Modified` status. Section 13 of "RFC 2616" specifies these rules in more detail.

By default, resources are cached. However, they are not cached if they were obtained using authentication, Hypertext Transfer Protocol Secure (HTTPS), or if the server said not to cache them.

Caching can be important on the iPhone because Apple bans applications that transfer too much data over the phone network.

HTTPS

Every request and response is sent over the network in plain text, which makes the HTTP traffic particularly easy to snoop on. HTTPS solves this problem by encrypting the TCP traffic to and from the server.

Another problem is that HTTP assumes it is talking to the right server, and not an impostor. HTTPS solves this problem by using digital certificates: The server knows how to sign messages with its private key. The client can verify that the server is who it says it is by checking the server's signature using the server's public key. The client obtains the server's public key from a certificate authority. The client verifies that the certificate authority is who it says it is in the same way: It contains the major certificate authorities' public keys.

Using Cocoa Touch to Access the Web

You'll be glad to hear that Cocoa Touch provides a lot of support for accessing the network using HTTP. It manages the TCP protocol, the HTTP protocol, pipelining, multiple connections, caching, and cookie handling for you. You just need to know what to ask it to do. Its `NSURL` class simplifies manipulating URLs. Its `NSURLRequest` class represents a request you can send to the server. The `NSURLConnection` class sends requests to the server and gathers the responses.

Using `NSURL`

The `NSURL` class constructs and parses URLs. `NSURL`s are either created directly from a string (`initWithString:`); created from a scheme, host, and path (`initWithScheme:host:path:`); created from a path relative to an existing URL (`initWithString:relativeToURL:`); or created from a local file path (`initFileURLWithPath` and `initFileURLWithPath:isDirectory:`). For convenience, these methods have autoreleased variants.

The `NSURL` class parses the resulting URL, letting you know its `scheme`, `user`, `password`, `host`, `port`, `path`, `parameterString`, `query`, and `fragment`. `NSURL` works fine for getting data, but URLs that use parameter strings, queries, and fragments can confuse its parser.

`NSURL` keeps track of the base URL and the relative path. For instance, if the base URL is `http://ansemond.com/iphone/tetratile.html` and the relative path is `../../mac/find_it_keep_it.html`, it will remember both parts. Figure 14.1 shows the results for `absoluteString`, `absoluteURL`, `baseURL`, `relativePath`, `relativeString`, and `resourceSpecifier` for these two URLs.

FIGURE 14.1
NSURL results

	URL: http://www.ansemond.com/iphone/tetratile.html relativePath: nil	URL: http://www.ansemond.com/iphone/tetratile.html relativePath: ../../mac/find_it_keep_it.html
absoluteString	http://www.ansemond.com/iphone/tetratile.html	http://www.ansemond.com/mac/find_it_keep_it.html
absoluteURL	http://www.ansemond.com/iphone/tetratile.html	http://www.ansemond.com/mac/find_it_keep_it.html
baseURL	nil	http://www.ansemond.com/iphone/tetratile.html
relativePath	/iphone/tetratile.html	../mac/find_it_keep_it.html
relativeString	http://www.ansemond.com/iphone/tetratile.html	../mac/find_it_keep_it.html
resourceSpecifier	//www.ansemond.com/iphone/tetratile.html	../mac/find_it_keep_it.html

Using `NSURLRequest` and `NSMutableURLRequest`

The `NSURLRequest` class lets you build the HTTP request to send to the server. `initWithURL:cachePolicy:timeoutInterval:` creates a `GET` request with the specified URL. The timeout interval specifies how long the client should wait after sending the request without receiving a response from the server before reporting an error.

HTTP data is often cached to reduce network traffic. The following three sources for each resource are queried in order: the local cache on the iPhone, zero or more caching proxies (or caching gateways) on the network between the iPhone and the server, and the server. If a source can provide the data, it does so; otherwise, it forwards the request to the next source. The iPhone's local cache contains a cache of resources that were recently loaded by the iPhone. Caching proxies (or gateways) are caches placed by network providers between your iPhone and the target server to reduce latency.

The cache policy specifies the possible sources of the response data. Figure 14.2 shows the caching options. In the table, `YES` means return the data if it is available; otherwise, pass the request on to the next source if there is one, or fail. `NO` means never use the local data, and forward the request. `IF VALID` means use the HTTP caching rules discussed in the previous section to determine whether the resource is valid, if possible without asking the server. `IF REVALIDATED` means always revalidate any locally cached data. Because `NSURLRequestReloadIgnoringCacheData` is a synonym for `NSURLRequestReloadIgnoringLocalCacheData`, I did not include it in Figure 14.2.

FIGURE 14.2
Caching options

	Local Cache	Internet Cache	Server
NSURLRequestUseProtocolCachePolicy	IF VALID	IF VALID	YES
NSURLRequestReloadIgnoringLocalCacheData	NO	IF VALID	YES
NSURLRequestReloadIgnoringLocalAndRemoteCacheData	NO	NO	YES
NSURLRequestReturnCacheDataElseLoad	YES	IF VALID	YES
NSURLRequestReturnCacheDataDontLoad	YES	NO	NO
NSURLRequestReloadRevalidatingCacheData	IF REVALIDATED	IF VALID	YES

HTTPMethod returns the HTTP method. To change it from the default GET, use setHTTPMethod:.

allHTTPHeaderFields and valueForHTTPHeaderField: return header values. Use setValue:forHTTPHeaderField:, addValue:forHTTPHeaderField:, and setAllHTTPHeaderFields: to change the headers. If you set HTTPShouldHandleCookies to NO using setHTTPShouldHandleCookies, you can create your own cookie headers. Otherwise, NSURLRequest will use the cookie store shared with all other applications to obtain cookie values. It uses the requestURL, or if set, the mainDocumentURL (as set by setMainDocumentURL:) to determine the cookies to send with the request.

HTTPBody returns the HTTP message body. The default GET request has no body. To create one, use setHTTPBody: (or setHTTPBodyStream:).

To create a URL request, create an NSMutableRequest that provides all the setting methods I just enumerated. To send the request to the server, create an NSURLConnection from it. NSURLConnection creates an immutable copy of the request because once a request is on its way to the server, it cannot be changed.

For instance, to send a tweet from user with password, create a POST request. The body of the POST request sets the key status to the text of the tweet.

```
// Create url http://user:password@twitter.com/statuses/update.xml

user     = [user stringByAddingPercentEscapesUsingEncoding:NSUTF8StringEncoding];
password
    = [password stringByAddingPercentEscapesUsingEncoding:NSUTF8StringEncoding];

NSString* urlString
   = [NSString stringWithFormat:@"http://%@:%@@twitter.com/statuses/update.xml",
                               user, password];
NSURL* url = [NSURL URLWithString:urlString];

// Create the Body

tweet  = [tweet stringByAddingPercentEscapesUsingEncoding:NSUTF8StringEncoding];
NSString *body = [NSString stringWithFormat:@"status=%@", tweet];

// Create POST request

NSMutableURLRequest *request = [NSMutableURLRequest requestWithURL:url];
[request setHTTPMethod: @"POST"];
[request setHTTPBody:[body dataUsingEncoding:NSUTF8StringEncoding]];
[request           setValue:@"application/x-www-form-urlencoded"
        forHTTPHeaderField:@"Content-Type"];
```

Using NSURLConnection

NSURLConnection sends the request to the server and waits for the response. It informs a delegate about its progress receiving the server's response. The delegate is responsible for collecting the received data into a buffer and processing it. NSURLConnection uses secondary threads to communicate with the server, but invokes the delegate methods on the thread that created the connection. To do this, delegate methods are invoked from the run loop, which was explained in Hour 7: Because delegate methods are invoked from the run loop, your code must either return to the run loop or use enough one-shot run loop invocations.

NSURLConnection provides limited support for the FTP protocol. However, this discussion of NSURLConnection focuses on HTTP because most applications use HTTP. If you need full FTP support, read Apple's Core Foundation's FTP stream documentation (keyword: CFFTPStream).

Sending a Request

To send a request, simply create an NSURLConnection using initWithRequest:delegate:. The *request* is an NSURLRequest. The *delegate* is an object you create to receive the server's responses. By default, connections are started as soon as they are created.

However, you can use initWithRequest:delegate:startImmediately: to create a connection without starting it. Invoke start to start the transfer. Do not invoke start on a connection that has already started—doing so can dereference a bad pointer and terminate your application with EXC_BAD_ACCESS.

Receiving the Response

As soon as the response status line and headers are received, the delegate method connection:didReceiveResponse: is invoked. connection is the NSURLConnection that caused the response. response is an NSURLHTTPResponse object (for HTTP requests, an NSURLResponse otherwise). It contains information derived from the response headers:

- allHeaderFields—A dictionary of the response's header fields.
- expectedContentLength—The content length as reported by the Content-Length header. This is NSURLResponseUnknownLength if the response had no Content-Length header.
- MIMEType—The MIME type of the content. Often, this is specified by the headers, but NSURLConnection corrects this field if it deems the server is wrong.
- statusCode—The response's status field.

- `suggestedFilename`—A filename based on the URL and `MIMEType` of the data.
- `textEncodingName`—Returns the IANA (Internet Assigned Numbers Authority) character set used to encode the text. This is explained in more detail in the following section, "Receiving Data."
- `URL`—Returns the request's URL.

Because HTTP uses responses to report errors, HTTP errors should be handled here. `NSURLHTTPResponse` provides a class convenience method, `localizedStringForStatusCode:`, which converts the status code into a baffling error message. For instance, status 406 is rendered as "unacceptable," which only makes sense if you understand RFC 2616.

```
- (void) connection:(NSURLConnection*)c didReceiveResponse:(NSURLResponse*)r
{

  if ([r respondsToSelector:@selector(statusCode)])
  {
    int statusCode = [((NSHTTPURLResponse*)r) statusCode];

    // HTTP errors have the status codes 4xx and 5xx

    if (statusCode >= 400)
    {
      [connection cancel];

      // Handle the error

      return;
    }
  }


  response = r;
  [self displayData:data]; // to display multipart/x-mixed-replace streams
  [data setLength:0];      // in case of multiple responses
}
```

Usually, a single response is received for each request. However, there are two cases where you'll receive multiple responses: `multipart/x-mixed-replace` streaming and redirections. Redirections are discussed further in the section "Redirections" later in this hour.

HTTP's `multipart/x-mixed-replace` header is used for simple streaming: The response contains multiple message bodies, each of which replaces the previous one. By displaying each message body as it is received, you can create an animation. To do this, your `connection:didReceiveResponse:` should display any previously received data and wipe clean the buffer it uses to receive new data. Because few connections require multipart header support, you will rarely implement `displayData:`.

Receiving Data

As soon as data is received, the `connection:didReceiveData:` delegate method is invoked. *data* contains the newly available data. Add it to your delegate's data buffer:

```
- (void) connection:(NSURLConnection*)c didReceiveData:(NSData*)d
{ [data appendData:d]; }
```

Processing data as it arrives adds complexity but can improve performance.

Completing the Request

As soon as the response is complete, the `connectionDidFinishLoading:` delegate method is called. Your delegate method should release the connection and its buffer:

```
- (void) connectionDidFinishLoading:(NSURLConnection*)c
{
  // Do something with the data

  [c    release];
  [data release]; data = nil;
};
```

If the data is text, you'll probably want to put it in an `NSString`. This is surprisingly complicated because Unicode was invented after the Internet. To specify the encoding of text returned by the server, the `Content-Type:` header specifies the character set as named by IANA. The Core Foundation function `CFStringConvertIANACharSetNameToEncoding` creates an `NSStringEncoding` from an IANA character set name. `NSString`'s `initWithData:encoding:` uses this encoding to convert the response's data into its internal Unicode format. For instance, the following header says the text uses the Latin4 encoding.

```
Content-Type: text/html; charset=ISO-8859-4
```

To convert the data to a string, you'd write the following:

```
NSString* ianaName = [response textEncodingName];
CFStringEncoding cfsEncoding
              = CFStringConvertIANACharSetNameToEncoding((CFStringRef)ianaName);
NSStringEncoding nssEncoding
              = CFStringConvertEncodingToNSStringEncoding(cfsEncoding);
NSString* string   = [[NSString alloc] initWithData:data encoding:nssEncoding];
```

TCP Errors

If a TCP error occurs (such as a timeout), the connection ends with an invocation of the `connection:didFailWithError:` delegate method. You must release the connection and data as you did in `connectionDidFinishLoading:`. The *error* message contains the URL of the failed connection in its `[error userInfo]` dictionary under the key `NSErrorFailingURLStringKey`.

```
- (void) connection:(NSURLConnection*)connection
   didFailWithError:(NSError*)error
{
  [connection release];
  [data       release]; data = nil;

  // Do something to inform the user or try again
}
```

Most applications simply display an error message if there is a problem. This is not a bad idea as Apple does not accept applications that fail silently. Another option is to try again. If you decide your application should try again silently, create the new connection after a delay (for example, a minute). Each time the connection fails, double the delay up to a preset limit. This is called exponential back off and it helps servers that have many pending requests service them all.

Redirections

If the connection receives a redirection response, the `connection:willSendRequest:redirectResponse:` delegate method is invoked. The *response* argument contains the server's response. *request* is a request generated by `NSURLConnection` that should satisfy the redirection request. Most of the time, you'll want to accept the redirection and return *request*. You can, however, choose to redirect elsewhere by returning a new `NSURLRequest`. Return `nil` if you want to receive the data that came with the redirection, or `cancel` the connection.

```
- (NSURLRequest*) connection:(NSURLConnection*)connection
             willSendRequest:(NSURLRequest*)    request
            redirectResponse:(NSURLResponse*)   redirectResponse
{ return request; }
```

Authentications and Caching

Because most applications don't need to support authentication or control the caching of responses, this section is brief.

If the server responds with a 401 status, the `connection:didReceiveAuthenticationChallenge:` delegate method is invoked. Use it to request authentication information from the user and create an

NSURLCredential containing the account details to give the challenge argument. Cocoa Touch can also store authentication details in NSURLCredentialStorage.

When NSURLConnection decides to cache responses locally, it will invoke the connection:willCacheResponse: delegate method. You can change the response that will be cached. For instance, if you return nil, the response will not be cached. Alternatively, you can change its cacheability so that it is not saved to disk.

Synchronous API

NSURLConnection also provides a synchronous application programming interface (API) to request data from a URL: sendSynchronousRequest:returningResponse:error: will block until it receives the response. Use it to prototype or debug a program. For instance, you can use it to check that a request works. Blocking any thread creates inflexibility you will almost always regret. To download data synchronously, write the following:

```
NSError*        error    = nil;
NSURLResponse* response = nil;
NSData* data = [NSURLConnection sendSynchronousRequest:request
                                  returningResponse:&response error:&error];
```

Making the Twitter Application Deal with Errors

Currently, your Twitter application fails on error. There are two steps to make it more robust. We can alert the user if the network is unavailable. We can also retry downloading data after an error.

Checking If the Network Is Available

Apple rejects applications that fail silently due to network errors. There is no point even trying to create a network request if the iPhone has no network connection. To find out whether the iPhone is connected to the network, call SCNetworkReachabilityCreateWithAddress with the IP address 0.0.0.0. This function belongs to a CoreFoundation like framework called the SystemConfiguration framework, which must be added to your project's set of frameworks.

```
#import <SystemConfiguration/SystemConfiguration.h>
#include <netinet/in.h>

BOOL networkAvailable()
{
  SCNetworkReachabilityFlags flags;
  struct sockaddr_in zeroAddress;
```

```
  zeroAddress.sin_family      = AF_INET;
  zeroAddress.sin_len         = sizeof(zeroAddress);
  zeroAddress.sin_addr.s_addr = 0;
  SCNetworkReachabilityRef reachability
    = SCNetworkReachabilityCreateWithAddress(NULL,
                                    (struct sockaddr*)&zeroAddress);
  BOOL hasFlags = SCNetworkReachabilityGetFlags(reachability, &flags);

  if (!hasFlags)
    return NO;

  int isReachable     = flags & kSCNetworkFlagsReachable;
  int needsConnection = flags & kSCNetworkFlagsConnectionRequired;
  return (isReachable && !needsConnection) ? YES : NO;
}
```

The `return` statement converts from C's Boolean convention (0 is false, anything else is true) to Objective-C's Boolean convention (`NO` is 0, and `YES` is 1). When this difference matters, the bugs it causes are extremely difficult to find.

To create an alert, create a `UIAlertView` and show it. Showing it adds it to the view hierarchy, which means it can be released. If you care when or how the alert is dismissed, you must create a delegate that obeys the `UIAlertViewDelegate` protocol. Add the following to `applicationDidFinishLaunching`:

```
if (!networkAvailable())
{
  UIAlertView* alert = [[UIAlertView alloc]
                              initWithTitle:@"No Internet connection"
                                    message:@"Try again later!"
                                   delegate:self
                          cancelButtonTitle:@"OK"
                          otherButtonTitles:nil];
  [alert show];
  [alert release];
  return;
}
```

We'll terminate the application when the user taps the button. Many people wonder how to exit applications cleanly because Apple does not document it: Apple's Human Interface Guidelines prohibit applications from exiting without the user clicking the Home button.

```
- (void)alertView:(UIAlertView*)a didDismissWithButtonIndex:(NSInteger)b
{ [[UIApplication sharedApplication] terminate]; }
```

Error Handling

`MGTwitterEngine` is a wrapper around `NSURLConnection`. If you look inside `MGTwitterEngine.m`, you'll see that `connection:didReceiveResponse:` checks the status and if it is greater than 400, invokes the `requestFailed:withError:` method.

The `User` class downloads two kinds of data: user images and tweets. `requestFailed:withError:` is called if either type of request fails. The example source code of this hour shows how to handle errors. `TwitterAppDelegate` forwards this error to `requestFailedWithError:forConnection:`.

`requestFailedWithError:forConnection:` starts a timer to retry reading data after `retryInterval` seconds. Each time there is an error, it doubles the `retryInterval` to reduce server load. It also shows an alert to inform the user of the failure.

```
- (void) requestFailedWithError:(NSError*)e forConnection:(NSString*)cID
{
  if (retryInterval > MAX_RETRY_INTERVAL)
    retryInterval = MAX_RETRY_INTERVAL;


  SEL s= [cID isEqualToString:imageConnectionID] ? @selector(sendImageRequest:)
                                                 : @selector(sendTweetRequest:);
  timer = [[NSTimer scheduledTimerWithTimeInterval:retryInterval target:self
                                    selector:s userInfo:nil repeats:NO]
retain];

  NSString*    title = [NSString stringWithFormat:@"Cannot reach Twitter"];
  NSString*   errMsg = [NSString stringWithFormat:@"%@\nWill retry in %g
minutes",
                                   [e localizedDescription],
retryInterval/60.0];
  UIAlertView* alert = [[UIAlertView alloc] initWithTitle:title message:errMsg
                        delegate:nil cancelButtonTitle:@"OK"
otherButtonTitles:nil];
  [alert show];
  retryInterval *= 2.0;
}
```

`imageReceived:forConnection:` and `statusesReceived:forConnection:` are called on success. They reset the `retryInterval`.

Summary

Networking protocols are inherently full of errors. Packets can be lost or discarded by the network at any time. Successive packets need not take the same path to the server and can arrive out of order. By using layered protocols, networks of different capabilities (Ethernet, Wi-Fi, 3G) are made interoperable, creating the Internet. Each layer introduces new capabilities and limitations. The main trade-off is robustness versus speed and latency. The HTTP protocol built upon TCP is now the most used protocol. `NSURLConnection` hides most of the complexities of the HTTP protocol behind an easy-to-use API. Nevertheless, as you'll learn in the second part of Hour 16, "Adding Application Preferences," writing transparent robust network clients is still quite difficult.

To learn more about TCP/IP and the HTTP protocols, read *The TCP/IP Guide* by Charles M. Kozierok and *TCP/IP Illustrated, Volume 1: The Protocols* by W. Richard Stevens.

Q&A

Q. ***Can I use*** `NSURLConnection`***s as keys to a dictionary so that I can add state to them so as to avoid using many delegates?***

A. No, the dictionary copies its keys, and `NSURLConnection` does not support copying. But you can use its pointer as a key (using `NSValue`'s `valueWithPointer:`).

Q. ***I don't like*** `NSURLConnection`***. What are my alternatives?***

A. `CFNetwork` may provide the functionality you need. Alternatively, `libcurl` is quite popular.

Q. ***Why do I see a memory leak in system libraries on the iPhone but not in the simulator?***

A. The implementation of Cocoa libraries may differ on the iPhone and the Mac, even if they share the same API.

Workshop

The Workshop consists of quiz questions and answers to help you solidify your understanding of the material covered in this hour. You should try to answer the questions before checking the answers.

Quiz Questions

1. What are the four main layers of TCP/IP and what do they do?
2. What is an HTTP cache?
3. What is a URL?
4. What is an HTTP request?

5. What are HTTP headers?

6. When you create an `NSURLConnection`, does it start immediately?

7. How does `NSURLConnection` handle caching?

Quiz Answers

1. The Physical layer transmits packets between two computers. The Data Link layer assigns unique addresses to computers so that they can form a network. The Network layer provides methods to create bridges between different networks, to create an internetwork (also known as an Internet). The Transport layer adds ports to packets so that a single computer can provide multiple network services. It also adds connection-oriented protocols, which automatically deal with many networking errors at the cost of losing a little speed.

2. An HTTP cache saves responses to HTTP requests to avoid reissuing the request to the server. This reduces latency.

3. A URL is a unique address for a resource (usually a file).

4. An HTTP request is a command sent to the server. Usually, the command is `GET` to return some data, but it can be `PUT` or `POST` to upload data.

5. HTTP headers are sideband information sent in the response. They specify such things as caching, cookies, or whether to close the connection.

6. Yes, unless explicitly told not to, `NSURLConnection`s send their request immediately.

7. `NSURLConnection` follows the caching behavior specified by its `NSURLRequest` argument (set by `initWithURL:cachePolicy:timeoutInterval:`'s `cachePolicy` argument).

Exercises

- **Simple:** Because of the 140-character limit, many people use URL shortening services in their tweets. Because the resulting URLs all follow the pattern http://service.com/rubbish, it is hard to know where a page links. For each tweet, find the URLs (look for *http://* in the tweet text), and use the redirection code of this hour to determine the redirection. At first display the original link, but replace it by the redirected link as soon as it is resolved.

- **Advanced:** Implement your own Twitter download engine. Downloading tweets is quite easy, but to parse them, you'll need to use an Extensible Markup Language (XML) parser. Cocoa Touch provides `NSXMLParser`. You can also use `libXML`, which is faster. `NSXMLParser` is an event-driven parser: As it steps through the XML file, it invokes delegate methods signaling the opening or closing of each tag. By keeping track of the method invocations, the delegate can build a tree for the XML, or extract meaning from the XML. For the Twitter application, you'd be extracting message properties such as `id`, `created_at`, and `text`, as shown at http://apiwiki.twitter.com/Twitter-REST-API-Method%3A-statuses-user_timeline.

HOUR 15
Showing a Web Page

What You'll Learn in This Hour:

- Understanding `UIWebView`
- Using `UIWebView`
- Using WebKit extensions

To display web content, Cocoa Touch provides a built-in web browser that can render documents in HTML, PDF, RTF, RTFD, Microsoft Office or iWork formats. You can also use the web browser to to execute JavaScript code from your application, for instance to support JavaScript only APIs. In this hour, you'll learn the capabilities of `UIWebView`, use it to dynamically update web pages, and learn how to run JavaScript code using its JavaScript interpreter.

Understanding `UIWebView`

`UIWebView` is a user-interface element that displays web content. This not only includes Hypertext Markup Language (HTML) and static pictures, but also PDFs and documents in Microsoft Office (Excel `.xls`, Word `.doc`, and Powerpoint `.ppt`) and iWork formats (Keynote `.key.zip`, Numbers `.numbers.zip`, and Pages `.pages.zip`). However, Flash and Java are not supported.

To be displayed, a web view must be added to the view hierarchy. Conceptually displaying web content involves two phases. First, the data must be downloaded from a server. Second, it must be parsed and rendered.

Creating a UIWebView

UIWebViews are views like any others. They are simply created and added to the view hierarchy:

```
CGRect screenFrame = [[UIScreen mainScreen] applicationFrame];
UIWebView* webView = [[UIWebView alloc] initWithFrame:screenFrame];
[self.view addSubview:webView];
```

Fetching Documents

UIWebView can download HTML data from a server. Internally, it uses NSURLConnection. The address of the web page is called the base URL. It uniquely identifies a file that may include references to other files that must be downloaded (such as images) to display the web page. These references may be absolute (a full URL) or relative paths (must be resolved using the base URL). Hour 14, "Accessing the Network," discussed NSURL's support for base URLs and relative paths.

```
CGRect screenFrame = [[UIScreen mainScreen] applicationFrame];
UIWebView* webView = [[UIWebView alloc] initWithFrame:screenFrame];
[self.view addSubview:webView];

NSURLRequest* request = [NSURLRequest requestWithURL:url];
[webView loadRequest:request];
```

Alternatively, you can load an HTML string (htmlString) directly into the web view. If the string was loaded from a local file, baseURL should point to that file, so that images are loaded from your bundle. If you need to jump to an anchor, append the anchor to the fileURL to create baseURL.

```
CGRect screenFrame = [[UIScreen mainScreen] applicationFrame];
UIWebView* webView = [[UIWebView alloc] initWithFrame:screenFrame];
[self.view addSubview:webView];

[webView loadHTMLString:htmlString baseURL:baseURL];
```

To show a document in a file which is in PDF, RTF, RTFD Microsoft Office, or iWork format, use the following code:

```
NSBundle*      bundle  = [NSBundle mainBundle];
NSString*      path = [bundle pathForResource:@"climate-change" ofType:@"pdf"];
NSURL*         fileURL = [NSURL fileURLWithPath:path];
NSURLRequest* request = [NSURLRequest requestWithURL:fileURL];
[webView loadRequest:request];
```

Parsing Documents

HTML stands for **Hypertext Markup Language**. Text that provides navigation links to other text is called **hypertext**. A **markup language** is a language that specifies a structure for the text it marks up. The markup language consists of tags: text surrounded by angle brackets. Most types of tags provide a start tag and an end tag. Just as parentheses form a tree of bracketed content, the markup of HTML documents forms a tree. This tree is called the **Document Object Model tree** (DOM tree).

An HTML parser is responsible for creating the DOM tree from the HTML text. Because people write HTML documents by hand, HTML parsers are very forgiving of malformed HTML and build correct DOM trees even when faced with missing or misordered tags. Most web page incompatibilities you'll encounter with `UIWebView` are caused by malformed HTML, which just happens to render correctly on Microsoft Internet Explorer (which is still dominant with approximately two thirds of the market share).

As the `UIWebView` receives the HTML page from the network, it parses it and creates a DOM tree for it. Some of the tags specify page content such as images that must be fetched separately. The `UIWebView` issues Hypertext Transfer Protocol (HTTP) requests to fetch this content. Web browsers try to schedule requests so that they can start rendering the page as soon as possible.

> **Did you Know?**
>
> Web pages are large—often requiring half a megabyte of data to be downloaded. Many websites rely heavily on HTTP caching and page compression to reduce the time users wait to see a page. Therefore, using `UIWebView` often leads to memory warnings.

Rendering Documents

CSS (Cascading Style Sheets) provides a mapping from tags to renderable properties. Browsers contain a default Cascading Style Sheet, which specifies, for instance, that text surrounded by `<B>` and `</B>` tags should be rendered in bold. The properties of an element are specified by the types of its ancestors in the DOM tree: Each node of the tree is the equivalent of a function that is applied to all its descendents. CSS is equivalent to the set of function definitions. Browsers have a default Cascading Style Sheet, which defines the appearance of common tags. For instance, this default sheet specifies that descendents of the DOM tree node of type `<B>` are rendered in bold. HTML documents can override the defaults by including their own CSS definitions to customize the appearance of a page. For instance, links to other pages are rendered as blue, underlined text by default, but their CSS can be overridden to display them in orange italic instead.

The `UIWebView` traverses the DOM tree, applying CSS to determine how to render the page given the aspect ratio of the screen and the constraints specified by the CSS and content. Then, it draws the content to the screen. The DOM tree is also used to provide intelligent zooming and cut-and-copy functionality. For instance, double-tapping a paragraph on the web view zooms to show that paragraph.

JavaScript

HTML and CSS provide a mostly static web browsing experience. Although CSS can change the appearance of elements as your finger "hovers" over them, pages are mainly static. JavaScript is an interpreted prototype-based programming language that is used to add dynamic behavior to web pages. Its name causes it to be confused with Java, although it is semantically very different. Netscape chose this name to cash in on hype surrounding Java at the time. JavaScript changes the DOM tree to render content. Because each change to the DOM tree causes a redraw, you should minimize the number of changes made to the DOM tree. JavaScript can build separate DOM trees and add them to the rendered DOM tree when they are complete. The rendered DOM tree is accessible via the `document` JavaScript variable. JavaScript now has capabilities beyond changing the DOM tree. It has access to the document's cookies. Advertisers use cookies to track you and show you advertisements that reflect your tastes according to the web pages you've visited. This additional complexity often causes pages to load slowly. JavaScript can also download Extensible Markup Language (XML) data using `XMLHTTPRequests`. Despite JavaScript's growing capabilities, remember that it is interpreted and the iPhone is a relatively slow device.

To execute JavaScript in a web view, simply invoke `UIWebView`'s `stringByEvaluatingJavaScriptFromString:` function with valid JavaScript as an argument.

```
[webview stringByEvaluatingJavaScriptFromString:@"alert('This is an alert!');"];
```

Contractually, JavaScript is the only interpreted language allowed to run in applications distributed by the App Store. However, applications openly using the Lua interpreter have been shipped.

Bypassing the App Store review process by downloading JavaScript updates for your application violates the software development kit (SDK) agreement and will result in your application being banned.

UIWebView Limitations

Because the iPhone is a constrained device, UIWebView imposes limitations on resource sizes and JavaScript runtimes.

Size Limitations

Individual HTML, CSS, and JavaScript files must not be larger than 10Mb.

GIFs, PNGs, and TIFFs must not require more than 2Mb of storage when decompressed. (They may only contain 512*1024 pixels as each pixel takes 4 bytes.) If an animated GIF requires more than 2Mb decompressed, only its first frame will be shown. Similarly, the canvas JavaScript can draw to is limited to 2Mb. JPEG images of up to 32 megapixels are allowed, but they will be rendered at a lower resolution when decompressed.

Apple gives as a rule of thumb that UIWebView should be able to display pages that take less than 30Mb when saved as a web archive by Safari on the Mac.

Runtime Limitations

JavaScript functions invoked by your code (or the run loop) are terminated after 10 seconds to prevent the main thread from hanging. My understanding is that JavaScript is run on a separate thread, but the DOM is rendered on the main thread. Because JavaScript can change the DOM (forcing it to be rerendered) and can query the position of rendered elements on the screen, it can monopolize the main thread. Web page editing is hindered (`document.body.contentEditable='on'`) because tapping on editable HTML elements does not show the keyboard. This prevents web-based rich text editors from working with the iPhone.

Using UIWebViews

To learn about displaying a web page, we'll use UIWebView to display a web page, which we'll dynamically update. To learn about using UIWebView's JavaScript interpreter, we'll create a JSON (JavaScript Object Notation) parser using a UIWebView.

Showing a Web Page

We'll create a web page for the About page. To demonstrate updating the content of the web page dynamically, this page provides an application programming interface (API) to create a running count of the number of network errors encountered so far.

Add the two files in Listings 15.1 and 15.2 to your project.

LISTING 15.1 WebViewController.h

```
#import <UIKit/UIKit.h>

@interface WebViewController : UIViewController
{}
@end
```

LISTING 15.2 WebViewController.m

```
#import "WebViewController.h"

@implementation WebViewController

- (void)viewDidLoad
{
  [super viewDidLoad];
  NSBundle*     bundle = [NSBundle mainBundle];
  NSString*     path    = [bundle pathForResource:@"Information" ofType:@"html"];
  NSURL*        fileURL = [NSURL fileURLWithPath:path];
  NSURLRequest* request = [NSURLRequest requestWithURL:fileURL];
  [self.view loadRequest:request];
  [self performSelector:@selector(setErrorCount:)
                            withObject:[NSNumber numberWithInt:20] afterDelay:2];
}

- (void) setErrorCount:(NSNumber*)number
{
  int       n    = [number intValue];
  NSString* str = [NSString stringWithFormat:@"updateErrorCount(%d);", n];
  [self.view stringByEvaluatingJavaScriptFromString:str];
}
@end
```

viewDidLoad simply loads the Information.html file, which shows the About page, and defines a JavaScript updateErrorCount function to update the errorCount. To test the update function, viewDidLoad simply invokes setErrorCount: after 20 seconds.

```
<html><head><meta name="viewport"
             content="width=device-width, initial-scale=1, user-scalable=no"/>
<script type="application/x-javascript">
function updateErrorCount(n)
{
  var errorCount = document.getElementById("errorCount");
  errorCount.innerHTML = n;
}
</script>
</head>
<body style="background-image:url('AboutPage.png')">
```

```
<div style="width:300; height:340; text-align:center; display:table-cell;
➥vertical-align:middle; font-size:24px; color:#400000;">
<b>Error Count: <span id="errorCount">0</span></b>
</div>
</body>
</html>
```

First create a new NIB file **WebView.xib** where the `File's Owner` is a `UITabBarController` and its `view` is a `Web View` (after reading the `WebViewController.h` class file from Interface Builder). Set the `Web View`'s size to **320** width by **416** height. Open `MainWindow.xib` and change the About tab's view controller NIB to **WebView**.

Now when you select the About tab, a web view is displayed. After 20 seconds, the error message is updated to 20. You could use notifications to update the error count: The `WebViewController` can register for them and update the error count, without requiring the network functions to know about it.

Parsing JSON

XML and JSON are the two main formats used by JavaScript applications to communicate with servers. Cocoa Touch provides an XML parser but not a JSON parser. You could use the third-party YAJL C library or the SB-JSON Objective-C library, but to illustrate communicating between Objective-C and JavaScript, we'll use a hidden web view to perform a search on Twitter. Rather than integrating it into Twitter, it's a standalone application that uses NSLog to print results to the Console: Small, simple test applications are often easier to play with.

Creating the Project

Create a new window-based project called **JsonSearchTest**. Change the `main.m` file as follows:

```
int retVal = UIApplicationMain(argc, argv, nil, nil);
int retVal = UIApplicationMain(argc, argv, nil, @"JsonSearchTestAppDelegate");
```

Now edit `JsonSearchTestAppDelegate.h` as follows:

```
#import <UIKit/UIKit.h>

@interface JsonSearchTestAppDelegate : NSObject <UIApplicationDelegate,
                                                 UIWebViewDelegate>
{
  NSString*   result;
  BOOL        waiting;
  UITextView* textView;
  UIWebView*  webview;
```

```
  UIWindow*   window;
}

@property (nonatomic, retain) IBOutlet UIWindow *window;

@end
```

Creating a Print Method

This is essentially a text-only application. `textView` is the text view that will display text. We'll create our own `print:` function that appends data to the text view. Objective-C methods support C's standard `va_args` variable argument notation.

```
#import "JsonSearchTestAppDelegate.h"

@implementation JsonSearchTestAppDelegate

@synthesize window;

- (void) print:(NSString*) formatString, ...
{
  va_list arguments;
  va_start(arguments, formatString);
  NSString* str;
  str = [[NSString alloc] initWithFormat:formatString arguments:arguments];
  textView.text = [NSString stringWithFormat:@"%@%@\n", textView.text, str];
  [str release];
}
```

Parsing JSON with a Web View

To parse JSON, we'll use the JavaScript interpreter. JSON serializes data as JavaScript dictionaries, arrays, or values. A set of keys form an index path that can retrieve a single value. We will define a `parseJson:forKeys:` method that returns the correct element for a variable argument list of keys.

First, we tidy up the JSON so that it does not cause any errors when we give it to `UIWebView`'s JavaScript interpreter: We escape Unicode, backslashes, and double quotes. The next step is to step through the argument list and create the index path. Finally, we run the JavaScript interpreter.

Because `UIWebKit` runs the JavaScript interpreter in a different thread, the JavaScript code creates a request (`document.location = url;`) by creating a `myapp:result` URL. The request is captured by the `webView:shouldStartLoadWithRequest:navigationType:` delegate method, which saves the result. To provide a more agreeable programming interface, I run the run loop until the request is captured. In a real application, you'd probably want to add a timeout and change the alert in the catch block to create a fail: request for errors.

```
- (NSString*) parseJson:(NSString*)json forKeys:(NSString*) keyStr,...
{
  // Clean up the json
  #define r NSMakeRange(0, [j length])
  NSMutableString* j = [NSMutableString stringWithString:json];
  [j replaceOccurrencesOfString:@"\\u" withString:@"\\\\u" options:0 range:r];
  [j replaceOccurrencesOfString:@"\\"  withString:@"\\\\"  options:0 range:r];
  [j replaceOccurrencesOfString:@"\"" withString:@"\\\"" options:0 range:r];
  #undef r

  // Make index

  va_list arguments;
  va_start(arguments, keyStr);

  NSMutableString* key = [NSMutableString stringWithFormat:@"[\"%@\"]", keyStr];
  for (;;)
  {
    NSString* p = va_arg(arguments, NSString*);
    if (p == nil)
      break;
    [key appendFormat:@"[\"%@\"]", p];
  }

  // Run

  waiting = YES;
  result  = nil;
  NSString* js = [NSString stringWithFormat:
                         @"try"
                         @"{ var json=\"%@\";"
                         @"  var result = eval('('+json+')');"
                         @"  var url=\"myapp:\"+escape(\"\" + result%@);"
                         @"  document.location = url;"
                         @"} catch(e) { alert (''+e); };", j, key];
  [webview stringByEvaluatingJavaScriptFromString:js];

  while (waiting)
    [[NSRunLoop currentRunLoop] runUntilDate: [NSDate distantPast]];

  NSArray *components = [result componentsSeparatedByString:@":"];
  [result release]; result = nil;
  return [components lastObject];
}

- (BOOL)                     webView:(UIWebView*)wv
        shouldStartLoadWithRequest:(NSURLRequest*)request
                    navigationType:(UIWebViewNavigationType)t
{
  result  = [[[request URL] absoluteString] retain];
  waiting = NO;
  return NO;
}
```

Downloading the JSON from twitter.com

As this is test code, I'm using `sendSynchronousRequest:returningResponse:error:`. As explained in Hour 14, I only recommend using this method for tests, and not real application code, because it blocks.

```
- (NSString*) queryTwitter:(NSString*)query
{
  NSString*      urlStr
    = [NSString stringWithFormat:@"http://search.twitter.com/search.json?q=%@",
        [query stringByAddingPercentEscapesUsingEncoding:NSUTF8StringEncoding]];

  NSURL*         url      = [NSURL        URLWithString:urlStr];
  NSURLRequest*  request  = [NSURLRequest requestWithURL:url];


  NSError*       error    = nil;
  NSURLResponse* response = nil;
  NSData* data = [NSURLConnection sendSynchronousRequest:request
                          returningResponse:&response error:&error];

  NSString* ianaName = [response textEncodingName];
  CFStringEncoding cfsEncoding
    = CFStringConvertIANACharSetNameToEncoding((CFStringRef)ianaName);
  NSStringEncoding nssEncoding
    = CFStringConvertEncodingToNSStringEncoding(cfsEncoding);
  NSString* string   =[[NSString alloc] initWithData:data encoding:nssEncoding];

  return string;
}
```

Setting Up the Web View and the Text View

Now that we've done all the hard work, we just need to set things up in `applicationDidFinishLaunching:`. We create a `UITextView` and add it to the view hierarchy. Then, we create a web view, but we don't need to add it to the view hierarchy as we won't be displaying anything. Finally, we send a request for the most recent tweets about the iPhone, and print them out.

```
- (void) applicationDidFinishLaunching:(UIApplication*) application
{
  window   = [[UIWindow alloc] initWithFrame:[[UIScreen mainScreen] bounds]];
  textView = [[UITextView alloc] initWithFrame:CGRectMake(0, 20, 320, 460)];
  textView.editable = NO;
  [window addSubview:textView];
  [window makeKeyAndVisible];

  webview  = [[UIWebView alloc] initWithFrame:CGRectMake(0, 0, 1, 1)];
  [webview setDelegate:self];

  NSString* twitter = [self queryTwitter:@"iphone"];
  // [self print:@"Got %@", string];
```

```
  NSString* rCount = [self parseJson:twitter forKeys:@"results_per_page", nil];
  [self print:@"Got %@ results", rCount];

  for (int i = 0; i < [rCount intValue]; ++i)
  {
    NSString* t;
    NSString* n = [NSString stringWithFormat:@"%d", i];
    t = [self parseJson:twitter forKeys:@"results", n, @"text", nil];
    t = [t stringByReplacingPercentEscapesUsingEncoding:NSUTF8StringEncoding];
    [self print:[t stringByReplacingOccurrencesOfString:@"%" withString:@"%%"]];

    [self print:@""];
  }
}
```

The results from `parseJson:forKeys:` are percent encoded (it's a URL) and must be decoded.

```
- (void) dealloc
{
  [result   release]; result   = nil;
  [webview  release]; webview  = nil;
  [textView release]; textView = nil;
  [window   release]; window   = nil;
  [super    dealloc];
}

@end
```

Did you Know?

In this case of JSON, it would be faster to parse the file natively. However, using a `UIWebView` in this manner is useful if you must interact with JavaScript code, for instance to use a JavaScript-only API.

Using WebKit Extensions

`UIWebView` is based on WebKit. Officially, it supports "a large subset" of HTML 4.01. Apple's *Safari HTML Reference* contains all the details. The *Safari CSS Reference* specifies all the CSS declarations supported by `UIWebView`. `UIWebView` supports a subset of the features supported by Safari on the Mac.

Apple and Google are driving the HTML 5 specification. Although HTML 5 is still being developed, WebKit implements the following proposed HTML 5 features:

- 2D drawing to a canvas
- Extended drawing and animation attributes
- Draggable elements

- audio and video elements to play audio and show H264 video
- SQL Database access from JavaScript
- Geo location
- An application cache that lets applications be started while the iPhone is offline

The last topics are not of much interest to Cocoa Touch programmers, who have native APIs for these tasks. However, the first three features allow you to customize content embedded within a web view.

Canvas Tag

A canvas is declared in the HTML document. By default, it will be 300 pixels wide and 150 pixels high, but you can adjust these with the height and width attributes. <CANVAS> tags are usually declared with an id attribute so that JavaScript can easily find them in the DOM tree. UIWebView supports a 2D context that lets you draw 2D images. The following HTML creates a canvas.

```
<html><head>
<meta name="viewport"
      content="width=device-width, initial-scale=1, user-scalable=no"/>
<script type="application/x-javascript">
function draw()
{
  var canvas = document.getElementById("canvas");

  if (canvas.getContext)
  { var ctx = canvas.getContext("2d");
    // draw stuff
  }
}
</script></head>
<body>
<img src="http://ansemond.com/Squirrel.png" onload="draw();" id="squirrel"/>
<canvas id="canvas"></canvas>
</body></html>
```

The strange meta statement forces WebKit not to scale the web page. Because the 2D context is extremely similar to the Core Graphics context, as you learned in Hour 8, "Drawing User-Interface Elements," I'll list the correspondences so that you can apply your knowledge from that chapter directly to the canvas element.

The origin of the canvas element's coordinate system is at the upper-left corner of the screen. Drawing is based on defining paths that can then be stroked or filled.

Paths are created as in Core Graphics:

- rect (CGContextAddRect).
- beginPath (CGContextBeginPath).
- moveTo (CGContextMoveToPoint).
- lineTo (CGContextAddLineToPoint).
- quadraticCurveTo (CGContextAddQuadCurveToPoint).
- bezierCurveTo (CGContextAddCurveToPoint).
- arc differs from CGContextAddArcToPoint: It takes a single-point coordinate and draws part of a circle from a starting angle to an ending angle, of specified radius.
- closePath (CGContextClosePath).

Once a path has been created, it can be drawn as a line using stroke (CGContextStrokePath) or filled using fill (CGContextFillPath). Lines are drawn straddling the path with half of their width lying on either side. strokeStyle (CGContextSetStrokeColorWithColor) and fillStyle (CGContextSetFillColorWithColor) specify the color to be drawn. As this is HTML, the color is specified as a CSS3 color value.

createLinearGradient (CGContextDrawLinearGradient) and createRadialGradient (CGContextDrawRadialGradient) are used to create gradients. addColorStop specifies colors to be placed along the gradient.

Lines are styled with lineWidth (CGContextSetLineWidth), lineCap (CGContextSetLineCap), lineJoin (CGContextSetLineJoin), and miterLimit (CGContextSetMiterLimit).

The canvas supports globalAlpha (CGContextSetAlpha), blend modes using globalCompositionOperation (CGContextSetBlendMode), and using paths to clip areas (CGContextClip).

fillText (CGContextShowTextAtPoint) renders text in the font (font) and color (fillStyle) of your choice. Fonts are specified as in CSS.

The canvas provides a 2D transformation matrix analogous to the Core Graphics' current transformation matrix (CTM). It provides rotate (CGContextRotateCTM), scale (CGContextScaleCTM), translate (CGTranslateCTM), setTransform (CGContextConcatCTM), save (CGContextSaveGState), and restore (CGContextRestoreGState).

drawImage is used to draw images to the canvas (CGContextDrawImage). For instance, to create a reflection from an image, as illustrated in Figure 15.1, you'd write the following:

FIGURE 15.1
Using the <CANVAS> tag

```
<html><head>
<meta name="viewport" content="width=device-width, initial-scale=1,
                               user-scalable=no"/>
<script type="application/x-javascript">
function draw()
{
  var canvas = document.getElementById("canvas");

  if (canvas.getContext)
  { var ctx = canvas.getContext("2d");
    var img = document.getElementById("squirrel");

    canvas.width  = img.width;
    canvas.height = img.height;

    // Draw an upside-down image

    ctx.save();
    ctx.translate(0, img.height - 1);
    ctx.scale(1, -1);
    ctx.drawImage(img, 0, 0, img.width, img.height);
    ctx.restore();

    // Draw a gradient whose opacity changes over the canvas to make the
    // reflection fade out. The resulting canvas changes opacity.
```

```
    ctx.globalCompositeOperation = "destination-out";

    var gradient = ctx.createLinearGradient(0, 0, 0, img.height);
    gradient.addColorStop(1, "rgba(255, 255, 255, 1.0)");
    gradient.addColorStop(0, "rgba(255, 255, 255, 0.0)");
    ctx.fillStyle = gradient;
    ctx.fillRect(0, 0, img.width, img.height);

    img.style.position = "absolute";
    img.style.left = "0px";
    img.style.top  = "0px";

    canvas.style.position = "absolute";
    canvas.style.left     = "0px";
    canvas.style.top      = Math.round(img.height).toString() + "px";
  }
}
</script></head>
<body>
<img src="http://ansemond.com/Squirrel.png" onload="draw();" id="squirrel"/>
<canvas id="canvas"></canvas>
</body></html>
```

2D and 3D Transformations

WebKit leverages CALayer's ability to be placed anywhere in 3D space to provide two types of transformations.

2D transformations use the same coordinate system as Core Graphics (with the x-axis growing right and the y-axis growing upward). An element accumulates its DOM tree ancestors' 2D transformations just as subviews accumulate their ancestors' 2D transformations in the view hierarchy.

3D transformations use the same coordinate system as Core Animation layers do, positioning elements in 3D space. Although elements can be positioned to intersect in 3D space, one element will be drawn above the other.

There are two ways of setting transformations: CSS and JavaScript.

CSS Transformations

To set most transformations in CSS, use the `-webkit-transform:` property. This corresponds to the `transform` property of a layer. It takes a list of transformations to apply to the element consecutively. The transformations are specified by CSS property functions.

For 2D transforms, use `matrix`, `rotate`, `scale`, and `translate`, which correspond to the `CGContextConcatCTM`, `CGContextRotateCTM`, `CGContextScaleCTM`, and `CGTranslateCTM` functions of Core Graphics.

The 3D CSS property functions matrix3D, rotate3d, scale3d, and translate3d correspond to creating a CATransform3D and using CATransform3DConcat, CATransform3DRotate, CATransform3DScale, and CATransform3DTranslate, respectively. The perspective CSS property function is used to set the m34 component of the CATransform3D matrix. Recall the m34 component specifies the distance of the viewer's face from the iPhone screen in pixels. skewX and skewY skew the HTML element by an angle.

To set the layer's sublayerTransform's m34 component, use -webkit-perspective:.

-webkit-transform-origin: and -webkit-perspective-origin: specify the origin of the transformation with respect to their HTML element. By default, they are set to its center. These properties are needed because you often do not know what size the rendered element will have.

JavaScript Transformations

Every element of the DOM tree has a style property, which specifies the CSS styling specifically applied to it. To obtain an element's computed CSS styling (which in the case of transformations includes all the ancestors' transformations), use getComputedStyle.

```
var element       = document.getElementById("some_id");
var computedStyle = window.getComputedStyle(element);
```

The style's webkitTransform is a string that specifies a 2D matrix (matrix(a,b,c,d,e,f)) or a 3D matrix (matrix3d(m11, m12, ..., m44)). The WebKitCSSMatrix JavaScript object's constructor takes this string to create a 4x4 matrix representing a 3D transform. You can inverse, multiply, rotate, scale, or translate these matrices. Setting the element's style.webkitTransform property to this matrix will reposition the element in 3D space.

```
var matrix = new WebKitCSSMatrix(computedStyle.webkitTransform);
element.style.webkitTransform = matrix.scale(2.0, 2.0, 2.0);
```

Animations

Just as the canvas leverages Core Graphics, and the 2D/3D transformations leverage CALayer's spatial properties, animations leverage Core Animation. The same limitations exist in terms of which properties are animatable, and the same classes are used for animation.

Basic animations use CATransition and linear interpolation (CABasicAnimation). To define a transition, use the -webkit-transition CSS properties. For instance, to change the opacity, specify that the property to change is the `opacity` with the `-webkit-transition-property` CSS property, and set the duration of the transition with `-webkit-transition-duration`. You can add a delay with `-webkit-transition-delay`, and replace the linear animation using `-webkit-transition-timing-function`. The standard `ease-in` and `ease-out` transitions are available. As soon as you change the opacity, the animation is started:

```
<html><head><style type="text/css">
div { -webkit-transition-property: opacity;
      -webkit-transition-duration: 2s; }
div.disappear { opacity:0; }
</style>
<meta name="viewport"
      content="width=device-width, initial-scale=1, user-scalable=no"/>
</head>
<body>
<div id="div" style="width:300; height:340; text-align:center;
➥display:table-cell; vertical-align:middle; background-color:green"
➥onclick="className='disappear'">Tap me!</div>
<script type="application/x-javascript">
var div = document.getElementById("div");
div.addEventListener( 'webkitTransitionEnd',
                      function( event ) { alert( "Finished transition!" ); },
                      false );
</script>
</body></html>
```

By setting `className` to `disappear` in the `onclick` handler, the `div` element's style is changed when the `div` is tapped. The `-web-transition` property groups the above web transition properties into a single statement. Transitions end with a `webkitTransitionEnd` event, which your JavaScript can listen to with `addEventListener`.

You'll find analogs to the rest of `CAAnimation`, including animation properties (`-webkit-animation-delay`, `-webkit-animation-direction`, `-webkit-animation-duration`, `-webkit-animation-iteration-count`), keyframes (`-webkit-keyframes`), and timing functions (`-webkit-animation-timing-function`), such as cubic Bézier curves, and so on. Animations are defined by name (`-webkit-animation-name`). JavaScript can start an animation by setting the `webkitAnimationName` of the style of an element. Animations end with a `webkitAnimationEnd` event.

CSS does not report errors, but silently ignores them, which makes debugging animations difficult. Although you can create animations with JavaScript, it's not easy because updating CSS from JavaScript is difficult. Furthermore, because Core Animation is used, you will encounter the same end-of-animation problems as were discussed in Hour 9, "Layers and Core Animation: Creating a Cover Flow Clone." You'll need to manage `webkitAnimationEnd` event handlers. These problems might explain why CSS animations have not proven popular.

Rendering Extensions

WebKit introduces a number of rendering extensions:

- -webkit-border-radius lets you create boxes with rounded corners.
- -webkit-box-shadow lets you add a shadow to the border box of an element.
- The -webkit-margin properties and -webkit-padding-start help improve layout.
- -webkit-box-reflect lets you create a reflection in CSS (including a gradient like the previous canvas example).

Draggable Items

The iPhone uses dragging to scroll, which means the usual JavaScript drag-and-drop methods do not work. However, you can register for the touchstart, touchmove, touchend, and touchcancel events to receive touches. To recognize touch events, the iPhone requires you to make elements "clickable" by creating a dummy onclick handler: onclick = "void(0)".

Summary

UIWebView provides a simple way to integrate your own browser into an application. Furthermore, you can use it to display a wide variety of images, documents, and HTML. However, UIWebView is performance intensive, and should be used sparingly. Rendering is slow because it involves downloading a lot of data, parsing it, and computing a layout. Javascript is slow because it must be parsed, and interpreted.

UIWebView contains a JavaScript interpreter that you can use from your application. For instance, you can leverage existing JavaScript libraries to interface with web services. However, do not attempt to update your application using the JavaScript interpreter if you distribute your application using the App Store. You can leverage CoreGraphics and CoreAnimation capabilities from JavaScript.

Q&A

Q. ***Can I use* UIWebView *to play MP3 audio files?***

A. Yes, simply create a UIWebView and make it load an MP3 file (using loadRequest).

Q. ***Can I use* `UIWebView` *to play YouTube videos?***

A. Playing YouTube videos using `MPMoviePlayerController` starts the YouTube application and quits your application. However, if you use the appropriate `embed` tag in a `UIWebView`, you can create a link that when tapped opens the YouTube application while keeping your application running in the background. Once the user leaves the YouTube video player, your application resumes, just like watching m.youtube.com on Safari.

Workshop

The Workshop consists of quiz questions and answers to help you solidify your understanding of the material covered in this hour. You should try to answer the questions before checking the answers.

Quiz Questions

1. How do you add a `UIWebView` to the view hierarchy?
2. Does `UIWebView` support `contentEditable`?
3. What are `UIWebView`'s resource limitations?
4. How long may JavaScript functions run?
5. What extensions do `UIWebViews` support?

Quiz Answers

1. Adding a `UIWebView` to the view hierarchy is no different from other views. Just add it to the view hierarchy.
2. No, `UIWebView` does not support `contentEditable`.
3. Resources may not be larger than 10Mb, 30Mb total in `UIWebView`. Bitmap images other than JPEGs must use less than 2 megapixels, and JPEGs must not exceed 32 megapixels.
4. JavaScript functions are limited to 10 seconds running time.
5. `UIWebViews` support rendering extensions such as rounded boxes and shadows, the `canvas` tag, the ability to place objects in 3D space, and to animate their CSS properties.

Exercises

- Change `TwitterViewController` so that tapping a tweet containing a web page link opens the web page within the application.
- Integrate the JSON search routines into the Twitter application.

HOUR 16
Adding Application Preferences

What You'll Learn in This Hour:

- Retrieving settings set by the Settings application
- Creating a settings bundle for the Settings application
- Dynamically updating data from the network

The Settings application provides a central location for users to change their application preferences. This hour, you'll learn how to create a settings bundle that will display your application's settings.

Providing settings in the Settings application simplifies your user interface and reduces the amount of code you must write to provide a standard user interface. The disadvantage of using the Settings application is that users must exit your application to change a setting. You might be able to provide a better end-user experience by creating a Settings page within your application. For instance, some applications let users change their appearance. Users will find it easier to make a choice if they see the effect of each setting immediately.

As more and more users expect their data to be seamlessly available on all their devices, transparently synchronizing data from other sources is becoming increasingly important. The third part of this hour discusses extending the Twitter application to transparently update the tables of tweets it displays each time a friend adds tweets.

Retrieving Settings Set by the Settings Application

The Settings application reads settings from and writes them to your application's user defaults. As you learned in Hour 12, "Adding Navigation and Tab Bar Controllers," user defaults behave like a dictionary associating values with keys. You saved the user's name to the user defaults using the key username. Similarly, all the other settings are associated with a key.

To illustrate the variety of settings you can use with the Settings application, you'll add the following options to the Twitter application:

- A username text field
- A password secure text field
- An On/Off switch for redirection resolution
- A multiple-choice questionnaire to specify the rate at which Twitter should try to update your friends tweets
- A slider for the number of tweets Twitter should save

The On/Off switch will result in a Boolean. Use the key redirects to access it:

```
NSUserDefaults *userDefaults = [NSUserDefaults standardUserDefaults];
BOOL resolveRedirects = [userDefaults boolForKey:@"redirects"];
```

The multiple-choice questionnaire will result in numerical values. Use the key refreshRate to access it.

```
int refreshRate = [userDefaults integerForKey:@"refreshRate"];
```

This hour's example source code uses this refresh rate.

The slider will result in a numerical value. Use the key cacheSize to access it. An exercise in Hour 17, "Using the SQLite Database," discusses how to create this functionality.

Hour 12 introduced two strings, `username` and `password`:

```
NSString *username = [userDefaults stringForKey:@"username"];
NSString *password = [userDefaults stringForKey:@"password"];
```

Creating a Settings Bundle for the Settings Application

Settings bundles specify the layout and keys of the settings for your application. The Settings application uses this information to show your application's settings. In this section you'll create a Settings bundle for the Twitter application.

How the Settings Application Works

The Settings application can modify other application's settings. This makes it a security risk. Bundles protect users from possible security breaches, while letting your application create its own custom Settings page.

Settings Bundles Specify User-Editable Settings

To show the settings of each application, the Settings application obtains a list of the installed applications. Then, it checks each installed application to see whether the application provides user-editable settings. Recall that in Hour 10, "Using View Controllers," you learned that applications are bundles: They contain executable code, NIB files, and resources such as pictures or sounds. They can also contain a `Settings.bundle` bundle. The settings bundle of applications specifies their user-editable settings. The Settings application assumes that applications that do not contain a settings bundle have no user-editable settings.

iPhone Application Security and Sandboxes

Your iPhone is a security risk. It contains your friends' contact information. It could spy on you. It knows your location. It can record audio and video and stream it anywhere on the Web in real time. Teaching third-party developers how to write software for it only increases this risk. Therefore, the iPhone OS runs all third-party software in a **sandbox**.

Sandboxes prevent unsigned applications from running on the iPhone. Should an application prove to be malicious, Apple can revoke its signature and prevent it from running on the iPhone. The sandbox also prevents applications from accessing files and directories belonging to other applications, and prevents applications from sharing data in unauthorized ways. For instance, applications cannot sabotage their competitors' files. Because applications can only access certain directories, the iPhone OS can delete an application's data when it deletes the application. Similarly, sandboxes enable iTunes to back up individual applications' files to the user's computer.

Jailbreaking is the process of disabling the sandbox. Software running on jailbroken phones is not limited by the sandbox. For instance, applications for jailbroken phones provided Multimedia Messaging Service (MMS) and video support before iPhone OS 3.0 appeared. Jailbroken phones also support tethering and running applications in the background. The disadvantage of jailbreaking your iPhone is that nothing prevents malicious software from being installed. In practice, nobody seems to have written malicious software targeting jailbroken phones.

Because jailbroken iPhones can run any software, their users can install software from the App Store without paying for it by removing Apple's protection mechanism. Because many people do this, some applications now refuse to run on jailbroken phones.

> You can see the simulators' sandboxes in the Library/Application Support/iPhone Simulator/User/Applications directory accessed from your home directory. They are the files that end with `.sb`

The Settings application needs special permissions to change other applications' user defaults because the sandbox prevents applications from changing files belonging to other applications. Code running within the Settings application must, therefore, be trusted. On the Mac, the Systems Preferences application provides a central location for application settings. Applications that tie into System Preferences provide executable code that lays out the settings view and responds to user interaction. If the iPhone Settings application adopted this solution, it would enable potentially malicious code to run in a nonsandboxed environment. Therefore, the Settings application uses a different solution based on property lists.

Customizing Settings with a Property List

Each settings bundle contains a property list file named `Root.plist` that serves much the same purpose as a NIB file does: It contains layout information for each setting, the type of each setting, and the key to use to save the setting's value to the application's user defaults.

The Settings application reads the property list and builds a table view showing the settings that can be changed.

The property list is a dictionary containing two elements: The value associated with the PreferenceSpecifiers key is an array of the settings items to display. The value associated with the StringsTable key is the name of an optional file that specifies translations of the strings in the property list for multilingual applications.

Each item of PreferenceSpecifiers is a dictionary. Every item has a `Type` entry, which specifies the type of user-interface element to display. Items that have a title have a `Title` entry that specifies the title to use.

Items that display a value from the user defaults file have a `Key` entry, which specifies the key to read from the user defaults, and a `DefaultValue` entry, which specifies the value to use should the user defaults file not have a value associated with the specified key.

For instance, to display a field for the username to be entered on the first row of our Settings page, the first element of the property list's PreferenceSpecifiers would be a dictionary containing three items:

- `Title: User Name`
- `Type: PSTextFieldSpecifier`
- `Key: username`

Figure 16.1 shows the settings we'll create for the Twitter application.

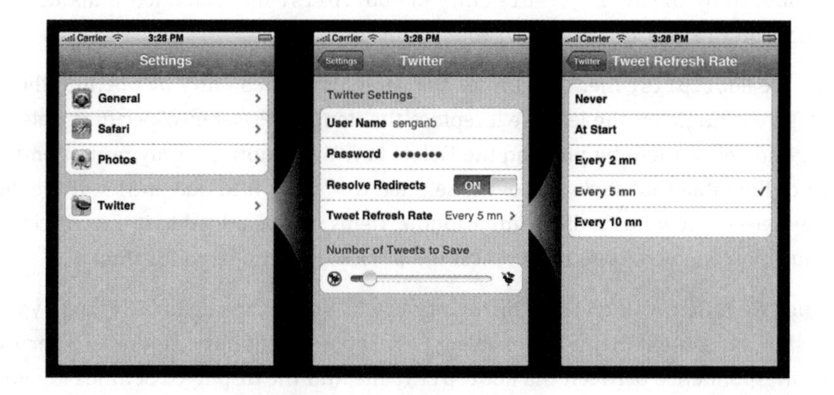

FIGURE 16.1
Settings for the Twitter application

Laying Out the Twitter Settings

Create the settings bundle by adding a new file to your projects' Resources: Ctrl-click the Resources section of your Groups & Files pane, choose Add, New File, select Settings in the right pane, and then Settings Bundle (see Figure 16.2). Don't change the default `Settings.bundle` name.

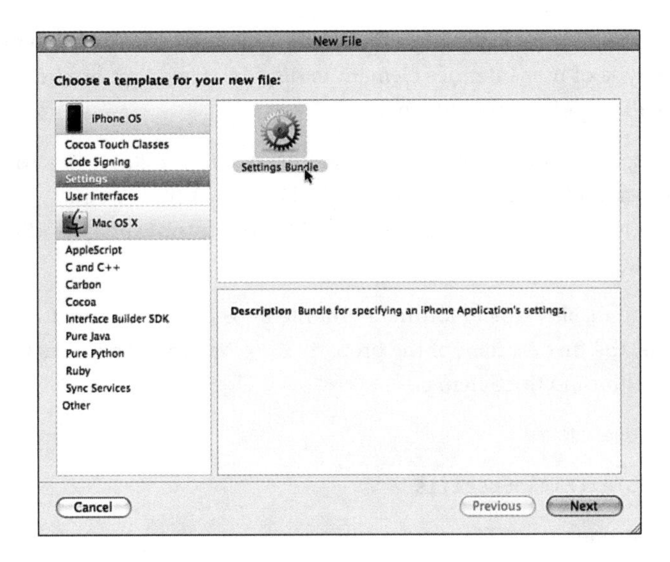

FIGURE 16.2
Creating a settings bundle

The bundle contains two files: `Root.plist` and `Root.strings`. The `Root.strings` file is loaded by the `StringsTable` entry of `Root.plist` file. You'll learn about localization in Hour 24, "Shipping Your Application."

Open the `Root.plist` file. You can see the contents of each entry by opening the disclosure triangle on the left. We'll replace the items of PreferenceSpecifiers: Select them and delete them by pressing the Delete key. You'll notice a gray button on the right of the table that sticks out of the selected row. Click it to add entries. If the item on the selected row has a disclosure triangle, items will be added to it if its disclosure triangle points down, or to its parent if the disclosure triangle points right.

Change each item you add to a dictionary by clicking on the default `String` `Type`. This shows a context menu of possible types. Choose Dictionary. Figure 16.3 shows the correspondence between the `Root.plist` file and the displayed Settings layout.

Application Name

If your application contains a `Settings.bundle`, the Settings application will display its title and your application's icon scaled down to 29x29 pixels. To use your own 29x29 pixel file, name it `Icon-Settings.png` and add it to your application bundle.

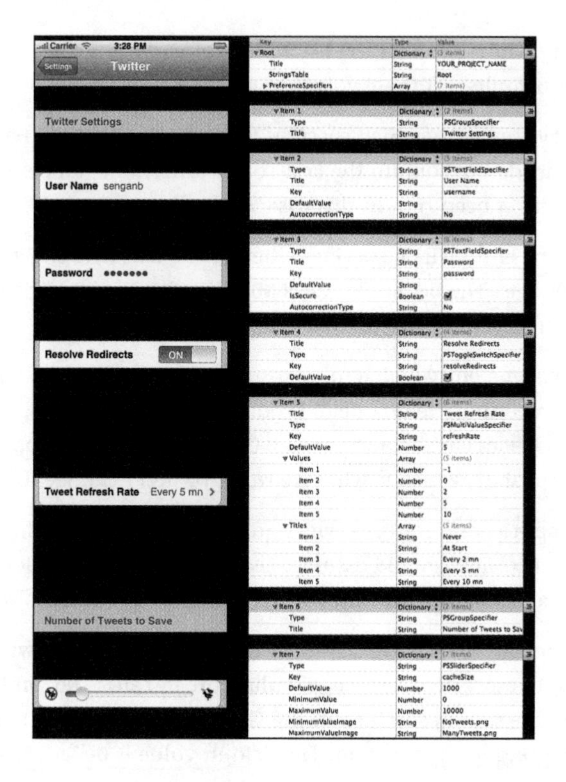

FIGURE 16.3
Settings layout

Group Items

The group item has the Type `PSGroupSpecifier`. The Settings application uses grouped tables to display settings. The group item specifies the section header, and creates a new section in the table. Its only property is its `Title`. Create an item of this type, and set the `Title` to `Twitter Settings`, as shown in Figure 16.4.

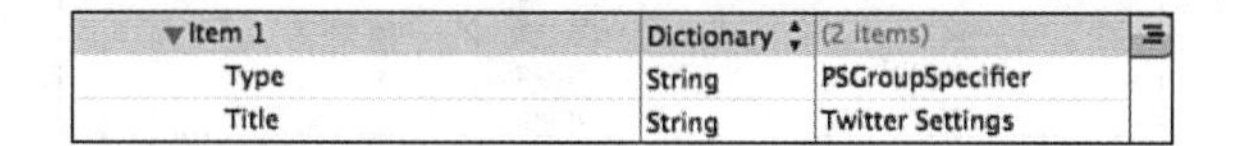

▾Item 1	Dictionary	(2 items)
Type	String	PSGroupSpecifier
Title	String	Twitter Settings

FIGURE 16.4
Group: Twitter Settings title

Text Field Items: User-Editable Text

The text field item has the Type `PSTextFieldSpecifier`. It provides a user-editable text field. Create two items of this type to set the username and password. Each item has the following:

- A `Title` entry which specifies the text to place on the left of the row. Set the title of the first item to **`User Name`** and the title of the second to **`Password`**.

- A `Key` entry which specifies the key to use to read this value from the application's user defaults. Set these values to **`username`** and **`password`**, respectively.
- A `DefaultValue` entry which specifies the value that should be used if the user defaults do not contain the key. For instance, this happens if the application has not yet been run. In this case, set both entries to empty strings.
- An `IsSecure` entry which specifies whether the text field shows the text you typed or bullets. The default value is `NO`. Therefore, only create an entry for the password item. Set its value to **`YES`**.
- A `KeyboardType` entry which takes a string that specifies the type of keyboard to use when editing the text field. Legal values are `Alphabet`, `NumbersAndPunctuation`, `NumberPad`, `URL`, and `EmailAddress`. The default value is `Alphabet`, which is what we want, so don't change it.
- An `AutocapitalizationType` which takes a string that specifies the capitalization the text field should assume. Legal values are `None`, `Sentences`, `Words`, and `AllCharacters`. The default value is `None`. Again, this is what we want.
- An `AutocorrectionType` which takes a string that specifies whether the text field should autocorrect text. Legal values are `Default`, `No`, and `Yes`. `Default` means use the setting specified in the General, Keyboard, Auto-Capitalization item of the Settings application. The default value is `Default`. Autocorrecting account names and passwords is a bad idea. Create entries for this type, and set them to **`No`**.

The final items should look like Figures 16.5 and 16.6.

FIGURE 16.5 Text Field: User Name

▾Item 2	Dictionary	(5 items)
Type	String	PSTextFieldSpecifier
Title	String	User Name
Key	String	username
DefaultValue	String	
AutocorrectionType	String	No

FIGURE 16.6 Text Field: Password

▾Item 3	Dictionary	(6 items)
Type	String	PSTextFieldSpecifier
Title	String	Password
Key	String	password
DefaultValue	String	
IsSecure	Boolean	☑
AutocorrectionType	String	No

Toggle Switches: On/Off Switches

The toggle switch item has the Type `PSToggleSwitchSpecifier`. It provides an On/Off switch. Create an item of this type to enable URL redirection resolution.

`Title` specifies the text to place on the left of the row, and `Key` or `DefaultValue` specifies the value to place on the right of the row. Set the `Title` to **`Resolve Redirects`**, the `Key` to **`resolveRedirects`**, and the `DefaultValue` to a check marked Boolean (**`YES`**), as shown in Figure 16.7.

The switch is shown to be on if the value from the user defaults matches the value specified by `TrueValue`, and is shown to be off if it matches the value specified by `FalseValue`. `TrueValue` and `FalseValue` may be any scalar type (Boolean, string, number, date, or data). `TrueValue`'s default is Boolean `YES`, and `FalseValue`'s default is Boolean `NO`.

▼Item 4	Dictionary	(4 items)
Title	String	Resolve Redirects
Type	String	PSToggleSwitchSpecifier
Key	String	resolveRedirects
DefaultValue	Boolean	☑

FIGURE 16.7
Toggle switch: Resolve Redirects

Multivalue Items: Multiple-Choice Questionnaires

The multivalue item has the Type `PSMultiValueSpecifier`. It shows a title and a modifiable value. Create an item of this type to decide how often your friends' tweets should be checked.

The `Title` entry specifies the text to place on the left of the row. Set this value to **`Tweet Refresh Rate`**

The `Key` entry specifies the key it should read from your user defaults. Set this value to **`refreshRate`**.

If the user defaults file does not have a value for the key, it uses the value specified by `DefaultValue`. Set the value to **`5`**.

It looks up the resulting value in its `Values` entry and displays the corresponding text from its `Titles` entry. This value is displayed on the right of the row. Editing its value opens a new page, which shows its possible values. Set `Values` to **`-1`**, **`0`**, **`2`**, **`5`**, **`10`**. Set `Titles` to **`Never`**, **`At Start`**, **`Every 2 minutes`**, **`Every 5 minutes`**, **`Every 10 minutes`**, as shown in Figure 16.8.

Because only the strings specified in `Titles` can be displayed, the Settings application can easily support localization: Looking up the string in a user-provided dictionary is sufficient to translate the text.

▼Item 5	Dictionary	(6 items)
Title	String	Tweet Refresh Rate
Type	String	PSMultiValueSpecifier
Key	String	refreshRate
DefaultValue	Number	5
▼Values	Array	(5 items)
Item 1	Number	-1
Item 2	Number	0
Item 3	Number	2
Item 4	Number	5
Item 5	Number	10
▼Titles	Array	(5 items)
Item 1	String	Never
Item 2	String	At Start
Item 3	String	Every 2 mn
Item 4	String	Every 5 mn
Item 5	String	Every 10 mn

FIGURE 16.8
Multivalue: Refresh Rate

Titles: Read-Only Text

The title item has the Type `PSTitleValueSpecifier`. It provides read-only information about your application's configuration. Its only difference to `PSMultiValueSpecifier` is that it does not let users edit the value.

Slider Items

The slider item has the Type `PSSliderSpecifier`. It provides a slider.

The slider has no title. Create a new group and set its `Title` to **`Number of Tweets to Save`**, as shown in Figure 16.9.

Create a slider item, as shown in Figure 16.10. Its `Key` or `DefaultValue` specifies the current position of the slider. Set the `Key` to **`cacheSize`**. Set the `DefaultValue` to **`1000`**.

The value must be between the real value of `MinimumValue` and `MaximumValue`. Set `MinimumValue` to **`0`** and `MaximumValue` to **`10000`**.

`MinimumValueImage` specifies the filename of an image to place at the left of the slider and `MaximumValueImage` specifies the filename of an image to place at the right of the slider. These images should be 21 pixels high and wide. The images are saved in the `Settings.bundle`. Unfortunately, as of version 3.12, Xcode is unable to add images to the `Settings.bundle` file so you must use `Finder` (choose the `Show Package Contents` context menu item) or the `Terminal` to put them there.

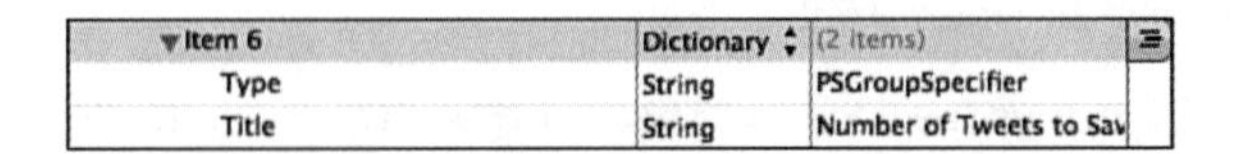

▼Item 6	Dictionary	(2 items)
Type	String	PSGroupSpecifier
Title	String	Number of Tweets to Sav

FIGURE 16.9
Group Item: Number of Tweets to Save

▾Item 7	Dictionary	(7 items)
Type	String	PSSliderSpecifier
Key	String	cacheSize
DefaultValue	Number	1000
MinimumValue	Number	0
MaximumValue	Number	10000
MinimumValueImage	String	NoTweets.png
MaximumValueImage	String	ManyTweets.png

FIGURE 16.10 Slider: Number of tweets

Child Panes

The child pane item has the Type `PSChildPaneSpecifier`. It is used to create subpages of settings.

Its `Title` property specifies the text displayed in the row the user must tap to see the subpage.

Its `File` property specifies the filename of the property list that the Settings application should use to build the subpage of settings. The filename should not contain any path information or file extension: If `File`'s value is `Twitter`, the Settings application will look for the `Twitter.plist` file in the top level of the settings bundle. The file should follow the same format as the `Root.plist` file.

Testing the Settings Bundle

To test the settings bundle, simply build and start the application from Xcode to install it on the iPhone. Leave the application, and open the Settings application.

Dynamically Updating Data from the Network

Internet connectivity has enabled new collaboration applications: Content is dynamically updated by users elsewhere on the network. The main difficulty lies in hiding the asynchronous behavior of networks and users to create the illusion of a consistent workspace. For instance, online games try to provide a consistent experience for the players, even if Frodo killed Gandalf half a minute ago, but Gandalf didn't know because his network connection dropped a packet. Simply properly keeping track of tweets requires a significant amount of work.

Dynamically Loading Tweets

Efficiently dynamically loading tweets is hard and involves solving a number of problems, which we've ignored so far. This section lists the problems and provides a solution.

The Problems

When a user posts a tweet, Twitter inserts the new tweet at the top of the stream of tweets. To reduce network traffic, clients load spans of consecutive tweets, which I'll call tweet pages. Tweet pages have a user-definable length. The first tweet page always includes the most recent tweets. Even if your client is loading the hundredth tweet page, each time a user tweets, the message will be inserted into the top tweet page, causing the last tweet of every tweet page to become the first tweet of the next tweet page. If the client loads the 99th tweet page of a user who then tweets, the 100th tweet page will contain the last message of the 99th page.

Any number of pages may be inserted between downloads of successive tweet pages. For instance, four pages can be loaded between the time the client loads the first and second page. Therefore, the client cannot just filter out tweets it has seen before. Instead, it must detect that new tweets were inserted, and resynchronize: Load as many tweet pages as necessary from the top of the stream of tweets until the client reaches the previous top of the tweet stream, and then resume loading the original tweet page. New tweets may be inserted while resynchronizing.

The table of tweets is generated by interleaving multiple users' streams. On a desktop computer, you could probably achieve reasonable performance by resetting all the user stream iterators, and reloading the table. On the iPhone, this is slow if the user is looking far down into the table. Therefore, it is better to add the new information to the top of the table. Because tweet streams might not be updated in order, and because Twitter is often unavailable, some tweets that are already in the table cache may be interleaved with tweets yet to be downloaded. This must be processed correctly.

Periodically checking for new tweets is similar: New tweets are loaded from the top of the stream, but should not affect the display of new tweets being loaded by the user who's scrolling down to see more tweets.

Failed connections must be detected, reported wherever the user might become confused, and retried after a delay.

As before, the table view is only updated every 10th of a second to coalesce updates. Displaying new tweets causes data to be prefetched, but only one request for a tweet page should be issued.

Finally, a good architecture should support saving downloaded tweets to a database and reloading them later.

A Solution

The solution is to encapsulate each span of consecutive tweets in a Page object. When users scroll down, they add new tweets to the end of the current Page. If a page that is appending new tweets detects that the tweet to be appended precedes the last tweet of the page, it resynchronizes the stream: It sets a flag to say it must be reloaded once the stream has been synchronized, and it creates a new Page that starts downloading the most recent tweets. It continues downloading the contents of the new Page until one of two things happen. If it detects that the synchronizing process was overtaken by events and needs to be resynchronized, it performs the same resynchronization procedure again. If it detects that a tweet it downloaded is the first tweet of an existing page, it merges the two pages, and restarts the old Page's download if necessary.

The Page architecture works well for saved tweets. For instance, if the users checked their Twitter accounts two days ago, and today, yesterday's tweets might not have been saved and might need to be downloaded.

The TweetViewController still expects to use a UserIterator to interleave the different streams of tweets. UserIterators must hide the details of Pages. For instance, they must maintain their position within the stream of tweets even as Pages are merged. To assist them, UserIterators use PageLocations. A PageLocation is an offset offset within a Page and a pointer page to that Page. When two Pages are merged, the PageLocations' page and offset are updated to point to the same tweet as before the merger. Each PageLocation keeps track of the UserIterators that use it, to inform them when pages are merged. They inform their delegates about the page merger. TwitterViewController uses UserIterator delegates to add newly received tweets to the top of its table.

Example Source Code

The example source code for this hour implements solution. Page contains the downloaded tweets for a given User. The tweets are saved as Message objects in Page's messages array. Each Page keeps track of the stream of tweets of a User and is responsible for creating a new Page as soon as it detects it is no longer synchronized with the stream of tweets from twitter.com. Pages may be syncing pages (created to resynchronize the tweet stream) or non-syncing pages (created to download the next pending tweets). They may be in the following states:

- Downloading tweets (pending=YES, a transfer is active, halted = NO, and no timer is active)

- Done downloading tweets (`pending` = `halted` = `syncing` = `NO`, and no transfer or timer is active)
- Paused (`pending=halted=YES`, no transfer is active, no timer is active)
- Waiting (`pending=YES`, no transfer is active, but the timer is active)

The components of these states are the following:

- `pending` specifies whether tweets have been requested from twitter.com. It ensures only one request is sent at a time.
- `halted` specifies whether the tweet transfer was halted because the received tweets indicated that the tweet stream needed resynchronization.
- `syncing` specifies whether the `Page` was created to resynchronize tweets.
- A request might have been sent to the server and be pending.
- A timer might be running to rerequest data after a failed load.

Once enough tweets have been received to resynchronize the stream, a `syncing` `Page` restarts the original transfer that detected the need for synchronization.

Asynchronous Programming in Cocoa

Asynchronous programming is difficult in Cocoa. The example code is complicated because each callback implicitly implements a set of transitions of a finite state machine. We encountered this same problem in Hour 5, "Adding Variables to the Calculator." For the calculator, we solved it by building expressions, which were parsed later: Implementing the finite state machine as a parser clarified the possible state transitions, in two ways:

- By grouping related functionality in the code, rather than scattering it over the delegates that implement it
- By moving state transitions from the data domain (conditions on variables) to the control domain (explicit code)

Summary

Settings are easy to create, but might confuse your users. Provide as few settings as possible, and as many as necessary. Most of the settings we created for the Twitter application are unnecessary. For instance, the application should refresh users' tweets as often as possible without exceeding twitter.com's API limits.

This hour's source code shows you how to write a real application that transparently synchronizes its state with a server. Requiring the user to wait while downloading data and limiting the amount of data the user can see would simplify the code, but would provide a less-compelling user experience. In the next hour, you'll save the tweets to a database so that they are accessible even without Internet access.

Q&A

Q. ***Is there a way to write more comprehensible networking code?***

A. Message passing languages like Erlang let you write networking code like you'd write a parser: Erlang was devised for telephone switches, a highly asynchronous domain. Each state in the state transition graph is modeled as its own run loop. Switching state is implemented by switching run loop. Messages are sent to run loops in the order they were received. Run loops can refuse certain types of messages. These messages are kept and given to the next active run loop. To learn more about Erlang, read *Programming Erlang* by Joe Armstrong.

This architecture can be simulated in Objective-C and results in much clearer code, separating concerns cleanly. For instance, `Page` no longer would maintain any networking state as `pending`, `halted`, `syncing`, and `timer` are all replaced by run loop state. Even `retryInterval` becomes part of a queued message.

Workshop

The Workshop consists of quiz questions and answers to help you solidify your understanding of the material covered in this hour. You should try to answer the questions before checking the answers.

Quiz Questions

1. How does your application retrieve the settings that `Settings` set?
2. How does `Settings` know what settings to show?
3. How do you add an image to the slider?
4. What is a sandbox?
5. What difficulty is encountered programming complex networking applications in Cocoa?

Quiz Answers

1. `Settings` saves user-changed settings to the application's user defaults file.
2. `Settings` scans all applications to find all those with a `Settings.bundle`. This contains a property list `Root.plist`, which specifies the layout and keys of your settings.
3. You must add them to your `Settings.bundle` using the `Finder` or the `Terminal`.
4. Applications can only access certain files: The set of these files constitutes their sandbox.
5. The finite state machine expressing legal transitions is scattered over many delegates and is expressed as conditions on state, rather than as code.

Exercises

- Add an `updateTweets` method, which lets users manually reload the tweets each time they tap the tab bar item of the currently displayed view controller.
- If you leave the Twitter application running, each network error results in an alert panel. Hundreds of alert panels might be queued up after a few hours. Once more than one error has occurred, the Twitter application should replace the currently shown alert panel with a single alert panel mentioning the number of errors encountered so far.
- If you follow many people on Twitter, and set a high refresh rate, you'll soon reach the 150 API calls limit because you're making an API call per user. Twitter supports a friends timeline, which merges all your friends' tweets into a single timeline and filters out their responses to other users. Because this book is not about Twitter, it introduces as few Twitter API calls as possible for its examples. `MGTwitterEngine` provides a `getFollowedTimelineSinceID:startingAtPage:count:` method to read the friends' timelines. Use this method and the Twitter API documentation at http://apiwiki.twitter.com/Twitter-API-Documentation to create your own `FriendTweetIterator` to display your friends' status. A real-world problem such as this one should take a day to work out, as it will involve rearchitecting some of the Twitter application.

HOUR 17
Using the SQLite Database

What You'll Learn in This Hour:

- **Saving and reading data from files**
- **Saving and reading data from an SQLite database**

In this hour, you'll learn about data persistence: saving data to a file or a database so that it can be retrieved later. Files are flat data structures without inbuilt indexing capabilities, whereas databases associate data with indexes to enable fast data retrieval.

Saving and Reading Data from Files

The iPhone provides a standard POSIX C API for file access. However, recall that your application runs inside a sandbox, which prevents it from writing to any path. Cocoa Touch provides functions which return the paths you can access. Cocoa Touch also wraps the POSIX C API in a more pleasant to use Objective-C API that lets you manipulate paths and access files.

Obtaining Legal File Paths

To obtain a path you can use, call `NSSearchPathForDirectoriesInDomains`. Paths you can write to all use the `NSUserDomainMask`. This mask supports three paths:

- `NSDocumentDirectory`—A directory for documents
- `NSCachesDirectory`—A directory for caches
- `NSApplicationSupportDirectory`—A directory for things like preferences

```
NSArray* paths = NSSearchPathForDirectoriesInDomains(NSDocumentDirectory,
                                                     NSUserDomainMask, YES);
NSString* documentsDirectory = [paths objectAtIndex:0];
```

Recall that you can also obtain your applications' resource with NSBundle's pathForResource:ofType: method.

```
NSBundle*     bundle  = [NSBundle mainBundle];
NSString*     path    =[bundle pathForResource:@"climate-change" ofType:@"pdf"];
```

Path Manipulation

pathComponents returns an array of the path components down a path. For instance, it returns @"/", @"tmp", and "foo" for @"/tmp/foo".

fileSystemRepresentation generates a valid filename for the string. For instance, filenames may not contain the 0xc4 character. Note that the C string returned by fileSystemRepresentation is autoreleased and must be copied to be kept.

```
NSLog(@"%s", [@"\u00c4" fileSystemRepresentation]);
AA~à
```

stringByDeletingPathExtension removes file extensions, and stringByStandardizingPath simplifies the path. The results will differ on the iPhone and the simulator.

```
NSLog([@"~/foo/bar/../test.gif" stringByStandardizingPath]);
```

Reading and Writing Cocoa Objects

NSArray, NSDictionary, NSData, and UIImage all support a number of file methods. They can be read from a file using initWithContentsOfFile:. They can also be read from a file (or http) URL using initWithContentsOfURL:. These functions return nil on error. To create a file URL from a path, use NSURL's fileURLWithPath: method.

```
NSURL*        u = [NSURL fileURLWithPath:path];
NSDictionary* d = [[NSDictionary alloc] initWithContentsOfURL:u];
```

Similarly, objects of these classes (except UIImage) can be written to a file using writeToFile:atomically: or writeToURL:atomically:. These functions return NO on failure. If atomically is set to YES, the file is first written with a different name and then is renamed. This prevents any possibility that it could be read in an incomplete state.

NSString has similar methods, but because text has many encodings for text (see Hour 14, "Accessing the Network"), NSString's methods have an argument to specify the encoding. Generally speaking, you'll use UTF-8. Another argument is used to record errors. You can pass nil if you do not care to decode errors.

```
NSError*  err;
NSString* string = [NSString stringWithContentsOfURL:url
                             encoding:NSUTF8StringEncoding error:nil];
BOOL         ok = [string writeToFile:path atomically:NO
                          encoding:NSUTF8StringEncoding error:&err];
```

Many of these functions have `autorelease` equivalents, such as `stringWithContentsOfURL:encoding:error:`.

> Many new Cocoa programmers expect `writeToURL:url` to write the string to any *url*, such as an FTP site or a web sever. It doesn't. It only saves strings to URLs that use the `file` scheme.

Saving and Reading Data from an SQLite Database

The SQLite database provides a small but reliable and relatively efficient database implementation. It uses the standard SQL language for queries, and saves databases as single files.

SQLite Is a Database

The problem with flat-file schemas is that you must load the entire file into memory to read its contents. Instead, you often only want part of a file. A simple way of doing this is to save data as a table, where each row is a set length. To calculate the offset of the *n*th row of data, simply multiply the row's index by its length. Then use `lseek` to skip to the relevant place in the file. This solution works well for densely indexed tables. However, for sparsely indexed tables, a lot of file space is wasted.

To find a better solution, you must first know that storage is divided into pages whose access times depend on the storage medium. Reading or writing a page on a hard-drive is relatively fast, but accessing it is slow because the disk head must move to the correct track and the disk must rotate to the correct sector until it can be read. Reading and accessing a page in flash memory is fast, but writing to a page requires it first to be erased, which is slow. File systems can hide this effect by writing new pages to unused blocks until they run out of them. Once they run out, they must erase freed but previously used blocks before they can write to flash memory. The data structures used to find data given an index must also take into account file system page size to reduce the number of pages they access.

Balanced binary trees provide a good indexing solution for read-only files. For instance, navigation systems save the road network in such indexed read-only files: The data associated with an index is found in at most O(log(*N*)) steps. Multiple tree nodes are saved in a page, to reduce the number of pages that must be read. The indexed data can either be stored with the tree nodes or in a large data block: It depends on the ratio of data size to page size. However, because balanced binary trees must be rebalanced every time a new element is inserted, each update requires many writes. This makes balanced binary trees a poor indexing solution for files that are updated.

B-trees pack data less densely than binary trees, as shown in Figure 17.1. This reduces the number of times they must be rebalanced: They store multiple keys and values in a single node. Only when adding or removing data causes a node to have fewer or more keys than allowed is the B-tree rebalanced. Rebalancing takes at most O(log(*N*)) operations but occurs much more rarely than it does for binary trees. Moreover, when rebalancing, most balanced binary tree algorithms reorder which nodes are parents and which nodes are children. In RAM, this is not a problem because memory access is fast. However reordering parents and children on disk causes more pages to be read and written than necessary. B-trees minimize this problem. B-trees have been the standard data structure for databases since the early 1970s. Like other balanced trees, B-trees are organized using the numerical order of nodes' keys.

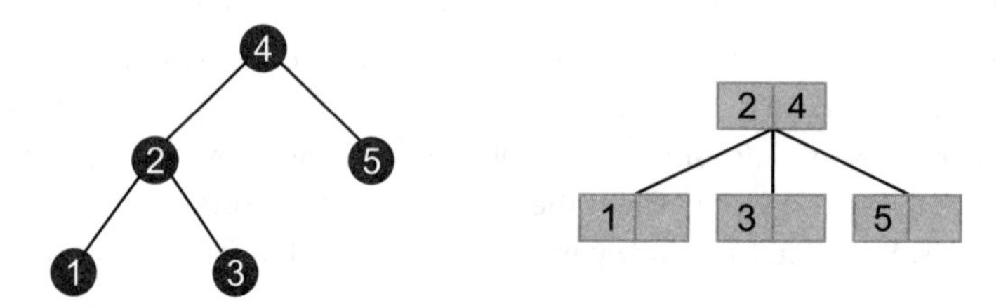
4
2
5
1
3
2 4
1
3
5
Every node of a binary tree only has 0, 1 or 2 children.
Every Node of a 2-3 B-Tree has 0, 2 or 3 children

FIGURE 17.1 Binary trees and B-trees

The SQLite database provides B-tree algorithms you can use via SQL.

SQL

If SQLite only provided a low-level interface to its B-tree data structures, your code would have to decide the order in which data should be retrieved or written. This would be suboptimal because the order of data on disk determines the program's performance. Because saving data to disk is SQLite's responsibility, it is SQLite that knows how data is organized on disk. Therefore your program should only specify the data it wishes to read or write and leave the mechanics up to SQLite.

The **SQL** language (**Structured Query Language**) provides a way for a program to specify the data it desires to read or write without specifying the order in which to fetch it. SQLite parses the SQL query and converts it to bytecode, which it optimizes to create an optimal sequence of file system accesses to the data. A cache further reduces the number of necessary reads and writes.

SQL supports creating multiple tables in a database. Each table consists of rows consisting of a primary key and values. The primary key uniquely identifies a row. The row consists of one or more **components**. Just like a data field of C structures, a component has a name (by which it can be accessed), a type, and a value. In terms of the B-tree, the primary key is the B-tree key, and the values are combined to form the B-tree value.

SQL makes it easy to combine the data from many tables together dynamically: Your table design can separate concerns without making your implementation more complicated. Thus, for instance, you can use different tables to represent the medical history, current insurer, and ward assignment of patients. However, it is important to remember that each of these tables is backed by a B-tree that will need to be traversed. The more tables accessed, the slower the resulting query.

Table Design

If you have multiple copies of the same information, the database can easily become inconsistent. This is not unique to databases. Keeping information consistent requires keeping track of every copy. The Don't Repeat Yourself (DRY) principle applies here as well. Database normalization strives to eliminate data duplication and to structure data so that it can be usefully manipulated using SQL queries.

SQL differs from C in that data fields cannot be arrays. This can confuse people who try to replicate arrays, either by putting items into comma-separated strings or by creating a column for each element of the array. Both of these solutions prevent SQL statements from usefully manipulating the data. Instead, each column of a table should have an unambiguous meaning and the number of rows should be increased to accommodate the data. Tables should use atomic values and only have one column per type of item.

Tables are best used to express relationships: If each table expresses a relationship, each row of the table states items for which the relationship is true. For instance, a table might state Social Security holders' dates of birth. The table consists of a column of Social Security numbers and a column of birth dates. Each row states that it is true that the person who has the Social Security number of the row has the date of birth of the row. Keeping independent relationships in different tables reduces the chance of data duplication. For instance, a Social Security number can be associated with multiple names (as people get married, divorced, and so on), each of which is valid for some time. If this information is in the date of birth table, there will be as many rows per person as the person had names. The date of birth information will be repeated on each row for the person because it does not change. Using a separate table associating Social Security numbers to names avoids duplicating the date of birth information (see Figure 17.2).

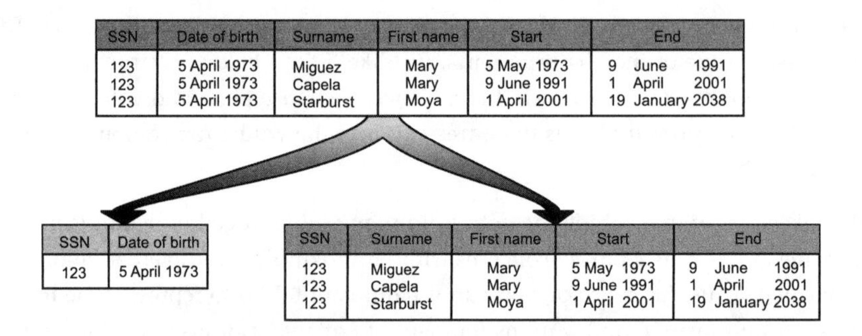

FIGURE 17.2 Normalization reduces duplicated information (date of birth) by splitting tables.

Often, a single update to a database involves updating a number of entries in different tables. If an exception occurs between those updates, the database is left in an inconsistent state. For instance, if a hospital keeps track of surgeries by bed numbers, and Mary was sent to bed 778, but bed 778's surgery was not correctly updated because of a network error, Mary might suffer the wrong surgery. To prevent this from happening, SQL statements can be grouped into transactions: Either the entire transaction completes, or the database is not updated, guaranteeing database consistency.

Normalization is a pragmatic issue. Although normalization reduces data size, it also increases the number of B-trees that must be read. If your performance bottleneck is reading data, you might find that creating additional tables containing all the data you need for a given request improves performance: You are creating a data cache.

Using SQLite from the Command Line

SQLite has a command-line tool that you can run on your Mac to manipulate databases or test out SQL statements. Databases created on your Mac will work on your iPhone: Simply add them to your project's Resources folder. We'll create a simple database to store tweets.

A Table of Tweets

We save each tweet in a row as a tweet identifier, a date, a message, and a user identifier. The table expresses the relationship "User said message at date". As we want to fetch tweets by identifier, we'll use the tweet identifier as the primary key.

Creating a Table

To open a new database, open the Terminal application, and type the following:

```
sqlite3 test.db
SQLite version 3.4.0
Enter ".help" for instructions
sqlite>
```

By the Way

You can exit SQLite at any time by typing `.quit`.

SQL commands resemble English: They start with a verb (`create`, `select`, ...), followed by an object (`table tweets`, `id from tweets`) and then one or more noun or verb phrases (`where ...`, `having ...`, `ordered by ...`).

To create a table, you must specify the components' names and types. For instance, we'll assign the component `id` to tweet identifiers. It will be an integer and the primary key. `SQLite` supports the following types: `INTEGER` (1,2,4,6, or 8 bytes), `REAL` (8 bytes), `TEXT` (UTF-8 or UTF-16, of any length), `BLOB` (binary data of any length), and `NULL`.

```
sqlite> CREATE TABLE tweets ( id INTEGER PRIMARY KEY, date DOUBLE, user
➥INTEGER, message TEXT );
```

The B-tree SQLite uses for the table uses an integer key. If you specify an integer primary key when you create the table, it will use that key. Otherwise, it will create a hidden component for the B-tree key. If you specify a noninteger primary key, it uses an index to map your primary key to the B-tree key (requiring a second lookup). The primary key of each row must be unique.

The primary key is a column constraint. Other column constraints include `UNIQUE` (the value of the component in each row is unique), `DEFAULT` (the default value to insert if no value is specified by the `INSERT` command), and `CHECK` constraints (a condition that must be satisfied for the column to accept the data being inserted). A unique feature of SQLite is that it lets you specify what the database should do if a constraint (such as uniqueness, or a check statement) is violated. It does this by introducing an `ON CONFLICT` statement. You can specify that the database should:

- `ROLLBACK`—End the current transaction and roll back;
- `ABORT`—Roll back this statement, but not the entire transaction;

- FAIL—Keep the changes made by this statement on other rows but give up;
- IGNORE—Don't change this row, but continue the operation for other pending rows;
- REPLACE—If the statement violated uniqueness, just replace the offending row.

For instance, you could write the following:

```
sqlite> CREATE TABLE tweets ( id INTEGER PRIMARY KEY ON CONFLICT REPLACE,
➥date DOUBLE, user INTEGER, message TEXT );
```

Did you Know?

> The definition of every table in a database can be accessed using
>
> sqlite> **SELECT * FROM sqlite_master;**.

Creating an Index

An index is a secondary B-tree, which provides a fast path to finding a row given a search on one or more components. For instance, to search faster by date, you'd create an index:

```
sqlite> CREATE INDEX date_index ON tweets (date);
```

Indexes are implemented as B-trees. If there is enough space to fit the row data in the index, it is added to each B-tree node. Otherwise, the index references the table's primary key (requiring a second lookup to return the data). Indexes are updated each time information is added to their table, and should only be used when the performance gains outweigh their costs.

Inserting Information

INSERT is used to add rows to a table. If you insert all the row's columns in the same order as they are defined in the table, you do not need to mention them by name.

```
sqlite> INSERT INTO tweets(id, date, user, message) VALUES(1234,
➥1249670633.87004, 56, 'This is a message');
```

Strings are enclosed by single quotes. Represent single quotes within the string by two single quotes in a row. Blobs are encoded in hexadecimal, enclosed by single quotes, and preceded by X.

> Instead of VALUES, you can use a SELECT statement to copy data from one table to another.

Updating and Deleting Rows

UPDATE lets you assign a value to the component of every row that matches the WHERE expression. UPDATEs without a WHERE update every row of the table. For instance, to change the user of a tweet, type the following:

```
sqlite> UPDATE tweets SET user=99 WHERE id=1234;
```

Similarly, DELETE deletes rows that match the WHERE expression. DELETEs without a WHERE expression delete every row:

```
sqlite> DELETE FROM tweets WHERE user=99;
```

Unless you set PRAGMA auto_vacuum = 1; before you created the database, SQLite will not shrink your database when you delete information. This improves write speed, at the cost of read speed. The VACCUUM command builds a new database file from the data in the current file, and then swaps them.

Did you Know?

You can delete an entire table or index by using DROP TABLE *table_name* and DROP INDEX *index_name*.

Transactions

SQLite logs transactions in a transaction file. If you do not explicitly enclose SQL statements in a transaction between BEGIN and COMMIT (or ROLLBACK), SQLite will create a transaction for each SQL statement, causing the transaction file to be updated for each statement. Because this is slow, you should group statements into single transactions whenever possible.

Selecting Information

The SELECT statement returns rows of data from one or more table. You can specify the components you want and their order. Similarly, a WHERE clause allows you to filter the rows you want to see. For instance, to retrieve all tweets since 17th April 2009, write the following (date is the number of seconds since January 1, 1970):

```
sqlite> SELECT message FROM tweets WHERE date > 1240000000;
```

Some WHERE clauses can be optimized using the underlying B-tree: Because the numerical order of B-tree keys determines the structure of the B-tree, WHERE clauses expressed in terms of inequalities or equalities on B-tree keys can find the first row to return in $O(\log(N))$ steps. Because successive rows are stored on data pages, and successive data pages form a linked list, successive rows can be streamed quickly from a table.

Did you Know?

Because each column may have a lot of data associated with it, tables are actually a special type of B-trees called B+trees: They do not store values on the nodes, but require an additional page read to get the data. To support data of any size, SQLite uses additional overflow pages if a row does not fit in a page. These pages will only be read if the data's component is read. Indexes are B-trees.

Other WHERE clauses cannot be optimized using the underlying B-tree: They require the entire table to be scanned through. For instance, the LIKE expression performs regular expression matching on strings. SELECT statements that filter rows using LIKE must traverse the entire table to find the strings that match. The same is true for GLOB, which matches filenames using slightly different rules.

LIKE only supports simple regular expressions:

- Each underscore (_) matches any single character.
- Each percent (%) matches any string of one or more characters.
- All other characters only match themselves. Thus, "fish" is LIKE '__s_' and '%h', but is not LIKE '__'.

SELECT statements can also return data from tables that are created on the fly with a JOIN statement.

The simplest form of JOIN statement is a cross join: Every row of one table is associated with every row of the other table. If the two tables have *N* and *M* rows, the resulting table has *N**M* rows. Cross joins are not particularly useful as they assume the two tables are independent (in which case, there is no need to combine them).

Usually, you will want to combine two tables to gain information about shared components. For instance, you might want to know the date of birth and all the names of known Social Security holders. In this case, you want to generate every combination of rows from the date of birth and names tables that share the same Social Security holder component. This is called an inner join. There are two variants of inner joins: NATURAL JOINs and INNER JOINs. Natural joins assume joined tables should share any components that have the same name. Inner joins let you specify the components you want to share in a WHERE or an ON expression:

```
sqlite> SELECT dob.ssn, dob.dob, name.surname, name.firstname, name.start,
➥name.end FROM dob INNER JOIN name WHERE dob.ssn = name.ssn;
```

If two components of two tables share the same name, you can distinguish them by prefixing them with their table name and a period.

Inner joins only return rows that share the same component value in both tables: In our example, Social Security holders who do not have a known birthday will not be returned by the preceding SELECT statement. Outer joins were invented to solve this problem. Outer joins behave like inner joins for components that are shared between both tables. However, rows whose shared component does not have a counterpart in the other table are also returned. The main kinds of join are illustrated in Figure 17.3

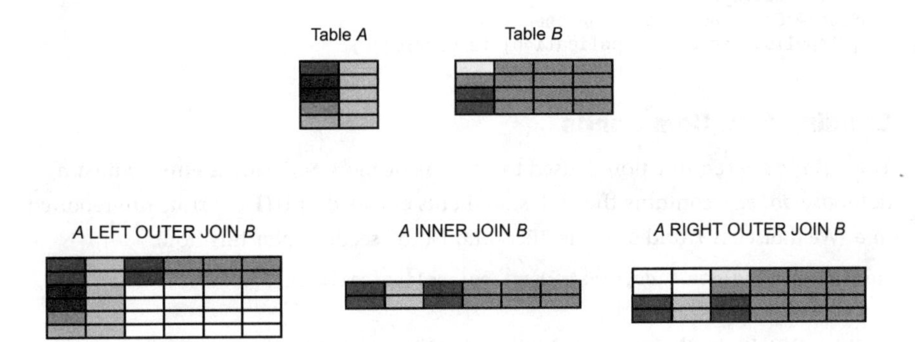

FIGURE 17.3 Inner and outer joins

SQLite only supports LEFT OUTER JOINs, which guarantee every row of the left table will be returned. Simply swap the two tables to create a RIGHT OUTER JOIN. To create a FULL OUTER JOIN, which includes all the elements of both tables, you can combine two LEFT OUTER JOIN SELECT statements with a UNION:

```
sqlite> SELECT dob.ssn, dob.dob, name.surname, name.firstname, name.start,
➥name.end FROM dob LEFT OUTER JOIN name WHERE dob.ssn = name.ssn;
```

SELECT statements provide other functionality such as ordering returned rows, guaranteeing rows are distinct, and grouping; however, space limitations preclude further discussion. Because these functions are implemented by postprocessing, they do not affect how data is fetched: You can implement equivalent functionality in Objective-C without using SQL.

Using SQLite from Your Application

To use SQLite from your application, you must link in the library by adding a new framework to the Frameworks section of your Groups & Files pane and choosing /usr/lib/libsqlite3.0.dylib at the top level of your iPhone software development kit (SDK). The headers are declared in <sqlite3.h>.

Opening and Closing a Database

To open a database, call `sqlite3_open(char* filename, sqlite3 **db);`. Using `NULL` for the *filename* creates a database in memory. If all goes well, *db* contains a handle (connection) to the database. To close the database, call `sqlite3_close(*db);`.

```
sqlite3* db = NULL;
int r = sqlite3_open("test.db", &db);
if (r != SQLITE_OK)
{ NSLog(@"Could not create or open test.db");
  [[UIApplication sharedApplication] terminate]; };
```

Sending SQL Commands

The `sqlite3_exec` function is used to run one or more SQL statements against a database *db*. *sql* contains the SQL statements encoded in UTF-8. Errors are reported in *e*. We'll discuss *f* and *d* in the "Reading Data" section later this hour.

```
sqlite3_exec(sqlite3* db,const char* sql,sqlite_callback f,void* d,char** e);
```

For instance, to create the table, you'd write the following:

```
char*     errMsg = NULL;
NSString* sql    = @"create table tweets (id integer primary key, date double,"
                   @"user integer, message text);";
r = sqlite3_exec(db, [sql UTF8String], NULL, NULL, &errMsg);
if ((r != SQLITE_OK) && (errMsg != NULL))
{ NSLog(@"SQLite error for %@ : %s", sql, errMsg);
  sqlite3_free(errMsg); }
```

Some SQLite commands only work with newer versions of SQLite. You can check the version of SQLite using gdb. Start an application and type the following:

```
(gdb) print (char*) sqlite3_libversion()
$1 = 0x927560d4 "3.4.0"
```

Escaping Strings

SQL commands are identical to the strings you typed directly into `sqlite3`. `sqlite_mprintf` provides a `printf` replacement that can add the proper escapes for your strings. Use `%q` to add string escapes and `%Q` to also enclose the resulting string with single quotes. You must free the string `sqlite_mprintf` returns by calling `sqlite3_free`.

```
char* sql     = "insert into tweets values (%lld, %lld, %g, %Q);";
char* escaped = sqlite3_mprintf(sql, id, userID, date, message);
r = sqlite3_exec(db, escaped, NULL, NULL, &errMsg);
if ((r != SQLITE_OK) && (errMsg != NULL))
{ NSLog(@"SQLite error for %s : %s", escaped, errMsg);
  sqlite3_free(errMsg); }
sqlite3_free(escaped);
```

Reading Data

Because SQLite knows how data is ordered, it is in the driver's seat and calls your application's callback `f` for each row. Use the data parameter (*d*) to uniquely identify the `SELECT` statement returning the data. The callback function returns a Boolean to stop the read. The headers and values are strings.

```
char* sql = "select * from tweets;";
r = sqlite3_exec(db, sql, callback, @"Tweet", &errMsg);
if ((r != SQLITE_OK) && (errMsg != NULL))
{ NSLog(@"SQLite error for %s : %s", sql, errMsg);
  sqlite3_free(errMsg); }


int callback(void* d, int ncols, char** values, char** headers )
{
  NSLog(@"%@:");
  for (int i = 0; i < ncols; ++i)
    NSLog(@"  %s : %s", headers[i], values[i]);
  return 0;
}
```

A shorthand to dump the entire content of a table to an array of C strings is provided by `sqlite3_get_table`. The resulting table must be released by `sqlite3_free_table`:

```
char  *errMsg, **table;
int   nrows, ncols;
int   rc    = sqlite3_get_table(db, "select * from tweets;",
                                &table, &nrows, &ncols, &errMsg);
...
sqlite3_free_table(table);
```

Compiling Commands

SQLite compiles queries to optimized bytecode. To convert an SQL statement to bytecode, call `sqlite3_prepare()`. The `sqlTail` will point to the next statement.

```
int sqlite3_prepare(sqlite3* db, const char* sql,     int byteCount,
                                 sqlite3_stmt** stmt, const char** sqlTail);
```

You can specify a statement's arguments using the `sqlite3_bind_`*xxx* functions, which takes a statement, an argument index, and a value. *xxx* may be `int`, `double`, `int64`, `null`, `blob`, `text`, and `text16`. The `text`, `text16`, and `blob` variants take two additional arguments (a length and a cleanup handler).

```
int   n   = [msg lengthOfBytesUsingEncoding:NSUTF8StringEncoding];
char* m   = (char*) malloc(n);
strcpy(m, [msg UTF8String]);

char* sql = "insert into tweets values(?,?,?,?);";
int   rc  = sqlite3_prepare(db, sql, strlen(sql), &stmt, &tail);
```

```
sqlite3_bind_int64 (stmt, 1, id);
sqlite3_bind_int64 (stmt, 2, userID);
sqlite3_bind_double(stmt, 3, date);
sqlite3_bind_text  (stmt, 4, m, n, free);
sqlite3_step(stmt);
```

Once the query is compiled, you can run it using `sqlite3_step`.

Statements contain a **cursor**, which serves the same purpose as an iterator: It points to the next row. Each invocation of `sqlite3_step` moves to the next row. `sqlite3_step` will return `SQLITE_BUSY` if the database is locked. It will return `SQLITE_ROW` if there is another row and `SQLITE_DONE` if the rows have been exhausted.

`sqlite3_column_count` returns the number of columns the statement will return, while `sqlite_data_count` returns the number of columns the row has.

To access the content of a row, use the `sqlite3_column_`*`xxx`* functions. *`xxx`* may be `int`, `double`, `int64`, `blob`, `text`, and `text16`. `sqlite3_column_bytes` returns the number of bytes in the blob. Each of these functions takes a statement and a column index, and returns data of the appropriate type (after a conversion, if necessary).

To reset the iterator back to the first row, use `sqlite3_reset`. To free the statement's resources, call `sqlite3_finalize`. If any statements are in progress, they are committed or rolled back.

```
char* sql = "select * from tweets;";
sqlite3_prepare(db, sql, strlen(sql), &stmt, &tail);

while (sqlite3_step(stmt) == SQLITE_ROW)
{
  int n = sqlite3_data_count(stmt);
  for (int i = 0; i < n; ++i)
    NSLog(@"%s : %s", sqlite3_column_name(stmt, i), sqlite3_column_text(stmt,
i));
}

sqlite3_finalize(stmt);
```

Did you Know?

> You can obtain the database connection for a statement by calling `sqlite3_db_handle(stmt)`.

Summary

The iPhone provides a full range of file-manipulation capabilities. It also provides a small general-purpose database based on B-trees. Obviously, B-trees are not ideal for all purposes. Text-completion algorithms or spell checkers based on B-trees are very slow. Instead, you should use a Trie or a Bloom filter, respectively.

We have only scratched the surface of SQLite's capabilities. For instance, SQLite adds a `TRIGGER` command to trigger actions when a value of a table is inserted, updated, or deleted. This can be used to update tables that serve as caches for improved performance, and reduce the amount of work required to maintain consistency. SQLite also has limitations: Its optimizer is limited to simpler SQL statements and it cannot drop columns, alter columns, or do either right outer joins or full outer joins. To learn more about SQLite, I strongly recommend *The DefinitiveGuide to SQLite* by Michael Owens. A good reference to SQL in general is *SQL* by Chris Fehily.

Q&A

Q. ***Is there an easy way to encrypt data?***

A. The SQLCipher variant of SQLite saves data to disk transparently, encrypting it with AES-256 encryption. The performance loss is only 5%. It is available at http://zetetic.net/software/sqlcipher.

Q. ***Can I use SQLite in multithreaded programs?***

A. Yes. Although SQLite authors believe that threads are evil (see the SQLite FAQ for their reasons), you can compile SQLite to be thread safe. You must open the database in each thread, and you cannot share `sqlite3` or `sqlite3_stmt` structures between threads. The application can suffer conflicting lock errors if threads try to read and write the database simultaneously.

Workshop

The Workshop consists of quiz questions and answers to help you solidify your understanding of the material covered in this hour. You should try to answer the questions before checking the answers.

Quiz Questions

1. When should you use a database?
2. How do you retrieve information from an SQL table?
3. How does SQLite process SQL statements?

Quiz Answers

1. Use a database whenever you need good-enough performance to access data whose indexes are sparse or whenever SQL will simplify development without causing performance problems.
2. Use the `SELECT` command to retrieve information from an SQL table.
3. SQLite processes SQL statements by compiling them to bytecode, which it optimizes and then runs.

Exercise

- Change the Twitter program to save received data to the database and read saved tweets from the database.

HOUR 18

Using Core Data

What You'll Learn in This Hour:

- Using NSSortDescriptor and NSPredicate
- Using Core Data
- Using Xcode to design objects

Core Data lets you load and save objects to storage transparently by providing a single object definition instead of writing your own classes and your own serialization code. Core Data can use SQLite as a storage medium, letting you easily write iPhone tools that manipulate databases that would not fit in memory. In this hour, you'll learn how Core Data works so that you understand its performance characteristics.

Using NSSortDescriptor and NSPredicate

Core Data relies heavily on NSSortDescriptor and NSPredicate. Hour 17, "Using the SQLite Database," pointed out that using code to directly access B-trees creates a form of strong coupling: Code not only specifies the desired data but also the order in which to fetch it. By moving requests to SQL, we were able to specify the data to read without specifying the order in which it should be fetched. NSSortDescriptor and NSPredicate provide a way of specifying the data to return and its order, so that data-fetching code can optimize its requests. You can also use these classes to sort and filter NSArrays. Both classes rely on Key-Value Coding to extract a key for sorting or filtering, and will cause an exception if reference keys cannot be accessed via Key-Value Coding.

NSSortDescriptor

NSSortDescriptor provides a representation for expressing ordering relationships. A sort specifies an order (ascending), and the key path of the variable to use for comparison (key). Creating a sort descriptor is easy. For instance, to sort people by their seniority (oldest first), you'd write the following:

```
NSSortDescriptor* sort
        = [[NSNSSortDescriptor alloc] initWithKey:@"dateOfBirth" ascending:YES];
```

Multiple sort descriptors can be combined to sort information according to primary, secondary, and so on keys. Thus, we can sort an array so that people are sorted by last name, but any people who share the same last name are then sorted by first name. You can sort an array with multiple descriptors using `sortedArrayUsingDescriptors:`.

NSPredicate

`NSPredicate` provides a representation for logic statements: When you apply a predicate to an object using its `evaluateWithObject:` method, the result is either true or false.

The Building Blocks of NSPredicates

`NSPredicate` uses three classes to build its statements:

- `NSCompoundPredicate` lets you combine a number of subpredicates using logical AND (&& in C) or OR (|| in C) into a compound statement. It also lets you negate the result of a subpredicate (`!` in C).
- `NSComparisonPredicate` combines two expressions returning a truth value. Predefined comparisons include <, <=, >, >=, ==, !=, `matches`, `like`, `beginswith`, `endswith`, `in`, `contains`, and `between`. `matches` performs ICU-style regular expression matching. (ICU stands for International Components for Unicode.) `like` performs simpler regular expression matching, which only recognizes single-character (?) and multiple-character (*) wildcards. `beginswith` and `endswith` check prefixes and suffixes. `in` is true if the element on its left appears in the collection on its right. You can also use a custom selector to perform the comparison.
- `NSExpression` specifies the items to be compared: constants or key paths. The special key path `SELF` refers to the object itself. Expressions also can apply predefined functions to their variables. For instance, `count` returns the number of items in a key path.

Using NSPredicate's Parser

Although you can build `NSPredicates` directly from their constituent classes, you can also use `NSPredicate`'s `predicateWithFormat:` to parse a string specifying the predicate. For instance, the following predicate checks whether an object's lastName matches searchString and its dateOfBirth follows searchDate:

```
NSPredicate* predicate = [NSPredicate predicateWithFormat:
    @"(lastName like[cd] %@) AND (dateOfBirth > %@)", searchString, searchDate];
```

The lastName comparison is case-insensitive and is diacritic-insensitive (as specified by [cd]). Diacritics are accents, umlauts, and the like, which are added to a character.

By default, NSString arguments to %@ will be substituted between quotes, whereas %K won't: Use %K to substitute for keys.

You can also create predicates with substitution variables, to be specified by a dictionary later. Prefix your variables with $. Then, when you know their values, substitute them using predicateWithSubstitutionVariables:. Its argument is an NSDictionary whose keys are the variable names and whose values are the values to substitute.

NSPredicate also lets you create conditions on collections with ANY and ALL. For instance, to find the departments whose employees are all paid more than a certain salary, you'd write the following:

```
NSPredicate *predicate
       = [NSPredicate predicateWithFormat:@"ALL employees.salary > %f", salary];
```

Using Predicates

Apply a predicate with evaluateWithObject::

```
BOOL ok = [predicate evaluateWithObject:identity];
```

Predicates can be used to filter the elements of an NSArray:

```
NSArray* r = [array filterUsingPredicate:predicate];
```

To learn more about NSPredicate, read Apple's "Predicate Programming Guide." It's simple but has many features.

Using Predicates for SQL

Core Data can use SQLite to save data to storage. To fetch data, it converts the NSPredicate you supply into a SQL WHERE statement. Because of SQL limitations, the conversion is only possible for a subset of all predicates. For instance, NSComparisonPredicates that use a custom selector would not work because there is no way to represent the custom selector in SQL. Because there is no support for regular expressions in SQL, predicates using it will fail. Similarly, the use of ALL, ANY, and IN mirrors SQLite's limitations (namely that there may only be one operator from ALL, ANY, and IN).

Generally speaking, use simple predicates that you can easily translate into SQL. To debug predicates faster, test them against a test NSArray before using them with a Core Data SQL persistent store: This will help you differentiate your misunderstandings of NSPredicate from the limitations of the conversion of NSPredicate to SQL.

Using Core Data

So far, adding the ability to load and save data has required two ways of representing the same data: objects in memory and objects serialized to storage. Sometimes, it is appropriate to have two representations because storage and memory have significantly different performance and size characteristics. Often, however, the bulk of your innovation lies elsewhere, and writing a storage layer is grunt work that simply replicates the off-disk layout: a violation of the "Don't Repeat Yourself" (or DRY) principle. Core Data, introduced in iPhone OS 3.0, provides a solution for this case. Figure 18.1 shows the constituents of Core Data.

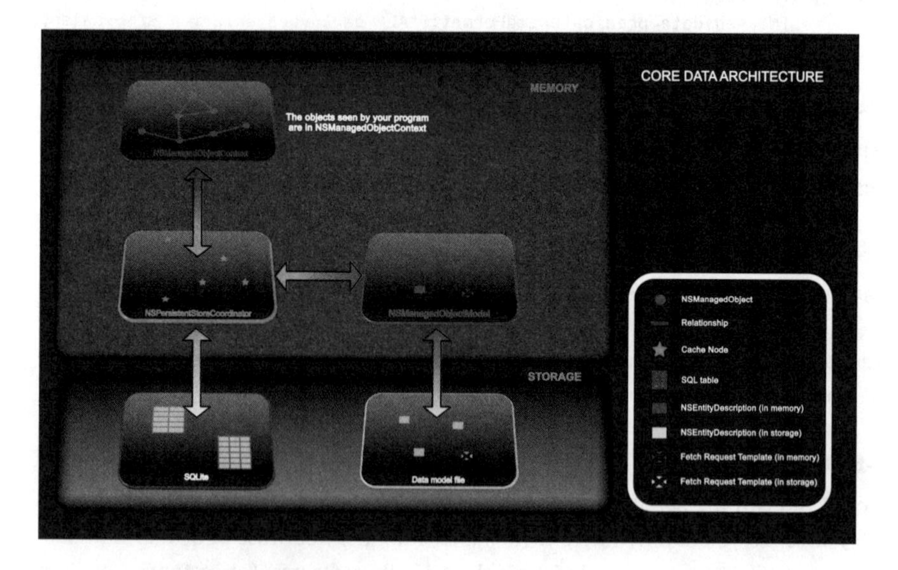

FIGURE 18.1
The components of Core Data

Creating a Data Model

Interface Builder replaces GUI glue code with a small interpreter that dynamically builds objects in memory and sets up their outlets from the specifications in a NIB file. Core Data provides a similar interpreter that interprets a data model file. Because objects' layouts are defined as data, two different classes can use them to create objects in memory and to serialize them to storage.

Defining Objects' Properties

The objects Core Data can model have two kinds of properties: attributes and relationships. Attributes are properties that contain values (numbers, Booleans, strings, dates). Relationships are properties that point to other `NSManagedObjects`. To specify these properties, Core Data provides three classes:

- `NSPropertyDescription`—A class that specifies features common to all properties
- `NSAttributeDescription`—A subclass of `NSPropertyDescription` for attributes
- `NSRelationshipDescription`—A subclass of `NSPropertyDescription` for relationships

To create an attribute description, specify its name and its type. You can also specify if it is optional and its default value.

```
NSAttributeDescription* firstName = [[NSAttributeDescription alloc] init];
[firstName setName:@"firstName"];
[firstName setAttributeType:NSStringAttributeType];
[firstName setOptional:NO];
[firstName autorelease];
```

To create a relationship description, specify its name, destination entity, inverse relationship, and counts. Every person only has one Social Security number and date of birth, although they might have many identities.

```
NSRelationshipDescription* person = [[NSRelationshipDescription alloc] init];
[person setName:@"person"];
[person setDestinationEntity:personEntity];
[person setInverseRelationship:personToIdentityRelationship];
[person setMinCount:1];
[person setMaxCount:1];
[person autorelease];
```

These objects become nonmutable after they have been used to create an in-memory object (an `NSManagedObject`).

Using NSEntityDescription

NSEntityDescriptions encapsulate the data model of an object: They specify an object's class, properties, and inheritance hierarchy (sub- and superentities corresponding to sub- and superclasses).

To create NSManagedObjects, you must create NSEntityDescriptions to describe the objects you want to create. You can change NSEntityDescription's properties dynamically, defining the properties of the object you want to build on the fly. For instance, invoke setProperties: to set the desired properties and setManagedObjectClassName: to decide the class of the object that will be created by NSEntityDescription. The NSEntityDescription hierarchy must be built from the top down. This is enforced programmatically by only providing a setSubentities: method.

```
NSMutableArray* identityProperties
  = [NSArray arrayWithObjects:firstName, lastName, nameStart, nameEnd,
                              person, nil];

NSEntityDescription* identityEntity = [[NSEntityDescription alloc] init];
[identityEntity setName:@"Identity"];
[identityEntity setManagedObjectClassName:@"Identity"];
[identityEntity setProperties:identityProperties];
```

After an NSManagedObject has been created, the NSEntityDescription that was used to create it becomes nonmutable. You can, however, create a mutable copy of it, modify it, and create a new NSManagedObject with it. For this reason, NSEntityDescription's isEqual: simply checks pointer equality and is unsuitable for use as an NSDictionary key.

Creating an NSManagedObjectModel

NSManagedObjectModel represents a data model. It contains the model's NSEntityDescriptions. To build an NSManagedObjectModel in code, you'd write the following:

```
NSManagedObjectModel* mom = [[NSManagedObjectModel alloc] init];
[mom setEntities:[NSArray arrayWithObjects:identityEntity, personEntity, nil]];
```

Alternatively, load a data model you created in Xcode using initWithContentsOfURL::

```
NSManagedObjectModel* mom
  = [[NSManagedObjectModel alloc] initWithContentsOfURL:modelFileURL];
```

entities and entitiesByName return the model's entities (in an array or a dictionary keyed by names). Note that modifying an entity creates a new version of the NSManagedObjectModel, which will be incompatible with any files saved using the original data model. Only the following changes do not create an incompatible `NSManagedModel`:

- Adding transient properties
- Changing the managed class name
- Changing validation predicates
- Adding default values
- Changing user info dictionaries

Multiple Model Versions

Upgrading your application might involve changing the data model. Core Data persistent stores are not backward compatible: You must provide the old data model to load data saved by an older version of your application. One approach to this problem is to save a version number in `NSPersistentStore`'s `metadata`. Use this version number to determine the data model to use. To upgrade the data model, create a new managed object context with the next version of the data model. Traverse all the data, and copy the objects and their attributes over to the new managed object context, changing them as required. Repeat this process until the data is in the newest data format. Iterating in this way reduces the number of data migrators you must build. (You'll learn about managed object contexts later in this hour.)

Because data models are often changed, Core Data provides a means to automate much of this process, using a data migration mapping model you can create in Xcode. Rather than explicitly saving version numbers, Core Data creates hashes (`versionHash`) of the various entities' descriptions, which are used to decide whether a data model is compatible. If automated data migration is enabled, Core Data can find the appropriate data models and mapping models and perform the process outlined earlier itself. Core Data's **automatic migration** only works for a subset of all mappings between data models, and must transform the entire database in a single pass—requiring a significant amount of memory. For these reasons, it might not always be suitable.

Did you Know?

Because you might change the data model often while developing an application, Core Data can now automatically migrate simple data model changes (for example, adding a property, changing a property name, changing whether a property is optional). This is called **lightweight migration** and is particularly fast when using a SQLite store.

Because explaining this topic in more detail would take an hour to itself, I'll refer you to Apple's "Core Data Model Versioning and Data Migration Programming Guide" and the NSEntityMapping, NSEntityMigrationPolicy, NSMappingModel, and NSMigrationManager classes.

Creating In-Memory Objects

NSManagedObjects are in-memory objects built from NSEntityDescriptions. Key-Value Coding, dynamic properties, and dynamically generated subclasses created with Objective-C runtime make NSManagedObjects look like standard Objective-C objects.

Key-Value Coding

As you learned with Key-Value Coding, accessing objects' properties and accessing a dictionary's keys are no different. Therefore, we just need to create an object that reads a data model, and builds a dictionary from it to respond to the Key-Value Coding methods valueForKey: and setValue:forKey: (see Hour 5, "Adding Variables to the Calculator"). The NSManagedObject class does just that, using the data model specified by NSEntityDescription.

Dynamic Properties

Dictionaries are somewhat cumbersome to use. All the valueForKey: and setValue:forKey: invocations make for verbose code, and bypass static type checking. Direct property access would improve NSManagedObject; the first line is more readable than the second in the following code:

```
newIdentity.person = oldIdentity.person;
[newIdentity setValue:[oldIdentity valueForKey:@"person"] forKey:@"person"];
```

The mechanisms that power Objective-C's forwardInvocation: make this possible (see Hour 13, "Adding Undo and Redo Functionality"). NSManagedObject can use the Key-Value Coding rules to override method lookup and ensure that missing methods get or set data for the appropriate key.

Overriding dynamic dispatch does not fix static typing. To do this, Objective-C introduces the notion of @dynamic properties. Declare the properties as usual in the @interface definition: The compiler can use the declared types to perform static type checking. Instead of implementing the properties in the @implementation, declare them to be @dynamic (which tells the compiler not to warn that they were not implemented).

```
@interface Identity : NSManagedObject
@property (assign) NSString* firstName;
```

```
@property (assign) NSString* lastName;
@property (assign) double    nameStart;
@property (assign) double    nameEnd;
@property (assign) Person*   person;
@end

@implementation Identity
@dynamic firstName, lastName, nameStart, nameEnd, person;
@end
```

Your objects can define methods as usual.

Dynamic Subclassing

To create an `NSManagedObject`, invoke its `initWithEntity:insertIntoManagedObjectContext:` method. This method looks up the `managedObjectClassName` of the entity you defined, and dynamically generates a subclass of it, which has methods and instance variables for the properties specified by the `NSEntityDescription`: Accessing `NSManagedObject` properties takes *O(1)* access time.

`NSManagedObject` also redefines its inheritance hierarchy methods to ensure it inherits the methods and instance variables of whichever class was deemed to be its superclass. Do not override the following methods yourself: `class`, `superclass`, `isKindOfClass:`, `isMemberOfClass:`, `conformsToProtocol:`, `respondsToSelector:`, `instancesRespondToSelector:`, `instanceMethodForSelector:`, `methodForSelector:`, `methodSignatureForSelector:`, `instanceMethodSignatureForSelector:`, and `isSubclassOfClass:`.

Persistent Storage

Use `NSPersistentStore` to specify the storage Core Data should save objects to. `NSPersistentStoreCoordinator` is responsible for converting `NSManagedObjects` to a storage appropriate format. `NSPropertyDescription` properties specify whether `NSManagedObject`'s properties should be saved to storage and whether an index should be built for them.

`NSPersistentStore`

Instances of `NSPersistentStore` represent the storage to which `NSManagedObjects` are saved. The iPhone supports three forms of storage:

- Atomic uses a binary file representation, which requires loading the entire object graph into memory.

- SQLite uses the SQLite database to load objects from the database on demand.
- In-memory lets you create object models on the fly without saving them to storage.

Because SQLite lets you reduce memory consumption, it is a good choice for the iPhone. The `NSPersistentStore` layer is responsible for converting object updates and fetches to the appropriate SQL commands, or for generating the appropriate binary file.

Did you Know?

> You can create your own `NSPersistentStore`, which supports lazy loading. Read Apple's "Atomic Store Programming Topics" to learn how.

`NSPersistentStoreCoordinator`

`NSPersistentStoreCoordinator` is responsible for converting the data model to the cache-node representation different `NSPersistentStores` can easily use: To build an `NSPersistentStoreCoordinator`, specify its managed object model, and then create its `NSPersistentStore(s)`:

```
NSPersistentStoreCoordinator* coordinator
  = [[NSPersistentStoreCoordinator alloc] initWithManagedObjectModel: mom];

NSPersistentStore* store
  = [coordinator addPersistentStoreWithType: NSSQLiteStoreType
                              configuration: nil
                                        URL: coreDataFileURL
                                    options: nil
                                      error: &error];
```

When you attach an `NSPersistentStore`, you can specify a number of options in the `options` argument. The options control the performance of specific stores. For instance, you can specify `SQLite` pragma options. They also let you specify stores to be read-only.

`NSPersistentStoreCoordinator` can attach to multiple `NSPersistentStores` to create an aggregate store. Core Data does not support creating relationships between objects in different stores. If you open more than one `NSPersistentStore`, you must specify the persistent store you want each newly added object to be saved to by invoking `NSManagedObjectContext`'s method.

`NSPersistentStoreCoordinator` provides a number of methods to return each persistent store's location and metadata.

Specifying Properties' Storage Properties

NSPropertyDescription lets you specify a number of properties that are useful to persistent storage. If you recall, SQLite can create a B-tree for any column that has unique values. A property is guaranteed to have unique values if its NSPropertyDescription's maxCount is 1.

If your code often performs searches using a unique property, consider requesting SQLite to create an index for it by setting its NSPropertyDescription's indexed property to YES. Just as with SQL, indexes lower write performance to improve read performance.

To create properties that are accessible from NSManagedObject instances, but will not be saved to the database, set their transient property to YES. For instance, if you want to find the shortest path to route a package and your objects represent mail depots, it is convenient to annotate each mail depot with its shortest distance from the package's initial position. However, you would not want to save these annotations.

Putting It All Together with Managed Object Contexts

Creating objects in a context makes it clear which context is responsible for keeping track of their changes, saving them, and loading them. The NSManagedObjectContext provides this functionality.

Creating a Managed Object Context

Because NSManagedObjectContexts access their data model through their persistent store coordinator, you must set their persistent store coordinator after creating them.

```
NSManagedObjectContext* moc
  = [[NSManagedObjectContext alloc] init];

[moc setPersistentStoreCoordinator:coordinator];
```

Managing Objects in Memory

NSManagedObjectContext keeps track of objects in memory so that it can synchronize object state in storage with the objects changed in memory.

Adding Objects to a Managed Object Context

NSManagedObjects can only be built within a managed object context.

```
NSDictionary*        entityDict     = [mom entitiesByName];
NSEntityDescription* identityEntity = [entityDict objectForKey:@"Identity"];
NSManagedObject*     identity
  = [[NSManagedObject alloc] initWithEntity:identityEntity
           insertIntoManagedObjectContext:moc];
```

Alternatively, invoke NSEntityDescription's insertNewObjectForEntityForName:inManagedObjectContext: method:

```
[NSEntityDescription insertNewObjectForEntityForName:@"Identity"
                              inManagedObjectContext:moc];
```

To delete an object, invoke NSManagedContext's deleteObject: method.

Changing Object Properties

The NSManagedObjectContext tracks the changes made to its NSManagedObjects:

- NSManagedObject's willAccessValueForKey: and didAccessValueForKey: methods inform it of data loads.
- It registers for KVO (Key-Value Observing) notifications to keep track of changes.

KVO causes a notification to occur each time a property changes. Sometimes, you'll want to update a whole set of properties in a single atomic step. To do this, invoke willChangeValueForKey: methods for the properties you want to change, change the properties with setPrimitiveValue:forKey:, and then invoke the didChangeValueForKey: methods. Core Data also lets you group read accesses by invoking many invocations of primitiveValueForKey: (placed between the appropriate invocations of willAccessValueForKey: and didAccessValueForKey:).

To avoid interfering with NSManagedObject's correct operation, do not override primitiveValueForKey: or setPrimitiveValue:forKey:.

willAccessValueForKey: loads unloaded data. willChangeValueForKey: records a property's value before it is changed. didChangeValueForKey: records a property's value after it is changed...But what does didAccessValueForKey: do? This question bothered me so much that I reverse engineered it. The answer is... It doesn't do anything right now.

Managing Objects in Storage

NSManagedObjectContext also keeps track of objects in storage to synchronize object state in memory with the objects stored in storage.

Fetching Objects from Storage

Every object in storage has a unique ID, which lets it be retrieved from storage at a later date. If your application knows the objectID of an object, it can load it by invoking NSManagedContext's objectWithID: method. The returned object is autoreleased. If you want to keep it in memory, you must retain it. By checking objects' existence in memory, objectWithID ensures a single object is created for each object on disk. Core Data calls this "uniquing."

To search for objects, create an NSFetchRequest. At the very least, you must specify the entity description of requested objects by using NSFetchRequest's setEntity: method. Then execute the fetch by invoking NSManagedObjectContext's executeFetchRequest:error: method. This returns an NSArray of results or nil if there was an error. For instance, to return all people, you'd write the following:

```
NSError* error;
NSFetchRequest* fetchRequest = [[[NSFetchRequest alloc] init] autorelease];
[fetchRequest setEntity:identityEntity];
NSArray* people = [moc executeFetchRequest:fetchRequest error:&error];
```

By default, executeFetchRequest:error: includes any objects that have been changed or inserted and now match fetchRequest. To only return objects in storage that match fetchRequest, invoke its setIncludesPendingChanges: method with NO as the argument.

Use NSPredicate to add conditions fetched objects must obey. For instance, to find the people whose first name is John, using a case-insensitive search, you'd write the following:

```
NSPredicate* johnPredicate
  = [NSPredicate predicateWithFormat:@"firstName LIKE[c] 'John'];
[fetchRequest setPredicate:predicate];
```

The SQLite persistent store converts predicates into the corresponding SQL statement, benefiting from SQLite's optimizations whenever possible. Because fetches are applied to data in the persistent store, it is an error to reference transient properties in a predicate.

You can also sort the results by setting the fetch request's sort descriptors. To sort people by last name, and then by first name, you'd write the following (people who share a last name would be further sorted by first name):

```
NSSortDescriptor* firstNameSort
  = [[NSSortDescriptor alloc] initWithKey:@"firstName" ascending:YES];
NSSortDescriptor* lastNameSort
  = [[NSSortDescriptor alloc] initWithKey:@"lastName" ascending:YES];

[fetchRequest setSortDescriptors:
                    [NSArray arrayWithObjects:lastNameSort, firstNameSort, nil]];
[firstNameSort release];
[lastNameSort release];
```

When fetching data to show in a table view, you only need a limited number of objects from an offset within the results. Use `setFetchLimit:` and `setFetchOffset:` to limit the results in this manner. `NSManagedObjectContext`'s `countForFetchRequest:error:` returns the total number of objects that would have been fetched.

By default, the `NSFetchRequest` returns instances of the entity you requested, including any subentities it might have. To only return entities (and not subentities), invoke `NSFetchRequest`'s `setIncludesSubentities:` method with `NO` as the argument. The SQL persistent store implements this by storing every entity and its subentities in a single table. A single `SELECT` statement will return all of them. Unfortunately, this means that fetching entities of a particular type involves loading them all from storage, and then discarding those that do not match the requirement.

Fetch requests can be stored in the data model file and retrieved using `fetchRequestTemplateForName` or `fetchRequestTemplatesByName`.

Did you Know?

Because Core Data is often used with `UITableView` objects, Cocoa Touch provides an `NSFetchedResultsController` object, which automatically manages the objects to show in the table view: It minimizes the number of objects in memory while keeping track of modified objects and updating the table view with any changes. It provides methods to simplify `UITableView`'s data source methods: `numberOfSectionsInTableView:`, `tableView:numberOfRowsInSection:`, `tableView:cellForRowAtIndexPath:`, `tableView:titleForHeaderInSection:`, `sectionIndexTitlesForTableView:`, and `tableView:sectionForSectionIndexTitle:atIndex:` The details are available in Apple's "NSFetchedResultsController Class Reference."

Transparently Loading Objects

To reduce the number of objects that must be loaded, and to avoid requiring that client programs issue explicit loads, Core Data loads objects in relationship properties transparently: Object relationships form connected graphs. The simple approach to loading an object would load every object its relationship properties reference. Loading these objects would load other objects until the entire connected graph is loaded into memory.

Loading an entire graph of objects just to edit an object is inefficient and unnecessary. Instead, the objects appearing in an object's relationships can be replaced by proxies. Editing a single object only requires loading that object, and each proxy only needs to know which object it is standing in for.

Instead of literally creating proxy objects, `NSManagedObject` uses internal state to indicate whether it has loaded its properties from disk: It has not if `isFault` is `YES`. Because `isFault` does not cause objects to be loaded, diagnostic code can use it to ensure that it only checks the properties of loaded objects.

Accessing any property of a faulted object will cause the properties of the entire object to be loaded. However, directly accessing the property's instance variables will not: Methods added to an `NSManagedObject` must invoke `willAccessValueForKey:` before reading the corresponding instance variable. After reading it, invoke `didAccessValueForKey:` in case it does something in the future. Similarly, writes to instance variables must occur between the Key-Value Observation pair `willChangeValueForKey:` and `didChangeValueForKey:`. Loading objects from disk cause Key-Value Observation notifications.

Objects' relationships are loaded from disk as `objectIDs` and are converted to `NSManagedObjects` by `objectWithID:`. The `NSManagedObjects` are faulted, but are only retained by the relationships. Core Data only retains objects that have been changed until they are saved or unloaded from memory.

Did you Know?

To unload an object's properties from memory, invoke the `NSManagedObjectContext`'s `refreshObject:mergeChanges:`, with *merge* set to `NO`. This will discard any changes you have made to the object. To check whether an object has been changed, you can invoke its `isUpdated` and `isDeleted` methods. Unloading an object releases the objects its relationship properties referenced (breaking retain cycles).

You can override the `awakeFromFetch:` and `awakeFromInsert:` methods to set up transient properties. Subclasses must invoke their parents' methods before performing their own initialization. `willTurnIntoFault` and `didTurnIntoFault` are called before and after objects are unloaded from memory, allowing your code to release any transient properties it set up. Use these methods instead of overriding `init` and `dealloc`.

Saving and Validating Data

Core Data performs data validation before saving the managed object context. If the data fails its consistency test, or another error occurs, `save:` returns `NO` and sets its argument reference to point to an `NSError` it creates.

Alternatively, you can invoke the validation methods at times that make sense for your UI. `NSManagedObjectContext` validates its data's consistency using three methods. Each property's `NSPropertyDescription` can specify one or more validation predicates (`validationPredicates`). Second, each managed object can implement validation methods of the form `validate`*`Key`*`:error:`, which return `NO` on error. Finally, to define validation rules that combine multiple properties (for instance, to reject people with a driver's license and a date of birth less than 16 years ago), `NSManagedObjects` can define `validateForInsert:` and `validateForUpdate:` methods that invoke their parents' methods and combine the result with additional validation rules.

```
- (BOOL) validateForInsert:(NSError**)error
{
  BOOL noPropertyErrors = [super validateForInsert:error];
  BOOL noOverallErrors  = [self  validateConsistency:error];
  return (noPropertyErrors && noOverallErrors);
}
```

Multiple errors can be combined into a single message using `NSError`'s `NSValidationMultipleErrorsError` code.

Advanced Usage

Although Core Data reduces the amount of code you must write to save objects to a persistent store, understanding how it works is key to using it efficiently. Similarly, by understanding the limitations of its undo and redo functionality, you can decide whether you want to use it.

Undo/Redo

Core Data can support undo and redo if `NSManagedObjectContext`'s `undoManager` is set to the current undo manager. Core Data adds a runloop observer that invokes `processPendingChanges` to batch up the changes into a single undoable action. This works well for simple programs that only update the managed object context in response to user updates.

However, if you need to update managed objects asynchronously (for instance, downloading data from the Web), Core Data will include these non–user caused changes in the undo stack: `processPendingChanges` simply saves a time stamp. Invoking undo on Core Data rolls the data back to its state prior to the time stamp, discarding all changes made in between. The simplest solution is to avoid using Core Data's undo functionality, and write the undo management code yourself.

Efficiency

Although Core Data provides a pleasant object-oriented API, it is important to remember that its objects are stored in the rows of a B-tree. Everything you learned about optimizing SQL databases also applies to Core Data. For instance, when designing the data model, avoid saving large objects in your properties. If your managed objects are tweets, do not create an `image` property for them: A copy of the image will be loaded for each tweet. Instead, use an image identifier and define the image property as a transient property of the subclass. Similarly, avoid executing fetches unless necessary and structure your data model to return all the information you need with a single request.

Avoid saving large objects to frequently used tables, as SQLite will have to load more data for each row. Profile to determine whether to save data to a database table or whether to save it to the file system.

By default, the properties of the objects returned by `executeFetchRequest:error:` are loaded into memory. For efficiency, they are loaded into the `NSPersistentStore`, but not into the `NSManagedObject`. To reduce memory consumption, ensure only their `objectIDs` are loaded into memory: Invoke `NSFetchRequest`'s `setIncludesPropertyValues:` method with `NO` as the argument.

By default, objects do not load objects their relationship properties reference. You can change this by invoking `NSFetchRequest`'s `setRelationshipKeyPathsForPrefetching:` method with an array of key-path strings specifying the objects to preload. Key paths let you load all the objects along their path.

Prefetching data will improve your application's performance at the cost of more memory usage. Similarly, saving contexts must be done rarely enough to prevent your application from being sluggish, but must be done sufficiently often to guarantee your application terminates promptly and can easily be restarted.

Using Xcode to Design Objects

This section shows you how to use Xcode's data modeling tool to create a data model file and how to load the data model file from your code.

Creating a Core Data Project

iPhone OS 3.0 introduces a new `Options` check mark item when creating a new project. Checking this check mark adds an `.xcdatamodel` file to your project and adds a build phase to compile it. Name your project `CoreData`, and open the `CoreData.xcdatamodel` file (see Figure 18.2).

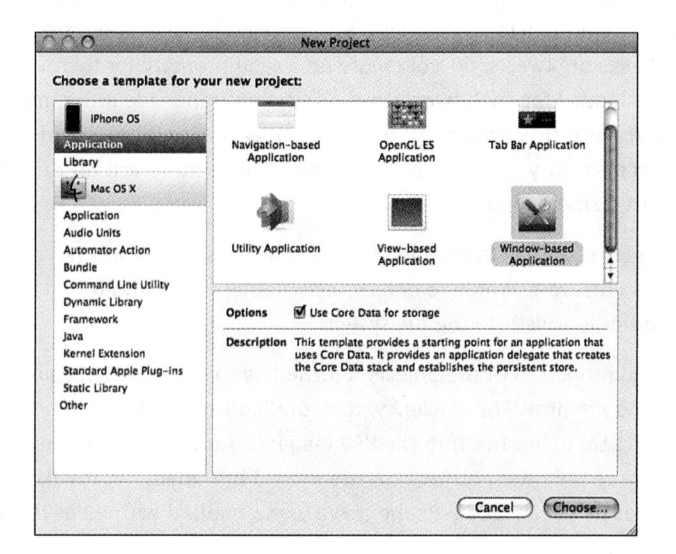

FIGURE 18.2 Creating a Core Data project

Creating a Data Model

To create an entity, select Design, Data Model, Add Entity. An `Entity` will appear in the canvas below. Click it to select it. The upper-right pane lets you change its `Name`, `Class`, and `Parent`. Change its name to **`Identity`**. When an entity is selected, you can add attributes and relationships using the Design, Data Model menu. Add the attributes: **`firstName`**, **`lastName`**, **`nameStart`**, and **`nameEnd`** of types `NSString` (two occurrences) and `NSDate` (x2). By default, attributes are optional. Uncheck the Optional check marks.

Create a new **`Person`** entity, and give it the attributes **`ssn`** (`NSString`), **`dateOfBirth`** (`NSDate`), and **`dateOfDeath`** (`NSDate`). Make the last attribute optional (see Figure 18.3).

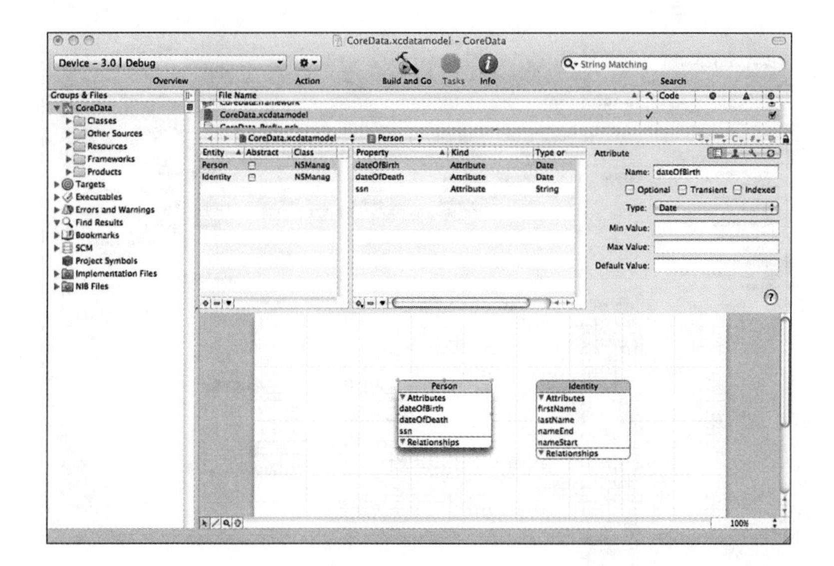

FIGURE 18.3
Two disconnected entities

Add a one-to-many **`identities`** relationship from `Person` to `Identity`. This results in a double arrow from `Person` to `Identity`. You must leave the Inverse pull-down menu set to `No Inverse Relationship` as shown (see Figure 18.4). Now create an inverse one-to-one `person` relationship from `Identity` to `Person`. When you choose `identities` as an inverse relation, the relations are merged into a single arrow (see Figure 18.5).

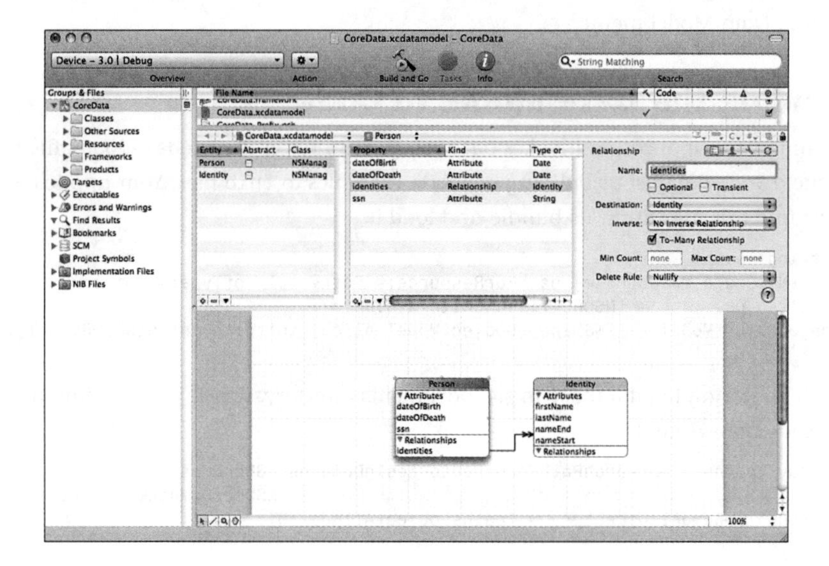

FIGURE 18.4
Adding a one-to-many relationship

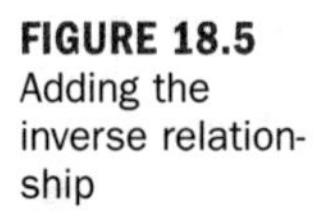

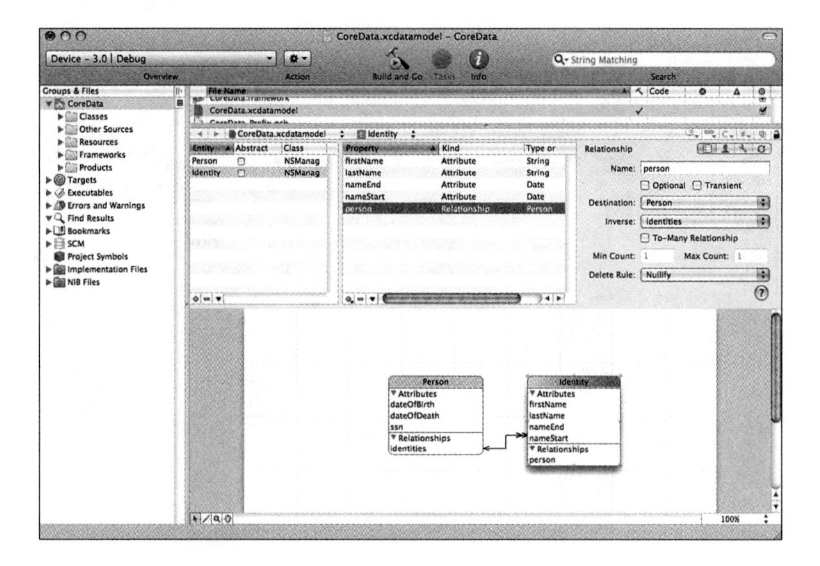

FIGURE 18.5
Adding the inverse relationship

The delete rule specifies what Core Data should do if the target object of a relationship is deleted. Deleting a person should delete his identities, so set the delete rule for `identities` to `Cascade`. However, deleting an identity should not delete the person, so set the delete rule for `person` to `Nullify`.

Notice the small tab selector at the top of the upper-right pane: Click on the small head to change user info information. You can also add Fetch Requests from the Design, Data Model menu.

Loading the Data Model in Code

Building your application invokes `DataModelCompile` on the `.xcdatamodel` file to create a `.mom` file, just as building converts `.xib` files to `.nib` files. Your application must find this file within its bundle and load it.

```
NSString* path
  = [[NSBundle mainBundle] pathForResource:@"DataModel" ofType:@"mom"];
NSURL*    url       = [NSURL fileURLWithPath:path];
managedObjectModel = [[NSManagedObjectModel alloc] initWithContentsOfURL:url];
```

You'll be storing the database in the documents directory, which you can find using the code from Hour 17:

```
NSArray* paths = NSSearchPathForDirectoriesInDomains(NSDocumentDirectory,
                                                     NSUserDomainMask, YES);
NSString* documentsDirectory = [paths objectAtIndex:0];
```

Create the persistent store coordinator, persistent store, and managed object context, as explained earlier. The file extension of your persistent store does not matter.

Did you Know?

`mom` files are property lists. You can open them with the Property List Editor application that came with your development tools.

Summary

Core Data lets you define the in-memory and in-storage representation of the objects your application uses, and provides support for only loading part of the object graph in storage. Unfortunately, I know of no definitive guide to Core Data. Apple's "Core Data Programming Guide" is instructive, as is Marcus Zarra's *Core Data* if you would like to delve deeper into the topic.

Q&A

Q. ***Can I create Core Data files on the Mac, and deploy them to the iPhone?***

A. Yes, if you use the SQLite persistent store.

Q. ***Should I provide an inverse relationship for each relationship I create?***

A. Yes, because it prevents the graph from becoming inconsistent. For instance, if `person` were a unidirectional link from an `Identity` to a `Person` object, deleting a `Person` would not update the `Identity` objects that referenced it. Dereferencing those objects' `person` properties produces objects that cannot fault correctly.

Workshop

The Workshop consists of quiz questions and answers to help you solidify your understanding of the material covered in this hour. You should try to answer the questions before checking the answers.

Quiz Questions

1. What is a predicate?
2. What is a managed object?

3. What is a managed object context?
4. What is a managed object model?
5. What is a persistent store?

Quiz Answers

1. A predicate is a logical statement that can be tested against an object's state.
2. A managed object is the in-memory representation of a data-model object.
3. A managed object context is a context that associates in-memory objects with their in-storage counterparts.
4. A managed object model contains the entity descriptions required to build managed objects.
5. Managed objects are saved to storage in a persistent store.

Exercises

- Read up on `NSFetchedResultsController` and create a simple application that uses it to display data in a Core Data store.
- Save some data to a Core Data store and open in with SQLite. Explore it. Recall that `select * from sqlite_master;` shows you its tables.
- Create a version of the Twitter application that stores tweets to Core Data.

HOUR 19
Playing and Recording Media

What You'll Learn in This Hour:

- Playing and recording audio
- Playing video files

In this hour, you'll learn to use Core Audio's Audio Toolbox and Audio File Services, which let you play and record sounds and music. You'll start by synthesizing your own sound to help you understand how sound is produced. Then, you'll learn to play compressed audio from an MP3 file and record your own audio. Finally, you'll learn how video compression works, and you'll learn about the API that you can use to show your own videos.

Playing and Recording Audio

The iPhone and iPod touch are inherently audio devices. You'd expect them to have good audio capabilities, and you won't be disappointed.

What Is Audio?

Sounds are oscillations of air pressure. They travel as compression waves from a source. By recording the local air pressure many times per second, a microphone can record the sound at that point. The number of times the measurement is performed per second is the sampling frequency. Air pressure is a continuous phenomenon: Each sample could require an infinite number of bits. However, it is sufficient to quantize (approximate) each sample to a limited number of bits. CD-quality audio uses only 16 bits per sample at a sampling frequency of 44.1Khz (44,100 samples per second). The sound is reproduced by converting it back to an analog signal and feeding it to a loudspeaker to re-create the same pressure waves as were recorded (see Figure 19.1).

FIGURE 19.1
Recording sound and playing it back

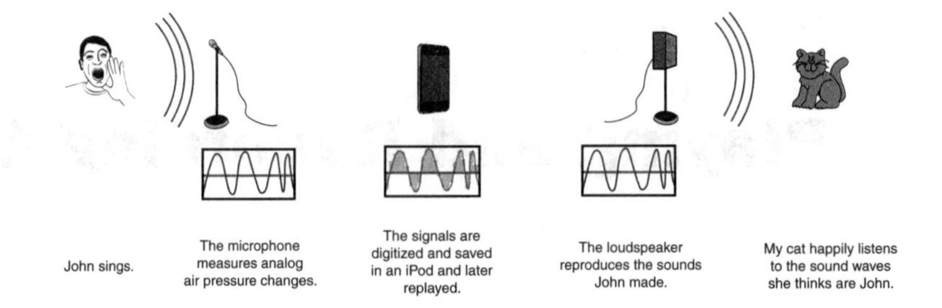

John sings.
The microphone measures analog air pressure changes.
The signals are digitized and saved in an iPod and later replayed.
The loudspeaker reproduces the sounds John made.
My cat happily listens to the sound waves she thinks are John.

People determine the horizontal location of a sound using the difference in time between the time it reaches one of their ears and the other (see Figure 19.2). This can be simulated by sending two different audio streams to two loudspeakers: stereophonic sound. The OpenAL API lets you place sounds in space using the same matrices as you use to place objects in 3D space.

FIGURE 19.2
The location of a sound source determines when the sound arrives at each ear.

Sound from the trumpet on the friar's left side
reaches his left ear before it reaches his right ear.
(Aerial view)

Did you Know?

People determine the vertical location of a sound by using the times between the microechoes produced by the sound bouncing off the different structures of your ear. They determine sound is behind them because their ears filter sound in a characteristic way. The so-called HRTF (head-related transfer function) can reproduce the microechoes and filtering to give the impression sounds are above or below you. When tuned for specific ears, this works well. Because people have differently shaped ears, an "average" ear is used, which only works well for people with average ears. The iPhone OS does not provide native support for HRTF.

Playing a Sound with the Software API

Core Audio represents sounds as audio streams. It uses audio queues to transfer sounds between memory and sound peripherals (for example, speakers, headphones, microphones). This section shows you how to put these elements together to make sounds.

Audio Streams

Playing sound requires data to be fetched from memory at a precise rate and dispatched to the loudspeaker (similar to recording). Core Audio calls this data an audio stream. The `AudioStreamBasicDescription` C structure specifies the characteristics of the audio stream. Obvious things include the sampling frequency (`mSampleRate`) and bits per sample (`mBitsPerChannel`).

```
struct AudioStreamBasicDescription
{
  Float64 mSampleRate;
  UInt32  mFormatID;
  UInt32  mFormatFlags;
  UInt32  mBytesPerPacket;
  UInt32  mFramesPerPacket;
  UInt32  mBytesPerFrame;
  UInt32  mChannelsPerFrame;
  UInt32  mBitsPerChannel;
  UInt32  mReserved;
};
```

Did you Know?

Frequencies are measured in Hertz (Hz). If something happens *n* times per second, its frequency is *n* Hertz. A Kilohertz (Khz) is 1000 Hertz.

When the iPhone plays stereophonic sounds, at each moment in time there are two samples to output. The set of samples to play at each moment is called a frame. `mChannelsPerFrame` specifies the number of samples per frame, `mBytesPerFrame` specifies the number of bytes per frame, and the `kAudioFormatFlagIsNonInterleaved` flag of `mFormatFlags` specifies whether each frame's samples are placed consecutively in memory (interleaved), or whether each of the channel's samples are placed consecutively in memory. `mBytesPerPacket` and `mFramesPerPacket` specify packet lengths. Compressed audio groups many frames into a packet. For uncompressed audio, packets can be as small as a single frame.

`mFormatID` specifies the format of the sound samples: Although each sound sample is a measurement of the pressure of the air at a point in time, you can measure it using a linear scale or a logarithmic scale. Because people perceive loudness as the logarithm of air pressure, using a logarithmic scale can reduce sample sizes significantly with only a small loss of quality. The `kAudioFormatLinearPCM` and `kAudioFormatULaw`/`kAudioFormatALaw` use linear and logarithmic scales, respectively. Other formats use compression (discussed later in this hour).

`mFormatFlags` specifies secondary aspects of the samples. The most common flags are as follows:

- Are samples integers or floats? (`kAudioFormatFlagIsFloat`)
- Are samples in big or little endian format? (`kAudioFormatFlagIsBigEndian`)
- Are samples signed or unsigned integers? (`kAudioFormatFlagIsSignedInteger`)
- Do samples use all the bits reserved for them, or do they need to be masked off in any way? (`kAudioFormatFlagIsPacked`, `kAudioFormatFlagIsAlignedHigh`)

Did you Know?

Loudspeakers use electromagnets to move a membrane in and out. The membrane's central position corresponds to 0 (for signed samples) or 0x8000 (for 16-bit unsigned samples); the membrane is fully sucked in for -0x8000 (signed 16-bit samples) or 0 (unsigned samples). The membrane is fully out for 0x7fff (signed 16-bit samples) or 0xffff (16-bit unsigned samples). By moving the membrane in and out fast enough, the loudspeaker increases and decreases the air pressure, creating compression waves.

Audio Queues

As sounds are unlimited in length, they are split into pieces to minimize memory usage. Pieces can be dynamically loaded from a file or the network. Each piece is converted by the iPhone OS into a format the iPhone hardware understands (for example, 16-bit integer 44.1KHz linear scale samples) and is saved to a buffer (see Figure 19.3). The hardware reads samples from this buffer and ensures that the loudspeaker receives a new sample regularly (at the sampling rate, for example, 44.1KHz). Audio queues are the software interface to this hardware.

As pieces are played, the hardware creates interrupts to request new pieces to be prepared, so that they are ready to be played when needed: If new pieces are not provided on time, the sound will suffer from gaps (or distortion). During playback, when this interrupt occurs, audio queues invoke a callback function to place more sound into the audio buffers. When recording, the callback must save the contents of the audio buffers. To minimize threading concerns, the callback is called from whichever runtime loop you specify.

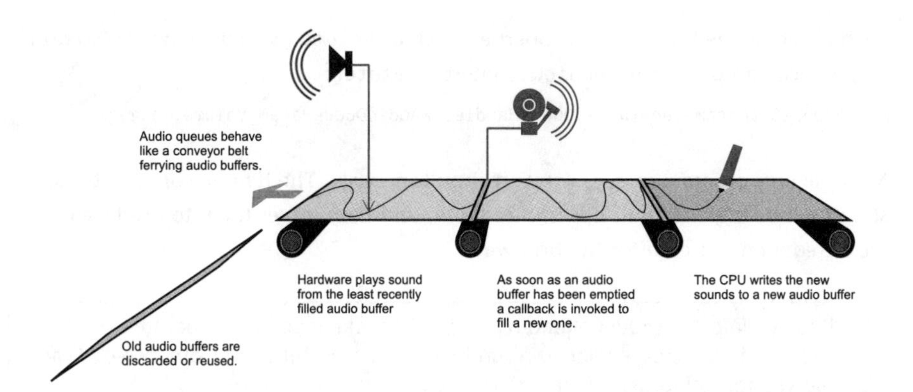
Audio queues behave
like a conveyor belt
ferrying audio buffers.
Hardware plays sound
from the least recently
filled audio buffer
As soon as an audio
buffer has been emptied
a callback is invoked to
fill a new one.
The CPU writes the new
sounds to a new audio buffer
Old audio buffers are
discarded or reused.

FIGURE 19.3
Audio Queues behave like conveyor belts.

Increasing the length of buffers reduces the urgency for new pieces at the cost of increasing sound latency, which can be a problem in games or when playing video. Similarly, increasing the number of buffers also reduces the chance of skipping samples, as the iPhone OS can read from one while another is being prepared. Commonly, three buffers are used. Your code must create the buffers using `AudioQueueAllocateBuffer`.

```
for (int i = 0; i < bufferCount; ++i)
  AudioQueueAllocateBuffer(audioQueueHandle, bufferLength, &buffer[i]);
```

Each audio queue needs to know the format of the frames, as specified by the `AudioStreamBasicDescription` structure, and the direction of the transfer, as specified by the function name `AudioQueueNewInput` or `AudioQueueNewOutput`.

```
OSStatus AudioQueueNewOutput
(
  const AudioStreamBasicDescription* streamFormat,
  AudioQueueOutputCallback           callbackFunction,
  void*                              callbackUserData,
  CFRunLoopRef                       callbackRunLoop,
  CFStringRef                        callbackRunLoopMode,
  UInt32                             flags,
  AudioQueueRef*                     audioQueueHandle
);
```

The callback function takes `callbackUserData` (specified when calling `AudioQueueNewInput` or `AudioQueueNewOutput`), `audioQueueHandle` (returned by `AudioQueueNewInput` or `AudioQueueNewOutput`), and `audioQueueBuffer` as arguments. The `audioQueueBuffer` is a buffer for the sample data. The buffer size is specified by `streamFormat`'s `mBytesPerPacket`.

```
void callback( void *callbackUserData, AudioQueueRef        audioQueueHandle,
                                       AudioQueueBufferRef audioQueueBuffer)
```

Each audio queue has its own properties, such as *volume* (a value between 0.0 and 1.0), which can be set with AudioQueueSetParameter:

```
AudioQueueSetParameter (audioQueueHandle, kAudioQueueParam_Volume, 1.0);
```

Multiple output audio queues can run simultaneously: The iPhone converts these streams to a single format, upsamples them, and then mixes them to produce a single stereophonic stream for the hardware.

By the Way

I did not explain AudioQueueNewOutput's callbackRunLoopMode parameter: It only applies if you create your own run loop modes. Set it to nil otherwise. flags is reserved for future uses (set it to 0).

Putting It All Together

To show how sound data is laid out, we'll synthesize a 440Hz sine wave (sinusoid), which moves between left and right speakers (see Figure 19.4). The sound phase corresponds to how far you are into the wave. The volume phase is how far you are into moving between the left and right speaker. Invoke AudioQueueStart to start playing.

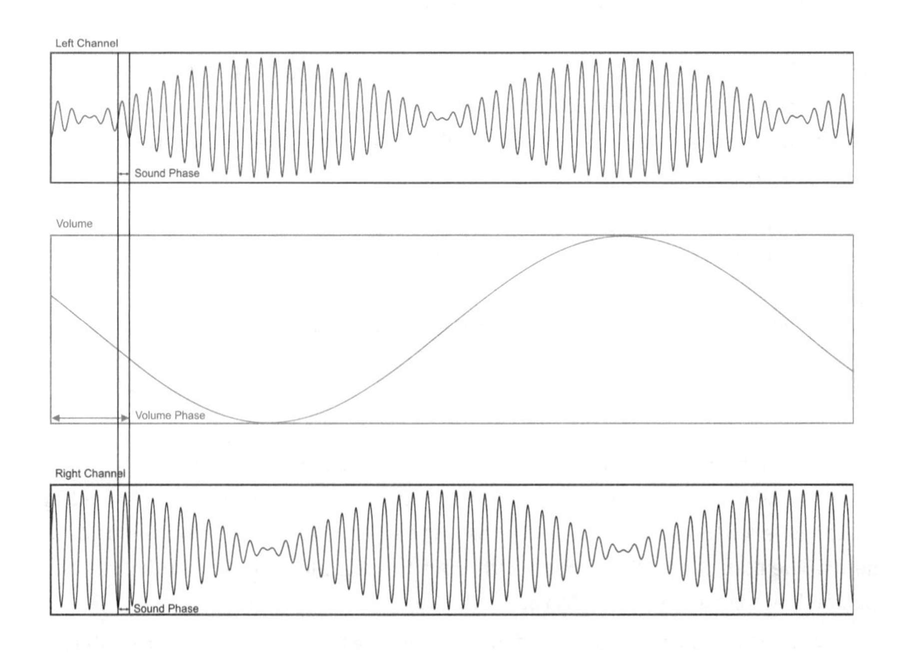

FIGURE 19.4 Synthesizing a sound that oscillates between the left and right channels.

```
- (void) applicationDidFinishLaunching:(UIApplication*) application
{
  volPhase    = 0;
  soundPhase = 0;
  [self createStream];
  [self createQueueWithBuffers:3 withPacketCount:44100/3.0];
  AudioQueueStart(queue, NULL);
}
```

We'll create two channels (left and right) and use 16-bit signed samples.

```
- (void) createStream
{
  stream.mSampleRate       = 44100;
  stream.mFormatID         = kAudioFormatLinearPCM;
  stream.mFormatFlags      = kLinearPCMFormatFlagIsSignedInteger
                           | kAudioFormatFlagIsPacked;
  stream.mBitsPerChannel   = 8 * sizeof(short);
  stream.mChannelsPerFrame = 2;
  stream.mBytesPerPacket   = sizeof(short) * stream.mChannelsPerFrame;
  stream.mFramesPerPacket  = 1;
  stream.mBytesPerFrame    = stream.mBytesPerPacket;
}
```

We'll synthesize the sound using a fast Taylor series approximation of the sine function (see http://www.coranac.com/2009/07/sines/).

```
int fast_sine(int x)
{
  x = x << 17;
  if ((x^(x << 1)) < 0)
    x = (1 << 31) - x;
  x = x >> 17;
  return x * ( (3 << 15) - (x*x >> 11) ) >> 17;
}
```

The `AudioQueueBuffer`'s `mAudioData` points to the sample buffer, and `mAudioDataBytesCapacity` specifies its size. As you can see, in this example, left and right samples are interleaved to create frames.

`mAudioDataByteSize` tells Core Audio how many samples were placed into the sample buffer: If it is zero, Core Audio will stop playing. Don't forget to tell Core Audio to play the buffer with `AudioQueueEnqueueBuffer`!

```
- (void) synthesizeWithHandle:(AudioQueueRef)handle
                       buffer:(AudioQueueBufferRef)buffer
{
  short*    b = (short*) buffer->mAudioData;
  short* endB = (short*) ((int)b + buffer->mAudioDataBytesCapacity);

  int volPhaseChange = 0xffffffff / (stream.mSampleRate * 4);
  int phaseChange    = (1 << 16 - 1) / (stream.mSampleRate / 440.0);
```

```
  while (b < endB)
  {
    // Calculate left/right volume
    const int  leftVol = 0x4000 + (fast_sine(volPhase >> 16) << 2);
    const int rightVol = 0x8000 - leftVol;
    volPhase += volPhaseChange;

    // Calculate sine wave
    int sample = fast_sine(soundPhase);
    *b++ = (sample * leftVol)  >> 12;
    *b++ = (sample * rightVol) >> 12;
    soundPhase += phaseChange;
  }

  buffer->mAudioDataByteSize = buffer->mAudioDataBytesCapacity;
  AudioQueueEnqueueBuffer(handle, buffer, 0, NULL);
}
```

Before starting to play, each buffer must be created, filled with valid data, and added to Core Audio's queue of buffers to play. For brevity, this code ignores errors that `AudioQueueNewOutput` and `AudioQueueAllocateBuffer` can produce.

```
- (void) createQueueWithBuffers:(int)n withPacketCount:(int)m
{
  AudioQueueNewOutput(&stream, cCallback, (void*)self, NULL, NULL, 0, &queue);
  AudioQueueSetParameter(queue, kAudioQueueParam_Volume, 1.0);

  buffers        = [[NSMutableArray alloc] init];
  int bufferSize  = stream.mBytesPerPacket * m;

  for (int i = 0; i < n; ++i)
  {
    AudioQueueBufferRef buffer;
    AudioQueueAllocateBuffer(queue, bufferSize, &buffer);
    [self    synthesizeWithHandle:queue buffer:buffer];
    [buffers addObject:[NSValue valueWithPointer:buffer]];
  }
}
```

Although Audio Toolbox expects a C callback, your callback can invoke Objective-C methods.

```
void cCallback(void* userData, AudioQueueRef       handle,
                               AudioQueueBufferRef buffer)
{[((SineWaveAppDelegate*) userData) synthesizeWithHandle:handle buffer:buffer];}
```

Stop playing with `AudioQueueStop`, whose second parameter means "stop immediately." To free buffers, invoke `AudioQueueFreeBuffer`. To free the queue, invoke `AudioQueueDispose`.

```
- (void) freeQueueAndBuffers
{
  if (queue == NULL) return;
```

```
    AudioQueueStop(queue, YES);
    for (NSValue* v in buffers)
      AudioQueueFreeBuffer(queue, [v pointerValue]);

    [buffers release]; buffers = nil;

    AudioQueueDispose(queue, YES);
    queue = NULL;
}
```

Don't forget to link against the AudioToolbox framework, and include it:

```
#import <AudioToolbox/AudioToolbox.h>

@interface SineWaveAppDelegate : NSObject <UIApplicationDelegate>
{
    AudioStreamBasicDescription  stream;
    AudioQueueRef                queue;
    NSMutableArray*              buffers;
    short                        soundPhase;
    int                          volPhase;
//...
```

Saved Audio

Because raw audio takes a lot of space, a number of lossy compression formats have been developed: Lossily compressed audio sounds very similar to the original while using much less memory. This information is then saved in standard file formats. Conveniently, Core Audio provides file services to decode them.

Compression

To compress audio, you express it in terms of more natural primitives. For instance, it takes an infinite number of circles to make a perfect square. However, it only takes a single square.

Simple forms of compression essentially save the difference between successive samples. Slightly more complex variants such as ADPCM (adaptive differential pulse-code modulation) use a model to predict the next sample, and then save the difference (error) between their prediction and the signal's sample. ADPCM also quantizes the error, achieving up to a 4:1 compression ratio at little computational cost.

A number of formats like MP3 use the fact that any digitized wave can be analyzed into a sum of a limited number of sine waves of varying amplitude. Your ear performs this same analysis: The hair cells that are responsible for detecting sound respond to sine waves of different frequencies, but do not respond to the sine wave's phase. We can discard the phase data, and only save the amplitude of each wave, halving the amount of data. Furthermore, the amplitude of each frequency often varies slowly, further reducing the amount of data to be saved. The sound is split into packets, which encode the sine waves' amplitudes for a small period of time. Furthermore, hair cells are not equally sensitive to amplitude, so we can quantize the amplitudes of some frequencies with less detail. Finally, just like a bus roaring past can drown out conversation, some sine waves when loud enough drown out others, which can simply be dropped from the compressed file. The compression ratio is approximately doubled (8:1), at the cost of more computation.

Other formats only compress speech. They use a model of the organs involved in speech and essentially transmit only the necessary parameters to resynthesize the sound at the other end. They achieve even higher compression (26:1 for LPC10—a 10 linear-parameter speech codec), but fare poorly when compressing music.

On the iPhone, audio queues can play any number of AMR (Adaptive Multi-Rate, a speech codec), iLBC (Internet Low Bitrate Codec, a speech codec), IMA-4 (ADPCM), or raw data streams. Raw data streams consist of samples created with a linear or logarithmic scale (linear, aLaw, or μLaw). Because MP3, AAC (MPEG-4 advanced audio), and Apple's Lossless formats require more computational power, they are off-loaded to a hardware decoder. Because there is only one hardware decoder per iPhone, only one stream of data in these formats can play at a time.

Audio queues can record in any of the following formats: Apple Lossless, iLBC, IMA-4, or raw.

Creating Audio Files

Use the `afconvert` tool from the Terminal application to generate CAF (Core Audio Format) files. Using the little endian 16-bit file format reduces the amount of decoding work the iPhone must do:

```
/usr/bin/afconvert -f caff -d LEI16 input_file output_file
```

To save space at the cost of some CPU usage, while not using the hardware MP3 decoder, use the IMA4 format:

```
/usr/bin/afconvert -f caff -d ima4 input_file output_file
```

`afconvert` does not convert to MP3. However, iTunes does.

Playing Saved Audio

Audio files do not just contain a sound's samples, but also metadata such as the name of the track, its sample rate, and its samples format. Core Audio's Audio File Services provide functions to parse (or create) files of the formats: AIFF files, Microsoft Wave files, MPEG audio layer 1/2/3 files, MPEG-4 files, AC-3 files, and CAF files (and a number of other rarely used formats).

AudioFileOpenURL opens a sound file of the specified file type (kAudioFileMP3Type for MP3 files). AudioFileGetProperty returns many properties extracted from the file. For playback, we need to know the sound's AudioStreamBasicDescription, which we can access with the kAudioFilePropertyDataFormat property. For instance, to load an MP3, we'd open the file as follows:

```
- (void) createStream:(NSURL*) fileURL
{
  UInt32 size = sizeof(AudioStreamBasicDescription);
  AudioFileOpenURL((CFURLRef) fileURL,  kAudioFileReadPermission,
                                        kAudioFileMP3Type, &audioFileHandle);
  AudioFileGetProperty(audioFileHandle, kAudioFilePropertyDataFormat,
                                        &size, &stream);
}
```

Because the iPhone hardware is responsible for decoding compressed formats such as MP3, audio queues can handle compressed data in packets. Because packet data is compressed differently for MP3, AAC, and Apple's Lossless format, the audio queue also needs to know the format and length of each packet. This information is saved in packet descriptors associated with the audio queue buffers: Use AudioQueueAllocateBufferWithPacketDescriptions to allocate the buffers with the correct number of packet descriptions. The buffer must contain enough space for all its packets, so we need to know the maximum size of packets: the kAudioFilePropertyPacketSizeUpperBound property provides this information.

```
- (void) createQueueWithBuffers:(int)n withPacketCount:(int)m
{
  AudioQueueNewOutput(&stream, cCallback, (void*)self, NULL, NULL, 0, &queue);
  AudioQueueSetParameter(queue, kAudioQueueParam_Volume, 1.0);

  done              = NO;
  packetsPerCallback = m;
  currentPacket     = 0;

  UInt32 maxPacketSize   = 0;
  UInt32 size = sizeof(maxPacketSize);
  AudioFileGetProperty(audioFileHandle, kAudioFilePropertyPacketSizeUpperBound,
                                                       &size, &maxPacketSize);
  buffers           = [[NSMutableArray alloc] init];
  int bufferSize    = maxPacketSize * m;

  for (int i = 0; i < n; ++i)
  {
    AudioQueueBufferRef buffer;
    AudioQueueAllocateBufferWithPacketDescriptions(queue,bufferSize,m,&buffer);
    [self    synthesizeWithHandle:queue buffer:buffer];
    [buffers addObject:[NSValue valueWithPointer:buffer]];
  }
}
```

The callback handler keeps track of the position within the file (`currentPacket`) and fills the buffer and packet descriptors obtained from the file by `AudioFileReadPackets`.

```
- (void) synthesizeWithHandle:(AudioQueueRef)handle
                        buffer:(AudioQueueBufferRef)buffer
{
  if (done) return;

  void*  b                = buffer->mAudioData;
  UInt32 outputByteCount = 0;
  UInt32 packetCount     = packetsPerCallback;
  AudioFileReadPackets(audioFileHandle, NO, &outputByteCount,
                   buffer->mPacketDescriptions, currentPacket, &packetCount, b);

  if (packetCount <= 0)
  { AudioQueueStop(handle, NO);
    done = YES;
    return; };

  currentPacket += packetCount;
  buffer->mAudioDataByteSize       = outputByteCount;
  buffer->mPacketDescriptionCount = packetCount;
  AudioQueueEnqueueBuffer(handle, buffer, 0, NULL);
}
```

Audio File Services also let you write files, but do not provide the CPU-intensive compression required by formats such as MP3.

Recording Audio

Recording audio works in much the same way. You can query the audio hardware to determine an appropriate sampling rate for recording. We'll compress to ADPCM.

```
- (void) createStream
{
  UInt32 c = kAudioSessionCategory_RecordAudio;
  AudioSessionSetProperty(kAudioSessionProperty_AudioCategory, sizeof(c), &c);
  AudioSessionSetActive(YES);

  UInt32 size = sizeof(stream.mSampleRate);
  AudioSessionGetProperty(kAudioSessionProperty_CurrentHardwareSampleRate,
                                                  &size, &stream.mSampleRate);

  // The simulator returns 0 here...
  if (stream.mSampleRate == 0) stream.mSampleRate = 8000;

  stream.mFormatID         = kAudioFormatAppleIMA4;
  stream.mChannelsPerFrame = 1;
}
```

To create a new input audio queue, use AudioQueueNewInput, which can fill in more fields of the AudioStreamBasicDescription structure. Use the result to create a file with AudioFileCreateWithURL.

```
- (void) createQueueForFile:(NSURL*)url
{
  AudioQueueNewInput(&stream, cCallback, (void*)self, NULL, NULL, 0, &queue);
  UInt32 size = sizeof(stream);
  AudioQueueGetProperty(queue, kAudioQueueProperty_StreamDescription,
                                                             &stream, &size);
  AudioFileCreateWithURL((CFURLRef)url, kAudioFileCAFType, &stream,
                                   kAudioFileFlags_EraseFile, &audioFileHandle);
  [self copyCookie]; // See next section
}
```

Buffers are created and enqueued as before, but not filled:

```
- (void) createBuffers:(int)n withSize:(int)bufferSize
{
  buffers         = [[NSMutableArray alloc] init];

  for (int i = 0; i < n; ++i)
  {
    AudioQueueBufferRef buffer;
    AudioQueueAllocateBuffer(queue, bufferSize, &buffer);
    AudioQueueEnqueueBuffer(queue, buffer, 0, NULL);
    [buffers addObject:[NSValue valueWithPointer:buffer]];
  }
}
```

The callback is responsible for saving data:

```
- (void) record:(AudioQueueRef)queueHandle buffer:(AudioQueueBufferRef)buffer
      packetCount:(UInt32)packetCount
      packetDescriptions:(const AudioStreamPacketDescription*)packetDescriptions
{
  if (packetCount == 0)
    return;

  AudioFileWritePackets(audioFileHandle, NO, buffer->mAudioDataByteSize,
                 packetDescriptions, packet, &packetCount, buffer->mAudioData);
  packet += packetCount;

  if (!stop)
    AudioQueueEnqueueBuffer(queueHandle, buffer, 0, NULL);
}
```

As before, we use a C callback to forward data.

```
void cCallback(void*                                userData,
               AudioQueueRef                        handle,
               AudioQueueBufferRef                  buffer,
               const AudioTimeStamp*                startTime,
               UInt32                               packetCount,
               const AudioStreamPacketDescription*  packetDescriptions)
{ [((RecorderAppDelegate*) userData) record:handle buffer:buffer
               packetCount:packetCount packetDescriptions:packetDescriptions]; }
```

Stopping closes the file:

```
- (void) stopRecording
{
  stop = YES;
  AudioQueueStop(queue, YES);
  [self copyCookie];
  AudioFileClose(audioFileHandle);
  AudioSessionSetActive(NO);
}
```

Magic Cookies

Some compression formats require you to set a "magic cookie," which is supposed to be an obscure type that you're just supposed to use. However, it's hard to remember things that don't make sense, and it's even harder to test them.

MP3 files do not require magic cookies. However, AAC files do: Their "magic cookie" describes the way in which packet data is laid out in the file, and corresponds to the ESDS (elementary stream descriptors) field. For more information, refer to Apple's *Universal container for audio data* patent.

To support these formats, your code must pass magic cookies from files to queues and vice versa. Most generic code simply checks whether there is a cookie and copies it over:

```
AudioFileGetPropertyInfo(audioFile,kAudioFilePropertyMagicCookieData,&size,nil);
if (size > 0)
{
 void* cookie = malloc(sizeof(char) * size);
 AudioFileGetProperty(audioFile,kAudioFilePropertyMagicCookieData,&size,cookie);
 AudioQueueSetProperty(queue, kAudioQueueProperty_MagicCookie, cookie, size);
 free(cookie);
}
```

Audio Sessions

Audio sessions provide a way to contextualize your application's use of audio, without changing all your code. The three kinds of context that affect your application are as follows:

- Whether other applications such as the Music application may play in the background
- A phone call interrupting your application
- Hardware configuration (whether headphones are plugged into the iPhone and whether a microphone is connected to a second-generation iPod touch)

The `AudioSession` singleton lets you customize your application's behavior.

Mixing Audio

By default, the first time your application makes a sound, any other sources of audio running in the background will be silenced. However, your users might want to listen to their own music. Inform AudioSession of your application's sound category to change this behavior.

There are two categories of sounds that let you mix your application's sounds with those of the iPod application: kAudioSessionCategory_UserInterfaceSoundEffects and kAudioSessionCategory_AmbientSound.

There are three categories of sounds that specify that when the Ring/Silent button is set to silent, your applications' sounds will be muted: kAudioSessionCategory_UserInterfaceSoundEffects, kAudioSessionCategory_AmbientSound, and kAudioSessionCategory_SoloAmbientSound. This allows your users to play a game during a boring meeting without offending the presenter, and control the sound by setting their ringer to silent.

One category specifies sounds are short and respond to user-interface actions: kAudioSessionCategory_UserInterfaceSoundEffects. Both kAudioSessionCategory_AmbientSound and kAudioSessionCategory_SoloAmbientSound specify longer ambient sounds such as game music.

kAudioSessionCategory_MediaPlayback allows audio to continue playing even if the screen locks.

Use kAudioSessionCategory_LiveAudio for music applications playing back your compositions and kAudioSessionCategory_RecordAudio for recording audio.

Using kAudioSessionCategory_PlayAndRecord disables the speaker at the bottom of the iPhone (next to the microphone), to reduce feedback, but still outputs sound through the receiver (the loudspeaker you place next to your ear at the top of the iPhone).

```
uint32 c = kAudioSessionCategory_AmbientSound;
AudioSessionSetProperty(kAudioSessionProperty_AudioCategory, sizeof(c), &c);
```

Responding to Interruptions

Because the iPhone is a phone, your application cannot prevent phone calls from being received. Users can enable Airport mode to block phone calls from being received. When a phone call is received, users can choose not to answer the phone.

While they make this choice, your application's audio is disabled. It is not automatically re-enabled if users decline the call. AudioSessionInitialize registers a callback for the interruption handler:

```
OSStatus AudioSessionInitialize(CFRunLoopRef callbackRunLoop,
                                CFStringRef  callbackRunLoopMode,
            AudioSessionInterruptionListener callbackFunction,
                                void*        callbackUserData);
```

The interruption handler is informed of interruptions starting (kAudioSessionBeginInterruption) and ending (kAudioSessionEndInterruption). For instance, to reactivate the session once it is done, use the following code:

```
void callBack(void* callbackUserData, uint32 interruptionState)
{
  if (interruptionState == kAudioSessionEndInterruption)
  {
    AudioSessionSetActive(YES);
    // Code to start playing whatever streams were running
  }

  else if (interruptionState == kAudioSessionBeginInterruption)
  {
    // Code to stop playing whatever streams are running
    AudioSessionSetActive(NO);
  }
}
```

Audio Session Property Changes

Use AudioSessionAddPropertyListener to add a property listener, which will be called if an audio property changes. The main properties that can be monitored are as follows:

- kAudioSessionProperty_AudioRouteChange specifies the audio route changed. The audio route specifies whether audio is sent to the headphone, receiver, or speaker, and where it comes from.
- AudioSessionProperty_CurrentHardwareInputVolume specifies the volume of input audio.
- AudioSessionProperty_CurrentHardwareOutputVolume specifies the volume of output audio.
- kAudioSessionProperty_AudioInputAvailable tells you if a microphone is available (for second-generation iPod touches).

The callback had the type signature:

```
void callbackFunction(void*                   userData,
                      AudioSessionPropertyID changedPropertyIdentifier,
                      UInt32 changeDataSize, censt void* changeData);
```

You can set the following properties with `AudioSessionSetProperty`: `kAudioSessionProperty_PreferredHardwareSampleRate`, `kAudioSessionProperty_PreferredHardwareIOBufferDuration`, `kAudioSessionProperty_AudioCategory`, and `kAudioSessionProperty_OverrideAudioRoute`. By default, recording when sound plays outputs sound to the receiver but not to the speaker. `kAudioSessionProperty_OverrideAudioRoute` lets you change this.

The following important properties can be read with `AudioSessionGetProperty`:

- `kAudioSessionProperty_AudioRoute` specifies whether audio is sent to the headphone, receiver, or speaker, and where it comes from.
- `kAudioSessionProperty_OtherAudioIsPlaying` tells you whether another application is currently playing audio.
- `kAudioSessionProperty_AudioInputAvailable` tells you if a microphone is available (for second-generation iPod touches).

Apple recommends that you monitor the audio route and stop recording whenever users plug or unplug the headset. Similarly, they would like your application to continue playing sounds if a headset is plugged in, but to pause output when the headset is disconnected.

Did you Know?

`kAudioSessionProperty_AudioInputAvailable` does not work unless you call `AudioSessionInitialize` first. You can set all the parameters to `NULL`:

```
- (void) checkMicrophone
{
  AudioSessionInitialize( NULL, NULL, NULL, NULL );
  UInt32   microphone = 0;
  UInt32 size = sizeof(microphone);
  AudioSessionGetProperty(kAudioSessionProperty_AudioInputAvailable,
                                                  &size, &microphone);
  NSLog(@"I did %@detect a microphone", microphone ? @"" : @"not ");
}
```

Playing Audio with `AVAudioPlayer`

To reduce the amount of code needed to play sounds, iPhone OS 2.2 introduced the `AVAudioPlayer` class, which provides an Objective-C API to Core Audio's audio queues, making it easier to play (but not record) sounds. Sounds can be loaded from a file (`initWithContentsOfURL:error:`) or created in memory (`initWithData:error:`). In both cases, the sound must be in one of the formats Audio File Services understands.

The `volume` property sets the volume, and the `numberOfLoops` property lets you loop the sound. Start it by invoking its `play` method, pause it by invoking its `pause` method, and stop it by invoking its `stop` method. Two delegate methods inform you if an error was encountered (`audioPlayerDecodeErrorDidOccur:error:`), when the sound finished playing (`audioPlayerDidFinishPlaying:successfully:`), and if the audio session is interrupted (`audioPlayerBeginInterruption:`) or resumed (`audioPlayerEndInterruption:`). `AVAudioPlayer` automatically reactivates the audio session for you.

All the limitations that applied to Core Audio apply to `AVAudioPlayer`. For instance, it is unable to play more than one MP3 sound at a time. To create a sequence of MP3s, implement `audioPlayerDidFinishPlaying:successfully:` to play the next MP3.

Playing Video Files

Video files are even larger than sound files. Keeping hours of high-quality video on as small a device as the iPod touch would have been science fiction 20 years ago. Advances in physics (reducing the size of transistors on chips) and video compression algorithms (motion compensation) have made it possible. The iPhone supports two forms of video compression: H.264's baseline profile and MPEG-4's simple profile.

Video Compression

Like audio compression, video compression works by finding and removing redundant information in the frequency, spatial, and temporal domains. Video consists of a series of pictures. Because the human brain can only process a limited number of pictures per second, showing successive images fast enough creates the impression of movement.

Most people's eyes have three color receptors (some have two, some have four), which is why any color can be made from three primary colors (RGB: red, green, blue). However, people perceive luminance more accurately than color. RGB can be converted without loss of information to luminance (Y: a weighted sum of the R, G, and B components) and two color components (U and V). The YUV image produced by halving the horizontal and vertical resolutions of U and V components does not look substantially different from the original but only uses a quarter the number of bits.

Pictures have long been compressed by transforming them into the frequency domain and quantizing their high-frequency components to fewer bits (reducing detail). Most high-frequency components are quantized to zero (sequences of the same number are easily compressed). The JPEG format does this, as do H264 and MPEG-4 for the initial images (and resynchronization images).

Because video does not change much from frame to frame, you can assume the previous frame looks like the current one: We only need to determine the differences and save those. Because the differences mainly consist of movement, they will look like parts of previous picture(s). Motion compensation computes the vectors required to move blocks of pixels from previous pictures to patch up the previous picture and make it look like the current one. Using many block sizes reduces the number of vectors required. Using vectors that can move blocks by quarter pixels (and interpolating the resulting block) improves the result.

Image frames do not need to be transmitted in order, as long as they are shown in order. By transmitting future images before they are shown, motion compensation can use blocks of pixels from both future and past images, further improving the quality of the patched-up image.

After motion compensation, there is still a residual error between the patched-up picture and the picture we want to show. The residual error can be compressed and quantized in the frequency domain. A camera that takes fewer pictures per second suffers from motion blur. This turns out to be a good thing as it lets you lower the frame rate without creating the impression of stuttering. Video compression can use the same trick, reducing how much error residual data it must transmit.

Because decoding video is even more performance intensive than decoding audio, the iPhone uses its video hardware to decode videos. Although the main and extended profiles can use motion compensation taking blocks from up to 16 past and future pictures, the iPhone's hardware is limited to using 2 images. This is why the iPhone only supports H.264's Baseline Profile Level 3.0 and MPEG-4 Part 2 video's Simple Profile. Furthermore, the hardware only supports displaying video using the entire screen, which is why the iPhone only displays video in Full Screen mode.

Using MPMoviePlayerController

The MPMoviePlayerController class provides an API to play movies. When you start it, it will take over the entire screen. To create a movie player and load the movie, specify its location as a URL (either as a file or a website URL).

```
MPMoviePlayerController* player = nil;
player                 = [[MPMoviePlayerController alloc] initWithContentURL:url];
player.scalingMode     = MPMovieScalingModeAspectFill;
player.movieControlMode = MPMovieControlModeDefault;
```

After creating the movie player, you can customize how it scales the movie, whether any controls are visible, and its background color.

The aspect ratio, specified by scalingMode, may be:

- MPMovieScalingModeNone—No scaling.
- MPMovieScalingModeAspectFit—Maintain aspect ratio, but try to use the entire screen without clipping.
- MPMovieScalingModeAspectFill—Maintain aspect ratio, but clip so that the movie fits the entire screen.
- MPMovieScalingModeFill—Scale the movie so that it fills the entire screen without clipping (distorting the movie).

Set movieControlMode to specify the control panel that is overlaid over the movie:

- MPMovieControlModeDefault shows the standard controls for playback (play, pause, volume slider, and timeline control).
- MPMovieControlModeVolumeOnly shows a small panel for volume controls only.
- MPMovieControlModeHidden hides the control panel.

To show the movie and start playing it, invoke play. play returns immediately, so you must register for notifications to know when it starts playing. You can set up the following notifications:

- MPMoviePlayerContentPreloadDidFinishNotification—The movie is now ready to play (or will not play due to an error).
- MPMoviePlayerPlaybackDidFinishNotification—The movie has finished playing.

- `MPMoviePlayerScalingModeDidChangeNotification`—The movie's scaling changed. You can release the movie (and its notifications) in the `MPMoviePlayerPlaybackDidFinishNotification` handler.

To pause and hide the movie, invoke `stop`.

> **Did you Know?**
> Apple recommends that you release any OpenGL ES contexts and surfaces you created before playing video.

Summary

The iPhone provides a very powerful audio API. This power comes at the price of complexity. The `AVAudioPlayer` class provides an easy-to-use alternative when you do not need all the capabilities of CoreAudio. In fact, we only brushed the surface of CoreAudio. For instance, OpenAL lets you place sounds in 3D, which is useful for game developers: It lets them associate sounds with the objects in their games. Core Audio also lets you create graphs of audio units to process sound in real time. At the time of writing, I know of no good book about Core Audio, so you'll have to rely on Apple's documentation to learn more:

- "Core Audio Overview"
- "Audio Queue Services Programming Guide"
- "Audio Session Programming Guide"

You can also play video files using the `MPMoviePlayerController` class. This simple class provides relatively limited opportunities for customization because video is decoded in Landscape mode and Full Screen mode by the iPhone's hardware. Nevertheless, it makes adding video to your application easy.

To learn more about video compression, read *H.264 and MPEG-4 Video Compression* by Iain E. G. Richardson. It's a fascinating topic.

Q&A

Q. ***Can I use*** `MPMoviePlayerController` ***to play audio?***

A. Yes, surprisingly you can. However, doing so will show `MPMoviePlayerController`'s user interface.

Q. ***Can I write my own video decoder in software?***

A. Yes you can, but you might find it difficult to run at acceptable performance levels. Part of the problem is that the iPhone SDK does not provide a documented API to access 3D texture memory directly. The documented APIs require you to write to an image, which is copied to texture memory at the iPhone's leisure. The undocumented `CoreSurface` API lets you access texture memory directly. Apple does not accept applications that access `CoreSurface` for distribution on the App Store, which explains why the VLC video player is only available on jailbroken iPhones. VLC's source code is available at http://github.com/zodttd/. Jonathan Zdziarski's book *IPhone Open Application Development* explains how to use `CoreSurface`.

Workshop

The Workshop consists of quiz questions and answers to help you solidify your understanding of the material covered in this hour. You should try to answer the questions before checking the answers.

Quiz Questions

1. How many MP3-encoded sounds can the iPhone play simultaneously?
2. Can you use `AVAudioPlayer` to record sounds?
3. Must you decode audio files and provide raw samples to play, as on other platforms?

Quiz Answers

1. The hardware can only decode one MP3 sound at a time.
2. No, you must use Core Audio to record sounds.
3. No, Audio File Services provides an interface to decode and encode audio files.

Exercises

- Use `AVAudioPlayer` to play an MP3 file. Run the Music application and play a tune. Run your application. What happens to the music the Music application was playing? Now convert the file to the IMA4 format using `afconvert`. Change your application to play the IMA4 file. Does the ADPCM sound now overlay the music the Music application is playing?

- Change the sine wave player to play "Au Clair De La Lune". The 440Hz tone it currently plays is the musical note A above C4. To obtain the A an octave higher, multiply the frequency by 2. Each octave consists of 12 notes, so you can obtain all the frequencies of all the notes by multiplying the base frequency by the 12th root of 2 as many times as necessary. Thus, the frequencies of C4, C4#, D4, D4#, E4, F4, F#4, G4, G#4, A4, A#4, and B4 are 261.63, 277.18, 293.66, 311.13, 329.63, 349.23, 369.99, 392.00, 415.30, 440.00, 466.16, and 493.88 Hertz.

  To improve the sound, you can change the sounds volumes to rise quickly, decay, sustain, and then release. You can also add some vibrato to your notes by varying their frequency around the note being played.

Exercises

HOUR 20

Sensing the World

What You'll Learn in This Hour:

- Using the iPhone's accelerometer
- Determining the iPhone's location
- Taking photos and making short videos

The main difference between iPhones and standard computers is their portability and the number of sensors they come with, which creates a new user experience. In this hour, you'll learn to use the accelerometer, which reports the angle at which your iPhone is tilted, Core Location, which tells you the location of your iPhone, and the camera, which lets you take pictures and short videos.

Using the iPhone's Accelerometer

The iPhone was the first mass-market device to use accelerometers for user-interface interaction: switching between Landscape and Portrait modes. The iPhone provides a remarkably easy-to-use API.

How Accelerometers Work

Accelerometers measure the acceleration they experience. For instance, if you're sitting in a plane that's taking off, you feel your back pressed into the chair in the direction opposite to the one you're traveling in. Accelerometers measure this force. If you lie on your back, you'll also feel your back pushing into the bed. Accelerometers also measure this force.

The iPhone has three accelerometers, which measure acceleration along the three axes:

- The x-axis grows right when you hold your iPhone vertical in Portrait mode.
- The y-axis grows upward when you hold your iPhone vertical in Portrait mode.
- The z-axis sticks out of your iPhone's screen. When you hold your iPhone's screen facing you, the z-axis grows toward you.

Therefore, when your iPhone is lying flat, screen pointing up, on a horizontal surface, the x and y accelerometers will report no force, but the z-axis accelerometer will report a -1.0 force corresponding to the force of gravity. As you pick your iPhone up, it will experience acceleration, and then it will experience deceleration as you stop moving it.

The accelerometer in your iPhone is a micromachine built of tiny components (0.001 mm). It is built using the same lithographic process as is used to manufacture computer chips. Although lithography is usually used to build connected components, it can be used to create build wires that are only connected on one side: tiny cantilever beams. As these wires bend due to the acceleration they experience, their capacitance changes. (Capacitance is a device's ability to hold electric charge.) This capacitance can be measured and quantized into numbers.

Did you Know?

The lithographic processes used to manufacture computer chips create stencils on the chips to control where substances such as metals are deposited on the chip. They use the following steps:

1. To create the stencil:
    1. First coat a chip with a chemical solution that is sensitive to light.
    2. Shine light through a mask. The mask prevents light from hitting certain areas of the chip. Wherever the light hits, the solution becomes solid (see Figure 20.1).
    3. Wash away the liquid solution, leaving the solid part of the stencil: Only the stencil's holes are washed away.
2. To deposit the substances such as metals on the chip:
    1. Spray onto the chip whatever substance you want to place on the chip (such as metal for wires) (see Figure 20.1).
    2. Dilute the stencil. Only metal on the surface of the chip remains as shown in Figure 20.1.

This process is repeated as many times as necessary to produce the chip. Figure 20.1 shows an accelerometer's tiny cantilever beam.

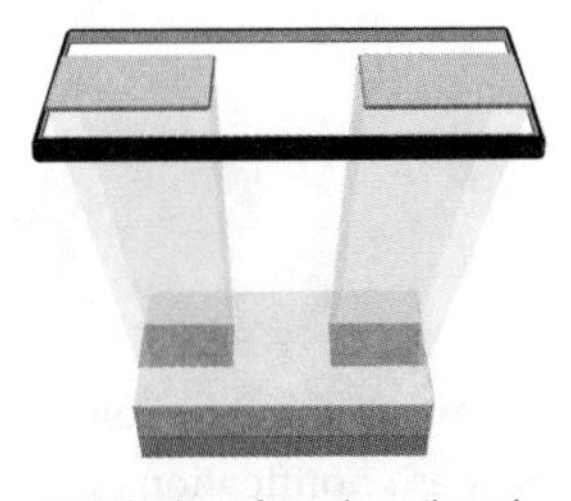

Light is shone from above through a mask to solidify a light sensitive chemical creating a stencil (yellow) on the suface of the chip (orange).

Metal is deposited in the holes of the stencil.

The stencil is removed leaving metal on the surface of the chip.

A tiny cantilever beam on the surface of the chip is used to measure acceleration.

FIGURE 20.1 Lithographic process.

Measuring the Acceleration

The accelerometer measures instantaneous force, just like the iPhone's microphone measures instantaneous air pressure. In both cases, we quantize each sample and record them at a sampling rate. The sampling rate for accelerometers is much lower than for sound (100Hz versus 44Khz). Because the rate is lower, the iPhoneOS forwards individual measurements to your application's callback function.

Using `UIAccelerometer`

The accelerometer is represented by a singleton in the software API. Invoke `sharedAccelerometer` on `UIAccelerometer` to retrieve it. Set its sampling rate with `updateInterval`. Apple suggests three frequency ranges:

- 10–20Hz (to determine the current orientation of the device)
- 30–60Hz (for games that are controlled by tilting the iPhone)
- 70–100Hz (for precise measurements)

By default, the accelerometer is off (to preserve power). Setting the delegate turns it on. The higher the frequency, the more battery is consumed.

```
- (void) setupAccelerometer
{
  UIAccelerometer*  accelerometer = [UIAccelerometer sharedAccelerometer];
  accelerometer.updateInterval    = 1.0 / 50.0;    // 50 Hz
  accelerometer.delegate          = self;
}
```

The `accelerometer:didAccelerate:` delegate method is invoked from the run loop each time a sample arrives.

```
- (void) accelerometer:(UIAccelerometer*)accelerometer
         didAccelerate:(UIAcceleration*)acceleration
{
```

```
  float xAxisAcceleration = acceleration.x;
  float yAxisAcceleration = acceleration.y;
  float zAxisAcceleration = acceleration.z;

  // Do something
}
```

Because you can only have one delegate per accelerometer, `UIDevice` provides low-frequency device-orientation notifications. You can register for these notifications with `NotificationCenter` using the notification name `UIDeviceOrientationDidChangeNotification`. To turn the accelerometer on, you must invoke `UIDevice`'s `beginGeneratingDeviceOrientationNotifications` method. Now the `orientation` method of `UIDevice` returns the current orientation. For example, `UIViewController` registers for these notifications to be informed of orientation changes.

Building Apple's AccelerometerGraph Example

Apple's software development kit (SDK) provides a nice interactive example of using the accelerometer called AccelerometerGraph (see Figure 20.2). It displays three constantly updated graphs, showing the last three seconds of measurements obtained from the accelerometer along the three axes. This lets you wave your iPhone around and see the effect.

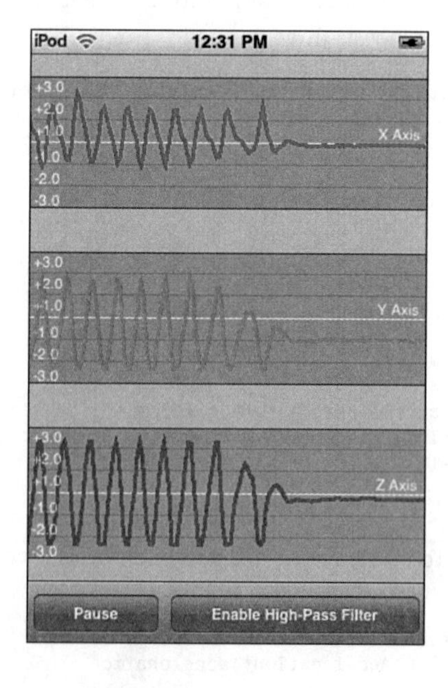

FIGURE 20.2 Apple's AccelerometerGraph example

Find the AccelerometerGraph example in the SDK (go to Xcode's iPhone documentation and search by name).

Build it. Run it on the simulator. Notice that the graphs stay flat: The simulator does not use your Mac's accelerometer. Now run it on your device (after setting the Bundle identifier in `Info.plist` and your iPhone Developer identity in the Code Signing Identity part of the Build settings—see Appendix B, "Troubleshooting Xcode," for details). If your iPhone is lying flat, with its screen up, you'll see -1 on the z-axis graph. Wave your iPhone around to see measurements on all axes.

Filtering the Measurements

The measurements from each axis of the accelerometer form a wave, just like a sound wave. Just like a sound wave, these waves can be built from a sum of sine waves of different frequencies.

You can show mathematically that you only need half as many sine waves as there are samples. The lowest frequency sine wave makes no oscillations over the entire range of samples: It's a constant. The next higher frequency sine wave makes a single oscillation over the entire range of samples—then 2, 3... up to N/2-1 oscillations over the entire range of samples. Because the number of oscillations (frequency) of each sine wave is fixed, its important characteristics are its phase and amplitude.

If you were to shake your phone creating a sine wave at precisely 1 Hz, and if the number of samples we analyzed corresponded to one second's worth of data, a single sine wave would have a nonzero amplitude. If you were to double, triple, or quadruple (and so on) the frequency, a different single sine wave would have a nonzero amplitude. However, if you did not quite double the frequency, more than one sine wave would have a nonzero amplitude.

The lowest frequency sine wave does not oscillate at all—rather like the earth's gravitational field. Lower frequencies correspond to slow oscillations, such as the movements caused when you pick the phone up. Higher frequencies correspond to tremors, for instance your hand shaking when holding the phone (something that worsens with age). Digital filters provide a computationally efficient way of selectively boosting the amplitude of sine waves belonging to a range of frequencies and dampening the others. By applying a digital filter to the sampled accelerometer data, you can isolate the effect of gravity from large voluntary movements and small involuntary movements, tuning your application to best respond to users' input.

Apple recommends the following recursive filter to isolate the effect of gravity. To obtain the high-frequency component, they simply subtract the low-frequency component from the instantaneous acceleration.

```
const float kFilteringFactor = 0.1;
lowFrequencyX  =    (acceleration.x * kFilteringFactor)
                  + (lowFrequencyX * (1.0 - kFilteringFactor));
highFrequencyX =  acceleration.x - lowFrequencyX;
```

If you tap the Enable High-Pass Filter button of the AccelerometerGraph example, you'll see this filter in action. It is good enough for most applications, and you can always reduce `kFilteringFactor` to increase the number of low frequencies that are included in `highFrequencyX`. `kFilteringFactor` is only valid between 0 and 1!

By the Way

> Your iPhone's iPod application comes with a set of equalizer settings (to boost bass, and so on). These settings are implemented by digital filters.

For more accuracy, increase the sampling rate. This will use more battery. The maximum sampling rate depends on the device (currently 400Hz). To measure it, you can vary the sampling rate and notice when samples are repeated (because of noise, you'll always get some nonzero samples). You can ask users to leave the phone on a stable surface for a few minutes, to calibrate the noise level.

Did you Know?

> If you need particularly precise measurements, you should be aware that because of variations in manufacturing, the accelerometer's axes might not line up precisely with the body of the iPhone. You can calibrate this by requesting the user to place each edge of the iPhone against a horizontal surface. Finding a perfectly horizontal surface can be a challenge.
>
> Early iPhones used the LIS302DL accelerometer, whereas newer ones use the LIS331DL. Their sensitivity varies by up to 10%, but because the earth's gravitational field is constant, you can calibrate for that. Similarly, each device has a "zero" level, which can be off by +/- 50mg. You can measure it over time. Quantization reduces the dynamic range to 256 unique values (18mg per unit out of a possible range of +/- 2.3g). To learn more about these devices, read their specifications at their manufacturer's website.
>
> http://www.st.com/stonline/products/literature/ds/12726.pdf
> http://www.st.com/stonline/products/literature/ds/13951/lis331dl.pdf

Determining the iPhone's Location

Many times, you might want to know information about your current location (for example, to find the nearest metro station). The iPhone is a good reference tool for these situations because most people carry it with them and it has Internet connectivity. 3G iPhones can determine their location using GPS, vastly improving user experience.

Location Technologies

To provide good location information everywhere, the iPhone combines three sources of information: GPS, nearby cell phone tower IDs, and local Wi-Fi access point IDs.

The U.S. military created the Global Positioning System (GPS) to allow precise targeting. After the Soviet Union shot down a Korean civilian airliner that had strayed into prohibited airspace, the United States decided to make GPS available to civilians. GPS provides an accuracy of around 50 feet (18 meters). GPS uses a constellation of 31 satellites, which constantly transmit their location and the time of their onboard atomic clock. The iPhone's position can be computed by triangulating the time it takes signals from the different satellites to reach it. The satellites' atomic clocks are only a few nanoseconds out of sync because they are constantly resynchronized by Earth-based stations. The more satellites are in line of sight, the better GPS' accuracy. Buildings, mountains, and even trees can block or reflect GPS signals making GPS less accurate in cities. GPS is only available on 3G iPhones.

Every cell phone tower has a unique ID. Cell phones connect to the closest cell phone tower. However, when you are talking on the phone in a moving vehicle, your connection is handed from cell phone tower to cell phone tower. The cell phone keeps track of the nearby towers and their distance, so that it knows when to switch. Your iPhone can use this information to triangulate its position (after querying the position of the cell phone towers). In rural areas, where GPS works well, cell phone towers can be as far apart as 50 miles. In suburbs, they are spaced 2 miles apart. In dense urban areas, they might be spaced as close as every quarter mile, providing for better accuracy. However, buildings also block cell phone signals. Cell phone tower positioning is only available on iPhones (and not iPod touches).

Every Wi-Fi access point has a MAC address (a Data Link layer identifier as explained in Hour 14, "Accessing the Network"). If the iPhone can detect multiple Wi-Fi access points whose location is known, it can triangulate its position to within 30 meters. Because Wi-Fi access points work within buildings, this provides coverage where cell phone towers and GPS do not. However, it only works if the location of the Wi-Fi access point is known. If the location of the Wi-Fi access point isn't known, the iPhone uses IP address geolocation, which is inaccurate (40 miles off where I live).

Because every cell phone has a unique ID, cell phone towers can triangulate every cell phone's position. Police can subpoena this information from cell phone tower operators.

Using the Location API

CLLocationManager hides the details of fetching locations by providing a unified API regardless of the location's source. First, you must create a location manager. (Don't forget to add the CoreLocation framework to your project.)

```
#import <CoreLocation/CoreLocation.h>
locator = [[CLLocationManager alloc] init];
```

You can specify the accuracy you want for your location data. The higher the desired accuracy, the longer the measurement will take and the more battery power it will consume. Your options are kCLLocationAccuracyBest, kCLLocationAccuracyNearestTenMeters, kCLLocationAccuracyHundredMeters, kCLLocationAccuracyKilometer, and kCLLocationAccuracyThreeKilometers. The default accuracy is kCLLocationAccuracyBest.

```
locator.desiredAccuracy = kCLLocationAccuracyBest;
```

To start gathering locations, invoke startUpdatingLocation. It is a good idea not to invoke it unless absolutely necessary if CLLocationManager's locationServicesEnabled property is false: Starting updates when the user has disabled location services causes an alert panel to appear asking them to turn location services back on (leaving your application). To stop gathering data, invoke stopUpdatingLocation.

```
locator.delegate         = self;
if (locator.locationServicesEnabled)
  [locator startUpdatingLocation];
```

Because querying location takes time, CLLocationManager invokes delegate methods when it has something to report. When a location is received, the locationManager:didUpdateToLocation:fromLocation: delegate method is invoked. Both locations are instances of the CLLocation class. Because this object can express all the location information available on any device, you must test to see which information is valid:

- coordinate (a C structure for latitude and longitude) is valid if horizontalAccuracy is positive.
- altitude is valid if verticalAccuracy is positive.

- `course` represents the direction of travel and is only valid if positive. 0 represents north, 90 represents east, and so on.
- `speed` represents the speed of travel in meters per second and is only valid if positive.
- `timestamp` represents the time at which the location was determined (not when it was received). For instance, only GPS can estimate `altitude`. Similarly, `course` is computed from location changes (requiring your iPhone to move).

`locationManager:didUpdateToLocation:fromLocation:` can receive location data out of order: GPS can determine the current location before the Internet returns the result of looking up Wi-Fi MAC addresses. Use `timestamp` to sort the locations appropriately.

```
- (void) locationManager:(CLLocationManager*)locator
         didUpdateToLocation:(CLLocation*)newLoc
         fromLocation:(CLLocation*)oldLoc
{
  [print @"Date: %@" [dateFormatter stringFromDate:[newLocation timestamp]]];

  if (newLoc.horizontalAccuracy >= 0)
  {
    CLLocationCoordinate2D ll = newLoc.coordinate;
    [self print:@"Coordinates at (%g, %g)", ll.latitude, ll.longitude];

    if (oldLoc)
      [self print:@"Moved: %g meters", [newLoc getDistanceFrom:oldLoc]];
  }

  if (newLoc.verticalAccuracy >= 0)
    [self print:@"Altitude %g", newLoc.altitude];
}
```

If no location can be found, the delegate's `locationManager:didFailWithError:` method is called.

```
- (void) locationManager:(CLLocationManager*)locator
        didFailWithError:(NSError*)error
{
  switch ([error code])
  {
    case kCLErrorDenied:
      [self print:@"Location access denied"];
      break;

    case kCLErrorLocationUnknown:
      [self print:@"Your location could not be determined"];
      break;

    default:
      [self print:@"Unknown error!"];
```

```
        break;
    }
}
```

If `kCLErrorDenied` occurs, no more location events will be gathered until the application is quit.

Because radios consume power, the iPhone turns them off whenever possible. To reduce the number of updates requested, set `CLLocationManager`'s `distanceFilter` property to the minimum distance the iPhone must move in the horizontal plane before an event is generated. By default, this value is `kCLDistanceFilterNone`: Any movement will cause an event.

Unfortunately, the simulator provides very little Core Location simulation functionality.

`CLLocation`'s `getDistanceFrom:` method computes an approximation of the distance between two `CLLocations`' `coordinates`, not taking into account altitude. This distance is the great-circle distance: This approximation assumes the Earth is a spheroid and that all points of the Earth are at sea-level.

Compass

The earth has a magnetic field and two magnetic poles. The field is currently almost aligned with the earth's axis of rotation, giving an approximate north-south direction. The magnetic poles wander around by a few degrees of latitude or longitude each year. Currently, the magnetic northern pole is in northern Canada, and the magnetic southern pole is at the northern edge of Antarctica near Australia.

The new iPhone 3GS contains a **magnetometer** (the AK8973). This device measures the direction of the earth's magnetic field with an accuracy of around 5%. It consists of three **Hall effect** devices, which measure the magnetic field along three axes. When an electron passes through a magnetic field, it is slightly deflected. For instance, if the magnetic field has the north-south direction, and the electron goes from east to west, it will be deflected slightly down. If the electron is in a wire, the top of the wire will go slightly positive, and the bottom of the wire will go slightly negative as electrons travel through it. Measuring the difference in charge between the top and bottom of the wire along three axes determines the direction of the field. Just like classical compasses, strong magnetic fields (such as a magnet placed nearby) will dominate.

As of iPhoneOS 3.0, the CLLocationManager object has a headingAvailable method, to tell you whether the device has a compass. If it does, you can invoke startUpdatingHeading. Your delegate's locationManager:didUpdateHeading: method will be invoked whenever a change of angle of more than headingFilter degrees occurs. By default, headingFilter is set to kCLHeadingFilterNone, which means any change of heading will cause the locationManager:didUpdateHeading: to be invoked. To stop receiving heading updates, invoke stopUpdatingHeading.

```
if (locator.headingAvailable)
{ locator.headingFilter = 5;
  [locator startUpdatingHeading]; }
```

Headings are represented by a CLHeading object, which is valid if its headingAccuracy is positive. The magneticHeading tells you the computed heading of the field, and x, y, z tell you the raw microteslas measured in each direction. This has been used to detect the magnetic field due to live wires in walls. If the iPhone knows its coordinate on the planet, it can compute the direction of the North Pole: trueHeading. 0 is true north, 90 is east, and so on. If you do not enable location updates, or if no location has been found, trueHeading will be negative.

```
- (void) locationManager:(CLLocationManager*)locator
       didUpdateHeading:(CLHeading*)heading
{
   if (heading.headingAccuracy >= 0)
   {
     [self print:@"Magnetic heading %@", heading.magneticHeading];
     [self print:@"x,y,z %g %g %g", heading.x, heading.y, heading.z];
     if (heading.trueHeading >= 0)
       [self print:@"True heading %g", heading.trueHeading];
   }
}
```

The earth's magnetic field is not uniform in strength or direction. If it is weak, or suddenly changes direction, the iPhone might display an alert panel requesting the user to wave it around to recalibrate it. The iPhone can separate internal and external magnetic fields when it is waved around: Internal magnetic fields will not move; external ones move with respect to the iPhone, but will stay stable with respect to the frame of reference provided by the accelerometers. For instance, the iPhone's components generate magnetic fields that must be filtered out. The alert panel will only be shown if you implement the optional locationManagerShouldDisplayHeadingCalibration: delegate method to return YES. Otherwise, headingAccuracy will be degraded until the iPhone detects a strong magnetic field or you move it around enough for it to recalibrate.

Taking Photos and Making Short Videos

The original iPhone has a fixed focus lens and a 2.0 megapixel camera (1600×1200 pixels). Although Apple does not provide a software interface for it, the hardware can take 15 pictures per second at a resolution of 384×288 pixels. The iPhone 3GS has a 3.0 megapixel camera (1536x2048 pixels) with an autofocus lens that can take 30 pictures per second at a resolution of 640×480 pixels. By taking a sequence of pictures, an iPhone can create a video. iPod touches have no camera.

Apple provides a unified high-level API, `UIImagePickerController`, to access users' photos and the camera. Your application can check whether the device it is running on supports a source type by invoking `UIImagePickerController`'s `isSourceTypeAvailable:` class method. The possible source types are as follows:

- `UIImagePickerControllerSourceTypePhotoLibrary`—The photo library, which is supported by all devices
- `UIImagePickerControllerSourceTypeCamera`—The device's camera, if it has one
- `UIImagePickerControllerSourceTypeSavedPhotosAlbum`—The Saved Photos folder for devices without a camera, the camera roll otherwise

iPhoneOS 3.0 adds an `availableMediaTypesForSourceType:` class method that lists the types of media a source can return: `kUTTypeImage` for pictures and `kUTTypeMovie` for 10 seconds or less movies (on the iPhone 3GS). By default, `UIImagePickerController` only takes photos. If you also want to take short videos, your application must add `kUTTypeMovie` to the `mediaTypes` array (if it is running on a 3GS).

Because the controller supports multiple sources, it builds all the views it needs, including its own navigation bar. The App Store rejects applications that access the view representing the camera interface directly.

`UIImagePickerController` requires you to provide a delegate, which responds to the `UINavigationControllerProtocol` as well as its own `UIImagePickerControllerDelegate` protocol. Once you have set up the picker, invoke `presentModalViewController:animated:` to add the picker to the hierarchy.

```
UIImagePickerController* picker = [[UIImagePickerController alloc] init];

#define CAMERA UIImagePickerControllerSourceTypeCamera
#define ALBUM  UIImagePickerControllerSourceTypeSavedPhotosAlbum
```

```
if ([UIImagePickerController isSourceTypeAvailable:CAMERA])
  picker.sourceType = CAMERA;
else if ([UIImagePickerController isSourceTypeAvailable:ALBUM])
  picker.sourceType = ALBUM;
else
  return NO;

picker.delegate = self;
[picker presentModalViewController:picker animated:YES];
[picker release];
return YES;
```

Your delegate is informed when a picture was taken by `imagePickerController:didFinishPickingImage:editingInfo:`. At that time, you can dismiss the picker, and save the picture.

```
- (void) imagePickerController:(UIImagePickerController*)picker
       didFinishPickingImage:(UIImage*)image
       editingInfo:(NSDictionary*)editingInfo
{
  // Do something with the image
  [picker dismissModalViewController:YES];
}
```

For instance, you can save the image to your photo album with `UIImageWriteToSavedPhotosAlbum`, which was discussed in Hour 9, "Layers and Core Animation: Creating a Cover Flow Clone."

`UIImagePickerController` lets users crop images if you set its `allowsImageEditing` property to `YES`. In this case, `image` will be the edited picture, and `editingInfo` will be a dictionary containing the original image (`UIImagePickerControllerOriginalImage`) and the cropping rectangle (`UIImagePickerControllerCropRect`).

As of iPhoneOS 3.0, `imagePickerController:didFinishPickingImage:editingInfo:` is deprecated—use `imagePickerController:didFinishPickingMediaWithInfo:` instead. Its `info` argument is a dictionary. For images, it contains the original (`UIImagePickerControllerOriginalImage`). If the image was edited, it also contains the edited image (`UIImagePickerControllerEditedImage`) and its crop rectangle (`UIImagePickerControllerCropRect`). For videos, it contains a URL to the video (`UIImagePickerControllerMediaURL`), which you can save or play with `MPMoviePlayerController` (described in Hour 19, "Playing and Recording Media").

If no image is taken or selected, `imagePickerControllerDidCancel:` is invoked. You can use it to `dimissModalViewController:`.

Did you Know?

Unfortunately, you cannot test the camera in the simulator even though most Macs have a camera. If you only have an iPod touch, you can easily populate your photo album to test your non–camera related `UIImagePickerController` code: Hold the Power key down and tap the Home key. The screen will flash to show a screenshot was taken.

Summary

Arthur C. Clarke once said that any sufficiently advanced technology is indistinguishable from magic. It's amazing to think that cell phones have only really taken off in the last 10 years. The first widespread cell phones with cameras appeared 8 years ago. Mobile GPS and magnetometers only appeared 5 years ago. The use of accelerometers as a user interface occurred within the last 2 years. The convergence of these technologies into one device makes for remarkable capabilities, which we have yet to see fully exploited.

Using these devices is remarkably simple. However, because the simulator does not support them, your testing must be done on the device (uploading takes time).

Q&A

Q. ***How do you record video on non-3GS iPhones?***

A. Before you take a picture, the iPhone camera interface shows a viewfinder to help you find your subject. By using the undocumented `CoreSurface` API, you can read the contents of the screen and save it as it is updated. This method can only capture video at low frame rates. Cycorder obtains better quality video by directly interfacing with the camera hardware. Remember that the App Store rejects all applications that use undocumented APIs!

Workshop

The Workshop consists of quiz questions and answers to help you solidify your understanding of the material covered in this hour. You should try to answer the questions before checking the answers.

Quiz Questions

1. What is the maximum acceleration the iPhone can detect?
2. Why does Core Location use multiple services to determine my location?
3. How accurate is Core Location?
4. What software API is used to take pictures?

Quiz Answers

1. 2.3g is the maximum acceleration the iPhone can detect.
2. Core Location uses multiple services because each service works in different situations: GPS requires a clear view of the sky, cell phone tower triangulation works in urban settings with a high density of cell phone towers, and Wi-Fi only works near Wi-Fi access points whose location is known.
3. Core Location can determine your location to within 20 meters.
4. `UIImagePickerController` is the software API used to take pictures.

Exercises

- Create an animation of a ball on a table. Make the ball accelerate in the direction of your iPhone's tilt. Change the ball so that it paints a color onto the screen where it has been. Detect when the iPod is tapped (sudden movements along the z-axis) and change the color.
- After coming back from vacation, it can be difficult to remember where you left your car. Create an application to save your car's GPS location. Then use Core Location functionality to show the car's direction and distance, so you can find it on your return. You might even want to run the application while on vacation, to know just how far you went to get away from it all.
- If you know some Physics, create an application to correlate the acceleration your car experiences with its current speed as measured by GPS. Plot the predicted speed (obtained from the accelerometer) versus the speed measured by GPS. Try to reduce possible sources of error using filters and calibration.

HOUR 21
Sharing Data

What You'll Learn in This Hour:

- Using custom URLs
- Using pasteboards
- Exporting data

In this hour, you'll learn how to share data between applications and how to share data with the outside world. Custom URLs let you start other applications. Pasteboards were introduced in iPhone OS 3.0 to support copy and paste, but provide a general mechanism for sharing data between applications. Finally, you'll learn to export data by sending email and creating a tiny web server.

Using Custom URLs

A URL's scheme specifies its protocol. In Hour 14, "Accessing the Network," you learned about the `http`, `ftp`, and `file` schemes. Mail has its own `mailto` scheme, which is used to open an email, and the iPhone introduces its own `tel` scheme to dial a number. Springboard (the application launcher which provides the home page's user interface) could hard-code which application should be opened for each scheme, but that would be inflexible. Instead, each application specifies the schemes it supports. Springboard collects this information and uses it to decide which application it should launch to service a URL request. This lets you create a protocol for other applications to start your application.

Starting Apple iPhone Applications

Many of the applications shipped with the iPhone support URL schemes. For instance, `http` opens Safari, `mailto` opens the Mail application, and `tel` opens the telephone application.

Starting the Mail Application

The standard `mailto:` URL handler is supported. To open a URL, write the following:

```
[[UIApplication sharedApplication] openURL:url];
```

The `mailto:` protocol lets you specify a `subject`, an addressee (`to`), a carbon copy addressee (`cc`), and a message `body`. It does not support attachments. The URL you create should follow the format:

```
mailto:?to=addressee&subject=subject&body=body
```

For the URL to be correctly parsed, *addressee*, *body*, and *subject* cannot contain the characters ?, =, and &. These are some of the reserved characters you should not use within the *addressee*, the *body*, or the *subject*: You must escape these characters. Although `NSString` provides `stringByAddingPercentEscapesUsingEncoding:` for URL encoding, it does not encode characters such as &. Instead, use the following category to encode your text:

```
@interface NSString (NSStringURLEncoder)
- (NSString*) urlEscape;
- (NSString*) urlUnescape;
@end

@implementation NSString (NSStringURLEncoder)
- (NSString*) urlEscape
{
  CFStringRef result
    = CFURLCreateStringByAddingPercentEscapes(kCFAllocatorDefault,
                                             (CFStringRef)self,
                                             NULL,
                                             (CFStringRef)@";/?:@&=+$,",
                                             kCFStringEncodingUTF8);
  return [((NSString*) result) autorelease];
}

- (NSString*) urlUnescape
{
  CFStringRef result
    = CFURLCreateStringByReplacingPercentEscapes(kCFAllocatorDefault,
                                                (CFStringRef)self,
                                                CFSTR(""));
  return [((NSString*) result) autorelease];
}

@end
```

Thus, to send an email, you'd write the following:

```
- (void) sendEmailTo:(NSString*)to subject:(NSString*)subj body:(NSString*)body
{
  NSString* url = [NSString stringWithFormat:@"mailto:?to=%@&subject=%@&body=%@"
                             [to urlEscape], [subj urlEscape], [body urlEscape]];
  [[UIApplication sharedApplication] openURL:[NSURL URLWithString:url]];
}
```

Phone and SMS

To dial a number, open a URL starting with the `tel` scheme. The phone number should not contain spaces or brackets:

```
NSString* url = @"tel:9876543210";
```

Similarly, you can open the Messages application to send an SMS (Short Message Service) tool with (or without) a telephone number:

```
NSString* url = @"sms:9876543210";
```

Safari, Maps, iTunes, Apple Store, and YouTube

Open Safari with a standard `http:` URL. However, if the URL is a Google maps URL (http://maps.google.com), an iTunes URL (http://itunes.apple.com), an App Store URL (http://phobos.apple.com), or a Youtube URL (http://www.youtube.com), those applications will open instead.

Did you Know?

> As of iPhone OS 3.0, Map Kit lets you display maps within your application. Alternatively, you can use `route-me` (http://code.google.com/p/route-me/), which can display maps from Microsoft Virtual World and open street maps.

Creating Your Own URL Handler

Creating your own URL handler requires informing the Springboard application of the URLs your application processes by changing the `Info.plist` file and adding a handler method to your application delegate.

Adding URL Schemes to the `Info.plist` File

To start your application, the iPhone OS needs to know which schemes are associated with which applications. Each application specifies the URL schemes to which it responds in its `Info.plist` file.

Create a `URL types` entry in your `Info.plist` file. This will create a `URL Identifier` child item. Set it to your application's bundle. Then create an array of `URL Schemes` containing the scheme names to which your application responds by clicking the plus icon (see Figure 21.1).

FIGURE 21.1
Adding a URL scheme to the `Info.plist` file

Key	Value
▼URL types	(1 item)
▼Item 1	(2 items)
URL identifier	com.ansemond.samsBook
▼URL Schemes	(1 item)
Item 1	say

Handling Requests

The iPhone OS informs your application of the URL that caused it to be started by invoking the `application:handleOpenURL:` method. Obtain the query and parse it. To remove percent escapes, use `urlUnescape` defined earlier this hour.

```
- (BOOL) application:(UIApplication*)application handleOpenURL:(NSURL*)url
{ /* Parse the URL and do something with it */ }
```

Return `NO` if your application fails to handle the URL.

Creating a Return Handler

Application authors are reluctant to use URL schemes because URL schemes do not provide a way to return to their applications. To encourage other applications to invoke your application, add a `returnto` parameter for your application's URL scheme:

```
myapp://...&returnto=returnToURL
```

Once your application has provided the service requested from it, it can restart the application that called it on exit.

```
- (void) applicationWillTerminate:(UIApplication*) application
{ [[UIApplication sharedApplication] openURL:returnToURL]; }
```

In this way, a number of small applications can work together, sharing data as needed.

Once you have defined your URL scheme, don't forget to register it at http://wiki.akosma.com/IPhone_URL_Schemes so that other application authors can use it.

Using Pasteboards

The sandbox prevents applications from accessing each other's files, to prevent malicious applications from destroying other applications' files. Pasteboards provide a controlled means for applications to share data while preventing them from destroying each other's files.

Pasteboard Architecture

The iPhone OS supports many pasteboards. Each pasteboard is uniquely identified by name. To retrieve a pasteboard, invoke `UIPasteboard`'s `pasteboardWithName:create:` class method. If the pasteboard does not exist, but the `create` argument is `YES`, a pasteboard will be created.

There are two kinds of pasteboards: The content of `persistent` pasteboards persists after application termination. To make a pasteboard persistent, set its `persistent` property to `YES`. Deleting an application deletes the pasteboards it made.

You may recall from Hour 12, "Adding Navigation and Tab Bar Controllers," that property lists are only able to support a subset of data types. Pasteboards can represent any of the types supported by property lists (`NSNumber`, `NSDate`, `NSString`, `NSArray`, `NSDictionary`, and `NSData`). However, they can also include other types as specified by Uniform Type Identifiers (UTIs). **Uniform Type Identifiers** are Apple-defined strings that identify types and are organized into a conformance hierarchy. The conformance hierarchy expresses specialization (`Is-a` relationships). For instance, it expresses the specialization that HTML is a form of text. This means that anything that can manipulate text can manipulate HTML. Thus, if a value is saved to a pasteboard as `public.text` or `public.html`, it can be retrieved as a string, but not as an image.

Pasteboards are implemented as an array of items. Each item may have multiple representations, and is represented by a dictionary. For instance, a URL can have a number of representations:

- A text representation (`kUTTypeUTF8PlainText`) for text editors
- A URL representation (`kUTTypeURL`) for tools that accept URLs
- An image representation (`kUTTypePNG` or `kUTTypeJPEG`) for tools that accept images

To retrieve a pasteboard's items, invoke `items`. To add an item, create the appropriate dictionary and add it to the pasteboard with `addItems:`.

```
NSDictionary* item
  = [NSDictionary dictionaryWithObjectsAndKeys: string, kUTTypeUTF8PlainText,
                                                url, kUTTypeURL,
                                                png, kUTTypePNG, nil];
[pasteboard addItems:[NSArray arrayWithObject:item]];
```

To help you extract data, `UIPasteboard` provides `valuesForPasteboardType:inItemSet:`, which returns an array of objects that match the requested type matching the input *`itemSet`* argument (an `NSIndexedSet`). If *`itemSet`* is `nil`, an object for each item will be returned. If no object matches the requested type, `NSNull` is returned. Otherwise, if possible the object is decoded to one of the following types: `NSNumber`, `NSDate`, `NSString`, `NSArray`, `NSDictionary`, `NSData`, or `NSURL`. Otherwise, it is returned as an `NSData`. Alternatively, you can simply retrieve it as an `NSData` with `dataForPasteboardType:inItemSet:`.

Copy and Paste

Every application that is able to copy or paste uses the general pasteboard, accessible using the name `UIPasteboardNameGeneral`. The general pasteboard is a persistent pasteboard, allowing copy and paste between applications. Only one item is used, and because copy and paste are the main use of pasteboards, `UIPasteboard` defines methods to allow quick access to the item's data: `dataForPasteboardType:`, `valueForPasteboardType:`, `setData:forPasteboardType:`, `setValue:forPasteboardType:`, `string`, `image`, `URL`, and `color`. You can also retrieve the pasteboard directly with the `generalPasteboard` class method.

The `UITextView`, `UITextField`, and `UIWebView` classes implement copy and paste. In all other cases, you must implement it yourself. `UIKit` provides a `UIMenuController` class to show a pop-up menu for the Cut, Copy, Paste, and Select commands. If the user selects an item from `UIMenuController`'s menu, its corresponding method is invoked on the `firstResponder`, propagating the message up the responder chain until a responder services it (see Hour 7, "Understanding How Events Are Processed").

The methods `UIMenuController` can invoke are the `UIResponderStandardEditActions` informal protocol's methods: `copy:`, `cut:`, `paste:`, `select:`, and `selectAll:`. To implement these methods yourself, override them in a `UIResponder` along the `UIResponder` chain. To enable or disable user-interface commands based on the context, override the `UIResponder`'s `canPerformAction:withSender:` method. To force `UIMenuController` to update available user-interface commands, invoke its `update` method. By default, `update` is invoked each time the menu is displayed or a menu item is selected.

Another system pasteboard, `UIPasteboardNameFind`, contains the most recent string value from the search bar. `UISearchBar` does not automatically display it, or set it, but you can do so in your applications.

Exporting Data

Although the iPhone provides `http` access to import data, it does not provide a way to export data. In this section, you'll learn to do this using email and creating a small web server. You could also upload it to a website.

Exporting Data in an Email

Sending data to your email address in an attachment provides a simple solution for your data-sharing needs. The advantage is that it works over the cellular network. The disadvantage is that attachments might be limited in size by your email provider. On the other hand, `gmail.com` provides free accounts able to receive and transmit 25Mb files, which should be enough for most purposes.

IPhone OS 3.0 provides a class, `MFMailComposeViewController`, that provides a user interface for creating emails and lets you attach data. However, if the task is sharing data, you might just want to transfer a file, not write a message.

The `SKPSMTPMessage` library available at http://code.google.com/p/skpsmtpmessage/source/checkout provides a good solution. Its main disadvantage is that it does not have access to your users' account settings. At the very least, your users will have to enter their email address, even if you supply an SMTP server for your application.

Just like the HTTP protocol, email is composed of a header and a body. The header specifies the addressees, the sender, and the subject.

```
SKPSMTPMessage *msg = [[SKPSMTPMessage alloc] init];
msg.fromEmail = @"you@yourserver.com";
msg.toEmail   = @"you@yourserver.com";
msg.subject   = @"Your file";
```

To contain an attachment, the body must be in MIME format: MIME lets you concatenate a number of submessages, each in MIME format. Each submessage, or part, has its own content type and encoding information. `SKPSMTPMessage` builds the MIME headers for you from a dictionary. For instance, straight text has the "text/plain" MIME type.

```
NSDictionary *text = [NSDictionary dictionaryWithObjectsAndKeys:
                           @"text/plain", kSKPSMTPPartContentTypeKey,
                  @"This is your file.", kSKPSMTPPartMessageKey,
                                 @"7bit", kSKPSMTPPartContentTransferEncodingKey,
                                                                          nil];
```

Many mail systems do not support characters whose eighth bit is set. Therefore, you must encode your attachment in base64:

```
NSString* path   = [[NSBundle mainBundle] pathForResource:@"a-file"
                                                   ofType:@"jpg"];
NSData*   data   = [NSData dataWithContentsOfFile:path];
NSString* base64 = [data encodeBase64ForData];

NSString* contentType
  = @"application/octet-stream;\r\n\tx-unix-mode=0644;\r\n\tname=\"test.jpg\"";
NSString* contentDisposition
  = @"attachment;\r\n\tfilename=\"test.jpg\"";

NSDictionary *attachment = [NSDictionary dictionaryWithObjectsAndKeys:
                             contentType, kSKPSMTPPartContentTypeKey,
                      contentDisposition, kSKPSMTPPartContentDispositionKey,
                                  base64, kSKPSMTPPartMessageKey,
                               @"base64", kSKPSMTPPartContentTransferEncodingKey,
                                                                            nil];

testMsg.parts = [NSArray arrayWithObjects:text, attachment, nil];
```

You must also set the SMTP host and account details to send email and a delegate, which will be told if the message was successfully sent.

```
msg.relayHost     = @"smtp.yoursever.com";
msg.login         = @"you@yourserver.com";
msg.requiresAuth = YES;
msg.pass          = @"yourpassword";
msg.wantsSecure  = YES;
msg.delegate      = self;
[msg send];
```

The two delegate methods are `messageSent:` and `messageFailed:error:`. They expect you to release the message passed as an argument.

HTTP Server

If your iPhone is connected to the same Wi-Fi network as your computer, you can point your computer's browser to an IP address to connect to a web server running within an iPhone application. The nice thing about using an Internet address is it works with any computer that has a browser. In this section, we'll create a very simple server so that you can understand how it is done.

If you recall from Hour 14, your server listens to port 80 for commands. We'll use port 8080 here because it does not require root access (ports below 1024 require root access).

```
const int port80 = 8080;

- (BOOL) startWebServer
{
```

```
  // Create a socket
  int sock = socket(AF_INET, SOCK_STREAM, 0);
  if (sock < 0)
    return NO;

  // Make the socket non-blocking
  int flags = fcntl(sock, F_GETFL, NULL);
  if (flags < 0) return NO;
  flags = O_NONBLOCK;
  if (fcntl(sock, F_SETFL, flags) < 0)
    return NO;

  // Assign it to port 80
  struct sockaddr_in server_port;
  memset(&server_port, 0, sizeof(server_port));
  server_port.sin_len         = sizeof(server_port);
  server_port.sin_family      = AF_INET;
  server_port.sin_addr.s_addr = htonl(INADDR_ANY);
  server_port.sin_port        = htons(port80);

  if (bind(sock, (struct sockaddr *) &server_port, sizeof(server_port)) < 0)
    return NO;

  // Queue up to 5 connections
  if (listen(sock, 5) < 0)     return NO;
  if (![self informUserOfIP]) return NO;

  // Loop waiting for connections
  serving = YES;
  while (serving)
  {
#if TARGET_IPHONE_SIMULATOR
    usleep(100000);
#endif
    errno = 0;
    // Accept the connection
    int stream = accept(sock, NULL, NULL);
    if ((stream < 0) && (errno != EWOULDBLOCK))
      break;

    if (errno != EWOULDBLOCK)
    { [self handleWebRequest:stream];
      close(stream); }

    [[NSRunLoop currentRunLoop] runUntilDate: [NSDate distantPast]];
  }

  return YES;
}
```

Handling web requests is a matter of parsing the only command we accept (GET) and returning the appropriate file.

```
- (void) handleWebRequest:(int)stream
{
  char crequest[4096];
```

```
  read(stream, crequest, sizeof(crequest));
  crequest[sizeof(crequest)-1] = '\0';

  // Only accept "GET path HTTP/..." requests
  NSString* request = [NSString stringWithCString:crequest];
  request = [[request componentsSeparatedByString:@"\n"] objectAtIndex:0];
  if (![request hasPrefix:@"GET"])
  { [self send:stream
        content:@"HTTP/1.0 501 Not Supported\r\n\r\nNot Supported!"]; return; };

  // Find the path
  NSRange range = [request rangeOfString:@"HTTP/"];
  range.location += 4;
  range.length   -= 4;
  NSString* path = [[request substringWithRange:range]
       stringByTrimmingCharactersInSet:[NSCharacterSet whitespaceCharacterSet]];

  // Return the file
  path               = [path isEqualToString:@"/"] ? @"index.html" : path;
  NSString* fullPath = [documentsDirectory stringByAppendingPathComponent:path];
  NSData*   data     = [NSData dataWithContentsOfFile:fullPath];
  if (!data) { [self send:stream
                 content:@"HTTP/1.0 404 Not Found\r\n\r\nNot Found!"]; return; };

  NSString* mime = [mimeDictionary objectForKey:[fullPath pathExtension]];
  mime = mime ? mime : @"application/octet-stream";

  NSString* header = [NSString stringWithFormat:
                          @"HTTP/1.0 200 OK\r\nContent-Type: %@\r\n\r\n", mime];
  [self send:stream content:header];
  write(stream, [data bytes], [data length]);
}

- (void) send:(int)stream content:(NSString*)str
{ write(stream, [str UTF8String], [str length]); };
```

We must inform the user of your iPhone's IP address. Unfortunately, there does not seem to be an easy documented way of doing this: `NSHost` is undocumented. The solutions based on getting the host's name, adding ".local" to it, and performing a DNS lookup with `gethostbyname` do not work on my Wi-Fi network. http://zach-waugh.com/2009/03/programmatically-retrieving-ip-address-of-iphone/ provides a solution that only uses documented methods, but it relies on knowing that Wi-Fi uses the `en0` interface.

```
- (BOOL) informUserOfIP
{
  NSArray*  addresses = [[NSHost currentHost] addresses];
  NSString* address   = nil;

  for (NSString* s in addresses)
    if (![s isEqualToString:@"127.0.0.1"])
    { address = s; break; }
```

```
  if (!address)
    return NO;

  NSString*    title = @"Started web server";
  NSString*    msg
             = [NSString stringWithFormat:@"Connect to %@:%d", address, port80];
  UIAlertView* alert = [[UIAlertView alloc] initWithTitle:title message:msg
                       delegate:nil cancelButtonTitle:@"OK" otherButtonTitles:nil];
  [alert show];
  [alert release];
  return YES;
}
```

The nice thing about web servers is that you can provide as sophisticated an interface as you'd like. You can even use the Cocoa-based Cappuccino web framework (http://cappuccino.org/) to create a full-blown application that runs within a web browser. For instance, you could provide a full financial application for your accounts over the web interface, which users can also take with them to clients.

For more advanced projects requiring encryption or a Bonjour interface, consider using the Cocoa HTTP Server at http://code.google.com/p/cocoahttpserver/.

Summary

Although the iPhone only runs one application at a time, you can create a rich environment of cooperating applications using custom URLs and pasteboards. Because the iPhone provides solid UNIX foundations, you can also send emails to export your data or run a tiny web server. The small web server option lets you add a desktop experience to your application.

Q&A

Q. ***Does Bonjour, Apple's Zeroconf service discovery protocol, work on the iPhone?***

A. Yes. You can read a tutorial on how to use it at http://www.mobileorchard.com/tutorial-networking-and-bonjour-on-iphone/. Microsoft Windows users can download Bonjour for Windows to enjoy the same ease of use.

Q. ***Is there a way to share data between nearby devices without requiring an Internet connection?***

A. Devices that support Bluetooth can use iPhoneOS 3.0's `GameKit` framework to exchange data over Bluetooth. The original iPhone and the first generation iPod touch lack Bluetooth hardware. The simulator doesn't harness your Mac's Bluetooth functionality for testing.

Workshop

The Workshop consists of quiz questions and answers to help you solidify your understanding of the material covered in this hour. You should try to answer the questions before checking the answers.

Quiz Questions

1. How can your application start another application?
2. Can applications share data despite the sandbox? How?
3. How can you create an application that returns to the invoking application?
4. Can you add copy-and-paste support to your own widgets?
5. How can your application export data?

Quiz Answers

1. Your application can start any applications that define a custom URL by invoking `UIApplication's openURL:` method with the custom URL as argument.
2. Yes, applications can share data by encoding it in a custom URL or by sharing a pasteboard.
3. You can create an application that returns to the invoking application by adding a return parameter to your application's custom URL schema. Once your application is finished, it can use the return parameter to return to the application that invoked it.
4. Yes, you can add copy and paste to your own widgets by using the general pasteboard.

5. Your application can export data by email, by uploading it to a website, by implementing a small FTP or web server, by implementing Bonjour, or by using `GameKit` to send it to a peer.

Exercises

- Add copy to the Twitter application: Copy the last selected message to the general pasteboard. Make sure you can paste it into the `Mail` application.
- Add the web server to the Calculator application so that it can show the history of calculations made so far.
- Add the web server to the Twitter application and create a full in-browser Twitter application using the Cappuccino framework.

HOUR 22
Debugging

What You'll Learn in This Hour:

- Using gdb, dtrace, valgrind, and nib2objc
- Resolving Cocoa misunderstandings

Bugs are misunderstandings. Design bugs happen when you have misunderstood the problem or misunderstood the tools you are using such as the Cocoa libraries. Implementation bugs happen when your implementation does not match your design. The four debugging tools introduced in this hour help you analyze where the program's behavior diverges from your expectations. A prerequisite to debugging is, therefore, to clearly define your expectations. The second part of this hour will help you resolve problems encountered with the Cocoa frameworks. By the end of this hour, you'll know how to reverse engineer a troublesome Cocoa framework if you need to.

Using gdb, dtrace, valgrind, and nib2objc

The main tool for studying an application's behavior is gdb. Use dtrace to study the system functions your application invokes. Use valgrind to study your application's memory usage. Use nib2objc to gain more visibility into NIB files built with Interface Builder.

Using gdb

gdb is a powerful debugger. Debuggers are able to show you program state and let you start and stop your program. They work by sending a signal to the target program, requesting its signal handler to accept ptrace commands. ptrace system calls let the debugger examine the target process's memory and register state, set breakpoints, and resume running code. Apple wrapped the command-line gdb debugger in a graphical user interface (GUI), making it similar to other debuggers you might have used. To see the GUI debugger, select Run, Debugger. To see the command-line tool, select Run, Console.

GUI Debugger

The GUI debugger shows different panes for the current stack trace, the current registers or variables, and the source code or assembly code of the function at which the target is paused. Source code is shown unless none is available, in which case assembly code is shown. Run, Debugger Display lets you change this behavior (see Figure 22.1).

The buttons in the toolbar let you control program execution:

- Continue continues running the program until you pause it, you terminate it, a breakpoint is reached, or an exception occurs (including hardware exceptions such as null pointer dereferences).
- Step Into executes the current instruction (or source line) and stops at the next one. If the executed line is a function call, the debugger stops at the first instruction (or source line) of the function.
- Step Over sets a breakpoint at the next instruction (or source line), and continues your program. If no exception occurs and no breakpoint is reached, the debugger will stop at that instruction (or source line). Use Step Over to avoid stepping into functions.
- Step Out sets a breakpoint at the next instruction (or source line) of the current function's caller, and continues your program. If no exception occurs and no breakpoint is reached, the debugger will stop at that instruction. Use Step Out to exit functions.

To set a breakpoint, click the left border of your source code at the line you want to stop at. A blue arrow will appear to show the breakpoint. Clicking the arrow a second time disables it. Dragging the arrow off the left border deletes it. Alternatively, use the Breakpoints window (Run, Show, Breakpoints). You can also enable and disable all breakpoints using the Activate/Deactivate button on the Debugger window.

Playing to `gdb`'s Strengths

Use many temporary variables: Because they are shown by the GUI, you'll see your application's temporary variables change as you step through code, improving your chances of noticing a bug. There is no performance cost to using temporary variables as the compiler has no problems optimizing them away in Release mode.

Use assertions to detect failure as close as possible to its cause. Assertions state your expectations, helping `gdb` find bugs for you.

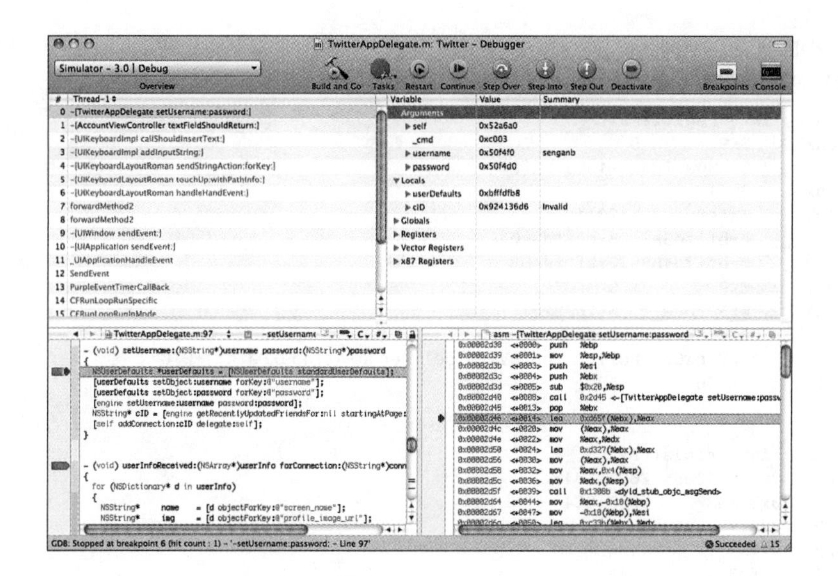

FIGURE 22.1
Xcode's Debugger Window.

Using gdb's Command Line

Although Apple has provided a GUI debugger, you'll only truly benefit from gdb's power if you learn to use its command line.

To display data, use print and po (print object). Note that gdb can invoke C and Objective-C functions from the command line.

```
(gdb) print (int) row
$1 = 9

(gdb) po messages
<NSCFArray 0x521e10> (
  Message
    ID : 3129275833
    Text : Xbox 360: Rock Band 2 + Drumkit + AC/DC track pack for $49
➥https://www.rockband49.com/
    Date : 1249411241
    User : User (codinghorror, <UIImage: 0x5e1c60>),
...
```

You can set variables using the set command:

```
(gdb) set row = 3
(gdb) print (int) row
$3 = 3
```

To display the registers, use `info registers`, which shows their values in hexadecimal and decimal:

```
(gdb) info registers
eax      0x9        9
ecx      0xa00a8760  -1609922720
edx      0x11        17
ebx      0x4e8e      20110
esp      0xbfffd3a0  0xbfffd3a0
ebp      0xbfffd488  0xbfffd488
esi      0x9         9
edi      0x538ba0    5475232
eip      0x4f8b      0x4f8b
<-[TwitterViewController tableView:cellForRowAtIndexPath:]+270>
eflags   0x246       582
...

(gdb) info registers
r0   0x10004005  268451845
r1   0x3000006   50331654
r2   0x0         0
r3   0x450       1104
r4   0xf03       3843
r5   0x0         0
r6   0x0         0
r7   0x2fffefd8  805302232
r8   0x0         0
r9   0x394306d0  960693968
sl   0xf03       3843
fp   0x450       1104
ip   0xffffffe1  -31
sp   0x2fffef9c  805302172
lr   0x31464b78  826690424
pc   0x31467aa4  826702500
...
```

You can move the "current statement" by dragging the red arrow next to the current statement in the GUI view or by setting the appropriate register (`eip` on the Mac, `pc` on the iPhone):

```
set $eip=0x4f8b
set $pc=0x20bc
```

On the simulator, function arguments are built on the stack. On the iPhone, the first four arguments are passed in the registers `r0` through `r3`. The rest are spilled to the stack.

The `x` command lets you see the content of memory. After the backslash, specify the type of object you expect to see. It follows the `printf` argument format (`s` stands for strings, `d` for decimal, and so forth), but adds `i` to show instructions:

```
(gdb) x/s $eax
0x92649324 <__FUNCTION__.12370+257988>:  "row"
```

bt shows you the stack backtrace, and disas shows you the assembly code of the function or method your code is paused within.

si lets you step into an instruction. s steps into the next source line. Similarly, ni steps over the next call instruction, and n steps over subroutines to the next source line.

gdb supports automatically running commands at breakpoints. For instance, you can use this to change function return values depending on the situation. The **commands** section, finished by an **end**, contains the commands to run at each breakpoint. The following gdb commands print the class of every method being invoked:

```
(gdb) b objc_msgSend
Breakpoint 5 at 0x92608670
(gdb) commands
>call (char *)class_getName($eax)
>c
>end
(gdb) c
Continuing.
$6 = 0x0
Continuing.
$7 = 0x90bb005c "NSRecursiveLock"
Continuing.
$8 = 0x90bb005c "NSRecursiveLock"
Continuing.
$9 = 0x90bb005c "NSRecursiveLock"
```

To save typing, add gdb commands such as this breakpoint to a text file, and load it with **source *path***.

On exceptions, you'll get errors with symbol numbers. To decode these error messages, you must convert these symbol numbers to the corresponding symbol names. To perform this conversion, type **info symbols *number***. The following example shows an error message, and what you would type to decode it:

```
2009-08-04 13:37:06.392 Twitter[45493:20b] Stack: (
    ...
    2436820778,
    10828,
    816111650,
    ...)

(gdb) info symbol 10828
-[TwitterAppDelegate applicationDidFinishLaunching:] + 65 in section
➥LC_SEGMENT.__TEXT.__text ...
```

To learn more about gdb, there are many online references. The "GDB QUICK REFERENCE" card at http://users.ece.utexas.edu/~adnan/gdb-refcard.pdf provides a good summary.

Debugging Failures Within `objc_msgSend`

To illustrate debugging failures within `objc_msgSend`, cast your mind back to your first debugging exercise in Hour 3, "Simplifying Your Code."

```
int main(int argc, char *argv[])
{
  NSLog(@"Was passed %@ arguments", argc);
  sleep(1);
  return 0;
}
```

Run the debugger until you hit the failure. Recall that the crash occurs within `objc_msgSend`, which was trying to invoke `[obj respondsToSelector:@selector(descriptionWithLocale:)]` with an invalid object (`argc`). Suppose you want to know what the next call to `objc_msgSend` would have been if the current one had completed.

Click on `_NSDescriptionWithLocaleFunc`. Scroll to the top of the code window. Notice the instructions.

```
0x909a8379  <+0009>  call    0x909a837e <_NSDescriptionWithLocaleFunc+14>
0x909a837e  <+0014>  pop     %ebx
```

`call` *`functionAddress`* is the assembly language instruction to perform function invocation. It places the address of the instruction following it onto the stack, and then jumps to *`functionAddress`*. The function ends with a `ret` instruction that takes the address following the call off the stack and jumps to it, thereby completing the function invocation.

Here, however, *`functionAddress`* is the address of the instruction following the call. The address is placed on the stack. Then, the `pop %ebx` instruction takes it off the stack. Now, the `%ebx` register contains the address of the instruction following the call, in this case `0x909a837e`.

The instruction before the red arrow is as follows:

```
0x909a83ac  <+0060>  call    0xa0a19d2e
```

The red arrow points to the return address from the call to `objc_msgSend`, so the instruction preceding the red arrow must be calling `objc_msgSend`. To check, type the following:

```
(gdb) x/i 0xa0a19d2e
0xa0a19d2e:    jmp    0x92608670 <objc_msgSend>
```

`x/i 0xa0a19d2e` shows the instruction at the address `0xa0a19d2e`. It's a jump to `objc_msgSend` as we thought.

Looking again at _NSDescriptionWithLocaleFunc, you can see there's another call to 0xa0a19d2e, another method invocation:

```
0x909a83b9  <+0073>  mov    0xf6fd52e(%ebx),%eax
0x909a83bf  <+0079>  mov    %esi,(%esp)
0x909a83c2  <+0082>  mov    %eax,0x4(%esp)
0x909a83c6  <+0086>  call   0xa0a19d2e
```

The first instruction is taking the value of %ebx, adding 0xf6fd52e to it, and then reading the value of that memory location into %eax. It then places %esi onto the stack at %esp. Then, it places %eax onto the stack at %esp+4. call 0xa0a19d2e decrements $esp by 4 when it places the return address on the stack. So %esi is at position 1 on the stack, corresponding to the object we can print with:

```
(gdb) print (char *) object_getClassName(((int*)($esp))[1])
```

%eax is at position 2 on the stack, corresponding to the selector we print with:

```
(gdb) print (char*)(((int*)($esp))[2])
```

So we know that the value at 0xf6fd52e + %ebx (which is 0x909a837e) must be a selector:

```
(gdb) print *((char**)(0x909a837e + 0xf6fd52e))
$5 = 0x926a38e0 "descriptionWithLocale:"
```

This makes sense. The previous call to objc_msgSend was checking whether the object could respond to a descriptionWithLocale: message. If it can, _NSDescriptionWithLocaleFunc will try to call it.

Using dtrace

The dtrace tool lets you instrument any code (including the kernel and system frameworks) with probes written in a language called D. (This is a different language from the compiled D language.) dtrace is quite amazing in that you can instrument a live system without restarting any software. It's particularly useful for profiling. In the next hour, "Optimizing Performance," you'll learn about Instruments, a profiling application built on top of it.

Leopard comes with a number of canned probes you can use with the simulator. The entire list is given by man -k dtrace. To determine the process identifier of your running application, use ps. For instance, to find the running instance of Twitter, type the following into the Terminal application:

```
ps x | grep Twitter
46248   ?? S      0:05.75 path/Twitter.app/Twitter
```

The first number is the process identifier. Now I can invoke dtruss (a script that uses dtrace):

```
sudo dtruss -p 46248
         ...
         ...
open("path/Twitter.app/TwitterViewController.nib0", 0x0, 0x1B6) = 9 0
open("path/Twitter.app/TwitterViewController.nib0", 0x0, 0x1B6) = 9 0
fstat(0x9, 0xBFFFDF10, 0x1B6)   = 0 0
fstat(0x9, 0xBFFFDF10, 0x1B6)   = 0 0
read(0x9, "bplist00324001002003004005006017020X$versionT$topY$archiverX$
➥objects0220", 0x6E0) = 1760 0
read(0x9, "bplist00324001002003004005006017020X$versionT$topY$archiverX$
➥objects0220", 0x6E0) = 1760 0
close(0x9)   = 0 0
close(0x9)   = 0 0
```

Did you Know?

Mac OS X is a multi-user system: It lets more than one user log into a single machine. Because dtrace can trace the system calls of any application, a user could use it to snoop on the activities of other users. To prevent this, only root may use dtrace. The sudo command lets you run the command that follows it as root. In this example dtruss is run as root. sudo will ask you for your root password (your password if you have an administrator account).

Here, you can see the NIB file being loaded. You must know your computer's root password to use dtrace. To learn more about dtrace, read "Exploring Leopard with DTrace" by Greg Miller, in MacTech (available online at http://www.mactech.com/articles/mactech/Vol.23/23.11/ExploringLeopardwithDTrace/index.html).

Using valgrind

valgrind is one of my favorite UNIX tools that has only just been ported to the Mac. You cannot run it on the iPhone, but you can on the simulator. Because it runs your program on an emulated CPU, it is able to keep track of each memory access. This means it can detect a number of classic C program errors, including the following:

- Using uninitialized memory
- Accessing memory that was freed
- Reading or writing beyond the end of a malloc'd buffer
- Memory leaks

valgrind is currently only available as source code. Download and compile it from the Terminal application as follows. Again you're using svn, which was introduced in Hour 11, "Displaying Tables." I place tools I compile myself in /opt to make them easy to remove.

```
svn co svn://svn.valgrind.org/valgrind/trunk valgrind
cd valgrind
./autogen.sh
./configure --prefix=/opt
make
sudo make install
```

The simulator starts your application. However, valgrind also needs to start your application. The solution is to start valgrind from your application.

```
static const char* valgrind = "/opt/bin/valgrind";

int main(int argc, char *argv[])
{
  if (argc < 2 || (argc >= 2 && strcmp(argv[1], "-valgrind") != 0))
    execl(valgrind, valgrind, "--leak-check=full", argv[0], "-valgrind", NULL);

  NSAutoreleasePool * pool = [[NSAutoreleasePool alloc] init];
  int retVal = UIApplicationMain(argc, argv, nil, @"ValgrindExampleAppDelegate");
  [pool release];
  return retVal;
}
```

Ensure your application is compiled in Debug mode so that valgrind can tell you which function caused a problem, but run the application (do not debug it), because gdb will get confused. For instance, let's allocate some memory, and write off the end of the buffer.

```
- (void) applicationDidFinishLaunching:(UIApplication*)application
{
  char* buffer = (char*) malloc(12);
  buffer[12]   = '\0';
}
```

Build and go. Open the Console Window. valgrind will print a lot of text. But the following lines show our bug:

```
  ==324== Invalid write of size 1
  ==324==  at 0x2AF4: -[ValgrindExampleAppDelegate
applicationDidFinishLaunching:]
                                                          (in path)
  ...
  ==324==  Address 0x2717cbc is 0 bytes after a block of size 12 alloc'd
  ...
```

valgrind also finds a leak: we never freed the memory we malloc'd.

```
==324== 12 bytes in 1 blocks are definitely lost in loss record 42 of 466
==324==    at 0x12516: malloc (vg_replace_malloc.c:193)
==324==    by 0x2AEA: -[ValgrindExampleAppDelegate
applicationDidFinishLaunching:]
                                                          (in path)
```

You'll notice valgrind finds Apple's leaks too: Sometimes the cost of tracking a small constant piece of memory is greater than simply leaking it. valgrind is mainly useful for leaks due to malloc and free because Objective-C uses its own allocator. To learn more about valgrind, visit http://valgrind.org.

By the Way

At the time of writing, valgrind does not work with Snow Leopard.

Using nib2obj

nib2objc is a tool that converts NIB files to Objective-C. It's available at http://github.com/akosma/nib2objc/tree/master. Its main use is to improve the performance of your application by avoiding NIB deserialization. However, I sometimes get lost inside Interface Builder and forget how I set things up. Converting my NIB files to source code often makes it simpler to find the missing setting.

Resolving Cocoa Misunderstandings

At first, Cocoa can be quite confusing. This book has given you a strong foundation, but you will still encounter problems. The next few sections will show you ways to approach these problems.

First Steps

The first step is to read Apple's documentation. It might be long-winded, it might assume you're new to programming, but it often contains the answer, buried somewhere deep down. Apple's developer mailing lists are good, and Apple's engineers sometimes respond to questions on them. Websites like http://cocoadev.com and http://stackoverflow.com provide good information, or at least valuable search keywords.

Take time to study other people's source code. You can sometimes find tricks you might have never found otherwise, and other people have often solved the very problems you have encountered.

Apple software has bugs. A good resource is http://openradar.appspot.com/page/1, where many third-party software developers log the bugs they have encountered and submitted to Apple at http://bugreport.apple.com.

Historically, Cocoa developers have helped others with the problems they encounter: There were few developers on the Mac, and scratching each others' backs worked well. More recently, the number of Cocoa programmers has swelled, putting strains on this system. If you ask a question and expect an answer, explain what you did, how you think it should work, and what actually happened. Requests for "sample code" will fall on deaf ears.

Unfortunately, Cocoa is not open source. The next best thing is the cocotron source code available at http://cocotron.org. It is simple and gives a good idea how much of Cocoa is implemented. GnuStep is another open source implementation. Studying them will help you understand the details of the more mature parts of Cocoa.

Studying Behavior Without Disassembly

Placing breakpoints in your delegates and looking at the stack trace also helps you understand Cocoa's architecture. The problem with breakpoints is that they are like a microscope. They overwhelm your mind with the detail of the entire state of the application at a point in time, rather than showing the evolution of relevant state over time. Although logging requires you to specify the state you care about, you don't have to worry about losing state because you clicked Continue.

Python makes it very easy for functions to log their stack traces. When writing Objective-C code, I realized how much I missed this power. In the June 2009 issue of the *MacTech* magazine, you'll find an implementation of a replacement of `NSLog()` called `debugLog()` that I wrote. It is able to print stack traces containing C, C++, and Objective-C functions, as well as a debug message like `NSLog()` can. It works both on the Mac and on the iPhone.

In Hour 11, you learned about swizzling methods: replacing a class's existing implementation with your own. Combining `debugLog()` with swizzling provides a particularly powerful scalpel to unravel Cocoa's behavior: You can log methods arguments, their return values, and their stack trace.

Reverse Engineering Frameworks

Sometimes you encounter a problem that cannot be solved without reverse engineering a framework. The iPhone frameworks are in the /Developer/Platforms directory. You'll notice an iPhoneSimulator.platform and an iPhoneOS.platform directory. The libraries in iPhoneSimulator.platform are compiled for the x86 architecture used by your Mac, while the libraries in iPhoneOS.platform are compiled for ARM CPUs. Although the libraries are not identical, they are very similar.

Listing the C Functions and Data in the Framework

The UNIX `nm` command lists the C functions and their addresses in a library. For instance, you can run `nm` on the `Foundation` framework (from the Terminal application):

```
cd /Developer/Platforms/iPhoneOS.platform/Developer/SDKs/
cd iPhoneOSnumber.sdk/System/Library/Frameworks/Foundation.framework
nm Foundation
```

Each line specifies a resource (code or data) and the symbol that identifies it (the string at the end of each line). If a line starts with a hexadecimal number, it means the file contains the resource. Otherwise, the file contains code or data that references that symbol. It is the job of the dynamic linker to ensure that all references to symbols are bound to the relevant resource at load time. My article about `debugLog` explains this in more detail.

Listing the Objective-C Classes and Methods

Some of the C data structures represent the Class objects used by objc_msgSend to dispatch messages to objects in the class hierarchy. They include a list of the methods and instance variables of each class as used by the Objective-C runtime. The class-dump tool available from http://www.codethecode.com/projects/class-dump/ extracts this information from the library binary and converts it to Objective-C interface declarations. This makes it particularly easy to reverse engineer Cocoa frameworks. To save you the trouble of making them, Erica Sadun maintains a full list of the resulting class dump files at http://ericasadun.com/iPhoneDocs300/files.html. Often, simply reading these files will give you a good idea of how things work.

Did you Know?

Apple doesn't like you using methods discovered with `class-dump`! They recently added the following method to iPhone OS 3.0:

```
@interface UIViewController (UIViewControllerClassDumpWarning)
- (void)                          attentionClassDumpUser:(id)fp8
                                         yesItsUsAgain:(id)fp12
       althoughSwizzlingAndOverridingPrivateMethodsIsFun:(id)fp16
                 itWasntMuchFunWhenYourAppStoppedWorking:(id)fp20
        pleaseRefrainFromDoingSoInTheFutureOkayThanksBye:(id)fp24;
@end
```

The method doesn't actually do anything, so a bug was filed against it (http://openradar.appspot.com/7044974).

Disassembling Objective-C Code in a Framework

The `otool` utility in /usr/bin disassembles frameworks. Use it with the `-Vvt` option to retrieve disassembled code. Alternatively, download the `otx` tool from http://otx.osxninja.com/. It provides better disassembly because it figures out the selector being sent to `objc_msgSend` when `objc_msgSend` is invoked by `calll` (but not when it is invoked by `jmpl`).

Objective-C frameworks are built of segments each consisting of sections. You can list the segments and sections with **`otool -l`**. The dynamic libraries (and frameworks) the framework depends on are listed at the end. Then, you can display the content of a section with **`otool -s`** ***`segment section filename`***.

Disassembling `UIView`'s `nextResponder` Method

`otool` and `otx` disassemble most but not all selectors. You might remember from Hour 7, "Understanding How Events Are Processed," that `UIView`'s `nextResponder` method invokes the method's view controller if it has one (by calling `UIViewController`'s `viewControllerForView:` class method) or the view's `superview` otherwise. Find the `UIKit` simulator binary, and disassemble it with `otx`.

Also look at the reverse engineered class declaration of `UIView` that you obtained from `class-dump` (or use http://ericasadun.com/iPhoneDocs300/_u_i_view_8h-source.html). Now open the disassembly file in your favorite text editor, and search for `UIView nextResponder`. Because disassembly changes between OS revisions, I'll walk you through what you should see:

1. First, there is some stack manipulation.
2. Then, there's a `call` to the next instruction, which is a `popl`. This sequence of instructions loads the current instruction pointer into a register: the only way for x86 CPUs to use PC-relative addressing. PC stands for **Program Counter**. PC-relative addressing lets you move code around in memory without modifying it. For instance, in iPhone OS 2.2.1, the line on which `popl` appears looks like this:

   ```
   +20  30a6fac5 5b             popl %ebx
   ```

   This tells you that the register `%ebx` now contains the value `0x30a6fac5`. Whichever register is `popl'd` is the PC-relative register.
3. Next, you should see a `testb` instruction testing a bit of a data structure. This data structure is the receiver, that is, a `UIView` object. The mask and the offset into the object correspond to the `hasViewController` bit. If this bit is clear, the code skips an invocation of `[UIViewController viewControllerForView:]`. The `jmpl` has the same destination address as the `calll` (`objc_msgSend`). The

result of the invocation is in %eax. If it's not zero (nil), it skips the next block of code.

4. Next, the code jumps to objc_msgSend. Because it's a jump, otx does not find the selector. To find the correct selector, recall that arguments to functions are placed in reverse order on the stack: The first argument that appears in the C function argument list is pushed last. This is required for variable argument list functions such as printf. objc_msgSend's first argument is the receiver and its second argument is the selector. The selector is computed by adding an offset to the PC-relative register. For instance,

```
+59  30a6faec  8b83cfee2900  movl 0x0029eecf(%ebx), %eax
```

Adding these numbers produces the pointer address *p*. In this case, *p* = 0x30a6fac5 + 0x29eecf = 0x30d0e994. In a different version of the OS, the numbers will be different, so sum them yourself. Now recall that the selector is a pointer to a C string. We'd expect to see a pointer at *p*. However, the disassembly ends before that address: The pointer is stored in the __message_refs section of the __OBJC segment. To display this section, type the following:

```
otool -s __OBJC __message_refs path/UIKit | less
```

This shows you many pointers. In this case, the data at *p* (30d0e994) is bc 42 c6 30: 0x30c642bc in little endian format. This tells you the selector's address is *sel*=0x30c642bc. Again calculate your own value. To see the C string, we need to find *sel*, which is in the __cstring section of the __TEXT segment.

```
otool -s __TEXT __cstring path/UIKit | less
```

Recall that C strings end with a zero character. You should see 73 75 70 65 72 76 69 65 77 00 at *sel*. This is the ASCII encoding of "superview."

Now we know that [UIView nextResponder] checks a cached bit hasViewController. If this is set, it invokes [UIViewController viewControllerForView:]. If the result of [UIViewController viewControllerForView:] was nil or hasViewController was clear, it invokes [self superview]. In Objective-C:

```
- (id) nextResponder
{
  id result = nil;
  if (hasViewController) result = [UIViewController viewControllerForView:self]
  if (!result)           result = [self             superView];
  return result;
}
```

Now that you understand how to reverse engineer Objective-C, there should be no barriers to understanding the frameworks.

Summary

In this hour, you learned about four tools that can help you debug your application. `gdb` and `valgrind` are particularly powerful, and well worth studying in more detail than this chapter allows. You've probably realized that it is worth learning assembly language if you don't already know it, because Apple does not provide the source code to their proprietary frameworks. I've provided you with a list of resources that should help you if you are stuck, and you can feel confident that you can solve any problem you encounter, because you have the weapon of last resort: If no one can help you, you know how to reverse engineer the offending framework.

Q&A

Q. ***Are there any other tools to reverse engineer?***

A. Yes, if you have access to Windows, you have access to the well-known reverse engineering tool, IDA Pro from http://hex-rays.com.

Q. ***Is reverse engineering legal?***

A. It depends on your intent and where you live. Consult a lawyer. For U.S. readers, the DMCA has an exemption for interoperability (17 U.S.C. § 1201(f) (2006)), which you can find on the Internet. The "Rethinking 'Anticircumvention' Interoperability Policy" paper by Aaron K. Perzanowski provides an interesting discussion. It is available at http://works.bepress.com/perzanowski/. Security researchers, OS providers, and chip manufacturers all use reverse engineering either to maintain their products' software compatibility or to find security flaws to fix. The Electronic Freedom Foundation is currently fighting Apple about the legality of jailbreaking iPhones. The EFF's complaint and information about jailbreaking is at http://www.eff.org/files/filenode/dmca_2009/EFF2009replycomment_0.pdf. Apple's counterargument is at http://www.wired.com/images_blogs/threatlevel/2009/07/applejailbreakresponse.pdf.

Workshop

The Workshop consists of quiz questions and answers to help you solidify your understanding of the material covered in this hour. You should try to answer the questions before checking the answers.

Quiz Questions

1. What is gdb?
2. What coding style is best suited to being debugged?
3. What is valgrind?
4. What source code can you consult if you do not understand Cocoa behavior?

Quiz Answers

1. gdb is a debugger.
2. Using many temporary variables which the debugger's GUI can display is the coding style best suited to being debugged.
3. valgrind helps you find use of uninitialized memory, memory leaks, and buffer overflows.
4. Look at cocotron's source code if you do not understand Cocoa behavior.

Exercise

- To familiarize yourself with the debugger, step through the Calculator application. Determine the appropriate breakpoints to step through code invoked from the run loop. For instance, you'd set breakpoints at the press*something* methods of the Calculator. Use Step Into and Step Over to understand the difference. Do the same with the Twitter Application. Because the control paths are more complex, you'll notice that it is harder to keep track of what's happening: Debuggers are like microscopes. They help you with details with not with the larger picture.

HOUR 23
Optimizing Performance

What You'll Learn in This Hour:

- Profiling your code
- Optimizing your memory usage
- Optimizing your code's speed

Profiling your code tells you where it is spending the most resources (memory and time). Although most people profile their code to improve its performance, profiling also serves as a good check to ensure the program is behaving as expected. Once you understand your program's behavior, you can more effectively optimize its memory usage and speed. Low memory usage is particularly important on the iPhone, which is memory limited. In this hour, you'll learn to profile your application, reduce memory usage, find leaks, and boost your code's speed.

Profiling Your Code

First, profile your application to see where it is spending the most time or using the most memory. For simplicity, this discussion talks about time usage, but the points it makes also apply to memory usage.

Profiling your application requires careful thought: 90% of the resource needs of many applications lie in 10% of the code. However, your application consists of a number of algorithms. If you only profile it once, you'll see the code that took the longest on that run. However, if the code that took half the time processed 10 times the amount of data the rest of the code did, it might be more effective to optimize the rest of the code.

To fully understand the performance behavior of a program, you must determine the sources of data input to each algorithm in your program: The amount of time used by an algorithm depends on the amount of data it must process. This is called the algorithmic time complexity. For instance, if an algorithm takes N^2 steps to process N pieces of data, the algorithm is said to have $O(N^2)$ time complexity. By varying the amount of data for each data source, you can determine the behavior of each algorithm of your program.

Theoretically, measuring the time used to process three quantities of data for each data source will tell you whether its algorithms have sublinear, linear, or superlinear complexity. However, because the speed of memory access depends on the memory hierarchy, you'll need to take many more measurements to discount these effects. Because your target device is the iPhone, and the iPhone has a different memory hierarchy than the Mac, perform your measurements on the iPhone. The iPhone's memory hierarchy is discussed in more detail later in this hour.

Once you know the behavior of each algorithm, you'll know which one to optimize. If an algorithm takes a lot of resources, and processes a lot of data, you'll get the biggest bang for the buck by replacing it with a better algorithm. However, even if an algorithm has terrible complexity behavior, if it is used on very few data elements and uses very few resources, changing the algorithm won't help.

Creating Your own Profiling Tools

The simplest way of profiling the time taken by any particular part of your code is to use the Mach timing functions. Because your code has full access to its own state, you can specify when profiling should occur by writing your own profiling code. In this way, you can capture specific program behavior and filter out undesirable measurements. `mach_absolute_time()` returns an `unsigned long long int` representing the current time. By recording the time before and after running your code, and subtracting the latter from the former, you can measure the time taken. Because the iPhone is a multithreaded device, you should measure the time taken a number of times, and use the fastest time you obtain: On a single core CPU such as the iPhone's, threads are implemented by interrupts, which interleave the execution of different threads.

`mach_absolute_time()` returns in units, which must be converted to seconds using the conversion information provided by `mach_timebase_info()`:

```
#include <mach/mach.h>

mach_timebase_info_data_t info;
mach_timebase_info(&info);
double divisor = ( (double)info.numer / (double)info.denom) / 1000000000L;

uint64_t before = mach_absolute_time();

// Your code goes here

uint64_t after = mach_absolute_time();
NSLog(@"took %g seconds", (after-before) * divisor);
```

This code is particularly useful when optimizing a key routine: Extract it from your code, create a test bench with representative data to run it in, and repeatedly measure the time it takes. The test bench lets you control the data your function receives, in a way that is difficult in a full-blown program. My test benches run inside `main`, and do not call `UIApplicationMain`, so that I can minimize the amount of other system activity.

The Mach functions also let you determine your application's memory usage and the amount of free memory on the iPhone. You can use this information to record the memory warnings your beta testers encounter, and provide them with an easy means to send it to you.

```
#include <mach/mach.h>

struct task_basic_info info;
mach_msg_type_number_t count = TASK_BASIC_INFO_COUNT;
kern_return_t kerr
    = task_info(mach_task_self(), TASK_BASIC_INFO, (task_info_t)&info, &count);
long my_memory_use = (kerr == KERN_SUCCESS) ? info.resident_size : -1;
```

Mach functions also let you measure the amount of free and used memory on your device:

```
#include <mach/mach.h>

mach_port_t host = mach_host_self();

vm_statistics_data_t   stats;
mach_msg_type_number_t count = HOST_VM_INFO_COUNT;
kern_return_t kerr
             = host_statistics(host, HOST_VM_INFO, (host_info_t)&stats, &count);

if (kerr == KERN_SUCCESS)
{
  vm_size_t pagesize;
  host_page_size(host, &pagesize);

  natural_t used
    = (stats.active_count + stats.inactive_count + stats.wire_count) * pagesize;
  natural_t free  = stats.free_count * pagesize;
  natural_t total = used + free;
  NSLog(@"used: %u free: %u total: %u", used, free, total);
}
```

For instance, if you place the preceding code into `applicationDidReceiveMemoryWarning:`, you might see the following line printed by a low-memory notification. (`me:` prints out `my_memory_use` above.)

```
me: 34623488 used: 59154432 free: 2351104 total: 61505536
...
me: 45244416 used: 45019136 free: 10289152 total: 55308288
me: 45596672 used: 45379584 free: 9785344 total: 55164928
```

As a general rule, if the free memory falls below 1Mb, your application should save the user's state, jettison as many data structures as possible, and load as little data as necessary to continue running: Your application will likely soon be terminated. To learn more about Mach, read *Mac OS X Internals: A Systems Approach* by Amit Singh.

Using Shark

Shark is a time-usage profiler. It interrupts your program regularly and records the stack trace. By sampling the program execution state in this way, it can show you the time each function takes: The 'self' time is the time the function itself took, subtracting the time taken by the functions it called. The 'total' time is the time the function took, including the time taken by the functions it called.

To profile your application on the iPhone, start Shark (in the /Developer/Applications/Performance Tools/ directory) and choose Sampling, Network/iPhone Profiling menu item (see Figure 23.1). Place a breakpoint on `main` and start the application from the debugger. Now choose it as a target from Shark, and click Start in Shark. Click Stop when you are done. You should see an `Analyzing samples...` message after a while. If the candy bar with the message `Shared Devices Processing Samples` does not go away after a few minutes, Shark might need to be restarted. I've had little success taking traces longer than a few seconds, as Shark will crash or not start analyzing its data. You must leave your application running until Shark has finished analyzing data. Pausing the program from the debugger will crash Shark. Running Shark on the iPhone is unusually finicky. Rebooting the iPhone seems to help.

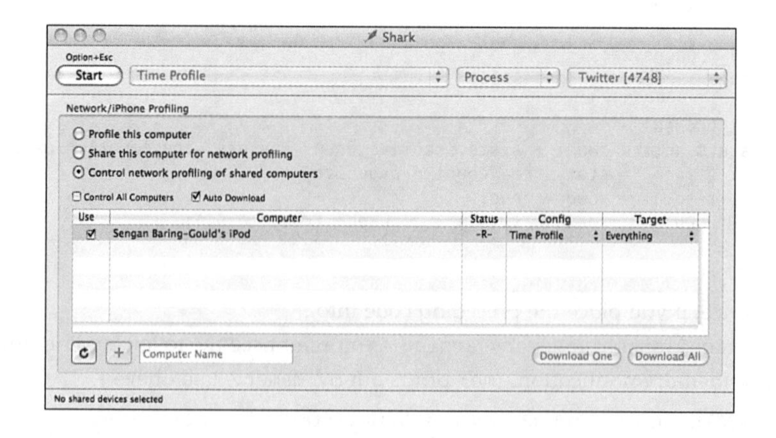

FIGURE 23.1
Using Shark on the iPhone

The iPhone runs a stripped-down version of the Shark profiler on the iPhone, which does not capture symbol information on the iPhone. You might need to select File, Symbolicate to add symbol information. Recall that your executable will be in the build/Debug-iphoneos or build/Release-iphoneos directory of your project.

As you can see from Figure 23.2, 60% of the Twitter application's time is taken by `NSXMLParser` and its subroutines. In particular, `NSDate`'s `dateWithNaturalLanguageString:` method takes 35% of the time. `NSAutoreleasePool`'s `drain` method takes 40% of the time, which tells you the application is wasting a lot of time creating and discarding objects.

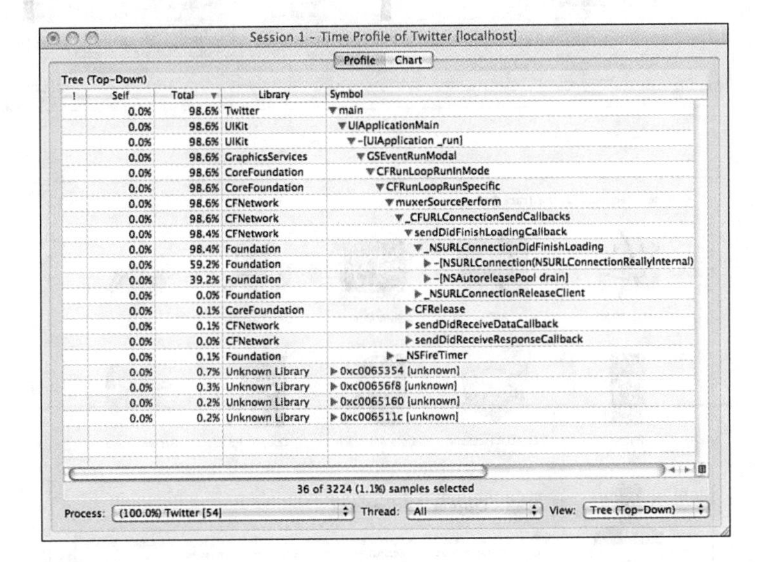

FIGURE 23.2
Shark's profile data

By double-clicking on a line in the Profile, you can see the function's source and assembly code, as shown in Figure 23.3.

Using Instruments

Instruments is a tool that provides an easy-to-use GUI to display data from `DTrace` probes. In particular, it can be used for memory profiling. You can start the Instruments application from Xcode, or from /Developer/Applications. The latter option will let you choose a template you'd like to run (see Figure 23.4).

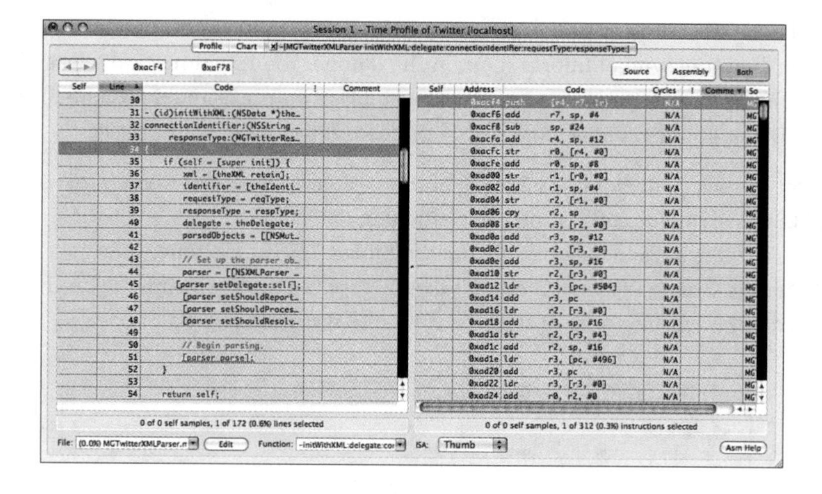

FIGURE 23.3
Shark showing program code

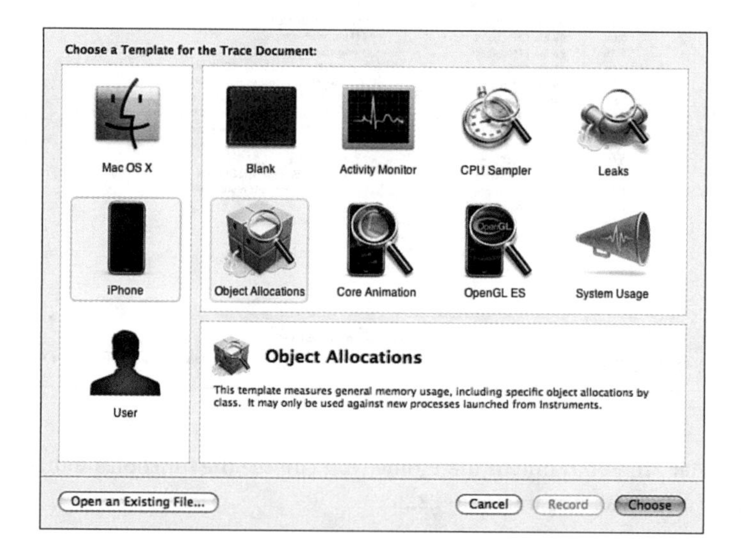

FIGURE 23.4
Instruments template panel

If you are running a memory profile, a good approximation is to run the application on the simulator. Instruments is very good at showing you how many allocations your program is making over time with its object allocations template. For instance, this will show us that `MGTwitterEngine` allocates tons of memory only to release it soon after. At the end of the trace in Figure 23.5, I am looking at different friends' tweet streams. This increases the application's memory usage when it should not, a sure sign of a leak. By clicking the small arrow next to All Allocations, you can examine which functions were responsible for allocating memory (see Figure

23.6). The Extended Detail pane on the right shows you a full call stack colored by the libraries each routine is inside. Double-clicking on a routine shows its source code, if available. To show the Extended Detail pane, click the View button on the upper right of the window.

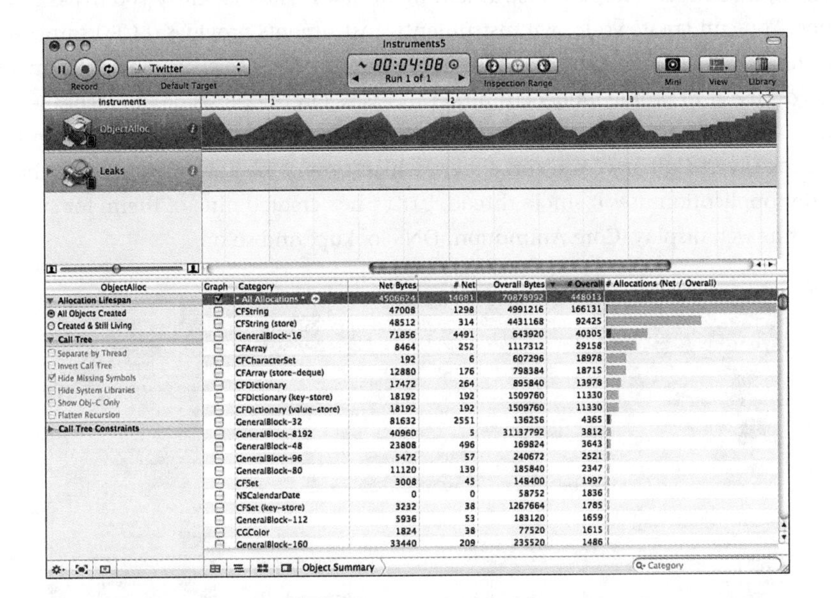

FIGURE 23.5 Instruments: Memory allocations

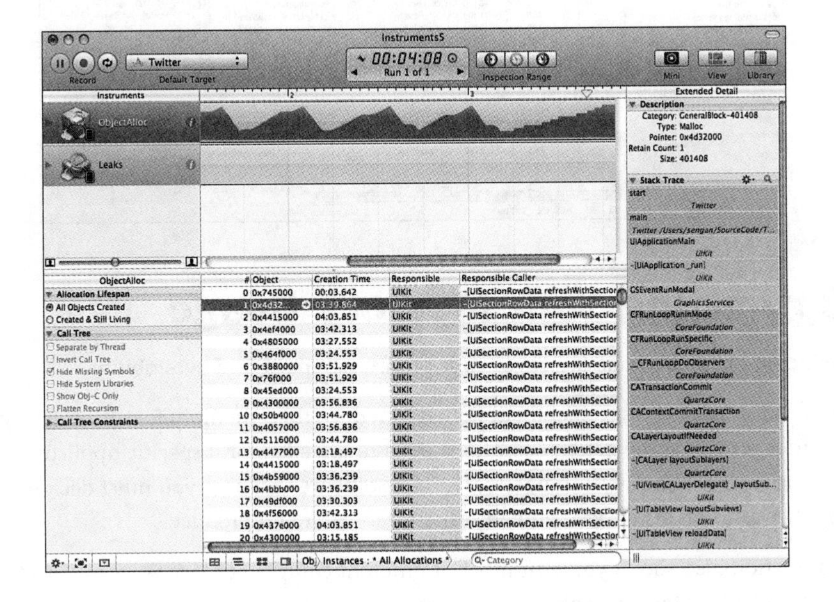

FIGURE 23.6 Instruments: Stack trace for each allocation

In this case, the friends' `TwitterViewControllers` are being kept. These are small data structures, but they cause `UITableView` data structures to be kept in memory.

To add an instrument, click the button that looks like a cog at the bottom of the window, and choose the Add Instrument menu item. The first entry is a `DTrace` probe: You can create your own instruments. Instruments provides a CPU sampler, which works like `Shark` but at a lower sampling rate (10ms versus 1ms). This means you can use it to profile longer-running processes. On the plus side, it crashes less often. Make sure to choose Running Sample Times, as shown in Figure 23.7, and to uncheck Invert Call Tree. You can choose which thread to show: Even though the Twitter application uses a single thread, `UIKit` has created nine of them, for such things as web display, Core Animation, DNS lookup, and so on.

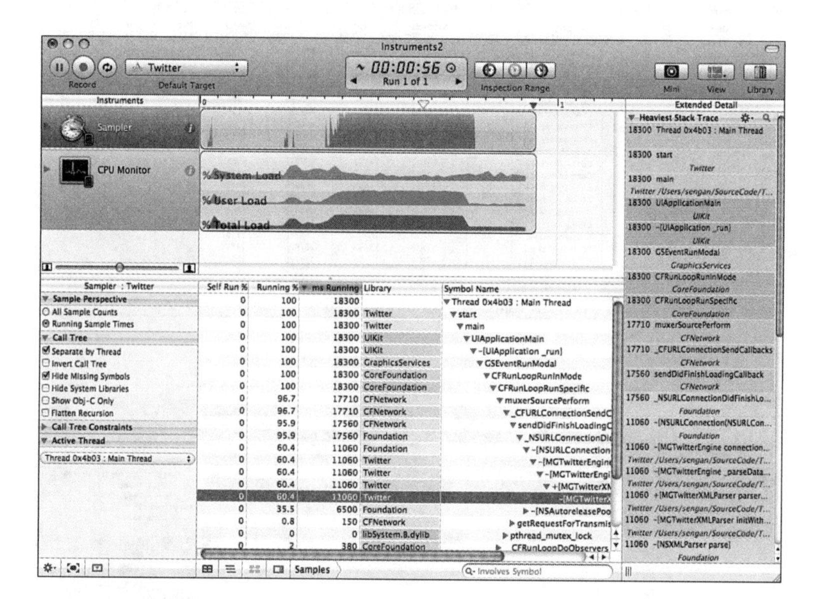

FIGURE 23.7
CPU sampler

Optimizing Your Memory Usage

Reducing memory usage improves your programs' speed and availability.

Programs have to be specifically designed to reduce their memory footprint: Because libraries provide more general solutions than are needed for a specific application, they use more memory than necessary. As a software engineer you must decide whether to trade faster development time for a faster end product.

This section also shows you a number of different complementary ways to detect memory leaks. Memory leaks are programming errors that involve your application losing track of the memory that was assigned to it.

Reducing Memory Usage

The iPhone has a limited amount of memory, so the iPhone OS terminates applications that use too much memory. At most, your program may use 25Mb of memory, but if the user has opened eight tabs, in Safari, and a few very large emails, the available memory can be as low as 5Mb. Apple keeps Safari and Mail running in the background to reduce the latency of starting them up again.

Reducing memory usage and encapsulation are diametrically opposed. For instance, the Twitter application is highly memory inefficient: `MGTwitterEngine` downloads each tweet stream into a large buffer. It has to wait for the entire buffer to be downloaded before giving it to `NSXMLParser` because `NSXMLParser` does not support being streamed data. Because twitter.com only accepts 150 API requests per hour, and because network access is power intensive, it's better to download many tweets at a time. Once the tweets have been downloaded, `MGTwitterEngine` uses `NSXMLParser` to convert them to an array of easy-to-use `NSDictionary`s, including `NSDate`s for the dates. This reduces the coupling to `MGTwitterEngine` because most client code need only know about Cocoa containers (`NSDictionary` and `NSArray`). There is, however, a large cost: Two thirds of the Twitter application's memory usage comes from this design (8Mb out of 12Mb). Although the memory is soon freed, each time the application downloads more tweets, it could be terminated.

To use significantly less memory, your application could parse tweets as they arrive, and only keep the data it needs: The tweet identifier (a 64-bit number), the date (a 32-bit number), and 140 characters of text. This change would reduce the amount of memory used by each downloaded set of tweets from 8Gb to only 7.5Kb. Using a handwritten parser would also significantly boost application speed as the parser only needs to look for a few tags. Of course, a hand written parser is less flexible.

To further reduce memory usage, you can use real-time compression. For instance, `LZO` can compress data to 60% of its original size while only taking 40% more time than a memory copy.

Responding to Memory Warnings

Computers commonly cache data to avoid fetching it again, improving latency, but increasing memory consumption. Because most computers use virtual memory, this is not a big problem: If another application needs more RAM, the least recently accessed data is saved to disk (or discarded if it's already on disk). This slows applications down, but does not terminate them.

On slow, memory-limited devices, such as the iPhone, caching also improves speed. However, once little memory is left, it is preferable to discard cached data than to terminate the program. The iPhone OS provides your application with an opportunity to discard its cached data whenever there is memory pressure by sending it a notification. Any object can register for this notification by registering for the `UIApplicationDidReceiveMemoryWarningNotification`. Your application delegate's `applicationDidReceiveMemoryWarning:` method is invoked as are the `didReceiveMemoryWarning` methods of any `UIViewController` classes.

`UIImage` uses low-memory notifications to release cached images. When `UIImages` are created using filenames, they can be flushed from memory and reloaded transparently. If `UIImages` are created with data, they are not cached:

```
UIImageView* v = [[UIImageView alloc] initWithImage:
                                  [UIImage imageWithContentsOfFile:path]];
```

`UIViewController` uses low-memory notifications to release views that are currently not being shown. When the view controller needs to show the view, it reloads the NIB file, which can cause memory leaks. If a NIB file defines objects other than a view, new copies of these objects will be created each time the NIB file is reloaded. Unless a setter method is defined for an instance variable referenced by the NIB file, the NIB loader directly assigns the instance variable to the new object's pointer, without releasing the old object, causing a leak.. Until iPhone 3.0, people would override `UIViewController`'s `setView:` method to release other objects. As of iPhone OS 3.0, you can define `viewDidUnload:` to do this.

It is important to reduce your application's footprint when you receive a memory warning. Design your applications so that they can reduce their memory footprint by saving their data to flash memory. Design storage protocols to minimize the amount of data that must be accessed to load any specific piece of data.

Virtual Memory

A computer's memory maps physical addresses to unique bytes. Modern CPUs add a level of indirection called virtual memory. The addresses your program uses are virtual: They are looked up in a page table to find the corresponding physical address. To reduce the size of the page table while maintaining its flexibility, only the top 20 bits of virtual address are looked up in the page table. Thus, each consecutive 4Kb page may be mapped to a different area of physical memory. Many useful tricks can be performed with the page table. In particular, it allows different processes to share memory, a faster implementation of `malloc`, the ability to map files into memory, and the ability to create the illusion of more computer memory by evicting written pages to storage.

The iPhone OS provides a full virtual memory implementation, just like the Mac. The only difference is that the program that evicts written pages to flash memory is disabled. Flash memory can only be written to a limited number of times (around 100,000 times). To reduce wear and tear, software tries to distribute writes over the entire flash memory. Because evicting pages to storage such as flash memory is write intensive (in normal usage, my Mac, which has 2Gb of RAM, pages out around 300,000 pages per day), most mobile devices avoid doing so.

Virtual memory allows the iPhone to share libraries and frameworks between simultaneously running applications. For instance, `UIKit` may be shared between Safari, the Springboard, and your application. This technique is called copy-on-write: Pages are only assigned their own copy of shared data if the shared page is written to. `malloc` also uses this technique: Unwritten memory pages are all shared. It is only once a page is written to that it is given a page in physical memory.

Because the iPhone supports virtual memory, you can use `mmap` to map a file's content into memory. Because only the pages that are accessed are read from flash memory, this lets you access a file as if it were in memory, without loading most of it. `mmap` also lets you write to the file, and written pages are evicted back to disk when memory gets tight. By storing large C data structures in `mmap`'d space, you can reduce your memory consumption, at the cost of using more battery charge and reducing flash memory life. `malloc` zone restrictions also apply to placing Objective-C structures in `mmap`'d space.

`Malloc` Zones

Hour 4, "Making the Calculator Calculate," discussed memory zones (represented by `NSZone`). By using memory from different zones, `malloc_zone_malloc` can reduce memory fragmentation. You can create a zone with `malloc_create_zone`, print information about it with `malloc_zone_print`, and delete the entire zone with `malloc_zone_destroy`. This can be useful for caching C data: `malloc_zone_destroy` frees an entire zone, without requiring individual resources to be freed. Unfortunately, the Objective-C runtime no longer supports placing objects in zones other than the default zone. You can probably trick it to work, but at the cost of future compatibility.

Detecting Leaks at Compile Time

The Clang static analyzer tool is able to detect programming errors, including leaks. It is used internally by Apple. For each function, it builds a graph corresponding to the paths through the function and checks whether the number of invocations of `retain` match the number of invocations of `release` along every path through the graph. It also tracks potential NULL pointer dereferences. It can find errors you would not otherwise see because it checks all paths through your program, not just the common ones.

First, download the analyzer from http://clang-analyzer.llvm.org/. It is in a tar.bz2 file. To untar it, open the Terminal application, go to the directory you downloaded it to, and type the following:

```
tar jxvf checker-number.tar.bz2
```

Now, enter the directory, and add it to your path:

```
cd checker-number
export PATH=`pwd`:$PATH
```

Clang uses the xcodebuild command-line tool to determine the files to analyze. xcodebuild is the tool that Xcode uses to build your application. It understands project files and invokes the compiler appropriately. Clang is not yet compatible with ARM compilers, so you should set your project's Base SDK for all Configurations to a simulator SDK. You'll find it in the project preferences (the Get Info context menu item of the topmost item of the Groups & Files pane, on the General tab). In Xcode, click Build, Clean so that xcodebuild tries to rebuild all the files for Clang. Invoke the static checker from your project directory with the following:

```
scan-build xcodebuild -configuration Debug
...
** BUILD SUCCEEDED **
scan-build: 11 bugs found.
scan-build: Run 'scan-view /var/folders/kH/kH-PrTYHHAmt4LleRDWwpU+++TI/-Tmp-
➥/scan-build-2009-08-02-2' to examine bug reports.
```

Run scan-view as it suggests, and Safari will open showing you the errors. Figure 23.8 shows the errors it found for the Twitter application:

- Two subtle errors where I forgot I was returning an unsigned long long, and assumed that invoking the method on nil would return 0—which is true on x86 (the simulator) but not on ARM (the iPhone). Figure 23.9 shows this error in more detail.
- One real leak (in an error alert).
- Nine errors because I did not follow Objective-C naming conventions: Any method that starts with new or contains the word copy should return a retained object. I returned autoreleased objects, which was intentional, but I should have named the methods differently. The poorly chosen names were newPageLocation, newIterators, and resetCopy.

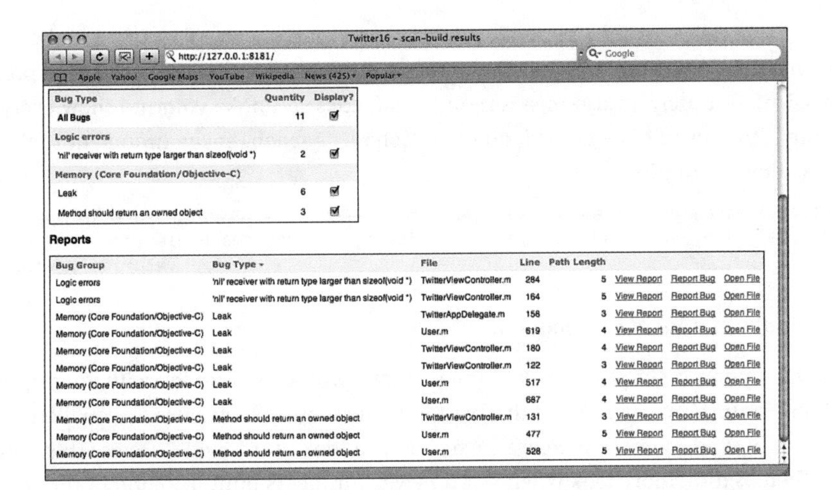

Bug Type	Quantity	Display?
All Bugs	11	☑
Logic errors		
'nil' receiver with return type larger than sizeof(void *)	2	☑
Memory (Core Foundation/Objective-C)		
Leak	6	☑
Method should return an owned object	3	☑

Reports

Bug Group	Bug Type	File	Line	Path Length			
Logic errors	'nil' receiver with return type larger than sizeof(void *)	TwitterViewController.m	284	5	View Report	Report Bug	Open File
Logic errors	'nil' receiver with return type larger than sizeof(void *)	TwitterViewController.m	164	5	View Report	Report Bug	Open File
Memory (Core Foundation/Objective-C)	Leak	TwitterAppDelegate.m	158	3	View Report	Report Bug	Open File
Memory (Core Foundation/Objective-C)	Leak	User.m	619	4	View Report	Report Bug	Open File
Memory (Core Foundation/Objective-C)	Leak	TwitterViewController.m	180	4	View Report	Report Bug	Open File
Memory (Core Foundation/Objective-C)	Leak	TwitterViewController.m	122	3	View Report	Report Bug	Open File
Memory (Core Foundation/Objective-C)	Leak	User.m	517	4	View Report	Report Bug	Open File
Memory (Core Foundation/Objective-C)	Leak	User.m	687	4	View Report	Report Bug	Open File
Memory (Core Foundation/Objective-C)	Method should return an owned object	TwitterViewController.m	131	3	View Report	Report Bug	Open File
Memory (Core Foundation/Objective-C)	Method should return an owned object	User.m	477	5	View Report	Report Bug	Open File
Memory (Core Foundation/Objective-C)	Method should return an owned object	User.m	528	5	View Report	Report Bug	Open File

FIGURE 23.8 The errors in the Twitter application

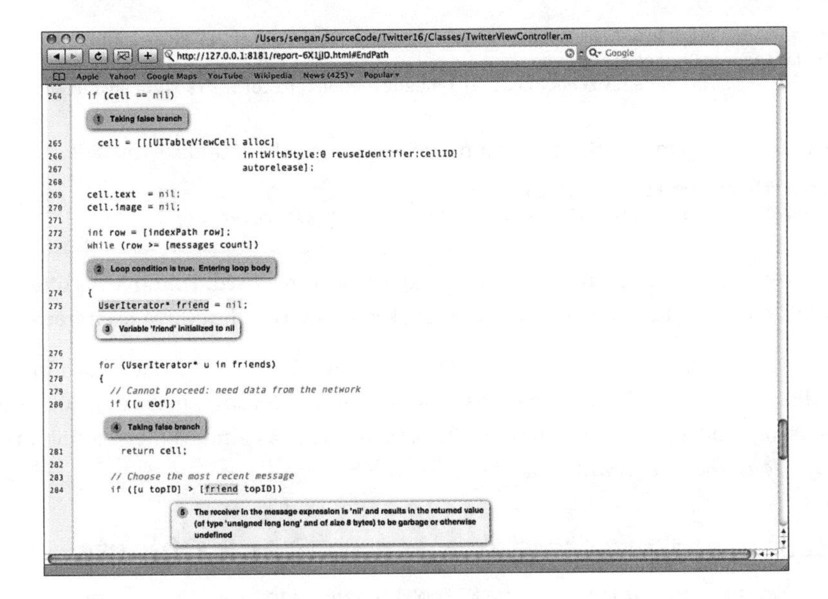

FIGURE 23.9 Clang shows you the path taken to cause the error

Detecting Leaks at Runtime

A number of tools are available to help you find leaks. For instance, both valgrind and Instruments report leaks. They keep track of each address returned by `malloc` and ensure that it is `free`'d.

By default, valgrind and Instruments discount addresses that still have a pointer pointing to them because the program could theoretically have `free`'d them. To detect these pointers, they scan allocated memory and assume that any number that matches a `malloc`'d pointer is a pointer. This reduces the number of false positives. Unfortunately, it also misses many valid leaks. To make valgrind show every pointer that has not been free'd, add the `--show-reachable=yes` argument to the invocation of valgrind:

```
execl(valgrind, valgrind, "--leak-check=full", argv[0], "-valgrind", NULL);
execl(valgrind, valgrind, "--leak-check=full", "--show-reachable=yes", argv[0],
                                                              "-valgrind", NULL);
```

This results in a lot of information.

Another option is simply to look at the memory profile as you play with your application. For instance, if you run the Twitter application in Instruments, you'll see the amount of used memory increase each time you look at a friend's tweets. This tells you there is a memory leak whenever a new controller is built. Looking at the code, we see:

```
TwitterViewController* friendVC = [[TwitterViewController alloc] init];
[(UINavigationController*)
          [self parentViewController] pushViewController:friendVC animated:YES];
```

There is nothing to free the view controller. Changing the line fixes the leak:

```
TwitterViewController* friendVC = nil;
friendVC = [[[TwitterViewController alloc] init] autorelease];
```

However, it causes a crash after the view controller is released. Fixing leaks often reveals bugs because now methods are invoked on objects that have been freed.

There is no magic bullet for detecting memory leaks. You have to audit each memory allocation you make. As programs grow larger, this becomes more difficult. Even in garbage-collected systems, resource leaks still occur: As long as there is still a reference to a resource, it will be kept.

`NSZombie`: Detecting Access to Freed Objects

If you set the environment variable `NSZombieEnabled` to `YES`, released objects are not `free`'d. Instead, they are assigned the `NSZombie` class. When a method is invoked on the released object, `NSZombie` throws an exception you can detect in the debugger:

```
  *** -[TwitterViewController setFriends:]: message sent to deallocated instance
➥0x5973f90
```

The stack trace shows you the code that invoked a method of the released object. This will help us determine any pointers to the deallocated object. However, if the object should not have been released, we'd like to know the sequence of `retains` and `releases` that led the object to be discarded. Because `NSZombieEnabled` ensures each new Objective-C object allocation receives a new address, if we can record every memory method message (`retain` and `release`), we can search using that address to determine the sequence of memory method messages the object received. The Instruments application lets you record these messages.

To record every memory management message, click on the *i* in the `ObjectAlloc` item of the Instruments pane. This shows an information panel: Click the Record Reference Counts check box (see Figure 23.10).

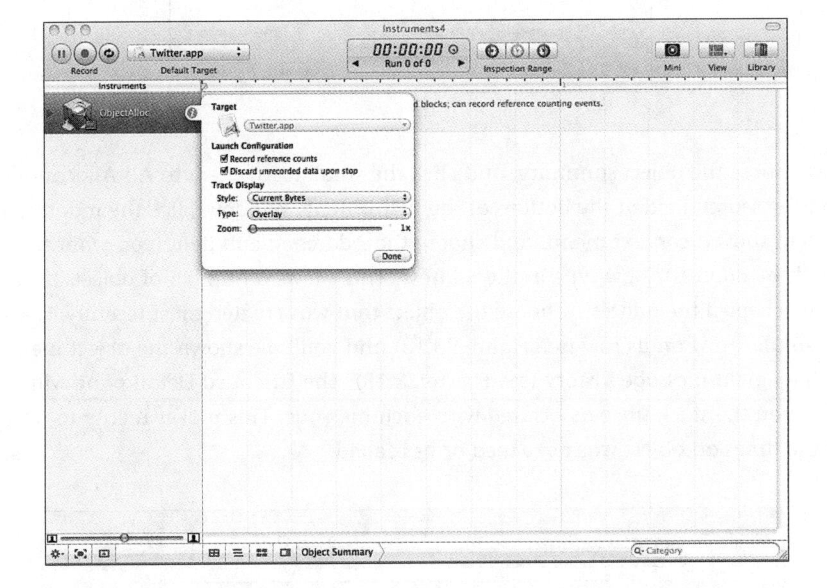

FIGURE 23.10 Instruments: Record Reference Counts

To run Instruments with the `NSZombieEnabled` variable set, you must set it when choosing the executable to launch (from Launch Executable), as shown in Figure 23.11. Run a simulator executable.

Click Record. Once your application stops due to an exception, run the Console application (in /Applications/Utilities). Choose the `system.log` file and look for the last message from your application. This should be `NSZombie`'s exception. Write down the address of the deallocated instance. For instance, you might see the following:

```
*** -[TwitterViewController setFriends:]: message sent to deallocated instance
➥0x8f16940
```

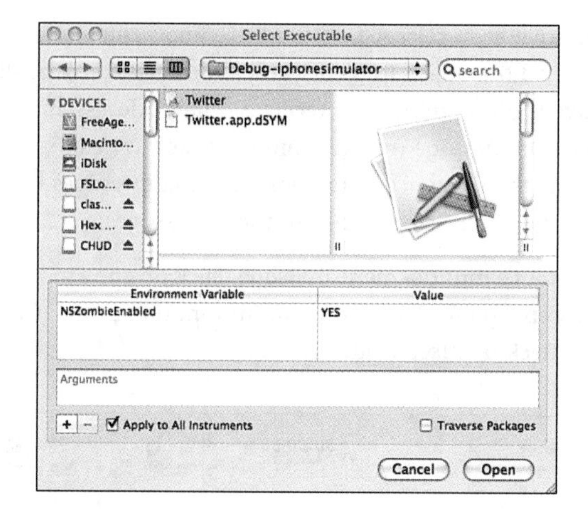

FIGURE 23.11 Instruments: Setting the `NSZombieEnabled` variable

Now choose the object summary, and click the small arrow next to All Allocations. Find the search field at the bottom of the Instruments Window, click the magnifying glass to show a context menu, and choose the Address menu item (you want to search by address). Now type in the address. This shows a number of objects that have occupied the address. Choose the object that was created most recently. Click the small arrow on its row (see Figure 23.12) and you'll be shown the object memory management message history (see Figure 23.13). The Extended Detail pane will show you the stack trace associated with each message. This makes it easy to find all the times an object was `retained` or `released`.

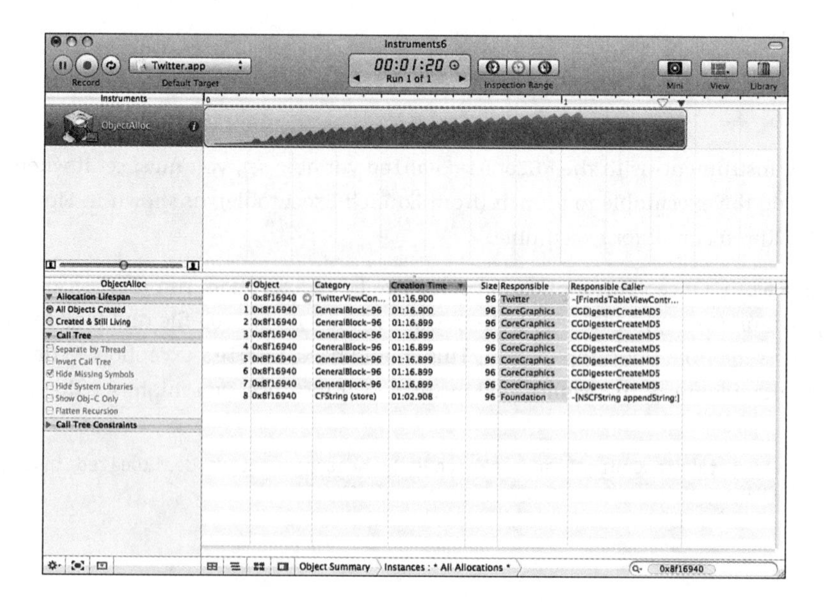

FIGURE 23.12 All allocations for an address

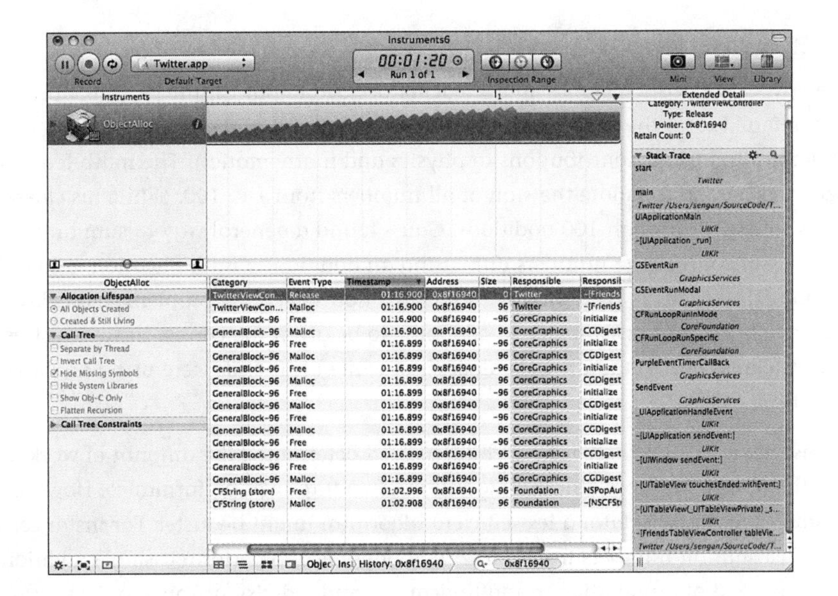

FIGURE 23.13
The failing stack trace

The OpenGL Instrument

The Instruments application lets you profile OpenGL behavior on the device. In particular, you can measure frame rate and memory usage. Recall that the iPhone only has 24Mb of texture memory. If your application uses more than 24Mb of texture memory, its performance will drop suddenly. The OpenGL `GARTResident Object Size` option shows you the amount of texture memory allocated. To set this option, click the *i* button of the `OpenGL ES` item of the Instruments pane.

Recall that querying OpenGL state also stalls rendering. Instead, you can use the `CATransform3D` matrix functions to compute matrices before sending them to OpenGL, and avoid any calls to `glGetFloatv`.

Optimizing Your Code's Speed

Once you have identified a problematic piece of code, the first step is to replace it with a more efficient algorithm. If this proves insufficient, ensure that your program data access patterns are efficient. A few small changes to your coding style and compiler settings might prove valuable. Then, if nothing else works, consider using assembly. Writing optimized assembly code can be fun, but it is very time consuming, and is not portable.

Changing Algorithms

One day, Carl Friedrich Gauss' math teacher decided to punish the class. (Gauss is often referred to as the greatest mathematician since antiquity because of his numerous important contributions to physics and mathematics). The math teacher asked the class to calculate the sum of all numbers from 1 to 100. While his classmates struggled through 100 additions, Gauss found a general way to sum any sequence of consecutive numbers only using an addition, a multiplication, and a division. The teacher was unhappy that Gauss had solved the problem so quickly, and gave him another sequence to add, only to be given the correct answer just as quickly. Gauss had found an O(1) algorithm, while his friends were using an O(*N*) algorithm.

Just as the algorithm these school children used determined the amount of work it took them, using a more efficient algorithm often improves performance. However, for small amounts of data, a less-efficient algorithm might be faster. For instance, if you must sum all numbers from 1 to 2, you only need to perform a single addition (1 + 2) instead of an addition, a multiplication, and a division. You should, therefore, measure any performance benefits you obtain from changing algorithms.

The basic idea behind improving algorithmic complexity is to find shareable units of work. Any time a computational result is reused by other parts of the algorithm, it reduces the algorithm's workload. For instance, insertion-sort sorts arrays by searching through the entire array to find where to place each element. If an array has *N* elements, this takes N^2 steps: It takes *N* steps for each element to find its place by searching the entire array, and this must be performed *N* times for each of the elements. Merge-sort splits the array into unit-sized subarrays, which are sorted because they only have one element. Then, it recursively merges all the subarrays, ensuring at each step that the resultant array is sorted: Merging two sorted arrays to produce another sorted array is a simple linear process. The work of sorting a subarray is shared by every recursion of merge-sort that uses the data from the subarray. Merge-sort is an O(*N *log N*) algorithm.

There are many books about algorithms. I like *Purely Functional Data Structures*, by Chris Okasaki, but it assumes knowledge of Haskell or ML. These days, many common algorithms are documented on Wikipedia (http://en.wikipedia.org/wiki/List_of_algorithms). If you want to create your own algorithms, it is useful to study a large number of algorithms. Over time, you'll develop an intuitive sense of good approaches.

Taking Account of the Memory Hierarchy

Computer memory is called RAM, which stands for random access memory. Random access means that any piece of data in memory is accessible in constant time. This distinguishes RAM from other forms of storage, such as magnetic tape or hard drives, whose time to fetch a piece of data depends on the data's physical location. Twenty years ago, when CPUs ran at a few megahertz, RAM access times truly were constant, and CPUs ran at sufficiently low speeds that accessing data from memory was essentially instantaneous. In those days, you could easily trade memory usage for speed: If you had enough memory, time-intensive computations could be replaced by lookup tables. Nowadays, physics constrains memory bus speeds to be much lower than the speed of the CPU. This means accessing data is not instantaneous.

Each time the CPU requests data, it must wait until it receives it. This is called a stall. Obviously, the more a CPU stalls, the slower software runs. Two different solutions are employed to reduce the number of stalls: caches and memory pipelining.

A cache is memory on the CPU where data can be temporarily stored for fast access. The cache consists of ways and cache lines. Because memory is accessed randomly, caches store memory for as many addresses as they have cache lines. For instance, a 16Kb cache with a 32-byte cache line can store 512 32-byte cache lines of memory at 32-byte aligned addresses. Because cache lines store 32 bytes at a time, if any byte at addresses 0 to 31 is cached, the cache contains the 32 bytes corresponding to addresses 0 thru 31.

To increase cache speed and reduce the size of the cache on the chip, only a few cache lines may store the data of any given address. For instance, the ARM processor in all iPhones other than the 3GS uses a four-way cache design: Any address can only be stored in one of four ways. Thus, a 16Kb cache using 32-byte cache lines is a 128 row by 4 column table. When the cache receives a request for data at an address, it uses bits 5 through 11 of the address to determine the cache row. Each cache row consists of four cache lines. Each cache line has a tag corresponding to the top 20 bits of the address of the data it caches. If a cache line's tag matches the top 20 bits of the requested address, the cache line contains the requested data. If none of the four cache lines' tags match the requested address, the data must be fetched from memory. Finally, the bottom address bits (0 to 4) are used to find data within a cache line. To improve performance, ensure your data fits in cache. Because caches divide memory into ways, you cannot just assume that your data will fit if it takes less space than the cache size: You must ensure that the addresses of cached data do not conflict. The iPhone 3G has two level 1 caches: a 16Kb four-way 32-byte cache line Instruction Cache and a 16Kb four-way 32-byte cache line

Data Cache. The iPhone 3GS has three caches: a 32Kb level 1 Instruction Cache, a 32kb level 1 Data Cache, and a 256Kb level 2 Cache. Instruction Caches store program instructions, whereas Data Caches store data. Level 2 caches are slower caches between memory and the CPU, which store both instructions and data, but take longer to access than level 1 caches. valgrind can simulate your application's cache behavior.

Because it takes time for requests to be sent to RAM and responses to return, memory access is pipelined. That is to say, once you make a request from an address, memory will stream the data starting at that address back to the CPU. Requesting data from another address requires sending a new request and waiting for the data to return. Thus, applications that stream data from consecutive addresses will run faster.

Improving memory access patterns provides a significant boost without requiring you to program in assembly. I optimized third-party software at AMD to run better on our CPUs: For instance, I was able to boost a key video codec routine's speed five times, mostly by improving its caching and memory access patterns. Similarly, I boosted the speed of my game Tetratile by ensuring the code and data it uses to search for winning moves fits within the iPhone's 16Kb caches.

Disabling Thumb Mode

The ARM CPU has two instruction encodings: 32-bit ARM instructions and 16-bit Thumb instructions. The Thumb instruction set is a subset of all ARM instructions. However, because Thumb instructions are smaller, they occupy less cache and are faster to read from memory. On average, Thumb code is 65% the size of 32-bit ARM code, and runs at almost the same speed. The Thumb instruction set does not include floating-point operations. To perform a floating-point operation, the CPU must call an ARM mode routine, which performs the floating-point instruction, and then returns to Thumb mode. This is much slower than using floating-point instructions directly. To improve floating-point intensive code's performance, compile it directly to ARM code by setting the target to the device, opening the project's properties (using the Get Info context menu item of the topmost item of the Groups & Files pane), and unchecking Compile for Thumb.

ARM Peculiarities

When targeting the ARM processor in C, consider the following facts:

- ARM processors natively manipulate 32-bit registers. Use `long` data types instead of `char`s or `short`s for values kept in registers: The compiler adds instructions to simulate `char` and `short` behavior.

- ARM processors have 12 registers available for your code to use. Try to use fewer than 12 local variables at a time inside performance-intensive loops.
- ARM processors prefer `for` loops that end when the variable is zero. For instance, to perform 256 iterations, write the following:

```
for (unsigned int i = 256; i != 0; --i)
  *x++ = *y++;
```

- ARM processors benefit from loop unrolling (reducing the number of iterations the `for` loop must perform by copying the loop body a number of times) because it reduces the number of times the loop control code must be executed. Measure performance gains to decide on the best number of times to unroll the loop. For instance, we can unroll the previous loop four times by writing the following code:

```
for (unsigned int i = 64; i != 0; --i)
{ *x++ = *y++;
  *x++ = *y++;
  *x++ = *y++;
  *x++ = *y++; }
```

- Avoid passing many arguments to functions. (They must be pushed onto the stack and retrieved at some point.)
- Use local variables to avoid pointer aliasing: If your program updates target data of a pointer, it must assume that any other target data was updated by this operation and it must reload it from memory.
- Integer division is performed in software. Division by a constant is converted to the equivalent shifts whenever possible.

Pushing Further: Assembly and Vector Processing

Although it is often said that compilers are better at writing assembly code than people, it is simply not true. However, it is true that to write fast assembly code, you can no longer simply count instruction cycles: The order in which your instructions flow through the CPU matters. When I write highly optimized code, I often write a small pipe simulator to simulate the flow of instructions through the CPU. If you're working at this level, be aware that Shark provides access to the ARM processor's performance counters, which include cycle counts, cache miss counts, TLB miss counts, branch misprediction counts, and pipe stalls.

Because you cannot run ARM code on the simulator, any assembly must be conditionally compiled using the `TARGET_IPHONE_SIMULATOR` macro to distinguish compilation for the simulator from compilation for the iPhone. Unfortunately, a discussion of ARM assembly is beyond the scope of this book.

All iPhones until the iPhone 3GS have a VFP vector processing unit. The iPhone 3GS has a NEON vector processing unit, and appears to emulate VFP instructions, making them slow. Writing VFP and NEON code is beyond the scope of this book, but if you are interested, start by looking at the VFP math library at http://code.google.com/p/vfpmathlibrary/ and the *ARM1176JZF-S Technical Reference Manual*.

Summary

Apple's development environment provides a wealth of tools to understand most of the performance problems you are likely to encounter. Careful design will avoid most problems. However, because adding new features can destroy a design's assumptions, it is important to keep code as simple as possible and test performance regularly. For example, Apple has long had a policy of rejecting any contribution to WebKit that slows it down. WebKit is now one of the fastest browsers. Remember that even the slowest iPhone released in 2007 has similar computational power to a year 2000 Mac.

Q&A

Q. *Should I use debug or release configurations when I profile?*

A. Memory profiles can be performed in the debug configuration, which will give you the best detail. Code built in a debug configuration lacks certain optimizations (like inlining), which make code run faster but also make it harder to debug. On the other hand, the debug configuration provides more precise debug information. Code built in a release configuration can lack symbol information (if the build stripped the executable), but will include all relevant optimizations. Initially, use debug configuration to understand your program: Inlining won't change the complexity of your algorithms. Later, once you are optimizing specific pieces of code, you can switch to Release mode, although Mach functions are the way to go to tune specific routines.

Workshop

The Workshop consists of quiz questions and answers to help you solidify your understanding of the material covered in this hour. You should try to answer the questions before checking the answers.

Quiz Questions

1. How do you determine what to optimize?
2. What tool should you use for time profiles?
3. What tool should you use for memory profiles?
4. What tool should you use for memory leaks?
5. How can you debug messages being sent to released objects?
6. What system behavior affects your program's performance?

Quiz Answers

1. You profile your code to understand its behavior. This will give you a better idea of what functions need improvement. Sometimes, an entire section of code is best replaced. For instance, you could replace `MGTwitterEngine`'s tweet parser with a more-efficient but less-flexible solution.
2. `Shark` provides more accurate time profiles, and is good for testing a few seconds of behavior. Instruments provides coarser profiling over longer times.
3. Instruments shows you memory allocations.
4. Looking at the memory allocations in Instruments will help find memory leaks. Clang uses static analysis to find many memory leaks. valgrind finds most memory leaks but reports so many that it takes time to examine its report.
5. Debug messages being sent to released objects by using `NSZombie` and Instruments.
6. The memory hierarchy is a nonobvious but substantial contributor to program performance.

Exercise

- Use Shark and Instruments to find leaks in the Twitter example. Fix the leaks and debug any resulting bugs. For instance, after adding autorelease to friendVC, and running for a while, I get the following error in gdb:

```
  *** -[TwitterViewController updateIterator:delta:]: message sent to
deallocated
➥instance 0x47f34f0
```

  To reproduce it, you'll need to subscribe to fast-updating Twitter services like CombatSI and BreakingNews, and look at a number of friends' tweet streams. Use the Instruments application and NSZombie to isolate and fix the bug.

HOUR 24

Shipping Your Application

What You'll Learn in This Hour:

- Polishing your application for submission
- Localizing your application
- Submitting your application to the App Store

You've built an application, and are ready to submit it to the App Store. You're probably feeling exhilaration, trepidation, and anticipation. But...you're not done yet. There are a few more steps to take. You must polish it (add a distinctive icon, improve its appearance when launching, beta test it) and choose a price point. If you intend to sell your application worldwide, consider localizing it. Finally, you must submit it to Apple and await its verdict. I provide a digest of the reasons for which applications have been rejected from Apple's App Store to help you avoid rejection.

Polishing Your Application for Submission

Polishing your application is a key phase. Having honest beta testers might be hard for your ego, but it does result in a better product. To help your users quickly recognize your application amid all the clutter on their Home screen, use a distinctive icon. I often confuse the Safari and iTunes icons on my Mac because they are both gray, blue, and round. Try to design an icon that is related to the topic, but different yet simple.

Adding an Application Icon

Each application has three icons:

- A 29x29 pixel PNG icon named `Icon-Settings.png` used by the Settings application and Spotlight.

- A 57x57 pixel PNG icon named `Icon.png` used as the application icon and shown on a Home screen.
- A 512x512 pixel JPEG icon used by the App Store and iTunes. Upload this icon with your application.

The three icons should match. By default, the application icon is automatically given a shine, a drop shadow, and rounded corners. However, the shine might be too strong for your application icon. You can render your own shine in your bitmap editor. To turn off the default shine, add the `UIPrerenderedIcon` key to your application's `Info.plist` property list file. Set its value to true.

For ad hoc distributions, name the 512x512 pixel icon `iTunesArtwork` (without a file extension) and add it to the top level of your application bundle. Be aware that Xcode will not run ad hoc distribution files that include `iTuneArtwork` files.

Adding `Default.png`

Launching your application takes time on slower devices. To create the impression that your application is loaded more quickly, you can add a `Default.png` file to your application's resources. This file will be loaded and displayed with a 3D animation, reducing the apparent lag starting your application.

Many games use `Default.png` to show a splash screen. This is a simple solution that provides the user with something to look at while the application loads. My game, Tetratile, shows the game board, and then displays the most recent game configuration once it has loaded. Another option is to show an empty skeleton of the application's UI. For instance, with the calculator application, we can take a screenshot of the calculator, and use it. By the time the user is ready to start tapping keys, the calculator is ready to use.

To take a picture of the calculator application as first launched, start it from Xcode. Choose Window, Organizer. This will show an organizer window. Choose the Screenshot tab and click the Capture button. You can then click the Save As Default Image button, which will save it and add it to your project (see Figure 24.1).

If you use Apple's Notes application, you'll notice that it takes a screenshot when it exits. When it is next opened, it shows this screenshot until it is ready to accept input. It can do this because it is not sandboxed and is not subject to cryptographic signing. As of iPhoneOS 3.0, there is no method to create this effect for third-party applications.

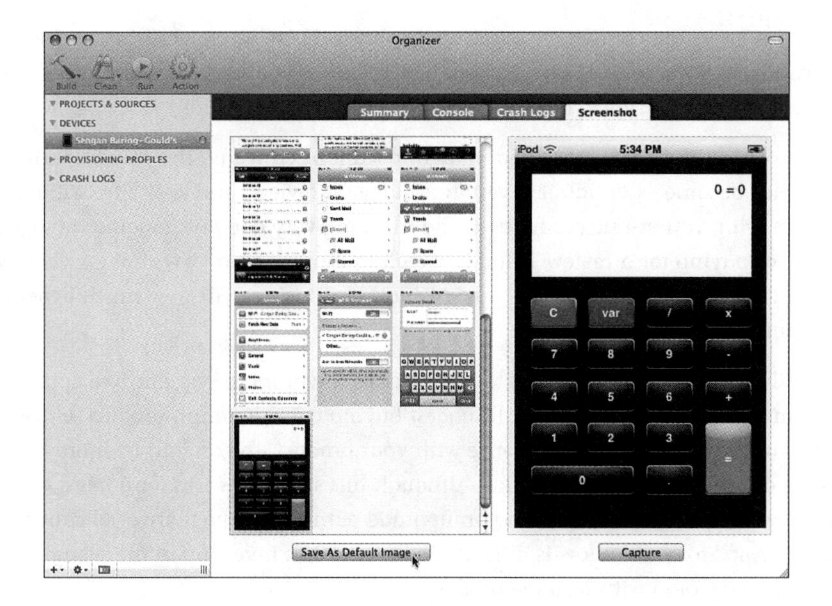

FIGURE 24.1
Capturing a default image

Adding Beta Testers

Before shipping your application, it is a good idea to ask for help testing it. For people to test your application, they must send you their device UDIDs (unique device identifiers). The developer portal only lets you register up to 100 devices for ad hoc tests, so use them wisely: Require serious beta tester commitment, as deleting devices from the developer portal does not free up space for new devices for a year.

Erica Sadun has published a useful iPhone tool called Ad Hoc Helper to help potential beta testers send you their device UDID for ad hoc tests.

Testing on other devices makes you realize that older iPhones are slow, and that there are significant color brightness differences between different iPhone and iPod touch models. Beta testers help find bugs (installation problems, crashes, incompatibilities) and provide valuable feedback (the sounds are too loud. I can't move the tiles easily, the game's too hard/easy).

Once your application has been approved, use promo codes to send free copies to reviewers or charities or friends.

Choosing a Price Point

This is probably the most difficult nontechnical decision you'll have to make. There has been a steady decline in the price that users are willing to pay for applications, and many users are content with free applications. There are advertising partners you can work with, but the rewards will be low unless your users compulsively check your application every few minutes (such as a Twitter application).

On the other hand, with more and more applications crowding the App Store, marketing has become essential. It is very hard to get a review on review sites without either proving you are successful beforehand, being very good at nagging the right people, or paying for a review. I find it revealing that many review sites expect payment, either for the review or for "advertising," but it is unclear how much benefit you gain from this kind of exposure.

Currently, the best strategy seems to be to create one or more popular free applications and a free lite version that all suggest buying your premium product. Once users have had a pleasant experience with your product, they might be more likely to shell out their hard-earned dollar. Although this strategy works for games, which can have only a few levels, finding an upgrade path for productivity applications that the App Store will allow is difficult. It also requires investing in more engineering than you would with a single product.

Localizing Your Application

In the early days of personal computers, most software and manuals were written in English. At the time, I lived in France, and I remember my French friends asking me to translate sentences and commands. Had the software been using hieroglyphics, the result would have been no different. They had a marked preference for French software, even when it was less powerful. Times have changed: Most European children now learn English at school, and much more software is available in other languages.

Cocoa Touch provides tools to help you localize your application, but does not perform the translation for you. In this section, you'll convert it to German and French, two of the main target markets. Spanish and Japanese are other key languages as many potential customers speak those languages. Figure 24.2 shows the completed application.

Localizing NIB Files

Cocoa uses the concept of locale to format numbers, dates, and currencies and to return localized error messages. A **locale** combines a set of conventions with a language. The conventions specify things like how people write dates and numbers. For instance, the meanings of decimal point and the comma decimal separator are inversed in France: Whereas an American would write 10,000, a French person would write 10.000. When users set the `Region Format` and `Language` in the Settings application, they also set the locale seen by all applications.

FIGURE 24.2
German localization

Locales combine a two or three lowercase letter language code (`en` for English, `fr` for French, `gsw` for Alemannic, Alsatian, and Swiss German) and a two uppercase letter country code (`US` for USA, `GB` for Great Britain, `CA` for Canada, `FR` for France). Locales can distinguish between American spellings (`en_US`: color) and British spellings (`en_GB`: colour). They also model countries that use two different languages (`en_CA` versus `fr_CA`).

The NIB files you've created so far are in the `English.lproj` directory (a synonym of `en_US.lproj`). To create German and French localizations, choose `MainWindow.xib` from the Groups & Files pane and select Get Info from the context menu. This will open the Info window shown in Figure 24.3. Click the Make File Localizable button. This opens a Localized Group "`MainWindow.xib`" Info window. Choose the General tab, and click the Add Localization button. Add **`fr`** for French (as spoken in France or Canada), and **`de_DE`** for German (as spoken in Germany but not Austria). The capitalization matters. The result should look like Figure 24.4.

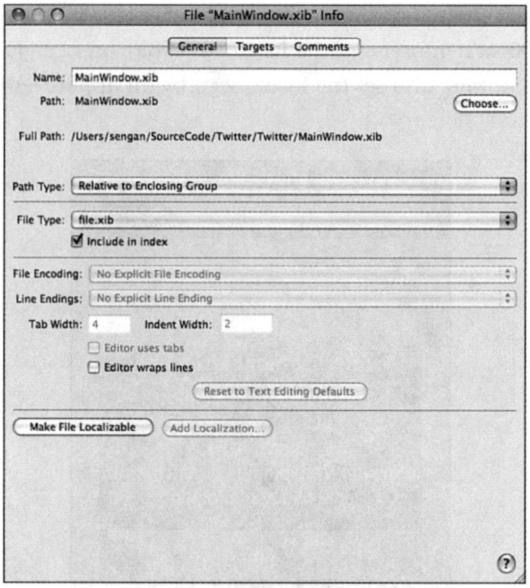

FIGURE 24.3
MainWindow.xib's Info window

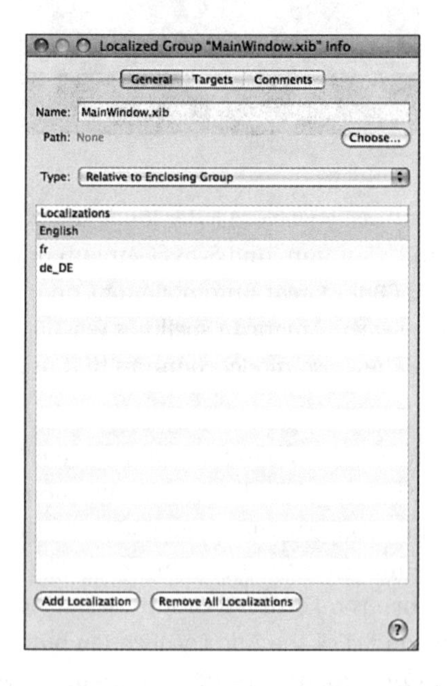

FIGURE 24.4
Localized Group "MainWindow.xib" Info window

Looking at the Groups & Files pane, you'll see `MainWindow.xib` has a disclosure triangle next to it. Open it to see three items: `English`, `fr`, and `de_DE`. Because languages such as German use longer words, you might have to change the layout of your user interface. Using separate NIB files for each language makes this possible. Double-click `fr` to open it in Interface Builder for localization. Change the Tab Item titles and Navigation Item titles, as shown in Figure 24.5. Do the same for the German window, as shown in Figure 24.6.

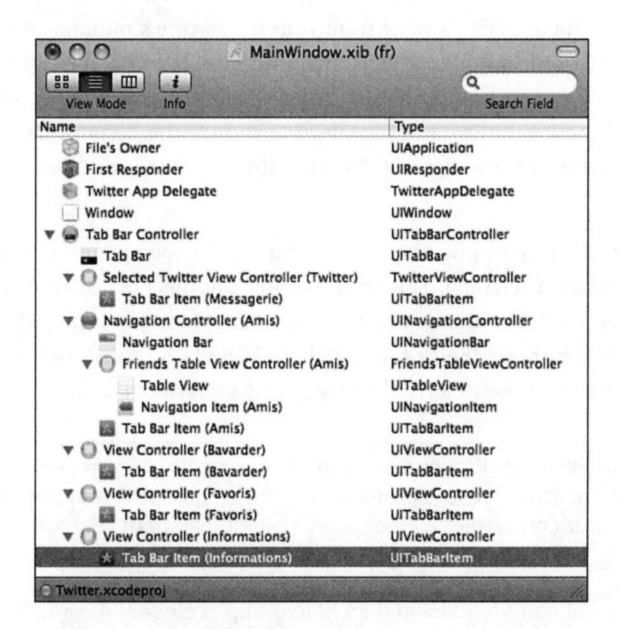

FIGURE 24.5
Localized `MainWindow.xib` (fr) Interface Builder Document Window

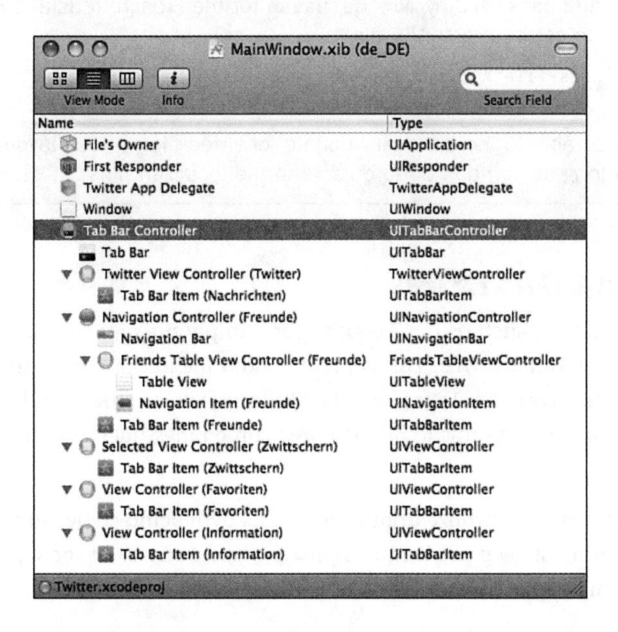

FIGURE 24.6
Localized `MainWindow.xib` (de_DE) Interface Builder Document Window

Run the Settings application. Change the language to Français and the regional format (Format régional) to France. The Settings application is called Réglages. You might have to leave the Settings application and return to see the regional format change.

Now clean all targets, delete Twitter from your target (the simulator or the iPhone), rebuild, and run. You should see the French interface. If you don't, delete the application from your target, and try again. Unfortunately, that will delete your user defaults. You'll notice that we will also need to change the account details page. However, the keyboard has replaced "Next" with "Suivant" and "Done" with "Terminer".

Go back to the Settings application and change the Language and Region Format to Deutsch and Deutschland. The Settings application is now called Einstellungen (and the International section is titled Landeseinstellungen in the Allgemein section). Cocoa Touch shows the closest matching NIB file, so Austrian users will see the de_DE NIB file even if their Region Format is set to Österreich.

Did you Know?

If you provide many localizations and you change a NIB file, you must now update all the other NIB files. Apple provides ibtool, a command-line tool to help mitigate this cost. It can extract all the user-visible strings from your XIB files:

```
ibtool —generate-strings-file AccountView.strings AccountView.xib
```

The resulting file can be translated as before (replace user name with mot d'utilisateur and password by mot de passe for the French translation), and merged back to create a new NIB file:

```
ibtool —strings-file AccountView.strings —write fr.lproj/AccountView.xib \
                                                         AccountView.xib
```

ibtool is also able to incrementally update localized files whose layout was adjusted as long as you don't add objects to the localized files.

Localizing Data Files

To localize data files, such as the About screen, simply make them localizable in the same way as you did for NIBs. This copies the data file into the relevant project directories (in this case, fr.lproj and de_DE.lproj) where they can be modified. For instance, you can use this to provide prerecorded messages in different languages.

Although you can also localize application icons by placing copies in the project directories, you must keep the default Icon.png and Icon-Settings.png files at the top level of your application bundle.

To localize your application's name, create an `InfoPlist.strings` file and provide the appropriate translations.

Localizing Code

Your application retrieves the current locale by using the `NSLocale` class. Cocoa Touch automatically ensures numbers, dates, and currencies are appropriately set, but it is up to you to translate any user-visible text that appears in the UI.

Using the `NSLocale` Class

The `NSLocale` class provides a `currentLocale` class method to retrieve the current locale. An `NSLocale` object has an `objectForKey:` method, which returns locale properties that the `NSNumberFormatter` and `NSDateFormatter` classes use to customize their output. For instance, to retrieve the current locale identifier, write the following:

```
NSLocale* locale              = [NSLocale currentLocale];
NSString* localeIdentifier = [locale localeIdentifier];
```

This will return `en_US` if your Language is set to English and your Region Format is set to United States. The first component is the language, and the second component corresponds to the formatting convention used in the chosen country.

The language component of the `localeIdentifier` is used to provide translations. The `NSLocalizedString` macro converts a string to its localized variant using `NSBundle`'s `localizedStringForKey:value:table:` method, which reads a localization table. `NSLocalizedString` is configured to return an empty string if a translation is missing and to use the `Localizable.strings` file (as specified by the `nil table` argument).

```
#define NSLocalizedString(key, comment) \
   [[NSBundle mainBundle] localizedStringForKey:(key) value:@"" table:nil]
```

Like `IBOutlet`, the `NSLocalizedString` macro is used by an external tool (`genstrings`) to generate a `Localizable.strings` file that contains all the strings of the project that need localizations. The file consists of key-value pairs each preceded by `NSLocalizedString`'s comment. Use the comment to help translators understand the intent of a string.

Updating the Twitter Application

The Twitter application's error messages are written in English. Add the necessary `NSLocalizedString` statements. Be careful: Some of the error messages appear twice in `User.m`, and others appear in `TwitterAppDelegate.m`. I've taken the opportunity to simplify the messages.

```
NSString*    title = @"Cannot reach Twitter";
NSString*    title = NSLocalizedString(@"Cannot reach Twitter", @"Alert title");
NSString* title=[NSString stringWithFormat:@"Cannot reach Twitter for %@",name];
NSString*    title = NSLocalizedString(@"Cannot reach Twitter", @"Alert title");

NSString*    errMsg = [NSString stringWithFormat:@"%@\nWill retry in %g minutes",
                                  [error localizedDescription], retryInterval/60.0];
NSString*     eMsg = NSLocalizedString(@"%@\nWill retry in %g minutes",
                                       @"Alert message. %@ is a localized \
                                         error message. %g is a number");
NSString*   errMsg = [NSString stringWithFormat:eMsg,
                                  [error localizedDescription], retryInterval/60.0];
NSString*    errMsg = [NSString stringWithFormat:@"%@\nWill retry in %g minutes",
                                        [error localizedDescription], retryIn/60.0];
NSString*     eMsg = NSLocalizedString(@"%@\nWill retry in %g minutes",
                                       @"Alert message. %@ is a localized \
                                         error message. %g is a number");
NSString*   errMsg = [NSString stringWithFormat:eMsg,
                                        [error localizedDescription], retryIn/60.0];
UIAlertView* alert=[[UIAlertView alloc] initWithTitle:title message:errMsg
                    delegate:nil cancelButtonTitle:@"OK" otherButtonTitles:nil];
NSString*    okMsg = NSLocalizedString(@"OK", @"Alert panel button");
UIAlertView* alert = [[UIAlertView alloc] initWithTitle:title message:errMsg
                    delegate:nil cancelButtonTitle:okMsg otherButtonTitles:nil];
```

Now open the Terminal application, change the directory to your source code, and run `genstrings` on your source code. Mine is in `SourceCode/Twitter/Classes` in my home directory, so I would type the following:

```
cd SourceCode/Twitter
genstrings Classes/*.m
```

Did you Know?

> If you don't know the UNIX path of a directory, you can simply drag and drop the directory onto the Terminal application. It will append the path to your current command. Therefore, you can type **cd** followed by a space, and then drop the folder onto the Terminal application.

This will generate a `Localizable.strings` file. The file is unusual because it uses the `UTF-16` encoding. Add the file to the resources of your project, but make sure to set the encoding to `Unicode (UTF-16)` (see Figure 24.7). Now make it localizable as you did with the NIB file.

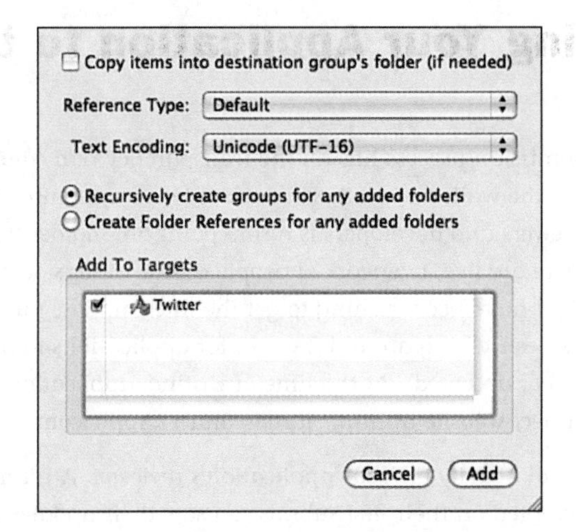

FIGURE 24.7
Localizable.s trings

To create the German translation, change the `de_DE` copy of the application as follows:

```
/* Alert message. %@ is a localized error message. %g is a number */
"%@\nWill retry in %g minutes"
            = "%$@\nErneuter Verbindungs Versuch wird in %2$g Minuten erfolgen";

/* Alert title */
"Cannot reach Twitter" = "Twitter ist nicht erreichbar";

/* Alert panel button */
"OK" = "OK";
```

Clean all targets, rebuild, and launch. The odd `$@` and `$g` strings specify the type of the operand for your translators. I find it helpful to set a breakpoint on `[NSBundle localizedStringForKey:value:table:` to make sure localization functions are being called when I expect them: It is easy to forget to invoke `NSLocalizedString`. Also make sure that each `Localizable.strings` file has the correct UTF-16 type. (Running `hexdump` on a UTF-16 file in the Terminal application should show you that the first two characters are `ff fe`.)

Localizing Settings

Settings are localized in the same way. The translation file is called `Root.strings` and is in `en.lproj` in your settings bundle by default.

Submitting Your Application to the App Store

The App Store submission process has all the transparency of a concrete wall. You throw the ball over the wall, and wait. The lack of two-way communication between the App Store reviewers and developers is a sore point among developers. Try to remember that there are live, overworked people on the other side of the wall. Although you might have been rushing to get the latest update out, patience will serve you well: It's been taking around 2 weeks for applications to be reviewed (and then either rejected or accepted). At the time of writing, applications are submitted via the iTunes connect website at http://itunesconnect.apple.com.

Your chances depend heavily on your application's reviewer. A number of applications that were accepted on their first submission saw their updates rejected because of concerns that would have applied to the first version. However, the following tips will help minimize your application's chances of being rejected.

By the Way

> On one hand, regularly submitting a new version of your application does result in a few more sales. On the other hand, if the author of every one of the 65,000 applications created did that, the App Store review process would grind to a halt. Don't forget that each application upgrade also requires user intervention, possibly annoying users who'll delete your application.

Apple Must be Able to Run the Application

Many applications do not work when shipped to Apple. One reason is Apple's hard-to-use mobile provisioning system. Appendix B, "Troubleshooting Xcode," should help you debug problems you encounter with it. Do follow the steps specified at Apple's developer portal, and use the AppLoader described in Appendix B.

Test the application with every version of the OS that you claim to support before submitting it. Apple will undoubtedly be using a different version than you.

Applications Must Enhance, not Sully Apple's Image

Applications that reduce the user's impression of Apple quality are banned. Apple is concerned about maintaining its image with its customers and worries what they might consider offensive. Steve Jobs answered an email from Alex Vance of Juggleware, whose application containing political satire had been rejected, by saying: "*...I think this app will be offensive to roughly half our customers. What's the point?*"

- Misusing standard UI elements creates an inconsistent user experience. Do not leave table view rows selected to indicate state. Do not use any standard control or icon in any way that is different from the way Apple uses it. Always place toolbars at the bottom of the screen so that they are not confused with tab bars. Do not use vibration to enhance a game: It is only for alerts.
- Applications that do not provide enough value are banned.
- Applications that need to connect to the network but cannot must explicitly say the network is down, so as not to reflect poorly on Apple hardware.
- Applications that need to connect to a network service but cannot must detect the error and tell the user the service is unavailable.
- Applications that need to use Core Location but cannot determine your location must explicitly report an error.
- Applications that provide customization for vibration must hide that customization for iPod touches that lack vibration.
- Applications' release notes should not confuse users. (This includes references to unreleased versions of iPhone OS.)
- Applications may not place a price in the description as it would confuse customers using different currencies.
- Applications that do not appeal to enough potential customers are banned.
- Applications may not simulate a broken iPhone and may not encourage iPhones to be damaged.
- Applications may not offend users (political satire, obscenity, demeaning public figures or creeds, shaking crying babies).
- Applications that users might think are Apple products are banned. For instance, Apple is extremely touchy about their trademarks and proprietary images. If you use any visual depiction of anything that looks like one of their products, your application will be rejected. Similarly, if your website uses a trademarked term inappropriately (for example, "iPhone Games"), your application will be rejected. Instead, use terminology that does not suggest Apple created your application (for example, "Games for iPhone").
- Applications may not use undocumented frameworks as they can crash when Apple updates its OS, casting an unfavorable light on Apple. It doesn't matter whether the framework is documented on the Mac, it must be documented on the iPhone. It's unclear how Apple detects undocumented framework usage.

For instance, a reimplementation of Cover Flow was at first rejected because App Store reviewers thought it used an undocumented framework. On the other hand, many Wi-Fi finder applications are sold that cannot be implemented without using undocumented frameworks.

- The first version of applications must be 1.0.
- Any sales model that might be considered bait and switch is banned. This includes the venerable shareware model of distribution, giveaways, prizes, and contests.
- Every version of the application icon (29x29, 57x57, and 512x512) should represent the same icon.
- Applications that show unfiltered web content must be given a 17+ rating. Incredibly, this includes the Twitter application developed in this book.

Unfortunately, it is difficult to guess what applications will be rejected as being offensive. For instance, there are many disgusting bodily noise applications, some of which sell very well, yet the Eucalyptus e-book reader was at first rejected because it enabled you to download books from the Project Gutenberg, one of which contained a Sanskrit word for human genitalia. The new rating system might help alleviate some of these issues.

Did you Know?

When I submitted my application, Tetratile, there were only 6,000 apps in the App Store. It was rejected because I created a small icon representing an iPod, to represent playing against the game's Artificial Intelligence. Apple's response was a form reminding me how important it is that I respect their trademarks. By resubmitting the application within a few hours, having simply removed the offending iPod icon, I was able to expedite my submission.

In a way, many of these restrictions make sense, as a user's perception of quality is the sum of all his experiences using his iPhone, not just Apple's applications. On the other hand, software developers put a lot of time and effort into writing applications only to see them rejected. Apple is clearly aware of the deficiencies in its App Store process. At the recent Worldwide Developers Conference (WWDC), the App Store session was the only session to end without an opportunity to ask questions.

Applications that interfere with Apple's business plans are banned:

- The PodCaster application was rejected for duplicating with future iTunes functionality.

- iKaraoke was rejected as soon as Apple published a patent for a Karaoke application on the iPhone.
- Drivetrain, a remote control tool for the desktop Transmission BitTorrent application was rejected because BitTorrent is sometimes used to violate copyright.
- To download the software development kit (SDK), you must agree to a contract that specifically prohibits distributing software developed with these tools outside of the App Store or ad hoc distribution.

Avoid Creating Applications That Interfere with AT&T's Business Plans

Apple bans applications that might degrade AT&T's network service:

- Applications, such as NetShare, that let users' computers share their iPhone data connection were banned.
- The 3G version the SlingPlayer application was banned because AT&T changed its terms of services to ban redirecting TV audio or video signals over its network to reduce congestion.
- Voice over Internet Protocol applications such as Skype are limited to Wi-Fi so as not to compete with AT&T.
- Applications that use "excessive" cellular bandwidth are banned.

Respect User Privacy and U.S. Export Laws

Any application that uploads data must inform the user that it will do so, at least once. For instance, uploading game scores to a server requires this. However, if Apple does not detect that users' data is being collected, they don't ban the application.

Any application that includes encryption must be submitted with a U.S. CCATS encryption license.

Summary

Congratulations! You now have a firm grasp of Cocoa Touch. You now understand most of the patterns used by Objective-C frameworks, so that learning new frameworks will be easy. Cocoa and Objective-C have been in development for over 20 years...I remember...Twenty years ago, my best friend won a prize and spent his winnings on a beautiful NeXT computer. I remember visiting his house and drooling over it. It was amazing. But it's equally amazing that what was a workstation class operating system now runs on a phone that you can keep in your pocket. Yet if you were to be transported back in time, you would recognize the technology.

Despite 20 years of development, Cocoa is still changing. Apple introduced Core Animation only two years ago to the Mac. Grand-Central will be introduced in September of 2009 to the Mac, and I expect it will trickle down to a future generation of iPhone because the next generation ARM CPU is multicore. A good way of staying abreast of Cocoa developments is to pay attention to Mac Cocoa.

Now that you know Cocoa Touch, learning Cocoa for the Mac should be easy. There are some differences, just as there is between the British and American variants of English, for much the same reason: history. Cocoa is also available on UNIXes as GnuStep, and on Windows as Cocotron. Both of these are slightly different again, sometimes lacking support for features available in Mac Cocoa, but both have been used for shipping products.

Cappuccino is a JavaScript-based version of Cocoa using an Objective variant of JavaScript called Objective-J. Cappuccino code looks very similar to Cocoa, square brackets and all, but can run inside a browser. You can see it in action at http://280slides.com. Because you can run a web server on your iPhone, and develop Cappuccino applications using Interface Builder and Objective-J, I expect Cappuccino to enable a new form of iPhone application: portable applications that have an iPhone interface for when you are away from a computer and an in-browser interface for when you are sitting at a computer.

In the meantime, consult Apple's "Human Interface Guidelines" to learn how to create a compelling user interface, and get busy!

Q&A

Q. ***How many reviewers does Apple employ?***

A. In its answer to the FCC's investigation, Apple claims it employs "more than 40 full-time trained reviewers."

Q. ***How many reviewers will check my application?***

A. In its answer to the FCC, Apple claims two reviewers check every submitted application.

Q. ***How long do the Apple reviewers test my application?***

A. In its answer to the FCC, Apple says it receives 8500 applications and updates per week to review. With 40 employees, working 40 hours a week, each application only has approximately 10 minutes to be reviewed. In reality, you may get a few more minutes because "full-time" means 40 hours or more.

Workshop

The Workshop consists of quiz questions and answers to help you solidify your understanding of the material covered in this hour. You should try to answer the questions before checking the answers.

Quiz Questions

1. What sizes icon should your application provide?
2. How does localization work?
3. What should you keep in mind when designing an application for the App Store?
4. Does the iPhone SDK contract allow you to create applications to be distributed on jailbroken devices?

Quiz Answers

1. Your application should provide three icons sized at 29x29, 57x57, and 512x512 pixels.
2. The localized NIB, icon and `.strings` files are placed in directories with a `.lproj` extension. The directories' names specify the language and region format to use. When the application requests a file, it is automatically from the appropriate directory based on the current `Language` and `Region Format` settings.
3. Ensure that your applications do not sully Apple's image.
4. No, Apple forbids you from doing so. The legality of jailbreaking is as yet unclear. Because Apple does not own the compiler (it uses the GPL'd gcc compiler), there are legal ways of developing applications for jailbroken devices.

Exercise

- Localize the Twitter application to some other language you might speak, or, failing that, to pig latin.

APPENDIX C
Resources

Appendixes A, B, and D are online-only bonus materials. You can access them at www.informit.com/title/9780672331251.

Because Cocoa is a vast subject, there are no one-stop sources of information. In this appendix, I list sources of information that I think will be useful to you.

I list books and papers first because they are better able to provide a broader treatment of their subjects. Many of the books are Mac specific, but, because the iPhone and the Mac share a common heritage, most of what they teach also applies to the iPhone. I also list other books that will help you with non-iPhone-specific subjects such as SQL or Object Oriented design.

I also list the web-based resources I often refer to while developing or to stay abreast of the latest developments. Although books generally excel at teaching the larger picture, websites provide useful details about specific topics.

This Book's Website

You can download the source code at this book's website. It also provides any errata discovered after publication: http://www.informit.com/title/9780672331251.

Books and Papers

There are a number of books about Cocoa or the Mac that are relevant to the iPhone. Most of these books will help you deepen your understanding of particular topics. Whereas this book covers how Cocoa works, giving you a firm grasp of the how Cocoa is designed, Erica Sadun's book (included in the following list) provides lots of sample code and serves as a good reminder of how specific classes are used.

Apple Computer. 2009. *The Objective-C 2.0 Programming Language*. Cupertino, California: Apple Computer

Dalrymple, Mark, and Aaron Hillegass. 2005. *Advanced Mac OS X Programming*. Atlanta, Georgia: Big Nerd Ranch Inc.

Dudney, Bill. 2008. *Core Animation for Mac OS X and the iPhone*. Raleigh, North Carolina: Pragmatic Programmers

Gelphman, David, and Bunny Laden. 2005. *Programming with Quartz: 2D and PDF Graphics in Mac OS X*. San Francisco: Morgan Kaufmann

Miller, Greg. "Exploring Leopard with Dtrace," *MacTech magazine*, Volume 23 (2007)

Sadun, Erica. 2008. *The iPhone Developer's Cookbook: Building Applications with the iPhone SDK*. Boston: Addison-Wesley Professional.

Singh, Amit. 2006. *Mac OS X Internals: A Systems Approach*. Boston: Addison-Wesley

Zarra, Marcus S. 2009. Core Data: *Apple's API for Persisting Data under Mac OS X*, Raleigh, North Carolina: Pragmatic Programmers

Zdziarski, Jonathan. 2008. *IPhone Open Application Development,* Sebastopol, California: O'Reilly

If you ever decide to learn to program for the Mac, the following book is good for beginners. However, it covers a lot of similar ground to this book.

Hillegass, Aaron. 2008. *Cocoa Programming for Mac OS X*. 3rd ed. Boston: Addison-Wesley Professional.

If you find yourself confused using a Mac, the following book might help:

Pogue, David. 2007. *Mac OS X: The Missing Manual*, 2007, Sebastopol, California: O'Reilly Media.

The following books are not about the iPhone per se, but will be valuable if you develop software. For instance, you might never use Erlang, but its philosophy is interesting if you write a lot of networking code.

ARM1176JZF-S Technical Reference Manual (currently at http://infocenter.arm.com/help/topic/com.arm.doc.ddi0301g/DDI0301G_arm1176jzfs_r0p7_trm.pdf)

Armstrong, Joe. 2007. *Programming Erlang*. Raleigh, North Carolina: Pragmatic Programmers

Butenhof, David R. 1997. *Programming with POSIX(R) Threads*. Reading, Massachusetts: Addison-Wesley

Fehily, Chris. 2005. *SQL*. Berkeley, California: Peachpit Press

Fowler, Martin. 1999. *Refactoring: Improving the Design of Existing Code*. Reading, Massachusetts: Addison-Wesley

Gamma, Erich, Richard Helm, Ralph Johnson, and John Vlissides. 1994. *Design Patterns*. Reading, Massachusetts: Addison-Wesley

Kernighan, Brian W., and Dennis M. Ritchie. 1988. *The C Programming Language*. 2nd ed. London: Prentice Hall

Kozierok, Charles M. 2005. *The TCP/IP Guide*. San Francisco: No Starch Press

Lee, Edward A. "The Problem with Threads," at http://www.eecs.berkeley.edu/Pubs/TechRpts/2006/EECS-2006-1.pdf

Okasaki, Chris. 1998. *Purely Functional Data Structures*. Cambridge, UK: Cambridge University Press

Owens, Michael. 2006. *The Definite Guide to SQLite*. Berkeley, California: Apress

Paeth, Alan. W. 1995. *Graphics Gems V*. No. 5. London: Academic Press

RFC2616 http://www.ietf.org/rfc/rfc2616.txt

Richardson, Iain E.G. 2003. *H.264 and MPEG-4 Video Compression*. Chichester, England: John Wiley & Sons Ltd

Sloss, Andrew N., Dominic Symes, and Chris Wright. 2004. *Arm System's Developer Guide*. San Francisco: Morgan Kaufmann

Stevens, W. Richard. 1994. *TCP/IP Illustrated, Volume 1: The Protocols*. Indianapolis, Indiana: Addison-Wesley

Web Resources

Apple's developer websites and mailing lists are a primary source of information: http://developer.apple.com. Unfortunately, Apple tends to write additional documents or tech notes on a subject rather than integrating the information together and clearly targeting it. Fortunately, Apple is not the sole repository of information.

The http://www.cocoadev.com website is a repository of information about Mac Cocoa. In many ways, Cocoa Touch is similar, and its advice is pertinent.

Good developer blogs are another resource. The difficulty here lies in that, as a beginner, it is hard to distinguish between experts and newbies who write well. For finding blogs, Google is your friend. More recently, the http://www.stackoverflow.com and http://www.iphonedevsdb.com websites, where people ask and answer questions, have become more valuable resources.

For more predigested technical information, read articles on http://bill.dudney.net and http://iphonedevelopment.blogspot.com. They present information in a conversational style. http://www.drobnik.com discusses common development problems, and http://iphonesdkdev.blogspot.com provides useful tips.

For technical information, I highly recommend Matt Gallagher's http://cocoawithlove.com website, Mike Ash's http://www.mikeash.com, and Scott Stevenson's http://theocacao.com. You'll always learn something by reading them.

The http://www.cimgf.com website has a lot of Core Animation and Core Data information. The http://cocoasamurai.blogspot.com blog also has some solid articles.

The Mac Tech magazine has featured a number of highly technical Cocoa articles over the years. You can purchase a DVD of their back issues. Many respected blog authors have written for it.

For deeper technical information, Erica Sadun's articles appear in many different venues. She writes from the reverse engineering perspective, which means she also writes about undocumented frameworks you should not use for the App Store. Other good resources include http://ridiculousfish.com/blog/, http://www.mulle-kybernetik.com/artikel/Optimization/, http://www.kernelthread.com, http://www.osxbook.com/blog/, and http://googlemac.blogspot.com. Although many of these resources have a Mac slant, you'll find the ideas translate over to the iPhone.

The http://daringfireball.net, http://tuaw.com, http://tidbits.com, and http://mobileorchard.com websites provide relevant daily news. Mobile orchard also has tutorials. http://148apps.biz provides iPhone business-related news.

Index

This index intentionally begins on page 567; Appendix D (pages 547-566) is located online.

Page numbers prefixed with PDF: refer to topics found in the online appendixes accessible at www.informit.com/title/9780672331251.

Symbols

A

B

C

F

G

H

I

J–K

N

P

Q–R

S

T

U

V

W

X–Z

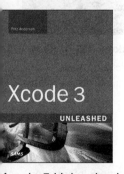

Your purchase of ***Sams Teach Yourself Cocoa Touch™ Programming in 24 Hours*** includes access to a free online edition for 45 days through the Safari Books Online subscription service. Nearly every Sams book is available online through Safari Books Online, along with more than 5,000 other technical books and videos from publishers such as Addison-Wesley Professional, Cisco Press, Exam Cram, IBM Press, O'Reilly, Prentice Hall, and Que.

SAFARI BOOKS ONLINE allows you to search for a specific answer, cut and paste code, download chapters, and stay current with emerging technologies.

Activate your FREE Online Edition at www.informit.com/safarifree

STEP 1: Enter the coupon code: VTWHPXA.

STEP 2: New Safari users, complete the brief registration form. Safari subscribers, just log in.

If you have difficulty registering on Safari or accessing the online edition, please e-mail customer-service@safaribooksonline.com

AdobePress

Cisco Press